PRAISE FOR PLAY HARD REST EASY GUIDES

"One great guidebook...We wish all guidebooks were as good."
– Tara Mandy, *New York* magazine

"Indispensable to anyone planning a trip to New England and may
convince those who are not to rethink their vacation plans.
Recommended for all public libraries and essential for those
in and around New England."
– Thomas O'Connell, *Library Journal*

"Presented in an easy-to-read, quick-to-digest format that makes the
book perfect for planning a quick escape or a longer vacation."
– Jerry Morris, *The Boston Globe*

"If you're an outdoor enthusiast who loves to combine the rugged
and the Ritz, don't leave home without the Play Hard, Rest Easy
guidebook series."
– Carole Jacobs, *Shape* magazine

"Covers hundreds of outdoor options, from mountain biking
...to sea kayaking...(coupled with)...classy restaurants
(and) well-appointed lodges."
– Dianna Delling, *Outside* magazine

"...a useful and practical guide for those who seek an active vacation
but have no qualms about pampering themselves."
– June Sawyers, *The Chicago Tribune*

"The only guidebook you'll need."
– Scott Jagow, National Public Radio

ALSO FROM WALKABOUT PRESS

Play Hard Rest Easy: New England by Malcolm Campbell
Rock Solid Golf: A Foundation for a Lifetime by Dana Rader

COMING FALL 2004
Play Hard Rest Easy: New Mexico & Arizona by Katie Showalter

COMING 2005-2006
Play Hard Rest Easy: Northern California
Play Hard Rest Easy: Washington DC, Virginia, Maryland & Delaware
Play Hard Rest Easy: New England, Second Edition

WALKABOUT PRESS, INC.

PLAY HARD
REST EASY™

Carolinas & Georgia

The Ultimate Active Getaway Guide

by Malcolm Campbell & Deron Nardo

WALKABOUT PRESS

Walkabout Press, Inc.

P.O. Box 11329
Charlotte, NC 28220–1329

Find us online at **www.walkaboutpress.com**

ISBN: 1-931339-01-5

Library of Congress Card Number: 2004104032

Library of Congress Cataloguing-in-Publication Data is available.

EDITORS: Sandy Kolman, Malcolm Campbell
ASSOCIATE EDITORS: Ryan Croxton, Rick Thurmond
ART DIRECTOR: Tess Gadwa, Tess Gadwa Design & Content Services
TRAVEL-RESEARCH WRITERS: Melissa Stone, Erin Lyman, Sandy Kolman
DIGITAL CARTOGRAPHY: Brandon Ray, Mapesthetics; Matt Hoffman, Lost Man Maps
FRONT COVER PHOTO: Steve McBride, Picturesque, 1997
BACK COVER PHOTO CREDITS: Sea kayaking (GA Dept. of Tourism); Mountain biking (Asheville Convention & Visitors Bureau); Beach Picnic/Lodge on Little St. Simons Island, GA (Randall Perry Photography); Inn exterior (GA Dept. of Tourism)
INTERIOR PHOTOGRAPHS by Deron Nardo or Malcolm Campbell, unless otherwise noted.

Special Sales

Corporations, organizations, mail-order catalogs, institutions, and charities may make bulk purchases (15+ copies) of this guidebook at special discounts. Walkabout Press can produce custom editions of this book for use as premiums or incentives in sales promotions. This content is available for private-label imprints. Contact Malcolm Campbell, Walkabout Press, P.O. Box 11329, Charlotte, NC 28220-1329, or call 1–800–231–3949.

Printed in the United States of America: First Edition/First Printing B

For Lauren, McLean, & Elliott:
It's time to get outside and play.
– mc

For my mother, whose love and support
was invaluable in my life,
and who I miss every day.
– dn

Dear Readers:

Every effort was made to make this the most accurate, informative, and easy-to-use guidebook on the planet. Any comments, suggestions, and corrections regarding this guide are welcome and should be sent to:

Walkabout Press, Inc.
P.O. Box 11329
Charlotte, NC 28220-1329
comments@walkaboutpress.com

We'd love to hear from you so we can make future editions and future guides even better. Keep checking our website, *www.walkaboutpress.com,* for updates to our existing guides.

Acknowledgments

I'm grateful for the guidance from and friendship of Chip Barrett, Mike Purkey, Pete Chepul, Cliff Jarrett, Jon Buchan, Ryan Croxton, Scott Adams, and my father and business mentor, George Campbell. Thanks to Melissa Stone and Erin Lyman for thorough research and writing assistance; to Rick Thurmond for the ready-fire!-aim editing; to Brandon Ray and Matt Hoffman for fine map-making; to Tess Gadwa for her steady hand at design; to Deron Nardo, for his dedication to seeing this through; and to our editor, Sandy Kolman, who did a bit of everything, did it all well, and maintained a sense of humor.

Without our posse of proofreaders—Connie Brush, Katie Wagner, Hank Griffin, Ellie Wiater, Camille Griffin, Emily Repede, Lauren Campbell, and most of all, Bobbie Campbell—you'd be reeding wordz like these'uns. Thanks to Carolyn Sakowski, Anne Waters, Ed Southern, and the crew at John F. Blair for guidance; to Frye Gaillard & Amy Rogers for camaraderie; to Frank Burgess, Sr., for warehousing my inventory; to Sally Brewster and the staff at Park Road Books for the retail-reality checks; and to all the innkeepers, business owners, folks at the various chambers of commerce, and fellow travelers I met along the way. May we meet again as we revise this book.

To Mom, Dad, Duncan, Kim, Frank, Barbara, Allen, Sally, and Frank Sr: thanks for your love and support.

And to Lauren, McLean, and Elliott: I love you "to infinity and back."

—Malcolm Campbell

First and foremost, I must thank my family and friends, who guided me through the roughest patch of my life and without whom I could not have finished this book.

Thanks to my family: Guy and Kim, who have provided me two little jewels to treasure; my Pop, who tirelessly supported my pseudo-athletic career and my education; Uncle Lou, whose wisdom is invaluable; Aunt Theresa, whose continued motherly support has become irreplaceable; and Wally, Aunt Karen, Uncle Duke, Steve, Aunt Rose and Uncle Anteo; Mr. and Mrs. DiTanna, who feel very much like family; and my dog Fiya, who is quite un-dog-like and who is a big part of my ongoing battle with sanity.

My friends, who came to my rescue and who I am eternally grateful to call my friends: Jeff, Jeff, Brian, Danny, Laura, Joseph, Beef, Kim, Tara, Tanya, Sarcanda, Jon, Chris, Pat, Brian C., Todd, Phil, Tony, Tom, Steve, Russell, Julie, Anna, Andrea, Katie, Lizzy, Alan, Frank, Jason, Kurt, Jess, Aaron, Enzo, Grattan, Drew, Carrington, Tom, Kate, and Bill.

Thanks to all of the innkeepers, restaurateurs, outfitters, shopkeepers, and members of travel and tourism departments who were patient with my inquiries, particularly Connie Nelson and Erica Backus. Final thanks to all those I befriended on my travels. Thank you, Malcolm, for the opportunity, and Sandy, for pointing out the nuances of proper grammar.

—Deron Nardo

Contents

List of Maps

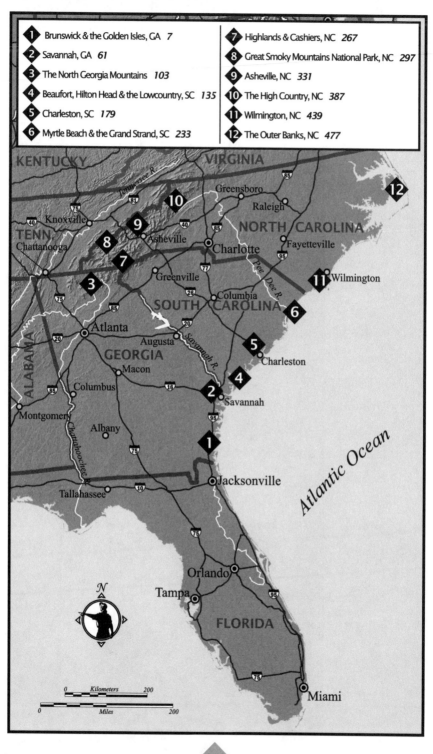

1 Brunswick & the Golden Isles, GA 7
2 Savannah, GA 61
3 The North Georgia Mountains 103
4 Beaufort, Hilton Head & the Lowcountry, SC 135
5 Charleston, SC 179
6 Myrtle Beach & the Grand Strand, SC 233
7 Highlands & Cashiers, NC 267
8 Great Smoky Mountains National Park, NC 297
9 Asheville, NC 331
10 The High Country, NC 387
11 Wilmington, NC 439
12 The Outer Banks, NC 477

xv

Preface

Since childhood, I've spent a lot of time outdoors in the woods—much of it strapped to a 50-pound backpack. I've pitched plenty of tents, eaten hundreds of freeze-dried meals, and extinguished loads of campfires, but here's an admission I don't make very often. With apologies to my former scoutmasters, I don't like to sleep outdoors. Give me a comfortable bed any night over a tent set upon the rock- and root-strewn earth.

Even when I'm exhausted from backpacking, getting a good night's sleep in a constrictive sleeping bag is nearly impossible. By the end of a three-day camping trip, I'm usually so sleep-deprived, dirty, and sore that I'm counting steps to the car. The splendor of the land goes unnoticed.

I married someone who also loves the outdoors but who would rather wrestle a Grizzly than sleep in a tent. Together, Lauren and I have found a great way to satisfy our need to get outside and not lose any sleep. We call our trips soft-adventure vacations. For us, the ideal, long-weekend getaway involves visiting a place of exceptional scenic beauty and spending our days exploring the area by hiking, biking, paddling, swimming, or snowshoeing. Since neither of us has completed—or *started*, for that matter—a triathlon, we rest in between physical activities by shopping; visiting museums, historic sites, and art galleries; or catching a play or a concert. At day's end, we return to the comfort of an inn or B&B to soak in the hot tub, shower, and depart for a relaxing dinner and evening out. Then, it's back to a comfortable bed—which someone else makes—for a deep, restful sleep. The next day? The very same thing.

Of course, we didn't invent the soft-adventure vacation. We merely discovered the physical, mental, and spiritual benefits that others have enjoyed for years from this type of travel. On every trip, we always meet another couple, group, or individual out doing the same thing. It's easy to spot them—they're the travelers juggling two or three guidebooks at once.

It's frustrating to plan a trip from several guidebooks, but that's what it takes to get the information you need for an enjoyable, soft-adventure vacation. I've found B&B and country inn guidebooks helpful for accurate descriptions of lodgings—the rooms, quality of the breakfast, and personalities of the owners. But few B&B/inn guidebooks offer much in the way of directions to good hiking trails and other adventurous activities. Likewise, good hiking, mountain biking, and paddling guidebooks rarely provide accommodation descriptions beyond campgrounds and budget lodgings. In my experience, both lodging and outdoor-sport guidebooks offer limited suggestions for dining and such excursions as shopping, antiquing, driving the back roads, and exploring a destination's cultural and historical heritage. Finally, travel guides that attempt to cover an entire area like New England, or even an entire state, fall short in their information for all four areas—lodging, dining, outdoor recreation, and interesting things to do.

The book you're reading combines all of the above for 12 vacation destinations in the Carolinas & Georgia. It's the second title in the **Play Hard Rest Easy** soft-adventure guidebook series. The first title, *Play Hard Rest Easy: New England*, will be completely updated and released as a second edition in 2005. Look for titles to New Mexico & Arizona in fall 2004; Northern California in spring 2005; and Washington, D.C., Virginia, Delaware, and Maryland in spring 2006. We're expanding the series to include many more scenic vacation regions—Florida, the Pacific Northwest, and the Caribbean, among them—so check our website (*www.walkaboutpress.com*) regularly for updates.

What else might you expect from Walkabout Press? An expanded publishing program, including more travel, outdoor, and sport titles. We're also on the lookout for good ideas that can be published according to our mission: *to produce and sell outstanding books that deliver exactly what they promise to the reader; continue to sell year after year; and earn our competition's respect.*

Our books do something else that's critically important: They promote the cause of adult and family literacy. Walkabout Press is a proud supporter of **Onepercentforward.com**, meaning that each year in which we make money, we give 1% of the pre-tax profit to the National Center for Family Literacy (*www.famlit.org*), an organization dedicated to fostering parents reading to children. (In years that we do not make a profit, we provide a baseline donation.)

It takes a village to run a small company. We rely on your critical feedback and would love to hear from you anytime. Drop us a note (my email is below) or call (1-800-231-3949). Meanwhile, have a great time out there, and whatever you do, be sure to...

Play hard and rest easy,

Malcolm Campbell
Publisher, Walkabout Press
malcolm@walkaboutpress.com

Introduction

Who says playing hard means roughing it? High-energy recreation, stylish lodgings, superb dining, and civilized relaxation make the ultimate getaway mix. If you like to play hard during the day—hiking, biking, paddling, skiing, sightseeing, or shopping (yes, there's sport in shopping)—but rest easy at night—dining in an elegant restaurant and sleeping in an upscale inn—you'll find this guide indispensable.

This book profiles the top 12 vacation towns or regions in which to play hard and rest easy. How were the destinations selected? We chose destinations or regions that are exceptionally scenic with a lot of public land and bodies of water open for multi-sport exploration. We've included areas that are popular with travelers in all four seasons and that offer a variety of interesting things to do when the weather is bad or when you're too tired to pedal or paddle another inch. Each region had to be easily accessible from the major cities of Atlanta, Charlotte, and Raleigh. Finally, we wanted places with dozens of upscale dining and lodging establishments.

To share with you only the finest trails, mountain vistas, lakes, rivers and streams, as well as the most interesting excursions and best country inns, B&Bs, and restaurants, we visited and revisited these places many times. In addition to our exploration, we befriended an untold number of residents and spoke with fellow travelers about their favorite places. Then, from three large cabinet-file drawers crammed with notes, brochures, restaurant menus, and directions scribbled on everything from napkins to CD covers, we began to whittle and write.

How Each Chapter Flows

Each chapter begins with an overview of the destination, including its geography, history and what makes it especially appealing to active travelers. You'll also find a digitally drawn map depicting all of the villages, roadways, major rivers, lakes, mountains, ski resorts, wildlife refuges, and national and state parks covered in the chapter. In *The Way Around*, there are brief descriptions of each town or village in the area, as well as a rundown of the local interstates, highways, and roadways. What to expect of the region's weather follows, and each chapter introduction ends with directions on how to get to the area by plane and automobile, including specific driving directions and estimated travel times from Atlanta, Charlotte, and Raleigh.

Following the introduction, there are four major elements to each chapter: *Play Hard*, which details the area's outdoor offerings and other interesting excursions; *Rest Easy*, which covers lodging and dining recommendations; A *Long-Weekend Itinerary*, which provides a suggested itinerary for two and a half days; and *Additional Information*, which provides the major sources for supplemental travel information.

Play Hard

This section is divided into *Wide Open*, which covers the active, physical pursuits, and *Kick Back*, which suggests more laid-back activities suitable for poor weather or for when your energy level wanes. **Wide Open** begins with a thorough description of the region's open spaces, including national and state parks and forests, large bodies of water, and major rivers. You'll find directions to these places as well as contact addresses, phone numbers, and websites (when available).

Dayhiking is the first *Play Hard* sport in each chapter and receives the most coverage because it is the most popular and accessible form of outdoor recreation. For each destination, you'll find a number of suggested hikes, ranging in length and difficulty from short, easy jaunts you can do in less than hour to long, grueling treks that take a full day to complete. While we recommend that you not venture into unfamiliar wilderness without an accurate topographical map, we've included only well marked and maintained trails that are easy to follow. Each hike description includes the trail's distance, route directions, spur trails to notable vistas, items of interest about the trail or terrain, and directions to the trailhead.

Mountain Biking covers places to ride off the pavement on public land, including state forest and logging roads, snowmobile and carriage paths, cross-country trails, and singletrack. (Singletrack is the most narrow of mountain bike trails and typically runs through the most-challenging terrain.) Novice to intermediate mountain bikers will be able to ride most routes listed in this book. We have not gone in search of routes that carry a good chance of ending in an orthopedic surgeon's office. If you're an experienced rider and want to find the wicked, local mountain biking terrain, stop by any of the bike shops and rental sources listed at the end of *Mountain Biking* for directions and the latest trail conditions. More and more downhill ski areas are opening their trails and providing lift access to mountain bikers in the summer for a nominal day-use fee. Many resorts also rent mountain bikes, and you'll also find a rundown of such places in each chapter.

Road Biking suggests the best routes through the scenic countryside on the paved paths and roadways in and around the destination. (You'll find road routes with occasional unpaved stretches included to create loops or add particularly noteworthy sections to the ride.) For the most part, the Southeast's back roads and rural highways are safe for pedaling, and local drivers are courteous and expect to encounter you on the roads. Regardless, wear bright clothing and never assume a driver sees you just because you see or hear him.

Unless you're a cyclist who sports endorsement logos on your Lycra® outfits or who is accustomed to riding a road bike that weighs less than a postage stamp, you'll find the rental offerings of the bike stores more than adequate. (Few bike stores rent professional road bikes.) In general, you'll have your choice between a mountain bike (with or without suspension) and a hybrid bike, which is a cross between a mountain and road bike. Hybrid bikes, with their more-upright positioning, tend to be better suited for casual, sightseeing rides. Mountain bikes do fine on paved roads, and, likewise, hybrid bikes handle most unpaved roads and paths with ease. Regardless of what type of bike you own or rent, be sure to wear a helmet. Most bike rentals include the use of a helmet in the rate.

Paddling presents the best waterways in each destination for flatwater, quickwater, and whitewater action. Whether you wish to meditate while gliding silently across a mountain pond or scream from primal fear while paddling frantically through frothy, ferocious rapids—you'll find options for each. This section lists businesses that rent canoes, kayaks, and sea kayaks, as well as outfitters that run one-stop river-running operations, including guide and shuttle services. If a river's flow depends upon dam releases, you'll find the appropriate contact phone numbers to call for release information. In general, spring is the best time for whitewater action in the Carolinas & Georgia.

A beautiful summer day feels incomplete if you fail to take a dip in a refreshing lake, stream, or river. Under **Swimming**, you'll find directions to the best swimming holes each region has to offer. If the storm clouds are out and you need your workout fix, **Rainy Day Workout** lists area gyms and health clubs that offer day passes for a reasonable fee. Sections like **Fly Fishing**, **Horseback Riding**, **Sailing**, **Scuba Diving**, and **Rock Climbing** appear in chapters where these activities are accessible to the general public. These sections provide everything you need—names, addresses, websites, and phone numbers of the outfitters—to help you plan such an adventure on your vacation.

While snow-cover in the southern Appalachian Mountains is never a sure thing, the region's ski resorts are proficient in making snow and typically operate from Thanksgiving until late March, cold-weather permitting. **Downhill Skiing** gives you the lowdown on the alpine ski areas, including everything from the percentage of beginner, intermediate, and expert trails to the number of chairlifts waiting to whisk you to the top. In a of couple chapters, **Cross-country Skiing & Snowshoeing** suggests backcountry terrain for you to explore on public land.

Wide Open ends with **Local Outdoor Advice**, a compilation of the best sources for current trail or river conditions. These are most often outdoor retailers, staffed by friendly folks who spend time hiking, biking, paddling, and skiing the area. Learning of any recent developments ahead of time will help you avoid the disappointment of driving to a trailhead only to learn that it's closed due to washouts or to protect nesting peregrine falcons.

Your legs, arms, and back will only go so far before it's time to slow the pace and **Kick Back**. This section details all of the more relaxing excursions available in each destination, from antiquing to zooming along the backcountry roads in your car. Here you'll find mention of each area's historic sites, museums, spas, wineries, microbreweries, cool movie houses, interesting shops and boutiques, as well as cultural outlets, including summer theater, music festivals, opera houses, and art galleries. The diversions are a mix of the quintessential, when-in-Rome-type activities with the more-eclectic diversions known primarily to the locals.

Rest Easy

Resting easy is all about dining and sleeping well. **Sleep Well** presents a select group of recommended country inns, hotels, and B&Bs in each area. (We selected these properties; no fees were accepted for inclusion.) This section is not meant to be an exhaustive list of all the lodging options in the area; rather, it's limited to upscale properties with extensive experience hosting active travelers. Innkeepers who regularly welcome hikers, mountain bikers, and skiers will serve as an additional resource for you in finding secluded swimming holes and hidden trails. Wondering what the difference is between a B&B and country inn? Technically, a country inn is supposed to have a restaurant onsite that serves dinner; however, this distinction is fading, and you'll find plenty of properties called "country inns" that serve only breakfast. Except where noted (primarily in the larger hotels), breakfast is included in the rates of nearly every property listed in this book.

You'll find brief descriptions of the property, including any unique architectural details; mentions of amenities like a pool, a sauna, or bikes available for guest use; the number of rooms; whether or not there are any shared baths; and the quality of breakfast. Be sure to call ahead or use the property's website to make reservations well in advance to avoid disappointment. Note that many smaller properties require a two-night minimum stay on weekends and during the high seasons (generally during foliage, winter ski season, and summer).

In **Dine Well**, you'll find descriptions of a handful of restaurants in each destination representing a variety of cuisine. In general, these restaurants are upscale in service and quality of food but few require jacket and tie. Many serve only dinner. Two other sections fall under *Dine Well*. **Cafés & Picnic Packing** provides suggestions for casual lunch spots or gourmet delis where you can pick up a filling picnic to tote on a hike, bike ride, or paddling excursion. If you've exercised a good bit on your vacation (and even if you haven't), you're entitled to your **Just Desserts**. You'll have little trouble finding the region's sweet spots from the ice cream shops and candy stores mentioned under this section.

Long Weekend Itineraries & Additional Information

Following *Kick Back*, you'll find either one or two recommended itineraries for a long weekend. (There are two itineraries for the chapters that cover a larger area.) The itineraries provide suggestions on how you might fill a typical long-weekend vacation, assuming you arrive late on Thursday night and leave mid day Sunday to return home. Finally, each chapter ends with a list of the primary sources for additional travel information, including chambers of commerce and tourism bureaus.

How to Use This Book

This book is designed to be the only guide you'll need to plan an active vacation. Start with the introductions to each chapter to determine which destination you'd like to visit and during what season. Turn next to accommodations and visit each property's website to see pictures of rooms, check availability, and learn if the inn offers special Internet rates. Book your reservations as far in advance as possible to secure availability and ask for the best room. Type-A travelers, you may wish to use the book and all of the listed websites to plan the perfect vacation right up until departure. Type-B travelers, you can feel safe throwing the book in your bag the night before leaving to plan your activities on the fly. Either way, be sure to bring this book! Share with the innkeepers, restaurateurs, and retailers how you learned about their business since we'll be traveling ahead of you promoting the book and asking if they'll reward Play Hard Rest Easy readers with special attention.

Travel is a unique experience, and while you can use this book to help you make every right or left turn, I hope you'll be ready to put the book away at a moment's notice to wander down an inviting road not mentioned in these pages. (But not a *private* road, of course.) Use this book as you would any guidebook—as a guide and not a tether. Travel is intensely personal and rewarding, especially when you discover something for the first time, something no one told you to expect. Be safe, have fun, and drop us a line to tell us how your vacation went. Write to *comments@walkaboutpress.com*.

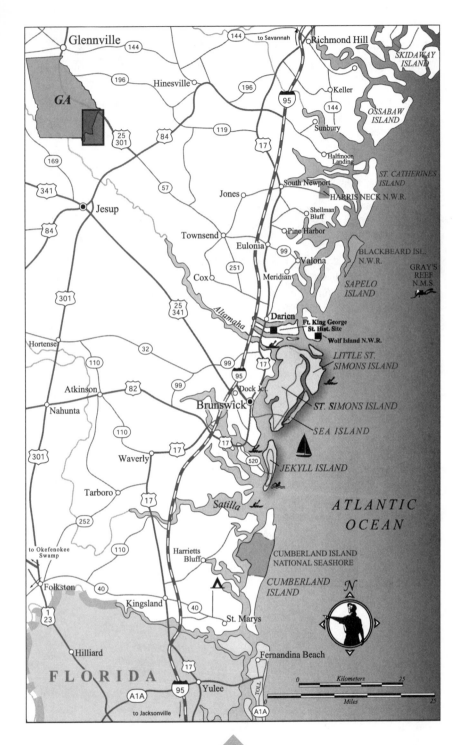

Glennville
144 to Savannah
Richmond Hill
SKIDAWAY
ISLAND
GA
144
196
Hinesville
196
95
Keller
144
OSSABAW
ISLAND
25
301
84
119
17
Sunbury
169
57
Halfmoon
Landing
ST. CATHERINES
ISLAND
341
Jesup
Jones
South Newport
HARRIS NECK N.W.R.
84
Shellman
Bluff
Townsend
Pine Harbor
BLACKBEARD ISL.
N.W.R.
Eulonia
99
Valona
GRAY'S
REEF
N.M.S.
251
Meridian
Cox
SAPELO
ISLAND
301
25
341
Altamaha
Darien
Ft. King George
St. Hist. Site
Wolf Island N.W.R.
Hortense
32
LITTLE ST.
SIMONS ISLAND
110
99
95
17
Atkinson
82
99
Dock Jct.
Nahunta
Brunswick
ST. SIMONS ISLAND
110
SEA ISLAND
301
17
520
JEKYLL ISLAND
Waverly
Tarboro
17
Satilla
ATLANTIC
OCEAN
252
to Okefenokee
Swamp
110
Harrietts
Bluff
CUMBERLAND ISLAND
NATIONAL SEASHORE
Folkston
40
CUMBERLAND
ISLAND
N
Kingsland
40
1
23
St. Marys
Hilliard
Fernandina Beach
FLORIDA
17
95
Yulee
TOLL
Kilometers
25
A1A
0
Miles
25
to Jacksonville
A1A

Brunswick and the Golden Isles, Georgia

Including St. Simons Island, Little St. Simons Island, Sea Island, and Jekyll Island

G eorgia's coastal mainland is low, flat, and rippled by creeks and rivers that wander toward the Atlantic through hardy vegetation, swamps, and fertile plains. As the land approaches the sea it gives way to marsh, where fresh and salt water mix with soil and river-delivered nutrients to produce a fertile nursing ground for hundreds of ocean-bound species, including shrimp, sharks, and loggerhead turtles. Waist-high marsh grass—green in the summer and golden in the fall—crowns the broad estuaries that separate the mainland from the gems of the state's tourism industry—the barrier islands.

Relative to its immediate neighbors—Florida to the south and South Carolina to the north—Georgia claims only a modest amount of Atlantic coastline, a mere 100 miles. But along this stretch are 12 of the most-pristine barrier islands found on the Eastern seaboard. Forming the state's eastern-most land boundary, these barrier islands greet and beat the Atlantic swells into submission, sending the ocean's subdued flow around them into harbors, coastal marshes, tidal creeks, and sounds. The islands are geological upstarts. Geologists believe they range in age from 3,000 to 30,000 years old, making them mere toddlers compared to the mainland.

George Gardner © Little St. Simons Island

Little St. Simons is a fraction of the mainland's age

7

Despite their youth, Georgia's barrier islands have a long, exciting settlement history, beginning with Native Americans, whom historians think settled here as many as 11,000 years ago. The coastal region was prime grounds for hunting, fishing, and farming and supported dozens of agrarian chiefdoms. Native American tribes included the Muskogee, Guale, and Mocama, all of whom belonged to the powerful Creek Nation. Soon after Christopher Columbus' 1492 Bahamian landfall, Spanish ships began exploring the Florida and Georga coasts, and by the 1520s, the Spaniards were regularly raiding the indigenous tribes, abducting natives to serve as slave labor. By the mid 16th Century, Spanish colonial and missionary settlements dotted the coastlines of Florida and Georgia; French and British colonists followed soon after.

However valiantly the Native Americans fought slave hunters or humored the Christian missionaries, their ultimate undoing were European-borne diseases, against which they had no natural defense. After thousands of years of settlement, it took less than 200 years from the arrival of the Europeans for 95% of the indigenous population to disappear. The majority perished from illness.

Brunswick-Golden Isles CVB

Situated along a valuable trade route between the Caribbean islands and Europe, Georgia's coast was a logical place to build forts to protect shipping interests. The race was on to lay claim to the New World, and the 18th Century saw much fighting among the Spanish, French, and British for control of the land. The see-sawing of ownership continued until American patriots beat the English in the Revolutionary

Established on St. Simons in 1736, Fort Frederica was built to protect Savannah from the Spanish forces at St. Augustine

War and named Georgia one of the 13 original states. The ensuing calm began a prosperous period in Georgia's coastal history. The rise of the plantation economy generated great wealth for the region's white land and slave owners, as area plantations produced rice, sugar, cotton, and indigo for sale in the larger Eastern U.S. cities and for export to Europe.

Plantation society crumbled after the Civil War, and it was another 30 years before the region saw the flicker of economic activity return. In the late 19th Century, the nation's wealthiest families—including the Rockefellers, Astors, and Pulitzers—"discovered" the region and formed the Jekyll Island Club, an ultra-exclusive, winter hunting club on Jekyll Island. It was the start of the resort era.

This highly social, wealthy tribe was nomadic, spending spring and fall in New York City and Philadelphia; summer in Newport, Bar Harbor, and the Berkshires; and winter on Jekyll Island. They built mansions, humbly called "cottages," and brought their butlers, maids, and chefs to aid in their enjoyment of country life. The good times lasted until the Great Depression, after which the number of fabulously rich wintering on the coast declined steadily. During World War II, the government suggested vacating the islands to reduce the risk of Japanese or German attack by sea. The ultra-rich never returned in earnest, and in 1947, the State of Georgia purchased the island as public land.

During the past 50 years, families and couples seeking the ultimate beach vacation have been the economic mainstay for Georgia's barrier islands. While the population still swells from June through August with traditional sun seekers, vacationers are increasingly getting up from the beach towel to sample the area's more adventurous activities. Here the outdoor pursuits are as varied as the species of South and Central American birds passing through each season. You can spend your days exploring a primal swamp, mountain biking through thick coastal forests, or diving along a natural reef loaded with colorful

Once the world's most-exclusive club, the Jekyll Island Club is now a hotel

fish. Certainly, there are wide, golden beaches perfect for reading a spy thriller, but there are also serpentine tidal creeks inviting exploration by canoe or kayak.

When your energy wanes, plenty of laid-back diversions await, from touring the back roads and photographing giant, live oak trees with shawls of Spanish moss to visiting historic forts and learning the story of the five nations that vied for ownership of the land. Why else should you visit? Shopping opportunities that will impress the pros, dining options from beach burger shacks to restaurants serving gourmet cuisine, and lodging choices from rustic cabins to historic plantations-turned-five-star resorts. Ultimately, whatever you do on your vacation, you're never far from the area's most-prominent feature: the Atlantic Ocean and her mesmerizing, meditative sight, sound, and smell.

The Way Around

Situated mid-way between Savannah and Jacksonville, FL, **Brunswick** is the commercial center for and gateway to the Golden Isles. The town straddles a small peninsula with a sheltered seaport on its western side. You'll encounter Brunswick shortly after exiting Interstate 95 at Exit #38, but rest assured that the long stretch of motels, gas stations, strip shopping centers, and fast food restaurants is not the Brunswick you'll be visiting. These "Anywhere, USA" accoutrements make up the town's commercial district, but not its soul. Venture off Route 17 by following the signs to the historic district and you'll find a much more-appealing scene. **Old Town Brunswick** is a National Historic District, comfortably nestled away from the bustle of the interstate and its unattractive access roads. (An alter-

Brunswick-Golden Isles CVB

Shrimp boats in port in Brunswick

native route into Historic Brunswick is to take Exit #36A off Interstate 95 and follow Route 341 south, which becomes Newcastle Street.)

An ideal walking destination, Brunswick's historic district features a waterfront park, wide, shaded streets, gorgeous old oak trees—including Lover's Oak, a legendary behemoth said to be 900 years old—and a bustling harbor with an armada of ocean-going vessels. Shrimp boats comprise much of the fleet. Brunswick is the home port for most of the ever-present shrimp boats trawling off the beaches of the Golden Isles. The historic portion of Brunswick also features numerous attractive Victorian buildings lining town squares, as well as grand residential homes and dozens of antiques dealers, shops, and restaurants.

Directly east of Brunswick, the **Marshes of Glynn** separate the mainland from the barrier islands. Immortalized by poet Sidney Lanier in the 1878 poem "The Marshes of Glynn," the vast coastal marshes stretch to the horizon, broken only by the greenery of the barrier islands in the distance. Prepare yourself for a few visual blots on the scene: A pulp mill spews acrid smoke into the air at the causeway to St. Simons, and a massive, concrete bridge farther south on Route 17 arches high above the St. Simons Sound.

Ye marshes, how candid and simple and nothing-withholding and free
Ye publish yourselves to the sky and offer yourselves to the sea!

– Sidney Lanier, The Marshes of Glynn

A cluster of four barrier islands comprise the **Golden Isles:** St. Simons Island, Little St. Simons Island, Jekyll Island, and Sea Island.

From Brunswick, off Route 17, the **F.J. Torras Causeway** connects St. Simons Island to the mainland. At roughly 12,000 acres, **St. Simons Island** is the largest of the Golden Isles, comparable to the island of Manhattan. There's plenty of room to spread out: With fewer than 20,000 residents, St. Simons has only three percent of the total residential population of Manhattan.

Home to many of the area's historic sites, including pre-Revolutionary War forts and battlefields, antebellum plantations, and a 19th-century lighthouse, St. Simons features plenty of tourist draws. In addition, there are first-class resorts, inns, restaurants, golf courses, upscale boutiques, and a small jetport. The island has its blemishes. Small strip shopping centers, subdivisions, and condominium complexes are common, especially on the southern, more-commercial end of the island, known as **the Village**. Here you'll find surf shops, cheap eats, nightspots, and the public pier. The northern end of St. Simons, once the site of several large antebellum plantations, is more residential and slower-paced,

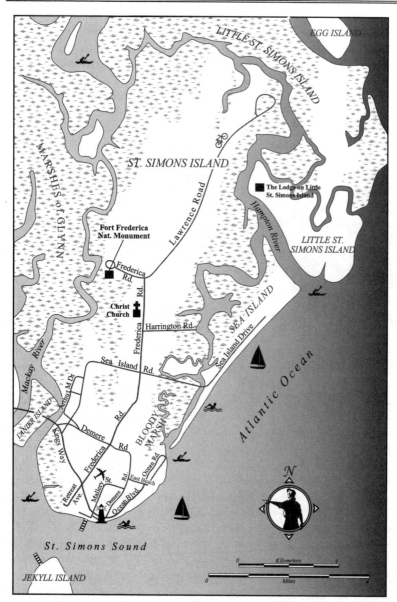

St. Simons, Little St. Simons, Sea Island

though commercial development is slowly encroaching north.

Sea Island shelters much of St. Simons' east coast from the sea, but there are several miles of public beach along the southeast tip of the island, off **Ocean Boulevard.** The major roadways on the island include **Kings Way,** which departs south (right) at the island's first traffic intersection from the Torras Causeway and leads to the Village. From that same intersection, **Sea Island Road** is on the left and travels north before turning east, bisecting the island, and becoming the short causeway to Sea Island. **Frederica Road** is the primary north-south blacktop, running from the Village through the middle of the island to the historic attractions Christ Church and Fort Frederica. The northern portion of the island is primarily residential but there remain numerous historic markers noting the grand plantations that once thrived here. **Lawrence Road** bears right off Frederica Road before reaching Christ Church and continuing to the northern tip of the island where the Hampton River Club Marina and the launch to Little St. Simons Island are located.

Brunswick-Golden Isles CVB

The Cloister's 1928 entrance is being replaced with a new building

Sea Island, located due east of the middle of St. Simons Island, is largely residential and also home to The Cloister, an exclusive and historic resort. **Sea Island Drive,** which is the name for Sea Island Road after it crosses the causeway, runs straight through the middle of the island, passing The Cloister and then row after row of stubby residential streets ending at either the sound (to the left) or Atlantic Ocean (to the right). In addition to numeric names (1st, 2nd, 3rd streets, etc.), many streets bear names of famous Spaniards, Native Americans, Revolutionary heroes, and seafaring pirates who played roles in local history. Gorgeous live oaks twist and turn along Sea Island Drive, creating a thick canopy above the road, sidewalks, and gracious homes—not one of which has sold for less than a million since 1999. In fact, Sea Island recently was ranked as the sixth-richest community in the United States by *Worth* magazine.

Sea Island is the smallest of the Golden Isles, but it looms large in its guest list of visiting dignitaries. The Cloister opened in 1928, founded by Ohio auto magnate Howard Coffin, and quickly developed a reputation as one of the world's great resorts. Past guests include Jimmy Carter, Woodrow Wilson, Calvin Coolidge, Somerset Maugham, Hopalong Cassidy, Carol Burnett, and Jimmy Stewart. In June, 2004, the resort held the G8 Summit of leaders from the world's major industrial democracies. President George W. Bush hosted the event. The resort is currently undergoing a five-year improvement plan, involving replacing the original, Addison Mizner-designed main hotel with a similarly designed facility.

© Little St. Simons Island

Tom Vargo

An egret on Little St. Simons

Accessible only by boat, **Little St. Simons Island** is situated along the northeastern tip of St. Simons Island. The island is a private retreat (see *Rest Easy*), and the resort limits overnight guests to just 30. At various times during the year, the public is welcome for the day to visit the island's 10,000 acres of wild beauty, including seven miles of beach. Originally part of the Hampton Rice Plantation on St. Simons, Little St. Simons remained untouched between the collapse of the Southern plantation economy and the island's purchase by the Eagle Pencil Company in 1908. The company planned to harvest the island's trees to manufacture pencils, but Eagle's owner decided instead to turn the island into a private retreat for family and friends. In 1979, the resort opened to the public. Except for the resort's rustic but refined buildings, Little St. Simons is not developed. It remains a natural habitat for dozens of animal species, including subtropical birds, deer, waterfowl, and alligators.

From Brunswick, if you continue south on Route 17, you'll cross the bridge over St. Simons Sound and arrive at the causeway entrance to **Jekyll Island,** the southernmost of the Golden Isles, located directly below St. Simons Island. Access Jekyll Island by driving the six-mile **Downing Musgrove Causeway** over marsh and mud flats to the island. (A toll booth at the island's entrance charges $3 per car.) Owned by the State of Georgia and protected by legislation limiting commercial development, this nine-mile-long by 1.5-mile-wide island features marshes, maritime forests of pine, palm, and twisted, live-oak trees, and a pristine public beach.

Jekyll was originally home to the Mocama Indians before the Spanish occupied the island in 1566 and named it Isla de Ballenas, or "whale island." (The Atlantic Ocean around Jekyll contained—and contains—vital breeding grounds for the right whale, a species nearly extinct today.) The British arrived 70 years later and rechristened the island Jekyll after a benefactor of General James Oglethorpe. At the end of the 18th Century, a French family purchased the island and held it until 1886, when the founding members of the Jekyll Island Club purchased it for $125,000.

Jekyll Island became an important part of the American social scene from the late 1880s through the 1920s, serving as the

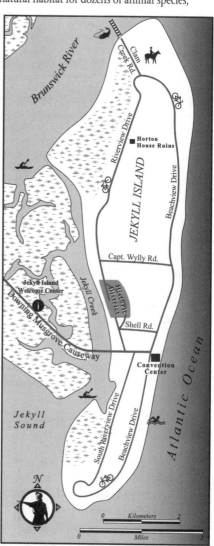

Jekyll Island

Where's the beach?

Beach erosion along portions of Sea, Jekyll, and St. Simons islands' coastlines makes passage by foot at high tide impossible. The incessant winds and tides shape the barrier islands, but no element is as instrumental in eroding the beaches as the ocean currents. Flowing north-to-south, Atlantic Ocean currents take sand from the mainland coast and the barrier  islands' eastern sides and deposit it elsewhere. On an undeveloped island, you'd be hard pressed to notice this natural give and take, but on islands with beachfront property, the erosion is hard to miss. Each year, the sea gets closer to the front porch. Many beach communities and resorts put a great deal of money and effort into replenishing their sand by dredging the ocean floor—which typically hastens beach erosion further south—but the re-nourishment works only long enough for a beach volleyball game or two, measured in geologic time. Ultimately, the Atlantic gets what the Atlantic wants.

winter vacation site for the nation's wealthiest families. In 1947, Georgia took possession of the island, offering a settlement to the remaining members of the Jekyll Island Club.

Today the island has golf courses, parks, picnic grounds, 10 hotels, residential areas, and a 240-acre National Historic District, located around the original, Queen Anne-style Jekyll Island Club building. Sixty-five percent of the island's 5,000 acres will remain a nature preserve forever. The roads, **Riverview** and **South Riverview drives**, skirt the western side of the island, while **Beachview Drive** runs the length of the eastern side facing the Atlantic. Together, the roads form a loop around Jekyll Island.

Weather

You can play hard outdoors in the Golden Isles all year long, thanks to a climate that produces short, mild winters with average temperatures in the mid 50s. Spring arrives around the first of March and warms steadily toward summer, which essentially lasts into October when average highs remain in the 70s. July, August, and September can be hot, with stretches in the upper 90s, but ocean breezes help sweep away any unpleasantness. Fall is perhaps the most-brilliant time to visit. Clear days with low humidity make the golden hue of the marsh grass appear all the more vivid.

Getting to Brunswick

By Air: Savannah International Airport, ☎ (912) 964-0514, *www.savannahairport.com*, is 75 miles north of Brunswick and **Jacksonville International Airport**, (904) 741-2723, *www.jaxairports.org*, is 60 miles south of Brunswick. Both airports host numerous airline carriers, ground transportation, and car rental services. Brunswick's **Glynco Jetport,** 1-800-235-0859 or (912) 265-2070, offers regular service by Atlantic Southeast Airlines (ASA/Delta Connection) out of Atlanta. Several national car rental companies are onsite.

By Car: From Atlanta, take Interstate 75 south to Interstate 16 east to Interstate 95 south, which you follow roughly 60 miles south of Savannah to Exit #38. From Exit #38, follow the Golden Isles Parkway east four miles before merging right onto Route 17 south. The drive should take about five hours. **From Charlotte**, take Interstate 77 south to Columbia, then Interstate 26 east to Interstate 95, which you follow south 60 miles past Savannah. Take Exit #38 and follow the Golden Isles Parkway east four miles before merging right onto Route 17 south. Expect a five-hour drive. **From Raleigh,** take Interstate 40 east to Interstate 95 south, which you follow to Exit #38 as explained above. Expect a six- to seven-hour drive.

Roll on, thou deep and dark blue
Ocean – roll!
Ten thousand fleet sweep over thee in vain;
Man marks the earth with ruin – his control
Stops with the shore

– Lord Byron, Childe Harold's Pilgramage

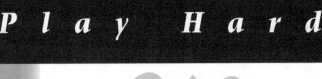

Wide Open

The Golden Isles region packs plenty of playgrounds for the outdoor adventurer, and the short, mild winters mean the action goes year-round. Hundreds of miles of inland and ocean-front shoreline make water sports—paddling, swimming, and fishing—king in these parts but expect regular insurrections from the unruly land subjects, including hiking, cycling, and horseback riding. The following are the region's major, multi-sport outdoor areas.

Sixty-five percent of **Jekyll Island's** 5,000 acres is protected, thanks to state legislation passed in 1950 designating much of the island a public nature preserve. There are 10 miles of beach, more than 20 miles of bike and walking paths beside the beach, marsh, and through maritime forest, as well as plenty of places to rent equipment for the sport of your choice.

St. Simons Island has several small public parks, but the biggest outdoor draw is its shoreline, including four miles of public beach on the southern end of the island. St. Simons is the most commercial of the islands and hosts a gaggle of adventure tour operators for horseback riding, fishing, sea kayaking, sailing, and diving. **Sea Island** and **Little St. Simons Island** have no public land, but if you're a guest of either The Cloister or the Lodge on Little St. Simons, the number of adventurous activities open to you is extensive.

Other multi-sport playgrounds in the region include **Cumberland Island,** (912) 882-4335 or 1-888-817-3421, *www.nps.gov/cuis/index.htm*, the largest and southernmost of Georgia's barrier islands, accessible only by ferry from the port village St. Marys, roughly one hour south of Brunswick. The 17.5-mile-long island covers more than 36,000 acres, of which roughly 17,000 acres are marsh, mud flats, and tidal creeks. Best of all, there are 17 miles of secluded, white-sand beaches. Cumberland Island is a federally protected National Seashore—the island will never be developed beyond its current state. Everywhere you look, there exists an amazing variety of wildlife. Reservations are required to visit Cumberland. Call the numbers listed above for more information.

Throughout the various *Wide Open* and *Kick Back* sections you'll find information about several more **barrier islands** that are easy daytrips from the Golden Isles. All of these islands offer multi-sport adventures for the active traveler but require advance reservations before visiting. ◆ About an hour's drive north from Brunswick, you can catch a ferry from the small town of Meridian to **Sapelo Island,** (912) 437-3224, a 10-mile-long by four-mile-wide spit of land accessible only by boat.

Tidal creeks and marshes off Sea Island

Just off the northeastern shores of Sapelo and accessible by boat, **Blackbeard Island National Wildlife Refuge,** (912) 652-4415, has 5,618 acres of maritime forest, salt marsh, freshwater marsh, and five miles of beach. The undeveloped island also has 3,000 acres designated as a National Wilderness Area. Named for the treacherous pirate, the island is believed to be one of the sites where Blackbeard anchored his boat. Rumors linger that he buried treasure here. Bring a shovel.

Situated on a mainland peninsula, the **Harris Neck National Wildlife Refuge,** Harris Neck Road, South Newport, (912) 652-4415, consists of more than 2,700 acres of woodland, saltwater marsh, grassland, and freshwater ponds spread over land that once served as the Harris Neck Army Airfield. The airfield shut down in 1944; little remains except concrete runways and several miles of paved roads. The site is excellent for boating, biking, hiking, and watching wildlife. The place teems with birds, animals, and reptiles, including endangered wood storks, peregrine falcons, bald eagles, and American alligators.

The **Okefenokee Swamp,** (912) 496-7836, *http://okefenokee.fws.gov*, is a vast wetland covering nearly 400,000 acres and is just more than an hour's drive west from Brunswick.

Designated a National Wildlife Refuge in 1937, the freshwater **Okefenokee Swamp** is a paddler's dream, with rivers, lakes, and winding canals. Here you'll pass moss-draped Cyprus trees and alligators so large and motionless you'll question whether they're real. (They are.) "Okefenokee" translates from Seminole to "land of the trembling earth," which refers to areas within the swamp's 700 square miles where you can jump and watch the earth, including the surrounding bushes and trees, rattle. In these places, deep layers of peat moss form the "ground," providing a soft cushion and resulting shockwave of instability.

The Okefenokee is open daily from a half-hour before sunrise to 5:30 P.M., November–February, and from a half-hour before sunrise to 7:30 P.M., the remainder of the year. Visitors may access the swamp at two major entrances within a reasonable drive from Brunswick. The **East Entrance,** located southwest of Folkston off Route 23/121, is the headquarters for the Okefenokee National Wildlife Refuge and features a large visitor center with educational displays. This entrance provides access to hiking trails, a swamp boardwalk, and two observation towers. You'll find numerous amenities, including bicycle rentals, at the East Entrance.

The **North Entrance** is located off Route 1 west of Waycross, but you must go through the **Okefenokee Swamp Park,** Route 1 South, Waycross, (912) 283-0583, *www.okeswamp.com,* a private, nonprofit attraction that charges a nominal admission fee. In exchange, there are numerous educational lectures and exhibits, animal habitats, a boardwalk, observation tower, and access to boat tours. Finally, the **Kingfisher Landing,** off Route 1 between Waycross and Folkston, provides access to the swamp and has a boat ramp and public parking.

What's bugging you?

Mosquitoes, horseflies, and sand gnats, that's what. It's a small problem, really, in the overall scheme of things, but no guidebook worth its salt should send you down to the Golden Isles without fair warning: In the spring, summer, and fall, biting bugs await. Your best defense? Liberal amounts of bug repellant with a healthy percentage (30 percent-plus) of DEET.

Dayhiking

The elevation changes little on the Golden Isles and Georgia's coastal plain—it's all nearly sea level—so exploration on foot means *walking* on trails rather than *hiking.* But don't let the lack of hills let you think you won't get a workout. Walking several miles on a beach provides outstanding exercise. Sand gives way underfoot and works more muscles in your legs than walking on a firm surface. In addition to many miles of public beach on the islands, there are trails and paths throughout the region.

St. Simons Island

◆ You can access **East Beach** on St. Simons Island from **Massengale Park,** off Ocean Boulevard on the southern tip of the island near the Coast Guard Station. Massengale is a popular public park and the beach tends to be crowded, but the throng thins the farther north you walk. In total, there are about four miles of beach on the island, all of which are on the southern end. If want to see it all, start your walk during a retreating tide. At high tide, the ocean swallows the beach whole in places, especially south of the King & Prince Resort on Arnold Street. Another benefit to walking at low tide: The sand is more firm at water's edge.

♦ The **St. Simons bike path** is a scenic asphalt path around the island, popular with cyclists, in-line skaters, and strollers alike. Winding under gorgeous, moss-draped live oaks, beside meditative beach and marsh scenes, and through the hubbub of the Village, this paved route stretches roughly 12.5 miles past the island's historic sites and landmarks, including Fort Frederica, Christ Church, the Bloody Marsh Historic Site, and the St. Simons Lighthouse. In places, the path starts and stops without clear direction, but any island map will keep you on track.

A couple of route ideas: From Retreat Village Shopping Center at the intersection of Demere and Frederica roads, follow the path north along the side of Frederica Road to its intersection with Lawrence Road. Follow Frederica to the left to explore Christ Church and Fort Frederica, and then return to Lawrence Road. Continue north on Lawrence to Hampton Point Drive, which forms a loop with Nevins Street, McBride Street, and Butler Lake Drive around the northern tip of the island before returning to Lawrence Road. Return south to the Village on Frederica Road.

♦ To tour the southern end of the island, you'd do well to pick up a map from any of the sources listed under *Additional Information* because there are many more streets than on the island's north end. An easy stroll (less than a mile) is along Retreat Avenue and the famed **Avenue of Oaks.** Park at the Retreat Village Shopping Center and follow Frederica Road south from the Retreat Village Shopping Center past the airport to the intersection with Retreat Avenue (the entrance to Sea Island Golf Club) straight ahead. Walk through

Tom Moran ©Little St. Simons Island

Walking the beach on Little St. Simons

the entrance and down beside the massive live oaks. Turn around at the gated entrance to Retreat Plantation and retrace your steps to the car. ◆ To get a feel for the varied boutiques open in the Village, stroll **Mallory Street** and then turn right onto **Beachview Drive** to pass the island's pier and lighthouse.

Sea Island

◆ The **Sea Island sidewalk**, which stretches from 1st Street at The Cloister to 36th Street and parallels Sea Island Drive, provides an outstanding, five-mile roundtrip walk beneath a canopy of live oaks and past elegant homes and gardens. Starting from the southern end of Sea Island, you pass The Cloister and then streets named for prominent historical figures, including buccaneers, Native Americans, and colonial Spanish, French, and British settlers. Examples of street names include Guale, DeSoto, Agramont, Teach (Blackbeard), Oglethorpe, and Rutledge. If you start your walk on St. Simons across the causeway and make it to the end of Sea Island Drive and back, you're looking at nearly a nine-mile walk.

Jekyll Island

◆ Some of the finest walks in the area are on **Jekyll Island,** where you can follow 22 miles of paved bicycle paths or stroll the 10 miles of sand beach. There's a nominal parking fee ($3 per car) to access the island, but once you've arrived, well...you've *arrived.* After passing the toll complex, continue straight to the end of the causeway road and head for the massive parking lot beside the convention center. The paved path and the beach are straight ahead. You can wander the beach in either direction, though at high tide, you'll find places where the beach disappears. (Carry or wear a pair of shoes or flip-flops to protect your feet from hot asphalt when you have to leave the beach.) The bicycle path passes through maritime forest, beside marshes and sand dunes, along rivers and the Atlantic Ocean, and through the 230-acre **National Historic District,** located around the Jekyll Island Club Hotel and surrounding cottages.

Life's a Beach

One of the majestic features of the Golden Isles is the wildlife you'll encounter along the area's beaches and walking paths. From the famous loggerhead turtles to the hundreds of species of brightly colored, unusual-looking birds, wildlife co-exists in a delicate relationship with humans. Do your part to protect this relationship by observing a few courtesies. First, **keep off of the sand dunes.** In addition to protecting the land from the sea, sand dunes are home to nesting birds and turtles. Second, **don't disturb resting birds.** Running or riding a bike through a flock of birds resting on the beach interrupts these creatures' valuable downtime. Proper rest gives them the energy to find food. Third, **lights out on the beach during turtle nesting season.** Starting in May, sea turtle hatchlings begin to make their way from nests in the dunes to the ocean. Artificial lights at night can disorient the baby turtles, leading them astray. Finally, **don't litter.** Trash can obstruct turtle paths and choke birds.

Cumberland Island

♦ Accessible only by boat, **Cumberland Island** is reached by driving an hour south on Route 17 to St. Marys, where the ferry departs for this large, pristine barrier island. Sixteen miles long and delightfully untouched by commercial interests, Cumberland Island features many miles of well-marked and maintained footpaths through the live-oak and pine tree-covered interior. The island also has more than 17 miles of beach. For a map, ferry information, and reservations to visit the island, contact the National Park Service in St. Marys, (912) 882-4335.

George Gardner ©Little St. Simons Island

Hiker in a maritime forest

Sapelo Island

♦ **Sapelo Island** is another walking destination about an hour's drive from Brunswick and accessible only by boat. (The ferry departs from Meridian, located off Route 17 north of Brunswick.) Roughly 10 miles long and four miles wide, Sapelo is the state's fourth largest barrier island. It features pristine natural settings, abundant wildlife, and a settlement history dating back more than 4,000 years.

The island is home to the Hog Hammock community, a group of approximately 60 descendants of the more than 400 slaves who lived and worked on Thomas Spalding's early 19th-century plantation. Today's residents of Hog Hammock speak Geechee (a Creole language that mixes English with African languages) and continue many of the artistic, spiritual, and cultural traditions of their ancestors. Like Cumberland, reservations are required to visit the island. Once there, you're free to explore the beaches. To protect wildlife, the island's interior is off limits, unless you've secured permission from the Sapelo Visitor Center. For more information and reservations, call the Sapelo Visitor Center, (912) 437-3224.

Blackbeard Island

♦ Additional hiking exists in the **Blackbeard Island National Wildlife Refuge** on Blackbeard Island, an undeveloped barrier island that's accessible only by boat. It features five miles of pristine beach and miles of trails through the adjacent forest of live oaks and pine trees. Bicycles are also permitted on the island. For access information, call the Savannah Coastal Refuges Office at (912) 652-4415.

On the mainland

♦ The **Earth Day Nature Trail,** located off Route 17 in Brunswick just north of the Sidney Lanier Bridge at Georgia's Division of Natural Resources Headquarters, (912) 264-7218, is actually two short trails, both of which take less than a half hour each. These two paths are outstanding educational walks through coastal marsh. They present good chances of seeing exotic birds and marine life, especially if you walk them in the early morning or late afternoon. A colorful brochure is available at the outdoor orientation center adjacent to the trail. The brochure and several displays on the trails explain the formation of Georgia's coastal marshes and the role that they play to the myriad species dependent upon them for sustenance and for nesting grounds.

◆ The **East Entrance** to the **Okefenokee Swamp National Wildlife Refuge,** has two and a half miles of hiking trails, plus a 4,000-foot boardwalk that provides outstanding wildlife viewing options. Stop by the visitor center, located just a few miles southwest of Folkston off Route 23/121. To get there from Brunswick, follow Interstate 95 south to Exit #3. Take Route 40 west to Folkston, then Route 23/121 south to the swamp entrance.

Mountain & Road Biking

Georgia Department of Tourism

Bicycling is a popular way to explore the Golden Isles

"Mountain" biking it's not. With terrain spread like pancakes in every direction, the Golden Isles do not encompass anything even remotely resembling a hill. But after a little *altitude* adjustment, cyclists will be pleased with the great exercise they get by pedaling along the region's hard-packed beaches, asphalt bike paths, and less-traveled roads. If you want to pedal a mountain bike, bring your own; most bike rentals are for single-speed beach cruisers. (Benjy's Bike Shop rents a limited number of mountain bikes. See "Rentals.")

St. Simons Island

The 12.5-mile, asphalt **St. Simons bike path** winds across much of the island, including scenic stretches, where Spanish moss spreads across stately live oaks, and not-so-scenic parts, where strip shopping centers line up next to the Golden Arches. Finding your way is easy, but any bike rental facility will happily provide a complimentary map of St. Simons and the bicycle path. In general, the paved portions of the bike path extend along the major roads of Kings Way, Frederica and Demere roads, Mallory Street, and the East Beach Causeway. Most of the remaining island roads are fine to ride on the far right side of the road. For specific route suggestions, including a brief description of a ride you can make along **Sea Island Drive,** follow the routes described under *Dayhiking.*

Jekyll Island

◆ Bikes are the most-popular means of transportation on Jekyll due in part to the 20 miles of paved bicycling paths circling the island. Those accustomed to riding off-road will find they can leave the pavement behind to explore various dirt roads and paths cutting across the island's interior. It is impossible to get lost on Jekyll Island, but maps come with your rental, just in case. The best way to get started? Mount up and start exploring. In warm weather, you can hit the Atlantic for a swim on the island's eastern side. Ride along the **beach** at low tide, or follow the **bike path**, which skirts the beach at times and moves inland at others. Along the western half of the island, the path swerves beneath canopies of large live oaks and beside the marsh. It passes an old plantation graveyard, several ruins of homes made from tabby (a building material made from sand, lime, and shells), and through the historic district. On the northern end of the island, you can leave the path to check out the **Clam Creek Picnic Area,** a heavily shaded area that includes a covered, concrete fishing pier overlooking St. Simons Sound and the southern tip of St. Simons. If you're riding late in the day, you may want to plan a picnic dinner at the southern end of the island, where the bike path ends at **St. Andrews Picnic Area.** This is a great place to watch the sun set.

Blackbeard Island

♦ Rent a bike and arrange passage to the **Blackbeard Island National Wildlife Refuge** on Blackbeard Island, where more than 20 miles of narrow, dirt roads through forests of live oak, scrub pine, magnolia, and palmetto await. Bring a bathing suit and pick your own private parcel of beach paradise from which to cool off in the surf. For access information, call Savannah Coastal Refuges Office at (912) 652-4415.

On the mainland

♦ Riding the streets of **Old Town Brunswick** provides plenty of interesting sights and the opportunity to stop for refreshments in one of the town's many cafés. Ride along the

Cyclists ride beside the beach on Jekyll Island

waterfront on **Newcastle Street,** turn into town on **Gloucester Street,** and explore the historic district's grid-design of streets, as laid out by General James Oglethorpe in 1771. (Oglethorpe also designed Savannah's grid of streets and squares.) Pedal along freely; you can't get lost. If you ride late in the day, end your ride at **Mary Ross Waterfront Park** at the intersection of Gloucester and Newcastle streets to watch the sunset and the shrimp boats come in with their daily catches.

♦ Roughly 30 miles north of Brunswick, the **Harris Neck National Wildlife Refuge,** (912) 652-4415, has more than 15 miles of paved roads perfect for exploration by bike. To get there, take Interstate 95 north from Brunswick to Exit #67 (South Newport), then take Route 17 south one mile to Harris Neck Road (Route 131), which you follow east seven miles to the refuge. Open daily during daylight hours.

♦ In addition to the nine-mile-long **Swamp Island Drive** at the **East Entrance** to the **Okefenokee Swamp National Wildlife Refuge,** located south of Folkston off Route 23/121, cyclists can pedal miles of country roads surrounding the swamp for flat, easy-going exercise through the gorgeous coastal plain.

Bike Rentals

In addition to the following rental locations, many of the region's hotels and resorts rent or provide bicycles to guests. In general, rentals are single-speed beach cruisers, unless otherwise noted. **Benjy's Bike Shop,** 130 Retreat Plaza (Winn Dixie Shopping Center), St. Simons, ☎ (912) 638-6766, rents both single-speed beach cruisers and mountain bikes; ♦ **Ocean Motion**, has two St. Simons locations: 1300 Ocean Boulevard, ☎ (912) 638-5225 or 1-800-669-5215; and 210-212 Mallory Street, St. Simons, ☎ (912) 638-4749; ♦ **Monkeywrench Bicycles**, 1700 Frederica Road, ☎ (912) 634-5551, rents and sells bicycles, and operates bicycle tours; ♦ **Okefenokee Adventures**, Route 2 at the end of the East Entrance road to the Okefenokee National Wildlife Road, Folkston, ☎ (912) 496-7156 or 1-866-843-7926; ♦ **Okefenokee Pastimes**, Route 23/121 across from the East Entrance to the Okefenokee National Wildlife Refuge, Folkston, ☎ (912) 496-4472; ♦ **Jekyll Island Bicycle Rentals**, at the Mini Golf, Beachview Drive, Jekyll Island, ☎ (912) 635-2648, rents beach cruisers and three-wheel bikes.

Paddling

Whereas skis and mountain bikes are must-have toys in the Appalachian Mountains, sea kayaks are the main instruments-of-fun in the Golden Isles. Sleek, stable, and able to navigate in mere inches of water, a sea kayak is your passage to the open ocean, broad sounds, local rivers, and coastal marshes. It's here—paddling silently at water level, observing dolphins, shore and aquatic birds, and other wildlife—that you get a full sense of how extensive and dynamic the coastal ecosystem is.

◆ The body of water most paddlers hit first is the broad **Marshes of Glynn**, the coastal plain separating the Golden Isles from the mainland. Throughout, you'll find serpentine channels perfect for paddling. The **St. Simons and Jekyll sounds** are fine waterways to explore and likely spots to catch a dolphin at play. Give a wide berth to ocean-going boats.

Popular daytrips by sea kayak include pad- dling the coastal marshes to the **Cumberland, Sapelo,** and **Blackbeard barrier islands**. Most tour operators also offer overnight trips.

◆ Paddling out into the **Atlantic Ocean**—assuming it's relatively calm—pre- sents a challenge for the more-experienced sea kayaker due to the potential for high winds, riptides, and sudden storms. If you've never been in open water before, you'd do well to make your first venture with an experienced guide. Open-water paddling requires better boat handling skills and experience in self-rescue maneu- vers like the "wet exit." You might also explore renting a sit-on-top kayak for pad- dling in the surf.

Tricky Tides

Unless you know the local waters well, start with a tour offered by one of the local pad- dling outfitters. The water can be tricky. Tides in the Golden Isles rise faster and higher than anywhere else in the Southeast due to the area's location at the end of a giant seafloor funnel that pushes and pulls the water six to eight feet, on average. That means you can get caught paddling against swift currents that will slow and perhaps stall your progress. More importantly, you'll want to avoid being stranded on a riverbank, sand bar, or oyster bed. Most sea kayak outfitters offer introduc- tory lessons and tours for paddlers with all lev- els of experience.

◆ The Altamaha and Satilla rivers are ideal for exploration by canoe or sea kayak. The **Altamaha River** features more than 100 miles of protected river corridor from Tattnall County to where it meets the sea at the historic seaport town of Darien, just a half-hour north of Brunswick. The river has

Photo by Altamaha Coastal Tours

dozens of tributaries, including the **Ohoopee River** and **Beards Creek,** allowing for a dazzling array of pad- dling options. Unless you plan to camp upriver, the majority of your exploration will be in the tidal creeks and swamps surrounding the river's mouth. This area includes the **Lewis Island Natural Area**, a tidal swamp full of centuries-old cypress trees.

◆ Peaceful and sublime, the black- water **Satilla River** moves slowly through the coastal plain more

Paddling on Blackbeard Creek

than 250 miles to its mouth at St. Andrew Sound, just south of Jekyll Island. Numerous swamps feed into the river, creating water that is clear but dark burgundy in color. (The distinct "blackwater" hue is from tannin, an acid released from decaying vegetation.) The water's color contrasts sharply with the white sand bars that build on the inside of some of the bends in the river. The farther you paddle upstream, the more the tree canopy closes in, as the marsh vegetation gives way to the jungle-like growth of coastal swampland.

♦ About an hour west of Brunswick lies the largest swamp in the United States, the **Okefenokee**. The only way to see its primal bounty is to dip the oars and paddle in. With more than 100 miles of canoe trails lining nearly 400,000 acres of wetland, the Okefenokee is to paddlers what Moab is to peddlers. The variety of plant and animal species is overwhelming, and visitors typically find themselves frustrated trying to capture the sights in words. Indeed, the Okefenokee is something you have to experience.

Expect plenty of blackwater in both wide and narrow channels, forests of cypress trees, stands of thick vegetation, and open prairies where the crosswinds may push your bow every way but straight. You may see such wildlife as deer, bears, snakes, and more than 200 species of birds. Insects buzz, creep, and crawl everywhere. Alligators, some of which are longer than a canoe, are the top wildlife draw. (See "Them Lizards Got Teeth.")

You need not be an experienced canoeist or sea kayaker to set off into the swamp because there's no quickwater to negotiate. You should, however, consider your fitness level before paddling too far from the put-in. There's very little dry land in the swamp on which to rest, so conserve energy for the return trip. By the end of the day, you're going to feel the work in your arms, back, shoulders, and rump (from sitting). Entrance hours to the refuge are from a half hour before sunrise to 5:30 P.M., November–February, and from

Tour Operators & Canoe/Sea Kayak Rentals

Altamaha Coastal Tours, 229 Fort King George Road, Darien, ☎ (912) 437-6010, *www.altamaha.com*, is on the historic waterfront in Darien and rents sea kayaks and canoes, provides instruction, runs shuttles, and offers day and overnight tours. ♦ **Ocean Motion**, 1300 Ocean Boulevard, St. Simons, ☎ (912) 638-5225 or 1-800-669-5215; and 210-212 Mallory Street, St. Simons, ☎ (912) 638-4749; *www.oceanmotion.biz*, rents sea kayaks, conducts tours, and provides instruction. ♦ **Okefenokee Adventures**, Route 2 at the end of the East Entrance road to the Okefenokee National Wildlife Road, Folkston, ☎ (912) 496-7156 or 1-866-843-7926, *www.okefenokeeadventures.com*, rents canoes and sea kayaks for self-guided or guided tours of the swamp. ♦ **Okefenokee Pastimes**, Route 23/121 across from the East Entrance to the Okefenokee National Wildlife Refuge, Folkston, ☎ (912) 496-4472, *www.okefenokee.com/pastimes.htm*, rents canoes and sea kayaks and offers guided tours of the swamp. ♦ **Southeast Adventure Outfitter**s, 313 Mallory Street, St. Simons, ☎ (912) 638-6732; and 1200 Glynn Avenue (Route 17 South), Brunswick, (912) 265-5292; *www.southeastadventure.com*, rents and sells sea kayaks and canoes, provides instruction, and operates day and overnight tours.

Them Lizards Got Teeth!

Alligators have changed very little in the last 65 million years, so perhaps no sight in the Golden Isles region is as primitive as spying one of these living dinosaurs sunning itself on a creek bed or floating patiently along a tidal river. The name *alligator* comes from the Spanish word for lizard, El Legarto, but the size of the largest lizard pales in comparison to a good-sized alligator. (An adult alligator can grow to more than 20 feet and weigh as much as 500 pounds.) A federal ban on hunting alligators has brought the species back from near extinction, and today gators flourish throughout the area. A few things to keep in mind about these spectacular reptiles: Never feed, tease, or harass an alligator. Keep small children and pets away from the edges of bodies of water in which there are alligators. Finally, keep a safe distance from alligators. They may look sleepy and slow, but they are surprisingly quick, even on land. Especially when they're hungry.

Tom Vargo ©Little St. Simons Island

a half hour before sunrise to 7:30 P.M., the remainder of the year. The canoe and kayak rental sources provide trail maps; most also offer guided expeditions, which are good ways to get oriented to the vast swamp. In general, rental rates run $20 a day for canoes, and $25 a day for sea kayaks. Guided tours average $12 per adult for an hour, and $20 per adult for two hours.

Fishing

Combine spectacular scenery with the potential for landing a shark, tarpon, or barracuda and you've got the salt-water essence of deep sea fishing off Georgia's coast. Local marinas feature many Coast Guard-licensed captains with sea-worthy vessels ready to diesel you 30 miles or more to the middle of mako, mackerel, or marlin waters. Deep-sea trips take at least half a day (a full day for the really big fish), but the journey offshore is one you'll never forget. (Fail to bring sunscreen and Dramamine™, and the memory might not be so fond.) The deep-sea season runs May–October. You can shop prices at the marinas but expect to spend between $200 to $400 for two people for half-day trips and up to $600 for full-day trips. Several particularly reputable outfits include: ♦ **Coastal Expeditions,** 3202 East 3rd Street, Brunswick, (912) 265-0392, run by Captain Vernon Reynolds; ♦ **Ducky II Charters,** 105 Marina Drive, St. Simons, (912) 634-0312, *www.duckyiicharters.com*, run by Captain Greg Smith; and ♦ **Captain Mark Noble's Fishing Center,** Golden Isles Marina, 206 Marina Drive, St. Simons Island (912)

634-1219, *www.georgiafishing.net*, run by Captain Mark Noble. Many more charters operate from the region's marinas.

◆ Don't have your sea legs but still want the thrill of a tug on the line? Fishing along the **Intracoastal Waterway** or in the area's countless tidal creeks and rivers presents the opportunity to reel in a variety of fish, including trout, bass, flounder, and sheepshead. The state requires a fishing license, which you can pick up at most marinas, bait and tackle shops, and hardware stores.

Marinas

Deep-sea charters set out from all of the major area marinas, including **Hampton River Club Marina**, 1000 Hampton River Club Drive, ☎ (912) 638-1210; ◆ **Village Creek Landing**, 526 S Harrington Road, ☎ (912) 634-9054; and ◆ **Golden Isles Marina**, 206 Marina Drive, ☎ (912) 634-1128, all on St. Simons Island. On Jekyll Island, try ◆ **Jekyll Harbor Marina**, 1 Harbor Road, ☎ (912) 635-3137; and ◆ **Jekyll Wharf Marina**, 1 Pier Road, ☎ (912) 635-3152. In Brunswick, marinas include ◆ **Brunswick Landing Marina**, 2429 Newcastle Street, ☎ (912) 262-9264; ◆ **Credle's Complete Marine**, 1455 Highway 17 South, ☎ (912) 261-1935; and ◆ **Two-Way Fish Camp**, 1400 Darien Highway, ☎ (912) 265-0410.

◆ You can fish from several local piers, including the **Clam Creek Fishing Pier** on the northern end of Jekyll Island, the **Village Pier** on the southern end of St. Simons, as well as from any public bridge or public beach.

◆ Interested in fly fishing? Head to **Bedford Sportsman South,** 3405 Frederica Road, St. Simons, (912) 638-5454, *www.stsimonsoutfitters.com*, a full-service outdoor store and fly fishing outfitter. The store offers an in-house, Orvis-endorsed guide service, fly tying and casting instruction, and invites anglers to stop by for free information on the best places to cast.

Horseback Riding

If the view of a beach and the ocean from high atop a sturdy steed sounds appealing, plan to meet up with the folks from **Victoria's Carriages & Beach Trail Rides,** Visitor Center, Stable Road, Jekyll Island, (912) 635-9500. With more than 50 horses and morning, afternoon, and sunset trail rides available, Victoria's is the way to ride through the forest, beside the salt marsh, and along Jekyll Island's beach. Reservations are required for the trail rides, but you may be able to catch a last-minute seat on one of the narrated carriage tours of the island's historic district. The carriage tours highlight the island's history and include interesting anecdotes about the wealthy, seasonal residents that once made Jekyll the most-exlusive island in the world. Sites you'll visit include the grand Rockefeller, Macy, and Goodyear cottages.

♦ Brunswick's **Sterling Equestrian Center,** 6924 New Jesup Highway, (912) 265-7799, is a full-service riding facility with a lighted arena for nighttime gallops. ♦ Guests of The Cloister or the Lodge at Sea Island, may ride at the full-service **Sea Island Stables,** at the intersection of Frederica and Sea Island roads, (912) 638-3611, where marsh and beach trail rides are offered, as well as advanced ring riding.

A guided horseback ride on Little St. Simons

Rainy Day Workout

If the rain clouds are out but you must get in your workout, you have several options for indoor fitness in the Golden Isles. The finest facility open to the public is the **St. Simons Health & Fitness Club,** 2929 Demere Road, St. Simons Island, (912) 638-5600, *www.stsimonshealthclub.com,* where there is a complete range of cardiovascular and strength-training equipment, free weights, aerobics classes, a gymnasium, racquetball courts, and locker room facilities with saunas, steam rooms, and showers. The health club also offers personal training and massage services. Nominal day-use fee.

♦ The **World Gym Fitness Center,** 4994 Altama Avenue, Brunswick, (912) 554-2151, offers a full lineup of cardiovascular and strength-training equipment and free weights, plus men's and women's locker rooms with showers. The facility offers day passes to the public for a nominal fee. ♦ Brunswick's **YMCA Family Center,** 144 Scranton Connector, (912) 265-4100, also provides day passes to guests who wish to use their lap pool, free weights, and cardiovascular and strength-training equipment. There are men's and women's locker rooms with showers onsite. Nominal day-use fee.

Sailing

Just a few tacks into the Atlantic from the Golden Isles and you'll be amongst dolphins, loggerhead sea turtles, and perhaps the very rare, official Georgian mammal, Northern right whales. While many private resorts, like The Cloister on Sea Island, rent catamarans or Sunfish for self-guided excursions from the beach, the best bet for catching sight of serious marine life is to board a chartered vessel. ♦ The 31-foot sloop *Weadore,* (912) 223-4419, *www.weadoresailing.com,* departs from the Jekyll Harbor Marina for daytime, sunset, and moonlight sails. Several other marinas, including the Golden Isles Marina just off the St. Simons Causeway, (912) 638-8573, have larger sail-

The Cloister

Hobie Cats off Sea Island

boats available for hire with a skipper.

If you prefer being closer to the water with the ocean spray in your face, you can rent a 14-foot Hobie Cat from one of several local sources to head out on your own. ◆ **Barry's Beach Service**, (912) 638-8053, rents sailboats to the public. Call for the location nearest you. ◆ **Ocean Motion's** two locations—210-212 Mallory Street, St. Simons, (912) 638-4749; and 1300 Ocean Boulevard, St. Simons, (912) 638-5225—rent Hobie Cats with or without skippers. The stores also offer sailing instruction.

Scuba Diving

Like to get to the bottom of things? If you're a certified diver, you can do just that off the Golden Isles' coast, where visibility is generally between 25 and 75 feet. Two of the surrounding dive sites are G Reef and Gray's Reef. ◆ **G Reef** is an artificial reef of three sunken ships 23 miles out to sea off Little Cumberland Island. The reef is comprised of two 100-foot tugboats and the 441-foot *E.S. Nettleton*, a Liberty Ship built in Brunswick during World War II. Dive depths at G Reef range from 35 feet to 70 feet. The reef attracts schools of angelfish and jacks, as well as the mafia bosses of the sea, barracuda. ◆ **Gray's Reef** sits 17 miles off Sapelo Island and is one of only 12 National Marine Sanctuaries. Angelfish, loggerhead turtles, mackerel, snapper, grouper, and barracuda are just some of the marine species you'll encounter along this 17-square-mile, live-bottom, natural reef. Dive depths range from 55 feet to 75 feet.

The Golden Isles have two well-respected dive outfits. ◆ **Island Dive Center**, Golden Isles Marina, 206 Marina Drive, St. Simons, (912) 638-6590 or 1-800-940-3483, *www.islanddivecenter.com;* and ◆ **Hammerhead Dive Center**, 1200 Glynn Avenue (Route 17 South), Brunswick, (912) 262-1778, *www.georgiascuba.com*. Both shops offer two- and three-tank dives to nearby sites, full equipment rental, as well as certification and instruction. Never been diving before? With advance reservations, Hammerhead's owner Adrian Wilson will arrange a resort certification, where you receive instruction and dive the same day at depths of up to 40 feet.

Swimming

This is, after all, part of why you're here, isn't it? To enjoy the beach and—temperatures permitting—take a dip in the sea? Swimming in the Atlantic Ocean is an exhilarating experience and an absolute must in the dead of summer when the mercury climbs into the 90s. You can swim year round, but it'll be a quick dip December–February, when water temperatures hover in the low 50s. Ocean temperatures typically stay above 70 degrees May–October, and in August the water is downright soupy, with an average temperature in the low 80s. Finding a spot on the sand is easy, with miles of shoreline accessible to the public. In general, expect wide beaches with hard-packed sand at low tide and narrow beaches with soft sand at high tide.

♦ If you're looking for easy access to largely uncrowded shores, **Jekyll Island's** 10 miles of white-sand beach is the best bet. In general, the beaches at the southern and northern ends of the island are the least crowded and developed.

♦ If you prefer a more-social beach scene, the beaches of **St. Simons** on the southern end of the island provide just that. Access the miles of sand on either side of the old U.S. Coast Guard Station from **Massengale Park**, located just off Ocean Boulevard in the Village. The park has restrooms and showers and is open daily, 7 A.M.–10 P.M.

The ocean is always just a few steps away in the Golden Isles

♦ If you're planning to visit any of the additional barrier islands for the day, including **Cumberland, Sapelo** and **Blackbeard** islands, be sure to pack your swimsuit. The desolate beaches of each island will have you fantasizing about owning your own island. And what good is your own island if you don't plan to swim from its beaches? For information on how to reach these islands, see *Island Hopping* under the *Kick Back* section.

Be aware that swimming in the ocean calls for common sense. Do not swim alone. Never enter very rough surf and keep an eye out for sudden lightning storms that are common in the summer. While shark attacks are rare, it's good common sense not to swim at dawn or dusk, when larger fish are feeding. Finally, riptides—fast-moving currents heading out to sea—can occur anywhere along the Golden Isles. For advice on what to do should you find yourself in a riptide, see "Keep Your Cool."

Keep Your Cool

Riptides—treacherous currents heading out to sea—can occur anywhere along the Golden Isles and can carry even the strongest swimmers quickly seaward. If you find yourself in a riptide, do not swim against it. Instead, swim parallel to the shore to reach the edge of the current, where you'll be able to swim back to shore.

Tennis

The **Jekyll Island Tennis Center**, Captain Wylly Road, Jekyll Island, (912) 635-3154, is one of the finest municipal tennis facilities in the nation. (*Tennis* magazine named it one of the top 25.) There are 13 "fast dry" courts, including seven lighted for night play. If you forgot your racquet, you can get into the swing of things with a rental from the full-service pro shop, open daily from 9 A.M.–6 P.M.

Local Outdoor Advice

Bedford Sportsman South • Owned and operated by Ellen and Larry Kennedy, Bedford Sportsman South is a full-service outdoor store, with a strong fly-fishing bent. You can purchase apparel, footgear, fly fishing and outdoor equipment, guidebooks, and canoes. Larry Kennedy is an Orvis-endorsed fishing guide, and the store offers fly tying and casting instruction. The store also rents sit-on-top kayaks, which are best used for fishing or for photography. • 3405 Frederica Road, St. Simons, ☎ (912) 638-5454, *www.stsimonsoutfitters.com*

Ocean Motion • This retail operation offers sportswear, footwear, swimwear, and travel gear. The 212 Mallory Street location is a full-service, outdoor outfitter, while the other locations have more surf-shop feels. Equipment rentals include kayaks, bikes, and sailboats. The knowledgeable staff is happy to point you to plenty of sites for outdoor adventure. Ocean Motion also operates various nature tours. • 1300 Ocean Boulevard, St. Simons, ☎ (912) 638-5225 or 1-800-669-5215; and 210-212 Mallory Street, St. Simons, (912) 638-4749; *www.oceanmotion.biz*

Bedford Sportsman South

Southeast Adventure Outfitters • This full-service outfitter and tour operator has a laid-back staff that is exceptionally helpful in offering advice on the outdoor scene. The store carries all manner of camping equipment, outdoor clothing, footwear, and paddling accessories, including a complete line of sea kayaks and canoes. The St. Simons location is open daily year-round and houses more outdoor merchandise than the Brunswick location. The Brunswick store is SEA's paddling headquarters on the water. • 313 Mallory Street, St. Simons, ☎ (912) 638-6732; and 1200 Glynn Avenue (Route 17 South), Brunswick, (912) 265-5292; *www.southeastadventure.com*

Kick Back

When the sun gets too hot or your ears become waterlogged, it's time to explore and enjoy the Golden Isles at a more-relaxed pace. From leisurely carriage tours of historic neighborhoods to some of the finest upscale shopping between Miami and Charleston, the Golden Isles offers numerous ways to kick back and enjoy life on "island time."

Antiques

Antiquing in the Golden Isles is more than a pastime; it's serious business. You'll find dealers throughout the region, but the majority is in **Old Town Brunswick,** where more than 50 dealers are located in 18 historic buildings within easy walking distance of one another. Brunswick's Downtown Development Authority offers a free brochure entitled, *Village of Antiques,* with a map showing the locations of nearly 15 dealers. (To request the brochure, call (912) 265-4098, or stop at any of the visitor centers listed under *Additional Information.*) Furniture, china, art, jewelry, coins, books, and glassware—it's all here. Many of the businesses operate out of restored Victorian homes or mansions just off Gloucester or Newcastle streets. ◆ One of the stops on the tour is the **Downtown Antiques & Collectibles Mall,** 1208 Gloucester Street, (912) 264-2322, which houses more than 45 dealers in 8,000 square feet of exhibition space.

Numerous antiques dealers operate on St. Simons Island. ◆ In the Village, stop at **Village Mews,** 504 Beachview Drive, (912) 634-1235, for an eclectic collection ranging from old photographs of St. Simons to furniture from faraway places like Africa, India, and Europe. ◆ In the attractive, upscale shopping complex Redfern Village, the **Royal Palm Trading Company,** 276 Redfern Village, (912) 638-7001, showcases colonial antiques from Europe, India, Africa, and the Orient. The shop also carries new merchandise, including Persian carpets, bedding, and home accessories. ◆ Similarly, **Oglethorpe Antiques & Interiors,** 3509 Frederica Road, St. Simons Island, (912) 638-8083, *www.oglethorpeantiques.com,* presents a mix of new and antique merchandise. The antiques are mostly 18th- and 19th-century English, French, and American furniture, porcelain, silver, and art. The new merchandise is primarily furniture and floor coverings.

If you prefer to amble along, stopping when the mood suits, keep your eyes open for the red and blue "Antiques" flag that most local dealers use to identify themselves with. ◆ In addition to the array of antiques dealers, the **Annual Safe Harbor Winter Antiques Show** brings together more than 30 dealers offering furniture, art, oriental rugs, porcelain, jewelry, silver, and more each January at the Jekyll Island Club Hotel, (912) 634-8768 or 1-800-535-9547.

Art Galleries

The **Left Bank Art Gallery**, 3600 Frederica Road, Suite 12, St. Simons Island, (912) 638-3017, *www.leftbankartgallery.com*, is one of the better-known art galleries in the Southeastern United States. Art aficionados recognize it as one of a handful of galleries known for finding and promoting talented but unknown artists. Begun in the 1940s by St. Simons' impressionistic painter Mildred Huie, the Left Bank Art Gallery features work from the United States and Europe, with a special concentration on paintings of local coastal scenes and of Paris. Since 1965, Huie's daughter, Mildred Huie Wilcox, has run the gallery. She manages the permanent collection and showcases new talent in rotating exhibits.

♦ Located at the Shops at Sea Island, artist Jill Goad's multi-faceted art business, **J. Goad Gallerie**, 600 Sea Island Road, St. Simons, (912) 634-1669, showcases oils, acrylics, and watercolors by well-known local, regional, and international artists. Goad also offers custom framing, photographic prints, hand-painted gifts, and pottery for sale. ♦ Father and son artists Jim and Addison Palmer present their original paintings of local beaches, marshes, and wildlife at the **Palmer Gallery**, 3414 Frederica Road, St. Simons, (912) 634-0045 or 1-888-821-0059. The Palmers are an artistic lot: Jim's brother, Walter and his daughter, Elise, are also well-known lowcountry artists. ♦ Check out the **Artshoppe**, 264 Redfern Village, (912) 638-6493, *www.muldowney-arts.com*, where you'll find watercolors, acrylics, pastels, and hand-painted items by owner Nancy Muldowney, as well as art pieces from around the world, including carved teak items from Thailand and soapstone from Kenya.

♦ The **Glynn Art Association** is an active nonprofit community art association that offers local members, residents, and visitors numerous artistic outlets, including the **Gallery on Mallory**, 319 Mallory Street, St. Simons (912) 638-8770, *www.glynnart.org*, which showcases drawings, paintings, pottery, sculptures, and photography from local and regional artists. The association also sponsors four annual events, including the **Golden Isles Art Festival** in October and the **Fine Arts & Fine Crafts Outdoor Festival by the Sea** each spring.

♦ On Jekyll Island in the Landmark Historic District, **Goodyear Cottage**, Riverside Drive, (912) 635-3920, houses the **Jekyll Island Arts Association** and features monthly art exhibits by local and visiting artists working in several mediums, including oil, acrylic, watercolors, and sculpture. There is also a gift shop onsite. Part of the draw is the cottage itself, built between 1903 and 1906 for Frank Goodyear, founder of Goodyear Tire Company.

Several Brunswick galleries are particularly noteworthy. ♦ **The Gallery on Newcastle**, 1626 Newcastle Street, Brunswick, (912) 554-0056, is in a historic building in Old Town Brunswick that local artist Janet Powers restored to showcase fine art and sculpture from more than a dozen local artists. ♦ Directly across from the Ritz Theater in historic Brunswick, the **Glenda Cason Gallery**, 1523 Newcastle Street, (912) 280-9352, houses oil paintings by local artist Glenda Cason, whose subjects are primarily historic Brunswick and St. Simons Island. ◆ Just a few doors away, **Galeria at the Port,** 1505 Newcastle Street, (912) 280-9777, showcases original art by pop-artist Peter Max and the late Russian painter/sculptor/fashion designer Erte'. There are also collections of Modern Masters lithographs by such artists as Pablo Picasso and Marc Chagall, and rotating exhibitions by local and regional artists.

Oldest Confederate Widows Tell All

They hail from a proud Southern line—one with deep roots—and they preside over the residents of the Georgian coast today as they have for hundreds of years. They are the region's **live oaks**, and their branches form much of the natural canopy above you as you drive along the Golden Isles. The live oak—so-called because it's an evergreen—is Georgia's state tree, but it grows throughout the southeastern coastal plain, from Virginia to Texas. Marked by a gnarly trunk, huge girth, and vast tentacles of twisting, twirling limbs, the live oak grows quickly, lives for centuries, and produces the heaviest wood of any tree in North America. Its strength and resistance to water made it crucial to early U.S. naval shipbuilding. The *USS Constitution*, affectionately known as "Old Ironsides," was built from live oaks taken from St. Simons.

The ultimate shade tree, the live oak decorates broad avenues throughout the South. On St. Simons, don't miss the **Avenue of Oaks**, leading to the Sea Island Golf Club from the intersection of Frederica and Kings Way. Planted in the early 19th Century, these live oaks line the entrance to the former plantation **Retreat**, once one of the more-prosperous plantations in the region. Today the Sea Island Company owns the property, but visitors are welcome to drive along Retreat Avenue and circle back at the private entrance. In Brunswick, two live oaks bear mentioning: **Lanier Oak**, just off Route 17 at Lanier Boulevard, is the tree under which poet Sidney Lanier felt moved to write *The Marshes of Glynn* in the 1870s. In Old Town Brunswick at Prince and Albany streets, **Lover's Oak** is a sprawling, centuries-old tree that comes with local legend: It was the site where Native-American braves would meet their maidens to profess their love.

If you're touring St. Simons, staring at the beautiful oak trees and you find one staring back, don't be alarmed. You've just passed one of the **Tree Spirits**, faces carved into live oaks throughout the island to honor sailors lost at sea aboard ships made from St. Simon's timber. You'll find some of these trees at the following locations: Demere Road at Skylane Drive; on Mallory Street next to Murphy's Tavern in the Village; and at Redfern Village at the Wine & Cheese Cellar off Frederica Road. For a complete list of locations, pick up the free brochure *The Tree Spirits of St. Simons Island* from any of the locations listed under *Additional Information*.

A tree spirit

Back Roads Touring

If the weather discourages outdoor activity but you still want to see some sights, hop in the car and explore some of the enchanting roads on the islands and along the coastal mainland. Start by stopping at any of the sources listed under *Additional Information* to pick up a copy of the free brochure ***Brunswick and the Golden Isles of Georgia Driving Tours***, published by Brunswick & the Golden Isles Visitors Bureau. (You can also call (912) 265-0620 to request the brochure, or access it online at *www.bgivb.com*.) The brochure, which provides maps of Brunswick, St. Simons Island, Sea Island, and Jekyll Island, includes sites of interest with descriptions and approximate mileages from point to point.

◆ While Interstate 95 is the most-expedient way to reach the Golden Isles from points north and south, it's far from the most scenic. **Route 17** follows the coastline and provides easy access to hundreds of country roads and state highways which lead you to the coves and along the peninsulas of Georgia's coast. There's no better way to take in the area's coastal hamlets, rural farms, tidal rivers, sprawling marshland, and historic churches (many of which have graveyards dating to the Revolutionary War). In addition to Route 17, check out **Route 99** from Darien (on Route 17 just north of Brunswick) through Meridian to where the road re-connects with Route 17 in Eulonia.

Boat Tours

Feeling Lucky?

The 190-foot, three-level ***Emerald Princess***, 1 Saint Andrews Court, ☎ (912) 265-3558 or 1-800-842-0115, *www.emeraldprincesscasino.com*, sets sail from Brunswick Landing Marina six nights a week for a buffet-style dinner cruise. Thrown into the mix of food, spirits, Vegas-style entertainment, and moonlit views of the mainland is a full casino, featuring a roulette wheel, blackjack, poker, craps, and rows-aplenty of slot machines. The cruises run Tuesday–Sunday, 7 P.M.–midnight during the week, and until 1 A.M. on the weekends. There are daytime depatures on Saturdays and Sundays. Call for current rates, which at press time were $15 per person during the week and for weekend day cruises, $25 per person for Friday and Saturday evenings. Pack some Dramamine™, just in case.

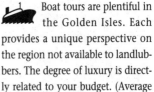

Boat tours are plentiful in the Golden Isles. Each provides a unique perspective on the region not available to landlubbers. The degree of luxury is directly related to your budget. (Average tour prices are $30 per person, per hour.)

◆ **Coastal Expeditions,** 3202 East 3rd Street, Brunswick, (912) 265-0392, offers sightseeing cruises, including dolphin and salt marsh tours, as well as sunset and moonlight cruises off Jekyll Island, St. Simons, and Brunswick. Captain Vernon Reynolds has more than 30 years of experience at the helm in local waters. ◆ **Captain Mark**

Noble's Fishing Center, Golden Isles Marina, 206 Marina Drive, St. Simons Island, (912) 634-1219, *www.georgiafishing.net*, also conducts dolphin and salt marsh tours. A native of St. Simons, Captain Mark Noble has spent his lifetime exploring the tidal creeks, rivers, and sounds of the Golden Isles and delights in sharing his knowledge. ◆ You can float close to wildlife in the tidal creeks around St. Simons and Little St. Simons on the shallow-draft pontoon boat, *The Marsh Hen* of **Salt Marsh Nature Tours**, (912) 638-9354, *www.marshtours.com*. Captain Jeanne Pleasants offers one-, two-, and three-hour tours, with binoculars for every passenger. You may encounter such wildlife as alligators, herons, egrets, kingfishers, and raccoons.

◆ Enough boat charters operate in area that you can visit any major marina and likely find a tour departing with seats available. The best places to stop include: **Hampton River Club Marina**, 1000 Hampton River Club Drive, (912) 638-1210; ◆ **Village Creek Landing**, 526 S. Harrington Road, (912) 634-9054; and ◆ **Golden Isles Marina**, 206 Marina Drive, (912) 634-1128, all on St. Simons Island; ◆ **Jekyll Harbor Marina**, 1 Harbor Road, (912) 635-3137, and ◆ **Jekyll Wharf Marina**, 1 Pier Road, (912) 635-3152, on Jekyll Island.

◆ In Brunswick: **Brunswick Landing Marina**, 2429 Newcastle Street, (912) 262-9264; ◆ **Credle's Complete Marine,** 1455 Route 17 South, (912) 261-1935; and ◆ **Two-Way Fish Camp**, 1400 Darien Highway, (912) 265-0410.

From Above

Given the pancake-flatness of the Golden Isles, the best way to gain perspective on the area is to gain altitude. **Captain Bill Buyan,** a former army officer and commercial pilot, conducts air tours above the region in his twin-engine Cessna Skyhawk. Departing from either the St. Simons or Jekyll Island airports, you'll fly over the surrounding barri-

Brunswick-Golden Isles CVB

Sea Island from the air

er islands. Buyan provides colorful narrative on the region's ecology and history en route. Expect plenty of photo opportunities. Advance reservations required by calling (912) 222-2448.

Historic Sites & Museums

The Brunswick & the Golden Isles Visitors Bureau proudly proclaims that the flags of five nations have flown over the region. Much of this history awaits the traveler interested in exploring the region's heritage. ◆ On the mainland, Brunswick—named for the German city of Braunsweig, home to England's King George II's ancestors—presents a potpourri of historical sites in charming **Old Town Brunswick**. (Best to park the car and

A home in Brunswick's Historic District

walk this district.) In 1771, British General James Oglethorpe designed Brunswick's streets based upon the grid pattern he used for Savannah. Brunswick is one of the few colonial towns that did not change its street names after the Revolutionary War, so you can park and walk streets with Anglican names like Newcastle, Gloucester, Albany, and Hillsborough, all named for English nobles. The grand Victorian buildings and homes in the historic district reflect the region's prosperity in the late 19th and early 20th centuries, when the logging, shipping, and resort industries flourished.

Developed beside a deep, natural harbor, Brunswick has an important maritime history. George Washington praised the port as an important point-of-entry for the original colonies, and during World War II, local shipyards built nearly 100 Liberty Ships. These 450-foot long, flat-bottom, flat-sided cargo ships were used to transport supplies to American troops in Europe and the Pacific. You can view a 23-foot replica of a Liberty Ship at the **Mary Ross Waterfront Park** located at the western end of Gloucester Street. ◆ For greater historical perspective on this port town, stop by the **Brunswick History Museum**, housed in the Listner House, 1327 Union Street, (912) 265-4032, to view archaeological and photographic exhibits. The museum is open Monday–Friday, 8 A.M–5 P.M. Nominal admission fee.

Bloody Marsh

In 1740, British General James Oglethorpe attempted to take St. Augustine in Florida from the Spanish but was easily turned away and forced to return to Fort Frederica on St. Simons Island. The Spanish couldn't let the line in the sand stand. Two years after Oglethorpe's excursion, the Spanish arrived on St. Simons with a force that dwarfed the British troops. Oglethorpe dispatched his army—comprised of British, Scottish Highlanders, and Native Americans—to points around the island to ambush the Spanish as they retreated from the fort's cannon fire. In an open marsh, the British caught the Spanish by surprise, and in the confusion of smoke, gunfire, and battle cries, the Spanish never realized that they greatly outnumbered their foes—until they no longer did. Today a plaque marks **Bloody Marsh,** located off Demere Road. It's hard to believe that this peaceful golden stretch once ran red with Spanish blood. It's not a typical tourist attraction—no admission fees, visitor center, or vending machines—it's just a place to contemplate how things might have been different today if the Spanish had taken Georgia. *Entienda?*

◆ Just north of Brunswick on Route 17 in the town of Darien sits the **Fort King George State Historic Site,** Fort King George Drive, Darien, (912) 437-4770. The fort was built in 1721 at the mouth of the Altamaha River as the southernmost outpost of the British Empire in the New World. The British, vying with the French and Spanish for control of Georgia, constructed Fort King George to protect Beaufort and Charleston and to lay claim on Georgia as their final colony. The fort consisted of soldiers' barracks, officers' quarters, a guard house, and a cypress-timber blockhouse atop a mud embankment. The British used the fort until 1733, at which point they officially colonized Georgia. Today, you can visit an accurate representation of the original fort and tour the museum, which presents coastal history from prehistoric times through the 20th Century, when Darien flourished as one of the country's greatest timber-processing centers. There's also a 10-minute film about the fort. Open Tuesday–Saturday, 9 A.M–5 P.M.; Sunday 2 P.M.–5:30 P.M. Nominal admission fee.

♦ Located on a hairpin turn in the Altamaha River on St. Simons, **Fort Frederica National Monument,** Route 9/Frederica Road, (912) 638-3639, *www.nps.gov/fofr,* commemorates the site where British General James Oglethorpe established Fort Frederica in 1736. The heavily fortified compound—built as a defensive post to protect Savannah and Darien from the Spanish—covered 40 acres and became a bustling, self-contained community with nearly 1,000 residents by 1743. After the Spanish threat receded with a treaty in 1748, the fort's usefulness to the British crown declined and it was abandoned. A fire ravaged what was left of the village in 1758. You can get a vivid idea of what life was like for residents through the onsite museum's interpretive displays and the 25-minute film entitled *This is Frederica,* shown continuously in the visitor center. Park rangers also lead tours of the site. The grounds are open daily, 8 A.M–5 P.M., and the museum is open 9 A.M–5 P.M. Nominal admission fee.

♦ As Frederica Road winds north on St. Simons from the Village, the road narrows and the live oak canopy thickens. Located on the left off Frederica Road, just past the Lawrence Road fork, is **Christ Church.** In the 1740s, Charles Wesley served as the minister to Fort Frederica and often preached to soldiers and Native Americans beneath a large oak tree on this site. Wesley hailed from the Church of England, the spiritual parent to the Episcopal Church, which formed in the colonies. Christ Church has the distinction of being the third Episcopal Church formed in the nation.

Christ Church at St. Simons

The first church on this site was built in 1820 but was destroyed by Union troops during the Civil War. In 1884, Anson Phelps Dodge, Jr. rebuilt Christ Church—the beautiful, wooden structure that stands today—in honor of his wife Ellen, who died of cholera on their honeymoon. The church's layout is that of a crucifix. The stained glass windows, which include one from Tiffanys, depict the early life of Christ and the Christian church. The adjacent cemetery holds the remains of most of the island's early settlers, as well as many notable residents. Buried here are Anson Dodge, his wife, Ellen, and author Eugenia Price (1916-1996), whose novels depicted life in the 19th-century South, including the Golden Isles region. Donations are required to visit the church,

Brunswick-Golden Isles CVB

The St. Simons Lighthouse

which is open daily, 2 P.M–5 P.M., in the summer, and from 1 P.M.–4 P.M. in the winter.

♦ The **St. Simons Island Lighthouse Museum**, 101 12th Street (off Beachview Drive), St. Simons, (912) 638-4666, *www.saintsimonslighthouse.org*, sits on the former site of Fort St. Simons, built in the 18th Century to protect the southern end of the island. The first lighthouse was built in 1807, but retreating Confederate forces destroyed it in 1862 to prevent Union forces from using it. Ten years later, the current lighthouse and adjacent cottage went up, making it one of the oldest, continuously operated lighthouses in the country. There is no longer a lighthouse keeper—the last full-time keeper retired in 1950—but the automated light still shines more than 18 miles out to sea, directing ships into St. Simons Sound. Visitors can climb the 129 steps to the top of the lighthouse for views of St. Simons and Jekyll Island. The museum offers a short video about the lighthouse and has period furniture in each room. The keepers' house also has a book and gift shop. Open Monday–Saturday, 10 A.M.–5 P.M., and Sunday, 1:30 P.M.–5 P.M. Nominal admission fee.

♦ To have 400 years of history presented in an hour and a half, catch a ride on the **St. Simons Trolley,** the Village Pier, St. Simons, (912) 638-8954, which travels to all of the island's major historic sites. Expect plenty of colorful anecdotes while you sit back and leave the driving to someone else. Tours depart from the pier at 11 A.M. and 1 P.M. daily, March 16–September 30; and at 1 P.M. daily, October 1–March 15.

♦ Want to know more about the club once proclaimed "the richest, the most exclusive, and most inaccessible club in the world?" Mosey on over to the museum at the **Jekyll Island Visitor Center,** 381 Riverview Drive, (912) 635-4036, for a glimpse of the island's history, including its gilded era as home to the **Jekyll Island Club,** a winter hunt club that counted amongst its members William Rockefeller, J.P. Morgan, and Vincent Astor. Housed in the former Jekyll Club Stable—built in 1897 with 46 horse stalls—the visitor center museum features free exhibits describing island history, from the earliest-known inhabitants to the present. The museum is open daily, 9 A.M.–5 P.M. There's a gift shop with an excellent book collection.

These Walls of Tabby

Throughout coastal Georgia, and especially in the Golden Isles, you'll run across new and historic buildings made of **tabby,** an indigenous building material made with sand, lime, and oyster shells. Historically, the manufacturing process was extensive. Builders extracted the lime by burning the oyster shells. Next, they removed salt—a weakening agent—from the shells and sand. Finally, they added the lime, clean sand, and crushed oyster shells together with water to make tabby.

♦ Catch a tram from the Jekyll Island Visitor Center for a narrated tour of the 240-acre **Jekyll Island Historical Landmark District.** The 1.5-hour tour includes visits inside three to four restored "cottages"—more accurately described as mansions—and anecdotes about the social gatherings the homes once hosted. Tours leave on the hour between 10 A.M.–3 P.M. Nominal admission fee. If you wish to explore the 200-acre historic district and its 33 buildings on your own, all you need is a fresh set of legs and an adventurous spirit.

The Horton House ruins

♦ Other historic sites worth visiting on Jekyll include the remains of the two-story **Horton House**, on the northwest end of the island on Riverview Drive, as well as the **Horton Brewery Site**, south of the home on Riverview Drive. The Horton in question was Major William Horton, one of General Oglethorpe's most-trusted underlings. He established a thriving plantation on Jekyll Island and Georgia's first brewery, which produced ale for the British troops at Fort Frederica. Informative historic markers designate each site.

Island Hopping

Active adventures on the neighboring islands are listed under the separate *Wide Open* sports sections, but Cumberland, Sapelo, Blackbeard, and Little St. Simons islands are also ideal for exploring at a butterfly's pace, visiting a museum, or taking a nap under the giant limbs of a live oak overlooking the ocean. Since each is accessible only by boat, you'll want to plan your excursion in advance and make reservations with the ferry service. Plan to bring everything you'll need, including food and drink, for a full day of exploring.

Your own private beach gazebo for a day on Little St. Simons

Little St. Simons

Officially part of the Golden Isles but privately owned, **Little St. Simons** affords the fortunate few—no more than 30 overnight guests and a handful of day-pass island hoppers—the opportunity to wander this 10,000-acre paradise with its seven miles of beaches, serpentine tidal creeks, golden marshes, and primal maritime forests. If you're a guest of the Lodge at Little St. Simons (see *Rest Easy*), you can wander this nirvana aimlessly without concern for time, but if you're visiting for the day, your boat departs Hampton Point Marina on St. Simons at 10:30 A.M. and returns at 4:00 P.M.

If there were ever a window of opportunity, the 5.5-hour **Little St. Simons Interpretive Day Trip** is it. The day begins with a 15-minute boat ride to the island, where a naturalist greets you and gives a narrated tour of Little St. Simons, covering the history and evolution of the island and the importance of barrier island ecology. After the tour, you're treated to a gourmet lunch with regional specialties. Then it's time for the beach. Whether you choose to fill your pockets with beautiful shells or simply to snooze on the white sand, the seven-mile beach satiates.

The day trips are subject to availability, and reservations are required. The $75 per person fee includes boat transportation, the guided interpretative tour, and lunch. To make reservations or to get more information, call the Lodge on Little St. Simons Island, (912) 638-7472 or 1-888-733-5774, *www.littlestsimonsisland.com.*

Sapelo Island

Sapelo Island is owned by the State of Georgia and hosts several state properties, including the University of Georgia Marine Institute, the Sapelo Island National Estuarine Research Reserve, and the R.J. Reynolds Wildlife Refuge. But it's the island's natural beauty and the unique community of **Hog Hammock** that bring most visitors here. Hog Hammock is a community of African Americans descended from slaves who worked on cotton planter Thomas Spalding's plantation. After the United States abolished slavery in 1865, Sapelo's slave trade continued for several years because the island's curvaceous coastline made smuggling easy. The isolation of island living preserved many of the West African traditions, and the slave descendents are closer to their roots than many other Southern coastal, African-American communities descended from slaves.

By the late 19th Century, nearly 900 people—many of them former slaves—lived on Sapelo on private land donated by the island's owners. Throughout the island's changes in ownership, the community of Hog Hammock has remained, though the population has declined as economic opportunities on the mainland pulled residents away. Today the approximately 60 remaining residents are gracious, kind, and proud people. They speak Geechie, a mix of English and African languages, and live in a series of brightly colored cottages and trailers along sandy roads. Tourism provides their economic livelihood.

Georgia Department Tourism

A traffic intersection on Sapelo Island

In addition to Hog Hammock, you'll find plenty of wide-open space on this 16,000-acre island, the fourth largest of Georgia's barrier islands. The land is largely pine and hardwood forest, salt marsh, and more than two miles of wide, sandy beach. Much of the island's interior is part of the **R.J. Reynolds Wildlife Refuge.** Reynolds—the last private owner of the island—sold it to the state in 1969.

Other interesting sites on the island include the ruins of **Le Chatelet**, a late 18th-century tabby home and estate owned by a French nobleman; and the **Sapelo Island Lighthouse**, a distinctive red and white-striped lighthouse on the southern end of the island. You'll see all of these landmarks on a tour of the island operated by the **Sapelo Visitor Center,** (912) 437-3224. Call the visitor center to make reservations to visit Sapelo. To protect the wildlife, visits to the island's interior without permission are prohibited. (You may wander the beaches.) For information on visiting the interior of the island, ask the staff at the visitor center. The ferry for Sapelo leaves from Meridian, a small village north of Brunswick on Route 17. To reach the ferry, take Route 17 north from the Golden Isles to Darien. In town, turn right onto Route 99 at the courthouse and follow signs for the eight-mile drive to the Sapelo Ferry dock.

Blackbeard Island

Separated from Sapelo Island by a saltwater marsh, **Blackbeard Island** is 5,600 acres of untouched barrier island, 3,000 acres of which are protected as a National Wilderness Area. The government acquired the island in 1800, making this one of the oldest national wildlife refuges in the country. The main dock area is the only manmade structure on Blackbeard. The rest of the island—maritime forest, salt marsh, freshwater marsh, and beach habitat—is undeveloped. The island is open to the public during daylight hours. Several private ferry services, departing from Shellman Bluff, provide access to the island. Shellman Bluff is a coastal community located an hour north of Brunswick off Route 17. Turn right onto Shellman Bluff Road from Route 17 north of the small town of Eulonia. For more information, call the **Savannah Coastal Refuges Office** at (912) 652-4415.

Cumberland Island

Prior to the 1996 wedding of the ill-fated couple, John F. Kennedy, Jr. and Carolyn Bessette, **Cumberland Island** existed below the radar of most American tourists. That's precisely why the celebrity couple chose the romantic **Greyfield Inn** (see *Rest Easy*), a grand and graceful mansion on Cumberland Island, as the location for their nuptials. Owned and operated by the National Park Service, Cumberland is the southernmost and largest of Georgia's barrier islands, accessible only by ferry from St. Marys, a village straddling the Florida State line. What else is on Cumberland? More than 17 miles of undeveloped beach. When you tire of relaxing on the sand, you can stroll the island's 36,000 acres and discover the ruins of **Dungeness,** a late 19th-century mansion built by Thomas Carnegie, brother of the steel industrialist, Andrew Carnegie. **Plum Orchard**, another Carnegie mansion, also stands on the island.

Highlights of visiting Cumberland include frequent wildlife encounters with wild horses, alligators, exotic birds, and the occasional wild hog. The National Park Service limits the number of island visitors to 300 per day, so advance reservations are required. If you miss your ferry—the last one pulls out at 4:45 P.M.—you'll be required to charter a boat back to shore. For a map, ferry information, and reservations to visit Cumberland, contact the National Park Service in St. Marys, (912) 882-4335, *www.nps.gov/cuis.*

Performing Arts

♪ Thanks to the **Golden Isles Arts & Humanities Association,** (912) 262-6934, *www.goldenislesarts.org,* a nonprofit organization dedicated to improving the quality of live music and theater events performed locally, you may get to add some culture to your coastal vacation. In addition to managing Brunswick's historic Ritz Theatre, the association plans and produces several annual events, including **Jazz in the Park,** a summer concert series held May–September on the lawn beside the St. Simons Lighthouse; and the **Annual Performing Art Series,** a series of theatrical and musical performances, ranging from Shakespeare to modern dance, held in Brunswick's Ritz Theatre. Call when you arrive for the entertainment lineup.

♦ Many of the GIAHA performances take place at the **Ritz Theatre,** 1530 Newcastle Street, Brunswick, (912) 262-6934. Originally built in 1898 with ornate brick and stone details, the theater housed the Grand Opera House, retail shops, and the offices for the Brunswick & Birmingham Railroad. Over time, the theater's fare expanded from opera to include vaudeville performances. In the 1930s, the building was retrofitted into a movie theater to show the increasingly popular motion pictures. The ground-level exterior brickwork was covered with Carrara glass, a pigmented surface popular in Art-Deco architecture. The theater recently underwent a complete renovation that restored parts of the original brickwork, storefronts, transoms, and glass.

♦ St. Simons is home to the community theater troupe, the **Island Players,** Casino Theatre, Neptune Park, (912) 638-3031, *www.islandplayers.com.* In existence since 1956, the troupe performs four annual productions, including two musicals. ♦ If you're in the Golden Isles between May and July, check out a production of the **Jekyll Island Musical Theatre Festival,** a professional repertory musical theater company that presents Broadway classics under the stars at the **Jekyll Island Amphitheatre.** A cooperative effort between Valdosta State College and the Jekyll Island Authority, the festival brings in more than 60 professional actors, musicians, and stagehands for three productions each summer. Recent American classics included *Annie Get Your Gun, My Fair Lady,* and *You're a Good Man, Charlie Brown.* Shows run Monday–Saturday. Call (912) 635-3636 or 1-877-453-5955 for information and tickets.

Plantations

Following the American Revolution, Georgia's coastal economy rebounded, as plantations on the islands and mainland used slave labor to produce such large-scale crops as cotton, sugar, and rice. The Civil War brought the plantation era to an end. With few exceptions, those plantations stand either in ruin or have been renovated for private interests. The following are the area's sites that provide a peek into the past. ♦ **Hamilton Plantation** once occupied the southwestern side of St. Simons on Gascoigne Bluff off Arthur J. Moore

Drive. The original home, built by James Hamilton, burned in 1890, but two well-preserved, tabby slave cabins still stand. Each cabin has a central chimney and windows and is open to the public at no cost. You'll find them just outside the gates of Epworth by the Sea, a United Methodist retreat center.

◆ The entrance to the former **Retreat Plantation**, now part of the Sea Island Golf Club, provides a sense of the plantation's former glory. Located at the intersection of Frederica and Kings Way roads on St. Simons, Retreat Avenue follows beside the famed **Avenue of the Oaks**, which leads to the Sea Island Golf Club. Unless you're a guest of The Cloister or Lodge at Sea Island, you'll have to circle back at the private entrance.

For a better look at what life was like on an antebellum plantation, visit the **Hofwyl-**

The famed Avenue of Oaks on St. Simons

Broadfield Plantation State Historic Site, 5556 Route 17 North, Brunswick, (912) 264-7333. The site, just north of Brunswick off Route 17 on the Altamaha River, was once a thriving, 7,000-acre rice plantation that belonged to the Troup family. Furnished with period antiques, including silver, furniture, and books, the antebellum home is open for tours, as is the barn, where 19th-century farm equipment is on display. The surrounding land, lined with live oaks and magnolias, features expansive views of the Altamaha delta. The museum features a brief slide show about the plantation's owners and the more than 350 slaves who worked the fields and in the home. Open Tuesday–Saturday, 9 A.M.–5 P.M; Sundays, 2 P.M.–5:30 P.M. Nominal admission fee.

The Okefenokee

The **Okefenokee Swamp**, (912) 496-7836, *http://okefenokee.fws.gov*, is a vast, freshwater wetland and wildlife preserve that supports an amazing ecosystem. It is essentially a 400,000-acre puddle. Eons ago, the bog was merely a depression on the ocean floor, which scientists speculate might have been created by an asteroid. When the ocean retreated, it left the swamp

The Okefenokee Swamp

you see today. In 1937, the government established the Okefenokee as a National Wildlife Refuge to preserve the then-438,000-acre swamp. In 1974, portions of the refuge were designated as a National Wilderness Area. As a result, the "Okie"—which extends 38 miles north to south and 25 miles east to west—remains one of the best-preserved bodies of freshwater in America.

As an alternative to paddling through this wonderbog (see *Paddling*), you can visit the **Okefenokee Swamp Park**, Route 1 South, Waycross, GA, (912) 283-0583, *www.okeswamp.com*, a private, nonprofit park, offering guided boat tours, wildlife shows, interpretive exhibits, and lectures. You'll find a boardwalk, an observation tower, and private paddling trails through parts of the swamp. (Note: The park's trails do not connect with the National Wildlife Refuge's trails.) There are several theme-park-like attractions, including a steam-engine train replica, *Lady Suwannee*—actually a diesel powered engine—that carries four cars around a 1.5-mile loop.

Shops & Stops

There are so many unique shops and boutiques in the area that some visitors spend their entire vacation listening to cash registers whir. If you're a pro, you probably have a methodical approach to scouting the values. If not, rest assured that one isn't needed. You can explore aimlessly and still find plenty of treasures.

Brunswick

The revitalization of the **Old Town district** has brought renewed vigor to the retail scene, where visitors wander along the streets and in and out of boutiques housed in historic Victorian-style buildings. There are many antiques shops and art galleries (described under *Antiques* and *Art Galleries*), but, increasingly, you'll find upscale gift shops, specialty retailers, and cafés in which you can order the nourishment necessary to continue your retail therapy.

Two shops worth mentioning: ◆ **A Snail's Pace,** 1430 Newcastle Street, (912) 466-0737 or 1-800-451-0743, *www.asnailspace.com*, is well-known in sewing circles as a complete source for needlepoint supplies, including hand-painted canvasses for just about every end-use you can imagine. Everything the store sells promotes needlepoint as an art form and as a component of interior design. ◆ Located across from the Ritz, **Hattie's Books,** 1527 Newcastle Street, (912) 554-8677, *www.hattiesbooks.com,* is a powerfully packed independent bookstore with fiction, nonfiction, and children's books. The shop also features a coffee bar.

St. Simons

As you drive across the causeway to St. Simons, you're entering serious shopping grounds. ◆ There are several concentrations of retail shops on the island, starting with the Village on the southern end. Here, especially along **Ocean Boulevard** and **Mallory Street,** the fare includes beach shops and pizza joints beside high-dollar sports- and resort-wear boutiques. ◆ There's a collection of small shopping centers along **Demere** and **Frederica** roads with a gem or two in each, but the greatest collection of upscale establishments exists in the more-recent development, **Redfern Village**, off Frederica Road just north of its intersection with Demere Road, *www.saintsimons.com/redfernvillage*. Redfern is a "mini-village" shopping complex with sidewalks and single-story shops under a live oak forest. Lined with numerous shops selling art, antiques, flowers, jewelry, men's and women's apparel, gifts, gourmet foods, and wine, Redfern Village could keep your attention for the better part of a day. A few standouts are: the **Royal Palm Trading Company** and the **Artshoppe** (described under *Antiques* and *Art Galleries* respectively); the **Beach Cottage,** 225 Redfern Village, (912) 634-2000, for high-end linens; **Thos. P. Dent Clothiers,** 206 Redfern Village, (912) 638-3118, *www.thospdent.com*, for fine men's apparel; and **Rarebbits & Pieces,** 295 Redfern Village, (912) 638-0718, *www.rarebbits.com*, for unique gifts, including hand-designed and hand-painted art pieces and such coastal-influenced gifts as mirrors with shell mosaics.

◆ **The Shops at Sea Island,** at the intersection of Frederica and Sea Island Drive, is an upscale strip shopping center with a Harris Teeter grocery store, CVS Pharmacy, and a movie theater as anchor tenants. Sandwiched in between are smaller treats like the **Goad Gallery** (see *Art Galleries*) and the independent bookstore, **G.J. Ford Bookshop**, (912) 634-6168, *www.gjfordbookshop.com*. Owner Mary Jane Reed and her well-read staff are adept at finding the right fiction or nonfiction title to take to the beach. ◆ You'll also find an excellent selection of fiction and nonfiction at **The Bookmark**, 1607 Frederica Road, (912) 634-2132, *www.bookmarkink.com*, located in Tabby Plaza at the intersection of Demere and Frederica roads. The store hosts regular author signings and carries a large selection of local and regional titles.

◆ **The Tabby House,** 105 Retreat Road, (912) 638-2257, is an especially interesting shop on St. Simons. Housed in a former slave home built in 1805 for laborers working on the nearby Retreat Plantation (today it's the Sea Island Golf Club), the Tabby House has been in operation for more than 45 years, selling gift items, books, fine pottery, and other decorative accessories. Closed Sundays.

Jekyll Island

On Jekyll Island, you'll find a few gift shops in the unattractive strip center at the intersection

The Tabby House is a gift shop housed in a former slave's home

of Beachview Drive and Fortson Parkway, directly across from the convention center. The unique shopping opportunities are in the **historic district**, where stores are housed in renovated historic buildings.

◆ Included in the mix is **The Cottage on Jekyll**, 32 Pier Road, (912) 635-2643, a small gift shop with wares from around the world, including works of art, games, dolls, afghans, and more. ◆ **Jekyll Books & Antiques,** 101 Old Plantation Road at the corner of Shell Road, (912) 635-3077, offers a mix of new and used books, plus dozens of collectibles in the historic Infirmary Building.

Spa & Massage

Looking to kick back by stretching yourself silly? Head to **Inner Source**, 1620 Frederica Road, St. Simons, (912) 638-7004, a unique business owned and operated by Lydia Aass. Inner Source offers yoga classes and massage therapy six days a week, from 7 A.M.–7 P.M. Walk-ins are welcome. ◆ Also on St. Simons, you can work your muscles into a quivering mass using the weights and machines at the **St. Simons Health & Fitness Club,** 2929 Demere Road, St. Simons Island, (912) 638-5600, *www.stsimonshealthclub.com*, and then meet up with one of the club's professional massage therapists to work the stress out.

◆ In Brunswick, massage therapists at **Coastal Stress Management,** 2560 Tara Lane, Brunswick, (912) 264-2118, offer neuromuscular, sports, tuinai, and general relaxation massages. ◆ If a major part of your stay is going to be seeking out spa treatments, you'd do well to book yourself a night at **The Cloister** on Sea Island (see *Rest Easy*). The resort's spa has been recognized by numerous publications as one of the finest in the nation. The spa is open only to resort guests.

R e s t   E a s y

S l e e p   W e l l

The great resort era in the Golden Isles began Jekyll Island's rise to prominence as an exclusive playground for the rich, but the other islands joined the rush to build resort hotels and comfortable accommodations to welcome vacationers and make available the area's beach bounty. The most-attractive lodging is at the larger resorts; this is not an area that's overflowing with smaller inns or B&Bs. (Brunswick has a few smaller properties, but for a real collection of small, historic B&Bs or inns, look to St. Marys just north of the Florida State line—see *Other Places to Stay*.)

From the beginning, the Golden Isles region has welcomed families. If you're not traveling with children and prefer not to share the pool or common areas with the energy and enthusiasm of a pack of seven-year-olds, you'll want to inquire with each property about their policies regarding quiet areas. In general, most resorts allow families full run of the property.

Accommodations Pricing

Less than $100	Inexpensive	$
$100-150	Moderate	$$
$151-200	Expensive	$$$
More than $200	Very Expensive	$$$$

Prices are per room, per night, based on double occupancy during peak seasons. Note that B&Bs and most country inns include breakfast in the rate.

Brunswick Manor • This handsome 1886 Victorian inn in the heart of Brunswick's historic district features more antique appointments than you can shake a stick at, but unless you've got a hefty wallet, you won't want to swing a stick anywhere inside: Everything is elegant. There are nine rooms—eight with a private bath—and each has period furnishings, a ceiling fan, refrigerator, and terrycloth robes. The inn's nautical-themed Romance of the Sea room received a prestigious Room of the Year award from *Country Inns* magazine. Other amenities/services include: a hot tub, wraparound veranda, and afternoon tea. Breakfasts are not only included, they're lit by candles. • *825 Egmont Street, Brunswick, GA 31520,* ☎ *(912) 265-6889, www.brunswickmanor.com* • *$$*

The Cloister • Combine gracious Southern hospitality with arresting Mediterranean architecture, luxurious accommodations, world-class dining, and exceptional service, and you have part of what makes The Cloister one of the best-known resorts in the nation. Add in a spa ranked first in the nation by readers of *Travel + Leisure*, as well as enough sporting amenities to dizzy the mind and exhaust the body, and you're closer to understanding the resort's appeal. The Cloister is a self-contained vacation destination. It typifies understated luxury, as well as discretion—for example, no one bats an eye when George Bush, Sr. walks by in his tennis whites. Since its opening in 1928, the venerable property has hosted political, literary, and cinematic dignitaries, including Woodrow Wilson, Somerset Maugham, and Jimmy Stewart. The original hotel—an Addison Mizner-designed stucco building with a distinctive, red terra cotta tile roof—was recently demolished as part of a five-year renovation plan. (The resort is building a new main hotel.) Guestrooms remain open in numerous buildings and cottages on the island. Each guestroom includes a private bath with plush terry bathrobes. While the property requests appropriate attire in the common areas, especially after sunset—jackets are required for dinner in the main dining room—The Cloister does not feel stuffy. You're here to play, after all, and play you will. You can tee up for 54 holes of world-class golf, head to the beach club and its two pools, learn to shoot or improve your aim at the shooting school, play tennis on one of 25 clay tennis courts, sail from the beach or the yacht club, or saddle up and ride from the resort's stables. Sure, the tab will build during your stay, but whatever pain the bill creates will fade long before your vacation memories will. • *P.O. Box 30351, Sea Island, GA 31561,* ☎ *(912) 638-3611 or 1-800-732-4752, www.seaisland.com* • *$$$$*

Greyfield Inn • Built in 1900 as a private home for the daughter of Thomas Carnegie and operated today by Carnegie descendants, the Greyfield Inn is a grand, colonial-style, white mansion with a square-columned front porch set in lush, live oak foliage. Old-wealth permeates the Greyfield: The dress is casual during the day, but gentlemen must wear jackets for dinner. Carnegie-owned antique furnishings are throughout the inn's common areas and 17 guestrooms and suites. (There are 11 main-house rooms and six rooms in two additional cottages. Note that several of the rooms in the main inn have shared baths.) You come to this inn to disconnect. Secluded on Cumberland Island—the largest of the barrier islands and made seemingly larger with strict limits on the number of day and overnight visitors—the Greyfield has one radio phone, used only for emergencies. So removed is this self-contained property that *Town & Country* magazine remarked that the inn "has become a favorite of notables, especially those seeking time off from being noted." Indeed, the late John F. Kennedy, Jr., once the world's most-watched bachelor, married Carolyn Bessette at the Greyfield in 1996, far from the public eye. You also come here to stay put. The inn requires a minimum two-night stay—three nights for holidays—and breakfast, lunch, and dinner are included in the rate, as is daily ferry service to and from Fernandina Beach, Florida. Other amenities include daily naturalist-led tours of the island and use of the inn's bicycles for your own exploration. • *8 North Second Street, P.O. Box 900, Fernandina Beach, Florida 32035-0900,* ☎ *(904) 261-6408, www.greyfieldinn.com* • *$$$$*

The Jekyll Island Club • Founded and built more than a century ago as a winter hunting retreat for the nation's power brokers—think Rockefeller, Astor, Gould, Pulitzer—this resort is a National Historic Landmark. Much of its storied past has been preserved through the careful renovation of the original 60-room, 1887 clubhouse, which is now the main hotel. The entrance to this 240-acre estate is a winding drive past live oaks and magnolia trees to the turreted, Queen Anne-style hotel. There are 134 rooms and suites between the main building and the Crane and Cherokee cottages. Each has a private bath and many have such elegant appointments as Victorian fireplaces, mahogany furnishings, and whirlpool tubs. From the Victorian grand dining room with Ionic columns and three fireplaces to the property's exquisitely tended lawns, the Jekyll Island Club sets the scene for Jay Gatsby and Daisy Buchanan to come strolling through on their way to afternoon tea. Popular with families, the hotel sits a quarter-mile from the beach (there's a surfside Beach Club). Other amenities include a heated swimming pool, a croquet lawn (bring your whites), putting green, and five gift shops. • *371 Riverview Drive, Jekyll Island, GA 31527,* ☎ *(912) 635-2600 or 1-800-535-9547, www.jekyllclub.com* • *$$$$*

The King & Prince Beach & Golf Resort • Built as a private club in 1935, the original structure of this property burned three months after opening, but the second structure—the Spanish Colonial building that stands today—went up soon after. Club members spared few expenses in creating a regal atmosphere, including the 1938 installation of stained-glass pictorials depicting scenes of St. Simons' history and natural beauty. The club remained private until 1941 when it opened to the public with 110 guestrooms, each with a private bath. After its first summer season as a public hotel, the King & Prince closed and became a radar post and living quarters for the United States Navy during World War II, when German U-boats lurked offshore. The hotel reopened in 1947 and has undergone many renovations, improvements, additions, and changes in ownership. Throughout it all, generations of satisfied vacationing families have returned each summer to this beachfront property. While a little worn in places, the King & Prince continues to undergo improvements, and the service is always friendly and attentive. There are 184 rooms, including two- and three-bedroom villas onsite. Amenities include five pools, two tennis courts, and an exercise room. • *201 Arnold Road, St Simons Island, GA 31522, ☎ (912) 638-3631 or 1-800-342-0212, www.kingandprince.com • $–$$$$*

The Lodge at Sea Island Golf Club •

As the most-recent, ultra-luxurious resort property to go up in the Golden Isles, the Lodge at Sea Island leaves little to be wished for. (Should you wish for something, expect it to arrive on a silver platter, thanks to the 24-hour a day butler service.) This $47-million, 40-room lodge earned the prestigious AAA Five Diamond Award just 10 months after opening in March 2001. That's a big deal. What makes for such distinction? Try its location (the grounds of the historic Retreat Plantation overlook the Atlantic Ocean) and the architecture (reminiscent of grand New England summer cottages from the early 20th Century). The interior common areas feature stone floors, stained wood ceilings, soft leather chairs, oriental rugs, and chandeliers. The spacious guestrooms feature views either of the Atlantic Ocean or of wide, green fairways from one of the resort's three world-class golf courses. The amenities include three dining options, 54 holes of championship golf, deluxe locker rooms, a fitness center, and full access to all of the amenities and services of The Cloister, including the Beach Club. Make no mistake: the Lodge is expensive, but if you're looking for complete indulgence, you'll get it here. • *100 Retreat Avenue, St. Simons Island, GA 31522, ☎ (912) 634-4300 or 1-866-465-3563, www.seaisland.com • $$$$*

The Lodge on Little St. Simons Island •

The Lodge on Little St. Simons distills what playing hard and resting easy is all about. With no more than 30 overnight guests and an occasional handful of day visitors, the island feels as if it's yours to conquer on foot, bike, horseback, or by kayak or canoe. You can tire yourself silly wandering the seven miles of beach or the forested paths through the island's interior, or you can pick the perfect live oak overlooking the ocean under which to plant yourself with a fat novel. But who has time to read when every activity on the island is included in your rate? Whether you hike, bike, fish, paddle or saddle your mount, you'll do it amidst the humbling beauty of the island's 10,000 acres of Atlantic beach, maritime forest, coastal marsh, and meandering tidal creeks. The readers of *Condé Nast Traveler* selected this island resort as the Best Small Hotel in North America, citing its rustic yet refined ambience, outstanding food, and exceptional service.

There are five cottages on the island with a total of 15 comfortable guestrooms and suites, each with private bath and air conditioning but not one with a TV or phone. Since the island was a hunting retreat for years, you'll find that many of the common areas feature animal trophies hanging on the walls, so be forewarned, if that makes you squeamish. Everything on the island, including cocktails and dinner, is casual, and all meals, snacks, and beverages are included in the rate. Note that a minimum two-night stay is required. Plan your trip well in advance: In addition to the lodge's popularity with individuals, the entire island is available for rent, and you'd be surprised at the number of folks who put forth the $6,500 nightly fee for the run of the place. • *P.O. Box 21078, Little St. Simons Island, GA 31522, ☎ (912) 638-7472 or 1-888-733-5774, www.littlestsimonsisland.com* • *$$$$*

Other Places to Stay

In addition to the above recommendations, the **McKinnon House,** 1001 Egmont Street, Brunswick, GA 31520, (912) 261-9100, is a gracious 1902 Victorian B&B bedecked in antiques from Charleston and New Orleans. There are three rooms, as well as two grand parlors and four porches overlooking Brunswick's historic district.

About an hour south of the Golden Isles, the centuries-old coastal village of **St. Marys** has a beautiful historic district with numerous B&Bs and country inns. As the gateway to Cumberland Island, St. Marys is a fine place to stay if you're planning to spend several days exploring Georgia's largest barrier island. For recommendations on local lodging, contact the **St. Marys Tourism Council**, P. O. Box 1291, St. Marys, Georgia 31558, ☎ (912) 882-4000 or 1-866-868-2199, or visit *www.stmaryswelcome.com.*

Dine Well

From seafood to Thai, cuisine is as diverse in the Golden Isles as the shells you'll collect along the area's beaches. Of course, seafood is the specialty, and nearly all restaurants serve crab cakes, plus three or four different dishes featuring fresh shrimp, the local staple. You'll also find native flounder, swordfish, and salmon to be plentiful on the menus. There are many fine restaurants in addition to those listed here, but the following sampling will remove any guesswork.

Barbara Jean's • Decidedly casual in everything but their approach to cuisine, Barbara Jean's is perfect for the night when your face wears salt lines from the ocean and you want to kick back without pretense and a hole blown in your wallet. Photos from early St. Simons' history adorn the walls of this small restaurant. With seating for only 50 or so patrons, Barbara Jean's is likely to have a wait, especially since every local resident directs visitors here for the crab cakes. (The five-ounce crab cakes—or the seven-ounce jumbos—are so popular that Barbara Jean's owners Jim and Barbara Barta do a solid business of overnighting the cakes all over the United States.) In addition to hearty seafood and fresh-water fish entrées, the menu includes country-cooking staples like meatloaf, chicken fried steak, turkey with dressing, and fried chicken. The regular entrées come with a choice of two fresh vegetables from 14 prepared fresh daily. The costs are so reasonable that you're not likely to believe that everything is made from scratch. (But it is.) • *214 Mallory Street, St. Simons Island,* ☎ *(912) 634-6500*

Bennie's Red Barn • Even on an island full of dining institutions, Bennie's Red Barn rules the roost, having served up steaks, chops, chicken, and seafood since 1954. You enter the cavernous dining room—it's a converted dairy barn—to find a sprawl of candle-lit tables filled with a contented dining crowd, their conversation and laughter rising up into the rafters. Working efficiently between the tables is an amazingly competent cadre of waiter captains, assistant waiters, and bus boys. The waiters—some of whom have worked here since the restaurant's early days—arrive and recite the nightly specials from memory—a remarkable feat given the number of daily specials—and before they're out of sight, your salads arrive. Freshly cut steaks and daily catches are the specialty. Save room for the cheesecake or the

Bennie's Red Barn

chocolate cake, both of which are outstanding. • *5514 Frederica Road, St. Simons Island,* ☎ *(912) 638-2844*

Brogen's Boathouse • If your approach to finding restaurants is to learn where the locals like to eat, you'll undoubtedly find yourself at one of the four Brogen's establishments on St. Simons: Brogen's Food & Spirits in the Pier Village; Brogen's North, in the middle of the island on Frederica Road; Brogen's Bait Shack at the Golden Isles Marina; and Brogen's Boathouse, also at the Golden Isles Marina. Each of the locations does a steady bar business, especially after dinner hours, but for dining, Brogen's Boathouse is particularly appealing with an inventive menu and great views overlooking the Frederica River. Appetizer options are plentiful and include grilled scallop dijon, which are scallops grilled and topped with a dijon tarragon cream, and a portobello mushroom tower, stacked with layers of goat cheese, pesto, and roasted sweet peppers. For entrées, check out the teriyaki-glazed yellowfin tuna served over stir-fried vegetables with rice pilaf, or the parmesan-crusted grouper served over a smoked red pepper with a cilantro-horseradish cream sauce. • *Golden Isles Marina, 206 Marina Drive, St. Simons Island,* ☎ *(912) 634-5940*

CARGO Portside Grill • Popular with visiting Atlantans who've discovered that chef Alix Kenagy was the tour de force behind the popular Atlanta eateries INDIGIO and Partners Morningside Café, this restaurant vies for top gourmet honors in the region. Trendy and all the rage with the Sea Island set looking for an alternative to dining at The Cloister, CARGO is situated in a three-story building that's more than a century old. The intimate, 68-seat dining room is on the main floor, and there's a private dining room on the second floor. (Kenagy restored the building and lives in a loft on the third floor.) Innovative décor includes tables made from 200-year-old heart pine, a bar made from the building's original floor joists, and large photographs of Brunswick's early shipping days. As attractive as the dining room is, it's the preparation and presentation of the cuisine that will linger the longest in your memory. The menu presents a combination of Southern cuisine (fried green tomatoes as an appetizer) and international (a rack of lamb entrée to make any Kiwi proud). Each arrives looking as if it should be photographed before eaten. For starters, try the grilled oysters "mood indigo:" a baker's half dozen grilled in their half-shells until the edges curl and then basted with a key lime, chipoltle, and bacon topping. Tired of seafood? Try the pasta "Vera Cruz," which is fresh red pepper and natural linguine served with grilled chicken breast and pablona peppers, smoked tomatoes, and caramelized onions in a Tequila-chipotle cream that includes seared corn, parmesan cheese, and cilantro. Dessert? It ought to be illegal to leave without trying the crème brulée. Closed Sundays and Mondays. • *1423 Newcastle Street, Brunswick,* ☎ *(912) 267-7330*

The Cloister Beach Club • The Cloister's "casual" dining experience is at the Beach Club on Sea Island, where sweeping views of the Atlantic Ocean await. The Beach Club serves creative Southeastern American cuisine from the menu or you can opt for the bountiful seafood buffet. Think: All the shrimp, oysters, crab claws,

and fish you can eat in an upscale setting. The dress code for the Beach Club calls for "casual elegant," which translates into collared shirts and slacks for men. • *The Cloister, Sea Island Road, Sea Island* ☎ *(912) 638-3611*

Colt & Alison's • The 2001 opening of Colt & Alison's brought the region its first upscale steakhouse on par with such national entities as Morton's of Chicago or Shula's Steakhouse. Specializing in premium cuts of steaks, chops, and Maine lobster, Colt & Alison's serves it all up in an intimate atmosphere with low, wood-paneled ceilings that make the dining area feel cozy and warm, especially after you sample a vintage from the wine list. (There are more than 800 unique selections of fine wines from around the world, including an extensive list of large-format wine bottles.) While you can have an intimate dinner here, you may find yourself with a large number of golfers reliving their exploits from the day's play, so come prepared for possible polite revelry. Jackets and collared shirts are required. • *The Lodge at Sea Island, 100 Retreat Avenue, St. Simons Island, GA 31522* ☎ *(912) 634-4300*

Frederica House • The dining experience at this casual restaurant is made all the more pleasant by the cool, worm-holed, white cedar interior walls. The walls were milled from logs originally used as fencing timbers to corral huge cypress logs floated downriver from the Florida swampland. The exterior siding was milled from cypress, a highly waterproof and durable wood. The cuisine is hearty and reasonably priced, and the service in this family-owned restaurant is especially friendly. For starters, order the

New Orleans-style seafood gumbo, and then any of the seafood entrées. Try the garlic shrimp, which is a generous portion of shrimp sautéed in garlic butter and white wine. All entrées come with the choice of two sides, ranging from a salad to cheese grits. • *3611 Frederica Road, St. Simons Island,* ☎ *(912) 638-6789*

George's Mediterranean Café • Located in Redfern Village, the cluster of shops off Frederica Road on St. Simons, George's presents an ambitious menu mix of American, Greek, French, and Italian cuisine. It all comes off nicely, but the best of the lot are the Greek dishes. With outside patio dining and an interior decorated to resemble a European café, this is the perfect setting to dig into appetizers like fried calamari or saganaki (imported Greek cheese sautéed tableside with brandy and lemon). For entrées, you'd do well to have the moussaka (eggplant layered with ground beef, parmesan cheese, spices, tomato sauce, and topped with a light Béchamel sauce). In addition to the international cuisine, you'll find numerous other dishes, including fresh seafood, steaks, black angus beef, lamb, and pasta. Each entrée includes vegetables and a choice of Greek, Caesar, or mixed green salads. Desserts are plentiful, but if you're looking for a sure thing, order the baklava. Closed Sundays. • *228 Redfern Village, St. Simons Island,* ☎ *(912) 634-9633*

J Macs • Located in the Village on St. Simons just a short walk from the pier, J Macs specializes in regional and coastal cuisine served in a posh setting. But don't let the décor make you feel unwelcome if you're not dressed in your finest. The restaurant invites those "on their way to the symphony or just off the sailboat" to dine. For starters, try the shrimp and ginger Asian pot stickers with Napa cabbage slaw and spicy soy dipping sauce, or the house-made potato chips baked with creamy blue cheese crumbles. Bet you can't eat just one. For dinner, try the herb-roasted pork loin over maple-whipped sweet potatoes, served with sauté haricot verts and Vidalia onion juice. Do not pass Go unless you've sampled the vanilla bean crème brulée for dessert. J Macs is also a piano and martini bar. Here you'll find such liquid concoctions as the Velvet Bunny, the Lady Godiva, and Picasso's Blue Period, which is perhaps how you'll feel in the morning should you sample all three. • *407 Mallory Street, St. Simons Island,* ☎ *(912) 634-0403*

Jekyll Island Club Main Dining Room • This grand Victorian dining room with Ionic columns, impressively carved woodwork, and three fireplaces hearkens back to the days when the Rockefellers, Astors, and Pulitzers dined here. White tabletops, lit by candles, and live piano music set the stage for a memorable evening. The cuisine and carefully selected wine list rise to the occasion. Start with the Blue Crab Cakes (local blue crab cooked with herbs and spices and served with a smoked apple relish and tarragon mustard cream) and then move on to Plantation Shrimp (Georgian white shrimp sauteed with grilled andouille sausage, black beans, grilled corn, peppers and onions, served with seasonal greens and white rice). Jackets requested for men. • *371 Riverview Drive, Jekyll Island, GA 31527* ☎ *(912) 635-2600 or 1-800-535-9547*

The Debate Stews

In this corner, with a slightly thicker consistency and purportedly first stewed in 1828: **Brunswick Stew** from Brunswick County, Virginia. In the next corner, arriving at the table in 1898 and with a stronger tomato and barbecue-oriented base: Brunswick Stew from Brunswick, Georgia. Who created this hearty, slow-cooked soup so thick with meat and vegetables that a fork does as well serving it as a spoon? Who knows and, frankly, one bite into it, who cares? All that matters is that it's there for the asking, on nearly every menu in the Golden Isles area.

If you've never had Brunswick Stew, head to one of the following eateries for their famed interpretations: **Spanky's Marsh Side Restaurant,** 1200 Glynn Avenue, Brunswick, ☎ (912) 267-6100; • **Twin Oaks Barbecue,** 2618 Norwich Street, Brunswick, ☎ (912) 265-3131; or • **Frannie's Place,** 318 Mallory Street, St. Simons Island, ☎ (912) 638-1001.

Picnic Packing

Pack for your day's active excursion by swinging by the **Wine & Cheese Cellar,** 211 Redfern Village, St. Simons Island, ☎ (912) 638-2465, where you'll find a dazzling array of wines and cheeses, deli sandwiches on specialty breads, and many delectable gourmet treats to slip into the picnic basket. • **Locos Deli & Pub,** 2463 Demere Road, St. Simons Island, ☎ (912) 634-2002, packs a mean sandwich to go. You'll get a workout just toting around their sandwich called "the biggest thing we've got," which is a half-pound of roast beef, ham, turkey, and American cheese plus fixings on a foot-long sub. • On Jekyll Island, stock up for the bike ride or beach excursion at **Café Solterra,** at the Jekyll Island Club Hotel, 371 Riverview Drive, ☎ (912) 635-2600, where there are plenty of deli items and treats to throw in the pack for a satisfying repast.

Just Desserts

How about an old-fashioned candy and ice cream shop with loads of great chocolate and freshly made fudge? Head to the **Island Sweets Shoppe,** 150 Old Plantation Road, Jekyll Island, ☎ (912) 635-3135, and leave your conscience behind.

A Long-Weekend Itinerary

Day One

After breakfast at your inn or B&B, swing by the **Wine & Cheese Cellar** (page 57) on St. Simons Island to purchase a picnic lunch and liquid refreshments for your day at the beach on **Jekyll Island.** Then take your supplies and fresh legs to **Jekyll Island Bicycle Rentals** (page 24) to rent bicycles. Explore the island by bike, being certain to stop and tour the **historic district** (page 41) and the **Horton House** (page 41) ruins. Then pedal your picnic to the southern end of the island to find your own stretch of beach on which to eat, nap, swim, and walk along the shore.

Turn in your bicycles and then return to your inn to prepare for an evening out. Head to Brunswick, park the car and stroll the streets of **Old Town Brunswick** (page 37) in the late afternoon light, stopping at **Mary Ross Waterfront Park** (page 38) to watch the shrimp boats return with the day's catches.

Enjoy cocktails and dinner at **CARGO Portside Grill** (page 54) in Brunswick.

Return to your inn to retire for the day.

Day Two

After an early breakfast, head to **Altamaha Coastal Tours** (page 26) to sign up for one of their half-day, sea-kayaking tours to Blackbeard Island. If you've never paddled before, don't worry. Part of the trip involves instruction. Once on the island, you can hike to your heart's content.

Back on land, head to **Barbara Jeans** (page 53) for their famous crab cakes. After lunch, visit the historic sights on St. Simons, including **Fort Frederica** (page 39), **Christ Church** (page 39), the **Avenue of Oaks** (page 45) and the **St. Simons Island Lighthouse Museum** (page 40).

As the sun wanes, head to **Brogan's Food & Spirits** (page 54) in the Village for a cocktail before returning to your inn to prepare for dinner. Dine at St. Simon's dinner institution, **Bennie's Red Barn** (page 54).

Day Three

After breakfast at your inn, spend the morning doing some serious retail therapy in the area's **antiques shops** (page 33), **art galleries** (page 34), and **shops** (page 46). Round out your therapy with the best way to end any vacation: a massage. Make an appointment with one of the professional massage therapists at the **St. Simons Health & Fitness Club** (page 48).

Return to the real world.

Additional Information

For additional dining, accommodations, and sightseeing information, including the dates of special events, contact:

The Brunswick & the Golden Isles Visitors Bureau, 4 Glynn Ave, Brunswick, GA 31520, (912) 265-0620 or 1-800-933-2627, *www.bgivb.com,* operates welcome centers at this location, as well as in Neptune Park, ☎ (912) 638-9014, on St. Simons Island; and on Jekyll Island on the causeway, ☎ (912) 635-3636 or 1-877-453-5955. All are open daily, 9 A.M.–5 P.M.

The St. Marys Tourism Council, 406 Osborne Street, St. Marys, Georgia 31558, ☎ (912) 882-4000 or 1-866-868-2199, *www.stmaryswelcome.com,* provides information about ferries to Cumberland Island and information about nearby lodging, dining, and activity options. Open Monday–Saturday, 9 A.M.–5 P.M.; Sunday, 1 P.M.–5 P.M.

Photo by Altamaha Coastal Tours

Paddling along Blackbeard Island

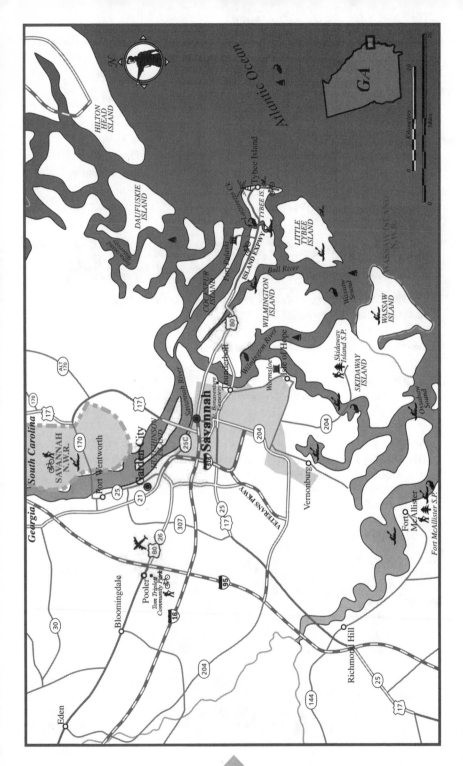

Savannah, Georgia

From its headwaters in the foothills of the Appalachian Mountains to its congress with the Atlantic Ocean, the Savannah River separates Georgia from its neighbor to the north, South Carolina. There are many scenic stretches along the river's 315-mile journey to the sea, but perhaps the most alluring is in the coastal region, an area of fertile marshes and winding tidal creeks. It's here, near the river's mouth, that the genteel and gracious City of Savannah sits, as she has for more than 270 years.

Savannah is roughly 18 miles from the Atlantic, though the broad river and surrounding maze of creeks give the impression of water everywhere. Protected by coastal marshes and barrier islands to the east, the city sits in an ecological paradise that has drawn people for as many as 4,000 years, beginning with Paleo-Indians who hunted and fished here. By the early 18th-century arrival of the first colonial settlers, the Yamacraw Indians (members of the Creek Nation) had lived beside the Savannah River for centuries. Their presence would play a crucial role in England's sucessful settlement of Georgia as the 13th and final colony in the New World.

British interest in establishing another colony arose, in part, from a report parliamentary member James Edward Oglethorpe prepared in 1732 on the condition of England's crowded prison system. Oglethorpe's findings—that prison

The Savannah riverfront

GA Department of Tourism

Oglethorpe's 1773 Savannah street design called for public squares

cells were overflowing with harmless debtors—led King George II to establish Georgia as a repository for England's debtors, as well as for its poor and unemployed. Another important role the Crown expected Georgia to play was to provide a cushion between Spanish settlements in Florida and British interests to the north, namely Beaufort and Charleston, South Carolina.

In 1733, Oglethorpe and 114 colonists crossed the Atlantic, sailed up the Savannah River, and started their village on Yamacraw Bluff, a high point on the south side of the river. Oglethorpe named the site "Savannah," the Creek word for *waterway*. While initial tensions were high between the Native Americans and settlers, Oglethorpe's fledgling colony avoided the disastrous warfare that beset other colonial settlements thanks to Mary Musgrove, the half-Yamacraw wife of English trader John Musgrove. Mary served as a liaison and interpreter between Oglethorpe and Chief Tomochichi, the Yamacraw leader. She was instrumental in fostering a friendship between the two men and in helping negotiate treaties between the English and the Creek Nation, which in turn, ensured the settlers' safety and secured their rights to settle the land.

Despite great difficulties—disease, weather, and skirmishes with the Spanish—Savannah continued to grow under Oglethorpe's direction. He returned to England in 1742 but not before working with Colonel William Bull to design the city's development according to a grid of squares framed by roads. As Savannah grew, the original four squares—Johnson, Telfair, Wright, and Ellis—expanded to six and then to 24. Of those 24, 21 remain today.

Savannah & SCAD

The 1978 founding of the **Savannah College of Art & Design (SCAD)**, 22 East Lathrop Avenue, Savannah, ☎ (912) 525-5100 or 1-800-869-7223, *www.scad.edu*, had a huge impact on Savannah's historic district. The school, which started with fewer than 100 students, purchased dilapidated buildings and converted them into classrooms. Today, SCAD is the largest art school in the country with more than 5,000 students working in some 50 buildings downtown. (Look for the SCAD initials.) The school hosts numerous annual events, including the Savannah Film & Video Festival and the Sidewalk Arts Festival, which make Savannah swell with both pride and visitors.

Deron Nardo

SCAD

The cultivation and exportation of rice drove Georgia's early economy and by the mid 1760s, the colony had grown six-fold. Tension developed between the increasingly wealthy planters and England over taxation and by the start of the American fight for independence, Georgia supported creating a new nation. Nonetheless, soon after the American Revolution began, the British overtook Savannah and occupied it from 1778 until Lord Charles Cornwallis' surrender at Yorktown in 1781.

Following the Revolutionary War, Savannah became one of the wealthiest port cities in the world. In 1793 on a

Savannah plantation, Eli Whitney, a schoolteacher and private tutor, invented the cotton gin, a machine that separated seeds from the fiber in cotton bolls. That development, combined with the booming slave trade, made Savannah landowners and merchants exceptionally wealthy and drove the city's growth—the results of which can be seen today—as elaborate homes, mansions, and civic buildings went up around the oak-shaded squares. But the good times did not last.

During the Civil War, Union ships blockaded Savannah's harbor, stopping the cotton trade and draining the city's cash stockpiles. In 1864, after burning Atlanta

BTB or ATB?

Savannah's history may be measured as Before the Book or After the Book. The book? John Berendt's *Midnight in the Garden of Good & Evil,* published in 1994. The steamy, nonfiction account of a murder in one of Savannah's opulent mansions introduced readers to a host of eccentric Savannahians, all the while casting the city in such an intriguing light that tourism has increased by nearly 50 percent since its publication. If you've read the book and want to see what Berendt describes, join any one of the numerous *Midnight*-themed tours. (See *Tours* under *Kick Back.*)

and every town east of it on his March to the Sea, Union General William Tecumseh Sherman entered Savannah, only to find it evacuated. Sherman was so taken with the city's beauty that he left it intact, writing to President Abraham Lincoln: "I beg to present you as a Christmas present, the city of Savannah." Despite the repeal of slavery, Savannah regained a brief measure of financial security, thanks to the efficient rebuilding of the South's rail system and a strong demand for cotton.

In the late 1890s, the boll weevil decimated more than half of Georgia's cotton fields, again triggering the collapse of Savannah's cotton industry. The city entered an economic decline that lasted nearly 50 years.

Meanwhile, many of Savannah's elegant homes fell into disrepair. Some were abandoned and others demolished. In the mid 1950s, a group of seven civic-minded women learned that the early 19th-century Isaiah Davenport House was to be torn down, and they set out to save it by forming the Historic Savannah Foundation. To date, the efforts of the foundation, along with those of the Savannah College of Art & Design, have helped preserve more than 1,700 historic structures, effectively kicking off what may be the city's most profitable and sustainable economic boom: *tourism.*

Today the national media regularly cites Savannah as one of the top places to vacation. The city's many charms—architecture, history, cultural outlets, and fine dining and lodging—afford her the well-earned moniker, "Hostess of the

Wealthy planters built elaborate homes in Savannah

GA Department of Tourism

South." Outdoor enthusiasts also find much to love. The network of tidal creeks and rivers surrounding Savannah are busy with adventurers kayaking, fishing, and sailing, while the nearby barrier islands offer ample space to explore on foot or by bike.

Why trek here? Because of the combination of a sophisticated, historic, riverside city with the sublime beauty of Georgia's coastal barrier islands. Whether you're seeking high-culture experiences, an afternoon sailing the Atlantic Ocean, or something in between, the buffet of possibilities is invigorating. You can begin your day with a cup of coffee or tea and decide whether to hike through a maritime forest, sea kayak a serpentine tidal creek, or visit a handful of museums. Start early enough and you can do all three.

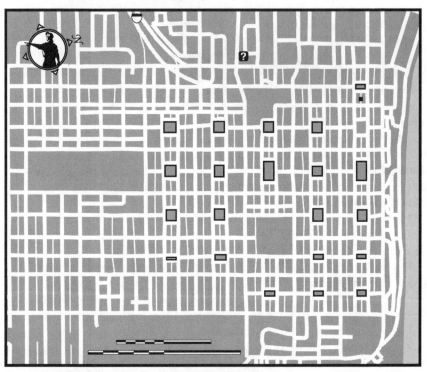

Downtown Savannah (see pages 66-67 for key to square names)

The Way Around

Considered America's first "planned city," Savannah has come a long way from the original grid pattern of streets and squares laid out by city founder, James Oglethorpe. Today Savannah sprawls across 65 square miles and is home to a quarter-million people. This chapter focuses primarily on the **National Historic Landmark District** downtown, a two-square-mile area bordered by the **Savannah River** to the north, **Gaston Street** to the south, **Martin Luther King, Jr. Boulevard** to the west, and **Broad Street** to the east. Within this district, you'll find the majority of the city's museums, galleries, and restaurants, as well as its historic inns, churches, parks, and much-heralded squares (see "Savannah, You're so Square").

While nearly every street in the historic district is worthy of your attention, several bear mentioning here. Cobblestone **River Street** fronts the Savannah River and is perhaps the most "touristy" of the city streets. Home to a string of souvenir shops, bars, and restaurants, River Street is the epicenter of the city's famed St. Patrick's Day celebration. Immediately south of River Street, **Factor's Walk** is a row of narrow buildings connected by a network of concrete and iron walkways. **Broughton Street**

River Street

runs east-west several blocks south of the river and is lined with shops, galleries, restaurants, and theaters. It provides the "Main-Street" feel that you'd expect in a historic district. Walking is the easiest way to explore the historic district; however, you'll undoubtedly drive through it at some point during your vacation. The following streets are the least impeded by squares and slow-moving traffic. **Whitaker Street** runs one-way north through downtown, and **Drayton Street** runs one-way south. For the smoothest east-west travel, use **Liberty** or **Oglethorpe streets**. Liberty Street traveling east becomes **Skidaway Road**, which leads to St. Bonaventure Cemetery. Oglethorpe Street traveling west connects with **Route 17** north over the Talmadge

> Downtown Savannah is the country's largest National Historic Landmark District.

Bridge, and heads to the Savannah National Wildlife Refuge in South Carolina. Just off the Savannah River, **Bay Street** traveling east becomes **President Street Extension/Island Expressway** and then **Route 80** en route to Tybee Island and Fort Pulaski.

There are detailed descriptions of downtown attractions throughout the chapter, but a few major sites worth mentioning here include **City Market** (on the west side of town between Franklin and Ellis squares), which contains the highest concentration of galleries, along with shops, restaurants, and bars; and **Colonial Park Cemetery** (at the corner of Oglethorpe and Abercorn streets), where many of Savannah's residents who died between 1750-1850 are buried.

Forsyth Park serves as a rough divider between the historic district and the **Victorian District,** which continues south from the park to **Anderson Lane**. The 20-acre park is down-

Forsyth Park

Savannah, You're so Square

Savannah's beautifully landscaped squares serve as delightful city parks, places ideal for sitting, resting your legs, and watching the world walk by. Here are the 21 surviving squares (of the original 24), listed west to east, working south from the river.

Franklin Square
Built in 1790 and named for Benjamin Franklin, who served as Georgia's colony agent in London.
Location: *Montgomery Street, between Bryan and Congress streets (#1 on downtown map)*

Johnson Square
The town's first square, paced by James Oglethorpe in 1733 and named for his friend, Robert Johnson, an early Governor of South Carolina.
Location: *Bull Street, between Bryan and Congress streets (#2 on map)*

Reynolds Square
Mapped in 1734 and named for John Reynolds, the first Royal Governor of Georgia.
Location: *Abercorn Street, between Bryan and Congress streets (#3 on map)*

Warren Square
Built in 1791 and named for Revolutionary War hero Joseph Warren, who died in the Battle of Bunker Hill.
Location: *Habersham Street, between Bryan and Congress streets (#4 on map)*

Washington Square
Laid out in 1790 and named for George Washington.
Location: *Houston Street, between Bryan and Congress streets (#5 on map)*

Telfair Square
Named for Edward Telfair, a Revolutionary patriot and Governor of Georgia, Telfair is one of the four original squares laid out in 1733.
Location: *Barnard Street, between York and State streets (#6 on map)*

Wright Square
Named for Royal Governor James Wright, this was one of the four original squares mapped in 1733.
Location: *Bull Street, between York and State streets (#7 on map)*

Oglethorpe Square
Built in 1742 and named for Georgia Colony founder, James Edward Oglethorpe.
Location: *Abercorn Street, between York and State streets (#8 on map)*

Columbia Square
Built in 1799 and named for the mythical goddess of Earth's fertility, Columbia.
Location: *Habersham Street, between York and State streets (#9 on map)*

Greene Square
Laid out in 1799 and named for Revolutionary War General Nathaniel Greene.
Location: *Houston Street, between York and State streets (#10 on map)*

Orleans Square
Built in 1815 and named in honor of Andrew Jackson's victory at the Battle of New Orleans during the War of 1812
Location: *Barnard Street, between Hull and Perry streets (#11 on map)*

Chippewa Square
Built in 1815 and named for the Battle of Chippewa in the War of 1812. Perhaps most famous for being the location of Forrest Gump's park-bench declaration, "Life is like a box of chocolates."
Location: *Bull Street, between Hull and Perry streets (#12 on map)*

Crawford Square
Built in 1841 and named for United States Senator William Harris Crawford.
Location: *Houston Street, between Hull and Perry streets (#13 on map)*

Pulaski Square
Built in 1837 and named for the Polish Count Casimir Pulaski, a Revolutionary War hero killed during the Siege of Savannah.
Location: *Barnard Street, between Harris and Charlton streets (#14 on map)*

Madison Square
Built in 1837 and named for President James Madison.
Location: *Bull Street, between Harris and Charlton streets (#15 on map)*

Lafayette Square
Built in 1837 and named for the Marquis de Lafayette.
Location: *Abercorn Street, between Harris and Charlton streets (#16 on map)*

Troup Square
Built in 1851 and named for former Georgia Governor George Michael Troup.
Location: *Habersham Street, between Harris and Charlton streets (#17 on map)*

Chatham Square
Built in 1847 and named for William Pitt, Earl of Chatham.
Location: *Barnard Street, between Taylor and Gordon streets (#18 on map)*

Monterey Square
Built in 1847 and named to commemorate the capture of Monterey, Mexico, by General Zachary Taylor during the Mexican War.
Location: *Bull Street, between Taylor and Gordon streets (#19 on map)*

Calhoun Square
Built in 1851 and named for South Carolinian John C. Calhoun.
Location: *Abercorn Street between Taylor and Gordon streets (#20 on map)*

Whitefield Square
Built in 1851 and named for Reverend George Whitefield, a Savannahian who founded the Bethesda Orphanage.
Location: *Habersham Street, between Taylor and Gordon streets (#21 on map)*

Silver Screen Savannah

Restore a historic city like Savannah, and the movie industry will come. Numerous films have been shot in and around Savannah. A sampling: *Forrest Gump*, whose title character (played by Tom Hanks) declared "Life is like a box of chocolates" from a bench in Chippewa Square; and Robert Redford's *The Legend of Bagger Vance*. Other major hits include *The General's Daughter* and *Midnight in the Garden of Good & Evil*.

town Savannah's major outdoor playground. Joggers, in-line skaters, and bicyclists flock here in pleasant weather. The park has several notable features, including the 1858 Forsyth Park Fountain. One of the most-photographed images of Savannah, this landmark was modeled after a fountain in the Place de la Concorde in Paris.

The Victorian District, which covers a square mile, is undergoing revitalization similar to the historic district with an increasing number of boutiques, inns, and restaurants opening. South of the Victorian District are two large sections of Savannah: **Midtown** and the **Southside**, both of which are full of "Anywhere, USA" elements like strip malls, car dealerships, and national-chain hotels, motels, and restaurants.

East of the historic district, Bay Street connects to President Street Extension/Island Expressway and then Route 80, which leads east to Tybee Island. The highway crosses a series of bridges connecting several barrier islands, the largest of which are **Wilmington** and **Whitmarsh islands** (both primarily residential) and then **Cockspur Island,** site of the Fort Pulaski National Monument. After crossing **Bull River** and **Lazaretto Creek**—the latter of which provides access to numerous kayak spots from its public boat launch—the road rolls beside the beautiful saltwater marshes that eventually give way to the beaches of Tybee Island.

Located 18 miles from Savannah, **Tybee Island** is a low-key beach resort area. It has a

GA Department of Tourism

Savannah's Victorian District

GA Department of Tourism

Tybee Island Beach

three-mile beach with ample public access. **Butler Avenue** is the island's main drag. The northern part of the island, home to the Tybee Lighthouse & Museum and Fort Screven, is primarily residential. Tybee's southern end is more commercial with numerous motels, hotels, restaurants, and beach-oriented businesses. This is also where you'll find the south-end pier and pavilion, the island's "hub."

Completely free from development and accessible only by boat, **Little Tybee Island** is actually larger than Tybee. Located directly south of its namesake, this barrier island is a haven for kayak and beach lovers drawn to its numerous tidal creeks, salt marshes, and several miles of sandy beach facing the Atlantic Ocean.

The communities of Thunderbolt and Isle of Hope are on the western bank of the **Wilmington River**, a narrow waterway that runs southeast from the Savannah River to Wassaw Sound. **Thunderbolt,** a quaint waterfront fishing village, is home to the mystical St. Bonaventure Cemetery, a must-see on any trip to Savannah. Here, beneath live oaks draped in Spanish moss, marble gravestones mark the final resting places for hundreds of Savannah's notable residents, including poet Conrad Aiken and songwriter Johnny Mercer.

Isle of Hope was once a protective garrison for Savannah and then a retreat for the city's wealthiest residents. It is now known for its stately homes, quiet streets, and rich history. Wormsloe State Historic Site, the tabby house built by early-settler Noble Jones in 1733, is located here.

Other areas of interest around Savannah include **Skidaway Island,** primarily a residential island but also home to Skidaway Island State Park, a 588-acre tract featuring a museum and nature trails. South of Skidaway Island and accessible only by boat, **Wassaw Island** is a 10,000-acre paradise. Much of the island is part of the Wassaw Island National Wildlife Refuge, making it an excellent daytrip destination.

GA Department of Tourism

St. Bonaventure Cemetery

A Footnote

Traffic in the historic district is heavy and parking is difficult, so you're better off leaving the car keys behind and exploring this section of town on foot or by bike. But exercise caution at night. Savannah's small-town feel belies a typical city's crime element. If you're unsure about walking back to your inn, play it safe and catch a cab.

Weather

Savannah enjoys a subtropical climate that makes outdoor activities possible year-round. The summers are hot, the winters mild. Average highs in the winter months range from the 50s to the 70s with overnight lows dipping into the 40s. Spring is the most-pleasant time to visit, as blooming azaleas add to the beauty of mild, mostly sunny days. Expect springtime highs in the 70s with lows in the upper 50s. Summer brings the most rain and humidity; it's not unusual for the heat index to climb into the triple digits for short stretches. Autumn is pleasant and dry, and its cool evenings make for wonderful strolls under the stars.

Getting to Savannah

By Air: Just outside of town, the **Savannah International Airport,** ☎ (912) 964-0514, *www.savannahairport.com,* hosts numerous major airlines and rental car companies.

By Car: From Atlanta, take Interstate 75 south roughly 80 miles to Interstate 16 east for approximately 165 miles to Savannah. Exit at the Montgomery Street Exit. Expect a 4.5-hour drive. **From Charlotte,** take Interstate 77 south to Columbia and then Interstate 26 east 50 miles to Interstate 95. Take Interstate 95 south roughly 80 miles to Exit #5 in Hardeeville, South Carolina, where you connect with Route 17 south. Take Route 17 south 15 miles to the Oglethorpe Avenue Exit. Expect a four-hour drive. **From Raleigh**, take Interstate 40 east to Interstate 95 south roughly 280 miles to Exit #5 mentioned in the directions from Charlotte. Expect a 5.5-hour drive.

P l a y   H a r d

W i d e   O p e n

The Savannah area's largest outdoor playgrounds are the **Atlantic Ocean** and **Savannah River,** with its many tributaries, but they are just the start. The following public lands are some of the region's best places to hike, bike, swim, sail, fish, and more. Any survey of Savannah's major outdoor venues has to include the **historic district**, given that the best way to explore this 2.5-square-mile area is on foot or by bike. Can't imagine much sport in exploring a downtown area? Make visiting all 21 squares your goal and see if you still feel that way.

Serving as the rough border between the historic and Victorian districts, **Forsyth Park** is workout central for joggers and cyclists who take to the perimeter sidewalk (bike riding inside the park is prohibited), as well as for tennis, basketball, and Frisbee players.

Just six miles southeast of Savannah, **Skidaway Island State Park,** 52 Diamond Causeway, Skidaway Island, (912) 598-2300, has 533 acres of maritime forest, salt marsh, and tidal estuary open to

Deron Nardo

Inside the Savannah National Wildlife Refuge

exploration by foot, bike, and kayak. The park has a visitor center at its entrance, as well as five-plus miles of interpretive trails with observation platforms. A boat launch just off Diamond Causeway provides access to Skidaway Narrows. To get to the park from Savannah, take Abercorn Street south to DeRenne Drive, where you turn left. Take DeRenne to Waters Avenue, where you turn right. Waters Avenue, which changes names twice—first to Whitfield Road and then to the Diamond Causeway—leads to the park.

Just a 15-minute drive from downtown, the **Savannah National Wildlife Refuge,** off Route 17 in South Carolina, (912) 652-4415, encompasses more than 28,000 acres of fresh-water marshes, tidal rivers and creeks, and bottomland hardwoods. Established in 1927, the refuge contains nearly four miles of gravel road available to hikers, bicyclists, and motorists. From Savannah, take Oglethorpe Avenue west to Route 17 north approximately eight miles to Route 170, onto which you turn left, heading west. Follow Route 170 west two miles to the refuge entrance on the left.

Located less than 10 miles west of Savannah, 200-acre **Tom Triplett Community Park,** Route 80 West, Pooler, (912) 652-6780, features a small lake; a 1.25-mile paved path for bik-ing, walking, and rollerblading; horseback riding trails; and several miles of mountain-bike singletrack. Access the park by taking Interstate 16 west from Savannah to the Dean Forest Road Exit. Turn right at the bottom of the ramp, drive two miles to Route 80 and turn left, heading west. Tom Triplett Community Park is a mile or so ahead on the left.

With nearly three miles of beach facing the Atlantic Ocean plus miles of protected shore-line facing the mainland, **Tybee Island,** 1-800-868-2322, *www.tybeevisit.com,* is popular with paddlers, beach combers, sailors, swimmers, surfers, and more.

Undeveloped **Little Tybee Island** features 7,000 acres of salt marsh, maritime forest, and beautiful beachfront popular with hikers and paddlers. Accessible only by boat, Little Tybee's draw is its isolation—even during the summer. The island and its waters contain alligators, dolphins, gray foxes, and deer, as well as an abundance of bird species.

No-seeums

Though humorously named—they *are* hard to see—these sand gnats are anything but funny when they cover your legs and begin to gnaw away. Primarily a problem in the summer, especial-ly early and late in the day, no-seeums are no match for a strong bug repellant, so be sure to pack plenty for your outdoor plans.

The 1,726-acre expanse at **Fort McAllister Historic Park,** 3894 Fort McAllister Road, Richmond Hill, (912) 727-2339, includes two hiking trails and a boat launch with access to Redbird Creek and the Ogeechee River. Both are mellow, tidal waterways where wildlife encoun-ters are plentiful. It's not unusual to paddle alongside playful dolphins. To get to Fort McAllister from down-town Savannah, take Martin Luther King, Jr. Boulevard to Route 16 west, which connects with Interstate 95. Take Interstate 95 south to Exit #15, where you connect with Route 144 east. From here, follow signs to the park.

Accessible only by boat, Wassaw Island is home to the **Wassaw National Wildlife Refuge,** (912) 652-4415, which features more than 10,000 acres of sand dunes, salt marshes, mud flats, and maritime forest perfect for exploration by foot or kayak. The prime attraction is the island's undeveloped, seven-mile beach. What's particularly cool about Wassaw Island is that its timber has never been harvested. The island looks just as it did to the first European settlers in the early 18th Century. To reach the refuge, you can paddle a kayak (see *Paddling*) or contact the Isle of Hope Marina, 50 Bluff Drive, Savannah, (912) 354-8187, *www.isleofhopemarina.com,* for a list of the charter boats that make the trip.

Dayhiking

Even without the slightest semblance of a mountain on the horizon, the area surrounding Savannah offers great diversity in its hiking/walking options. Area beaches provide excellent workouts, and many trail systems on public lands stretch through maritime forests and past marshlands full of wildlife. The following are some of the better walking options in and around Savannah.

♦ To mix cardio with culture, tour Savannah's **historic district** on foot. Using the city map in *The Way Around* or one of the maps available free from the sources listed under *Additional Information,* make it your goal to walk through all 21 squares, plus Colonial Cemetery and Forsyth Park. If you move at a quick pace, the journey takes a little more than an hour-and-a-half. Not only is this a fine workout, but it's also an excellent way to get oriented to Savannah.

♦ The 6.5-mile **Old Savannah-Tybee Railroad Historic & Scenic Trail,** Route 80 East, (912) 652-6780, skirts the Savannah River and slices through scenic coastal marshland. The trail is on the former railroad line that whisked vacationers from Savannah to Tybee Island in the late 19th and early 20th centuries until Route 80 was built in 1933. The parking area and trailhead are in the middle of the limestone-covered path, so whether you head left or right, you'll come to the end of the path and have to turn around. To see every foot of the trail, you'll hike or bike 13 miles. Stop at a few of the exercise stations along the way and you're looking at a world-class workout. To get to the trail from downtown Savannah, take Bay Street to President Street

Savannah's parks make for pleasant walks

GA Department of Tourism

Two short trails wind around Fort Pulaski

Extension/Island Expressway to Route 80 east toward Tybee Island. Just across the Intracoastal Waterway, the parking area is on the left (as the road curves right). A sign marks the trailhead.

◆ There are two trails at **Fort Pulaski National Monument,** Route 80, Cockspur Island, (912) 786-5787, which is located 15 miles east of Savannah on Cockspur Island. Built in the 19th Century to protect Savannah from ships sailing up the river, Fort Pulaski is surrounded by 5,623 acres of scenic marshes and uplands that support a variety of animal life, including white-tailed deer, alligators, and raccoons. The park features a quarter-mile, self-guiding nature trail and a two-mile path that travels around the fort's perimeter, providing visitors views of this imposing fort from every angle. From Savannah, take Bay Street east to President Street Extension/Island Expressway to Route 80 east toward Tybee Island. Before reaching Tybee Island, you'll encounter signs for Cockspur Island and Fort Pulaski. The park charges a nominal admission fee.

◆ Walking the beaches of **Tybee Island** is an excellent way to get your heart rate up and to work your legs into submission. Plus, you're never far from the water should you need to cool off. The **North Beach** area is a better bet for lonely strolls, while the **South Beach** area provides more people-watching opportunities. From Savannah, take Bay Street east to President Street Extension/Island Expressway to Route 80 east 18 miles to Tybee Island. For parking on the north end, follow signs to the Tybee Island Lighthouse, near which there's a public lot with metered parking. (Watch your time carefully; the town is vigorous in tending its meters and in levying fines for expired parking.) To park on the island's south end, follow Route 80 (Butler Avenue) to 14th Street, where you turn left to reach the beach pavilion's metered parking area.

◆ **Skidaway Island State Park,** 52 Diamond Causeway, Skidaway Island, (912) 598-2300, has more than five miles of hiking trails. Throughout the park, you'll find numerous observation towers from which to watch deer, raccoons, and the many species of birds that reside in this 588-acre wonderland of salt marsh, maritime forest, and tidal estuary. Warm up on the one-mile **Sandpiper Trail** before tackling the **Big Ferry Trail**, which can be hiked in a two- or three-mile loop. There is also a short trail linking the two, making for a total hike of 5.5 miles. The park, which borders a portion of the Intracoastal Waterway, is open 7 A.M.–10 P.M. and charges a nominal parking fee. Trail maps are available in the visitor center. Directions to the park are in *Wide Open*.

◆ In the **Savannah National Wildlife Refuge,** (912) 652-4415, you can join motorists and mountain bikers on the four-mile, gravel-surface **Laurel Hill Wildlife Drive,** but a better bet would be to hike along the more than 40 miles of dikes that criss-cross the 28,000 acres of swamp forest, freshwater marsh, and tidal rivers and creeks of this former rice-growing region. The farther you venture from the motorized traffic on Laurel Hill Drive, the more likely you are to see wildlife, including alligators and numerous bird species. All of the refuge paths are well marked, so you're safe to wander. Looking for a suggestion? **The**

Cistern Trail departs Laurel Hill Drive and heads through the woods to the edge of the marsh. There's a map of the refuge, along with other useful information, at the refuge entrance. See *Wide Open* for directions.

♦ For a short walk filled with abundant environmental-education opportunities, visit the **Oatland Island Education Center,** 711 Sandtown Road, Savannah, (912) 898-3980, *www.oatlandisland.org,* and take in the 1.75-mile interpretive trail. Stroll through oak and pine forests and enjoy some prime habitats for viewing indigenous wildlife, some species of which are extinct in

Tybee Island

Georgia's wilds. The path is bordered by fenced-in habitats that contain bison, bobcats, foxes, and panthers, among other animals. Owned and operated by the Savannah-Chatham County Public Schools, the center's budget is met chiefly from grants, gifts, and donations. With your nominal donation, you'll get exercise, some tutoring on the environment, and a good feeling from contributing to public school education. From Savannah, take Bay Street east across the Wilmington River drawbridge and proceed another mile to the education center on the right. Signs direct you to visitor parking.

♦ In **Fort McAllister Historic Park**, 3894 Fort McAllister Road, Richmond Hill, (912) 727-2339, the flat, 3.1-mile **Fort McAllister Nature Trail** winds through coastal forest and beside scenic marshland. The trail sets out from the group-shelter parking lot and reaches a bridge a little more than half a mile into the hike. Once over the bridge, head right and continue to an intersection, where you turn right to reach a lookout tower from which excellent views of wide-open marshland and Redbird Creek open up. Retrace your steps to the intersection, where you turn right to continue the hike. When you reach the bridge again, backtrack the final half-mile to the parking lot. There is a nominal fee for entry into the historic site. See *Wide Open* for directions.

Bicycling

Trail riding (versus mountain biking) better describes the two-wheeled adventures to be had around Savannah given the region's flat-as-a-pancake landscape. That said, the following rides should get your heart pumping, whether from incessant pedaling or from the sight of an alligator beside the trail. ♦ It won't take long in downtown Savannah to see a bicyclist exploring the **historic district.** Given the slow-moving

Deron Nardo

The scenic Savannah-Tybee Rail Trail

(and at times aggravating) traffic filling the city's live oak-shaded streets, a bicycle is perhaps the easiest way to move about town. (It's certainly the fastest way to visit the city's 21 squares.) To get in on the fun, check with the rental sources below.

◆ With several miles of singletrack, **Tom Triplett Community Park,** Route 80, Pooler, (912) 652-6783, is the city's big mountain-biking venue. There are three wooded trails—loops of 3.5 miles, five miles and 6.3 miles—that present enough challenges (rolling pitches and tree stumps, for example) to make up for the lack of long, grueling climbs. Access the trails from the park's main parking lot. See *Wide Open* for directions. ◆ The **Old Savannah-Tybee Railroad Historic & Scenic Trail,** Route 80 East, (912) 652-6780, is a fine route for riding, particularly when you consider the scenery of marshland and the South Fork of the Savannah River lining the path. The flat, 6.5-mile trail is wide enough to ride two bikes side-by-side. While much of the trail is protected by palm trees, strong winds—common locally around any wide body of water—periodically blow through and make pedaling more challenging. See *Dayhiking* for directions to the trailhead.

◆ The system of dikes and gravel roads in the **Savannah National Wildlife Refuge,** (912) 652-4415, makes for great riding. You can pedal at an easy pace to enjoy the sights or hoof it for an intense workout. If you're interested in observing wildlife, this is the place. Venture off from beside the canals and you may come face-to-snout with a 12-foot alligator. **Laurel Hill Wildlife Drive** is a 4.5-mile auto-loop through the refuge; the road is narrow, but traffic moves slowly, rarely posing a risk to mountain bikers. The surface varies from dirt to gravel. To pedal away from the auto-tourists, ride along any of the refuge's dikes, open only to foot and pedal traffic. The dikes are worth the adventure and provide the best chance for seeing gators, eagles, egrets, and more. These dirt and grass trails are typically in good condition, though if it has recently rained a lot, call the refuge's office for a report on conditions. See *Wide Open* for directions.

◆ Like many beach towns, **Tybee Island** is a fine place to explore atop a beach cruiser. When **Butler Avenue**, the primary road on the island, is congested, ride the less-busy streets that parallel it: **Jones, Second,** and **Lovell avenues.** You can also ride on the island's beach for a couple of hours on either side of low tide.

Rentals

Bicycle Link, 22 West Broughton Street, Savannah, ☎ (912) 233-9401; and 7064 Hodgsen Memorial Drive, Savannah, ☎ (912) 355-4771, *www.bicyclelinksav.com* ◆ **Jaime's Sundance Bike Shop**, 22 Tybrisa Street, Tybee Island, ☎ (912) 786-9469, *www.jaimesbikes.com* ◆ **The Pack Rat,** 14th and Butler Avenue, Tybee Island, ☎ (912) 786-4013 ◆ **Savannah Pedicab,** City Market, Savannah, ☎ (912) 447-0800 ◆ **Star Bike**, 127 East Montgomery Crossroads, Savannah, ☎ (912) 927-2430

Paddling

There's no better way to escape Savannah's weekend crowds than to slip into a sea kayak and put some water between you and the tourists. Here tidal creeks and rivers are around every bend, offering plenty of places to launch a boat. Your reward will be a sublime tour of a secluded waterway where the only sounds are the quiet splash of your paddle or the swoop of an egret, heron, or osprey taking flight. If you like open water, the ocean is your oyster. There are also plenty of well-traveled routes between the mainland and the region's barrier islands.

A few words of caution: Eight- to 10-foot tides and a dizzying array of routes in the creeks and rivers make this a challenging place to paddle without a guide. The dramatic tidal changes disorient your visual memory, and stories of capable kayakers abandoning their vessels or having to drag them through oyster-laden riverbeds are common. (Wear old sneakers, not flip flops or sandals.) Unless you know the area well, hire a guide or join a tour. Never paddled before? Tours typically include instruction as part of the package. Some of the most popular waters your tour may visit follow.

◆ There ought to be a law against paddling around Savannah without visiting **Little Tybee Island,** the 7,000-acre barrier island just south of Tybee Island. Actually comprised of many small islands intersected by creeks and marshes, Little Tybee is completely undeveloped and presents innumerable places to pull ashore and explore the island's desolate beach and maritime forest. Accessible only by boat, Little Tybee promises relative isolation on its shores. Once you've reached Little Tybee, be sure to paddle the many tidal creeks, including routes known as **Jack's Cut, Mosquito Ditch, Lynn's Cut,** and **MRS Cut,** each of which offers smooth waters, seclusion, and plenty of chances to view wildlife. Again, given tidal differentials, you're best off joining a tour, but if you decide to set out alone, **Sea Kayak Georgia** (see "Tour Operators & Canoe/Sea Kayak Rentals") will provide satellite photos of the island with highlighted paddling routes for a small fee. The most common point of departure for the island is from the **Back River Boat Launch,** located on Alley 3 off Chatham Avenue, near the south end of Tybee Island.

◆ From Tybee Island, paddling **Lazaretto Creek** south delivers you to the **Cockspur Lighthouse,** standing 46 feet tall at the mouth of the Savannah River's South Fork. When the winds are light, the half-mile trip to the lighthouse is relatively easy. From the lighthouse area, expect excellent views of cargo ships making their way to and from Savannah's commercial port. At high tide, the lighthouse is completely surrounded by water, but at low tide, oyster beds make getting out of the kayak dicey. The boat ramp at **Lazaretto Creek Marina** is located off Route 80 on the right (coming from Savannah) just after you cross the Lazaretto Creek Bridge onto Tybee Island. Look for signs for the public boat launch.

Coastal Georgia kayaking

♦ Famous for its bone yard—a grove of dead, sun-bleached oak trees jutting from the sand—the **Wassaw National Wildlife Refuge,** (912) 652-4415, on Wassaw Island has seven miles of pristine and protected beach waiting for your landfall. Add to that nearly 20 miles of dirt roads and you've got a recipe for a killer multi-sport day. Wassaw Island is a popular nesting area for endangered loggerhead turtles, which come ashore at night in the summer to lay eggs before returning to the sea. It's not uncommon to find turtle tracks in the sand. To reach Wassaw, you'll paddle to the right from Priest Landing on the Wilmington River, located on the northeast part of Skidaway Island. It is roughly six miles one-way—a trip of two hours with the tide flowing with you at a moderate clip. Timing the tides is essential to making the trip an adventure (versus disaster), so if you plan to paddle alone, stop by one of the paddling outfitters for guidance and directions to the put-in.

♦ Just 25 minutes from Savannah, **Ebenezer Creek** is a gentle blackwater creek lined with overhanging cypress trees. The slow-moving current allows you to paddle Ebenezer in either direction. To put in, head to the juncture of Ebenezer Creek and the Savannah River, where you'll find a boat launch. Take Route 21 north from Savannah roughly 20 miles to Ebenezer Road, where you turn right. Approximately five miles ahead, you'll reach the Savannah River and the boat launch.

♦ For some nice paddling on protected waters with ample opportunities to view ospreys and their nests, head for **Skidaway Narrows,** west of Skidaway Island. This waterway doubles as part of the Intracoastal Waterway and is prone to boat traffic, particularly on the weekends. The best put-in is at Butterbean Beach, located on the Diamond Causeway. (See directions to Skidaway Island State Park under *Wide Open.*) Just before you reach the bridge over Skidaway Narrows, you'll see a prominent pull-off to the right. From the put-in, paddle left under the bridge (north) toward Isle of Hope where you'll find a number of creeks worth exploring.

Tour Operators & Canoe/Sea Kayak Rentals

Sea Kayak Georgia, 1102 Route 80, Tybee Island, ☎ (912) 786-8732, *www.seakayakgeorgia.com,* is a full-service paddling outfitter that rents kayaks, provides instruction, and operates a number of tours, including day and overnight trips. They also sell sea kayaks, canoes, and every type of paddling gear you can imagine. ♦ **Alakai Outfitters,** 1213 Route 80, Tybee Island, ☎ (912) 786-4000, *www.alakaioutifitters.com,* rents and sells kayaks, and specializes in two-hour guided tours that depart from the small retail shop four times a day. ♦ **Savannah Canoe & Kayak,** ☎ (912) 341-9502, *www.savannahcanoeandkayak.com,* rents kayaks, provides instruction, and operates a variety of paddling tours.

Deron Nardo

Redbird Creek

◆ Numerous waterways wind through the 28,000 acres of coastal marsh and wetlands inside the **Savannah National Wildlife Refuge,** (912) 652-4415, making the area very popular with kayak tour operators. More than 100 species of native and migratory birds keep company with the alligators you're sure to see sunning themselves at water's edge in the summer. So many put-ins and paddling routes exist within the refuge that you'll do well to pick up a map from your rental outfit, assuming you're not joining a tour. If you're heading out without a guide, one of the better boat launches is at the Savannah River's Millstone Landing, located near Hardeeville, SC, where the tidal fluctuation is less than a foot. Take Route 17 north to Hardeeville, where you turn left onto Main Street West, which eventually becomes Church Road. Just past West Hardeeville School, you'll come to Old Charleston Road, onto which you turn left. Millstone Landing is ahead on the right.

◆ The ranger station at **Fort McAllister Historic Park,** 3894 Fort McAllister Road, Richmond Hill, (912) 727-2339, rents canoes and kayaks by the hour or for a full day for use on **Redbird Creek,** a wide waterway that makes up the southern border of the state park. Daily rentals stop at 2 P.M. See *Wide Open* for directions.

Fishing

The variety of fresh, brackish, and salt water around Savannah translates into the possibility of hooking anything from a catfish or a largemouth bass to a bluefish or a shark. Some of the more-popular inshore fishing spots include **Lazaretto Creek, Skidaway Narrows,** the **Savannah** and **Wilmington rivers,** and **Wassaw Sound,** where your catch may include trout, redfish, shark, tarpon, and whiting. The best advice on where to fish and what bait to use comes from area fishing shops, where you can retain the services of a local guide. One of the better stops is **Oak Bluff Outfitters,** 4501 Habersham Street, Savannah, (912) 691-1115, *www.oakbluffoutfitters.com,* a full-service fly-fishing and wing-shooting shop. In addition to all manner of gear, Oak Bluff offers fly-fishing instruction, operates a number of tours, and provides guide services.

◆ Offshore and deep-sea fishing in the Atlantic Ocean takes the better part of a day—expect a minimum of two hours motoring out to good fishing grounds—but if you're into the thrill of hooking a big one, the ride is worth it. **Snapper Banks** is a popular spot off Georgia's coast, where a number of big fish wait, including tuna, king mackerel, shark, wahoo, and marlin. To head offshore, sign up with one of the area's charter boats, of which there are many. The following are some of the better bets.

◆ **Amick's Deep Sea Fishing,** Lazaretto Creek Marina, #1 Old Highway 80, Tybee Island, (912) 897-6759, *www.amicksdeepseafishing.com,* offers six-, 10-, and 20-man charters and will accommodate any number in between for half- and full-day trips. ◆ **Miss Judy**

Charters, 124 Palmetto Drive, Savannah, (912) 897-4921, *www.missjudycharters.com,* has a fleet of boats for inshore and offshore charters. ◆ Captains Elizabeth and Cecil Johnson of **Tybee Island Charters,** Old Highway 80 East, Lazaretto Creek, Tybee Island, (912) 786-4801, *www.fishtybee.com,* have two boats that can accommodate from six to 28 people for inshore and offshore trips.

Horseback Riding

Cutter Ridge Ranch, 555 Squirrel Run, Rincon, (912) 826-0223, features miles of trails through more than 280 acres of land, including portions of a Cypress swamp. You can either trail ride or stay in the pen for a beginner lesson. Open seven days a week, 8 A.M.–5 P.M. Call ahead for reservations. For additional riding opportunities nearby, see *Horseback Riding* in the Beaufort & Hilton Head chapter.

Rainy Day Workout

When Mother Nature fails to cooperate with your outdoor plans, you can still get a workout in at any one of the Savannah-area fitness facilities, most of which accept guests for a nominal day-use fee. The **Downtown Athletic Club,** One East Broughton Street, Savannah, (912) 236-4874, *www.dacsavannah.com,* features Precor treadmills, stairclimbers, recumbent bikes, and ellipticals, as well as strength-training equipment and more than 15,000 pounds of free weights. Classes include aerobics, cardio kickboxing, Hatha yoga, and tae kwon do. There are locker rooms, shower facilities, a steam room, and a sauna. ◆ **The Fitness Club Lifequest of Savannah,** 1800 East Victory Drive, Savannah, (912) 447-0909, *www.thefitnessclubofsavannah.com,* has free weights, cardio machines, and circuit-training equipment, as well as a sauna and steam room accessible from both locker rooms.

GA Department of Tourism

Sailing off Georgia's coast

Sailing

Since hosting the sailing competition for the 1996 Olympic Games in Atlanta, the waters off Savannah have increased in stature as serious sailing grounds. While offshore sailing in the **Atlantic Ocean** is possible, most of the tacking takes place on the **Wilmington River** and on **Wassaw Sound,** which was the site of the Olympic sailing events. To get in on the fun, head to **Sail Harbor Marina,** 618 Wilmington Island Road,

Savannah, (912) 897-2896, where you'll find a 25-foot Catalina for rent. There's also a retail store with sailing merchandise, showers, and a sailing school for all levels of helmsmen, including beginners.

Swimming

Savannah can be downright blistering in the summer, with average July and August highs in the low 90s. Factor in the humidity common to the area, and you're looking at a formula that calls for a proven means of relief: a dip in the sea. There's no faster way to get wet than to head to **Tybee Island,** whose toll-free number—1-800-868-BEACH (2322)—says it all. The island's Atlantic-facing beach is split into two areas, each with a distinct feel. The **North Beach** is more popular with locals and is generally less crowded. You can park in the lot adjacent to the Tybee Island Lighthouse for a daily fee ($7) and access the beach directly from the parking area. **South Beach** is much more active, particularly around the pavilion, where there's a public parking area. (Fee is also $7 per day.) Lifeguards are on duty, Memorial Day–Labor Day.

Local Outdoor Advice

Bicycle Link • This full-service bike shop has all manner of two-wheeled machines for sale. Bicycle Link also rents single-speed cruisers and mountain bikes, and the staff is happy to provide directions to the best places to ride. • 22 West Broughton Street, Savannah, ☎ (912) 233-9401; and 7064 Hodgsen Memorial Drive, Savannah, ☎ (912) 355-4771, *www.bicyclelinksav.com*

Rec Arts • A full-service adventure retailer, Rec Arts sells outdoor gear, apparel, and footwear from a cool, two-story shop located in the historic district. Owner Jessica Tenenbaum is a former Sea Kayak Georgia guide, and she and her staff are exceptionally knowledgeable about local outdoor pursuits. • 15 East Broughton Street, Savannah, ☎ (912) 201-9393, *www.rec-arts.com*

Sea Kayak Georgia • This is the definitive stop for paddlers, as area kayakers bow to owner Dale Williams' expertise and knowledge of the local waters. The outfitter provides kayak instruction, guided tours, and rents and sells kayaks, canoes, and paddling gear. • 1102 Route 80, Tybee Island, ☎ (912) 786-8732, *www.seakayakgeorgia.com*

K i c k   B a c k

Savannah excels in laid-back offerings for the tired adventurer, so when the sun, sand, and salt spray have slowed your pace, check out some of the following easier-going activities.

Antiques

Antiques dealers comprise a large part of the local shopping scene; serious collectors know Savannah as one of the Southeast's finest markets. Even if you're not a collector, browsing the stores or admiring the pieces in local inns, restaurants, and homes open for touring is an excellent way to appreciate the city's past as a major cosmopolitan port. A good rule of thumb: If something—a clock, piece of furniture, or place setting, for example—looks old, it probably is. The main antiques action is in and around **Pulaski, Lafayette, Calhoun,** and **Chatham squares.** For a complete listing of the historic district's

offerings, pick up any one of the several antiques-oriented brochures available free from the sources listed under *Additional Information.* The following is just a sampling of Savannah's best stops. ◆ **Savannah Galleries,** 30 East Bryan Street, (912) 232-1234, focuses on high-end American, English, and

French antique furniture, as well as antique and modern oriental carpets, chandeliers, and mirrors. ◆ In a seemingly never-ending series of rooms, **Universe Trading,** 27 Montgomery Street, (912) 233-1585, displays smaller and more unique, antique-related items—an Egyptian mummy CD holder, for example—and will not empty the pocketbook like high-end antiques dealers will. ◆ **Portobello,** 413 East Liberty Street, (912) 651-1056, *www.portobello.com,* features collectibles from dealers across the Southeast and specializes in silver, linen, lighting, and art.

Art & Crafts Galleries

Due, in part, to the Savannah School of Art and Design (SCAD) and the pool of students and faculty it brings to the community, Savannah now boasts more than 50 artists' studios/galleries, cooperatives, and retail galleries spread throughout the historic district. The school itself showcases budding talent in its nine exhibition spaces around town. While there is no "art district," you'll find the highest concentration of galleries in **City Market** and on **Liberty Street,** between Abercorn and Whitaker streets. The following galleries are a few of the standouts.

◆ **Jack Leigh Gallery,** 132 East Oglethorpe Avenue, (912) 234-6449, *www.jackleigh.com,* features the photography of native Savannahian Jack Leigh, who's best known for the Bird Girl photograph gracing the cover of *Midnight in the Garden of Good & Evil.* Leigh's gallery also displays the work of local, regional, and national photographers. ◆ Another destination for photo enthusiasts, **Innerlight Gallery,** 309 West Saint Julian Street, (912) 234-0403, *www.emersonimages.com,* displays the powerful photography of Emerson Matabele, who spent his lifetime traveling the globe and shooting pictures. His color photographs focus on indigenous peoples. ◆ **Osibisa,** 305 West Saint Julian Street, (912) 236-4006, features market scenes and African imagery by Ghanaian artist William Kwamena-Poh. His realist watercolors are stunning in their expression, often capturing your gaze from across the room.

◆ A must-stop is the **Ray Ellis Gallery,** 205 West Congress Street, 1-800-752-4865, *www.rayellis.com,* where a collection of oils, watercolors, and bronzes ranges in subject from regional coastlines to golf. Ellis' work may be familiar to you. His paintings hang in studios around the world, and in the 1980s, he collaborated with Walter Cronkite on a series of fine art books depicting America's coastline. ◆ Like Impressionistic paintings? Visit the **Murphy Gallery,** 324 Habersham Street, (912) 232-1874, to view the fine work of Michelle Murphy, whose oil and watercolor paintings depict Savannah landscapes. ◆ Since 1902, art collectors have turned to **Friedman's Fine Art,** 28 West State Street, (912) 234-1322, *www.friedmansfineart.com,* for exquisite paintings by artists from Savannah and the Lowcountry. ◆ **Alix Baptiste's Art Gallery,** 307 West Saint Julian Street, City Market, (912) 232-0372, *www.alixbaptiste.com,* showcases the work of Baptiste, a self-taught Haitian immigrant, whose paintings offer a bright, colorful take on Caribbean village life. Word of warning: After viewing some of Baptiste's delightful Caribbean scenes, you may find yourself en route to Savannah International for a flight to the islands. ◆ There are three businesses under one roof at 12 West Liberty Street: **SOHO South Café,** (912) 233-1633; **Savannah Fine Arts,** (912) 234-1874; and the **Bookmeister.** Have lunch, grab a cup of coffee, and browse the books on the shelves and the art on the walls.

The Telfair Museum

GA Dept. of Tourism

The **Telfair Museum of Art,** 121 Barnard Street, ☎ (912) 232-1177, *www.telfair.org,* is housed in an English Regency-style mansion bequeathed to the Georgia Historical Society in 1875 by philanthropist Mary Telfair, who intended for it to operate as a museum. In 1886, the Telfair opened as the South's first public art museum. The Telfair has many impressive paintings, sculptures, and decorative arts but is perhaps best known for its outstanding examples of American Impressionism, with works by Childe Hassam and Frederick Frieseke. Don't miss: Julian Story's billboard-sized painting *Black Prince of Crecy,* which depicts a

The Telfair Museum

14th-century battle. Also on display: the original Bird Girl sculpture, made famous on the cover of John Berendt's *Midnight in the Garden of Good & Evil.* Open Sunday, 1 P.M.–5 P.M.; Monday, noon–5 P.M.; Tuesday–Saturday, 10 A.M.–5 P.M. Moderate admission fee.

Day Spas

You've worked hard and earned your vacation, right? So give yourself a good rub on the back from one of Savannah's top spa facilities. ◆ **Vanilla: A Downtown Day Spa**, One East Broughton Street, (912) 232-0040, *www.vanilladayspa.com*, offers a variety of spa treatments, from the "All Day Getaway," which includes a facial, Swedish massage, sea mud body wrap, manicure, and pedicure; to the "Socialite Delight," a deep pore-cleansing facial, chocolate-raspberry scrub, and Swedish massage. ◆ At **Savannah Day Spa,** 110 Barnard Street (inside the Banana Republic building), (912) 234-9100, the stress-relief specialists know how to soothe your body (and soul), whether providing facials, massages, tanning, or hydrotherapy services.

Gardens

Spring in Savannah dazzles with color and fragrance, particularly in the city's squares, where a multitude of flowers bursts into bloom. The city has numerous private gardens, many of which are open for tours during the annual **Savannah Garden Expo**, 601 West Harris Street, (912) 236-4795, *www.savannahgardenexpo.com*, which takes place the first weekend of April. ◆ The **Ships of the Sea Maritime Museum**, housed in the **Scarbrough House,** 41 Martin Luther King, Jr. Boulevard, (912) 232-1511, *www.shipsofthesea.org*, also happens to have the largest garden in the historic district. Open Tuesday–Sunday, 10 A.M.–5 P.M. Entry is free. ◆ The **Bamboo Farm and Coastal Gardens,** 2 Canebrake Road, Savannah, (912) 921-5460, has the largest public collection of bamboo in North America, with more than 140 varieties. There are also more than 600 types of daylilies and numerous magnolias on the grounds. Open Monday–Friday, 8 A.M.–5 P.M. Entry is free.

Historic Homes

Spared General William Tecumseh Sherman's torch at the end of the Civil War, Savannah's historic district features more than one thousand historic homes; however, only a handful are open to the public. Here are some of the best bets. ◆ Built in 1849, the **Andrew Low House,** 329 Abercorn Street, (912) 233-6854, is an excellent example of the Italianate style. Once the home of Girl Scouts founder Juliette Gordon Low and her husband Andrew, the house opened as a museum in 1952. Open Monday–Saturday, 10 A.M.–4:30 P.M.; Sunday, noon–4:30 P.M. Closed Thursday. Nominal admission fee. ◆ The **Juliette Gordon Low National Birthplace,** 10 East Oglethorpe Avenue, (912) 233-4501, was built around 1820, and is filled with the original furniture and belongings of William Washington Gordon's family. It is now run by the Girl Scouts of America as a program center. Open daily, 10 A.M.–4 P.M.; Sunday, 12:30 P.M.–4:30 P.M. Closed Wednesday. Nominal admission fee. ♦ The Federal-style **Davenport House,** 324 East State Street, (912) 236-8097, *www.davenportsavga.com,* was built between 1815–1820 by noted Southern builder Isaiah Davenport. It was the first house preserved by the Savannah Historic Foundation, and among its highlights are delicate plasterwork and woodwork; an open-well, cantilevered staircase; and Ionic-Tuscan columns. Open Monday–Saturday, 10 A.M.–4 P.M.; Sunday, 1 P.M.–4 P.M.. Nominal admission fee. ♦ Noted-author Flannery O'Connor was born in Savannah and spent her early years in what is now called the **Flannery O'Connor House,** 207 East Charlton Street, (912) 233-6014. One floor of the dwelling has been refurbished to represent the period of O'Connor's youth. Open Saturdays, 1 P.M.–5 P.M.; Sundays,1 P.M.–4 P.M. Free admission.

♦ Used as General Sherman's headquarters during the Union Army's occupation of Savannah beginning in 1864, the **Green-Meldrim House,** One West Macon Street, (912) 232-1251, is a gorgeous Gothic Revival-style home with stunning carving and plaster work. The building now serves as the parish house for St. John's Episcopal Church. Open Tuesday, Thursday, and Friday, 10 A.M.–4 P.M.; Saturday, 10 A.M.–1 P.M. Nominal admission fee. ♦ Built between 1816–1819, the **Owens-Thomas House,** 124 Abercorn Street, (912) 233-9743, is one of the country's leading examples of the English Regency style. The adjacent **Carriage House** once served as a slave quarters and is now home to a museum displaying tools and other items made and used by slaves. Open Monday, noon–5 P.M.;

Deron Nardo

Andrew Low House

An Architectural Primer

GA Department of Tourism

So varied are the well-preserved examples of various building styles in downtown Savannah that architectural buffs can wander for days and not grow bored. If your knowledge of architecture is rudimentary at best, the following primer will get you started. The **Federal style** (1790-1838) is marked by elongated columns, plaster interiors, and fanlight doorways. Example: the Davenport House on State Street. ♦ The **Victorian style** (1860-1915) features flowery carvings, multi-gabled roofs, and turrets on the exterior. Example: the King-Tisdell Cottage on East Huntington Street. ♦ The **English Regency style** (1811-1830) features semicircular stairs, alcove entrances, articulated window openings, and Ionic columns. Example: the Owens-Thomas House on Abercorn Street. ♦ Low-pitch roofs, thin first-floor windows, long porches, and cast-iron balconies highlight the **Italianate style** (1830-1900). Example: the Mercer House on Bull Street. ♦ The **Greek and Roman Revival style** (1820-1875) features long front porches supported by towering columns, and wide staircases. Example: First African Baptist Church on Montgomery Street. ♦ The **Gothic Revival style** (1830-1885) features steeply sloping roofs, pointed arches, and ribbed vaults. Example: the Green-Meldrim House on West Macon Street.

Mercer House

Tuesday–Saturday, 10 A.M.–5 P.M.; and Sunday, 2 P.M.–5 P.M. Nominal admission fee. ◆ Located at the west end of Montgomery Square, the 1869 **Mercer House**, 429 Bull Street, of *Midnight in the Garden of Good and Evil* fame, is the stunning Italianate mansion inside of which antiques dealer Jim Williams was believed to have murdered Danny Handsford. (Williams was accused, tried four times, and finally acquitted.) Today the home is the private residence of Williams' sister, who operates a gift shop around the corner at 430 Whitaker Street. The home is not open for tours.

Historic Sites & Museums

The past is very much present in Savannah—preserved in museums, on plaques marking important events, and in the city's 21 remaining squares, where you'll find a number of statues and fountains commemorating historic figures and events. The best place to start is at the **Savannah History Museum,** at the Savannah Visitor Center, 303 Martin Luther King, Jr. Boulevard, (912) 238-1779, which provides a comprehensive overview of the city's history from the arrival of Oglethorpe to the filming of *Forrest Gump*. Located in an old train station, the 20,000 square-foot museum also includes a theater that shows a brief film about Savannah. Open daily, 9 A.M.–5 P.M. Nominal admission fee. ◆ Located in the 1819 William Scarbrough house, the **Ships of the Sea Maritime Museum,** 41 Martin Luther King, Jr. Boulevard, (912) 232-1511, *www.shipsofthesea.org,* features a dazzling array of maritime antiques, paintings, and ship models, plus interpretative exhibits on Savannah's maritime history. There's also a wonderful garden where you can stop to smell the roses. Appropriately enough, the Scarbrough House was owned by one of the financiers of the *S.S. Savannah*, the first steamship to cross the Atlantic. The home itself is one of the earliest examples of the Greek Revival style in the South. From the 1870s until the mid 1900s, the house was used as a public school for children of African descent. Open Tuesday–Sunday, 10 A.M.–5 P.M. Nominal admission fee. ◆ Noble Jones, who arrived in Georgia with James Oglethorpe in 1733, settled what is now **Wormsloe State Historic Site,** 7601 Skidaway Road, Isle of Hope, (912) 353-3023, a plantation with a stone

Wormsloe State Historic Site

For Whom the Bell Tolls

Founded on the basis of religious tolerance, the Colony of Georgia became home to a wide variety of religious faiths. That tradition is reflected in Savannah's many historic churches. Some of the highlights include **Congregation Mickve Israel,** 20 East Gordon Street, ☎ (912) 233-1547, founded in 1733. The congregation's 1878 building on Montgomery Square is the only Gothic-style synagogue in the nation. ◆ Georgia's oldest Catholic congregation meets in the stunning, Gothic-style **Cathedral of St. John the Baptist,** 222 East Harris Street, ☎ (912) 233-4709, built in 1899 within the shell of an earlier building destroyed by fire. ◆ The **Wesley Monumental United Methodist Church,** 429 Abercorn Street, ☎ (912) 232-0191, was built in its current location on Telfair Square in 1862 and stands as a monument to John and Charles Wesley, founders of the Methodist Church. ◆ John Wesley lived in Savannah while serving as Rector to **Christ Episcopal Church,** 28 Bull Street, ☎ (912) 238-0434, the first church established in the new colony in 1733. The church building dates to 1840. ◆ Founded in part by George Liele, a slave who purchased his freedom, the 1777 **First African Baptist Church,** 23 Montgomery Street, ☎ (912) 233-6597, is the oldest black congregation in the nation. Reverend Liele helped raise funds to purchase the building on Franklin Square from a white church, and then the congregation of slaves rebuilt the church brick by brick, completing the current building in 1788.

Cathedral of St. John the Baptist

archway entrance and a 1.5-mile driveway lined with century-old live oaks. The onsite museum details Georgia's colonial history, as well as the history of Jones and his homestead. A nature trail winds past the tabby ruins of Jones' home and the fortification around it. As you drive down the avenue of oaks, you'll see an 1828 home on the left; however, the residence is privately owned and not open for tours. Wormsloe is 10 miles southeast of downtown Savannah. Open Tuesday–Saturday, 9 A.M.–5 P.M.; Sunday, 2 P.M.–5 P.M. Nominal admission fee.

◆ You can visit and climb the 178 steps of Georgia's oldest and tallest lighthouse at the **Tybee Island Museum and Light Station,** 30 Meddin Drive, Tybee Island, (912) 786-5801, housed within Fort Screven's Battery Garland. The first lighthouse on this site was constructed in 1736. The current lighthouse has been repaired several times, but stands on the base of a lighthouse built in 1773. An onsite museum has among its exhibits weapons from different eras of Tybee's history; a periscope from a vintage World War II submarine; and a history of Tybee's role in the Civil War and its growth as a resort town. Open daily, 9 A.M.–4:30 P.M. Closed Tuesday. Nominal admission fee.

Historic Forts

Fort Pulaski

The Savannah Region played major roles in the Revolutionary and Civil wars, and you can discover this rich military history by visiting the area's historic forts. ◆ Built after the War of 1812 as part of a coastal fortification system, the 1847 **Fort Pulaski**, which sits at the mouth of the Savannah River on Cockspur Island, was once deemed as "strong as the Rocky Mountains." Ultimately, the 7.5-foot-thick brick walls and surrounding moat proved weaker than the Rockies when the Union Army overtook Fort Pulaski in 1862 after 30 hours of shelling from Tybee Island. (The damage caused by those canon shots remains visible today.) Restoration of the fort began in 1933, and today you can visit the pentagon-shaped **Fort Pulaski National Monument**, Route 80, Cockspur Island, (912) 786-5787, where interesting historical exhibits, including audio stations, detail the region's military past. Open daily, 9 A.M.–5 P.M. Nominal admission fee.

◆ Just three miles outside of Savannah's historic district, **Old Fort Jackson**, One Fort Jackson Road, (912) 232-3945, is Georgia's oldest standing brick fort, garrisoned for the War of 1812. During the Civil War, Fort Jackson served as Savannah's riverfront headquarters. There are 13 exhibit areas detailing its history, along with periodic battle reenactments and blacksmithing demonstrations. Open daily, 8 A.M.–5 P.M. Nominal admission fee. ◆ Located roughly 20 miles south of Savannah on the Ogeechee River, **Fort McAllister Historic Park**, 3894 Fort McAllister Road, Richmond Hill, (912) 727-2339, was the last line of resistance for the Confederate Army in the face of General Sherman's March on Savannah. After bombardment from sea, the fort eventually succumbed to a land attack, whereby Confederate trade through Savannah's port shut down. The sand and mud fort is the nation's best-preserved,

What Lies Beneath

St. Bonaventure Cemetery

Cemeteries in the Savannah area are well worth visiting for their historic significance and ability to spook. ◆ Located at the corner of Abercorn and Oglethorpe streets, **Colonial Park Cemetery** is the final resting place for many notable Georgians, including most of Savannah's prominent historical figures like Button Gwinett, one of the signers of the Declaration of Independence. If you're looking for a place to lay your weary bones, you can forget Colonial; the cemetery hasn't had a new burial in nearly 150 years. ◆ Due to its prominence in *Midnight in the Garden of Good & Evil*, **St. Bonaventure Cemetery** is one of the nation's better-known burial grounds. Here you'll find a stunning collection of monuments to the dead. Don't forget your camera, particularly if you enjoy working in black and white, as the combination of stone monuments and moss-draped live oaks makes for truly haunting images. Of note: monuments to lyricist Johnny Mercer and poet Conrad Aiken, as well as the spine-chilling statue of "Little Gracie," who died as a child and whose monument is frighteningly life-like. Signs in the cemetery direct you to notable gravesites.

Confederate earthen fortification. The onsite museum displays Civil War artifacts, shows a brief video, and houses a gift shop. Open daily, 8 A.M.–5 P.M. Nominal admission fee.

Minor League Baseball

Looking for the way baseball used to be? Take yourself out to the ball game and root for the **Savannah Sand Gnats**, Victory Drive, (912) 351-9150, *www.sandgnats.com*, a minor-league affiliate of the Montreal Expos and member of the South Atlantic League. You can get a good seat for less than $10. The season runs April–September.

Performing Arts

The Lucas Theatre

♪ Nestled in the heart of the historic district, the **Lucas Theatre**, 32 Abercorn Street, (912) 525-5040, *www.lucastheatre.com*, is an icon of the bygone era of grand "moving picture" theaters. Built in 1921 and restored in 1987, the 1,250-seat theater features Italianate décor, including a 40-foot-wide ceiling dome. This gorgeous performing arts center offers musical theater, classical music performances, and concerts by top artists. Call the venue for a current schedule of events. ♦ **City Lights Theatre Company**, 316 East 55th Street, Savannah, (912) 234-9860, is a non-profit community theater that produces musicals and classic and contemporary plays for performance in the Lucas Theatre. Recent productions include *Cat on a Hot Tin Roof*; *Dinner with Friends*; and Neil Simon's *Rumors*. Annual productions of the popular **Savannah Shakespeare Festival** in Forsyth Park (held each May) and **Savannah Playwrights Festival** (held each July) provide excellent live theater for visitors and residents.

♦ SCAD's **Trustees Theater**, 216 East Broughton Street, (912) 525-5050, *www.trusteestheater.com*, was built in 1946 as the Weis Theater, an Art Moderne-style movie house. Restored and reopened in 1998 with a gala performance by Tony Bennett, Trustees Theater is a 1,105-seat performance venue that hosts a variety of fare, from plays and musicals to concerts and lectures. ♦ Billed as the oldest continuously

The Green Party

If your idea of the perfect weekend vacation includes throngs of intoxicated tourists, congested streets and sidewalks, the color green everywhere you look, and anything and everything Irish, make reservations early—up to a year in advance—to visit Savannah during the annual **St. Patrick's Day** celebration, essentially a four- to five-day bash around March 17. (Looking for cheap accommodations in or near the historic district? You're out of luck—Irish luck, that is. Expect to pay top dollar.) With one of the largest parades in the country—rivaling New York's and Chicago's—Savannah's celebration has become a major party, drawing more than 300,000 revelers to town each year. Fountains in the public squares are dyed green, as is much of the beer consumed in the city.

running theater in America, the **Savannah Theatre,** 222 Bull Street, (912) 233-7764, presents a wide range of performances, from musicals to dramas. There are five main-stage performances a year, and recent productions have included *Bus Stop* and *The Yellow Boat.* Ticket prices are particularly reasonable—around $15—for shows in the 450-seat theater, which was constructed around the back wall of the original 1818 theater.

Shops & Stops

You'll have little trouble entertaining your credit cards in Savannah's historic district, where the number of interesting boutiques boggles the mind. Here shops of every size and shape wait around each corner. The best approach is to lace up your sneakers, load up your wallet, and start walking. The major shopping areas include **River Street,** a nine-block area paralleling the Savannah River, where renovated warehouses hold everything from kitschytourist shops to upscale boutiques; and **City Market,** between Ellis and Franklin squares, (912) 232-4903, *www.savannahcitymarket.com,* a pedestrian-mall area spread over two blocks with galleries, shops, restaurants, and bars.

◆ Some recommended stops within City Market: **Moondance,** 306 West Saint Julian Street, (912) 236-9003, *www.moondancecenter.com,* which carries a selection of candles, soaps, silver jewelry, stone Buddhas, and spiritual self-help books. ◆ If you're particularly adept at sniffing out great shopping, poke your nose into **Scented by Nature,** 33 Jefferson Street, (912) 447-1817 or 1-800-486-9133, *www.europeanperfumery.com,* a boutique carrying his and her perfumes and a line of aromatherapy oils. ◆ With an eclectic offering—hats, shoes, paper lanterns, and retro lunchboxes, for example—**The Gypsy Moth,** 311 West Saint Julian Street, (912) 232-6800, is bound to have something to suit your interests.

◆ **Broughton Street** might as well be called "Main Street," as it's the heartbeat of the historic district and lined with restaurants, shops, and cultural spots that bustle six days a week. (Sundays are quiet all over Savannah.) **Wonderful Things,** 115 Broughton Street, (912) 447-0004, *www.wonderfulthingsinc.com,* carries perfumes, linens, and china, and pulls in passerby with window displays of Victorian wicker furniture and Murano glass figurines.

◆ Other shops around town: ◆ **E. Shaver, Bookseller,** 326 Bull Street, (912) 234-7257, is an outstanding independent bookseller of new and rare books housed in an 1843 antebellum home. Here, in a maze of rooms, you'll find an extensive selection of children's books, current and classic fiction, local history, and poetry titles. ◆ Part of the SCAD, **Ex Libris,** 228 Martin Luther King, Jr. Boulevard, (912) 525-7550, is a many-headed monster of a shop that sells books, music, coffee, gift items, and art supplies on three floors. ◆ If you felt *Midnight in the Garden of Good & Evil* was the book to end all books, make a bee-

GA Department of Tourism

City Market

line for **"The Book" Gift Shop and Midnight Museum**, 127 East Gordon Street, (912) 233-3867, *www.midnightinsavannah.com*, where you'll find all manner of memorabilia, from autographed copies of John Berendt's best seller to "Bird Girl" coasters.

Tea Rooms & Coffee Shops

Savannah's bustling pace may be due, in part, to an abundance of hip coffee and tea houses, many of which showcase local art. Follow your nose to the freshest roasts or head to one of these standouts. ◆ **Gallery Espresso,** Six East Liberty Street, (912) 233-5348, is a European coffee house and wine bar that features high-profile art exhibits. ◆ It's tough to beat the **Tea Room,** Seven East Broughton Street, (912) 239-9690, *www.thetearoomsavannah.com*, for atmosphere, where an intimate dining area with a small fireplace awaits. Choose from more than 50 kinds of tea. A lunch menu includes soups, crumpets, finger sandwiches, quiche, and more. ◆ Housed in an early 20th-century pharmacy, the **Gryphon Tea Room,** 337 Bull Street, (912) 525-5880, dispenses breakfast and lunch, along with a diverse assortment of fine teas.

Tours

One of the more-informative ways to see Savannah is through a professionally guided tour. There are ghost tours; Civil War tours; and church, graveyard, and architectural tours. There are even tours devoted exclusively to the sites and personalities profiled in *Midnight in the Garden of Good & Evil.* ◆ With the greatest variety of offerings, **The Savannah Walks,** 123 East Congress Street, (912) 238-9255 or 1-888-728-9255, *www.savannahwalks.com,* has walking tours leaving either Reynolds or Johnson Square in the morning, afternoon, and evening. A sampling of the company's tours: "Historic Homes;" "Savannah Stroll" (detailing general Savannah history); "Civil War;" "Churches & Graveyards;" "Midnight Tour;" "Gates & Gardens;" and "Lowcountry Ghosts." Admission ranges from $6–$13; reservations are required. ◆ **Old Savannah Tours,** 250 Martin Luther King Jr. Boulevard, (912) 234-8128 or 1-800-517-9007, *www.oldsavtour.com,* offers tours that combine land and water exploration. The *Savannah River Queen* explores the city from the Savannah River, and trolleys and buses guide you through its streets. ◆ For a boat tour of the Wassaw National Wildlife Refuge or of the Savannah National Wildlife Refuge, make an appointment with **Bull River Cruises,** 8005 Old Tybee Road, (912) 897-7300, whose narrated excursions provide interesting details about coastal ecosystems and allow ample opportunities for wildlife sightings. ◆ For sunset and dolphin cruises, **Captain Jim's Backriver Adventures,** 146 San Marco Drive, Tybee Island, (912) 786-8847, offers 1.5-hour tours of the local waters.

A horse and buggy tour

Rest Easy

Sleep Well

Make no mistake: Lodging in Savannah is a serious industry. Like Charleston to the north, Savannah has so many romantic inns and B&Bs that entire books focus on just the city's accommodations. There are more than 20 historic inns, where you can rest easy in a home that has sheltered people during many of America's critical times: the early days of a young nation; the antebellum period; the Civil War; the Roaring Twenties; and the Great Depression. Such lodging comes at a price. Restoration is expensive, and guest rates reflect this. The following inns are in Savannah's historic district, which puts you in the center of the city's action.

Accommodations Pricing

Less than $100	Inexpensive	$
$100-150	Moderate	$$
$151-200	Expensive	$$$
More than $200	Very Expensive	$$$$

Prices are per room, per night, based on double occupancy during peak seasons. Note that B&Bs and most country inns include breakfast in the rate.

17 Hundred 90 • Savannah's oldest inn sits a block from Oglethorpe Square and has it all: 14 rooms, a full-service restaurant and bar, and even its own ghost! Each guestroom features period furniture, a fireplace, CD radio, and a complimentary bottle of wine upon check-in. The reputed ghost is Anna Powers, a jilted lover who jumped to her death from the third-floor balcony. She's still hanging out, awaiting the return of her lover. To meet her, request Room 204. The inn will ask that you sign a waiver absolving them of blame for any nocturnal happenings, and regardless of what may (or may not) happen, your nerves will be tested. If you have a hard time sleeping, you'll be especially grateful when the smells of breakfast permeate the inn. Served in what was originally the kitchen—look for the original exposed crossbeams, brick walls, and stone floors—breakfast is buffet-style, with such offerings as sausage, pancakes, muffins, and fresh fruit. • *307 East President Street, Savannah, GA 31401,* ☎ *(912) 236-7122, www.17hundred90.com.* • *$$–$$$*

The Ballastone • The Ballastone features 16 guestrooms in a four-story, antebellum mansion built in 1838. The inn's rooms are individually decorated with period antiques and include rice poster and canopy beds so high you'll need a stool to climb into them. "Elegant Superior" rooms are located on the third and fourth floors and are worth asking for—they have fireplaces, whirlpool tubs, and excellent views. Best bets are the China Trade Suite and the Gazebo Suite. The hot breakfast is elegant—think Eggs Benedict—and can be served in your choice of the tea room, parlor, lounge, or garden courtyard. Savor afternoon tea and evening hors d'oeuvres in front of two roaring fires in the parlor. Of note: a gorgeous antique harp in the main lobby. Located in the heart of the historic district, the Ballastone is within walking distance of most attractions. • *14 East Oglethorpe Avenue, Savannah, GA 31401,* ☎ *(912) 236-1484 or 1-800-822-4553, www.ballastone.com* • *$$$–$$$$*

Bed & Breakfast Inn • Located one block from Forsyth Park, this inn—made up of two restored 1853 Federal-style row houses and a cottage house on Gordon Row—has 15 rooms and offers one of the rare lodging "deals" in Savannah. You get a great location, sacrifice little in amenities, and pay a fraction of the high-end prices. Guestrooms in the row houses have private baths, and many feature four-poster, queen-sized beds. The slightly larger rooms in the cottage feature private baths and share a small kitchenette. Breakfast is hearty—expect dishes like waffles or stuffed omelets—and afternoon tea is served daily. • *117 West Gordon Street, Chatham Square, Savannah, GA 31401,* ☎ *(912) 238-0518 or 1-888-238-0518, www.savannahbnb.com* • *$$–$$$*

Catherine Ward House • Featured in the book and movie, *Midnight in the Garden of Good & Evil*, this 1884 Italianate Victorian inn is full of antiques and artifacts from owner Alan Williams' world travels. There are 10 suites (three are in the carriage house), each with a different theme. For example, the China Trade Room features Asian and Egyptian art, and the Versailles Room has Baroque and Rocco furniture and a crystal chandelier. Each room has a queen- or king-sized bed (many of them hand-carved) and a private bath. All except the Blue Room have wood-burning fireplaces. An enticing breakfast—French toast topped with bananas foster, for example—is served on a sprawling mahogany table. After breakfast, enjoy the morning paper in the courtyard or on one of the house's many verandas. Situated in the heart of the Victorian District, the Catherine Ward House is just a block from Forsyth Park. • *118 East Waldburg Street, Savannah, GA 31401,* ☎ *(912) 234-8564, 1-800-327-4270, www.catherinewardhouseinn.com • $$-$$$$*

Eliza Thompson House • A wealthy cotton merchant gave this 1847 house to his wife, Eliza Thompson, and a stay here conveys a sense of just how much wealth "white gold" (cotton) generated. There are 25 rooms—12 in the main house, 13 in the carriage

house—all with private baths and furnished with period antiques. Request the J. Stephen Room for its four-poster canopy bed, ornate fireplace, whirlpool tub, and bay window overlooking the courtyard. Amenities include 24-hour concierge service, an enclosed patio, and grounds highlighted by a spacious courtyard with a fountain. Guests are treated to evening wine and hors d'oeuvres, as well as before-bed sweets and coffee. • *5 West Jones Street, Savannah, GA 31401,* ☎ *(912) 236-3620 or 1-800-348-9378, www.elizathompson-house.com • $$-$$$$*

Foley House Inn • Built in 1896, the Foley House Inn is an exceptionally romantic property—so much so that it was one of *Vacation Magazine*'s "Ten Most Romantic Inns in the Country." Located on Chippewa Square, the inn features 18 guestrooms, all restored to their original elegance and appointed with antiques and antique reproductions. Many rooms have oversized baths or Jacuzzis; 15 rooms have fireplaces. Want a private balcony? Request the Stafford or Suffolk rooms. The Essex Room is huge and has a king-sized canopy bed, two-person Jacuzzi, and sitting area. The hot breakfast—recent fare included strawberry-glazed French toast, fruit, and biscuits—is served downstairs or in your room; and wine, cheese, and hors d'oeuvres are served each evening in the parlor. Common areas include a double front parlor, library, dining room, wine room, and a large courtyard with a fountain. • *14 West Hull Street, Chippewa Square, Savannah, GA 31401,* ☎ *(912) 232-6622 or 1-800-647-3708, www.foleyinn.com • $$$-$$$$*

Hamilton-Turner Inn • A member of the upscale *Select Registry* lodging association, this centrally located inn shares beautiful

Deron Nardo

The morning paper on the Foley House patio

Lafayette Square with the Cathedral of St. John the Baptist, the Flannery O'Connor House, and the Andrew Low House. The Second French Empire-style home was built in 1873 for jeweler Samuel P. Hamilton. Eighteen rooms and suites make the Hamilton-Turner Inn large enough to afford its guests anonymity, but small enough to make them feel at home. Each room has a private bath and is decorated with Eastlake, Empire or Renaissance Revival antiques. Several rooms offer private balconies overlooking Lafayette Square, and some feature claw-foot or whirlpool-style tubs. Others have working fireplaces. The Noble Jones Room features all three. Public spaces include the parlor with its Italian marble fireplace, an artfully landscaped garden, and a floral-themed tea room. The inn serves a hearty Southern breakfast and high tea from 4 P.M.–5 P.M. • *330 Abercorn Street, Lafayette Square, Savannah, GA 31401,* ☎ *(912) 233-1833 or 1-888-448-8849, www.hamilton-turnerinn.com • $$$–$$$$*

Kehoe House • Built in 1892, the Renaissance Revival-style Kehoe House is located on beautiful Columbia Square. The inn has 13 rooms furnished in antiques and reproductions. The corner rooms feature large, rounded sitting areas. A hot breakfast of items like baked peach French toast and citrus pecan waffles is served in the dining area, and afternoon refreshments and evening hors d'oeuvres are served in the parlor. Don't be surprised if you hear the mysterious knocking some guests have heard coming from behind the inn's walls. Is this inn haunted? No one knows for sure, but the Kehoe House was once a funeral parlor. Supernatural occurrences or not, this inn is an excellent place to rest easy. The Kehoe House is a member of the distinguished *Select Registry* association. • *123 Habersham Street, Savannah, GA 31401,* ☎ *(912) 232-1020 or 1-800-820-1020, www.kehoehouse.com • $$$$*

The President's Quarters Inn and Guesthouse • This inn on Oglethorpe Square—made up of two 1855 town homes and an 1872 guesthouse—names its rooms after past presidents. In addition to a picture and short bio of the president, each of the inn's 19 rooms features period antiques, a working fireplace, and a writing desk with a data port. The Abraham Lincoln suite in the guesthouse boasts an enormous bathroom with a steam shower, Jacuzzi, and fireplace. In the main house, the Franklin D. Roosevelt room has 13-foot ceilings, a four-poster bed, a private balcony overlooking Oglethorpe Square, and a Jacuzzi tub in the bathroom. You can enjoy a full breakfast—sample fare includes Belgian pecan waffles and banana pancakes—in your room or on the inn's expansive brick patio with cast-iron tables, marble statues, and artful landscaping. The inn also has its own parking lot, a rare feature in the historic district. • *225 East President Street, Savannah, GA 31401,* ☎ *(912) 233-1600 or 1-888-592-1812, www.presidentsquarters.com • $$–$$$$*

Deron Nardo

The Kehoe House

Other Places to Stay

If you'd prefer a more laid-back atmosphere, consider heading to Tybee Island. • **The 17th Street Inn**, 12 17th Street, Tybee Island, GA 31328, ☎ (912) 786-0607 or 1-800-909-0607, *www.tybeeinn.com*, has eight suites, each with a full kitchen, sitting area, and queen-sized bed, plus access to either a common or private porch. The inn is situated on the south end of the island, just a half-block from the ocean and the pavilion. • **The Lighthouse Inn,** 16 Meddin Drive, Tybee Island, GA, 31328, ☎ (912) 786-0901 or 1-866-786-0901, *www.tybeebb.com*, has three rooms and a quiet front porch. Its location is just a few steps from the beach and the Tybee Lighthouse.

D i n e   W e l l

D ining in Savannah combines historic settings—many restaurants are housed in buildings dating back two centuries or more—with diverse cuisine. Fresh seafood takes top billing, but you'll also find traditional French, Italian, Greek, and Thai fare throughout the city. The following is just a sampling of the city's best bets. Note that reservations are required or recommended at most of these restaurants.

17 Hundred 90 • The dining room of 17 Hundred 90 is on the ground floor of Savannah's oldest inn and features low, exposed-beam ceilings, and brick floors and walls, all of which make you feel as if it is 1790. But the cuisine will tell you otherwise; food could not have been this delicately prepared two centuries ago. Appetizers include crab cakes and oysters Rockefeller, while entrées include such items as rack of lamb Dijon and filet mignon in a mushroom Madeira. Open for lunch and dinner. • *307 East President Street, Savannah,* ☎ *(912) 236-7122*

45 South • One of the finer dining experiences in Savannah, 45 South is part of the 1734 Pirate's House, the oldest building in Georgia. (Note: There's another restaurant, "The Pirate's House," inside the same build-ing.) Chef Brian Palefsky brings an artistic stroke to his contemporary Southern gourmet entrées, served in an elegant, romantic dining room. For starters, try the sautéed lump crab cakes with shrimp, endive, and radicchio, before moving on to the brie-stuffed filet served with Yukon gold potatoes. More than 150 wines (strong emphasis on Californian vintages) assure you'll find the perfect complement to your meal. The menu changes regularly. Open Monday–Saturday for dinner. Jackets rec-ommended. • *20 East Broad Street, Savannah,* ☎ *(912) 233-1881*

Bistro Savannah • Located a block from City Market, Bistro Savannah specializes in seafood with Southern, Thai, and Cajun influences. Start with the seared beef tender-loin tips served with scallions and shittake mushrooms over crisp corn pancakes. If they're on the menu, order the barbeque black grouper in peach and pear chutney or the potato-crusted salmon. The main dining area features exposed-brick walls with rotating exhibits of paintings by local artists. Open daily for dinner. • *309 West Congress Street, Savannah,* ☎ *(912) 233-6266*

Elizabeth on 37th • Executive chef Elizabeth Terry and her husband Michael opened Elizabeth on 37th in a turn-of-the-century mansion to serve classic Southern cooking with a contemporary twist. Appetizers include Southern fried grits with shrimp, country ham, and red eye gravy; and a black-eyed pea patty with greens and a curry cream. Entrées include broiled mustard-garlic-glazed salmon with steamed greens and rosemary potatoes; and spicy Savannah red rice with shrimp, clams, sausage, and okra. The menu, which changes seasonally, is accompanied by an award-winning wine list. Open daily for dinner. • *105 East 37th Street, Savannah,* ☎ *(912) 236-5547*

George's of Tybee • George's presents a small but diverse menu of regional cuisine, complemented by a great wine list. For starters try the blue crab and granny smith apple salad. If it's on the menu, which changes seasonally, order the half- or full-rack of lamb with spinach, mushrooms, and olives served over Israeli couscous in apricot chutney. In addition to the spacious dining room with its cozy, stone fireplace, there's an enclosed wraparound porch with seating. Open daily for dinner except Monday. • *1105 Route 80 East, Tybee Island,* ☎ *(912) 786-9730*

Il Pasticcio • In a large, full-windowed, corner storefront (a former department store), Il Pasticcio serves authentic Italian fare, including homemade pastas with a variety of savory sauces. Brush up on your Italian and order the ravioli ripieni d'aragosta (lobster-stuffed ravioli in a champagne cream sauce) appetizer, and follow it with the agnello grigniato (grilled lamb chops with a port wine reduction) or the filetto di manzo gratinato (grilled filet mignon encrusted with gorgonzola served with potato and pancetta gratin). If you think you might stumble over some of the dishes' pronunciations, just wait until you're halfway through a bottle of one of the restaurant's Italian reds. A rotating selection of paintings by local artists complements the contemporary interior. Open daily for dinner. • *2 East Broughton Street, Savannah,* ☎ *(912) 231-8888 or (912) 231-8813*

North Beach Grill • For lunch, you can wander in from the beach in little more than a bathing suit for North Beach Grill's bevy of Caribbean eats, all listed on a dry-erase board behind the counter. Dinner, which is only *slightly* more formal than lunch, is served either in a small dining room or outside on the patio. Owned by the same proprietors as George's of Tybee, North Beach Grill is located adjacent to the Tybee Lighthouse and just a few strides from the beach. The menu changes regularly but generally includes creative preparations of locally caught seafood, such as jerk salmon. The restaurant's crab cakes have garnered a number of fans. Open daily for lunch and dinner. Call for winter hours. • *41 A Meddin Drive, Tybee Island,* ☎ *(912) 786-9003*

The Olde Pink House • Located in the 1771 Habersham House, with its distinctive pink hue and deep history, this restaurant serves regional cuisine with Southern panache. Before dining, sit for a drink in the Planters Tavern, located in the cellar, with its two fireplaces, antique couches, and exposed-brick walls. Live piano music plays in the tavern six nights a week. Start with the sautéed local shrimp with country ham and a grits cake and follow it with the crispy scored flounder with apricot shallot sauce. The house was the private residence of James Habersham, Jr., a wealthy planter, until 1800, when the Planter's Bank, the first bank in Georgia, opened inside. The old vaults are now used as the wine cellar. After dining, stroll through Reynolds Square, just outside the restaurant. Open daily for dinner. • *23 Abercorn Street, Savannah,* ☎ *(912) 232-4286*

Sapphire Grill • From the modern stone bar to the hip art hanging on the walls, this trendy restaurant serves contemporary regional cuisine on two floors. The main floor is the more energetic, decorated with steel, glass, and sapphire hues, and the upper floor is more subdued and romantic. Regardless of where you sit, the food is con-sistently good. For starters, try the lobster, corn, and celery-heart bisque with lemon butter, and then order the grilled prime tenderloin served with golden potato mountain chevre gratin, wok-seared seasonal vegetables, and sweet onion rings. The immense wine list is sure to please even the most finicky connoisseur. Open daily for dinner. • *110 West Congress Street, Savannah,* ☎ *(912) 443-9962*

Suzabelle's • Remember the movie *Shine*? A brilliant pianist entertaining, food service paused, raucous applause, and then...back to your meal. Here dining and music come together; live entertainment appears Wednesday–Sunday evenings. While the piano is on a raised platform, the lowcountry cuisine deserves attention, too. Start with a platter of fried-green tomatoes and black-eyed pea fritters, before moving on to the grilled shrimp and scallops served with fried stone-ground grit cakes and fried okra, all touched off with a Cajun cream. Elegantly appointed décor, friendly service, and an award-winning wine list complement the food and music to make for a thoroughly memorable evening. Open daily for dinner. • *102 East Broad Street, Savannah,* ☎ *(912) 790-7888*

Cafés & Picnic Packing

Clary's Café, 404 Abercorn Street, ☎ (912) 233-0402, opened in 1903 and is still going strong as a popular Savannah stop for sandwiches, soups, salads, and sides, plus a collection of excellent desserts. Grab lunch to go and head for a shaded bench in nearby Forsyth Park. • **Parkers Market,** 222 Drayton Street, ☎ (912) 233-1000, sells sandwiches, salads, fruit, desserts, wine and beer, as well as prepared foods such as chicken salad and crab cakes. • At **Soho South Café,** 12 West Liberty Street, ☎ (912) 233-1633, expect a fusion of metro-bistro with Southern gourmet in their soups, salads, and sandwiches.

The tuna and chicken salad sandwiches are exceptional. • **Wall's Bar B Que,** 515 East York Street, ☎ (912) 232-9754, is a tiny, unpretentious restaurant famous for its bar-beque sandwiches and pecan and sweet potato pie.

Just Desserts

Café Gelatohhh, 202 West Saint Julian Street, ☎ (912) 234-2344, serves homemade Italian ice cream. • **River Street Sweets,** 13 East River Street, ☎ (912) 234-4608, serves a tempting array of pralines, taffy, chocolate, caramel, and more. • **Savannah Candy Kitchen,** 225 East River Street and 318 West Saint Julian Street, ☎ (912) 233-8411, *www.savannahcandy.com,* sells various decadent temptations, including brownies and fudge, cakes and pies, and assorted candies and nuts.

*Like music and art, love of nature
is a common language that can
transcend political or social boundaries.*

– President Jimmy Carter, a native Georgian

A Long-Weekend Itinerary

Day One

After breakfast, head to **Sea Kayak Georgia** (page 78) for a three-hour guided paddle tour of **Lazaretto Creek** and **Little Tybee Island.** For lunch, dine at **North Beach Grill** (page 97). To work off your lunch, climb the 178 steps of the **Tybee Island Lighthouse** (page 87) for a great view of the Atlantic, and then tour the light station's museum. Next, spread out your towel to catch some rays, take a dip in the surf, and then stroll the beach to look for shells. Head back to Savannah, recaffeinate at the **Gallery Expresso** (page 91) and then return to your inn to shower and to prepare for dinner at **The Olde Pink House** (page 98). After dinner, join **Savannah Walks** (page 91) for a late night ghost tour. Thoroughly spooked, head back to your inn for lights out...well, maybe leave one light on. BUMP. What was that?

Day Two

After breakfast, head to **Bicycle Link** (page 76) to rent mountain bikes and then drive to the **Savannah National Wildlife Refuge** (page 76). Park the car, unload the bikes, and set off along the refuge's miles of dikes in search of the largest alligator you can find. Return to Savannah, park your car, and cycle to **SoHo South Cafe** (page 98) to purchase a picnic lunch. Ride to **Forsyth Park** (page 71) off Bull

Street to eat and to people watch. Next climb back onto the bike and spend the afternoon exploring downtown Savannah. Can you ride through all 21 squares?

Return your bikes and then head to **River Street** (page 90) to browse the shops. Grab an early dinner at **Suzabelle's** (page 98) and then take in a live performance at the historic **Lucas Theatre** (page 89).

Day Three

Rise early, eat breakfast, and make a morning of visiting some of Savannah's **historic homes** (page 89). Stroll through **City Market** (page 90) to browse the shops.

The Tybee Lighthouse

Deron Nardo

Eat a light lunch at one of City Market's cafés and then walk to your massage appointment at **Vanilla: A Downtown Day Spa** (page 84). Thoroughly relaxed, wander through nearby **Johnson Square** (page 66) to savor your last moments in Savannah, and then climb into your car for the reluctant drive home.

Additional Information

For additional dining, accommodations, and sightseeing information including the dates of special events, contact:

Savannah Area Convention and Visitors Bureau, 101 East Bay Street, Savannah, GA 31401, ☎ (912) 644-6401 or 1-877-728-2662, *www.savannah-visit.com,* is open Monday–Friday, 8:30 A.M.–5 P.M.

Savannah Visitor Information Centers: Main Center, 301 Martin Luther King Jr. Boulevard, ☎ (912) 944-0455, is open Monday–Friday, 8:30 A.M.–5 P.M.; Saturday and Sunday, 9 A.M.–5 P.M.

The **River Street Hospitality Center,** One River Street, ☎ (912) 651-6662, is open daily, 10 A.M.–10 P.M.

Tybee Island Visitor Information Center, Campbell Avenue and Route 80, Tybee Island, GA 31328, ☎ (912) 786-5444 or 1-800-868-2322, *www.tybeevisit.com,* is open Monday–Friday, 8:30 A.M.–5 P.M.; Saturday and Sunday, 9 A.M.–5 P.M.

Savannah Airport Visitor Information Center, 464 Airways Avenue, Savannah, GA 31408, ☎ (912) 966-3743, is staffed daily, 9 A.M.–10 P.M.

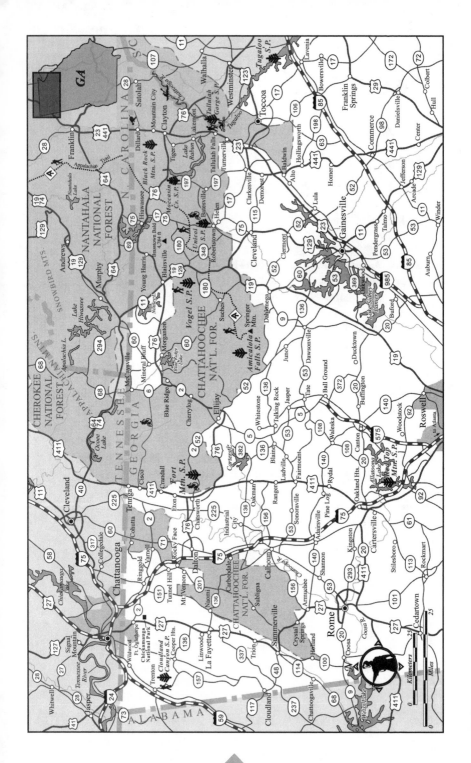

The North Georgia Mountains

North of Atlanta, Georgia becomes increasingly rural. The towns are fewer, hues of green replace concrete-gray, and the land rises slowly in elevation until foothills give way to the start of the Appalachian Mountain Range. Nowhere is Georgia's land as rugged and remote as it is in the north. Here you'll find ancient, rounded mountains, narrow valleys, clear lakes, and quick-moving streams, as well as small towns, time-honored traditions, and friendly people, most of whom can trace their local roots back many generations.

For the active traveler, the draw is the vast acreage of protected land open for four-season exploration. The 750,000-acre Chattahoochee National Forest spreads across 18 counties. Within its borders you'll find: the start of the Appalachian Trail, which extends 2,100 miles northeast to Maine; the state's highest peak, 4,784-foot Brasstown Bald; and a stretch of the mighty Chattooga, a National Wild and Scenic River. While hikers, anglers, mountain bikers, river runners, and back packers flock here in droves, you'll be darned if you see more than several. The forest is that big. It swallows the sports-minded and then spits them out, having plastered smiles on their faces.

For thousands of years prior to European settlement, the Cherokee lived in these mountains, farming the land and using the waterways and footpaths to trade with tribes from as far away as the Ohio Valley and Gulf Coast. Another tribe, the Etowah Moundbuilders, settled the western area of present-day Georgia. Named for unusual earthen mounds they built on which they erected temples, the

Rugged North Georgia

The first Indian Newspaper at New Echota

Moundbuilders developed a culture that included a sociopolitical system and complex trading network.

The powerful Cherokee Nation numbered perhaps 20,000 in the 16th Century when Hernando DeSoto trudged through in search of gold. Cherokee society, with its own government, laws of progeny, and rich mythology, was advanced, and while inter-tribal skirmishes broke out over hunting lands and trade practices, the tribe essentially lived in peace. That is, until the first white settlers made their way into the mountains in the 18th Century. Land negotiations favored the settlers and continually pushed the Cherokee west until the discovery of gold in present-day White County prompted the 1830 Removal Act, sending Native Americans east of the Mississippi to Oklahoma on the "Trail of Tears."

Gold had been discovered long before the nation's first "gold rush" in 1828. Native Americans and Spanish miners panned for it on the Chattahoochee River until the early 1700s, but the "official" discovery was made by Frank Logan. Get-rich-quick fever ensued, and prospectors arrived by the wagonful. The Georgia hills began producing more than 300 ounces of gold per day, prompting the government to establish a mint in Dahlonega in 1838. During 24 years of operation, the mint produced coins totaling $6.1 million.

The 1849 discovery of gold in California lured away many of the prospectors, but the void was soon filled by large corporations that used hydraulic mining equipment to rake the land over double-time. (Commercial mining for gold, iron, clay, coal, and marble continues today, albeit on a far lesser scale than during the late 19th Century.)

The area's permanent settlers were primarily Scotch-Irish farmers who valued the isolation bestowed by the rugged land. These hardy individualists subsisted off the land, making their own clothes and linens (quilt-making is an art); forging a fire-brand form of religion (snake handlers, while rare, still exist); and creating their own entertainment (impromptu bluegrass jams still occur today on front porches and in small general stores).

The Civil War did not interest North Georgians. Fewer than three percent of mountain settlers owned slaves. Though several important battles—Chickamauga, Missionary Ridge, and the Hell Hole, for example—were fought in the area, few settlers were involved in the fighting. Toward the end of the war, lawlessness ran rampant in North Georgia, as roving bands of both

Nacoochee Valley

Union and Confederate forces ransacked farms, destroying crops and stealing cattle.

Following the war, lumber companies built railroad lines deep into the mountains to transport lucrative timber to points south. From the 1880s to the early 1900s, thousands of acres of forest were clear cut. In 1911, President Taft signed the Weeks Act into law, allowing the U.S. Forest Service to purchase private land to manage timber supply and to generate hydroelectric power. The law eventually led to the establishment of the Chattahoochee National Forest in 1936.

Of all the destinations covered in this guide, North Georgia has perhaps the least amount of rest-easy refinery. Herein lays the region's appeal. You don't vacation here to shop expensive, upscale boutiques; dine on cosmopolitan haute cuisine; or order your pillow from a menu offering six varieties of down feathers. You come first and foremost to play in the forest. While there are indeed nice places to shop, stay, and eat, it's exploring Earth in all her rugged beauty that will fill your day's dance card.

The Way Around

The **Chattahoochee National Forest** stretches across North Georgia from the state's eastern border with South Carolina west along the North Carolina and Tennessee borders to Route 411. A small section of forest exists south of Chattanooga and west of Interstate 75 (which connects Atlanta and Chattanooga). Except for commercial development along the interstate and immediately south of Chattanooga, the region is primarily rural—full of small towns within the national forest and along its borders. This chapter focuses primarily on the towns in and immediately around the forest in the north-central and northeast regions of the state.

Located 65 miles north of Atlanta on Route 19, the historic gold-mining town of **Dahlonega** (pronounced de-LAW-ne-gah) mines its past for tourist traffic with a panful of consumer-oriented mining operations. The town's attractive town square with numerous antiques shops, galleries, and historic buildings. Northeast of Dahlonega (via Routes 19 and 129), **Cleveland** features several antiques and pottery shops surrounding the small town square. It was from this town that the Cabbage Patch dolls originated.

GA Dept. of Tourism

Dahlonega

Roughly 35 miles northwest of Dahlonega on Route 52, the state's "apple capital," **Ellijay** sits in the foothills of the Chattahoochee National Forest and serves as a gateway to the mountainous playground. In addition to the wealth of outdoor activity surrounding it, Ellijay is also home to numerous apple orchards, antiques shops, and historic sites.

North of Ellijay on Route 2 is **Blue Ridge**, an outdoor-oriented hamlet tucked into the mountain ridges of the Cohutta Wilderness Area of the Chattahoochee National Forest. There's a historic downtown with an old train depot and a smattering of restaurants, galleries, and shops that add to the fishing, hiking, and rafting outfitters. Lake Blue Ridge and the headwaters of the Toccoa River are also here.

Located in the center of Georgia's Blue Ridge Mountains, **Blairsville** is east of Blue Ridge on Route 76 and is the closest town to Georgia's highest peak, Brasstown Bald. Also nearby: the Appalachian Trail and numerous waterfalls. Despite this multitude of natural wonder, Blairsville is most famous for its sorghum (a molasses-like syrup you spread on biscuits), and

GA Dept. of Tourism

Alpine Helen

each October the town hosts the Sorghum Festival. Continuing northeast from Blairsville on Route 76, you'll enter an area Native Americans called the "enchanted valley" and the villages of **Young Harris** and **Hiawassee**. Located on Lake Chatuge, Hiawassee is the site of the Georgia Mountain Fair, an annual August celebration of mountain crafts and music.

Directly south of Hiawassee on Routes 17/75, **Helen** is an early 1900s lumber outpost that saved itself from anonymity after the logging industry departed. Local business leaders decided to turn the village into Alpine Helen, a replica of a Bavarian mountain town. The streets are lined with beer halls, cafés, cobblestone walkways, bakeries, and more than a few folks in lederhosen.

East of Helen on Route 17 in the Appalachian foothills, **Sautee Nacoochee** is home to the Sautee Nacoochee Center, a thriving cultural center housed in a restored rural schoolhouse. Here you'll find a theater, gallery, art studio, museum, and more, all of which helped the town earn a place in John Villani's book *The 100 Best Small Arts Towns in America*.

Clayton is the commercial center of Georgia's northeast corner and provides access to the Tallulah Gorge State Park and several Chattooga River running operations.

Weather

North Georgia enjoys a relatively mild climate. Summertime is practically mosquito-free, and daytime temperatures rarely reach beyond the upper 80s with evening lows in the lower 60s. Fall is spectacular and perfect fire weather with clear, crisp days and highs in the lower 60s and overnight lows around 40. The colder winter temperatures—January highs average in the upper 30s and overnight lows dip into the mid 20s—make for periodic snowfalls. Spring comes late and is temperate with daytime temperatures not reaching the 60s until late April.

Getting to North Georgia

✈ **By Air: Hartsfield-Jackson Atlanta International Airport,** ☎ 1-800-897-1910, *www.atlanta-airport.com,* services all major airlines and has ground transportation and rental cars available onsite. The drive from the airport to Dahlonega is roughly two hours.

🚗 **By Car: From Atlanta,** take Interstate 75 north to Dalton and Route 76 east into the forest. Expect about a two-hour drive. **From Charlotte,** take Interstate 85 south two hours to Exit #19B, where you take Route 76 west (toward Clemson) to Clayton and the Chattahoochee National Forest. Expect a 3.5- to four-hour drive. **From Raleigh,** take Interstate 40 west to Interstate 85 south and pick up directions from Charlotte. Expect a 6.5- to seven-hour drive.

P l a y   H a r d

W i d e   O p e n

I f you've come to North Georgia to hike, bike, paddle, ski, swim, climb, or ride horses, you'll have no trouble finding scenic public land on which to play. In addition to the Chattahoochee National Forest, numerous state parks provide access to the region's peaks, valleys, lakes, and rivers.

Consider the **Chattahoochee National Forest's** numbers: 750,000 acres; 450 miles of hiking trails; 1,600 miles of forest roads and scenic highways; more than 30 recreation areas; 10 wilderness areas (where the government leaves the land in its primal state); and 2,200 miles of rivers and streams. To manage this colossal territory, the National Forest Service has divided the Chattahoochee into **six ranger districts**—the Armuchee, Cohutta, Toccoa, Brasstown, Chattooga, and Tallulah—all of which operate offices (two are combined) providing recreation information. (Note: the Chattahoochee and Oconee national forests are officially combined into one forest system. The 113,000-acre **Oconee National Forest** is further south

Chattahoochee National Forest

in Georgia's rolling piedmont region and is not covered in this guide.)

The following lists the ranger districts west-to-east and provides district office information and brief highlights. Directions to individual trailheads and recommended activities appear in the individual sport sections. For more information, stop by any of the ranger offices, most of which are open weekdays, 8 A.M.–4 P.M. (Hours and days vary across offices, so call ahead.) ◆ Recently combined, the **Armuchee** and **Cohutta ranger districts,** 3941 Route 76, Chatsworth, (706) 695-6737, encompass more than 172,000 acres of the forest's western boundaries, including the stand-alone Armuchee section west of Interstate 75. Within the Cohutta section is the state's highest lake, 19-acre **Lake Conasauga,** which sits at an elevation of more than 3,100 feet and is surrounded by one of the more-popular recreation areas in the forest. ◆ The jewel of the 147,000-acre **Toccoa Ranger District,** East Main Street, Blue Ridge, (706) 632-3031, is 3,290-acre **Lake Blue Ridge,** a sparkling, manmade lake surrounded by scenic, rugged mountains. The **Aska Mountain Bike Trails System** lies within this district, as well as **Springer Mountain,** the southern terminus of the 2,100-mile Appalachian Trail.

◆ East of the Toccoa District, the 157,000-acre **Brasstown Ranger District,** 1881 Route 515, Blairsville, (706) 745-6928, includes Georgia's highest peak, 4,784-foot **Brasstown Bald,** and **Lake Winfield Scott,** an 18-acre, manmade lake popular for swimming, fishing, and boating. Also within Brasstown is 7,000-acre **Lake Chatuge,** which straddles the North Carolina-Georgia line. ◆ Encompassing more than 118,000 acres east of the Brasstown District, the **Chattooga Ranger District,** Burton Road, Clarksville, (706) 754-6221, includes **Anna Ruby Falls,** twin waterfalls that fall 150 feet from Curtis Creek and 50 feet from York Creek to form Smith Creek. Also within the Chatooga district is 100-acre **Lake Russell,** popular with anglers and swimmers, as well as hikers who make use of several challenging trails nearby.

◆ The **Tallulah Ranger District,** 809 Route 441 South, Clayton, (706) 782-3320, oversees more than 153,000 acres of the forest's easternmost region. Here you'll find **Rabun Beach,** the forest's most-developed recreation area, located on 835-acre Lake Rabun. Two rivers run through the district: the **Tallulah River,** popular with anglers, and the **Chattooga Wild and Scenic River,** which divides Georgia from South Carolina and is the area's major whitewater river.

The Chattooga

GA Dept. of Tourism

◆ There are roughly 10 state parks in North Georgia around the national forest, all of which provide opportunities for outdoor play. Parking fees range from $2 to $4 per car, and most are open 7 A.M.–10 P.M. Listed from west-to-east, the following are the major parks.

◆ Located in the extreme northwest corner of Georgia on the western edge of Lookout Mountain, **Cloudland Canyon State Park**, 122 Cloudland Canyon Park Road, Rising Fawn, (706) 657-4050, is a 3,485-acre park straddling a gorge that's between 800 and 1,980 feet deep. Sitton Gulch Creek flows through the gorge. Tremendous views into the gorge exist from the picnic parking area; however the footloose will want to hike the park's 4.5-mile West Rim and Waterfalls Trail to the base of two waterfalls in the canyon. Many Georgians consider this to be the state's most-scenic park. Located eight miles east of Trenton and Interstate 59 on Route 136.

◆ The 3,712-acre **Fort Mountain State Park,** 181 Fort Mountain Park Road, Chatsworth, (706) 695-2621, features 14 miles of hiking trails, 30 miles of mountain-bike trails ($2 trail fee), and 18 miles of equestrian trails, all through hardwood forests and blueberry thickets. There's also a pretty 17-acre lake with a sand beach. Located eight miles east of Chatsworth off Route 52.

◆ With the tallest waterfall east of the Mississippi, 729-foot Amicalola Falls, the 829-acre **Amicalola Falls State Park,** 240 Amicalola Falls State Park Road, Dawsonville, (706) 265-4703, features 12 miles of hiking trails, including an eight-mile trail to Springer Mountain and the start of the Appalachian Trail. The State of Georgia operates a lodge for overnight guests in the park. From Dahlonega, take Route 52 west roughly 18 miles to the park.

◆ Set at the base of Blood Mountain, 233-acre **Vogel State Park,** 7485 Vogel State Park Road, Blairsville, (706) 745-2628, is one of the state's oldest and most-popular parks. There are 17 miles of hiking trails and a 20-acre lake. From Blairsville, take Route 19/129 south for 11 miles. ◆ Located three miles west of Helen on Route 75-Alternate, the 5,664-acre **Smithgall Woods Conservation Area,** 61 Tsalaki Trail, Helen, (706) 878-3087, features four miles of hiking trails and 18 miles of forest roads for hiking and mountain biking. Dukes Creek, one of the state's best trout streams, runs through the property.

◆ The site of another state-owned lodge, **Unicoi State Park,** 1788 Route 356, Helen, 1-800-573-9659, is a 1,050-acre park with 12 miles of hiking trails, eight miles of mountain biking trails, and a 53-acre lake with fishing docks and seasonal canoe rentals. From Helen, take Route 356 northeast roughly two miles. ◆ Located on the shore of 2,800-acre Lake Burton, **Moccasin Creek State Park,** 3655

GA Dept. of Tourism

Winter in the Chattahoochee

GA Dept. of Tourism

Tallulah Gorge

Route 197, Clarkesville, (706) 947-3194, features two short hiking trails through the park's 32 acres of relatively flat land. Seasonal canoe rentals are available. From Clayton, take Route 76 roughly 14 miles west to Route 197 south to the park's entrance.

Straddling the Eastern Continental Divide at 3,640 feet and located three miles north of Clayton off Route 441, **Black Rock Mountain State Park,** Black Rock Mountain Parkway, Mountain City, (706) 746-2141, features 1,738 acres with a 17-acre lake and 10 miles of hiking trails. It's Georgia's highest state park.

You'll find the two-mile long and nearly 1,000-foot deep Tallulah Gorge inside 2,689-acre **Tallulah Gorge State Park,** 338 Jane Hurt Yarn Drive, Tallulah Falls, (706) 754-7970, where many overlooks exist along the 20 miles of hiking and mountain biking trails on the canyon's rim. (The park issues 100 free permits per day for access down into the canyon.) You can swim in a 63-acre lake, raft the Tallulah River Gorge, hike a 1.7-mile paved rail-trail, and cross an 80-foot suspension bridge. Located south of Clayton on Route 441 in Tallulah Falls.

Dayhiking

Often referred to as a hiker's paradise, North Georgia has so many trails that you'd need to hike 10 miles a day during a 45-day vacation to explore them all. There are trails of every type: short and long, steep and flat, wooded and open, and easy and difficult. The following recommendations are just a sampling of the region's offerings. For a much more thorough review, contact the Chattahoochee National Forest, 1755 Cleveland Highway, Gainseville, GA, (770) 297-3000, to request a copy of the pamphlet, *Trails of the Chattahoochee-Oconee National Forest,* or swing by any one of the ranger district offices listed under *Wide Open*. It's available for a nominal fee.

◆ The **Appalachian Trail** (AT) extends for more than 75 miles through the Chattahoochee National Forest, and many short dayhikes can be created with spur trails connecting to it. The following are a few options. In the Brasstown Ranger District, the four-mile out-and-back hike on the **Byron Herbert Reece Trail** and AT climbs to the summit of 4,458-foot Blood Mountain, the AT's highest point in Georgia. The summit offers stunning views. From the trailhead at the Byron Reece Memorial, follow the blue blazes through a mountain laurel and rhododendron thicket before crossing a fork of the Shanty Branch. The trail then veers away from the stream and climbs two switchbacks before entering an oak and white pine forest. This spur trail soon dead ends at a three-way intersection with the AT, just south of Flat Rock Gap. Turn right on the AT to climb 1,040 feet over roughly 1.5 miles to Blood Mountain. Retrace your steps to finish the hike. To

GA Dept. of Tourism

reach the trailhead, take Route 19/129 south 12 miles from Blairsville to the Byron Herbert Reece Memorial parking area on the right.

◆ One of several hikes beginning at the Brasstown Bald Visitor Center, the moderate-to-strenuous **Jacks Knob Trail** travels 4.5 miles to Chattahoochee Gap and the AT. The blue-blazed trail begins at the southern end of the parking lot, opposite the concession buildings, and heads immediately into dense rhododendrons. After a half-mile, the trial switch-backs down Wolfpen Ridge, past granite boulders and an exhilarating display of wildflowers that bloom in the spring. At Jacks Gap the trail crosses both Route 180 and the Route 180 Spur, before heading back into the forest for the second half of the trek. The trail then travels up, down, and around peaks along the Hiawassee Ridge as it makes its way to Chattahoochee Gap. At the AT, turn around and retrace your steps. See "Four-State Views" for directions to the trailhead.

◆ For some magnificent views without too much work, hike the **Desoto Falls Trail** from the Desoto Falls Recreation Area. This 1.6-mile out-and-back leads you past the two lower cascades of Desoto Falls, as well as an abundance of spring wildflowers. To get to the recreation area from Dahlonega, take Route 19 north roughly 18 miles.

◆ The Toccoa Ranger District's 13,276-acre **Rich Mountain Wilderness Area** contains a number of hiking trails featuring dense forest, rugged peaks, deep valleys, and ever-present wildflowers. An easy hike is the 0.6-mile trail that encircles **Lake Blue Ridge**, a stunning, 3,290-acre lake fed by the Toccoa River. To reach the lake from Blue Ridge, take Old Route 76 east 1.5 miles to Dry Branch Road, onto which you turn right and travel three miles to the entrance sign. The **Green Mountain, Flat Creek Loop, Stanley Gap,** and **Long Branch Loop trails** are also accessible from this recreation area. (These multi-use trails are part of the Aska Trails System. See *Mountain Biking*.)

Four-State Views

From the summit of 4,784-foot **Brasstown Bald,** views extend across four states: Georgia, Tennessee, and the two Carolinas. At the summit, the Brasstown Bald Visitor Information Center, ☎ (706) 896-2556, provides access to four great hiking trails. To get here, take Route 19/129 south eight miles from Blairsville to Route 180-Spur. Turn left and continue three miles to the parking area. (Nominal parking fee.) To reach the summit, either catch a shuttle for a nominal fee, or hike the steep, paved half-mile **Brasstown Bald Trail**. Other trails accessible from the summit are the 5.5-mile **Arkaquah Trail;** the six-mile **Wagon Train Trail;** and the 4.5-mile **Jacks Knob Trail.**

GA Dept. of Tourism

Go the Distance

Four long-distance hiking trails pass through North Georgia. The **Appalachian Trail (AT)** stretches from Georgia's Springer Mountain 2,100 miles north to Mount Katahdin in Maine. Each spring, thousands of thru-hikers set out to hike its length; most hike south to north, hoping to finish in Maine before autumn snows begin. ◆ Originally conceived by Benton MacKaye, the man who envisioned the AT, the 90-mile **Benton MacKaye Trail** extends from Springer Mountain to Route 64 in Tennessee. Eighty miles of the trail are in Chattahoochee's Toccoa and Armuchee-Cohutta districts. ◆ The 117-mile **Bartram Trail** follows the approximate route 18th-centry naturalist William Bartram took through Georgia and North Carolina, as documented in *The Travels of William Bartram*. There are 37 miles of the trail in the Chattahoochee's Tallulah Ranger District. ◆ The strenuous, 35-mile **Duncan Ridge Trail** sets out from an intersection with the Benton MacKaye Trail and the AT near Long Creek at Three Forks, crosses a 260-foot swinging bridge over the Toccoa River, and then proceeds along Duncan Ridge to rejoin the AT at Slaughter Gap.

◆ The Brasstown Ranger District's **Lake Winfield Scott Recreation Area** has an easy half-mile trail (the **Lake Winfield Scott Trail**) that follows the shore of the 18-acre mountain lake. Also here: the 1.2-mile **Jarrard Gap Trail,** which climbs to the AT just south of Jarrard Gap; and the 2.7-mile **Slaughter Creek Trail,** which ascends to Slaughter Gap on the AT. All trails set out from the campground parking area and are clearly signed. To reach the recreation area from Blairsville, take Route 19/129 south 10 miles to Route 180, onto which you turn right (west) to drive seven miles to the lake.

◆ The **Dockery Lake Recreation Area** is a scenic spot popular with anglers and hikers. Two trails set out from Dokery Lake's parking lot. The half-mile **Lakeshore Trail** encircles the lake and is particularly pretty in the spring and early summer when purple and white rhododendrons, dogwoods, and sourwoods bloom. The **Dockery Lake Trail** is a seven-mile out-and-back hike that intersects with the AT near Miller Gap. Its route, which follows and crosses numerous streams, is bordered by magnolias, wildflowers, delicate mosses, and strands of hemlock, white pine, and black walnut. To access the trailheads from Dahlonega, take Route 60 north roughly 12 miles to Forest Road 654, onto which you turn right and travel a mile to

Dockery Lake.

◆ The 35,000 acres of the **Cohutta Wilderness Area** feature flat-topped ridges and peaks covered in deep soil in which ferns and herbs thrive. Many miles of trails wind through the area, the majority of which leads to or follows the **Jacks** and **Conasauga rivers**. Both rivers are prone to powerful flows following heavy rain that make them impassable, so avoid this area if rain is forecast. The **Conasauga River Trail** is too long to hike in its entirety in a day (13 miles one way); however, you can start and turn back at any point. Bring a swimsuit along to cool off in one of many idyllic swimming holes. The moderately strenuous trail follows an old railroad bed, flanked by eastern hemlock trees, and crosses the river nearly 40 times. To reach the trailhead from Ellijay, follow Route 52 west roughly 9.5 miles to Forest Road 18, where you turn right

> **Buy the Book**
>
> The finest hiking guide to the region is Tim Homan's *The Hiking Trails of North Georgia* (Peachtree Books). You'll find this $15.95 book available in all local bookstores.

at the Lake Conasauga Recreation Area sign. Proceed to a fork and bear left over the one-lane bridge. Continue to Forest Road 68, turn right, and drive six miles to a three-way junction with Forest Road 64. Turn right and drive 1.4 miles to the signed trailhead.

♦ From the same parking area, the easy, 1.7-mile **Songbird Trail** loops around a scenic beaver pond and is particularly picturesque in the spring and early summer when wildflowers explode in fragrant color. ♦ The 1.7-mile **Chestnut Lead Trail** descends to the Conasauga River, where you'll find numerous swimming holes. The 3.4-mile out-and-back hike is easy hiking down and moderately strenuous on the return. To get to the trailhead, follow the directions for the Conasauga River Trail to the three-way intersection of Forest Roads 68 and 64. Turn left here and proceed two miles to the signed trailhead.

♦ Named for an 850-foot stone wall encircling the top of a mountain, **Fort Mountain State Park**, 181 Fort Mountain Park Road, Chatsworth, (706) 695-2621, features five trails, only one of which is longer than two miles. The short, scenic **Big Rock Nature Trail** is a half-mile loop that passes a boulder field, a pretty stream, and a cliff overlook with views of a forested valley. From the park's entrance—see *Wide Open* for directions—turn left at the camping/swimming sign, and drive 1.2 miles to the parking area on the left just past the dam. The signed trailhead is just across the road. ♦ From the same parking area, the blue-blazed **Lake Loop Trail** encircles 15-acre Fort Mountain Lake, providing mountain views including a giant boulder field along its 1.2 miles. ♦ Up for a challenge? The 8.2-mile, orange-blazed **Gahuti Trail** is a strenuous hike that loops around Fort Mountain, affording terrific views, vicious descents, and steep climbs along several ravines. To get to the trailhead from the park entrance, drive past the park office (pick up a trail map), following signs to

Anna Ruby Falls

Anna Ruby Falls are twin waterfalls, formed by Curtis Creek, which drops 150 feet, and York Creek, which drops 50 feet. A half-mile scenic trail takes you to the base of the falls. To get here, take Route 75 one mile northeast from Helen to Robertstown, where you turn right on Route 356 for 1.5 miles to a left turn at the Unicoi State Park sign. Follow signs for the falls through the park.

GA Dept. of Tourism

Anna Ruby Falls

GA Dept. of Tourism

the "Old Fort." At the sign for Cool Spring Overlook, turn right toward the gravel parking lot and the signed trailhead.

◆ So many more hiking trails exist in the region than are covered here; however, it's easy to hike without a specific trail in mind visiting any one of the region's state parks, where you can pick up a trail map that lists trails, directions to trailheads, route distances, and difficulty ratings. Of particular note: **Cloudland Canyon State Park,** 122 Cloudland Canyon Park Road, Rising Fawn, (706) 657-4050, in the western corner of North Georgia; and **Black Rock Mountain State Park,** Black Rock Mountain Parkway, Mountain City, (706) 746-2141, in the eastern corner of the state.

Amicalola Falls

The nation's highest waterfalls east of the Mississippi, 729-foot **Amicalola Falls** are easily reached via an exceptionally scenic and blessedly short (0.25-mile) trail to an observation tower. the trail sets out from the end of the park road in Amicalola Falls State Park. (See *Wide Open* for directions.) Other trails inside the park include the 2.6-mile **West Ridge Spring Trail** and the eight-mile **AT Approach Trail,** which climbs to the top of Springer Mountain.

Bicycling & Mountain Biking

While not as well known for mountain biking as North Carolina's Pisgah National Forest, the Chattahoochee offers similar terrain and more than one hundred miles of trails open to mountain bikes. In addition, there are roughly 1,600 miles of forest roads. The following are some of the highlights. For a complete list of trails, contact the Chattahoochee National Forest, 1755 Cleveland Highway, Gainseville, (770) 297-3000, to request a copy of the pamphlet, *Trails of the Chattahoochee-Oconee National Forest,* or swing by any one of the ranger district offices listed under *Wide Open.* It's available for a nominal fee.

◆ The **Aska Trail System** includes 17 miles of scenic hiking/mountain-biking trails of varying lengths and difficulties throughout the Toccoa Ranger District. Routes make use of singletrack and logging roads. Rides include the 5.5-mile **Stanley Gap Trail,** a challenging singletrack through a hardwood forest with strenuous climbs and screaming descents. In winter, there are fine views of Lake Blue Ridge. The spring and summer

GA Dept. of Tourism

seasons present a variety of blooming flora. To reach the trailhead from Blue Ridge, take Route 515 east roughly 0.7 miles past Route 5 to Windy Ridge Road, where you turn right. Drive to the dead end at Old Route 76. Turn left and travel 0.2 miles to Aska Road on the right. Take Aska Road roughly 4.5 miles to the Deep Gap parking area. The trail shares the first stretch with the Flat Creek Loop Trail and then departs right.

◆ The moderately difficult, 5.8-mile **Flat Creek Loop** departs from the Deep Gap parking area and forks within 100 yards. (The Stanley Gap Trail departs right.) Bear left and ride the gentle ascent on the old logging road, which after coming out of the woods, descends to Flat Creek. The trail switches from road to trail and back to road again. Cross the creek and then take a right roughly 50 yards further on an old woods road. Follow signs to complete the loop and return to the parking lot.

◆ A much easier trail, the two-mile **Long Branch Loop** consists of old logging roads with one stream crossing. To get to the trailhead, follow the directions to Aska Road (see the Stanley Gap Trail description). Take Aska Road six miles to Shady Falls Road. Turn left and go less than a half-mile to the next road on the left. At that road's fork, bear left to the parking area. The green-blazed trail departs from the parking lot on an old logging road. Veer right at the fork for a gradual descent. Stay on the road past the white and dark green-blazed **Green Mountain Trail** (a 3.3-mile trail also departing from the Deep Gap parking area). The route crosses a stream and then ascends a grassy road. Continue following the road as it bears left, winding to a ridgetop, where you turn left to reach the original fork. Turn right for the parking lot.

◆ Trails open to mountain bikes inside the Toccoa Ranger District near Dahlonega include the 11-mile **Bull Mountain,** four-mile **Turner Creek,** and 7.5-mile **Jake Mountain trails**. To reach them from Dahlonega, take Route 52 west eight miles to a right turn onto Nimblewill Road. Continue to Forest Road 28-1, turn right and then left on Forest Road 83, following signs to the Bull Mountain parking area.

◆ The Brasstown Ranger District's **Davenport Trail** is a moderate, five-mile route that circles Davenport Mountain with views of Lake Nottely. From Dahlonega take Route 19/129 north two miles to a left turn onto Pat Colwell Road. Drive eight miles to Forest Road 143 and turn right. The trailhead parking area is 0.75 miles ahead on the left.

GA Dept. of Tourism

Numerous dirt roads in North Georgia are ideal for mountain bikes

♦ Also in the Brasstown district, the 5.6-mile **Mountaintown Creek Trail** features many creek crossings, majestic waterfalls, and stands of white pine and hemlock. Numerous rocky, narrow, and steep sections make the ride suitable for intermediate to advanced mountain bikers. From Ellijay, take Route 52 west five miles to a right turn onto Gates Chapel Road. Take Gates Chapel five miles to a right turn onto Forest Road 90. At the junction with Forest Road 68, turn right and drive 3.3 miles to the T-intersection. Turn right on Forest Road 64 and drive seven miles to the trailhead.

♦ The Cohutta section of the **Armuchee-Cohutta Ranger District,** features several trail options, including **Bear Creek Trail,** a 6.7-mile double loop that follows Bear Creek through a hardwood forest and over several steep, narrow sections with numerous stream crossings. From Ellijay, take Route 52 west five miles to a right turn onto Gates Chapel Road (at the Bear Creek Campground sign). Drive 4.5 miles to a right turn onto Forest Road 241. The trailhead parking lot is two miles ahead.

♦ There are many more miles of mountain-bike trails in the forest, as well as in North Georgia's state parks. Try **Fort Mountain State Park,** 181 Fort Mountain Park Road, Chatsworth, (706) 695-2621, where four trails, ranging from easy to difficult, add up to 30 miles of pedaling pleasure. There's a $2 trail fee. ♦ Other good bets: **Tallulah Gorge State Park,** 338 Jane Hurt Yarn Drive, Tallulah Falls, (706) 754-7970, where there are 20 miles of trails; ♦ and the eight miles of trails at **Unicoi State Park,** 1788 Route 356, Helen, 1-800-573-9659. Stop at the park offices to get trail maps, as well as current trail conditions.

Bike Rentals

Woody's Mountain Bikes, 19 Clayton Road, Helen, ☎ (706) 878-3715, rents mountain bikes and operates guided tours.

Ride 'n Swim

At the **Ridgeway Recreation Area** on Carters Lake, a singletrack and logging-road trail system features a six-mile main loop, as well as many smaller trails that branch off through the park. While there are some technical sections—strenuous climbs, steep descents, and deep stream crossings—even beginners can ride the area, if they're willing to walk the tough stretches. It's worth the trip. Numerous high ridges overlook the deep, clear-water lake. The main loop, marked by orange arrows, can be accessed from several areas inside the park, including the boat ramp parking area. When you've built up a sweat, take a swim in the lake's cool, refreshing water. From Ellijay, take Route 282 west roughly eight miles to a left turn at the Ridgeway Recreation Area sign.

Paddling

North Georgia's big whitewater action occurs on the **Chattooga River,** one of the few free-flowing rivers in the southeast. Whitewater season runs mid March–October. Popularized by the movie *Deliverance,* the Chattooga defines the boundary between South Carolina and Georgia along a 40-mile stretch. The National Wild and Scenic River (federal designation given to exceptionally scenic, remote sections of river with recreational value) flows into Georgia's Tugaloo Lake.

The river's whitewater sections have lured many river-running businesses to the region. (See "River-Running Outfitters.") The following describes the river in Georgia; however, unless you're an expert paddler, don't venture onto the water without a guide. The Chattooga is exceptionally rugged, scenic, and in places, dangerous.

The river is open for boat traffic from the Route 28 Bridge in northeast Georgia south 31 miles to Tugaloo Lake. The first seven miles between Route

The Chattooga River

28 and Earl's Ford are fairly quiet with only one class III rapid. Shortly after Earls Ford, the Chattooga picks up speed as it flows through steep, narrow ravines and over numerous Class III–V rapids, including *Eye of the Needle, the Narrows,* and *Bull Sluice,* a tough Class V rapid. After passing the Route 76 Bridge, the Chattooga gets downright testy for its final seven miles. The river's most demanding rapid, *Woodall Shoals,* awaits, as well as a 500-yard stretch called *Five Falls,* where a series of Class III–V rapids exists in quick succession. The Chattooga then serenely empties into Tugaloo Lake.

◆ Other rivers with sections suitable for whitewater or quickwater paddling include the **Cartecay, Ellijay,** and **Coosawattee rivers,** and **Mountaintown** and **Turniptown creeks.** For directions to put-ins and for the latest flow information, stop by one of the paddling outfitters listed below. ◆ Two state parks feature seasonal canoe rentals: **Unicoi State Park,** 1788 Route 356, Helen, 1-800-573-9659, with a 53-acre lake; and **Moccasin Creek State Park,** 3655 Route 197, Clarkesville, (706) 947-3194, on the shore of 2,800-acre Lake Burton.

River-Running Outfitters

The following Georgia-based paddling outfits operate rafting tours on the Chattooga River and/or on other regional whitewater rivers, including the nearby Ocoee in Tennessee: **Appalachian Outfitters,** Route 60 South, Dahlonega, ☎ (706) 864-7117, *www.appoutga.com;* ◆ **Rolling Thunder River Company,** 20 Hughes Street, McCaysville, ☎ (706) 492-5752 or 1-800-408-7238, *www.rollingthunderriverco.com;* ◆ **Southeastern Expeditions,** 7350 Route 76 East, Clayton, ☎ (706) 782-4331 or 1-800-868-7328, *www.southeasternexpeditions.com;* and ◆ **Wildwood Outfitters,** 7272 South Main Street, Helen, ☎ (706) 878-1700, *www.wildwoodoutfitters.com.*

Fly Fishing

To anglers who practice fly fishing as a form of religion, North Georgia is their cathedral. A common sight here is of fishermen reverently pulling up waders by the road, preparing to step through the woods to a nearby stream. Popular fishing waters include **Rock Creek River** near the Chattahoochee National Fish Hatchery; the **Toccoa, Chattahoochee, Jacks** and **Conasauga rivers;** as well as **Frogtown** and **Cooper creeks.** But like a large trout breaking the water before a strike, these rivers hardly scratch the surface. In addition to numerous trout-stocked lakes—**Lake Blue Ridge** and **Lake Winfield Scott,** for example—there are more than 2,200 miles of rivers and streams throughout the forest.

GA Dept. of Tourism

Fly fishing on Dukes Creek

♦ How to make sense of all this water? Head for one of North Georgia's full-service fly shops, which carry equipment, apparel, and dizzying arrays of flies. Other services include fly-fishing instruction and guided trips, ranging from half- and full-day wading trips to full-day float trips.

Two full-service outfitters with outstanding reputations are **Unicoi Outfitters,** 7280 South Main Street, Helen, (706) 878-3083, *www.unicoioutfitters.com;* and ♦ **Upper Hi Fly Fishing and Outfitters,** Fieldstone Marina, 3375-A Route 76 West, Hiawassee, (706) 896-9075, *www.upper-hi-fly.com.* At both shops, you'll find free copies of the *Georgia Guide to Trout Fishing,* which lists season, creel limits, size restrictions, and fishing-license information.

Horseback Riding

Chattahoochee Backcountry Treks, 1420 Chester Road, Dahlonega, (706) 482-8302, *www.cbctreks.com,* offers half- and full-day rides through the national forest. ♦ **Gold City Corral & Carriage Company,** 49 Forest Hills Road, Dahlonega, (706) 867-9395, *www.goldcitycorral.com,* offers one-hour beginner rides on mountain trails, and two-hour rides for more-advanced riders. ♦ **Trackrock Stables,** 4890 Trackrock Camp Road, Blairsville, (706) 745-5252 or 1-800-826-0073, *www.trackrock.com,* offers one- and two-hour trail rides on 250 acres of private land bordering the Chattahoochee National Forest.

Swimming

The Chattahoochee National Forest has dozens of cool, clear mountain lakes perfect for cooling off after a vigorous hike or mountain-bike ride. The following are just a few of the region's great swimming holes. In the **Brasstown Ranger District**, 18-acre **Lake Winfield Scott** has a swimming beach and bathhouse with changing facilities. Open April–October; nominal day-use fee. Take Route 19/129 south 10 miles from Blairsville to a right turn onto Route 180, which you take west seven miles to the lake. ◆ Located at the base of Blood Mountain, **Vogel State Park**, 7485 Vogel State Park Road, Blairsville, (706) 745-2628, includes a swimming beach on 20-acre Lake Trahlyta. The park is 11 miles south of Blairsville via Route 19/129. Nominal day-use fee.

◆ In the Toccoa Ranger District, **Morganton Point Recreation Area** on Lake Blue Ridge has a swimming beach, as well as bathrooms, showers, and changing rooms. Nominal day-use fee. Take Route 515 south four miles from Blue Ridge to Route 60, onto which you turn right and drive three miles to Morganton. In Morganton, turn right onto County Road 616 and drive one mile to Morganton Point.

GA Dept. of Tourism

◆ Located near the summit of Grassy mountain at 3,150 feet, 19-acre **Lake Conasauga** is the highest lake in Georgia. There's a marked swimming area with a grassy ledge and dock. Take Route 411 north four miles from Chatsworth. Turn right at the traffic light in Eton onto Forest Road 18, which you take east 10 miles to a left turn on Forest Road 68. Lake Conasauga is 10 miles ahead. ◆ **Fort Mountain State Park,** 181 Fort Mountain Park Road, Chatsworth, (706) 695-2621, features a scenic 17-

An idyllic swimming hole

acre lake with a sand beach. Located eight miles east of Chatsworth off Route 52.

◆ **Rabun Beach,** in the Tallulah Ranger District, has a roped-off swimming area surrounded by beautiful mountain scenery. Picnic tables and restrooms are available. Take Route 23/441 south seven miles from Clayton to a right turn onto an unnumbered county road for one-tenth of a mile. Turn left on Route 15 for two miles, and then right on County Road 10 for five miles.

Skiing

Located in the northeast corner of Georgia, **Sky Valley Ski Slopes,** 1 Sky Valley Way, Dillard, (706) 746-5303, *www.skyvalley.com,* is the state's only ski mountain.

As far as ski mountains go, it's not much: four slopes, ranging from beginner to advanced (the longest run is a half-mile), and a 250-foot vertical drop. The bright spot? Lift tickets are more reasonable than at nearby North Carolina resorts. Lessons and ski and snowboard rentals onsite. Open weekends only. To reach Sky Valley from Clayton, take Route 23/441 north to Dillard, where you turn right at the only traffic signal onto Highlands Road and drive four miles to Sky Valley.

Local Outdoor Advice

Chattahoochee National Forest • The National Forest Service operates five ranger district offices, most of which are open weekdays from 8 A.M.–4 P.M. (Hours and days vary across offices, so call ahead.) See *Wide Open* for office locations. Another option, the National Forest Information Office, 13 South Park Street, Dahlonega, ☎ (706) 864-6173, is staffed weekdays and serves as a clearinghouse for recreation information. The Forest Supervisor's Office in Gainesville manages all of the ranger districts and serves as a good place to write or call for information. • 1755 Cleveland Highway, Gainseville, GA, ☎ (770) 297-3000, *www.fs.fed.us/conf/*

Wildwood Outfitters • This full-service outdoor retailer sells all manner of equipment, apparel, and accessories for canoeing, kayaking, hiking, and camping. Join one of their guided canoe, kayak, and raft trips, or stop in for suggestions on where to play. • 7272 South Main Street, Helen, ☎ (706) 878-1700, *www.wildwoodoutfitters.com*

Kick Back

When you've had your fill of adventurous, outdoor play or when the weather fails to cooperate, check out the following more laid-back pursuits to North Georgia.

Animal Parks

Interact with grizzlies, black bears, and other bear species from a viewing area 10-feet above at the **Black Forest Bear Park,** South Main Street, Helen, (706) 878-7043, *www.blackforestbearpark.com.* Also onsite: a snake exhibit with more than 20 snakes, including boa constrictors and pythons. Open Monday–Friday, 10 A.M.–7 P.M.; Saturday, 10 A.M.–9 P.M.; Sunday, 11 A.M.–6 P.M. Admission fee. ◆ More than 100 exotic animals roam 10 acres of gently rolling farmland at the **Chestatee Wildlife Preserve,** Old Dahlonega Highway, Dahlonega, (706) 864-941, *www.chestateewildlifepreserve.org.* See zebras, tigers, lions, leopards, kangaroos, baboons, and more. Open daily, 10 A.M.–4 P.M. Admission fee.

Antiques

A smattering of antiques dealers exists in North Georgia; expect plenty of country furniture, antique hardware, farm and garden tools, and Americana knick knacks. Some of the better stops include **Nacoochee Antiques,** 7091 South Main Street, Helen, (706) 878-4069, *www.nacoocheevillage.com*, located in Nacoochee Village, where you'll find books, paintings, china, kitchen and dining accessories, and oak and mahogany furniture. ◆ **Sycamore Crossing Antiques**, 531 East Main Street, Blue Ridge, (706) 632-3366, *www.sycamore-crossing.com*, has 25 rooms of art, books, furniture, crystal, wood carvings, and china. With items stacked everywhere, the shop will likely reward the deliberate shopper with something of value. ◆ **The Mountain Gallery**, 110 School Street, Blairsville, (706) 835-2765, *www.themountaingallery.com*, located one block off the town square, houses fine art and antiques, as well as an Irish Tea Room in which to relax, refresh, and contemplate your new find or potential acquisition. ◆ **Quigley's Rare Books & Antiques**, 104 Public Square North, Dahlonega, (706) 864-0161, *www.quigleysbooks.com*, has a big selection of rare books, including "the largest advertised collection of *Gone With The Wind* first editions for sale in the world."

Art & Crafts Galleries

Carriage House, 115 Cleveland Street, Suite A, Blairsville, (706) 745-9735, *www.carriagehouse-framing-gallery.com*, displays local and regional art in various mediums, including oil, watercolor, and acrylic paintings; photography; sculpture; blown glass; pottery; and mountain crafts. ◆ **High Country Art & Antique**, 715 East Main Street, Blue Ridge, (706) 632-6882, *www.highcountryart.com*, boasts 1,000 pieces of original art from local and regional artists. Work includes oil paintings, pottery, photography, and more. ◆ Located 10 miles north of Clarkesville in a restored mill on the Soque River, **Mark of the Potter**, 9982 Route 197 North, Clarkesville, (706) 947-3440, *www.markofthepotter.com*, sells contemporary, handmade crafts, including wood, metal, pottery, and blown glass.

◆ **Mathenas**, 21 River Street, Helen, (706) 878-3305 or 1-877-354-2691, *www.mathenas.com*, opened in 1981 as a woodworking shop. They've since added work from artists across a range of mediums, including crafts, picture frames, rugs, candles, painted glass, and weather vanes. ◆ Located on the public square in an 1858 building, **The Crimson Moon**, 24 North Park Street, Dahlonega, (706) 864-3982, *www.thecrimson-*

Funky Chicken
Founded in a dilapidated chicken house, the **Funky Chicken Art Project**, 1538 Wesley Chapel Road, Dahlonega, ☎ (706) 864-3938, *www.funkychickenartproject.com*, is a cool gallery filled with whimsical, fanciful creations, including jewelry, oil and acrylic paintings, fiber art, and sculptures. There's an outdoor sculpture garden and, of course, a collection of chickens clucking 'round.

The Funky Chicken Art Project

Apple Orchards

North Georgia is apple country, and nowhere is this more apparent than in Ellijay, which proudly proclaims itself "Georgia's apple capital." Numerous apple orchards are open to the public year-round, but fall is the best time to visit and pick your own. (You can also buy apples by the bushel, as well as such apple byproducts as jam, jelly, juice, and good 'ol apple pie.) Some of the better known orchards: **Hillcrest Orchards**, 9696 Route 52 East, Ellijay, ☎ (706) 273-3838, *www.hillcrestorchards.net;* **Mercier Orchards**, 8660 Blue Ridge Drive, Blue Ridge, ☎ (706) 632-3411 or 1-800-361-7731, *www.mercier-orchards.com;* and **Panorama Orchards**, 63 Talona Spur, Ellijay, ☎ (706) 276-3813.

moon.com, is an eclectic art gallery, coffee house, and acoustic venue founded with the mission "to support, promote, and reward creativity." Art on hand includes handmade jewelry, paintings, drawings, and photographs. Live music performed three or four nights a week.

Back Roads Touring

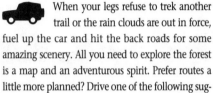

When your legs refuse to trek another trail or the rain clouds are out in force, fuel up the car and hit the back roads for some amazing scenery. All you need to explore the forest is a map and an adventurous spirit. Prefer routes a little more planned? Drive one of the following suggested tours. ◆ Atlantans driving north can connect with the **Georgia Mountain Parkway** in Pickens County—take Route 515 north from Interstate 575—and drive through Jasper, Talking Rock, Ellijay, Blue Ridge, McCaysville, Blairsville, Young Harris, and Hiawassee. Winding east through the Blue Ridge Mountains and the Chattahoochee National Forest, the parkway allows for easy driving without much traffic. Along with scenic views and access to numerous trails and mountain lakes, the road passes

Scenery along the Richard Russell Scenic Highway

shops, restaurants, and historic attractions. Request a free brochure from the Georgia High Country Tourism Association, 1-800-733-2280, *www.georgiahighcountry.org.*

◆ The 14-mile **Richard Russell Scenic Highway** (Route 348) serves up one scenic mountain vista after another at elevations ranging from 2,040 to 3,644 feet. To access the road, take Route 19/129 south five miles from Blairsville to a left turn onto Route 180. The highway, which twists and turns its way toward Helen, is a half-mile ahead on the right. ◆ Other scenic roads worthy of mention include **Route 17/75** between Helen and Hiawassee; **Route 76** between Blairsville and Blue Ridge; and **Route 19** between Dahlonega and Blairsville.

◆ The **Southern Highroads Trail,** a tourism association, publishes a free map for a driving tour through 13 counties in four states: the Carolinas, Georgia, and Tennessee. It covers the entire Chattahoochee National Forest. Call, write, or visit the organization online to request the brochure: Southern Highroads Trail, P.O. Box 1528, Blue Ridge, GA 30513, (706) 633-6706, *www.southernhighroads.org.*

GA Dept. of Tourism

Gem Mines

North Georgia mines its past—gold was discovered here in 1828—for tourist traffic with a panful of consumer-oriented mining operations, including the one-remaining commercial mine, **Gold 'n Gem Grubbin,** 75 Gold Nugget Lane, Cleveland, (706) 865-5454, *www.goldngem.com*. This mine also welcomes tourists hoping to strike gold or any of the other valuable gems found in the hills, including rubies, amethysts, quartz, and topaz. ◆ Other mines include **Consolidated Gold Mine,** 185 Consolidated Gold Mine Road, Dahlonega, (706) 864-8473, *www.consolidatedgoldmine.com*, which features gold panning and underground-mine tours; and ◆ **Crisson's Gold Mine,** 2736 Morrison Moore Parkway, Dahlonega, (706) 864-6363, features panning and has a gold stamp, a machine used to extract gold by crushing rock.

Historic Wanderings

Dahlonega's Chamber of Commerce has developed three walking tours highlighting various sections of town. The **Dahlonega Historic Commercial District,** located on the town square, is listed on the National Register of Historic Places. Buildings on this tour include the Old Lumpkin County Courthouse, built in 1836 and now the Gold Museum; Hall House, built in 1881 in the Victorian Mansardic style; and the 1897 Victorian-Italianate-style Price Building. Also listed on the National Register of Historic Places, **Hawkins Street Neighborhood** is two blocks northwest of the town square. Buildings on this tour are primarily private residences dating to the mid 1800s. The **South Park Street Tour** also highlights private residences built in the mid 1800s. Pick up free tour brochures from the Dahlonega-Lumpkin County Welcome Center, 13 South Park Street, (706) 864-3711 or 1-800-231-5543, *www.dahlonega.org*. Open daily, 9 A.M.–5:30 P.M.

◆ In Georgia's northwest corner in Fort Oglethorpe, the **Chickamauga and Chattanooga National Military Park,** (706) 866-9241, commemorates some of the Civil War's fiercest fighting. In 1863, Union forces numbering 60,000 fought against 43,000 Confederate troops for Chattanooga, a key railway center for the South. The result? Victory for the Federal Army, 30,000 casualties, and one of the final blows to the Confederacy. The 8,000-acre site includes two visitor centers, one in Georgia and one in Tennessee. There are numerous monuments and plaques explaining the battle and a seven-mile self-guiding tour of the Chickamauga Battlefield. Signs direct you to Chickamauga Battlefield Visitor Center, located one mile south of the intersection of Route 2 (Battlefield Parkway) and Route 27 in Fort Oglethorpe. Open daily, 8 A.M.–4:45 P.M. Nominal admission fee.

◆ From 1825–1838, **New Echota,** 1121 Chatsworth Highway, Calhoun, (706) 624-1321, served as the capital of the Cherokee Nation until the federal government forced the tribe to relocate to Oklahoma. During a 15-year span, the Cherokee developed the first written

GA Dept. of Tourism

Chief Vann House

Indian language, published a newspaper, and established a government modeled after the United States Constitution. Built on the site of the original capital, New Echota features such original and reconstructed buildings as the court house, council house, and print shop. There are also smokehouses, corn cribs, and barns onsite. The visitor center offers Native-American crafts and music for sale. Open Tuesday–Saturday, 9 A.M.–5 P.M.; Sunday, 2 P.M.–5:30 P.M. Nominal admission fee.

◆ Built in 1804 by James Vann, a significant Cherokee leader, the **Chief Vann House,** 82 Route 225 North, Chatsworth, (706) 695-2598, is a well-preserved brick home with intricate, hand-carved moldings, a floating staircase, and numerous antiques and Native-American artifacts. Vann did much to strengthen the fledgling Cherokee Nation; however, he was a volatile man who killed his brother-in-law in a duel, fired a pistol at dinner guests, and once shot at his own mother. Vann was shot and killed in a tavern fight in 1809. The home passed to his son, Joseph, who lived here until the Georgia Militia evicted him in 1835. Tours, crafts demonstrations, and historic exhibits are in the house. Open Tuesday–Saturday, 9 A.M.–5 P.M.; Sunday, 2 P.M.–5:30 P.M. Nominal admission fee.

The Chieftains Trail

A fascinating driving tour, the 200-mile **Chieftains Trail,** winds through Northwest Georgia and highlights the area's rich Native-American heritage at six stops. Historic sites include **Fort Mountain State Park,** where a mysterious wall stands atop the mountain; the ceremonial and burial mounds and museum at **Etowah Indian Mounds State Park;** the Cherokee homes of **Major Ridge** in Rome and **James Vann** in Chatsworth; the **Cherokee Capital of New Echota**; and the **Funk Heritage Center**, one of the nation's most-comprehensive Native-American museums, located in Waleska. The drive, undertaken in its entirety, takes 2.5 days to complete. For more information, contact Georgia's Historic High Country Travel Association, ☎ 1-800-733-2280.

Museums

Located in the old Lumpkin County Courthouse, the **Dahlonega Gold Museum,** Public Square, Dahlonega, (706) 864-2257, chronicles the nation's first gold rush following the discovery of gold nearby in 1828. The museum shows a short film. Exhibits include mining tools, gold nuggets, and minted gold coins. The building's bricks were cast from gold-rich Cane Creek, so if you look closely, you may catch a golden glimmer reflecting in the sunlight. ◆ The **Alpine Antique Auto and Buggy Museum,** 115 Escowee Drive, Helen, (706) 878-0072, displays vintage autos and horse-drawn buggies. Open daily, March–November, 10 A.M.–6 P.M. Call for winter hours. Nominal admission fee.

◆ Located in the Sautee Nacoochee Center, the **Sautee Nacoochee History Museum,** 283 Highway 255, Sautee Nacoochee, (706) 878-3300, *www.sauteena-coochee.org,* features changing exhibits dedicated to the history and culture of Sautee Nacoochee, an official historic district. Open Monday–Saturday, 10 A.M.–5 P.M. Free admission.

Dahlonega Gold Museum

◆ Home to the Union County Historical Society, the **Union County Courthouse Museum**, One Town Square, Blairsville, (706) 745-5493, chronicles life in Union County through a variety of exhibits, ranging from the personal items of a Union County poet to a 1960s parking meter. Open weekends only, 10 A.M.–4 P.M., May–October. Free admission.

Railroads

The **Blue Ridge Scenic Railway,** 241 Depot Street, Blue Ridge, (706) 632-9833 or 1-800-934-1898, *www.brscenic.com,* departs from Blue Ridge and travels through the mountains along the Toccoa River to McCaysville, Georgia and Copperhill, Tennessee. The 26-mile out-and-back trip takes 3.5 hours, including a 1.5-hour layover in McCaysville/Copperhill.

Shops & Stops

The villages of Ellijay, Blue Ridge, Dahlonega, and Clayton feature a number of small shops selling crafts, mountain goods, and tourist kitsch. Alpine Helen is full of Bavarian-themed souvenirs. A few stops worth checking out: **Mountain Scholar Books,** 679A East Main Street, Blue Ridge, (706) 632-1993, specializes in Southern titles, but also carries general fiction, nonfiction, and children's titles. Stop here for local hiking guides and nature books. ◆ **Twigs to Furniture,** 511 East Main Street, Blue Ridge, (706) 374-2811, *www.twigstofurniture.com,* sells twig furniture, accessories, and unique home furnishings. ◆ In Alpine Helen, head to **Wooden Shoe Dutch Café and Gifts,** 8520A South Main Street, (706) 878-3530, where you can shop for such Dutch imports as wooden shoes and windmills. ◆ A half-mile south of Alpine Helen, **Village News and Coffee House,** Nacoochee Village, Helen, (706) 878-8245, sells new and used books, and serves coffee, espresso, smoothies, soups, and bagels.

◆ Located at the intersection of the Sautee and Nacoochee valleys, the **Old Sautee Store,** Routes 17 & 255, Sautee, 1-888-463-

Shops along Dahlonega's public square

9853, *www.sauteestore.com*, opened in 1872 and today sells a wide selection of Appalachian and Scandinavian gifts. ◆ For one-stop shopping, head to **The Nostalgic Village Shoppes,** 3073 Chevy Drive, Blairsville, (706) 745-8871, *www.nostalgicvillage.com*, where you'll find nine shops, including candy, Christmas-collectible, and ladies-apparel stores, as well as an old-fashioned general store.

Spa & Massage

Located in a 19th-century cottage just off the square in Dahlonega, **Littlefield Cottage Healing Arts & Day Spa,** 78 North Meaders Street, Dahlonega, (706) 867-9229, *www.littlefieldcottage.com*, offers several forms of massage, aromatherapy, acupuncture, skin care, and reflexology. ◆ In a wooded setting on a hillside above the Nacoochee Valley, **Mandala Wellness Retreat & Day Spa,** 47 Wingo Drive, Sautee-Nacoochee, (706) 878-0036, *www.mandalaretreat.com*, provides an extensive range of spa treatments, including therapeutic and La Stone massages, facials, body treatments, bath therapies, hypnotherapies, and relaxation sessions. They also have a studio for yoga, Pilates, and tai chi classes.

Wineries

Diverse microclimates in North Georgia make for excellent grape cultivation, and a handful of local wineries produce a variety of reds and whites. ◆ In the shadow of Brasstown Bald, **Crane Creek Vineyards,** 916 Crane Creek Road, Young Harris, (706) 379-1236, *www.cranecreekvineyards.com*, produces intricate, bold chardonnays and other wines. Tasting room and vineyard tours available. ◆ **Frogtown Cellars,** 3300 Damascus Church Road, Dahlonega, (706) 865-0687, *www.frogtownwine.com*, produces wines from 14 grape varieties, including chardonnay, merlot, and cabernet sauvignon. Tasting room onsite. ◆ One of Georgia's oldest and largest wineries, **Habersham Winery,** Nacoochee Village, 7025 South Main Street, Helen, (706) 878-9463 or 1-770-983-1973, *www.habershamwinery.com*, has received more than 100 national and international medals for its cabernets, Rieslings, and chardonnays. Tasting room and vineyard tours available. ◆ **Three Sisters Vineyards,** 439 Vineyard Way, Dahlonega, (706) 865-9463, *www.threesistersvineyards.com*, grows cabernet franc, merlot, cabernet sauvignon, pinot noir, and three varieties of chardonnay grapes on 180 acres in the Chestatee River Valley. Tasting room and vineyard tours available. ◆ **Wolf Mountain Vineyards & Winery,** 180 Wolf Mountain Trail, Dahlonega, (706) 867-9862, *www.wolfmountainvineyards.com*, harvests cabernet sauvignon, syrah, mourvedre, and touriga grapes on 25 acres five miles north of Dahlonega's town square.

GA Dept. of Tourism

Three Sisters Vineyards

R e s t   E a s y

S l e e p   W e l l

With the mountains' proximity to Atlanta, you'll find a number of North Georgia resorts that specialize in corporate-retreat business; however, there are also a number of smaller inns and B&Bs in the area. Expect higher rates in the summer and fall.

Accommodations Pricing

Less than $100	Inexpensive	$
$100-150	Moderate	$$
$151-200	Expensive	$$$
More than $200	Very Expensive	$$$$

Prices are per room, per night, based on double occupancy during peak seasons. Note that B&Bs and most country inns include breakfast in the rate.

Brasstown Valley Resort • Situated high in the Blue Ridge Mountains on 503 acres, this resort features 102 main lodge rooms, many of which have balconies, gas log fireplaces, and mountain or valley views. They all contain hand-crafted twig furniture and cable TV. The lodge's centerpiece is the Great Room, which has a 72-foot stacked-stone fireplace, vaulted oak ceilings, pine floors, and large windows. There are also eight, four-bedroom cottages on the property, each with a covered deck, kitchen, parlor, and living room. Several have wood-burning fireplaces. Resort amenities include an award-winning golf course, indoor and outdoor heated swimming pools, more than nine miles of hiking trails, and a state-of-the-art fitness center. • *6321 Route 76, Young Harris, GA 30582,* ☎ *1-800-201-3205, www.brasstownvalley.com* • *$$$–$$$$*

The Fieldstone Resort and Conference Center • Set on 20 acres along the shoreline of Lake Chatuge, this resort features 66 rooms decorated in 19th-century reproduction cherry furnishings. Most have private balconies. Four executive suites have Jacuzzi tubs. A continental breakfast is served each morning, while the onsite Watercrest at Fieldstone restaurant serves fine dinners. Play-hard amenities include a pool, tennis court, walking trails, a wildlife sanctuary with almost 50 different species of birds, a fitness center with two outdoor whirlpools, a full spa, and a marina renting everything from pontoons to kayaks. • *3499 Route 76, Hiawassee, GA 30546,* ☎ *(706) 896-2262 or 1-888-834-4409, www.fieldstoneinn.com* • *$$–$$$$*

Glen-Ella Springs Inn • Listed on the National Register of Historic Places and a member of the *Select Registry*, this 1905 inn has 16 rooms. Decorated with period antiques, all rooms have heart-pine-paneled walls and ceilings, private baths, and access to common porches. Rooms are available in four types: eight feature queen-sized beds and views of the meadow; four have king-sized beds and wooded views; and two suites have queen-sized beds, whirlpool tubs, gas log fireplaces, and sitting rooms. Two penthouses, one with a king-sized bed and the other with two queen-sized beds, share a private sitting room and balcony. A full breakfast, including homemade granola, breads, fresh fruit, and a hot entrée, is served each morning. • *1789 Bear Gap Road, Clarkesville, GA 30523,* ☎ *(706) 754-7295 or 1-877-456-7527, www.glenella.com* • *$$$–$$$$*

Highland Falls Bed & Breakfast Inn • Snuggled in the Blue Ridge Mountains and completely surrounded by the Chattahoochee National Forest, Highland Falls is a reasonably priced mountain retreat. The striking stone-work exterior also features covered wraparound porches with rocking chairs. There are four antiques-filled, high-ceilinged rooms with private baths, Jacuzzi tubs, and satellite TVs. A gourmet breakfast, including fresh fruit, egg casserole, and homemade breads and pastries, is served each morning. • *4434 Highland Forge East, Blairsville, GA 30512,* ☎ *(706) 835-1926, www.blairsvillega.com* • *$–$$*

The Lodge at Smithgall Woods • Located on the Georgia State Parks-owned Smithgall Woods Conservation Area, this property is the epitome of rustic serenity. Five cottages come furnished with overstuffed chairs and sofas, oriental rugs, Native-American art, and stacked-stone fireplaces. The two-story

Smithgall Lodge is constructed of Montana lodge-pole pine and features four bedrooms; the three-bedroom Creekside Cottage hugs the banks of Dukes Creek, which Trout Unlimited calls "One of the Top 100 Trout Streams in the U.S."; the five-bedroom Dover Cottage overlooks the creek and a paddock; and the one-bedroom Garden and Laurel cottages have private decks with hot tubs. Chef Mac Parks prepares breakfast, lunch, and dinner with fresh trout and home-grown vegetables. Breakfast and dinner are served family style; lunches are picnic-packed for guests wishing to hike, bike, and fish on the 5,600-acre retreat. • 61 *Tsalaki Trail, Helen, GA 30545,* ☎ *(706) 878-3087 or 1-800-318-5248, www.smithgallwoods.com* • *$$$$*

Pura Vida USA Spa and Yoga Retreat • Set on 82 acres with walking trails, open pastures, and perennial gardens, this spa and yoga retreat is located in a reproduction 1920s-style farmhouse. There are 19 guestrooms, each with a private bath and decorated in high-country style. Three farmhouse rooms have queen-sized beds, eight barn rooms have king-sized beds, and eight cabin rooms have two queen-sized beds each. Amenities include a salt-water Jacuzzi, wraparound porch, and a spa with massage and bodywork services, and daily yoga classes. A full country breakfast is served each morning, complete with Costa Rican coffee and fresh fruit. • 400 *Blueberry Hill, Dahlonega, GA 30533,* ☎ *1-866-345-4900, www.puravidausa.com* • *$$–$$$*

Souther Country Inn • With 200 acres of private forest, wildflower-covered hiking trails, a creek, and a lake, you may have a hard time leaving the outdoors at the Souther Country Inn. However, the library, game table, living room with TV/VCR, and Norman Rockwell Poster and Memorabilia gallery might help persuade you. Decorated in the English Country style, each of the eight bedrooms has a private bath; seven have queen-sized beds. Also on the grounds: the three-bedroom, three-bath Yorkshire Cottage; and the three-bedroom, two full-, two half-bath ranch-style farmhouse. A full breakfast is served each morning. • *2592 Collins Lane, Blairsville, GA 30512,* ☎ *(706) 379-1603 or 1-800-297-1603, www.southercountryinn.com* • *$–$$*

Dine Well

The majority of fine dining in the mountains is found in the upscale resorts and inns; however, a few standout stand-alone restaurants exist as well.

Brasstown Valley Resort • The resort's restaurant features fine cuisine with fireside intimacy in the dining room and with scenic vistas on the veranda. The menu changes monthly but may include such entrees as grilled chicken breast with roasted chestnut and Frangelico veloute or antelope medallions with blackberry sage sauce. Open daily for breakfast, lunch, and dinner. If you're looking for a more-casual dining experience, check out McDivot's Sports Pub, also onsite. • *6321 Route 76, Young Harris,* ☎ *1-800-201-3205*

Colonel Poole's Bar-B-Q • In 1989 Oscar and Edna Poole opened their restaurant in a roadside shack. Today their reputation is known across the country. Currently housed in a modern cabin next door to the original shack, Colonel Poole's serves barbeque to everyone from senators and embassy officials to Olympic athletes and Miss America. The menu consists of pork, beef, chicken, and pork ribs, all with Poole's special BBQ sauce, as well as such sides as beans, slaw, potato salad, and Brunswick stew. Open for lunch and dinner, Thursday–Sunday. • *Route 515, East Ellijay, ☎ (706) 635-4100 or 1-888-632-8778*

Glen-Ella Springs Inn • Named the "best gourmet inn in the North Georgia mountains" by *Atlanta Magazine*, Glen Ella offers elegant, white-tablecloth dining in a historic inn. Johnson and Wales grad Dickie Smith creates such appetizers as marinated goat cheese with peppers, onions, olives, and herbs, and such entrées as a boneless filet of rainbow trout, sautéed with lime juice, fresh herbs, and pecans. Save room for one of the best pieces of key lime pie around. Open daily for dinner. • *1789 Bear Gap Road, Clarkesville, ☎ (706) 754-7295 or 1-877-456-7527*

Hofbrau International Restaurant • Overlooking the Chattahoochee River, the Hofbrau serves a variety of international cuisines in a cozy atmosphere. The menu changes but may include such dishes as Seafood Wellington—tender filets of orange roughy, topped with a paste of shrimp, scallops, and fresh mushrooms, then wrapped in a flaky pastry crust and baked—and Steak Lupe—tournedos of beef tenderloin, chargrilled and topped with a creamy parmesan-wine sauce, and served with marinated aspara-

gus spears and sea crab legs. Arrive early and relax with a drink in the riverfront lounge. Open daily for dinner. • *9001 Main Street, Helen, ☎ (706) 878-2248 or 1-800-830-3977*

Nacoochee Grill • Located in Nacoochee Village, this contemporary American bistro spit-roasts hand-carved Angus steaks, fresh gulf seafood, ribs, and chops over a "live-fire" grill with oak, hickory, and applewood chips. A wine list with vintages from nearby Habersham Winery complements the meals. To start, try the portabella stuffed with lump crab, artichoke hearts, and parmesan cheese, and then try the roasted duck with a chili-orange glaze. Open daily for lunch and dinner. • *7277 South Main Street, Helen, ☎ (706) 878-8020*

Toccoa Riverside Restaurant • This casual restaurant with a down-home menu features steaks, chicken, pasta, and more, but the house specialty is rainbow trout, which is prepared in a number of ways. Diners eat inside or out on the large, open deck overlooking the Toccoa River. Open for lunch and dinner, Wednesday–Sunday. • *8055 Aska Road, Blue Ridge, ☎ (706) 632-7891*

Watercrest at Fieldstone • On the shores of Lake Chatuge in a wood-paneled dining room, this restaurant serves fresh, innovative cuisine from a menu that changes seasonally. Options may include such appetizers as fried artichoke hearts, hand-breaded and served with roast garlic aioli, and such entrées as flounder filled with house crab stuffing and topped with fresh tomatoes and onions with herb butter. Open Tuesday–Saturday for dinner, and Sunday for brunch. • *3499 Route 76, Hiawassee, ☎ (706) 896-2262 or 1-888-834-4409*

Picnic Packing

Great Eats Deli, 611 East Main Street, Blue Ridge, ☎ (706) 632-3094, is a full-service deli, serving Boar's Head meats, cheeses, salads, soups, and desserts. Enjoy lunch on the outside patio or order takeout for the trail. • Located in downtown Ellijay, **River Street Café and Coffee House,** 28 River Street, Ellijay, ☎ (706) 635-6397, serves breakfast and lunch, plus homemade desserts. Specialty sandwiches can be packed for your hike.

Just Desserts

The Chocolate Express of Blue Ridge, 634 East Main Street, Blue Ridge, ☎ (706) 632-6517 or 1-866-860-6517, serves more than 20 different flavors of homemade fudge. Toffees, truffles, clusters, and creams are also available.• **Doodle's Coffee and Cream,** 7275 South Main Street, Helen, ☎ (706) 878-8245, is an old-fashioned ice cream parlor with more than 20 flavors of Blue Bell Ice Cream. • Order an ice-cream soda, coke float, or vanilla coke at **Lindsey's Malt Shop,** 644 East Main Street, Blue Ridge, ☎ (706) 632-1950, a true old-time soda fountain.

A Long-Weekend Itinerary

Day One

After breakfast at your inn, stop by **Woody's Mountain Bikes** (page 116) to rent mountain bikes and then head to nearby **Unicoi State Park** (page 116) to ride the park's eight miles of trails. After riding, rent a canoe to explore the park's scenic, 53-acre lake. Return the bikes, and head to **Nacoochee Grill** (page 130) for lunch. Spend an hour exploring Alpine Helen and then drive the picturesque **Richard Russell Scenic Highway** (page 122) to Route 180 and Route 9/60 to Dahlonega to walk one or two of the **historic walking tours** (page 123). Next explore the **Gold Museum** (page 124) before returning to your inn to shower and dress for dinner at **Glen-Ella Springs Inn** (page 130). Call it a day.

Day Two

After breakfast, head to **Great Eats Deli** (page 131) to grab a picnic lunch and then head to **Brasstown Bald** (page 111) to hike the nine-mile out-and-back **Jack's Knob Trail** (page 111). Eat lunch on the trail. When you return to Brasstown Bald (thoroughly exhausted), relax on the scenic mountain before getting in your car to spend the afternoon visiting the region's **wineries** (page 126). Return to your inn to shower and dress for dinner at **Watercrest at Fieldstone** (page 130). Return to your inn to hit the hay.

GA Dept. of Tourism

Day Three

After breakfast at your inn, spend the morning browsing North Georgia's **antiques shops** (page 120), **art & crafts galleries** (page 121), and **shops** (page 125).

Head to **Mandala Wellness Retreat & Day Spa** (page 126) for a massage before swinging by **Colonel Poole's Bar-B-Q** (page 130) for lunch and to purchase plenty of 'cue to take home.

Unicoi State Park

Additional Information

Dahlonega-Lumpkin County Chamber of Commerce, 13 South Park Street, Dahlonega, GA 30533, ☎ (706) 864-3711 or 1-800-231-5543, *www.dahlonega.org,* operates a welcome center open daily from 9 A.M.–5:30 P.M.

Fannin County Chamber of Commerce, 3990 Appalachian Highway, Blue Ridge, GA 30513, ☎ (706) 632-5680 or 1-800-899-6867, *www.blueridgemountains.com,* operates a visitor center open Monday–Friday, 8:30 A.M.–5:30 P.M., Saturday, 9 A.M.–5 P.M., and Sunday, 1 P.M.–5 P.M.

Gilmer County Chamber of Commerce, 368 Craig Street, East Ellijay, GA 30539, ☎ (706) 635-7400, *www.gilmerchamber.com,* operates a visitor center open Monday–Friday, 9 A.M.–5 P.M.

Rabun County Chamber of Commerce, 232 Highway 441, Clayton, GA 30525, ☎ (706) 782-4812, *www.gamountains.com,* operates a visitor center open Monday–Friday, 9 A.M.–5 P.M., year-round; Saturday, 9 A.M.–5 P.M., April–November.

Towns County Chamber of Commerce, 1411 Fuller Circle, Young Harris, GA 30582, ☎ (706) 896-4966 or 1-800-984-1543, *www.townscountytourism.com,* operates a visitor center open Monday–Friday, 9 A.M.–5 P.M., year-round; Saturday, 10 A.M.–4 P.M., April–December.

Union County Chamber of Commerce, 385 Welcome Center Lane, Blairsville, GA 30514, ☎ (706) 745-5789 or 1-877-745-5789, *www.blairsvillechamber.com,* operates a visitor center open Monday–Friday, 8:30 A.M.–4:30 P.M., year-round; Saturday, 10 A.M.–1 P.M., Memorial Day–October.

White County Chamber of Commerce, 122 North Main Street, Cleveland, GA 30528, ☎ (706) 865-5356, *www.whitecountychamber.org,* is open Monday–Friday, 8 A.M.–4:30 P.M.

The Helen Convention and Visitor's Bureau, 726 Bruckenstrasse, Helen, GA 30545, ☎ 1-800-858-8027, *www.helenga.org,* operates a welcome center open Monday–Saturday, 9 A.M.–5 P.M., and Sunday, 10 P.M.–4 P.M.

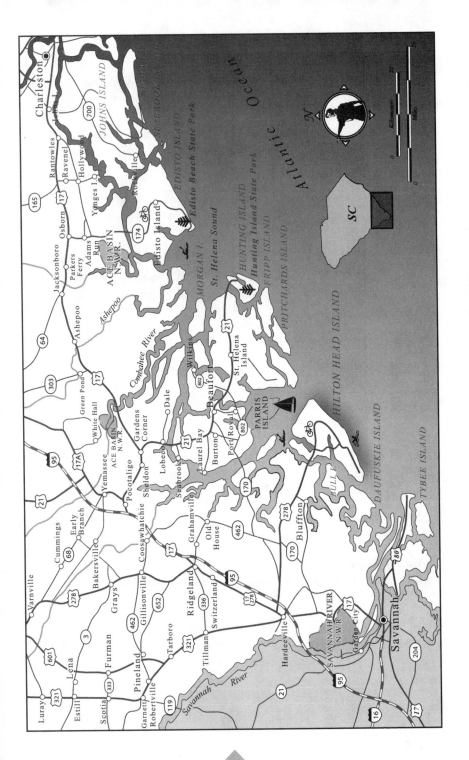

Beaufort, Hilton Head, & the Lowcountry, South Carolina

South Carolina's geography from northwest to southeast is like a gentle playground slide, a gradual fall from the Blue Ridge Mountains across the rolling hills of the Piedmont to the "fall line," a marked drop in elevation where rivers "fall" to the sea. At the base of this rocky step down, the state's vast coastal plain begins. Here broad rivers flow through flat pine forests and fertile fields to the inland swamps, blackwater creeks, tidal bays, and sandy marshlands of the South Carolina coast. This is the Lowcountry.

Whereas "Lowcountry" once referred to the entire coastal plain—an area equaling more than half the state—today it defines South Carolina's coastal region from Georgetown south to the Savannah River. In and around Beaufort, the Lowcountry best fulfills its image as a place of centuries-old live oaks with shawls of Spanish moss, antebellum plantations, abandoned rice fields, and isolated pockets of Gullah communities on rural barrier islands.

Here vast marshes crowned by golden cordgrass blur the lines between mainland and island. There are more than 60 barrier islands in Beaufort County—perhaps thousands, if you include the low-lying hummocks (mini-islands). Water is everywhere. The ACE Basin, a 350,000-acre estuary where three rivers (the Ashepoo, Combahee, and Edisto) meet in St. Helena Sound, fills much of the space between Charleston and Beaufort. The ACE is an important nursing ground for a variety of species, including

Vast marshes separate islands from the mainland

shrimp, crabs, oysters, plankton, and small fish. In turn, this estuary is a veritable seafood buffet for ospreys, bald eagles, raccoons, reptiles, bigger fish, and people.

Archaic Indians were the first people to live in the Lowcountry, but evidence of their presence is limited to a few mounds of discarded oyster shells that date to a pre-agricultural age more than 4,000 years ago. More is known about their descendants—Woodland tribes such as the Ashepoo, Combahee, Edisto, Kiawah, and Wimbee—that farmed, hunted, and fished on the mainland and barrier islands from Charleston south to the Savannah River.

The Spanish were the first Europeans to arrive in the Lowcountry, and they constructed a fort near present-day Port Royal in 1525. That settlement perished as did a subsequent French Huguenot fort on Parris Island. The Spanish returned in 1566 to build St. Elena on Parris Island. The fort flourished for 20 years as the capital of Spain's North American settlement before the Spanish departed to consolidate forces at the more defensible St. Augustine in Florida.

In 1663, British Captain William Hilton (for whom Hilton Head Island is named) sailed from Barbados to explore the Port Royal and St. Helena sounds. His favorable report piqued the interest of the Lords Proprietors, eight men who'd been granted land in the Carolinas by Charles II, and they began lining up colonists. In 1670, 148 English settlers arrived near present-day Port Royal, but hostile Indians and the proximity of the Spanish sent them north to the Ashley River where they founded Charles Town. To provide a buffer between the Spanish and growing port of Charles Town, the British established Beaufort, the second oldest town in South Carolina, in 1711.

The fledgling settlement survived raids by seafaring pirates, epidemics such as small pox, powerful hurricanes, and raids by hostile Indians to become a major trading center. Planters arrived from Europe and the Caribbean with African slaves to grow indigo and rice. By the start of the American Revolution, Beaufort's population numbered nearly 4,000, but despite its size, the city fell easily to the British during the war.

Following the war, the Lowcountry became the nation's wealthiest region from Sea Island cotton produced on local plantations. Planters and merchants built palatial summer homes in Beaufort. Meanwhile, the political discourse turned to secession over the issues of states' rights and slavery. In fact, South Carolina's Ordinance of Secession was drafted in a house on Beaufort's Craven Street. In 1861, soon after Confederates fired on Fort Sumter, more than 50 Federal Navy ships sailed into Port Royal Sound, forcing residents of Beaufort and the surrounding islands to flee.

The city remained in Union hands throughout the Civil War. As a result, its homes, churches, and buildings—used as barracks, hospitals, and administrative offices—were spared General Sherman's torch. During the war, the government levied a tax on the absentee landowners, knowing it would go unpaid. After con-

Charles N. Bayless, Library of Congress

South Carolina's Ordinance of Secession was drafted in this house

fiscating the property, the government subdivided the land and sold it to former slaves, Union soldiers, and Northern investors.

The Civil War decimated the lowcountry economy, and economic improvement came slowly. Farming and phosphate mining drove the recovery. In 1891, the United States built a naval yard on Parris Island to service and repair battleships. But hard times returned in 1893 when a monstrous hurricane struck, killing more than 2,000 people and devastating property. A subsequent yel-

Though Sherman spared Beaufort, he torched a nearby church in Sheldon

low-fever outbreak and a boll-weevil infestation sent the lowcountry economy into a tailspin that would last for decades.

During the first half of the 20th Century, the region's commercial shrimping industry and the expanding American-military presence on Parris Island kept the region afloat. Shortly thereafter, entrepreneurs realized the commercial value of the warm weather, the islands' beaches, and the immaculately preserved antebellum town of Beaufort. Tourism has been a major industry ever since.

The busy season here remains June through August when the influx of sun and sand seekers arrives for vacation. Increasingly however, people are visiting year-round to sea kayak the region's tidal creeks and rivers; to mountain bike the immense maritime forests; and to hike the upland marshes. When you've had your fill of active outdoor pursuits, a wide variety of laid-back diversions awaits, from touring Beaufort's historic sites to visiting the area's many impressive art galleries. What else will you find here? World-class shopping, delicious dining, and historic inns that have retained their 18th-century character while adding modern amenities.

The Way Around

South of Charleston on **Route 17**, the South Carolina Lowcountry becomes increasingly rural as the highway traverses the **ACE Basin** wetlands and crosses the **Edisto, Ashepoo,** and **Combahee rivers**. **Route 21** veers due south from Route 17 for Port Royal Island and **Beaufort**. Bordered on three sides by the Beaufort River, this historic city shimmers with light reflected off the water's surface. The city was spared the destruction that befell many other Southern cities during the Civil War. Through careful preservation and strict architectural-zoning laws, Beaufort has become a popular destination for tourists drawn to its serene, shady streets lined with elegant, antebellum homes and mansions.

As Route 21 enters Beaufort, it becomes **Boundary Street** and makes a hairpin turn to the right at the Beaufort River. Despite remaining Route 21, the road's name changes to

Water is everywhere in the Lowcountry

Carteret Street. Traveling south on Carteret, the historic downtown is to the right, and the **Old Point** neighborhood is to the left. Here you'll find numerous antebellum mansions, including Tidalholm, the 1856 home featured in the movies *The Big Chill* and *The Great Santini*. (Note that nearly all homes in Beaufort are privately owned.)

Beaufort's entire downtown forms the **historic district**, which measures roughly eight blocks by fourteen blocks. The streets adhere to a grid design. **Bay Street,** the town's primary commercial street, looks and feels like "Main Street, USA" until it reaches the **Henry C. Chambers Waterfront Park**, a seven-acre greenway beside the Beaufort River. The park has a public marina, a seawall promenade, and an ample supply of benches facing the water. Many of Beaufort's outdoor civic events, including crafts fairs, music events, and the annual Water Festival each July are held in the park. (The park is undergoing a two-year renovation that began January 2004.) Bay Street extends out of town past even more gracious mansions along the water.

Most of the city's shops, art galleries, restaurants, and inns are on or immediately off of Bay Street. To get oriented in Beaufort, pick up a map from the Greater Beaufort Chamber of Commerce Visitor Center, 1106 Carteret Street, park the car, and start walking.

A Tale of Two Beauforts

North and South Carolina both have port towns named Beaufort, but the pronunciations are different. South Carolina's Beaufort is pronounced "Bew-fort," whereas North Carolina's is pronounced "Bo-fort."

Moving east from Beaufort, **Sea Island Parkway** (Route 21) crosses the Beaufort River to **Lady's Island**, a large island where much of Beaufort County's residential development is occurring. The next stop on Sea Island Parkway is **St. Helena Island,** the largest of Beaufort County's sea islands and site of the **Penn Center**, a 50-acre National Historic Site and community center dedicated to preserving the history, language, and culture of the region's Gullah people. (See *Gullah Culture* under *Kick Back*.)

The remaining barrier islands on Sea Island Parkway are, in order of access: **Harbor Island,** a residential island; **Hunting Island,** home to the popular Hunting Island State Park; and **Fripp Island,** another upscale, residential island. Roads from St. Helena and Lady's Island connect to even more residential and resort-property islands like **Dataw, Spring,** and **Coosaw.**

Three miles south of Beaufort on **Route 281** is the historic town of **Port Royal,** a pleasant community with a public beach and wooden boardwalk along the Beaufort River. An increasing number of good restaurants and classy boutiques are opening here.

Greater Beaufort COC

Beaufort's Waterfront Park

Further south across Battery Creek and accessed by Route 802, the **Marine Corps Recruitment Depot** on **Parris Island** goes busily about its duty of training the young men and women of the United States Marine Corps. Visitors are welcome at the training base, including at graduations, held every week on Fridays. Traveling south from Beaufort toward Hilton Head on scenic **Route 170,** you come to **Route 278,** which is the highway to Hilton Head. As you approach the island, rural scenery gives way to the commercial development of **Bluffton,** once a sleepy town whose borders wrapped tightly around its downtown on the May River. As Hilton Head grew, so did economic opportunity, and many developers chose to construct shopping centers on the highway leading to the island. Technically, this commercial stretch of highway is Bluffton, but the line blurs and you'll find yourself following directions to a Hilton Head business, only to find it's off the island in Bluffton.

Downtown Bluffton is not the bustling retail scene of Route 278. Instead, the village center, accessible via **Route 46,** is much as it was when planters built the town as a summer retreat in the mid 19th Century. Set upon a bluff overlooking the May River, Bluffton receives cool ocean breezes. The historic downtown is a serene spread of antebellum and post-Civil War homes on quiet, oak-lined streets. Here one of the few remaining lowcountry oyster operations, the Bluffton Oyster Company, still harvests its crops from the May River. Once a good-sized industry in South Carolina, commercial oystering has fallen victim to increasingly polluted waters.

Route 278 crosses the J. Wilton Graves Bridge and becomes **William Hilton Parkway** on **Hilton Head Island.** This 12-mile-long, five-mile-wide island looks remarkably like a running shoe, and indeed, directions to the island may include references to the toe, heel, or instep.

Hilton Head is *trés chic.* The island is home to more than 30,000 full-time residents, many of whom live in upscale homes or condominiums inside one of the island's gated, plantation-style communities. Roughly 2.5 million tourists visit each year. The island hosts major tennis and golf events, including the WorldCom Classic golf tournament (formerly called the Heritage). Each New Year's, the Renaissance Weekend draws international thinkers, movers, and doers for an off-the-record, collective brainstorm. The participants try to envision solutions to the world's problems. President Clinton attended the Renaissance several times during his terms in office.

While development is tasteful and discretely tucked into live-oak forests, Hilton Head does suffer large shopping complexes, ubiquitous fast food chains, wicked traffic, and enough chintzy tourism brochures to rival vacation destinations such as Myrtle Beach. The draw is ultimately the beach, and while public access is limited, once you're on it, you have up to the high-tide mark to enjoy yourself at will. Golf is also a major pastime here. More than 20 championship-caliber,

A Wet 'n Wacky Good Time

With so much water surrounding Beaufort and the sea islands, it stands to reason that there ought to be a water festival. And is there ever. Fifty years old in 2005, the annual **Beaufort County Water Festival**, *www.waterfestival.com,* has grown from a small boat show into one of the largest festivals in the South. Held in July, the event draws thousands who help this town celebrate its relationship with the water. There are national music acts, a fishing tournament, crafts shows, power boat races, antique car shows, festival rides, and wacky events like a bed race down Bay Street.

Hilton Head Island CVB

Sunrise on Hilton Head Island

public-access courses are on the island. Four of them consistently rank among the nation's top 100 in key golf publications.

The 25-mile **William Hilton Parkway** (Route 278) is the island's main artery, providing access to all the communities and attractions on the island. An alternative to this heavily trafficked road is the **Cross Island Parkway**, a four-lane toll highway ($1 per car) that zips over the marshes and Broad Creek from near the mainland bridge to the south end of Hilton Head.

Just across **Calibogue Sound** and accessible only by boat, **Dafauskie Island** is what many consider Hilton Head to have been fifty years ago: largely rural and undeveloped. With a mere 300 residents—including a Gullah community comprised of descendants from freed slaves—and the posh Daufuskie Island Resort, Daufuskie is an unspoiled place ripe for exploration. Ferries depart from Hilton Head and land at Daufaskie's Freeport Marina, from which you can rent golf carts to explore the island.

Weather

The Lowcountry's climate is semi-tropical. You can swim comfortably seven months a year. Summers can be hot, with August temperatures typically in the 90s, but ocean breezes temper the heat. Winter is rarely frigid. Average high temperatures in February are 61 degrees with only occasional overnight dips into the 20s. The shoulder seasons of spring and fall are almost perfect with daytime highs in the mid 70s and lows at night in the upper 50s.

Getting to the Lowcountry

✈ **By Air: Savannah International Airport**, ☎ (912) 964-0514, *www.savannahairport.com*, hosts numerous major carriers, as well as car rental and ground transportation companies, and is a 45-minute drive from Beaufort. **Charleston International Airport,** (803) 767-1100, *www.chs-airport.com*, hosts most major carriers and car rental companies and is roughly a 1.5-hour drive from Beaufort. USAirways Express, a commuter airline, flies into the **Hilton Head Airport**, (843) 689-5400, *www.hiltonheadairport.com,* which has most major car rental companies onsite.

🚗 **By Car: From Atlanta,** take Interstate 75 south to Macon, then Interstate 16 east to Interstate 95 north, which you take roughly 20 miles to Exit # 8/Route 278. Follow

Route 278 east to Route 170, which you take roughly 20 miles into Beaufort. Route 170 ends at a right turn onto Route 21/Boundary Street. The drive is approximately six hours. **From Charlotte**, take Interstate 77 south to Columbia and then Interstate 26 east to Interstate 95. Take Interstate 95 south roughly 50 miles to Exit # 33/Route 17 north. Follow Route 17 north eight miles to Route 21, which you take south into Beaufort. Expect a 4.5-hour drive. **From Raleigh,** take Interstate 40 east to Interstate 95 south, which you follow for roughly 250 miles to Exit # 33. Follow directions above from Exit # 33. Expect a six-hour drive.

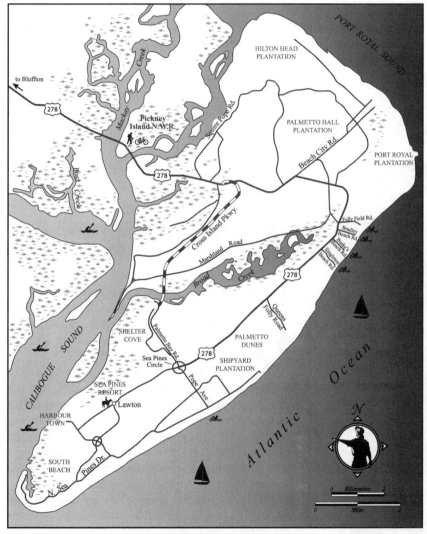

Hilton Head Island

Play Hard

Wide Open

Public land in the Lowcountry is abundant, offering many multi-sport playgrounds. The common denominator among most is water. Whether you enjoy paddling, swimming, sailing, or simply bicycling or walking beside bodies of water, the Lowcountry has H20 with buckets to spare.

The 12,000-acre **ACE Basin National Wildlife Refuge,** Grove Plantation Office, 8675 Willtown Road, Hollywood, SC (843) 889-3084, *http://acebasin.fws.gov,* is a federally protected section of the 350,000-acre basin where you can paddle, pedal, or hike. There are two sections to the refuge: one along the Combahee River and the other on the Edisto River, closer to Charleston. The refuge office is in the Edisto section in an antebellum plantation home. To get to the Grove Plantation office from Beaufort, take Route 21 north to Route 17 north to Osborn, where you turn right onto Route 174. Follow Route 174 through Adams Run. (Route 174 makes a right turn in Adams Run.) Continue on Route 174 to an intersection with a flashing light and a sign directing you to the refuge. Turn right at the light onto Willtown Road and proceed two miles to the entrance.

The state's most popular park, **Hunting Island State Park**, 2555 Sea Island Parkway, (843) 838-2011, *www.huntingisland.com*, encompasses the entire 5,000-acre Hunting Island, a barrier island of semi-tropical forest, salt marsh, and more than three miles of sand beach. Once used as hunting grounds by Native Americans and early Port Royal settlers, the island is now a nature preserve where wildlife encounters—with deer, alligators, rattlesnakes, and birds—are a distinct possibility. Here the sports go year round, from kayaking the island's lagoon and swimming in the Atlantic Ocean to hiking and mountain biking its trails. Also on the island are a historic, 1873 lighthouse (closed for repairs at press time); a visitor center with ecology exhibits; and a fishing pier. To reach the park from Beaufort, take Route 21 (Sea Island Parkway) south 15 miles. Expect a nominal admission fee ($3 for adults).

Just a half-mile west of Hilton Head Island on Route 278 (just across the J. Wilton Graves Bridge), **Pinckney Island National Wildlife Refuge,** (912) 452-4415, encompasses four islands—Pinckney, Corn, Big Harry, and Little Harry—and more than 4,000 acres of forestland, salt marsh, and tidal creek. Only Pinckney Island, the largest of the four, is open to the public. But you'll be well satisfied after exploring the island's 14 miles of trails. They provide access to five ponds—Ibis Pond and Osprey Pond are the most accessible—as they meander through Pinckney's forested interior and beside its salt marshes.

There are also many smaller state parks, wildlife management areas, and nature preserves in the Lowcountry described in the individual sport sections.

Tidal creeks run throughout the ACE Basin

Dayhiking

Because of the flat landscape, coastal areas in the South rarely offer much in the way of rigorous hiking. However, plenty of trails exist for those who enjoy walking in the woods or along the coast without punishing their lungs.

Beaufort & the Northern Lowcountry

The most popular walking destinations in the Lowcountry are the beaches, and none in the area around Beaufort rivals the three-mile stretch of sand at **Hunting Island State Park,** 2555 Sea Island Parkway, (843) 838-2011, *www.huntingisland.com*, where a nominal admission fee opens the gate to this coastal oasis. Park in Lot J and hit the beach. Walk left for North Beach or right for South Beach. ♦ In addition to the beach, you can hike a smattering of short trails inside the park. Pick up a trail map at the park's visitor center. The

Hilton Head Island CVB

Lowcountry beaches are perfect for walking

Campground Access Trail is a one-mile, out-and-back, dirt path from just outside the park's entrance to the campground at North Beach. This multi-use path (watch for bicyclists) winds through the maritime forest. To access the trailhead, walk outside the park, past the fee station to the trailhead on the right. ◆ From Parking Lot D at the Lighthouse, the three-quarter-mile **Lighthouse Trail** is a sandy path running along the coast to its terminus at North Beach. ◆ Another 0.3-mile trail in the state park is the **Marsh Boardwalk,** a wooden pathway built over the marsh to an upland piece of land. Look beneath the tall marsh grass to see fiddler crabs waving hello with their over-sized cruncher claws.

◆ The **Hunting Island Trail** is a four-mile foot and bicycle path that can be combined with park roads to create an eight-mile loop. Begin by parking in Lot J (the trailhead is marked) and follow the path south on the bluffs beside the lagoon. At the southern end of the island, walk the length of the 1,100-foot fishing pier, the longest, free-standing pier on the East Coast. Backtrack to the trail and continue north to a juncture on your left. Follow this to the Marsh Boardwalk, or continue straight on the Hunting Island Trail to the visitor center, where you follow the road back to Lot J.

◆ The **ACE Basin National Wildlife Refuge**, (843) 889-3084, has two separate units—one portion of the refuge is along the Combahee River; the other is along the Edisto River—and both sections are open for exploration on foot. The Combahee section is closer to Beaufort and has a pleasant three-mile hiking path that loops over marshes, along river dikes, beside irrigation canals, around ponds, and past former rice fields. In addition to plenty of interesting birds, including bald eagles, you may see an alligator swimming or simply sunning itself. To reach the trail from Beaufort, take Route 21 north to Route 17 north roughly five miles to River Road. Turn left on River Road and drive two miles to the parking area and trailhead on the left. ◆ As part of the colossal ACE Basin, the **Bear Island Wildlife Management Area,** State Road 26, Bennett's Point, (843) 844-8957, is a veritable wildlife wonderland spread across 11,000 acres of wetlands and maritime forest. Park the car and set out on the numerous marked trails along river dikes and through forested land. The area is closed to hikers November–January and on Sundays year-round.

Hilton Head & the Southern Lowcountry

◆ The Lowcountry's other good walking beaches are on **Hilton Head Island.** To get to them, head for one of the five public access areas, the most popular of which is at **Coligny Circle** beside the Holiday Inn. With ample parking (in a municipal lot beside the traffic circle) and public restrooms with showers, this spot is perfect for taking a break from shopping or sightseeing. You can pull up, walk on the beach, swim, and then shower before resuming your day. Parking fees are nominal. ◆ A short drive south of Coligny Circle off South Forest Drive, you'll find another public beach access area on **Alder Lane** near the Marriott Grand Resort. Alder Lane has metered parking spaces. ◆ The northern beach areas of Hilton Head are accessible from Route 278. From north to south, **Folly Field Road, Bradley Beach Road,** and **Burke's Beach Road** all offer public parking and easy access to the beach. For more information about the facilities available at each, see *Swimming*. In general, Hilton Head's northern beaches are less crowded, and parking typically isn't a problem. (Hilton Head takes parking very seriously, so be sure you're in a public space. If the side of a road is not marked as open to parking, don't risk it.)

◆ Hilton Head has 20 miles of paved **island pathways** that stretch across the island and are popular with cyclists and pedestrians. Stop at any of the sources listed under *Additional Information* to request the "Island Pathways" map. ◆ The 600-acre **Sea Pines Forest Preserve,** 175 Greenwood Drive, Hilton Head, (843) 363-4530, offers nearly eight miles of trails through maritime forest and over marshland. The paths and boardwalks, built on former rice-field dikes and logging paths, are clearly marked. The preserve also provides a map. Unless you're a guest of Sea Pines Plantation, you'll have to pay a nominal access fee.

◆ Also on Hilton Head, the **Audubon Newhall Preserve,** Palmetto Bay Road, (843) 785-5775, has two miles of easy walking trails through 50 acres of undeveloped land. Pick up a trail guide at the entrance for descriptions of the local plants and trees. To reach the preserve, take the Cross Island Expressway from the mainland bridge to Palmetto Bay Road. A sign on the right marks the entrance.

◆ More than 14 miles of trails provide access to the marsh, maritime forest, and freshwater ponds in the **Pinckney Island National Wildlife Refuge,** Route 278, (912) 452-4415. Island maps are available under the kiosk at the center of the parking area. They detail numerous hiking options, including the eight-mile roundtrip hike to **White Point,** where four waterways converge at the northern end of the island: Mackey's Creek, the Chechessee

River, Port Royal Sound, and Skull Creek (the Intracoastal Waterway). This was where General Charles Cotesworth Pinckney built his home in the late 1700s. (It no longer stands.) ◆ For a more moderate hike, the 2.7-mile roundtrip walk from the parking area around **Wood Stork Pond** provides ample opportunity to see (and smell) the island's flora and fauna. Keep an eye out for alligators, raccoons, and deer, as well as nesting platforms for ospreys.

◆ Located between Hilton Head and Bluffton, the **Victoria Bluff**

Hilton Head Island CVB

The Sea Pines Forest Preserve

Heritage Preserve, Sawmill Creek Road (off Route 278), (803) 625-3569, is an 1,100-acre parcel of land consisting of maritime forest and low-lying marshland. Firebreaks throughout the preserve make excellent hiking paths. Leaving Hilton Head on Route 278, you'll see the sign for Victoria Bluff on the right.

Mountain & Road Biking

With nary a mountain in sight, it's not *mountain* biking, but the Lowcountry does have a number of places where you can ride a mountain bike through forested terrain. Overall, singletrack trails are scarce and trails that do exist are often popular with hikers. Take care to avoid any close encounters of the pedestrian kind. A more popular form of bicycling in the Lowcountry, particularly on Hilton Head Island, is riding single-speed beach cruisers on the beach.

♦ Around Beaufort, head to **Hunting Island State Park,** 2555 Sea Island Parkway, (843) 838-2011, *www.huntingisland.com,* where you can make use of the park's roads and short sections of singletrack along the **Hunting Island Trail** to piece together an eight-mile circuit. The trail is relatively flat, but root-strewn and sandy sections may slow or stall the novice rider. What the park lacks in hardcore mountain biking, it compensates for with the continuous smell of and regular sightings of the sea. For the route description and directions to the trailhead, see the Hunting Island Trail listing under *Dayhiking.* ♦ At low tide, take a beach cruiser to the beach at Hunting Island State Park and ride the four miles of hard-packed sand near the water's edge. Surf fishing is popular on the beach; if you see a fisherman holding a pole, ride above him to avoid tangling his line.

♦ Hilton Head has more than 20 miles of paved, public **island pathways** that follow many of the island's major roads. Built with pedestrians and bicyclists in mind, these asphalt routes are tucked a safe distance from traffic. As you ride, remember that pedestrians have the right-of-way. For a map of the pathways, stop at any of the sources listed under *Additional Information* and request the "Island Pathways" map published by the Town of Hilton Head.

Bike Rentals

Most bike stores offer a variety of models, from single-speed beach cruisers to front-suspension mountain bikes. Rentals typically include a helmet and lock. In the more competitive bike rental market on Hilton Head, rentals also come with child carriers, baskets, and delivery to your hotel. Near Beaufort, visit **Low Country Bicycles,** 102 Sea Island Parkway, Beaufort, ☏ (843) 524-9585. ♦ A partial listing of the many bike rental shops on Hilton Head Island includes: **Coconut Bike Rentals,** 50 Yacht Cove Drive, ☏ (843) 686-5055; ♦ **Bicycle Billy's,** 101 Arrow Road, ☏ (843) 785-7851; ♦ **Hilton Head Bicycle Company,** 112 Arrow Road, ☏ (843) 686-6888; ♦ **Paradise Bike Rentals**, ☏ (843) 686-4146; and ♦ **Pedals,** 71 Pope Avenue, ☏ (843) 842-5522.

♦ The big bicycling draw on Hilton Head is the 12 miles of sandy beach. Within a couple of hours on either side of low tide, you can ride the hard-packed sand near the waterline. In fact, if you want to see the whole length of the island's beaches, a beach cruiser is the fastest and easiest way to do it. While the beach itself is public (up to the high-tide mark), access is not, so before you lug your cycle across the sand, make sure you're using one of the public beach access areas, detailed under *Swimming*.

♦ Also open to mountain bikes are the 14 miles of flat, easy, forested trails on Pinckney Island in the **Pinckney Island National Wildlife Refuge**, Route 278 just off Hilton Head Island, (912) 452-4415. There's a gravel road (closed to automobile traffic) that extends from one end of the island to the other and numerous paths that create loop possibilities. For an eight-mile roundtrip ride, pick up an island map from the kiosk at the parking area and set off for White Point on the northern end of the island.

Cycling Hilton Head's beach at low tide

Paddling

Visiting the Lowcountry and not slipping into a sea kayak is like visiting an amusement park and not riding the roller coaster. The thrill of sitting low in the water and gliding past alligators sunning themselves or dolphins at play is unforgettable. Sea kayaking is a booming industry here, and numerous tour operators offer a variety of trips, from two-hour nature tours to full-day paddles and overnight trips. Thinking of going it alone? Unless you're an experienced sea kayaker with knowledge of the local waters, think again. Rapid tides, ocean currents, wind, and sudden storms can make unguided paddling an unwelcome adventure.

The following provides general descriptions of the best paddling spots. Your outfitter will provide transportation to and from the put-in and take-out points. If you're alone, check with the rental sources below for directions to the best put-ins based on current conditions.

♦ The Big Kahuna of paddling spots in the Lowcountry is the **ACE Basin,** where route options amongst the rivers and tidal creek tributaries are infinite. The northernmost river that flows into the basin is the **Edisto,** the longest free-flowing blackwater river in the world. From its headwaters in the central part of South Carolina, the river runs the entire length of the state's coastal plain. As the Edisto nears

Sea kayaking the Lowcountry

the ACE, its broad, calm waters pass many former rice fields and plantations—Hope and Willtown Bluff plantations among them—that are reminders of the Lowcountry's past as a rice, cotton, and indigo-producing region. A particularly pleasant side-paddle from the Edisto is along the tree-canopied tributary, **Penny Creek.**

Marshlands, an 1814 Beaufort waterfront home, from the water

♦ With headwaters just a short distance west of Interstate 95, the **Ashepoo River** is much shorter than the Edisto. Upstream from Route 17, the Ashepoo passes several plantations, including White House plantation, before the river narrows and the tree cover closes in. From Route 17 downstream to the ACE Basin, the river passes several more plantations and former rice fields, full of such nesting birds as bald eagles. ♦ The **Combahee River** is formed from two rivers—the Salkahatchie and Little Salkahatchie—and is an especially nice paddle from Route 17 south to St. Helena Sound. One of the more popular paddles off the Combahee is a six-mile stretch along **Cuckold's Creek**, where gorgeous white spider lilies bloom in the spring.

♦ The **Beaufort River** is popular with paddlers hoping to see Beaufort from the water. Local tour operators plan trips around the tides to keep you from paddling against a swift current and to allow access to the many tidal creeks that intersect with the river. A popular trip involves paddling under the bridge to Lady's Island and past the grand, waterfront homes in Beaufort's Old Point neighborhood. ♦ The lagoon in **Hunting Island State Park** is a calm, protected waterway perfect for novice paddlers. High bluffs to the east protect the lagoon from winds off the Atlantic Ocean. The salt marshes surrounding Hunting Island are also perfect for exploration in a sea kayak.

♦ The **Port Royal Sound** around Hilton Head and the tidewater creeks and rivers between the sea islands and mainland provide ample playgrounds for the many paddling tour operators based on Hilton

The 350,000-acre, All-You-Can-Eat, Seafood Buffet

The ACE is full of nutrients that feed a dizzying array of wildlife species, including more than 15 endangered ones such as the bald eagle. It's practically impossible to paddle here without seeing the food chain in action. Look for sights such as a raccoon foraging for shellfish, an osprey flying with a wiggling fish in its talons, or a school of fish stirring and slapping the water in a frantic escape from something bigger.

Tour Operators & Canoe/Sea Kayak Rentals

Around Beaufort: **Beaufort Kayak Tours**, 2709 Oaklawn Street, Beaufort, ☎ (843) 525-0810, *www.beaufortkayaktours.com;* ♦ **The Kayak Farm**, 1289 Sea Island Parkway, St. Helena Island, ☎ (843) 838-2008; ♦ **Outpost Moe's**, Route 17 on the Ashepoo River, ☎ (843) 844-2514, *www.outpostmoes.com.* ♦ Around Hilton Head: **Outside Hilton Head**, Plaza at Shelter Cove, Hilton Head, ☎ (843) 686-6996, *www.outsidehiltonhead.com;* ♦ **Water-Dog Outfitters**, Broad Creek Marina, Hilton Head, ☎ (843) 686-3554, *www.waterdogoutfitter.com*

Head Island. Some of the more popular trips include: ◆ **Broad Creek,** the protected waterway that penetrates deep into Hilton Head Island; ◆ the marshes and creeks around **Pinckney Island National Wildlife Refuge;** ◆ the **Colleton River,** a protected waterway that flows past Spring Island and the banks of Victoria Bluff; ◆ **Bull Creek,** a popular place to meet and greet Atlantic bottlenose dolphins; ◆ the **May River,** leading past the historic town of Bluffton; ◆ and the tidal creeks and rivers surrounding **Daufuskie Island.**

Fishing

Saltwater fishing is more than a sport in the Lowcountry; it's a religion. From the Orvis-endorsed staff at locations like Beaufort's Bay Street Outfitters to the old men of the sea hanging at local marinas, you'll have little trouble finding a captain willing to take

you to the fruitful spots, both inshore and offshore. What might you catch? Depending upon the season, you may reel in redfish, Spanish and king mackerel, blue fish, dolphin, speckled trout, barracuda, tarpon, giant cobia, snapper, shark, and grouper, to name a few.

Fishing from shore on Hilton Head Island

◆ No fly-fishing operation in the region is as well-respected as **Bay Street Outfitters,** 815 Bay Street, (843) 524-5250 or 1-877-501-5001, *www.baystreetoutfitters.com,* in Beaufort. The shop operates the highly regarded Redfish School, which offers several classes, including a one-day experience for the intermediate to advanced angler interested in casting for redfish in the local salt marshes and flats. Fees include all fishing equipment, lunch, and a professional guide. Check the website for scheduled class dates.

Everywhere a Marina

Public marinas—seemingly on every protected cove in the Lowcountry—are the place to find fishing and sailing charters; sunset, dinner and nature tour cruises; boats for parasailing; and Wave Runners, Sunfish, or small motorboats for rent. The following are just some of the many public marinas: Beaufort's **Downtown Marina,** 1006 Bay Street, ☎ (843) 524-4422; ◆ **Port Royal Landing Marina,** 1 Landing Drive, Port Royal, ☎ (843) 525-6664; ◆ **Lady's Island Marina,** 73 Sea Island Parkway, Beaufort, ☎ (843) 522-04307. ◆ On Hilton Head: **Broad Creek Marina,** 18 Simmons Road, ☎ (843) 681-3625; ◆ **Harbour Town Yacht Basin,** 149 Lighthouse Road, ☎ (843) 671-2704; ◆ **Shelter Cove Harbour,** Palmetto Dunes Resort, ☎ (843) 842-7001; ◆ **Skull Creek Marina,** Hilton Head Plantation, ☎ (843) 681-4234.

Shelter Cove Harbour

♦ Chartering a boat with a seasoned captain is your ticket to the deep sea and big game fish like marlin, tuna, and wahoo. Should you opt to motor the 50 to 70 miles out to the Gulf Stream, you'll spend a minimum of eight hours on open water and roughly $500 for a guided charter for two people. Half-day rates are approximately $300. There are far too many charter operations in the Lowcountry to list; however, a few of the better bets around Beaufort include: **Sea Wolf Charters,** Port Royal Landing Marina, Beaufort, (843) 525-1174, *www.seawolfcharter.com;* and ♦ **Captain D's of Beaufort,** 2427 Boundary Street, (843) 522-3474. ♦ On Hilton Head: **Bonanza Sportfishing**, 3 Hudson Road, (843) 689-5873, *www.bonanzasportfishing.com;* and ♦ **Whipple Charterboat Company,** Skull Creek Marina, 22 Lenora Drive, (843) 681-8943, *www.whipplecharterboats.com.*

Horseback Riding

Climb into the saddle at **Lawton Stables,** 190 Greenwood Drive (in Sea Pines Plantation), Hilton Head, (843) 671-2586, for a guided ride through 600 acres of maritime forest and marshland in the Sea Pines Preserve. Lawton Stables also offers instruction, plus riding options for advanced equestrians. ♦ Also on Hilton Head, **Sea Horse Farms**, 34 Mitchelville Road, (843) 681-7746, offers guided trail rides through marsh paths and along the beach.

Trail horses in a maritime forest

Rainy Day Workout

If a steady rain keeps you in, you don't have to rule out a workout thanks to numerous area health clubs. Expect to pay a nominal day-use fee. Some of the better bets include **Omni Health & Fitness Center,** 1505 Salem Road, Beaufort, (843) 575-2424, where there's a complete fitness center with free weights, strength-building machines, cardio equipment, and a variety of aerobics classes. There's also a smoothie bar. ♦ On Hilton Head, head to **Breakthrough Fitness,** 130 Arrow Road, (843) 341-2166, to join in a variety of classes or to work out with free weights, resistance machines, and cardio equipment like the impact-free elliptical trainer. Breakthrough also has a stream room, sauna, and shower facilities.

Sailing

Evidenced by the sheer number of sloops docked in the region's marinas, sailing is a popular sport among lowcountry residents. The Port Royal and Calibogue sounds, the Beaufort River, and the wide-open Atlantic Ocean make ideal sailing grounds, and enough charter operations exist so that you won't be stuck watching all the fun from shore. While you can arrive at any of the major marinas in the area and find a licensed captain, the following operations will remove any guesswork: ◆ Captain Bill Wilkes, who owns and operates **Lowcountry Sailing,** Port Royal Landing Marina, (843) 252-7245, *www.lowcountrysailing.com,* offers instruction on the *Havodtee,* a 23-foot Compac sailboat, and advanced instruction and sailing tours on the *Harvest Moon,* a 30-foot Catalina.

◆ On Hilton Head, **Advanced Sail,** Palmetto Bay Marina, (843) 686-2582, operates several charter sailboats, including the *Flying Circus,* a 27-foot catamaran that accommodates six passengers, and *Pauhana,* a 53-foot catamaran that can carry 49 passengers. Why sail on a cat? It's more stable; the boat does not "heel," or tip to one side in heavy wind. ◆ For another unique sailing experience, climb aboard the *Schooner Welcome, www.schooner.net,* a gorgeous, 62-foot, wooden yacht capable of carrying 30 passengers. You can kick back and enjoy the complementary hors d'oeuvres or help raise the sails and steer the ship. The boat sails from Hilton Head's Shelter Cove Harbour. Call (843) 785-5566 for reservations.

◆ Want to be closer to the water with the ocean spray in your face? Rent a small sailboat such as a Hobie Cat or Sunfish and head out on your own. Try one of **Island Water Sports'** three Hilton Head locations: South Beach Marina, (843) 671-7007; Shelter Cove Harbor, (843) 842-8181; the Docks on Skull Creek, (843) 689-6800; or ◆ **Commander Zodiac,** South Beach Marina, (843) 671-3344.

Sail the *Stars & Stripes*

It's the real deal: the 12-meter racing yacht Dennis Connor skippered in the 1983 America's Cup trials. *Stars and Stripes* takes passengers out on Calibogue Sound for daytime dolphin sails or sunset cruises in the evenings. All trips last roughly ninety minutes. The ship sails from Harbour Town Marina in Sea Pines. To secure a seat on a piece of sailing history, call (843) 842-7933.

Swimming

Hundreds of rivers and creeks flow through the Lowcountry, but mud, alligators, and tidal currents make them far less appealing for swimming than the sea. Thanks to a temperate climate, you can swim in the Atlantic Ocean seven months a year. (Those who appreciate a quick, good-to-be-alive dip in the sea can swim year-round.) Beaufort's major swimming destination is **Hunting Island State Park**, where the three-mile public beach is wide, sandy, and designated "swimming only" in places. (See directions under *Wide Open.*) More often than not, the Atlantic Ocean is gentle, but you should always be careful, especially on days when the undertow is strong and the waves are large.

◆ The 12 miles of sandy coastline on **Hilton Head Island** afford ample space to drop a towel, heat up, and then cool off in the ocean. While the entire beach up to the high-tide mark is public land, beachfront property is not, and unless your inn or hotel has direct access, you'll have to use one of five public beach access areas. They are: ◆**Alder Lane Beach Access,** off South Forest Beach Drive, with restrooms and metered parking; ◆ **Coligny Beach Park,** off Coligny Circle, where there are restrooms, outdoor showers,

Hilton Head Island CVB

Summer on Hilton Head Island

metered parking spots, and life-guards on duty in the summer; ◆ **Driessen Beach Park**, at the end of Bradley Beach Road, where there are metered parking spots, restrooms, showers, a boardwalk, umbrellas for rent, a grill, and lifeguards on duty during beach season; ◆ **Folly Field Beach Park,** off Folly Field Road, with metered parking, seasonal life-guards, a boardwalk, restrooms, and the most locals (who know this public access area to be the least-crowded); and ◆ **Islanders Beach Park** off Folly Field Road, where you'll find restrooms and a boardwalk.

Local Outdoor Advice

Bay Street Outfitters • Though the store's emphasis is on fishing, Bay Street Outfitters employs a staff knowledgeable about outdoor activities in and around Beaufort and wel-comes visitors curious about good spots to explore. As a complete tackle and fly shop, the store stocks everything related to sport fishing, including apparel from such upscale brands as Orvis, Pendleton, and Patagonia. Also onsite: the outfitter's highly regarded Redfish School, Orvis-endorsed guides with extensive knowledge of the local waters, and a travel service specializing in adventure vacations. • 815 Bay Street, Beaufort, ☎ (843) 524-5250 or 1-877-501-5001, *www.baystreetoutfitters.com.*

Lowcountry Outfitters • This outfitter's primary emphasis is on hunting and fly fish-ing. In addition to an extensive lineup of high-quality fishing gear (Sage and G. Loomis rods, for example) and fine American and European shotguns, you'll find outdoor gear and apparel from trusted names like Patagonia, Columbia, Ex Officio, and Barbour. • Moss Creek Village (off Route 278 just off the bridge on the mainland), ☎ (843) 837-6100 or 1-800-935-9666, *www.lowcountryoutfitters.com*

Outside Hilton Head • This full-service outfitter carries all manner of outdoor clothing, gear, apparel, and footwear. Staff members are interpretative naturalists who undergo a four-day training course on local ecology and area outdoor opportunities before they work the retail floor. Outside Hilton Head is also a full-service paddle shop with kayaks for sale and rent. There are two shops. The main store in Shelter Cove is the region's premier ski shop in the winter. The smaller location at South Beach Marina (near the Salty Dog Café) is primarily a surf shop. • The Plaza at Shelter Cove, Route 278, Hilton Head, ☎ (843) 686-6996 or 1-800-686-6996, *www.outsidehiltonhead.com*

K i c k B a c k

Worn out from long walks on the beach or from paddling past dolphins at play? Or perhaps you're simply in the mood for an easier-going day? You'll have no trouble busying yourself with the following laid-back activities.

Antiques

As you'd expect from a seaport region with a richly preserved history, the antiques market in and around Beaufort is bustling. The majority of shops is in Beaufort, Port Royal, Bluffton, and on Hilton Head, but you'll find plenty of small shops along the region's back roads. A few good bets: **Michael Rainey Antiques,** 702 Craven Street, Beaufort, (843) 521- 4532, features 18th- and early 19th-century furniture and accessories. ◆ Also in Beaufort: **Legacy & Whimsey Antiques,** 812 Port Republic Street, (843) 524-2685, for French antiques and decorative accessories. ◆ **Canup Antiques,** 809 Bay Street, Beaufort, (843) 524-8914, *www.canupantiques.com,* for 18th- and 19th-century American country furniture, as well as early American folk art, antique frames, mirrors, and kitchen items.

◆ In Port Royal, the **Collectors Antique Mall** 1351-F Ribaut Road, (843) 524-2769, features a variety of antiques spread throughout the shop's 5,000 square feet, including furniture from all periods. A popular place with interior designers, this shop has an extensive array of china, glass, and Waterford crystal. ◆ Bluffton's many antiques shops include **Stock Farm Antiques,** 1263 May River Road, (843) 757-8046, where you'll find 18th- and 19th-century oriental rugs, paintings, prints, porcelain objects, and English and American furniture. ◆ On Hilton Head, head to **Guggenheim's Fine Antiques,** 72 Arrow Road, (843) 758-9580, for a great selection of furniture, art, porcelain, and silver.

Art Galleries

Art is big business in the Lowcountry. You'll find dozens of galleries, including many studio-galleries that present opportunities to meet the artists at work. ◆ The **Beaufort Art Association,** 905 Port Republic Street, (843) 379-2222, operates a gallery in a former bank where it showcases the diverse work of many of its members. Original oils, watercolors, prints, sculptures, photographs, decorative arts, and much more are on display and available for sale. ◆ For a mix of paintings, sculptures, and decorative arts by South Carolina artists, visit Beaufort's **I. Pinckney Simons Gallery,** 711 Bay Street, (843) 575-4774, *www.ipsgalleries.com;* ◆ The **Rhett Gallery**—two locations: 901 Bay Street, Beaufort, (843) 524-3339; 847-A Sea Island Parkway, St. Helena Island, (843) 838-1339, *www.rhettgallery.com*—sells prints, paintings, and decorative pieces by noted lowcountry artist Nancy Rhett.

◆ Exploring Hilton Head's galleries, which range in style from blue-blooded art houses to more laid-back, funky boutiques, can easily fill a day or more. For the island's quintessential gallery experience, head to the **Red Piano Art Gallery,** 220 Cordillo Parkway, (843) 785-2318, *www.redpianoartgallery.com,* which sits under a canopy of pine and palmetto trees just short of the Ocean Gate entrance to Sea Pines Plantation. For thirty-five years, the Red Piano has been one of the best-known art galleries in the South and has shown works by such celebrated artists as Andrew Wyeth. Founded by Alan and Mary Palmer in 1969, the gallery has changed hands several times but continues to exhibit the finest American art from the 19th and 20th centuries. ◆ With the tag, "Local Charm, Regional Flavor, Universal Appeal," **Crossroads Fine Art,** 107 Towne Center, Bluffton, (843) 757-5551, *www.crossroadsfineart.com,* delivers what it promises in an eclectic collection of work by both up-and-coming and nationally known artists. Crossroads displays original paintings, prints, crafts, and glass, much of it with a regional theme.

Back Roads Touring

The scenery along the rural highways of the Lowcountry—marsh grasses, blackwater creeks, and live oaks—is soothing to the eyes. While the stretch of **Route 17** between Charleston and Beaufort (particularly through the ACE Basin) is pretty, there are even more attractive roads to explore. If you have the time and enjoy driving without a destination in mind, grab a map and start exploring the region's rural roadways. If, on the other hand, you feel better knowing exactly where to go, check out this ACE Basin tour recommended by the Walterboro-Colleton Chamber of Commerce, (843) 549-9595, *www.walterboro.org.*

◆ A number of roads spiderweb through the **ACE Basin**, past antebellum plantations, beneath dense canopies of live oaks, and over blackwater tributaries of the Ashepoo, Edisto, and Combahee rivers. The following 50-mile route traverses the western side of the basin and takes less than two hours (more if you choose to stop en route). The drive begins 10 miles south of Jacksonboro on Route 17, where you take **Route 303** (Green Pond Highway) north. Follow Route 303 through Green Pond and over the upper Ashepoo River, which at this point

is a mere creek winding through a hardwood forest. Look for **Ritter Road** (State Road 15-41) on the left, which you follow across the Ashepoo again. During the spring and summer, a variety of flora, including blackberries, elderberries, arrow weed, and wisteria, blooms in the open fields.

You'll reach a bridge on Ritter Road that crosses a dark swamp full of cypress and tupelo trees. Continue on Ritter Road to the small township of Catholic Hill, site of the St. James Catholic Church, founded in 1832 by Irish immigrants. Two miles past Catholic Hill, turn left onto

Live oaks line many back roads in the Lowcountry

White Hall Road, which eventually passes White Hall Plantation, a former rice plantation. The property is private, but you can look down the avenue of live oaks leading toward the antebellum home as you drive past.

After a railroad crossing, look for the sign for Cuckhold's Creek Landing where you turn right onto **Combahee Road.** At a small church on the left, take the dirt road to the landing, just a short distance ahead. Here, in this pastoral scene, you'll find the creek lazily making its way toward the Combahee River. Return to Combahee Road by taking the dirt fork to the left. Turn left on Combahee and continue over the creek and past former rice fields overgrown with cattails, wild rice, and plume grass. Look for a canal on the right side of the road that was once used to flood the fields for rice cultivation.

This area was once owned by Nathaniel Heyward who, by the time of his death in 1851, had amassed more than 45,000 acres of land worked by more than 2,000 slaves. Today all of the plantations on this stretch, including Combahee, Bluff, and Cherokee plantations, are privately owned.

When the road reaches **Route 17A,** turn left and continue seven miles, crossing the Combahee River, to the town of Yemassee. In Yemassee, turn left at the flashing light onto State Road 13 and proceed 3/10 of a mile to a sharp left turn onto **Railroad Avenue** just before the double railroad tracks. Continue for less than a half-mile to River Road on your right. **River Road** skirts the western banks of the Combahee River and passes even more former rice plantations.

The road passes through the **ACE Basin National Wildlife Refuge** before coming to the Auld Brass Plantation, where there stands a home designed by Frank Lloyd Wright. Note the unusual fence style, also Wright's design. If you wish to stretch your legs and take in some scenery, turn left three miles beyond Auld Brass at the sign for **Sugar Hill Creek Public Landing**. This is a nice place to view the river. Continuing on River Road, you'll pass the entrance to Bonny Hall Plantation before the road intersects with Route 17, roughly eight miles south from the start of the tour.

◆ Another scenic drive recommended by the Walterboro-Colleton Chamber of Commerce is a 60-mile route along the eastern segment of the ACE Basin that takes half a day to complete. For directions, call the chamber at (843) 549-9595 or download the route from their website: *www.walterboro.org.* ◆ Other scenic stretches of road in the Lowcountry include **Route 170** from Beaufort toward Hilton Head; **Route 46** through Bluffton; and any of the public roads on **St. Helena** and **Edisto islands.**

Boat Tours

With so many narrated tours available to lowcountry visitors—horse-drawn carriage, bus, and walking tours, among them—you might be tempted to lump boat tours into the same category. Don't. While some overlap in topics exists with land-based tours (history of the region, for example), boat tours provide a unique perspective on Beaufort and Hilton Head. Even just half a mile from land, you get a sense of how wide the

Hilton Head Island CVB

A sunset sailing tour off Hilton Head Island

Port Royal and Calibogue sounds are, plus you stand a good chance of seeing dolphins at play or ospreys diving for fish.

◆ For a cruise from Beaufort south along the placid waters of the Beaufort River to the end of Parris Island, board the 125-passenger *Islander*, (843) 524-4000. This handsome, two-level ferryboat departs from the marina at Waterfront Park on Bay Street and motors slowly past many of Beaufort's historic homes, while a narrator shares stories of the city's past. The boat travels far enough out to catch sight of Land's End, Fripp Island, Hilton Head, and the Atlantic Ocean. Along the way, you'll learn about the ecology of the salt marshes and likely catch site of bottlenose dolphins.

◆ Given the general lack of public roads through the ACE Basin, the best way to see this massive estuary and its wild residents—herons, ospreys, egrets, minks, otters, eagles, and alligators, to name a few—is by boat. **Lowcountry Rafting Adventures**, (843) 986-1051 or 1-877-722-7238, *www.lowcountryraftingadventures.com*, operates the *Osprey*, a unique, 30-foot inflatable boat with an aluminum hull. Two tours are offered: the two-hour "ACE Express," which departs from Beaufort's downtown marina, and the four-hour "Ultimate Adventure" that combines a trip to the ACE Basin with time spent paddling on inflatable, sit-on-top kayaks.

◆ Boat tours departing from Hilton Head's nine public marinas are extensive. For nature or dolphin tours, take your pick of vessel, from small to large. Want to meet a dolphin eye-to-eye? Climb aboard a small craft like a Zodiac, an inflatable raft with a hard hull powered by

Across the Wide Water

A mile across Calibogue Sound from Hilton Head and accessible only by boat, Daufuskie is the barrier island made famous by Pat Conroy's book, *The Water Is Wide,* and the subsequent film *Conrack* starring Jon Voight. Conroy based the book upon his experience in the late 1960s teaching Gullah children in a one-room schoolhouse. At that time, Daufuskie was a poor, isolated island populated primarily by the descendants of freed slaves. Today the island has several developments, including the luxurious Daufuskie Island Club & Resort (see *Sleep Well*), but it remains largely rural. In addition to the school where Conroy taught, there's a 19th-century church with two front doors (one for men, the other for women), and a late 18th-century cemetery. Several boat tours and ferries depart from Hilton Head's marinas for Daufuskie. Once on the island, you can rent a golf cart to explore this five-mile-long, three-mile-wide island. To visit the island, call **Outside Hilton Head**, ☏ (843) 686-6996, *www.outsidehiltonhead.com;* or **Calibogue Cruises**, ☏ (843) 342-8687.

an outboard motor. Short of swimming, you can't get closer to the water. **Commander Zodiac,** South Beach Marina, (843) 671-3344, offers dolphin and nature tours on these three- to four-person crafts in Calibogue Sound. ◆ For a larger boat, board the *SS Pelican,* (843) 681-2522, which departs Broad Creek Marina for narrated, environmental tours of Calibogue Sound. The boat is a restored Navy Motor Whaler with a roof to keep you dry and shaded.

◆ Most sailing and touring charters offer sunset and cocktail cruises at day's end. The larger boats tend to have stocked galleys on board, while smaller operations may invite you to bring your own cooler. In general, all cruises—sunset cruises as well as dolphin tours—average 90 minutes in length and cost roughly $20 per adult, excluding beverages and snacks.

Gullah Culture

The unique Gullah culture that developed in the Lowcountry amongst slaves abducted from West Africa lives on in small communities on St. Helena and Hilton Head islands. From museums exhibiting Gullah history to shops and galleries carrying Gullah art and crafts, the culture is readily available for you to explore. The best place to begin is the **Penn Center,** Martin Luther King Drive, St. Helena Island, (843) 838-2432, *www.penncenter.com,* an organization dedicated to preserving and cultivating the African-American sea island culture.

Nearly 20 buildings sit beneath a live-oak and Spanish-moss canopy on the center's 50 acres of historic land. In 1862, abolitionists from Pennsylvania established the nation's first school for freed slaves here, and its first two teachers, Laura Towne and Ellen Murray, taught here for more than 40 years. During the Civil Rights Movement's early days, the center hosted Southern Christian Leadership Conference meetings, led by Dr. Martin Luther King, Jr. At these, the organization planned the non-violent movement to end the nation's Jim Crow laws.

Gilford Photography, Library of Congress

Historic buildings at the Penn Center include Gantt Cottage, where King stayed, and Darrah Hall, one of the school's first buildings and the oldest building at Penn Center.

Gantt Cottage, where Martin Luther King, Jr. stayed

The Penn Center's **York W. Bailey Museum & Cultural Center** features changing exhibits on the Gullah culture, plus a permanent exhibit, "Education for Freedom," which details the Penn School's history. The museum is open to the public, Monday–Saturday, 11 A.M.–4 P.M. Nominal admission fee. Also onsite: a gift shop with Gullah sweetgrass baskets, quilts, indigo-dyed fabrics, music, and books.

◆ Gullah art and crafts are available throughout the Lowcountry, but the greatest concentration is at the **Red Piano Too,** 870 Sea Island Parkway, (843) 838-2241, *www.redpianotoo.com,* in the town of Frogmore on St. Helena Island. (The shop is housed in a historic wooden grocery store at the intersection of Sea Island Parkway and Dr. Martin Luther King, Jr. Drive.)

The vibrant, colorful artwork includes paintings, quilts, crafts, and jewelry. Also onsite are a number of books about Gullah culture, plus the Pat Conroy Room, which houses a

Brian Corll

Gullah sweetgrass baskets

collection of books signed by the author and available for sale.

◆ For a more comprehensive exploration of the region's African-American culture, join a Gullah-themed tour. Nobody on St. Helena does this better than **Gullah-n-Geechie Mahn Tours,** (843) 838-7516, *www.gullah-ngeechietours.net*. This outfit provides narrated, 2.5-hour tours of the island, including the churches, cemeteries, and gathering places of the Gullah people.

◆ On Hilton Head, **Gullah Heritage Trail Tours**, (843) 689-9317, has a two-hour tour of Gullah sites and neighborhoods that have continued to exist despite the island's explosive resort growth. Tours depart from the Gullah Flea Market, 103 William Hilton Parkway, at 10 A.M. and 2 P.M., Wednesday–Saturday; Sunday at 2 P.M.

◆ To fashion your own tour, pick up the free brochure, **"Gullah Heritage Guide,"** from the Hilton Head Convention & Visitors Bureau, 100 William Hilton Parkway. The brochure tells an interesting history of lowcountry Gullah culture and gives directions to numerous points of interest.

Historic Buildings & Sites

History is ever-present in downtown Beaufort, as well as on the surrounding islands and mainland, and there are numerous ways to discover it. You can visit museums like the Beaufort Museum or the Parris Island Museum (see *Museums*), take a horse-drawn or walking tour (see *Tours)*; or set out on your own. The following sites and buildings are worth seeing.

◆ Beaufort is home to the majestic **Beaufort National Cemetery,** 1601 Boundary Street, (843) 524-3925, built in 1863 on orders from Abraham Lincoln to be the resting place for Union soldiers killed in the Civil War. Today more than 17,000 American soldiers—veterans of the Civil, Spanish-American, Korean, Vietnam, Persian Gulf, and Iraqi wars—are buried within this 33-acre cemetery. The cemetery also holds the remains of 19 soldiers from the famed Massachusetts 54th Infantry, a unit of African-American soldiers from the Lowcountry. Their bodies were discovered on Folly Island in 1987, and they were laid to rest with full military honors in 1989. Open daily, 8 A.M.–sunset.

A tombstone at St. Helena's Episcopal Church

◆ Beaufort's **St. Helena's Episcopal Church,** 507 Newcastle Street, was founded as a parish in 1712, making it one of the oldest, active churches in the nation. The first church was erected on this site in 1724. (The church's present appearance came from an 1842 renovation.) During the Civil War, the church served as a Union hospital; tombstones were pulled up and used as operating tables. With a silver communion set dating to the 1700s and an interesting history, the church and its live oak-shaded graveyard are fun to explore. Buried here are many of Beaufort's prominent citizens, including two Confederate Generals and one of Beaufort's founders, Colonel John Barnwell, better known as the Indian fighter, "Tuscarora Jack." (He's buried under the actual church.)

In general, the church is open Monday–Thursday, 10 A.M.–4 P.M.; Friday and Saturday, 10 A.M.–1 P.M. The church holds regular services on Sundays and is not open for sightseeing.

Semper Fi, O Great Santini

Interred in Section 62, Grave 182 of the Beaufort National Cemetery is one of the most famous American Marines: Colonel Donald Conroy, or as he referred to himself, "The Great Santini." Immortalized by his son, author Pat Conroy, in the novel *The Great Santini* (which became a movie of the same name), Colonel Don Conroy "lived life at full throttle, moved always in the fast lanes, gunned every engine, teetered on every edge, seized every moment and shook it like a terrier shaking a rat," said the novelist in a moving eulogy delivered at his father's funeral. "There's not a fighter pilot alive who does not lift his glass whenever Don Conroy's name is mentioned."

◆ Roughly a half-hour drive northwest of Beaufort, the **Sheldon Church Ruins** sit like a ghostly apparition amongst massive live oaks. All that remains of the stone building are some walls, large columns, and the cemetery. Originally built in 1753 as the Prince Williams Parish Church, this building is thought to be the first structure in the nation constructed in the Greek Revival style. It was burned by the British in 1779, rebuilt in 1826, and burned again by General Sherman in 1865.

Tombstones in the graveyard show history dating back to the Indian Wars in the early 18th Century. To reach the site, take Route 21 north from Beaufort to Route 17, turn left and follow Route 17 south for several hundred yards to State Road 21 (Old Sheldon Church Road) on the right. Take this road and follow signs to the ruins. The picturesque grounds have an area for picnics.

The Sheldon Church ruins

◆ Other notable historic churches in and around Beaufort include: **The First African Baptist Church,** 601 New Street, built in 1865 as a house of prayer for freed slaves; **The Beaufort Baptist Church,** 600 Charles Street, built in 1844 in the Greek Revival style and also used as a hospital during the Civil War; the ruins of the **Chapel of Ease**, Land's End Road, built in 1742 on St. Helena Island as a worship house for planters and destroyed by a forest fire in 1886; and the **Brick Baptist Church**, Land's End Road, St. Helena, built in 1855 for planters but given to freed slaves during the Civil War and now part of the Penn Center's historic district.

◆ As the site of the first school in the nation for freed slaves, the 50-acre **Penn Center,** Land's End Road, St. Helena, is designated a National Historic District. See *Gullah Culture* for more information.

An African-American Hero

As a slave with extensive experience on lowcountry waters, Robert Smalls was given the responsibility of piloting a Confederate supply ship (the *Planter*) in and around Charleston during the early months of the Civil War. One night, he and two other slaves stole the ship, picked up their families, and sailed past Fort Sumter into the arms of the Union Navy and a life of freedom. Smalls then served in the Union Army during the war before retiring with the rank of Major General. After the war, he returned to Beaufort and bought the home his masters had owned at 511 Prince Street. He learned to read and was elected to the U.S. House of Representatives, where he served five terms. Smalls, who lived 1839–1915, is buried in the churchyard of Beaufort's **Tabernacle Baptist Church,** 907 Craven Street, where a bronze bust memorializes his life and achievements.

Historic Homes & Neighborhoods

Beaufort is perhaps best known for her gracious homes and mansions, many of which represent the finest home construction in the Federal, Georgian, and Greek Revival styles. The city's oldest and grandest homes are found on **The Point**, east of Carteret Street, and on **Bay Street** west of Waterfront Park. Most of the old houses face due south to catch cool summer breezes and warm winter sunlight, and many were designed in a T-formation to allow back rooms ample ventilation and views of the water.

◆ Except for the John Mark Verdier House on Bay Street (see *Museums*), nearly all historic homes in Beaufort are private residences or inns and must be enjoyed from the sidewalk. (Please respect that families live in these homes.) Fortunately each fall, the **Historic Beaufort Association**, (843) 379-3331, *www.historic-beaufort.org*, sponsors a **Fall Festival of Houses and Gardens,** during which visitors are able to appreciate a number of private homes and gardens like the owners do: from inside. Tickets are reasonably priced. This event (typically held in October) is popular, so make inn reservations well in advance.

◆ If visiting at any other time of year, stop by the Beaufort Visitor Center (see *Additional Information*) to pick up a free map detailing the locations of 26 historic homes and buildings in town. You can easily walk past all of them in a day. The entire

The 1820 Rhett House is now an inn

list of homes is worth seeing, but if you're pressed for time, don't miss these: The **Thomas Hepworth House,** 214 New Street, is Beaufort's oldest house, built in 1717. It has musket slits in the walls of the raised basement. ◆ The 1786 **Thomas Fuller House,** 1211 Bay Street, also known as "Tabby Manse," has thick walls constructed of tabby—an oyster-shell, sand, and lime cement. ◆ The 1813 **Milton Maxcy House,** 113 Craven Street, became known as the "Secession House" because South Carolina's Ordinance of Secession was drafted here. ◆ The 1850 **Joseph Johnson House,** 411 Craven Street, also called "the Castle," is a waterfront mansion that resembles a medieval castle. The home and its gardens occupy an entire city block. ◆ The 1856 **Edgar Fripp House,** 1 Laurens Street, is also known as "Tidalholm." This gorgeous mansion figured prominently in the films, *The Great Santini* and *The Big Chill.*

◆ **Port Royal** publishes a brochure entitled **"Downtown Historic Walking Tour"** that showcases 40 historic homes and sites. Pick up a copy from Port Royal's Town Hall (the intersection of Paris Avenue and 8th Street) or from the Beaufort Visitor Center (1106 Carteret Street.) ◆ Similarly, the Hilton Head Island/Bluffton Chamber of Commerce, 100 William Hilton Parkway, 1-800-523-3373, publishes the pamphlet, **"Walking Tour Guide to Bluffton Township."** The tour passes 10 antebellum homes and nearly 20 post-Civil War buildings. You can also pick up a copy of the brochure at the Heyward House Historic Center (see below for listing).

◆ The **Heyward House Historic Center,** 52 Boundary Street, Bluffton, (843) 757-6293, *www.heywardhouse.org,* is located in the **Cole-Heyward House,** a summer home built around 1840 for a local plantation owner. It is one of only eight antebellum homes remaining in Bluffton and the only one open to the public. The simple, timber-framed house is particularly impressive because it has not been altered over the years. Also onsite are a slave cabin and the remains of an outdoor kitchen. The house serves as a small museum with exhibits on lowcountry lore and as a welcome center for the Town of Bluffton. Open Tuesday–Friday, 10 A.M.–3 P.M.; Saturday, 11 A.M.–2 P.M. There's a nominal fee for a guided house tour.

Museums

Beaufort's only historic house open to the public is the Federal-style **John Mark Verdier Museum House,** 801 Bay Street, (843) 542-6334, *www.historic-beaufort.org.* It was built in the late 1790s by John Mark Verdier, who fought in the Revolutionary War and then returned to Beaufort to continue a successful career as a cotton trader. His home stayed in the Verdier family for more than 100 years. Of note: The Marquis de Lafayette addressed the citizens of Beaufort from the front steps of this home late one night in 1825, and the house served as headquarters for Union officers occupying the city during the Civil War. The Historic Beaufort Foundation saved the house from destruction in 1940, and today it houses a museum exhibiting period antiques and information about

The John Mark Verdier House in 1940

Charles N. Bayless, Library of Congress

The Beaufort Museum

Beaufort's early days. Open Monday–Saturday, 11 A.M.–4 P.M. Nominal admission fee.

◆ Housed in the historic Beaufort Arsenal, a brick and tabby Gothic building, The **Beaufort Museum**, 713 Craven Street, (843) 525-7077, *www.historic-beaufort.org*, displays collections of fossils, plantation crafts, Civil War artifacts, and other items relating to Beaufort's history, including a desk that belonged to Robert Smalls, a former slave who served five terms in the U.S. House of Representatives. The building has a fascinating history. Built in 1798 to house one of the nation's early military regiments, the Beaufort Volunteer Artillery, and to serve as a laboratory for the production of gunpowder, the imposing building was occupied by the Union Army during the Civil War. Open Monday–Saturday, 11 A.M.–4 P.M. Nominal admission fee.

◆ Whether you're a military buff or not, you'll likely find the **Parris Island Museum,** Marine Corps Recruiting Depot, Parris Island, (843) 228-2951, a worthwhile visit. In addition to a compelling history of the Marine Corps and its training methods, the 10,000 square-foot museum depicts the history of Parris Island and the Port Royal area beginning with the arrival of French Huguenots in the mid 1500s. Interpretative exhibits show the evolution of Marine uniforms, weapons, and more, with a special emphasis on advances made in the 20th Century. Open daily, 10 A.M.–4:30 P.M. (until 7 P.M. Thursdays). Admission is free.

◆ At Hilton Head Island's **Coastal Discovery Museum**, 100 William Hilton Parkway, (843) 689-6767, *www.coastaldiscovery.org*, visitors get a hands-on education about the history, wildlife, and cultural heritage of the Lowcountry. The museum features both indoor and outdoor exhibits, and offers a variety of educational tours and cruises. There's a museum store on-site. Open Monday–Saturday, 9 A.M.–5 P.M.; Sunday, 10 A.M.–3 P.M. Admission is free.

Loggerhead Sea Turtles

At night in the Lowcountry between May and August, female turtles weighing as much as 200 pounds (or more) move slowly onshore and up to the dunes to dig nests into which they lay between 100 and 150 eggs. They use their giant flippers to cover the eggs with sand and then crawl back to the sea. Roughly two months later, if undisturbed, the turtle hatchlings break their shells and begin the slow crawl toward the surf. A startling 99 percent of these hatchlings won't make it to adulthood. They're picked off by birds, raccoons, and fish. Those that survive may live more than 100 years. If you'd like to witness this spectacle, contact Hilton Head's **Coastal Discovery Museum,** ☎ (843) 689-6767, *www.coastaldiscovery.org*, to ask about joining one of their late-night **Turtle Watch Walks.**

Performing Arts

♫ Performing arts offerings in and around Beaufort range from chamber music to modern dance. There are typically one or more performances to enjoy each week regardless of the time of year. To learn what's happening when you arrive, contact the Beaufort Visitor Center (see *Additional Information*), check with the individual arts organizations listed here, or contact the Grand Poohbah of regional arts activity, the **Arts Council of Beaufort County,** (843) 521-4145, *www.beaufortarts.com*, housed in the University of South Carolina at Beaufort's (USCB) Performing Arts Center, 801 Carteret Street.

◆ The full-sized **Beaufort Orchestra,** *www.beaufortorchestra.org,* presents four indoor concerts each year: classical concerts in October and February, a Christmas concert in December, and a Pops concert in May. Most shows are held in the USCB Performing Arts Center. The orchestra also performs an outdoor concert at the Waterfront Park in June. For ticket information, call (843) 379-2787. ◆ The University of South Carolina's Beaufort campus hosts **The USCB Festival Series,** (843) 521-4145, an annual five-concert program conducted by chamber-music maestro Charles Wadsworth. Wadsworth, a periodic host at New York's Lincoln Center, directs many of the world's greatest chamber musicians in these performances. Brochures detailing each season's performances are available from the Arts Council of Beaufort County.

◆ Beaufort's **Byrne Miller Dance Theater,** (843) 524-1117, brings professional dance companies to town from San Francisco, New York, and everywhere in between, and presents performances by local dancers. Formed in 1972 by the late Byrne Miller, the company's offerings range from classical ballet to modern dance. Call for a schedule and ticket prices.

◆ There are few theatrical performances in Beaufort, but what does appear on stage is worth seeing. If you happen to be in the area in October, catch one of the Bard's works by **Lowcountry Shakespeare,** (843) 522-0418, a troupe of professionally directed actors. Shows are free, but donations are gladly accepted. ◆ USCB's undergraduate theater troupe, the **Roges & Vacaboundes,** and the alumni troupe, the **Rafael Sabatini Players,** perform modern classics, from Sam Shepard's *True West* to Samuel Becket's *Waiting for Godot,* throughout the year in the USCB Performing Arts Center. Call (843) 521-4156 for show information.

◆ The primary performing arts venue on Hilton Head is the **Arts Center of Coastal Carolina,** 14 Shelter Cove Lane, 1-888-860-2787, *www.artscenter-hhi.org.* This impressive facility has a 350-seat theater, two smaller stages, and gallery space for art exhibits. The center produces five to six theatrical performances a year, including musicals, comedies, and dramas, and also hosts visiting musicians, dance troupes, vocalists, and more. Performances are ongoing, so call or check online to see what or who is playing when you're in town. ◆ Since its founding in 1992, the **South Carolina Repertory Company**, 136-B Beach City Road, (843) 681-5194, *www.hiltonheadtheatre.com,* has produced more than 40 critically acclaimed plays. The company draws patrons from across the region. South Carolina Rep performs in its own 80-seat theater, making for wonderfully intimate performances. Recent shows have included *Wit, Love Letters, Driving Miss Daisy,* and *A Midsummer Night's Dream.* Tickets are reasonably priced.

Arts in the Park(ing lot?)

Beaufort's annual **Arts in the Park,** ☎ (843) 521-0611, presents outdoor performances—music, dance, film, and more—in Waterfront Park. But in January 2004, Beaufort embarked on a two-year renovation of the park and, at press time, the Arts in the Park organization was unsure where performances would be held. To get the scoop, call the organization or check with the Beaufort Chamber of Commerce, ☎ (843) 524-3163.

Shops & Stops

In need of some retail therapy? You're in luck because the Lowcountry has more shops than you can wave a Ben Franklin at. (For a more comprehensive list than the following suggestions, pick up the free brochures and booklets available at the tourism offices listed under *Additional Information*.) Beaufort's shopping scene is downright sedate compared to the more than 300 retail establishments on Hilton Head Island. But rest assured the lack of quantity does not reflect a lack of quality. The primary shopping corridor in downtown Beaufort is **Bay Street,** where a collection of art galleries, clothing stores, bookstores, and gift shops awaits. Some notable establishments around town:

Shopping on Beaufort's Bay Street

◆ Two women's apparel shops in Beaufort are worth a visit: **Plumage,** 104 West Street, (843) 522-8807, carries elegant evening clothes, as well as upscale sportswear for women; and ◆ **Elizabeth's,** 1001 Charles Street, (843) 524-2734, for "dressy casual" apparel. ◆ If you're looking for a wedding gift, head to **Rossignol's,** 817 Bay Street, (843) 524-2175, where you'll find china, fine stationery, silver, picture frames, and other household gifts. ◆ **Lulu Burgess,** Old Bay Marketplace, 917 Bay Street, (843) 524-5858, carries an eclectic mix of gifts, jewelry, and home accessories. ◆ Housed in the basement of the historic John Mark Verdier House, the **Verdier House Gift Shop,** 801 Bay Street, (843) 542-6334, carries old-fashioned games, toys, and books, as well as note cards featuring historic homes, antique maps, and postcards with old Beaufort photographs.

◆ **WhatsinStore,** 853 Sea Island Parkway, St. Helena, (843) 838-7473, sells locally made pottery, artwork, furniture, and accessories for the home, beach, and garden. ◆ For the sommelier in you, head to Kim and Andrea Hunt's **Sea Island Wine & Provisions,** 403 Carteret Street, (843) 524-9463. This upscale wine and cheese shop carries a number of excellent vintages, as well as gourmet items to complement your selection.

◆ Vacationers on Hilton Head must be awfully serious about shopping, as the shopping centers are often packed. Nearly every major, national retailer—from Wal-Mart and Home Depot to upscale department stores—is located along Route 278's commercial sprawl in Bluffton and along William Hilton Parkway (Route 278) on the island. Sandwiched between these familiar stores are some true treasures. If you're looking for more unique shopping experiences, check out the following suggestions. ◆ In downtown Bluffton, **eggs 'n tricities,** 71 Calhoun Street, (843) 757-3446, is a delightfully wacky art and crafts shop housed in a renovated gas station. Promising "funky junk" and the "best artsy-craftsy collectibles around," eggs 'n tricities carries everything from a stuffed rooster to funny greeting cards.

◆ The **Audubon Nature Store,** the Village at Wexford, 1000 William Hilton Parkway, (843) 785-4311, *www.audubonnature.com,* is a stop worth making for anyone who loves the

Hilton Head Island CVB

The shops at Harbour Town

outdoors. With a complete selection of merchandise related to nature—books, garden décor, binoculars for bird watching, educational toys, tide clocks, and weather instruments—this shop is jam-packed with enough gift items to suit most everyone. Our favorite? The tide clock with a map of Hilton Head for when we look out across suburbia and our thoughts turn to the sea. ◆ The **Lilly Pulitzer Shop,** Village at Wexford, (843) 686-6161, sells the designer's bright, pastel-colored clothing for women and children.

◆ For anything and everything made with seashells, stop by **The Shell Shop,** Coligny Plaza, (843) 785-4900. Items on hand made with Atlantic Coast shells include jewelry, wind chimes, candles, figurines, boats, decorative accessories, and night lights.

◆ If you're in the mood to browse through a shopping complex, the most aesthetically pleasing collection of stores is at **Harbour Town,** 149 Lighthouse Road, in Sea Pines Plantation located near Hilton Head's distinctive red and white lighthouse. Expect a smattering of men's and women's apparel, toy, and gift shops, as well as a few galleries. ◆ One mile west of the island, the **Hilton Head Factory Stores,** off Highway 278, Bluffton, (843) 837-4339, has more than 75 retail shops in two large complexes (creatively named "1" and "2") selling apparel, home items, footwear, and accessories. A sampling: Banana Republic, Eddie Bauer, Polo, Dan River, Coach, and Dansk.

Beach Reading

A trip to the beach without a good book to read (or to use as camouflage for discreet people watching) is like a warm soda without ice. Fortunately, the area has plenty of independent and national-chain booksellers willing to help you find the right fiction or nonfiction title to tote to your towel. Independent booksellers around Beaufort include: ◆ **Bay Street Trading Company/The Book Shop**, 808 Bay Street, ☎ (843) 524-2000, for contemporary and classic fiction and nonfiction; ◆ **McIntosh Book Shoppe**, 917 Bay Street, ☎ (843) 524-1119, for new, used, and antiquarian books; ◆ **The Beaufort Bookstore** in Jean Ribaut Square, 2127 Boundary Street, ☎ (843) 525-1066, for bestselling fiction and nonfiction; ◆ **Firehouse Books & Espresso Bar**, 706 Craven Street, ☎ (843) 522-2665, for atmosphere (it's one-part coffee house, one-part bookstore, and one-part restored firehouse) and fiction, nonfiction, and regional titles. ◆ On Hilton Head, try the **Island Bookseller**, 71 Lighthouse Road, Sea Pines Center, ☎ (843) 671-3773; ◆ and **Port Royal Bookstore**, The Village at Wexford, ☎ (843) 842-6996, both of which stock current and classic fiction and nonfiction.

Spa & Masssage

When your muscles ache from paddling a sea kayak or from strenuous shopping excursions, you're an ideal candidate for a visit to one of the Lowcountry's myriad spas. ◆ In Beaufort, stop by the **Bayside Salon and Day Spa,** 310 Scotts Street, (843) 522-9095, to enjoy your choice of an array of botanical facials, massages, and body treatments, including the Essential Back Treatment and the Herbal Body Masque Wrap.

◆ **The European Spa,** Sea Pines Circle, (843) 842-9355, *www.european-spa.com*, offers holistic aromatherapy facial treatments designed by Elizabeth of London, as well as body treatments and massage therapies. You can even get a tan the way the folks in Hollywood do it: with an airbrush. ◆ The **Faces Day Spa & Boutique,** Village at Wexford, (843) 785-3075 or 1-888-443-2237, *www.hhfaces.com,* has been relieving the aching muscles of Hilton Head residents and vacationers since 1983. Included in the spa's huge facility are a chemical-free nail salon, steam room, sauna, wet room with hydrotherapy tub, and several massage and spa treatment rooms. ◆ Nearly all of Hilton Head's upscale resort properties have spas with fitness facilities, saunas, and more. Two worth calling: **Crowne Plaza Resort,** 130 Shipyard Drive, Shipyard Plantation, 1-800-334-1881, *www.crowneplazaresort.com;* and **The Westin Resort,** 2 Grasslawn Avenue, 1-866-846-9330, *www.westinhiltonhead.com*

Tours

You want tours? Beaufort's got tours: walking tours, horse-and-buggy tours, bus tours, and boat tours (listed in a separate section). And each comes with a knowledgeable, entertaining guide. For a nominal price, you get not only an overview of what's where, but you also learn the history of the town, anecdotes about grand houses and their owners, and plenty of good gossip about the many celebrities who've visited Beaufort while filming

movies. ◆ For a walking tour of Beaufort's historic district with a costumed guide, join **The Spirit of Old Beaufort,** 103 West Street Extension, (843) 525-0459.

◆ Carriage tours are ever-present in Beaufort, as you'll notice when you pull into town. Two of the operations are **Carolina Buggy Tours,** Charles & Craven streets, (843) 525-1300, *www.carolinabuggytours.com;* and ◆ **Southurn Rose Buggy Tours,** 1107 Boundary Street, Beaufort, (843) 524-2900.

◆ **Point Tours and Transportation,** (843) 522-3576, provides bus tours of Beaufort and the surrounding islands. ◆ Companies offering **Gullah tours** in the Lowcountry are listed under *Gullah Culture.*

Boo!

The **Ghosts of the South,** ☎ (843) 575-4967, a 90-minute, candle-lit walking tour departs at 8 P.M. every evening from Beaufort's Waterfront Park (at the West Street Extension) and takes you past houses purportedly haunted by jilted lovers, ticked-off Union soldiers, and a French Huguenot dwarf dressed in pink. (You read that correctly.) Tours typically run $10 for adults, $5 for children.

R e s t   E a s y

S l e e p   W e l l

L owcountry lodging options range from upscale, historic properties in Beaufort to modern properties on Hilton Head. Almost all
of Beaufort's grand, antebellum homes are privately owned, so
the best way to see inside is to stay in one of the city's historic inns
that has been converted from a private home. On Hilton Head, you'll
find every major resort hotel chain represented. As this guidebook
series focuses more on inns, B&Bs, and unique, independently owned
properties, we give more consideration to lodging choices in Beaufort.
At the end of these listings, you'll find a short list of some of Hilton
Head's premier resorts.

Accommodations Pricing

Less than $100	Inexpensive	$
$100-150	Moderate	$$
$151-200	Expensive	$$$
More than $200	Very Expensive	$$$$

Prices are per room, per night, based on double occupancy during peak seasons. Note that B&Bs and most country inns include breakfast in the rate.

Beaulieu House • Pronounced Byu-lee and translated, "beautiful place," this inn lives up to its name and then some. Located five miles beyond Beaufort's historic district, Beaulieu House is on Cat Island, a 322-acre snip of land that was once a nudist colony and then a Methodist ministers' retreat. The newly built inn is a cross between a Caribbean cottage and grandmother's house. Located on the edge of Port Royal Sound, Beaulieu House includes a main house with five rooms, a river cottage with two suites, and a carriage house suite with a sitting area and kitchenette. Innkeeper Diann Corsaro and her mother, Wanda, decorated the rooms and suites with island colors and simple décor that allow the tranquil marsh views to dominate. Each room is unique, yet common features include immense jet tubs, private porches, and hammocks. Breakfast is a delicious affair of fresh fruit and a hot entrée. Diann and Wanda are gracious hosts who go to great lengths to help plan excursions, meals out, shopping, and tours. • *3 Sheffield Court, Beaufort, SC 29902, ☎ (843) 770-0303 or 1-866-814-7833, www.beaulieuhouse.com • $$$–$$$$*

The Beaufort Inn • This Victorian inn, pink with white porches and lacy trim, is as pretty today as it must have been upon completion in 1897. Lavish furnishings accent the interior. Rooms are spacious and decorated with elegant fabrics and period reproductions. The nine unique rooms in the main house and 12 cottage suites include such amenities as fireplaces, wet bars, stocked refrigerators, four-poster beds, and luxurious, private baths. Of particular note is the inn's restaurant, respected far and wide as one of the finest in the region. The Beaufort Inn is in the heart of the historic district, steps away from dining, tours, and shopping. • *809 Port Republic Street, Beaufort, SC 29902, ☎ (843) 521-9000, www.beaufortinn.com • $$–$$$$*

The Craven Street Inn • A sunny welcome and easygoing atmosphere prevail at the Craven Street Inn. Immense live oaks swaying with Spanish moss and boxes of fragrant blossoms greet guests as they ascend the walk to this 1870 Victorian home. The four rooms in the main house blend period décor with contemporary touches. Behind the inn are four carriage rooms and two copper-roofed cottage suites. The suites are completely renovated in lowcountry style with modern conveniences like walk-in showers, whirlpool tubs, fireplaces, and kitchenettes. Rooms have front porches from which guests can watch horse-drawn carriages clip-clop past. A delicious, home-cooked breakfast satisfies even the heartiest eaters, and afternoon tea and baked goods are served daily. Head innkeeper Paige Solomon and her staff tend to every detail with warmth and good humor. • *1103 Craven Street, Beaufort, SC 29902, ☎ (843) 522-1668 or 1-888-522-0250, www.thecravenstreetinn.com • $$–$$$$*

Cuthbert House Inn • Built in 1790 for John Cuthbert, a Scottish planter, this Federal-style home overlooking the Beaufort River has a fascinating history etched into it–literally. The Eastlake Room's fireplace mantel has the names of Union soldiers who occupied the home scratched into the black marble. ("Joel D. Dudley, Brighton, Mass, Nov. 28th, 1862" reads one.) While he did not bother to scratch "Bill was here," General William Tecumseh Sherman did indeed spend a night in the house in 1865 during his firestorm march through the Confederacy. The inn features large rooms decorated in Southern-plantation style, 12-foot ceilings, elegantly carved trim everywhere, and large glass windows that flood the house with light. Innkeepers Sharon and Gary Groves' knowledge of the area precludes your need for a tour, and their outstanding hot breakfast precludes your need for lunch. Also of note: a meticulously tended formal garden and bicycles for use by inn guests. There are seven rooms with private baths, robes, comfortable sitting areas, and modern amenities like phones with data ports,

The Cuthbert House Inn

televisions, and mini-refrigerators. The inn is a favorite of the national media, so book well in advance. • *1203 Bay Street, Beaufort, SC 29902, ☎ (843) 521-1315, www.cuthberthouseinn.com • $$–$$$$*

The Inn at Harbour Town • Located in the pleasant marina village of Sea Pines on Hilton Head and just off the water, this full-service inn with 60 rooms is one of the preferred properties for the wealthy, international intelligentsia that arrives each New Year's for the annual Renaissance Weekend. There are four room configurations; all feature such luxury appointments as marble soaking tubs and walk-in showers. Should you need something, you can ring the 24-hour butler service for just about any reasonable service you can imagine. Also available: two swimming pools, a fitness facility, full-service spa, bicycles, golf, tennis, and much more. • *1 Lighthouse Lane, Hilton Head, SC 29928, ☎ (843) 524-9030 or 1-888-807-6873, www.seapines.com • $$–$$$$*

The Main Street Inn • A unique property amongst the high-rise resort properties of Hilton Head, this European-influenced inn looks like an Italian villa, with a Charleston-style garden and courtyard. Common areas are elegantly furnished with antiques, finely framed artwork, and heart-pine and stone-slab floors covered with Turkish rugs. There are 33 luxury rooms with several configurations from which to choose. All have private baths with porcelain sinks, Italian marble, and large tubs. Some have outdoor courtyards. Also onsite: an outdoor lap pool with fountains, a hot tub, a mahogany bar for afternoon cordials, and a comfortable library with numerous chairs and a fireplace. A hot breakfast is served each morning. • *2200 Main Street, Hilton Head, SC 29926,* ☎ *(843) 681-3001 or 1-800-471-3001, www.mainstreetinn.com* • *$$$–$$$$*

The Rhett House Inn • If the Rhett House Inn were clothed, it would be wearing a tuxedo. The 1820s antebellum, plantation-house exterior stands proud with fourteen fluted columns, upper and lower verandahs, and curving "bookend" steps. Tailored, orderly living spaces are accented in blacks, whites, and rich-brown velvets. The 17 main-house rooms and seven newer cottage rooms are uniquely decorated, yet common amenities include CD players, fireplaces, refrigerators, whirlpool baths, and fresh flowers. A favorite of guests is Room #10 with its private screened porch overlooking the quiet garden and fountain. You'll never go hungry at The Rhett House. First there's a full, hot breakfast served to order; then ever-present tea, lemonade, and cookies; next comes evening wine and cheese; and finally, home-baked desserts and coffee from 7 P.M.–10 P.M. All are complimentary. Of course, you'll find one last sweet on your pillow with the turndown service. Loaner bikes and beach towels are available to guests, and historic district shopping and dining are just a block away. • *1009 Craven Street, Beaufort, SC 29902,* ☎ *(843) 524-9030 or 1-888-480-9530, www.rhetthouseinn.com* • *$$$–$$$$*

Two-Suns Inn • Need a room with a view? You'd do well to stay in one of the six guestrooms of the brightly decorated Two-Suns Inn, where rooms feature incredible views of a bend in the Beaufort River. The inn, converted from a 1917 Neo-Classic Revival-style residence, features individually

appointed rooms, each with a private bath. In the Oriental Room, you'll find a brass, full-body shower that sprays 15-20 gallons of water per minute for an invigorating wash. The Skylight room has a 9' x 5' x 6' greenhouse-shaped skylight directly over two beds. Bi-lingual innkeepers Henri & Patricia Safran happily accommodate attempts at recollecting eighth-grade French while seeing to it that your needs are met. A hot breakfast cooked by a French chef starts each day. • *1705 Bay Street, Beaufort, SC 29902,* ☎ *(843) 522-1122 or 1-800-532-4244, www.twosunsinn.com* • *$$–$$$$*

Hilton Head Resorts

Hilton Head's large upscale resorts cater to every need with a wide array of services and amenities, including excellent beach-front locations. Some of the better bets: **Crowne Plaza Resort**, 130 Shipyard Drive, Shipyard Plantation, ☎ 1-800-334-1881, *www.crowneplazaresort.com*; • **Hilton Oceanfront Resort**, Palmetto Dunes, 23 Ocean Lane, ☎ 1-800-845-8001, *www.hiltonheadhilton.com*; • **The Westin Resort**, 2 Grasslawn Avenue, ☎ 1-866-846-9330, *www.westinhiltonhead.com*. • On Daufuskie Island, try the **Daufuskie Island Resort**, ☎ 1-800-648-6778, *www.daufuskieresort.com*.

Dine Well

Dining in the Lowcountry is a highlight for most visitors. Numerous fine restaurants with waterfront views are spread throughout Beaufort County, and most serve some variation of lowcountry cuisine, a style of cooking that blends seafood, fruits, and locally harvested vegetables. Expect rice, sweet onions, fish, crab, and oysters as common ingredients in dishes. Oh, and grits, of course. Grits aren't just for breakfast anymore, and you'll likely encounter dishes like shrimp and grits or salmon over grits. A few other lowcountry favorites: **Frogmore stew,** which is a broth filled with sausage, shrimp, corn, potatoes and onions; and **she-crab soup,** a rich, creamy soup with chunks of blue crab and a touch of sherry. The selection of fine dining around Beaufort is ample but minute in scale compared to the number of restaurants on Hilton Head.

Alexanders • Located in the Palmetto Dunes Resort, Alexanders is an upscale seafood restaurant and wine bar that's had its list of more than 100 wines recognized twice by the highly selective *Wine Spectator* magazine. Expect a nice variety of seafood, steak, and lamb dishes. Standouts include the lobster tempura (lightly battered lobster meat deep fried in a honey mustard sauce) appetizer and grilled yellowfin tuna, topped with a soy vinaigrette and served with wasabi-whipped potatoes and shitake mushrooms as an entrée. The facility includes the main dining room, a wine bar, and an enclosed porch overlooking a lagoon. Throughout the restaurant, you'll find a collection of vintage motorcycles. Open daily for dinner. • *76 Queens Folly Road, Hilton Head,* ☎ *(843) 785-4999*

Beaufort Inn & Grille Room • When you're ready for food so delectable that it stops conversation, go see what Executive Chef Chip Ulbrich is serving at the Beaufort Inn. This award-winning chef assembles meals that can only be called sublime. Appetizer offerings might include jumbo lump crab and crawfish tails tossed with lemon parsley mayonnaise and crusted in pecans, while entrée selections may include porcini-dusted seared salmon on ragout of bacon gnocchi, with artichoke hearts and basil; rack of lamb; maple duck breast; or "Frogmore" International (Ulbrich's take on Frogmore Stew). Beaufort Inn's impressive wine cellar features an excellent selection of vintages to complement the cuisine. The restaurant is situated in the heart of Beaufort's historic district, and diners can sit in the clubby Grille Room with a bar or in the formal dining room. Both overlook majestic live oaks trailing Spanish moss. Reservations suggested. Dinner served nightly. Sunday brunch. • *809 Port Republic Street, Beaufort,* ☎ *(843) 521-9000*

Emily's Restaurant & Tapas Bar • With a jovial clientele, Emily's is a cozy, narrow, wood-paneled restaurant that serves up tapas, the Spanish version of appetizers. (Several selections can be made into a meal.) Some recent dishes included garlic shrimp, chicken spring rolls, crab wontons, salmon paté, and alligator ribs. Traditional meals of steak and seafood are also available. Emily's serves dinner only and is closed on Sundays. • *906 Port Republic Street, Beaufort,* ☎ *(843) 522-1866*

Firehouse Books & Espresso Bar • Anyone who loves books and food in equal measure will love the Firehouse. Constructed in the original town square in 1911, the Firehouse—a brick building with wood beams, a cozy loft, and shelves of books—serves up a hearty lunch and dinner. Such homemade café selections as deli sandwiches, wraps, salads, quiches, and desserts are complemented by a splendid array of beverages. Choose from coffees, espressos, lattes, sodas, and juices, or frozen drinks like the mocha raspberry glacier, vanilla Oreo freeze, or mocha turtle latte. The Firehouse also offers ready-to-go boxed lunches. No reservations needed, but this is a popular spot, so arrive early. Firehouse closes at 7 P.M. every day except Sunday when it closes at 3 P.M. • *706 Craven Street, Beaufort,* ☎ *(843) 522-2665*

The Mad Tea Party • Expect a bit of England in this quiet little café at the corner of Port Republic and Scott streets, where lunch and afternoon tea are served daily in high style. Menu items refer to English literature—from the Lewis Carroll-influenced White Rabbit Salads to the Bard's Midsummer Night's Tea—and you can expect more than cute allusions. The food is excellent. If you indulge in the baked-daily Royal Quiche of the Day, or the Triple Decker Club, with Boars Head honey-smoked turkey, baked Virginia ham, Swiss cheese, and other fixings, you might need a nap right after lunch.

Perhaps that's why tea is served. Choose from more than a dozen types of black, oolong, green, and chai teas to pep up your step for an afternoon of exploration. Open daily from 11 A.M.–4:30 P.M.; and Sundays for brunch from 11 A.M.–3 P.M. • *223 Scott Street, Beaufort,* ☎ *(843) 982-0832*

The Original Steamer • Don't expect a romantic view from this simple restaurant beside Route 21. But with the lip-smacking platters of food, you won't know the difference. Old-style tables with holes in the middle for metal buckets let diners know they are in shellfish country. You'll hear the dull thunk of oyster shells hitting buckets as diners feast on heaps of either raw or cooked oysters. If you're not in the mood for fresh seafood steamed, grilled, or fried, choose from Steamer's steaks and burgers. Come casual to this wood and brick eatery and prepare to be generously fed. Open daily for lunch and dinner. • *168 Sea Island Parkway, Beaufort,* ☎ *(843) 384-2978*

La Maisonette • For one of the fancier dining experiences on Hilton Head, make reservations for the three-course, prix fixe dinner at this French restaurant. A true island tradition—La Maisonette has been in business since 1975—the restaurant serves traditional French fare, including such stalwarts as escargots and filet du boeuf. Recommended dishes include the appetizer crevettes maisonette (shrimp sautéed with herbs in a light butter sauce) and the Flétan Daufuskie (flounder stuffed with blue crabmeat and topped with a dill sauce). Dessert? Mais oui, la crème brulée. Appropriate dress suggested. Dinner only, Tuesday–Saturday.

• *20 Pope Executive Park Drive (in the RMC Building), Hilton Head,* ☎ *(843) 785-6000*

Old Oyster Factory • Surrounded by Broad Creek with outstanding views of water and marsh thanks to numerous large windows, the Old Oyster Factory is just the kind of casual restaurant to visit when you're hungry for great seafood. Two appetizers stand out: "Oyster Rockefeller," (oysters baked with spinach and Béarnaise sause), and "Oyster Savannah," (shrimp, crabmeat, and smoked bacon topped with cheddar cheese). For entrées, the Seafood Medley (broiled shrimp, scallops, Oyster Rockefeller, Oyster Savannah, and fish filet) is outstanding, as is the peppered mahi mahi. A vintage from the restaurant's extensive wine selection is recommended to complement each dish. If your day wraps up early, head here to enjoy happy hour and to watch the sun set over the water. Open daily for dinner. • *Marshland Road, Hilton Head,* ☎ *(843) 681-6040*

Plums Waterfront Cafe • This casual café serves up sophisticated food (as well as down-to-earth sandwiches). Depending on your mood, you can dine on grilled filet mignon with roasted garlic, artichoke hearts, caramelized onions, and brandy Maytag Chèvre sauce, or a blue crab cake sandwich. The lunch menu is easygoing, with ingredients from oysters to corned beef to bacon and brie. This small restaurant fills up fast with a festive crowd that spills out onto the terrace overlooking the Beaufort Rive. Sweatshirts and silk can be seen on any given night, so don't worry about neckties. Finally, save room for ice cream. Plums is famous for its many sinful flavors, each homemade by the owner's aunt. Plums is a little tricky to find. Just go along Bay Street looking for the address, and when you get to a narrow alley that looks like a back entrance, head down it to the café. Open daily for lunch and dinner. • *904 1/2 Bay Street, Beaufort,* ☎ *(843) 525-1946*

The Shrimp Shack • Over the bridge from Beaufort and south roughly 12 miles on the Sea Island Parkway is a building a little bigger than a shack. Out of a quick-order window, The Shrimp Shack serves fresh shrimp burgers, sweet potato sticks, and seafood dinners. Wash it all down with iced tea or lemonade and you have the lowcountry version of fast food. When not ordering take out, diners sit either on a screened porch or at picnic tables under shady live oaks. Call first because hours vary seasonally. • *1925 Sea Island Parkway, Beaufort,* ☎ *(843) 838-2962*

Picnic Packing

To pack a lunch for your paddling, pedaling, or hiking excursion, stop by **The Sandwich Shop,** 846 Sea Island Parkway, Beaufort, ☎ (843) 838-9838, run by Ghee Chee Girls, Inc. (aka, Alluette Jones). This tiny, easy-to-miss shop uses homemade breads and fresh, healthy ingredients to make mouthwatering sandwiches, salads, and soups served up with a smile. • For a more European flair try **Wine & Provisions**, 403 Carteret Street, Beaufort, ☎ (843) 524-9463. They make a mean focaccia-bread sandwich. Put together a picnic from a case of salamis, hams, cheeses, olives, breads, and similar market items. Add a bottle of wine and a checkered blanket to feast away. • Finally, **Firehouse Books & Espresso Bar**, 706 Craven Street, Beaufort, ☎ (843) 522-2665, creates three ready-to-go boxed lunches sure to please. Choose from deli sandwiches, specialty salads, or specialty wraps. Complete with sides and beverages.

Just Desserts

No question, when Beaufort gets warm, there's nothing like sitting down with a cold ice cream cone. **Southern Sweets Ice Cream Parlor,** ☎ (843) 575-0798, inside Beaufort's Old Bay Market Place, is very handy for a break from shopping or touring. In addition to nearly 20 flavors, this old-fashioned ice cream parlor offers coffees, sodas, and rich, smooth candy. • If your sweet tooth favors candy and fudge, check out **The Chocolate Tree** at 507 Carteret Street, Beaufort, ☎ (843) 524-7980, where an amazing variety of confections—milk chocolate, fudge, toffee, and truffles, to name a few—is made on the premises. • At **Renaissance Fine Chocolates**, 1001 Boundary Street, Suite B, Newcastle Square, Beaufort, ☎ (843) 525-1328, or 80 Baylor Drive, Suite 109, at the Bluffton Commons, ☎ (843) 706-3880, you'll find "American chocolates in the Belgian Tradition," along with an array of sweets, including brownies, cookies, and caramel popcorn, plus coffee and tea.

A Long-Weekend Itinerary

Day One

After breakfast at your inn or B&B, swing by **Wine & Provisions** (page 175) in Beaufort to purchase a gourmet picnic lunch, and then hit the Sea Island Parkway for **Hunting Island State Park** (page 143) to spend the morning exploring the various trails, including the **Marsh Boardwalk** (page 144), before spreading a blanket on the beach, swimming, collecting shells, and eating lunch.

Return to your inn to shower and dress comfortably to explore **historic Beaufort** (page 160). Visit **Firehouse Books & Espresso Bar** (page 165) for a cup of java to boost your energy level. Join a guided walking tour with **The Spirit of Old Beaufort** (page 166), or if you'd rather sit and watch the sites roll by, catch a carriage tour with **Carolina Buggy Tours** (page 166).

Return to your inn and prepare for dinner at the **Beaufort Inn** (page 171). Stroll Beaufort's waterfront before calling it a day.

Day Two

Linger over breakfast to soak in your vacation, and then head to **Outside Hilton Head** (page 148) to join one of their guided, two-hour nature tours in a sea kayak. Back on land, visit **Hilton Head Bicycle Company** (page 146) to rent beach cruisers and get thee to **Driessen Beach Park** (page 152) where you can order lunch at the grill, spread a towel on the sand, and relax. When the tide is low and your energy level is high, start pedaling to explore the island's seemingly endless beach.

After your ride and cool-off swim, shower at the beach pavilion, return your bikes and spend the afternoon exploring Hilton Head's **art galleries,** including the **Red Piano** (page 154), browsing its **shops** and **boutiques** (page 164), or wandering the

streets of historic **Bluffton** (page 161). As the afternoon fades, head to the Shelter Cove Harbour for a sunset sail with hors d'oeuvres and drinks aboard the *Schooner Welcome* (page 151).

Head to Hilton Head's **Old Oyster Factory** (page 173), and then put your thoroughly exhausted selves to bed.

Day Three

After breakfast at your inn, visit the **York W. Bailey Museum & Cultural Center** (page 157) at the historic Penn Center on St. Helena Island. As you return to Sea Island Parkway, stop at the **Red Piano Too** (page 157) in Frogmore to purchase some Gullah crafts. Then, continue further out Sea Island Parkway to have lunch at the **Shrimp Shack** (page 173). Return to Beaufort and spend the afternoon shopping the city's downtown **antiques shops and art galleries** (page 153) or visit the historic **John Mark Verdier Museum House** (page 161) and the **Beaufort Museum** (page 162).

Take a final, deep breath of the Lowcountry's salt air and reluctantly return to the real world.

Additional Information

For additional dining, accommodations, and sightseeing information, including the dates of special events, contact:

The Greater Beaufort Chamber of Commerce, 1106 Carteret Street, Beaufort, SC 29901, ☎ (843) 524-3163 or 1-800-638-3525, *www.beaufortsc.org*, operates a visitor center open daily, 9 A.M.–5:30 P.M.; and a smaller visitor center in the center of town at the John Mark Verdier House, 801 Bay Street, open Monday–Saturday, 10 A.M.–5:30 P.M.; Sunday, noon–4 P.M. Both centers are open year-round except for major holidays.

The Hilton Head Island Convention & Visitors Bureau, 100 William Hilton Parkway, Hilton Head Island, SC 29938, ☎ (843) 785-3673 or 1-800-523-3373, *www.hiltonheadisland.org*, operates a welcome center, open daily year round except major holidays, from 9 A.M.–6 P.M.

The Lowcountry & Resort Islands Tourism Commission, ☎ (843) 717-3090 or 1-800-528-6870, *www.southcarolinalowcountry.com*, operates a visitor center and museum off Interstate 95 at Exit # 33 and Route 17. The center is open daily, 9 A.M.–5:30 P.M.

So we came to Beaufort, a town I grew to love
with passion and without apology for its serenity
for its splendidly languid pace, and for its
profound and infinite beauty.

– Pat Conroy, *The Water is Wide*

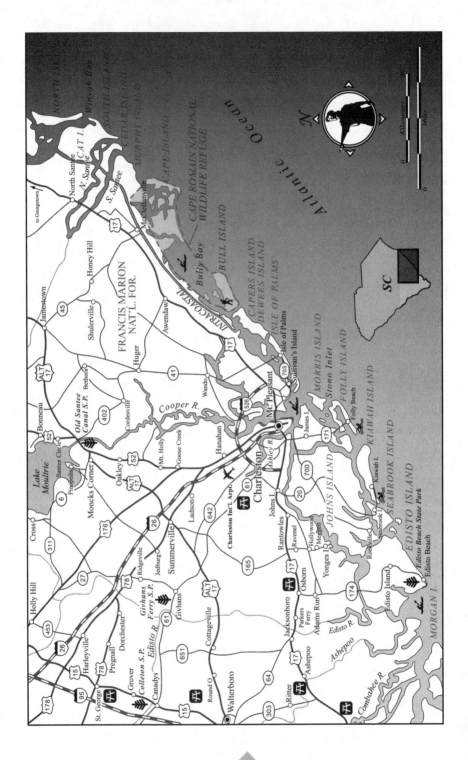

Charleston,
South Carolina

Surrounded on three sides by water—the Ashley River to the west, the Cooper River to the east, and Charleston Harbor to the south—downtown Charleston occupies a small peninsula of former marshland that points past a puzzle of barrier islands to the Atlantic Ocean. Yet to many native Charlestonians, the city occupies a position far beyond its physical location; the compact peninsula has long been the social and cultural capital of the Old South. Indeed, Charleston looms large in the minds of her citizens but also in the minds and memories of the more than five million people who visit each year.

Descriptive labels and superlatives abound. She's the Holy City (spires from many of the 180-plus churches rise above the low-profile skyline); the City of Gardens (wrought-iron gates cannot contain the myriad public and private gardens that spill over onto the sidewalks); and the Heart of the South (the first shots of the Civil War were fired here).

National media commendations include "the most romantic city;" "one of the nation's top 10 vacation destinations;" and "one of the top 25 cities in the world." Charleston's been called the "best place to vacation solo," as well as the "best place to vacation with your family." One ranking the city never tires of receiving is etiquette expert Marjabelle Young Stewart's "Most Mannerly City in America." (In 2003, Charleston took top honors for the ninth year in a row.) While such rankings may come and go, the designation on which Charleston has a lock is as the South's most historic city.

Charleston CVB

The Holy City

Paul Daniel Marriott

The Ashley River

Archaic Indians hunted and fished the Lowcountry around Charleston, but little remains of these earliest settlers save for a few mounds of discarded oyster shells dating back 4,000 years. (Shell mounds exist on Edisto Island south of Charleston and in the Francis Marion National Forest to the north.) More is known about the Woodland tribes—the Edistow, Kiawah, Wando, and Sewee—that lived on the mainland and barrier islands around the Ashley and Cooper rivers for centuries prior to the arrival of Spanish explorers in the 1500s. Though these agrarian tribes were generally peaceful, several factors lead to their violent demise: abduction (Spanish ships sailed north from Florida to raid Indian villages for slaves); inter-tribal warfare (more aggressive tribes from Florida aligned with the Spanish and moved north); and most devastatingly, European diseases against which the natives had no immunity. From 1600 to 1715, more than 85 percent of South Carolina's coastal Indians disappeared.

Harsh weather, malaria, and less-than-welcoming natives made the New World difficult to colonize. In the 16th Century, the Spanish and French attempted to establish permanent settlements in the Port Royal area (near present-day Beaufort), but their efforts failed. Meanwhile, England's Charles II rewarded eight English nobles—the Lords Proprietors—for their help in restoring him to the throne with land grants to Carolina, an amorphous swath of land from Virginia to Florida. Britain's race to capitalize on the region's rich raw materials had begun.

Preservatives Added

Charleston has one of the longest, most-interesting, and best-preserved histories of any American city, thanks in part to a motto the city adopted in 1783 (when Charles Town became Charleston): *She guards her customs, buildings and laws.* Indeed, after more than 333 years of hard living—wars, disease, hurricanes, earthquakes, and poverty—Charleston's historic district has more than 1,400 historically significant buildings still standing proud, thanks to the city's strong preservation ethic.

Charleston CVB

The English sailed into Port Royal in March 1670, but again the area proved unkind to settlement. The land was hard to defend, it was too close to the Spanish, and the Edistow Tribe wasn't interested in sharing space. Fate arrived in an invitation from the Kiawah Indians who, figuring the English would provide protection from the dreaded Spanish, invited the would-be colonists to settle beside the Ashley River.

In April 1670, 148 colonists, including several indentured servants and slaves, sailed up the Ashley River to Albemarle Point on the western bank. They named their settlement Charles Town in honor of King Charles. The following year, 130 Barbadians arrived. As more colonists turned up, a handful opted to build homesteads downstream on the tip of the peninsula between the Ashley and Cooper rivers. Oyster Point—so-called because Kiawah Indians had left behind huge piles of discarded shells—offered two key advantages over Albemarle Point: It was more defensible and could receive larger ships. By 1780, the entire settlement moved to the western tip of the peninsula fronting the Cooper River. They built a wall around the town and began a dense building pattern that continued through the 18th and 19th centuries.

The early years were a financial success for the colony. Exports to Europe and England included furs acquired from trade with Native Americans and naval stores—timber, tar, and turpentine, for example—harvested from the region's vast forests. Barbadian planters began moving up the Ashley and Cooper rivers to establish plantations to grow rice and eventually indigo and

The Battery sits on land Native Americans called Oyster Point

On Charleston & Her Citizens

Popular sayings you may hear in Charleston:
The Ashley and Cooper Rivers come together to form the Atlantic Ocean.
I'd rather be dead in Charleston than alive in Columbia or rich in Greenville.
We, like the Chinese, eat rice and worship our ancestors.

cotton. Crops were moved down the tidal rivers to the now-bustling port of Charles Town, where ships would unload supplies and luxuries from Europe, load the exports, and set sail. By 1740, more than 6,000 residents lived in Charles Town, making it the fourth-largest English settlement in the New World behind Boston, New York, and Philadelphia.

Wealthy planters, merchants, and slave traders, who imported human cargo from West Africa to work on area plantations, built large homes in town, filling them with European furniture, silk fabrics, china, and art. They hired the world's finest landscapers to build extravagant, formal gardens. The city's aristocracy modeled its increasingly cultured existence after London and French society, and in fact, a common nickname for Charles Town prior to the Revolutionary War was "Little London."

Despite the city's affinity for English society, considerable frustration grew with the Lords Proprietors, who proved ineffective, absentee leaders. The number of colonists loyal to England dwindled until the start of the Revolutionary War, when most resi-

The Holy City

From its founding, Charles Town drew settlers by adopting a tolerant attitude toward religious beliefs. All manner of non-Anglican-Church faiths—French Huguenot, Anabaptist, Presbyterian, Congregationalist, Lutheran, Roman Catholic, and Methodist—arrived to establish congregations. Of particular note is the city's Jewish heritage. Charleston has the nation's second-oldest synagogue, the Kahal Kadosh Beth Elohim Synagogue, established in 1749, and it was from this congregation that American Reform Judaism took root in the 19th Century. Today Charleston has more than 180 churches.

Charleston CVB

Wealthy Charlestonians built extravagant homes

dents supported independence. In 1776, a British fleet attacked Fort Moultrie on Sullivan's Island but was turned back in the first decisive patriot victory. Eventually, the British overtook Charles Town, occupying the valuable port city from 1780 until the end of the war in late 1782. In 1783, Charles Town established a municipal government and renamed itself Charleston.

Following the Revolutionary War, planters, merchants, and shippers continued to amass huge fortunes importing slaves and exporting rice, cotton, and indigo. Political tensions grew between wealthy lowcountry residents and the growing constituent of settlers in the Upcountry, resulting in the state's capital moving from Charleston to Columbia in 1788. Regardless, Charleston remained a powerful political den, and it was here that the Ordinance of Secession was signed in 1860, effectively making South Carolina an independent nation from the United States.

On April 12, 1861, Citadel cadets fired cannons at Fort Sumter in the middle of Charleston Harbor, marking the start of the Civil War. After a 34-hour barrage—Confederate forces also fired on Sumter from Fort Moultrie on Sullivan's Island and other points around Charleston Harbor—Union forces surrendered. Soon after, the Federal Navy blockaded Charleston Harbor, and the city's commerce diminished to a trickle. Blockade runners managed to slip in and out of the harbor, but the Union chokehold threw Charleston into a state of siege.

> *"The citizens of Charleston are requested to have ready at hand a tub of water on their premises so as to use immediately in the event of a bursting shell igniting."*
>
> – Notice in Charleston's *Post & Courier* during the Civil War

The Federal Army tried three times to take the city without success, so they settled for bombing Charleston into submission between 1863 and 1864. During this time, Confederate forces used the first submarine to sink an enemy ship when the *Hunley* left Charleston Harbor and sunk the *Housatonic*. After surfacing to signal the mission's success, the submarine sank and wasn't found until 1995. (See "Subversive History" under *Kick Back*.) Charleston's destruction was so thorough that General William Tecumseh Sherman bypassed the port city, dismissing it as "a mere desolated wreck... hardly worth the time to starve it out." In early 1865

Library of Congress

Fort Sumter

just prior to the end of the war, Confederate forces abandoned the nearly deserted city, and the Union Army pulled in and established headquarters at the Citadel.

Following the Civil War, Charleston's economic, physical, and emotional recovery took time. After two centuries as a cultural, financial, and political powerhouse, the city was suddenly poor—too poor, in fact, to renovate its downtown by wrecking old buildings and rebuilding, as many American cities were doing. By the 1920s, Charleston leaders realized preserving the city's historic buildings could be beneficial in attracting visitors. Preservation efforts began to save the old buildings, and civic boosters helped to fund the construction of large hotels.

Of Belles and Balls

Prior to the Civil War, Charleston was the playground of the planter aristocracy, who built lavish homes in which to entertain during the winter social season. There were balls, plays, concerts, fox hunts, dinners, and dances. Young men from prominent families were sent to Europe for education, while Southern belles received private tutoring in the arts. Meanwhile, patriarchs—and matriarchs, of course—plotted sensible marriages. The grand party came to an abrupt end following the Civil War; however, you'll find ample evidence of the good times preserved in the city's architecture and in the stories told by the city's many tour guides.

The United States Navy built a major base and shipyard on the Cooper River in 1912, which operated until the 1990s, when defense-budget cutbacks shut both down. Despite nearly 30,000 jobs lost, Charleston worked hard to attract new business. Continuous improvements to Charleston Harbor make the seaport the second-busiest cargo port on the East Coast. (New York is the busiest.) And of course, tourism is a major, year-round industry.

When it comes to playing hard and resting easy, Charleston is the Southeast's hostess-with-the-mostest. The toughest choices to make here are what pleasures to indulge. On any given day, will you discover the city's history on a guided tour, stroll along cobblestone streets, get lost in a museum, visit the aquarium, or shop the town's upscale boutiques and funky stores? Or perhaps the refinery of town can wait for the next day. Will you sea kayak Charleston Harbor, mountain bike the Francis Marion National Forest, or wander a desolate beach on an undeveloped barrier island?

However you play hard during the day, you can return to the Holy City for a downright sinful dinner and decadent evening out before returning to your historic inn for the sleep of a charmed traveler.

She Keeps Going and Going...

Consider Charleston's misfortunes over the years: five major fires; small pox and yellow fever epidemics; marauding pirates, including Blackbeard who used four ships to hold Charleston Harbor hostage in 1718; bombardment by Union cannons; a crippled economy following the Civil War; an estimated 7.7-Richter-scale earthquake that damaged more than 2,000 buildings; and a handful of serious hurricanes, including Hurricane Hugo in 1989, which rang up more than $8 billion in damages. Despite such setbacks, Charleston endured, recovered, and set sights on continued growth. As Charlestonians boasted after the 1886 earthquake, "Charleston has once more risen from her ashes."

The Way Around

As South Carolina's second-largest city—Columbia is bigger—**Charleston** spreads across 90 square miles. The bulk of this chapter focuses on the 8.5-square-mile **Charleston Peninsula,** located between the Ashley and Cooper rivers. This is quintessential Charleston—soaring steeples; gently waving palmetto trees; clip-clopping, horse-drawn carriages; pastel-colored row houses; gracious homes with wide porches on every level; and intricate, wrought-iron gates barely containing fragrant gardens of jasmine, honeysuckle, and gardenia.

To access downtown from Interstate 26 or from Route 17, follow signs to **"Meeting Street,"** which leads south to the center of town. Once on the peninsula, the streets are easy to navigate. Major downtown roads include **King Street** (Route 78) and **Meeting Street** (Route 52), which parallel one another the length of the peninsula. (King Street becomes one-way south of Calhoun Street.) Two long blocks east of Meeting Street, **East Bay Street** parallels the eastern shore of the peninsula south to White Point Gardens. (East Bay Street becomes **East Battery Street** along the Battery below Tradd Street.)

Wrought-iron gates barely contain Charleston's many gardens

Major roads running across the peninsula, more or less perpendicular to Meeting and King streets, include **Calhoun Street,** which runs from East Bay Street to the James Island Bridge, and **Broad Street,** which extends across the tip of the Peninsula from East Bay Street to the Ashley River. You'll find the bulk of historic sites and attractions south of Calhoun Street and the city's oldest homes and buildings south of Broad Street.

North of Route 17 on the peninsula, **North Charleston** is a separate city that is the region's commercial center. The Charleston International Airport, the Charleston Area Convention Center, and the *Hunley* submarine (housed inside the Warren Lasch Conservation Lab at the former Charleston Naval Base) are all here.

East Cooper

East of Charleston across the Cooper River Bridge on Route 17 (north), **Mount Pleasant** is an attractive river town settled in 1680, a mere ten years after Charles Town. A quick detour from the commercial sprawl along Route 17 brings you to the carefully preserved Old Village of Mount

The city's oldest homes are south of Broad Street

Pleasant, which is listed on the National Register of Historic Places. Popular area sites are Boone Hall Plantation and Patriot's Point, the world's largest naval museum aboard the aircraft carrier *Yorktown*.

Shem Creek in Mount Pleasant

South of Mount Pleasant on Route 703 and across the Intracoastal Waterway, **Sullivan's Island** is a residential barrier island with numerous beach homes, some of which date back to the 19th Century, when Charleston residents and lowcountry planters summered on the island's beach. Fort Moultrie, which played roles in the Revolutionary and Civil wars and remained in use through World War II, is also on the island.

Adjacent to Sullivan's Island, **Isle of Palms** was not settled until the 19th Century, when Charlestonians and lowcountry planters discovered the barrier island as an ideal place to escape the heat. In the 1970s, the Sea Pines Company (developer of Hilton Head Island) began to develop much of the island into Wild Dunes, a gated resort community. The fastest route to Isle of Palms from Charleston is via the Isle of Palms Connector, accessed off Route 17 in Mount Pleasant.

West Ashley

West across the Ashley River are James Island, Johns Island, Folly Beach, and Kiawah, Seabrook, and Edisto islands. From Charleston, Calhoun Street becomes the James Island Connector, crossing the James Island Bridge onto **James Island**, a residential area full of neighborhoods and small shopping centers. (You can also access the island by taking Route 17 south across the Ashley River

Numerous beaches surround Charleston

Bridge.) A few rural areas remain on the island, but increasingly the land is giving way to planned subdivisions, as Charleston's population shifts away from the peninsula toward outlying bedroom communities.

From James Island, Folly Road (Route 171) leads directly south to **Folly Beach,** a barrier island with various beach accommodations, from functional, single-family vacation cottages to newer, million-dollar homes that serve as year-round residences for Charleston commuters.

Johns Island is directly west of James Island and, though much more rural than James, is rapidly becoming another residential community for commuters working in the greater Charleston area. South of Johns Island are Kiawah and Seabrook islands, both of which are beach-vacation destinations unto themselves. **Kiawah Island** is a 10,000-acre barrier island with a 10-mile beach and thousands of acres of marshland and forest. Though the island is primarily private, the public can access the beach at Beachwalker County Park on the island's west end. **Seabrook Island** is an entirely private resort island; access to this island's beach is limited to residents, landowners, and guests renting vacation properties.

Though 45 miles south of Charleston, **Edisto Island** is worth the drive. In contrast to its well-dressed neighbors (Kiawah and Seabrook), Edisto is decidedly laid back. Named for the Edistow, a powerful tribe of Native Americans, the island is full of dense maritime forest, marshland, and beach. Separated from the mainland by the Edisto River, it remains largely rural and undeveloped. The biggest draw here is the beach and Edisto Island State Park. To reach Edisto, take Route 17 south to Route 174 south onto the island.

Weather

Charleston's temperate climate produces mild winters, nearly perfect shoulder seasons, and hot, often humid summers. Average highs in July are around 90, though it's not unusual to hit a few days throughout July and August with 100-degree readings. Ocean breezes help cool the peninsula and nighttime temperatures are typically in the low 70s. Fall weather is brilliant with less humidity and temperatures in the upper 70s during the day, dipping into the mid 50s at night. January highs average 59 degrees with overnight lows in the upper 30s. Spring is Charleston's finest season, with azaleas and dogwoods blooming from early March through early June. Like fall, average spring highs are in the upper 70s; overnight lows are in the mid 50s.

Getting to Charleston

- **By Air: Charleston International Airport,** (803) 767-1100, *www.chs-airport.com,* services most major air carriers and national car rental companies.
- **By Car: From Atlanta**, take Interstate 20 east to Interstate 26 east for the 5.5-hour drive into Charleston. **From Charlotte,** take Interstate 77 south to Interstate 26 in Columbia, which you take east into Charleston. The trip takes just more than three hours. **From Raleigh,** take Interstate 40 east to Interstate 95 south. Interstate 95 intersects with Interstate 26 in South Carolina, which you take east into Charleston. Expect a 5.5-hour drive.

P l a y   H a r d

W i d e   O p e n

The outdoor action goes year-round in the greater Charleston area, thanks to a mild climate and a wide variety of public lands on which to play. Water sports reign supreme, but there are also places to hike and mountain bike.

The **Charleston County Parks and Recreation Commission**, (843) 794-4386, *www.ccprc.com*, operates several public, multi-sport parks, including three beach parks—Folly Beach, Isle of Palms, and Beachwalker (on Kiawah Island). Each features restrooms, dressing areas, outdoor showers, boardwalks, and picnic areas, and rents beach chairs, umbrellas, and boogie boards. Lifeguards are on duty Memorial Day–Labor Day.

Located on the west end of Folly Beach, **Folly Beach County Park**, West Ashley Avenue, (843) 588-2426, is open daily and charges a nominal parking fee, except in the winter. To reach the park, take Calhoun Street west to the James Island Expressway (Route 30), which connects with Folly Road (Route 171). Take Folly Road south onto Folly Island and continue to Ashley Avenue. Turn

A maritime forest

right on West Ashley Avenue and continue to road's end.

Isle of Palms County Park, One 14th Avenue, (843) 886-3863, fronts the Atlantic Ocean on Isle of Palms and is also open daily with a nominal parking fee, except in the winter. To get to the park, take Route 17 north to Mount Pleasant, where you take the Isle of Palms Connector (Route 517) four miles across the Intracoastal Waterway onto the island. Continue straight through the light at Palm Boulevard and take the next left at the park gate.

The only public access to Kiawah Island's 10-mile beach is from **Beachwalker County Park**, Beachwalker Drive, (843) 768-2395, on the island's west end. Open daily, May–September, with a nominal parking fee. (Closed in the winter; open weekends only March, April, and October.) To get here, take Route 17 south onto James Island. Continue straight onto Folly Road (Route 171) to Route 700. Turn right on Route 700 for roughly seven miles to Bohicket Road, onto which you turn left to drive to Kiawah Island. Just before the Kiawah Island security gate, turn right on Beachwalker Drive, which leads to the park.

Other Charleston County parks include 643-acre **James Island County Park,** 871 Riverland Drive, (843) 795-7275, which features paved trails for walking, bicycling, and inline skating; a fishing dock on a tidal-creek; a 50-foot tall climbing wall; and a water park. Canoe, kayak, paddleboat, and bicycle rentals are available. Open daily; nominal admission fee. To get here, take Calhoun Street west onto James Island and to the intersection with Folly Road. Turn right onto Folly Road and immediately get in the left-hand lane to turn left onto Central Park Road. At the stop sign, turn left onto Riverland Road and drive 0.75 miles to the park on your right.

Mount Pleasant's **Palmetto Islands County Park,** 444 Needlerush Parkway, (843) 884-0832, is a wooded, 943-acre nature facility with a two-acre pond, bicycle paths, boardwalks, nature trails, a water park, and numerous picnic areas. Rentals include bicycles and paddle boats. Open daily; nominal admission fee. From Charleston, take Route 17 north to Mount Pleasant, and turn left on Long Point

Forecast: Hot and Buggy

In the hot summer months, a visit to the inland wilderness areas around Charleston quickly shows why lowcountry planters moved to the mountains from June–September. Biting bugs—mosquitoes, sand gnats, and horseflies—and the humid heat make for rough going. If you're headed into the backwoods, pack plenty of water and bug spray. Or head to the beach where ocean breezes keep the bugs at bay. The best time to visit the region's forests, swamps, and marshes is in the fall, when cool temperatures and relatively bug-free days prevail.

Road (marked by signs to Boone Hall Plantation). Roughly a half-mile past the entrance to Boone Hall, turn right on Needlerush Parkway and drive 1.2 miles to the park.

North Charleston's **Wannamaker County Park,** 8888 University Boulevard (Route 78), (843) 572-7275, encompasses more than 1,000 acres of woodlands and wetlands. There are two miles of paved trails and a five-acre lagoon system with two islands. Bicycle and paddleboat rentals are available. Open daily; nominal admission fee. To get here,

Tidal creeks abound in Cape Romain

take Interstate 26 west toward Columbia 12 miles to the Route 52 Exit toward Goose Greek/Moncks Corner. Follow signs toward Kingstree/Moncks Corner. Bear left onto Rivers Avenue and drive just more than a mile until University Boulevard/Route 78 bears left, which you take a half-mile ahead to the park on the right.

Northwest of Charleston, the **Cape Romain National Wildlife Refuge** stretches 22 miles along the coast, encompassing three bays, numerous barrier islands, a handful of small rivers, and vast stretches of marshland. Hikers take to the refuge's maritime forest and beaches, while paddlers and fishermen float on the miles of tidal creeks and open water. The highlight is primitive **Bull Island,** an 5,000-acre barrier island with a six-mile beach. There are 16 miles of hiking trails that cross the island's interior and provide the best chance of wildlife sightings. (Look for deer, alligators, snakes, and numerous species of birds.)

Bull Island is accessible only by boat. **Coastal Expeditions,** (843) 881-4582, *www.coastalexpeditions.com,* operates a ferry from Garris Landing. Take Route 17 north from Charleston 16 miles to Sewee Road on the right; take Sewee Road 3.5 miles to Bull Island Road on the right, which ends at the landing. From March–November, ferries depart for the three-mile trip on Tuesdays, Thursdays, Fridays, and Saturdays at 9 A.M. and 12:30 P.M. Return trips leave Bull Island at 12 P.M. and 4 P.M. In the winter, ferries depart Saturdays only at 10 A.M. and leave Bull Island at 3 P.M. The fare is $30 per adult.

Hugo Was Here

In 1989, Hurricane Hugo roared ashore near Charleston with 135 mph winds that flattened the Cape Romain National Wildlife Refuge and Francis Marion National Forest. Bull and Capers islands were ravaged by the wind and sea, and more than 70 percent of the national forest's trees were snapped or pulled from the earth. Surprisingly, despite such ferocious winds and a 12-to-17-foot storm surge, downtown Charleston fared reasonably well. Just 25 of the city's thousands of historic buildings were severely damaged.

Coastal Expeditions also offers ferry service (by demand only) to 2,100-acre **Capers Island,** an undeveloped barrier island roughly half the size of Bull Island. Managed by the Heritage Trust Preserve, Capers Island is located just south of Cape Romain National Wildlife Refuge and features more than 800 acres of maritime uplands, thousands of acres of salt marsh, and a three-mile beach. Surrounded by winding tidal creeks, the island is popular with paddlers, who make the three-mile trip, pull ashore, and hike the interior or collect seashells on the beach.

The region's largest multi-sport playground is north of Charleston, the 250,000-acre **Francis Marion National Forest**. Popular for hiking, paddling, fishing, mountain biking, and horseback riding, the forest has hundreds of miles of recreational trails, forest roads,

and waterways, ranging from vast swamps to slow-moving, blackwater creeks. There are four wilderness areas and seven recreational areas inside the forest. Located on a former rice plantation on the Intracoastal Waterway (roughly 25 miles northeast of the city off Route 17), the **Buck Hall Recreation Area** is the forest's most accessible recreation area to Charleston.

Information about all of the recreational activities inside the national forest and Cape Romain National Wildlife Refuge is available from the **Sewee Visitor & Environmental Education Center,** (843) 928-3368, located 16 miles north of Charleston on the right side of Route 17 in Awendaw.

Located 50 miles south of Charleston, **Edisto Beach State Park,** Route 174, Edisto Island, (803) 869-2756, is a popular draw year-round with hikers, fishermen, paddlers, and beachcombers looking for shells. You'll find plenty of campers, too, making use of the park's 100-plus campsites in the summertime. Encompassing nearly 1,300 acres of salt marsh, forest, and beachfront crowned by sky-reaching palmettos, the park is a historic place. Edistow is the name of a powerful tribe of Native Americans, and a trail in the park leads to an Indian mound several thousand years old. The park charges a nominal day-use fee. To get to Edisto Island from Charleston, take Route 17 south roughly 20 miles to Route 174, which leads directly to the island. Follow signs to the state park.

Dayhiking

From cobblestone streets and paved, county-park paths to sandy beaches and root-strewn forest trails, the Charleston area has many scenic places to explore on foot. Despite the lack of elevation gain—the region is flat—most of the following suggestions provide a healthy workout. Charleston's 1,000-acre **historic district** is a fine place to begin. The compact downtown with its broad streets, fragrant alleys, and cobblestone lanes is meant for walking. Either join a walking tour (see *Tours*) or grab a detailed street map from

Charleston's sidewalks make for great walks

the Charleston Visitor Center, 375 Meeting Street, and set out on your own.

♦ A long walk on the beach not only provides great exercise but also allows you to cool off in the surf. What's more, few sights are as meditative as the wide-open ocean. Three excellent beaches with public access are within a half-hour drive from downtown Charleston: **Isle of Palms, Folly Beach,** and **Kiawah Island.** Access Isle of Palms from Isle of Palms County Park, Folly Beach from Folly Beach County Park, and Kiawah Island from Beachwalker County Park. Directions to all three are under *Wide Open.*

♦ While the remaining Charleston County parks—James Island, Wannamaker, and Palmetto Islands—feature paved and unpaved nature trails (see *Wide Open*), the county's wildlife sanctuary and forest preserve, the **Caw Caw Interpretive Center,** 5200 Savannah Highway (Route 17 South), Ravenel, (843) 889-8898, features the longest and most-interesting trails. Eight self-guiding trails with interpretive kiosks wind through the preserve's various ecosystems, including fresh, brackish, and salt-water marsh; cypress-tupelo swamp; and maritime forest. To visit all of the property's habitats, hike the 3.1-mile **Habitat Loop,** which makes use of several trails. Expect to be wowed by the wildlife. There are more than 200 species of birds, 30 species of mammals, and 50 species of reptiles, including alligators and snakes. In addition to eight miles of trails, there's a 1,200-foot-plus

Safety During Hunting Season

The Francis Marion National Forest is open for deer hunting from mid August through December, so anyone venturing into the backwoods should wear orange or bright-yellow clothing.

boardwalk over swamp and marshland. Bring insect repellant. To get to Caw Caw, take Route 17 south roughly 20 miles to the center on the right. Open Tuesday–Sunday, year-round. Nominal admission fee.

♦ Located 25 miles north of Charleston, **Francis Marion National Forest** features miles of scenic hiking trails through primitive forest and swampland. The trails are flat and easy, but the payoff is pure wilderness and relatively few people. South Carolina's long-distance trail, the 425-mile (when complete) **Palmetto Trail** begins at Buck Hall Recreation Area (see "To the Sea!") and passes through the forest en route to the Appalachian Mountains. The **Swamp Fox Passage** section, which stretches 42 miles from Route 17 to the forest's western border at Canal Park Recreation Area, follows old railroad logging routes through a variety of habitats, including longleaf pine stands, swampland, and grassy savannah. The flat trail passes through an area hit particularly hard by Hurricane Hugo. (Trees are coming back, but it'll be 50 years or more before the forest regains its pre-Hugo appearance.) A number of forest roads intersects the path, but

---

few options exist for loops. It's best to hike this trail based on time. Hike two hours in and count on two hours back. Carry plenty of water and bug repellant. The best time to hike the trail is in the fall, when bugs and humidity are less bothersome. The trailhead is located in Awendaw on the left side of Route 17, roughly 20 miles north of Charleston and just beyond Steed Creek Road (also on the left).

♦ The two-mile, interpretative **I'on Swamp Trail** loops through a former rice plantation and provides a good chance of sighting alligators, river otters, turtles, and an amazing variety of birds, including the great blue heron. The path wanders over dikes built centuries ago, past ponds, and through wetlands with cypress trees and blackwater swampland. Signs en route explain the land's history. To get to the trailhead from Charleston, take Route 17 north roughly 15 miles to I'on Swamp Road (Forest Road 228) on the left. (If you pass the Sewee Visitor Center, you've overshot the road by 100 yards.) The trailhead is two miles down I'on Swamp Road on the left.

♦ For a short, fascinating hike loaded with Native-American history, the one-mile **Sewee Indian Shell Mounds Trail** passes through maritime forest and marshland. A spur trail leads to a 120-foot boardwalk overlooking a 4,000-year old mound of oyster shells, left behind by Sewee Indians. (Another spur trail leads to a less-distinct clam-shell mound.) Five interpretive stops explain the history of the land and shell rings. The boardwalk also features views of the surrounding marsh, tidal creeks, and Intracoastal Waterway. To get to the trailhead from Charleston, take Route 17 north roughly 18 miles to Doar Road (Route 432 S). Turn right and drive 2.5 miles to a right turn onto Salt Pond Road (Forest Road 243). Drive a half-mile to the trailhead.

♦ Roughly an hour's drive south from Charleston, the **Edisto Beach State Park**, Route 174, Edisto Island, (843) 869-2756, has a 1.5-mile beach ideal for walking, as well as the two-mile (one way) **Spanish Mount Trail**, which leads to a mound of discarded oyster shells left by Native Americans several thousand years ago. This trail is open to mountain bikes, so watch for endorphin-crazed cyclists. It winds through maritime forest crowned by towering palmetto and live oak trees and over marshland on a wooden boardwalk before reaching the mound at Scott Creek. To reach the

To the Sea!

The **Awendaw Passage** section of South Carolina's Palmetto Trail stretches seven miles from the Swamp Fox trailhead on Route 17 to the Intracoastal Waterway at Buck Hall Recreation Area. The trail crosses numerous tidal creeks, passes alongside Awendaw Creek, and through marshland and maritime forest to a scenic overlook of the Intracoastal Waterway and Cape Romain National Wildlife Refuge. The 14-mile out-and-back hike passes quickly (it's flat), particularly if the insects are biting and you forgot bug spray. Park at the Swamp Fox Trail parking area, located on the left side of Route 17, roughly 20 miles north of Charleston and just beyond Steed Creek Road (also on the left) in Awendaw. The Awendaw Passage trailhead is on the opposite side of Route 17. Cross the highway carefully.

Over the Water & Thru the Woods

Catch the ferry from Garris Landing—or sea kayak the three miles—to **Bull Island** in the Cape Romain National Wildlife Refuge (see *Wide Open* for ferry information), where you can hike the island's 16 miles of open, grassy roads and along its six-mile beach. Pick up a trail map at the Sewee Visitor Center (see *Local Outdoor Advice*) and plan to hike the two-mile **Bull Island Wildlife Trail,** a self-guided, National Recreation Trail that winds through forest, wetland, and along the beach. Two other trails— the 3.7-mile **Sheephead Ridge Loop** and the 6.6-mile **Old Fort Loop**—provide great opportunities for sighting some of the island's wildlife. Look for alligators, all manner of birds, snakes (watch your step), and possibly red wolves (introduced to the island in the 1990s). Pack plenty of water and bug spray, and bring a towel and change of clothes to enjoy the beach.

trailhead, take Route 174 into Edisto State Park and look carefully for the blue nature trail sign and dirt parking area on the right.

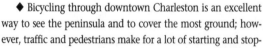

Bicycling & Mountain Biking

Unless you brought your own bike, bicycling in and around Charleston means renting a single-speed beach cruiser for sightseeing downtown or for riding on the nearby beaches. (In general, you can ride the hard-packed sand for a couple of hours on either side of low tide. For public access to the beaches, see *Wide Open* for directions to the county beach parks.) Mountain biking purists—those who believe mountains (or at least serious hills) must be involved—will be under-whelmed with the trails around Charleston. Technical singletrack is scarce, and the terrain is flat. But for most riders, the region's trails offer plenty of excitement, exercise, and outstanding lowcountry scenery.

◆ Bicycling through downtown Charleston is an excellent way to see the peninsula and to cover the most ground; however, traffic and pedestrians make for a lot of starting and stopping. If you're looking primarily for excercise, you'll want to take your rental to one of the area's outlying trails. The **West Ashley Greenway** is an excellent place to begin. This paved and unpaved rail-trail stretches 10 miles from the West Ashley River to Johns Island, loosely paralleling Route 17. It begins in a neighborhood and crosses several streets. Roughly five miles into the ride, you'll enter a pleasant, forested stretch before riding through a marsh. The ride ends at Route 20 on Johns Island. The 20-mile, out-and-back ride is lined with trees and offers several pleasant spots to spread a blanket and picnic. To get to the trailhead, take Route 17 south across the West Ashley Bridge. Roughly a half-mile after the bridge,

The Swamp Fox Passage trailhead

The Swamp Fox

The Francis Marion National Forest is named for Revolutionary War General Francis Marion, who earned the nickname "the Swamp Fox," because of his guerrilla attacks on the British and subsequent ability to disappear into the region's dense swamps without a trace. Marion was part of the model for Mel Gibson's character in the film *The Patriot*.

turn left onto Folly Road (Route 171) and continue to the second light. Turn right into South Windemere Shopping Center. The trail is behind the center on the right.

◆ There are several mountain-bike trails inside the **Francis Marion National Forest**. The **Awendaw Passage** of South Carolina's mountain-to-sea **Palmetto Trail** begins at the Intracoastal Waterway in Buck Hall Recreation Area (see *Wide Open* for directions) and stretches seven miles west to Route 17. This flat, easy section of trail passes through marshland and maritime forest. Across Route 17, the **Swamp Fox Passage** section of the Palmetto Trail begins, stretching 42 miles through bog, swamp, and grassland to the forest's western border at the Canal Recreation Area. The root-strewn trail can be muddy in places, particularly after heavy rains. Throughout the ride, the trail crosses forest roads, any one of which is ideal for exploration on a bike. The Swamp Fox Passage trailhead is on the left side of Route 17 just beyond Steed Creek Road in Awendaw roughly 20 miles north of Charleston. Pack plenty of water and insect repellant.

◆ Another eight miles beyond the Swamp Fox Passage trailhead on Route 17, the national forest's **South Tibwin Trail** consists of five miles of flat connecting trails that can be made into various loops. The terrain—marshland and maritime forest—provides a good chance of seeing wildlife, including alligators, water birds, and snakes. The trailhead is on the right side of Route 17, almost 30 miles north of Charleston. Look for the small forest sign to the parking area. An information kiosk has trail maps.

◆ To combine historic wandering with exercise, head northwest of Charleston to **Middleton Place**, 4300 Ashley River Road, (843) 556-6020 or 1-800-782-3608, *www.middletonplace.org*, on the banks of the Ashley River. Tour the plantation and gardens, and then rent a bike to ride the nature trails throughout the property's 200 acres. Trail maps are provided with your rental. The plantation charges a moderate entrance fee.

◆ Roughly an hour south of Charleston, the **Spanish Mount Trail** in **Edisto Beach State Park**, Route 174, Edisto Island, (843) 869-2756, is open to mountain bikers and hikers. This two-mile, out-and-back trail through maritime forest, over marshland, and beside Scott Creek reaches its end at a 4,000-year-old mound of oyster shells left behind by coastal Indians. While four miles roundtrip isn't exactly a marathon, you can combine the trail with the paved and unpaved roads of Edisto Island to piece together a great ride. Look for blue "Bike Trail" signs posted on the island's roadways for the best routes. To get to the trailhead, see the Spanish Mount Trail description under *Dayhiking*.

◆ Many more riding options exist, including trails in the **James Island**, **Palmetto Islands**, and **Wannamaker county parks**. (See *Wide Open* for directions to these parks.) If you brought your own mountain bike, you'll find the area's most-challenging terrain exists in **Marrington Plantation** on the grounds of the Naval Weapons Station in Goose Creek. There are 12 miles of double- and singletrack, but you'll want to stop at one of the area's bike shops before venturing here. (The site is near where terrorism detainees are held by the federal government and access rules may change after press time.)

Rentals

The following businesses rent beach cruisers. Currently, no area bicycle shop rents mountain bikes. ◆ **Bicycle Shoppe** has two locations: 280 Meeting Street, Charleston, ☎ (843) 722-8168; and 1539 Johnnie Dodds Boulevard, Mount Pleasant, ☎ (843) 884-7433; ◆ **Mike's Bikes & Backwoods,** *www.mikesbikescharleston.com,* has two locations: 709 Coleman Boulevard, Mount Pleasant, ☎ (843) 884-5884; and 808 Folly Road, James Island, ☎ (843) 795-3322. ◆ On Edisto Island, try **Island Bikes and Outfitters,** 140 Jungle Road, Edisto Beach, ☎ (843) 869-4444, *www.islandbikesandoutfitters.com.*

Paddling

Numerous Charleston-area sea kayaking outfitters offer paddling adventures, ranging from two-hour nature tours to full-day paddles and overnight trips. Thinking of going it alone? Unless you're an experienced sea kayaker with knowledge of the local waters, think again. Tidal fluctuations, large ships, ocean currents, wind, and sudden storms can make unguided paddling an unwelcome adventure. The following provides general descriptions of the best paddling spots. Your outfitter will provide transportation to and from the put-in and take-out points. If you're planning to paddle without a guide, check with the rental sources for directions to the best put-ins based on current conditions.

◆ One of the more-popular places to sea kayak is **Charleston Harbor,** best accessed from Shem Creek in Mount Pleasant. You can paddle past Crab Bank, a narrow island teeming with pelicans and aquatic birds; to Patriot's Point and alongside the aircraft carrier *Yorktown;* and out to Fort Sumter. Charleston's low skyline and historic waterfront homes make for picturesque views of the city. On warm, calm days, the harbor is generally a safe place to paddle, though boat traffic can be heavy. There's also a commercial shipping lane through which ocean tankers pass. ◆ There are intricate networks of marshland and tidal creeks on the western sides of the area's barrier islands. Some of the more-popular paddling spots include **the Narrows,** behind Sullivan's Island; **Folly Hammock Retreat,** behind Folly Beach; and **Morgan Creek,** behind Isle of Palms.

◆ As if created with the sea kayak in mind, **Cape Romain National Wildlife Refuge** offers a dizzying array of shallow, protected waterways along its 22-mile shoreline. With

Charleston CVB

more than 64,000 acres of preserved salt marsh, bay, and barrier islands between Charleston and Georgetown, the refuge allows paddlers the opportunity to slip silently across the water and to view hundreds of wildlife species, including birds, deer, and alligators. The water teems with fish, shrimp, and crabs, and the refuge's beaches are essential loggerhead turtle nesting grounds.

Popular paddling waters within the refuge include **Bulls Bay,** a 14-mile long bay too shallow for boats other than sea kayaks and john boats; and **Sewee Bay,** a smaller, protected bay to the east of Bull Island. A popular, full-day trip is to 5,000-acre **Bull Island**. The three-mile (one-way) trip departs Garris Landing and passes through the Intracoastal Waterway, various creeks, and Sewee Bay. Similarly, the three-mile paddle to **Capers Island** departs Garris Landing and includes passage through winding tidal creeks and open bays. (If you're paddling without a guide, see directions to Garris Landing under *Wide Open*.)

◆ The South Carolina Lowcountry is full of cypress swamps, blackwater creeks, tidal rivers, and former canals built by slaves in the 1700s. All of these waterways are in the 250,000-acre **Francis Marion National Forest**. One of the forest's better-known paddling spots is the **Wambaw Creek Wilderness Canoe Trail,** a nine-mile route along a tidal, blackwater tributary of the Santee River. The scenic, easy-going route passes through pine forests, swamps, and former rice fields. There are various access points to the creek, but your

Tour Operators & Canoe/Sea Kayak Rentals

Bohicket Boat Adventure & Tour Company, 1880 Andell Bluff Boulevard, Johns Island, ☎ (843) 768-7294, *www.bohicketboat.com,* rents kayaks and offers paddling tours. ◆ **Coastal Expeditions**, Shem Creek Maritime Center, 514-B Mill Street, Mount Pleasant, ☎ (843) 884-7684, *www.coastalexpeditions.com,* operates a full-service retail paddling shop that rents and sells kayaks, provides instruction, and operates a number of tours. ◆ **Island Bikes and Outfitters**, 140 Jungle Road, Edisto Island, ☎ (843) 869-4444, *www.islandbikesandoutfitters.com,* rents kayaks and canoes. ◆ **Lowcountry Kayak,** Isle of Palms Marina, 41st Avenue, Isle of Palms, ☎ (843) 886-8456, *www.tidalwavewatersports.com,* rents kayaks and offers tours. ◆ **Mike's Bikes & Backwoods** has two locations: 709 Coleman Boulevard, Mount Pleasant, ☎ (843) 884-5884; and 808 Folly Road, James Island, ☎ (843) 795-3322; *www.mikesbikescharleston.com,* that rent kayaks. ◆ **Nature Adventures Outfitters**, 1900 Iron Swamp Road, Awendaw, ☎ 1-800-673-0679, *www.natureadventuresoutfitters.com,* rents kayaks and canoes, provides instruction, and offers a number of paddling tours.

tour outfitter will most likely use a bridge off Route 45. (If you're paddling without a guide, take Route 17 north to McClellanville, turn left onto Route 45 and continue 6.5 miles to the bridge over Wambaw Creek.)

◆ On the **Ashley River,** you can paddle the route that rice, cotton, and other goods traveled from the plantations to Charleston. Either join an outfitter's tour

Canoes on the Ashley River

or rent kayaks and canoes from **Middleton Place,** 4300 Ashley River Road, (843) 556-6020 or 1-800-782-3608, *www.middletonplace.org.* ◆ South of Charleston, Edisto Island is a popular paddling destination. Sea kayakers explore the **South Edisto River** and marshes on the western side of the island. Further south and covered in the Beaufort chapter, the colossal **ACE Basin** is one of the East Coast's premier paddling spots with more than 350,000 acres of marshland, riddled with rivers and tidal creeks.

Fishing

Shallow marsh flats, hidden creeks, mellow bays, broad rivers, and the Atlantic Ocean make up the fertile waters around Charleston. Fishing—inshore and offshore—is a big business here. The area's marinas feature a number of Coast Guard-licensed captains and boats available for charter. The following are some of the most-respected operations. ◆ If you don't have the patience to sit in the boat, rod in hand, waiting for the fish to come to you, **Absolute Reel Screamer Charters,** 1027 Oceanview Road, Charleston, (843) 270-4464 or 1-888-349-4465, *www.charleston-fishing.com,* will help you wade your way to them. Captain Gresh Meggett prefers to walk the shallow marsh flats, hot on the trail of big red drum, which are plentiful in spring, fall, and winter. ◆ **Captain Rick Hiott's Inshore Fishing Charters,** 4131 Flynn Drive, North Charleston, (843) 412-6776 or (843) 554-9386, specializes in inshore and nearshore fishing for red drum, trout, ladyfish, black sea bass, and barracuda. ◆ Captain Legare Leland of **Head Shaker Charters,** 1496 Village Square, Mount Pleasant, (843) 810-0495, *www.headshakercharters.com,* offers inshore, light tackle, and fly fishing in Charleston Harbor and the waters around Edisto Island for red and black drum, spadefish, and Spanish mackerel.

◆ To head offshore, sign up with **Aqua Safaris,** (843) 886-8133 or 1-800-524-3444, *www.aqua-safaris.com,* which manages an entire armada of fishing vessels that set off from several marinas, including Charleston Harbor Marina and Isle of Palms Marina. Offshore charters generally take up to six passengers and may troll anywhere from 15 miles to more than 50 miles offshore. Depending upon the season and how far you head to sea, you may fish for sea bass, grouper, tuna, dolphin, wahoo, and marlin. ◆ If you weren't born with sea legs but won't be denied the pleasure of hooking a big one, head to one of the East Coast's longest piers, the **Edwin S. Taylor Fishing Pier,** 101 East Arctic Avenue, Folly Beach, (843) 762-2172, *www.follyfishingpier.com.* The pier extends more than 1,000 feet into the Atlantic, features a covered shelter, rod rentals, and a bait and tackle shop.

Horseback Riding

There are more than 200 acres of maritime forest to explore on the trail rides at **Stono River Stable,** 2962 Hut Road, Johns Island, (843) 559-0773 or 1-877-777-8951. ♦ Daytime and moonlight trail rides through the Francis Marion National Forest are offered by **M&M Farms,** 1859 Hoover Road, Huger, (843) 336-4886, *www.mmfarms.com,* located just 20 minutes from downtown Charleston. Call for directions. ♦ The **Seabrook Equestrian Center,** 1002 Landfall Way, Seabrook Island, (843) 768-7541, offers trail rides through scenic woods, marshland, and on Seabrook's North Beach. ♦ Located northwest of Charleston along the banks of the Ashley River, **Middleton Place,** 4300 Ashley River Road, (843) 556-6020 or 1-800-782-3608, *www.middletonplace.org,* operates a full equestrian center with guided trail rides on the plantation's 200 acres.

Rainy Day Workout

If rain clouds threaten your outdoor play, head to one of the numerous local gyms that accept guests for a nominal day-use fee. The largest and most-comprehensive workout facility in downtown Charleston is the Medical University of South Carolina's **Harper Student Center,** 45 Courtenay Drive, (843) 792-6611. This 100,000 square-foot facility features everything. The choices of how to get your heart pumping are staggering: free weights; rooms for aerobics, yoga, and Pilates; a full gym with basketball, racquetball, and squash courts; indoor and outdoor running tracks; and a seven-lane, junior Olympic-sized swimming pool. Men's and women's locker rooms feature showers, saunas, and steam rooms.

Scuba Diving

During the past three centuries, the floor of the **Atlantic Ocean** around Charleston has become the final resting place for a number of unlucky ships. Lucky for you, if you like to dive. The offshore diving season runs May–October to wrecks beneath 60–90 feet of water and to offshore ledges at depths of 45–70 feet. Fish you may encounter include amberjack, spadefish, barracuda, grouper, and many colorful tropical fish. Inshore, the **Cooper River** is popular for dives. Despite a fast-moving current and low visibility (five to 10 feet), the river is a great place to dive for fossilized teeth of the giant Megalodon shark. This pre-historic shark grew as large as a school bus and was similar to the great white shark in appearance and temperament. ◆ Several Charleston-area dive shops offer charters, equipment rentals, and instruction. Try **Charleston Scuba,** 335 Savannah Highway, Charleston, (843) 763-3483, *www.charlestonscuba.com;* or **Freedom at Depth,** 5121 Rivers Avenue, North Charleston, (843) 746-9896, *www.freedomatdepth.com.*

Swimming

Charleston's temperate climate makes swimming in the Atlantic Ocean possible eight months a year. The area's summer temperatures make swimming mandatory three months a year. The best places to swim are Charleston County's beach parks—**Folly Beach, Isle of Palms,** and **Beachwalker** at Kiawah—where there are changing rooms, restrooms, showers, designated swim areas, and lifeguards on duty Memorial Day–Labor Day. You can rent a beach chair, umbrella, or boogie board, if the surf looks inviting. Of these, Kiawah has the most-pristine beach. See *Wide Open* for directions to each park. **Sullivan's Island** also has a nice beach, but parking is limited to side streets marked open for parking. (Look carefully. The town tows cars parked illegally.)

Water Sports

Charleston and the surrounding beaches are playgrounds for many more sports than fishing, swimming, and paddling. Residents and visitors alike hit the water for sailing, surfing, windsurfing, jet skiing, wake boarding, water skiing, parasailing, and the latest rage, kiteboarding. (Imagine wake boarding in the surf, attached to a giant kite.) In fact, if a sport involves water, chances are you'll find it here.

◆ The best surf shops are on Folly Beach, in Mount Pleasant, and on Isle of Palms. The majority of the cutting-edge action occurs at Folly Beach, which is home to the area's finest surf spot, **the Washout,** located at the end of East Ashley Road. (The waves have their own surf cam: *www.follysurfcam.com.*)

An uplifting experience provided by Tidal Wave Water Sports

◆ Interested in renting a sailboat, Wave Runner, or your own Boston Whaler? You'll want to visit one of the area's many marinas, where you'll find companies like **Bohicket Boat Adventure & Tour Company,** 1880 Andell Bluff Boulevard, Johns Island, (843) 768-7294, *www.bohicketboat.com;* and ◆ **Tidal Wave Water Sports,** whose main operation is at Isle of Palms Marina, 41st Avenue, Isle of Palms, (843) 886-8456, *www.tidalwavewatersports.com.* (Tidal Wave operates four additional locations. Call for details.) ◆ You can arrange water adventures at other popular marinas, including **Ashley Marina,** 33 Lockwood Drive, Charleston, (843) 722-1996, *www.ashleymarina.com;* **City Marina,** 17 Lockwood Drive, Charleston, (843) 723-5098, *www.charlestoncity-*

marina.com; and **Charleston Harbor Marina,** 24 Patriots Point Road, Mount Pleasant, (843) 856-9996 or 1-888-856-9996, *www.charlestonharbormarina.com.*

Local Outdoor Advice

Coastal Expeditions • Located on Shem Creek in Mount Pleasant, this paddling super-center sells kayaks, gear, apparel, guidebooks, maps, and charts. Coastal Expeditions also rents kayaks and offers paddling instruction and numerous tours, ranging from three-hour nature trips to overnight, barrier-island excursions. • Shem Creek Maritime Center, 514-B Mill Street, Mount Pleasant, ☎ (843) 884-7684, *www.coastalexpeditions.com*

Half Moon Outfitters • Staffed by energetic, knowledgeable outdoor enthusiasts, this full-service gear, apparel, and footwear shop equips hikers, mountain bikers, paddlers, skiers, and serious alpinists. Half Moon also provides kite-boarding instruction. • 280 King Street, Charleston, ☎ (843) 853-0990; 425 Coleman Boulevard, Mount Pleasant, ☎ (843) 881-9472, *www.halfmoonoutfitters.com*

Outdoor Shoppe • The sister company to the Bicycle Shoppe, this outfitter sells gear, apparel, and footwear for most outdoor pursuits. The friendly staff will gladly suggest local outdoor excursions. • 280 Meeting Street, Charleston, ☎ (843) 722-0618; 1539 Johnnie Dodds Boulevard, Mount Pleasant, ☎ (843) 884-2999

Sewee Visitor and Environmental Education Center • This unique center educates visitors about the Francis Marion National Forest and the Cape Romain National Wildlife Refuge through exhibits about the land and its indigenous plants, animals, and fish. There's a three-dimensional map of the area, as well as an auditorium where a 10-minute film about the region is shown. Finally, an outdoor recreation information desk carries trail maps and is staffed by rangers who'll point you to nearby outdoor fun. A short nature trail onsite heads to a viewing area of a red-wolf habitat. Admission is free. • 5821 Route 17, Awendaw, ☎ (843) 928-3368, *www.seweecenter.fws.gov*

Kick Back

If there's a destination that excels in slower-paced activities, it's Charleston. When your shoulders are sore from paddling or your legs have had enough walking on the beach, enjoy the following pleasures of town.

Antiques

 You'll find antique treasures throughout the Lowcountry, but no Southern city compares to Charleston in its breadth and depth of antiques inventories. In fact, you could spend a week here and still need a return visit to hit every antiques dealer. What makes Charleston so great for antiquing? First, the city is an antique herself, with a 330-year history. Second, as a wealthy colonial port, Charleston received innumerable shipments of furniture, furnishings, decorative accessories, plumbing fixtures, tools, toys, clothing, and kitchen items. English antiques are the dominant fare, but you'll also find fine Americana, colonial Caribbean, and all manner of European items.

◆ The city's **"Antiques District"** is on lower King Street, between Queen and Beaufain streets, where you'll find more than 30 antiques dealers. Stop in at **A'riga IV,** 204 King Street, (843) 577-3075, which offers a selection of 17th–19th-century furniture. Of particular interest is the shop's array of antique medical and scientific instruments. ◆ **George C. Williams American Antiques,** 155 King Street, (843) 377-0290, *www.georgecwilliams.com,* specializes in early American furniture and accessories, including fireplace andirons, clocks, mirrors, and porcelain. ◆ With more than 80 years in business, **Croghan's Jewel Box,** 308 King Street, (843) 722-6730, *www.croghansjewelbox.com,* is a mainstay of the Charleston antiques community and where you'll find a variety of items, including estate jewelry, elegant silver, and crystal. This is a particularly good stop for wedding gifts. ◆ Another pre-owned, fine jewelry store is **Joint Venture Estate Jewelers,** 138 King Street, 1-800-722-6730, which, as a consignment shop, offers excellent prices.

◆ For one-stop antiques hunting, head to the **King Street Antique Mall,** 495 King Street, (843) 723-2211, *www.kingstantiquemall.com,* an 8,000 square-foot facility with more than 80 dealers offering furniture, art, china, collectibles, and more. ◆ **Chicora Antiques,** 102 Church Street, (843) 723-1711 or 1-888-343-8775, *www.chicoraantiques.com,* offers some the country's finest pieces of high-end, 18th- and 19th-century American antiques and decorative arts.

The many antiques shops around King Street is merely the start to Charleston's offerings. Dealers are located throughout the region, including in Mount Pleasant's Old Village and on James Island.

Take a Seat

For a more durable memento of your vacation, stop by **Geo. C. Birlant & Co.,** 191 King Street, ☎ (843) 722-3842 or 1-888-247-5268, *www.birlant.com,* to order a reproduction of the renowned Charleston Battery Bench. Geo. C. Birlant & Co. purchased the 1880 molds for the bench's cast-iron sides from the original manufacturer (the defunct Riley Iron Works Company) more than 50 years ago and has since been turning out stunning reproductions of the benches that line Charleston's Battery and public parks. Manufactured with durable cypress slats, the bench makes a great addition to gardens, lawns, and patios. The antiques shop also specializes in imported 18th- and 19th-century furniture, silver, crystal, brass, and more.

Aquarium

Inside the 330,000-gallon "Great Ocean Tank"

Anything and everything related to South Carolina's aquatic life can be found inside the sparkling, 93,000 square-foot **South Carolina Aquarium,** 100 Aquarium Wharf, (843) 720-1990, *www.scaquarium.org.* This impressive glass structure juts out over Charleston Harbor at the east end of Calhoun Street and is home to thousands of living creatures, including fish, river otters, fish, turtles, fish, snakes, fish, birds, fish, and of course, sharks. More than 60 exhibits reproduce the state's various aquatic habitats from mountain streams to the Atlantic Ocean. The 330,000-gallon "Great Ocean Tank" features huge viewing windows that bring guests face-to-face with beauties and oddities from the sea. (Some fish look as if they've had one-too-many collagen lip implants.) Did we mention the variety of fish you'll find here? From April 1–August 15, open Monday–Saturday, 9 A.M.–6 P.M.; Sunday, noon–6 P.M. From August 16–March 31, open Monday–Saturday, 9 A.M.–5 P.M., Sunday, noon–5 P.M. Moderate admission fee.

Art Galleries

Charleston loves art, as is evident by the large number of galleries exhibiting work by regional, national, and international artists. In 1999, a handful of fine-art galleries formed the **Charleston Fine Art Dealers' Association**, *www.cfada.com,* to grow Charleston as a world-class, visual-arts destination. Each November, the organization sponsors the **Charleston Fine Art Annual**, a weekend series of exhibits, lectures, and social gatherings held at the Gibbes Museum. The museum and nine galleries make up the association's membership. A few notable members: ◆ **Carolina Galleries,** 188 King Street, (843) 723-2266 or 1-

The Gibbes Museum

For an artistic perspective on Charleston and the Lowcountry, visit the **Gibbes Museum of Art,** 135 Meeting Street, ☏ (843) 722-2706, *www.gibbesmuseum.org,* one of the South's premier art museums. Founded in 1905, the Gibbes has more than 10,000 works. Its emphasis is on 18th-, 19th-, and 20th-century American paintings, prints, watercolors, photographs, and sculptures that reflect a Charleston perspective. If the enormity of the collection overwhelms you, scale down your visit by stepping into the Miniature Gallery, where there are more than 500 miniature portraits from the 18th Century to today. Also, check out the Rotunda with its green and yellow Tiffany-style dome. Open Tuesday–Saturday, 10 A.M.–5 P.M.; Sunday, 1 P.M.–5 P.M. Nominal admission fee.

800-328-6256, *www.carolinagalleries.com,* is Charleston's oldest art gallery. It specializes in work from the Charleston Renaissance (see "The Charleston Renaissance"). ◆ **The Bernie Horton Gallery,** 111 Church Street, (843) 958-0014, *www.berniehortongallery.com,* exhibits low-country landscapes by Bernie Horton and his brother, Mark Kelvin Horton. ◆ The **Charleston Renaissance Gallery,** 103 Church Street, (843) 723-0025, *www.fineartsouth.com,* features work from the Charleston Renaissance with art by such painters as West Fraser and Elizabeth O'Neill Verner. ◆ **Ann Long Fine Art,** 12 State Street, (843) 577-0447, *www.annlongfineart.com,* displays work by Realists, especially Americans who've lived, studied, and trained in Florence, including North Carolina fresco artist Ben Long.

◆ Another gallery group, the **French Quarter Gallery Association,** (843) 577-7100, *www.frenchquartergalleries.com,* includes roughly 30 galleries located in the city's French Quarter District, bounded by Lodge Alley and Cumberland, East Bay, and State streets. In total, you'll find work by more than 500 artists working in a variety of mediums and styles, ranging from traditional to contemporary. Stop by any gallery inside the district to pick up a map to the other galleries.

◆ There are many more noteworthy art galleries than those belonging to the aforementioned associations. A sampling: **Gallery Chuma,** 43 John Street, (843) 722-7568, *www.gallerychuma.com,* is the largest gallery in the South to exhibit the work of African-American artists. Here you'll find 2,900 square feet of fine-art exhibits in the historic Long Stable Building. In addition to permanent collections of work by such artists as Jonathan Green, John Jones, and James Denmark, the gallery hosts traveling exhibits. ◆ **The Verner Gallery,** 38 Tradd Street, (843) 722-4246, *www.vernergallery.com,* houses work by Elizabeth O'Neill Verner, as well as contemporary lowcountry painters and sculptors. Verner was one of Charleston's most famous and revered artists; her work hangs in the Metropolitan Museum of Art in New York and in Charleston's Gibbes Museum. The gallery is part of a property that was Verner's home and studio, dating back to 1938.

The Charleston Renaissance

The Civil War and Reconstruction eras left Charleston impoverished financially and spiritually. From this state, the city witnessed a cultural revival dubbed the Charleston Renaissance, which lasted from 1915 to 1940. Artists took pride in the city's rich heritage and began painting scenes that captured the architecture, landscape, and daily life of Charleston and the surrounding region. This body of work created by such artists as Alice Ravenel Huger Smith, Elizabeth O'Neill Verner, Alfred Hutty, and Anna Heyward Taylor brought national attention to Charleston and helped drive the city's preservation efforts.

Back Roads Touring

Walking the many streets of downtown Charleston provides one aspect of the region's history, but to get the entire picture, fuel up and drive off Charleston Peninsula to explore the back roads of the Lowcountry. One of America's oldest scenic drives is **Ashley River Road,** an 11-mile stretch of Route 61 from Church Creek to Bacons

Photo by Paul Daniel Marriott

The entrance to Drayton Hall off Ashley River Road

Bridge Road. Route 61, the state's oldest highway, developed from Native-American trading paths. In 1690, merely 20 years after Charleston's founding, the road was built to deliver goods arriving in port to the Ashley River plantations and settlements further inland. Today Ashley River Road passes through a National Register Historic District that includes historic churches, abandoned rice fields, former Confederate defense posts, and three of Charleston's original plantations.

Historic sites you'll pass in order, driving northwest from Charleston: **Springfield Baptist Church,** one of the few remaining, freely organized Black Baptist Churches in the area. Founded in 1863 as the St. Andrew's Baptist Church, the building sits on land donated by a local plantation owner in 1871. The oldest-remaining church in the Carolinas, **Old St. Andrew's Church** was founded in 1706 and was the worship house for the area's white plantation families. The building has been renovated many times since its original construction. The next three sites—**Drayton Hall, Magnolia Plantation and Gardens,** and **Middleton Place**—are described under *Plantations*.

Lined by massive live oaks, Ashley River Road took a huge hit from Hurricane Hugo in 1989 and lost a number of trees that had been protected by law since 1721. The least-affected section of road is between Middleton Place and Drayton Hall, where live oaks with Spanish moss create a canopy. The best time to drive this National Scenic Byway is in the spring or early summer, when blooming flowers intoxicate the senses.

Access the road from downtown Charleston by taking Route 17 west to the Ashley River Memorial Bridge. Stay in the right lane and exit onto Route 61/171 (St. Andrews Boulevard), which you follow two miles until Route 61 departs to the left. Take Route 61 roughly five miles to Church Creek, which marks the beginning of the 11-mile stretch. Signs mark the route.

◆ Other scenic drives in the area include **Route 17 south** from Charleston through the ACE Basin (see the Beaufort & Hilton Head chapter); **Route 17 north** from Charleston through the Francis Marion National Forest (note: the roadside scenery is rela-

Save a Little, See a Lot

Ring up the folks at **Best of Charleston,** 18-A Anson Street, ☎ 1-800-540-3919, *www.bestofcharleston.cc,* to purchase reduced admission rates to such sites as Middleton Place, Patriot's Point, Drayton Hall, and the South Carolina Aquarium. You can also score savings on tours from the Original Charleston Walks, Spirit Line Harbor Cruises, and Old South Carriage Company. Savings may exceed 20 percent, you pay only for the attractions and tours you choose, and the pass is good for two weeks. What's more, a number of shops and restaurants provide discounts to pass holders.

tively uninteresting but there are numerous picturesque sites at which to stop); and **Route 174 south** from Route 17 to Edisto Island. In general, all of the public roads on Edisto Island serve up classic, lowcountry scenery of centuries-old live oaks with shawls of Spanish moss.

Boat Tours

Whether you'd like to view Charleston's Rainbow Row from the water, visit historic Fort Sumter, or travel upriver on one of the Lowcountry's famed waterways, there's a boat tour—two or three, more likely—ready for you to board. Tour prices generally range from $12–$25 per adult; private charters are more. While merely a sampling, the following are good bets. ◆ **Fort Sumter Tours/Spirit Line Cruises**, 498 Wando Park Boulevard, Suite 200, Mount Pleasant, (843) 881-7337 or 1-800-789-3678, *www.spiritlinecruises.com*, offers the 2.25-hour tour to Fort Sumter, located in the middle of Charleston Harbor. Departing from either Aquarium Wharf downtown or from Patriot's Point in Mount Pleasant, the trip includes an hour at the fort, where National Park Service employees explain the fort's history and the role it played in the Civil War. The cruise includes a narrated tour of the harbor. Spirit Line also offers 1.5-hour harbor tours from both points of departure, and three-hour dinner cruises aboard the passenger yacht, *Spirit of Carolina*, departing from Patriot's Point.

◆ For a unique sailing experience, board the *Schooner Pride*, (843) 559-9686, *www.schoonerpride.com*, at Aquarium Wharf for a two-hour harbor cruise. This 84-foot, three-masted schooner was built to resemble ships that carried goods up and down the East Coast in the 19th Century. The *Pride* carries only 49 passengers, so make reservations in advance.

◆ **Barrier Island Eco-Tours,** Isle of Palms Marina, 41st Avenue, Isle of Palms, (843) 886-5000, *www.nature-tours.com*, offers interpretive cruises aboard a covered, shallow-draft pontoon boat. The "Capers Island Wildlife Exploration Trip" is led by naturalists who point out the dolphins, alligators, pelicans, clapper rails, oyster-catchers, and crabs that you'll see en route to and on pristine Capers Island. The company also offers creek-fishing, crabbing, and sunset-cruise tours.

◆ Located on Johns Island, **Bohicket Boat: Adventure & Tour Company,** 1880 Andell Bluff Boulevard, (843) 768-7294, *www.bohicketboat.com*, operates a number of tours and charters, including dolphin and sunset cruises, fishing charters, and barrier island tours. If you're having little luck shell hunting on Folly Beach or on Sullivan's Island, join Bohicket's shelling shuttle to a nearby barrier island, where thin crowds mean more shells.

A sunset sail in Charleston Harbor

Carriage Tours

Charleston CVB

For an excellent overview of Charleston and some witty, historical anecdotes told by well-informed guides, join one of the city's many horse-drawn carriage tours. There are several kinds of carriages—some built for two, others for 22—but all carriage companies offer group tours that depart at regular intervals throughout the day. Prices average $20 per adult for a one-hour tour. Private tours are more expensive and should be reserved in advance. The following are some of the more-established tour companies: ◆ **Carolina Polo & Carriage Company,** 16 Hayne Street, (843) 577-6767, *www.cpcc.com,* is owned by Charlestonians who trace their roots to the city's earliest days. ◆ **Charleston Carriage Company**, 14 Hayne Street, (843) 577-0042, is Charleston's oldest carriage tour company. ◆ Known for their beautiful Percheron Draft Horses, **Classic Carriage Tours**, 10 Guignard Street, (843) 853-3747, *www.classiccarriage.com,* uses restored 19th- and early 20th-century carriages and surreys. ◆ The carriage guides wearing red sashes and Confederate uniforms are with **Old South Carriage Company,** 14 Anson Street, (843) 723-9712, *www.oldsouthcarriagetours.com.* ◆ With tours that set out from a distinctive red barn on North Market Street, **Palmetto Carriage Works,** 40 North Market Street, (843) 723-8145, *www.charlestoncarriage.com,* is especially appealing to families with young children because the barn houses miniature horses and other small farm animals.

Cool Movie Houses

For a mainstream show in a 1940s Hollywood-glamour setting, hit the **American Theater**, 446 King Street, (843) 722-3456, *www.americantheater.com,* a refurbished Art-Deco theater that originally opened in 1942. There are small, pull-out table tops at each seat, so you can dine while watching a first-run flick. ◆ Looking for an independent, art-film house where you stand a chance of catching Citizen Kane or a for-

The Big Picture

Charleston is home to one of the nation's larger-than-life movie theaters, the **Charleston IMAX Theater,** 360 Concord Street, ☎ (843) 725-4629, *www.charlestonimax.com.* IMAX films are short—generally 45 minutes—but their impact is huge. We're talking five stories of screen, 12,000 watts of digital wrap-around sound, and footage of climbers ascending Everest, scuba divers descending into the dark sea, and astronauts floating weightless while orbiting Earth at 17,000 mph. Shoot for the middle seats toward the top. Call for show listings.

eign film? Try the **Roxy Theater**, 245 East Bay Street, (843) 853-7699, *www.charlestonartscreens.com,* which also offers in-your-seat café dining.

From Above

Given the flat terrain of the Lowcountry, the best way to gain perspective on the area is to gain altitude. Jim Ellison's **Flying High Over Charleston,** 202 Commons Way, Goose Creek, (843) 569-6148, puts you above it all, flying over the peninsula, up the Ashley and Cooper rivers, and along the coast. See the area's plantations, Fort Sumter, The Citadel, and the aircraft carrier *Yorktown* as the birds do. Flights depart from Mercury Air, just off Interstate 26 and only 15 minutes from downtown. Call for reservations.

Historic Forts & Sites

Located at Albemarle Point on the Ashley River's west bank, the **Charles Towne Landing State Historic Site,** 1500 Old Towne Road, (843) 852-4200, marks where the first 148 English settlers arrived in 1670 to found Charles Town. The 80-acre outdoor museum, set up in 1970 during the celebration of South Carolina's 300-year anniversary, recreates life as it might have been for the original settlement. Begin at the Interpretation Center, where exhibits feature a variety of artifacts from the colony's first 100 years. Then catch the 30-minute film, "Carolina," which enacts how the early settlement formed. Also onsite: a settler's homestead; a crop garden with indigo, cotton, and vegetables; a 20-acre animal forest; and the *Adventure,* a 53-foot replica of a 17th-century trading ship that's docked at Albemarle Point. You can walk the grounds, ride a tram, or rent bicycles. Open daily, 8:30 A.M.–6 P.M., Memorial Day–Labor Day; 8:30 A.M.–5 P.M., the rest of the year. Admission charged. The site is undergoing a $5 million improvement, expected to be complete in 2005. To get here take Route 17 south to Route 171.

◆ Also known as "Snee Farm," the **Charles Pinckney National Historic Site,** 1254 Long Point Road, Mount Pleasant, (843) 881-5516, was the residence of Charles Pinckney, a Revolutionary War officer, primary framer of the U.S. Constitution, and four-time governor of South Carolina, from 1757–1824. The visitor center is an 1828 cottage with exhibits about Pinckney's contributions to the emerging nation, the impact of slavery on the region, and archeological discoveries made on the plantation site. Throughout the 28 preserved acres, you'll find information about agricultural history, archeological excavations, and wetlands ecology. Open daily, 9 A.M.–5 P.M. Free admission. To get here, take Route 17 north through Mount Pleasant, past the Isle of Palms

Fort Sumter

Subversive History

Desperate times called for desperate measures, and the Union blockade of Charleston drove, in part, the dive toward innovation. On the night of February 17, 1864, a Confederate crew of eight sailors boarded the *Hunley,* an experimental submarine, and motored out of Charleston Harbor to sink the *USS Housatonic.* After ramming a torpedo into the *Housatonic's* hull, the *Hunley* surfaced to signal the mission's success to observers on shore. Moments after becoming the first submarine in history to sink an enemy ship, the *Hunley* mysteriously sank with her entire crew. In 1995, the submarine was discovered. It was raised from the ocean floor in 2000. Today the *Hunley* rests at the Warren Lasch Conservation Center on the former Charleston Navy Base, 1250 Supply Street, Building 255, North Charleston, ☎ 1-877-448-6539, *www.hunley.org.* Tours available every Saturday, 10 A.M.–5 P.M., and Sunday, noon–5 P.M. Tickets cost $10.

Connector to Long Point Road on the left. Follow signs.

◆ At **Fort Moultrie National Monument,** 1214 Middle Street, Sullivan's Island, (843) 883-3123, discover more than 170 years of seacoast defense history. Active until World War II, the fort was the site of decisive battles in the Revolutionary and Civil wars. The current structure is the site's third fort, built in 1809. The original palmetto-log fort repelled canon fire from British warships in 1776, thus making the palmetto the state tree. The visitor center details the fort's history and shows a 20-minute orientation film every half-hour. Seminole Chief Osceola, who was imprisoned here during the 19th-century Seminole Wars, is buried at Fort Moultrie. Also of interest, Edgar Allan Poe was stationed at the fort from 1827–1828. His experience inspired the short story, *The Gold Bug.* Open daily, 9 A.M.–5 P.M. Entrance to the visitor center is free. Nominal admission fee to the fort.

◆ As the target of the Civil War's first shots, **Fort Sumter National Monument,** in Charleston Harbor, (843) 722-1691, is an impressive manmade island. Exhibits and historical anecdotes told by National Park Service employees explain what it must have been like for the Union soldiers holed up inside during the 34 hours of continuous shelling. The favor was returned; once Confederates occupied Fort Sumter, the Union Army shelled it regularly for two years until Rebel forces abandoned it. Today you can explore the fort, visit the onsite museum, and take in some tremendous views of downtown Charleston from the harbor. Fort Sumter is accessible only by boat, with tours departing from Patriot's Point in Mount Pleasant and Charleston's City Marina. Departure times vary seasonally. In the summer, make a reservation in advance by calling (843) 881-7337 or 1-800-789-3678. Open daily, 10 A.M.–5:30 P.M., April–Labor Day; 10 A.M.–4 P.M., September–November, and March.

◆ The **Old Exchange and Provost Dungeon,** 122 East Bay Street, (843) 727-2165, *www.oldexchange.com,* is one of the most historically significant colonial buildings in the United States. Built by the British in 1771 as a customs and exchange house, the Provost served as a prison for various state offenders, including pirates and American Patriots, three of whom signed the Declaration of Independence. After the Revolutionary War, George Washington visited Charleston in 1791 and addressed citizens from the steps of

The Powder Magazine

the Old Exchange. Today you can tour the dungeon, as well as see portions of the city's original sea wall, discovered during a 1965 restoration. The upper two floors of the Old Exchange are home to an array of colonial artifacts. Open daily, 9 A.M.–5 P.M. Nominal admission fee.

♦ The 1703 **Powder Magazine,** 79 Cumberland Street, (843) 805-6730, is the oldest public building in Charleston and the only building still standing from the Lords Proprietors-era. It played an important role in defending Charleston from the Spanish in the early 1700s and was used to store gunpowder during the Revolutionary War. After 1820, the building fell into private hands and served a variety of uses, including as a printing house, storage facility, and livery stable. In the 1990s, the Powder Magazine was restored, and today it's a National Historic Site maintained by the Historic Charleston Foundation. Open Monday–Saturday, 10 A.M.–5 P.M.; Sunday, 2 P.M.–5 P.M. Nominal admission fee.

♦ **City Hall,** 80 Broad Street, (843) 577-6970, dates back to 1801, when the building held a branch of the First Bank of the United States. In 1818, the City of Charleston bought the building to use as City Hall, a role it's played ever since. Here you'll find the Council Chamber, the nation's second oldest in continuous use, with original black-walnut council members' desks. City Hall is also home to an array of historic paintings by renowned artists, including a portrait of George Washington by John Trumbull. Free admission. Open Monday–Friday, 8:30 A.M.–5 P.M.

Historic Homes

The three-story, brick **Joseph Manigault House,** 350 Meeting Street, (843) 723-2926, *www.charlestonmuseum.org,* is a National Historic Landmark and one of America's finest examples of the Federal style. Built in 1803, the house was designed by Gabriel Manigault, an amateur architect—or as called then, a "gentleman-architect"—for his brother, Joseph. The home features an elegant, curving staircase that ascends from the entry hall. Inside is an outstanding collection of 19th-century English, French, and American antiques. A Roman temple-inspired gatehouse opens to the gardens, designed by Joseph's wife. Open Monday–Saturday, 10 A.M.–5 P.M.; Sunday, 1 P.M.–5 P.M. (Last tours begin at 4:30 P.M.) Admission charged, though discounted combination tickets may be purchased for this and the Heyward-Washington House, as well as for admission to the Charleston Museum.

♦ Completed in 1808, the **Nathaniel Russell House,** 51 Meeting Street, (843) 724-8481, *www.historiccharleston.org,* was the residence of a wealthy shipping merchant who traded indigo, cotton, rice, and slaves. Considered one of the nation's most-impressive

Historic Charleston Foundation

The "free-flying" staircase in the Nathaniel Russell House

Neoclassical residences, the home features ornate plasterwork on the mantles and cornices, period antiques, historic works of art, and geometrically shaped rooms. The home's most-dramatic feature is the "free-flying" staircase, which ascends three floors without any visible support. The house museum interprets the lives of the Russells and their slaves. Impressive gardens surround the house. Open Monday–Saturday, 10 A.M.–5 P.M.; Sunday, 2 P.M.–5 P.M. Admission charged, though discounted combination tickets may be purchased for this and the Aiken-Rhett House.

◆ Built in 1818 by merchant John Robinson, the Federal-style **Aiken-Rhett House,** 48 Elizabeth Street, (843) 723-1159, *www.historiccharleston.org,* was expanded and redecorated to include Greek-Revival features by the subsequent owners, Governor and Mrs. William Aiken, Jr. The Aikens traveled throughout Europe to shop for home furnishings, including crystal and bronze chandeliers, classical sculptures, and paintings. Many of these are on display today. Considered an "urban plantation" because of the various surrounding outbuildings—the kitchens, slave quarters, stables, cattle sheds, and privies—the Aiken-Rhett House portrays life as it was in the mid 19th Century for the owners, servants, and slaves. Of historical note: The home served as Confederate General Beauregard's headquarters during the Civil War. Open Monday–Saturday, 10 A.M.–5 P.M.; Sunday, 2 P.M.–5 P.M. Admission charged, though discounted combination tickets may be purchased for this and the Nathaniel Russell House.

◆ One of the first homes built on Charleston's High Battery on land purchased by Charles Edmonston, a

George Washington Slept Here

Following the Revolutionary War, the nation's first president toured the South and spent time in Charleston in 1791. He stayed at the **Heyward-Washington House,** at 87 Church Street, ☎ (843) 722-0354, *www.charlestonmuseum.org,* a 1772 brick townhouse that belonged to Thomas Heyward, a rice planter and signer of the Declaration of Independence. Today it's the oldest of Charleston's grand homes open to the public. Located in the Cabbage Row district and made famous in Dubose Heyward's novel *Porgy,* the Heyward-Washington house features a collection of Charleston-made furniture, including the Holmes Bookcase, perhaps the most-impressive piece of historic, American-made furniture in existence. Tours include the small gardens, servants' quarters, and the restored, 18th-century kitchen building, the only of its kind in Charleston open to the public. Open Monday–Saturday, 10 A.M.–5 P.M.; Sunday, 1 P.M.–5 P.M. (Last tours begin at 4:30 P.M.) Admission charged, though discounted combination tickets may be purchased for this, the Joseph Manigault House, and the Charleston Museum. Call for details.

The Inside Scoop

Historic Charleston Foundation's annual **Festival of Homes and Gardens** runs mid March–mid April each year and provides entrance to many of the city's private, historic homes and gardens. Each year, approximately 150 homes are on the tour, held during the peak-blooming season. Make plans well in advance, as tickets sell out and lodging is scarce. For information, call ☎ (843) 722-3405 or visit *www.historiccharleston.org*. In September and October, the Preservation Society of Charleston hosts the annual **Fall Candlelight Tours of Homes and Gardens,** during which tour guides lead visitors through historic homes lit entirely by candlelight in the evening. Call ☎ (843) 722-4630 or 1-800-968-8175, or visit *www.preservationsociety.org* for more information.

Historic Charleston Foundation

prominent merchant, the **Edmonston-Alston House**, 21 East Battery, (843) 722-7171 or 1-800-782-3608, *www.middletonplace.org,* features a spectacular view of Charleston Harbor. Completed in 1825, Edmonston lived here until the late 1830s when his fortunes turned. Charles Alston, a member of one of South Carolina's most successful rice-planting families, purchased the home and made several additions, including the distinctive third-story piazza. Today this Greek-Revival house remains in the Alston family, though the first two floors are open for tours. Inside is an incredible array of Alston-family possessions, including silver, paintings, furniture, and a magnificent collection of books in the library. Of historical note: Confederate General Beauregard watched the 1864 firing upon Fort Sumter from the second-floor piazza, and General Robert E. Lee spent the night once when visiting Charleston. Open Tuesday–Saturday, 10 A.M.–4:30 P.M.; Sunday & Monday, 1:30 P.M.–4:30 P.M. Admission charged.

◆ One of Charleston's most-majestic homes, the **Calhoun Mansion**, 16 Meeting Street, (843) 722-8205, boasts 25 rooms, 35 fireplaces, and 14-foot ceilings throughout the building's 24,000 square feet. Built in 1876 by shipping merchant George Walton Williams for $200,000, the Calhoun Mansion remains Charleston's largest single-family home. Among the home's features are a 75-foot staircase, a ballroom with a glass-domed ceiling, elaborate oak and walnut woodwork, and gas chandeliers. It is Charleston's only Italianate-Victorian home. Sadly, the home fell into disre-

Charleston CVB

More than 1,400 historically significant buildings stand in Charleston

Steeple Chasing

The Holy City dazzles historic-church aficionados, who can fill an entire vacation visiting one church after another. A mere sampling: the 1751 **St. Michael's Episcopal Church**, Meeting and Broad streets, ☎ (843) 723-0603, the oldest-standing church in Charleston; ◆ the 1787 **Unitarian Church**, 4 Archdale Street, ☎ (843) 723-4617, the second-oldest church in Charleston and the South's oldest Unitarian Church; ◆ **St. Philip's Episcopal Church**, 142 Church Street, ☎ (843) 722-7734, the oldest congregation in Charleston, begun in the 17th Century; ◆ the **Emanuel African Methodist Episcopal Church**, 110 Calhoun Street, ☎ (843) 722-2561, the South's oldest AME church; ◆ and **Congregation Beth Elohim**, 90 Hassell Street, ☎ (843) 723-1090, the second-oldest synagogue in the nation and the birthplace of American Reform Judaism. Most churches welcome visitors, but request that you respect their posted worship hours and closing times.

St. Phillips is Charleston's oldest church

pair, passing through several hands until 1976, when an attorney saved the mansion from condemnation, buying it for the original $200,000 price and undertaking years of work, restoring it to its former grandeur. Admission is charged. Visiting hours vary, so call for information.

Museums

◆ Founded in 1773 by the Charleston Library Society, **The Charleston Museum**, 360 Meeting Street, (843) 722-2996, *www.charlestonmuseum.org*, deserves its own exhibit as the nation's oldest museum. On display are permanent exhibits on numerous subjects, including regional Native-American heritage, the Revolutionary War, the Civil War, the history and culture of plantation society, and regional African-American history. Of special interest is the internationally acclaimed Charleston Silver Exhibit, a collection of early colonial silver that includes George Washington's confirmation cup. Open Monday–Saturday, 9 A.M.–5 P.M.; Sunday, 1 P.M.–5 P.M. Admission charged, though discounted combination tickets may be purchased for this and the Heyward-Washington and Joseph Manigault houses.

◆ The College of Charleston's **Avery Research Center for African American History and Culture**, 125 Bull Street, (843) 953-7609, preserves the historic and cultural contributions African Americans have made to Charleston and the Lowcountry. Items on display include iron work by the legendary blacksmith, Philip Simmons, hand-woven fish and shrimp nets, coiled sweetgrass baskets, and hundreds of letters and documents. Also, you can tour a restored 19th-century classroom of the Avery Normal Institute, one of the first schools to educate freed slaves. Open Monday–Friday, noon–5 P.M. Free admission; donations accepted.

◆ Established by Confederate veterans in 1894, **The Confederate Museum,** Market Hall, 188 Meeting Street, (843) 723-1541, features a colossal collection of Confederate memorabilia, including uniforms, swords, guns, flags, and other unusual items such as a small lock of Robert E. Lee's hair. You'll also find men's and women's shoes,

Planes on the Yorktown's *deck*

letters, rare photographs of blockade runners, and Confederate currency. Open Tuesday–Saturday, 11 A.M.–3:30 P.M. Nominal admission fee.

◆ The **Karpeles Manuscript Museum,** 68 Spring Street, (843) 853-4651, is one of seven museums in the nation that houses philanthropist David Karpeles' collection of historically significant manuscripts. Karpeles rotates a portion of his more than one million documents from museum to museum every few months. At any given time in Charleston, you may catch the original draft of the Bill of Rights, Einstein's Theory of Relativity, the original manuscript of *The Wedding March*, or even Roget's *Thesaurus*. The museum's building has a fascinating history as well, dating back to 1791. Open Wednesday–Saturday, 11 A.M.–4 P.M. Free admission.

◆ Across the Cooper River from downtown Charleston, **Patriot's Point Naval & Maritime Museum,** 40 Patriots Point Road, Mount Pleasant, (843) 884-2727, is the world's largest naval museum. Hundreds of exhibits and interpretative displays are housed on the World War II aircraft carrier *Yorktown*, the submarine *Clagamore*, destroyer *Laffey*, and the Coast Guard cutter *Ingham*. Each vessel is a floating museum. The *Yorktown* is the most impressive, in part because of its size (you can get lost inside) and because of the fascinating black-and-white photographs throughout the ship that show the carrier in wartime action. In addition to the flotilla, there are more than two-dozen Navy and Air Force airplanes and helicopters, ranging in age from the World War II era to the first Gulf War. **The Medal of Honor Museum**, located on the *Yorktown's* hangar deck, details the names of all medal recipients from the Civil War onward. Open daily, 9 A.M.–6 P.M., October–March; 9 A.M.–7:30 P.M., April–September. Nominal admission.

Parks & Gardens

Visit Charleston in the spring and you'll find innumerable public and private gardens exploding in fragrance and color and overflowing their brick and wrought-iron borders onto the city's sidewalks. In addition to the following suggested gardens, many historic homes and plantations also feature gardens open to the public. (See *Historic Homes* and *Plantations*.)

Charleston CVB

♦ Located on the grounds of Magnolia Plantation, the **Audubon Swamp Garden,** 3550 Ashley River Road, (843) 571-1266 or 800-367-3517, *www.magnoliaplantation.com,* features hundreds of types of native and exotic plants that bloom year-round in a 60-acre, blackwater cypress and tupelo swamp. Boardwalks, dikes, and bridges

provide access through the swamp. In addition to the gorgeous plants, you'll encounter an array of wildlife, including blue herons, snowy egrets, otters, turtles, and alligators. Blinds along the boardwalk let you watch and photograph wildlife without being detected. Of historical note: bird artist and naturalist John J. Audubon visited the swamp to collect waterbird specimens in the mid 1800s. The site was also the location for the classic horror film, *Swamp Thing.* Load up on the bug spray for summer visits. Allow at least an hour for a self-guided tour. Open daily, 8 A.M.–dusk; winter hours vary. Call for details. Admission is charged; fee is separate from the admission rates to Magnolia Plantation.

♦ A quick 24 miles north of Charleston, **Cypress Gardens,** 3030 Cypress Gardens Road, Moncks Corner, (843) 553-0515, *www.cypressgardens.org,* is on the grounds of the former Dean Hall Plantation, a major, 18th-century rice plantation. In 1909, Benjamin

From This Point Forward

Shaded by oak and palmetto trees and lined with park benches, **White Point Gardens at the Battery** overlooks a tremendous view of Charleston Harbor. On this point, several notable moments in Charleston's history occured. In 1680, White

Library of Congress

The pavilion in White Point Gardens

Point was a giant oyster-shell dump for Native Americans (bleached-white shells gave the peninsula its name) that attracted settlers from the less-defensible Albemarle Point. In the 1700s, pirates—Stede Bonnet, among them—were executed here for sabotaging ships leaving the harbor and left to hang as warnings to other pirates. During the Civil War, residents gathered at the point to watch the shelling of Fort Sumter. And today the point rivals most downtown churches as a wedding site. On any given Saturday in May, you'll likely encounter a bride and groom nuptializing in the park's gazebo.

Kittredge purchased the property to use as a hunting preserve. He cleared trails through the swamp and planted thousands of azaleas, camellias, daffodils, and tea olives. In 1932, Cypress Gardens opened to the public, allowing visitors to board boats and float past the blooming plants. The gardens include a butterfly house, fresh-water aquarium, reptile center, antique-rose garden, and daylily display garden. If you're not up for paddling a flat-bottom boat through the swamp garden, opt for a guiding boat tour or view the gardens from the four miles of walking trails. Spring and fall are prime times to visit. Open daily, 9 A.M.–5 P.M. Nominal admission fee. Directions from Charleston: Take Interstate 26 west to Exit #208, where you take Route 52 west toward Goose Creek. After passing through Goose Creek, look for the intersection with Cypress Gardens Road. Turn right and drive to the road's end and the gardens' entrance.

Cypress Gardens

Performing Arts

♪ From the internationally renowned Spoleto festival (see *Spoleto*) to the city's resident theatrical and musical organizations, Charleston's arts scene is thriving. You'll have little trouble finding a performance to enjoy during your stay.

◆ The largest professional theater company in the state, the **Charleston Stage Company,** 135 Church Street, (843) 577-5967 or 1-800-454-7093, *www.charlestonstage.com,* produces plays and musicals on its home stage, the historic **Dock Street Theatre.** The 1736 Dock Street Theatre was the nation's first building constructed for the sole purpose of hosting theatrical performances. (The original building burned down and was replaced with an inn in 1800, which eventually fell into disrepair. In 1936, the inn was renovated to hold today's Dock Street Theatre, modeled after 18th-century, European playhouses.) In addition to performing classics such as *Romeo & Juliet* and *The Importance of Being Earnest,* Charleston Stage Company's productions include world premieres of original plays. Tickets are reasonable and shows often sell out.

◆ Founded in 1931, **The Footlight Players,** 20 Queen Street, (843) 722-4487, *www.footlightplayers.net,* is the state's longest continuously running theatre troupe. This group performs six productions each August–May in a renovated 1850s cotton warehouse. Productions have included *Master Class, Forever Plaid,* and *Sweet Charity.* Call for show times. ◆ The **College of Charleston Theatre Department,** 66 George Street, (843) 953-5604, supports five performing organizations, including Center Stage, which features student productions; Premiere Theatre, with faculty, student, and professional actors; and the Shakespeare Project, which produces one work by the Bard each summer. Most performances are in the Simons Center for the Arts on the college's beautiful, historic campus, located between Calhoun and Beaufain streets.

◆ The state's premiere ballet company, **Charleston Ballet Theater**, 477 King Street, (843) 723-7334, *www.charlestonballet.com,* touts itself as "not your run-of-the-mill ballet company." What that means is that alongside the requisite *Nutcracker Suite,* you may catch

Entrance to the Footlight Players' Theatre

a balletic rendition of the *Rocky Horror Picture Show.* Recent shows include *Peter Pan, Romeo & Juliet,* and *CBT Rocks,* a high-energy dance production featuring the music of Elvis and Elton John. The troupe's annual season runs October–June. In the spring, Charleston Ballet performs its highly praised production of *Rite of Spring* under the Angel Oak tree on Johns Island. Call or go online for performance schedule.

◆ The **Charleston Symphony Orchestra,** 77 Calhoun Street, (843) 723-7528, *www.charlestonsymphony.com,* performs five major concert series—the Masterworks, Sottile Chamber Orchestra, Charleston Pops, Saturdays in Town, and Small Fry series—that present a variety of musical styles to appeal to different audiences. Performance venues include Gaillard Auditorium on Calhoun Street, the Gibbes Museum, and historic Middleton Place. Call or check online for concert schedules and prices.

Plantations & Country Homes

Charleston CVB

Drayton Hall

Visiting Charleston without visiting the grand antebellum plantations and country homes along Ashley River Road is like vacationing in Paris and forgoing the Eiffel Tower. You don't do it. Here, then, are the area's major plantations and what you can expect to find at each. But first, directions to Ashley River Road: From downtown Charleston, take Route 17 west to the Ashley River Memorial Bridge. Stay in the right lane and exit onto Route 61/171 (St. Andrews Boulevard), which you follow for two miles until Route 61 departs to the left. Take Route 61/Ashley River Road north.

◆ You'll reach **Drayton Hall,** 3380 Ashley River Road, (843) 769-2600, *www.drayton-hall.org,* first. Set on the banks of the Ashley River and surrounded by 630 acres, this red-brick house is the oldest and one of the finest examples of Georgian-Palladian architecture in the South. It was built in 1742 as the country home of John Drayton, son of Thomas Drayton, Jr., who built Magnolia Plantation. Drayton Hall, which served as John Drayton's residence and not as a working plantation, has survived earthquakes, fires, and the Revolutionary and Civil wars completely intact. It stands today carefully preserved (not restored) almost exactly as it did on moving day in 1742: without electricity, running water, central heating, or furniture. Whatever emptiness you anticipate is quickly forgotten once the professional tour guides begin narrating the Drayton (family and building) history. Also on the grounds are two footpaths—the Marsh Walk and River Walk trails—which make for scenic strolls through the grounds. Open daily, 9:30 A.M.–4 P.M., March–October; 9:30 A.M.–3 P.M., November–February.

Library of Congress

Ceiling inside Drayton Hall

◆ Next on Ashley River Road: **Magnolia Plantation and Gardens**, 3550 Ashley River Road, (843) 571-1266 or 1-800-367-3517, *www.magnoliaplantation.com,* the ancestral home of the Drayton family for more than 325 years. Originally owned by Stephen Fox, a Barbadian who arrived on the banks of the Ashley River in the early 1670s, the plantation passed to Thomas Drayton, Jr., when he married Fox's daughter in 1676. It has remained in the Drayton family ever since. The first

Magnolia Plantation features a number of pleasant walking paths

home on the plantation burned in a fire, and Union troops set fire to the second home in 1865. The current building was a Drayton Family hunting lodge in Summerville that was dismantled, floated down the Ashley River, and reassembled here in 1873.

The house has an intriguing collection of antiques, but the plantation's gardens are the big attraction. Magnolia's 500 acres are home to the oldest gardens in America. Thomas and Ann Drayton (or more likely their slaves) kicked in the first spades to plant a Barbadian tropical garden. The gardens reached their current, natural glory in the mid 1800s under the watch of Reverend John Grimke Drayton, who brought the first imported azaleas to America. There's a topiary garden and a Biblical garden, featuring most of the plants identified in the Old and New testaments; a horticultural maze patterned from the one designed by England's Henry VIII for Hampton Court Palace; and the Audubon Swamp Garden (separate admission, see *Gardens.*) There are so many things to do—walking and biking paths, canoe rentals, a petting zoo, boat tours, and more—that admission is good for one return trip within seven days of purchase. Open daily, 8 A.M.–dusk, March–October. Call for winter hours. Admission fee charged for basic entry to plantation; house tours and other activities are extra.

◆ In 1741, Henry Middleton, a wealthy descendent of English planters who'd settled Charles Town in 1678, married Mary Williams and received in her dowry the 200-acre plantation and home they named **Middleton Place**, 4300 Ashley River Road, (843) 556-6020 or 1-800-782-3608, *www.middletonplace.org.* Middleton, who was President of the First Continental Congress, turned immediately to creating the plantation's gardens, modeled after 18th-century, formal English and European gardens. They feature walkways, lakes, grand terraces, and extended river and marshland vistas. Middleton descendents—including a signer of the Declaration of Independence, a South Carolina Governor, and a signer of the Ordinance of Secession—added to the gardens. Henry Middleton also built two "flanker" buildings adjacent to the original 1730, three-story plantation home. Union troops completely destroyed the original home in 1865, as well as the north flanker. In 1870, the family renovated the badly damaged south flanker, turning it into the main plantation resi-

Charleston CVB

Middleton Place Gardens

dence. Today the building houses a number of original family possessions. Visitors may tour the house, gardens, stables, and the small home that belonged to freed slaves, and hike, bike, kayak, and ride horseback on the grounds. Admission charged for stable, garden, and grounds tours; additional fees for house tours and sport activities. Open daily, 9 A.M.–5 P.M.

◆ Once one of the Lowcountry's largest cotton plantations with more than 17,000 acres, **Boone Hall Plantation,** Long Point Road (off Route 17 North), Mount Pleasant, (843) 884-4371, *www.boonehallplantation.com,* was settled by Major John Boone, who acquired the land in grants from the Lords Proprietors in the early 1680s. In 1743, his son, Captain Thomas Boone, planted the avenue of live oaks that line the half-mile drive toward the main house. In the 19th Century, ownership of Boone Hall passed to the Horlbeck family, who added pecan groves and brick and tile production to the plantation's revenue source. (In fact, the main home you see today, plus the cotton gin, slave cabins, and garden walls were built with original brick made at Boone Hall.) The setting for several films and television shows, including the "North and South" television miniseries, the plantation and 1930 estate home remain a private residence. (Only the first floor is open to visitors.) There are ample sites to explore, including a "slave street," where nine original slave cabins stand. Admission is charged. From Labor day–March, open 9 A.M.–5 P.M., Monday–Saturday; 1 P.M.–4 P.M., Sunday. From April–Labor Day, open 8:30 A.M.–6:30 P.M., Monday–Saturday; 1 P.M.–5 P.M., Sunday.

Shops & Stops

To gauge how extensive the shopping opportunities are in Charleston, consider that many national and regional travel agencies offer shopping trips to Charleston for visitors who wish to do nothing but browse and buy. The major retail thoroughfares are **King Street** and **Meeting Street,** but don't limit your retail therapy to those. The city's many side streets and alleys feature hundreds of unique shops. How to begin? Park the car and start walking. The following are shops you won't want to miss.

◆ The **Old City Market,** on North and South Market streets between Meeting and East Bay, is the city's most prominent shopping scene. Built in 1841, the brick buildings are home to an assortment of vendors whose wares include jewelry, Charleston prints, lowcountry cooking mixes, clothing, antiques, and Gullah sweetgrass baskets. ◆ The evolution of shopping is apparent across the street at the **Shops at Charleston Place,** 130 Market Street, (843) 722-4900 or 1-800-611-5545, *www.charlestonplaceshops.com,* a collection of high-end retailers

located on the ground level of Charleston Place Hotel. Here you'll find national retailers such as April Cornell, Gucci, Laura Ashley, Mont Blanc, and Yves Delorme Paris. Waldenbooks operates a bookstore inside Charleston Place with an outstanding collection of regional titles.

◆ Promising "department store variety in a boutique setting," **Worthwhile,** 268 King Street, (843) 723-4418 or 1-877-454-0876, *www.shopworthwhile.com,* is indeed worth a visit.

Shopping on King Street

Charleston CVB

Sweetgrass baskets in the Old City Market

You'll find women's, children's, and infant's apparel; fashion accessories; personal care gifts; bed and bath products; and items for the home. From soaps and candleholders to watering cans and gift books, the selection guarantees you'll find something for the friend who seems to have everything. ◆ For elegant, tasteful men's clothing and accessories, head to **Ben Silver Collection,** 149 King Street, (843) 231-7458 or 1-800-221-4671, *www.bensilver.com.* Famous for its striped and crested tie collection, as well as a massive array of blazer buttons, Ben Silver also carries women's clothing, jewelry, and fashion accessories. ◆ One of Charleston's oldest clothing stores, **Berlin's Clothiers,** 114 King Street, (843) 722-1665, *www.berlinsclothing.com,* opened in 1883 and has dressed generations of men, young and old. The family-owned retailer sells classic clothing and accessories. Ladies can step next door to **Berlin's for Women,** where they'll find sportswear and an assortment of evening dresses from recognized designers.

◆ **Charleston Gardens,** 61 Queen Street, (843) 723-0252 or 1-800-469-0118, *www.charlestongardens.com,* is such a welcoming shop, you'll be tempted to take a cup of complimentary tea and sit awhile amongst the collection of English and French garden merchandise or in the garden out back. The shop carries a selection of furniture and home and garden accents—think pots, tools, statuaries, fountains, and dining accessories—all selected and imported directly by the owners. They'll ship anywhere or hold purchases until you're ready to leave town. ◆ Looking for that special something for your four-legged pal? Stop in **Alpha Dog Omega Cat,** 40 Archdale Street, (843) 723-1579, *www.alphadogomega-cat.com,* for items ranging from designer collars and leashes to gourmet dog treats. You'll even find jewelry, clothes, and home accessories for pet lovers.

Spa & Massage

When your muscles ache from long hikes, strenuous golf matches, or hours on your feet shopping, make an appointment at one of Charleston's myriad spas, where you'll find a range of services, including facials, body wraps, hair and nail treatments, and massage. The following are some of the better bets. The **Charleston-Place Hotel European Spa**, 205 Meeting Street, (843) 722-4900, *www.charleston-place.com,* is a multi-million dollar facility with a complete fitness center. ◆ **Earthling Day Spa**, 334 East Bay Street, (843) 722-4737, *www.earthlingdayspa.com,* which bills itself as the Charleston area's first day spa, has a Pilates exercise studio in addition to its spa services. ◆ Repeatedly recognized by *Elle* magazine as one of the best in the Southeast, **Stella Nova Spa Salon,** 78 Society Street, (843) 723-0909, *www.stella-nova.com,* is located in an 1850s house. The full-service spa also operates a retail shop at 292 King Street, 1-800-577-6682.

Spoleto & Piccolo Spoleto

◆ Every spring from late May–mid June, many of the world's greatest musicians, dancers, actors, and visual artists converge in Charleston for **Spoleto Festival USA,** (843) 579-3100, *www.spoletousa.org,* a 17-day cultural extravaganza of exhibits and more than 100 performances. Founded in 1977 by Pulitzer Prize-winning composer Gian Carlo Menotti, Spoleto has become the largest, multi-dimensional arts festival in North America. More than 100,000 visitors attend the event, which showcases traditional and experimental arts, ranging from opera, modern dance, classical ballet, chamber and symphonic music, jazz, and theater to literary and visual arts. Past performers have included the Harlem Dance Theater, the Royal Shakespeare Company, the Westminster Choir, and Ireland's Gate Theatre. Performance venues across the city include historic churches, auditoriums, theaters, and homes. The grand opening is in front of the Old Exchange on East Bay Street and the concert finale is at Middleton Place.

◆ **Piccolo Spoleto,** 133 Church Street, (843) 724-7305, *www.piccolospoleto.com,* runs concurrently with Spoleto, but the emphasis is on performers and artists primarily from the Southeast. Organized by the City of Charleston, Piccolo Spoleto features more than 700 presentations, many of which are free. (Those that aren't cost far less than Spoleto's events.)

Walking & Bus Tours

◆ Whether your interests lean toward the Civil War, African-American heritage, architecture, churches, or haunted places, there's a walking or bus tour to suit. The following is just a sampling of the city's many reputable tour companies. (For an extensive list, swing by the Charleston Visitor Center on Meeting Street.) ◆ To learn about Charleston from a 12th-generation Charlestonian, join **Anna's House and Garden Tour,** 122 Queen Street, (843) 577-5931, *www.ghostwalk.net,* conducted by Anna Taylor Blythe. Ms. Blythe's walking tours depart from Charleston Gardens at 61 Queen Street, last approximately two hours, and include refreshments at the famous Palmer House on the Battery. She also operates a nightly ghost walk. Call for departure times. ◆ To learn the history of the local Gullah culture, join **Gullah Tours,** (843) 763-7551, *www.gullahtours.com,* for a two-hour journey on an air-conditioned bus to Charleston's many important African-American sites. Tours depart from the African American Museum of Art, 43 John Street. ◆ A one-stop shop for Charleston walking tours is **The Original Charleston Walks,** 58 ½ Broad Street, (843) 577-3800 or 1-800-729-3420, *www.charlestonwalks.com,* where the menu of tours includes: "The Original Charleston Walk," "Slavery & Freedom," "Pirates and Buccaneers," "Historic Homes Walk," "Lowcountry Ghost Walk," and "Wicked Charleston." Tour groups are limited to 15 people to keep the walks intimate and to encourage interaction between guide and guests. All tours depart from the company's Broad Street location.

Rest Easy

Sleep Well

Milk & cookies, wine & cheese, after-dinner cordials, turndown service...it's easy get accustomed to lowcountry pampering. With a long history of hosting discerning travelers, the majority of Charleston's inns has high standards (and prices that reflect them). There are dozens more outstanding properties than listed here; the following is merely a sampling, ranging from civilized cozy to the luxurious crème de la crème.

Accommodations Pricing

Less than $100	Inexpensive	$
$100-150	Moderate	$$
$151-200	Expensive	$$$
More than $200	Very Expensive	$$$$

Prices are per room, per night, based on double occupancy during peak seasons. Note that B&Bs and most country inns include breakfast in the rate.

Ansonborough Inn • If space to spread out appeals to you, the Ansonborough Inn's 37 suites, which range from 450 square feet all the way to 750 in the Admiral's Suite, make a great choice. (Ceilings range from 12 to 20 feet.) Housed in a 1901 stationer's warehouse in the historic district, the inn was recently renovated. Rooms feature high, canopied rice beds, plantation shutters, and nautical memorabilia in honor of sea captain, Lord Anson, for whom the inn is named. Expect a full range of amenities, including fold-out sofas, in-room safes, refrigerators, microwaves, fireplaces, and garden tubs. Huge beams and exposed brick remain in common areas and rooms, giving the flavor of an upscale lodge. Continental breakfast is included, as is an afternoon wine reception. Lemonade and cookies served throughout the day. • *21 Hasell Street, Charleston, SC 29401, ☎ (843) 723-1655 or 1-800-522-2073, www.ansonboroughinn.com • $$-$$$$*

Charleston Place • A favorite of seasoned, luxury travelers, Charleston Place has everything you'd expect (and a few things you wouldn't) from a world-class hotel, including elegant rooms; impeccable service; an excellent location; a private spa with massage and salon services, a hot tub, sauna, and steam room; a health club; a pool with retractable roof; and a four-star restaurant. This centrally located, grand hotel treats the eye with twin sweeping staircases, gleaming glass chandeliers, Italian marble floors topped with plush rugs, and rooms filled with period antiques. The hotel's lobby level includes 32 elegant shops, two restaurants, and a lounge. Above are 440 rooms, 46 luxury suites, and 80 concierge-level rooms, where treatment gets even more lavish. Breakfast, not included in the rate, is available in-room

or in the Palmetto Café. • *205 Meeting Street, Charleston, SC 29401, ☎ (843) 722-4900 or 1-800-611-5545, www.charlestonplacehotel.com • $$$$*

French Quarter Inn • A pillow menu with seven choices pretty much defines the level of luxury offered by the French Quarter Inn. Located in the heart of the historic district, this brand new inn, designed in French Urban architecture, features 50 elegantly appointed rooms and suites with fireplaces, whirlpool tubs, and private balconies. A smiling bellman greets guests and ushers them up the grand spiral, marble staircase to an expansive lobby, meticulously decorated and accented with armfuls of fresh orchids, calla lilies, and seasonal flowers. If you can't resist a bit of work while vacationing, the inn offers five suites complete with computer, Internet, printer, and fax. A Continental breakfast, served on silver in-room or in the lobby and adjoining terrace, is complimentary, as are champagne and ladyfingers at check-in, an afternoon wine reception, turndown service, and round-the-clock coffee, tea, and snacks. • *166 Church Street, Charleston, SC 29401, ☎ (843) 722-1900 or 1-866-812-1900, www.fqicharleston.com • $$$-$$$$*

The Governor's House • Upon entering this historic home, your eye is drawn to a majestic hardwood staircase that curves around and up with exquisite grace. Beyond the entry, common areas are filled with light, carved hardwood, and antiques reflecting the home's 240-year heritage. Seven rooms and four suites feature four-poster, arched-canopy beds, elegant baths, and fresh flowers. Some feature fireplaces and private porches. Innkeeper Karen Spell Shaw, full of enthusiasm and quick to smile, takes great pride in the high level of service provided by her inn. A native Charlestonian, she's an invaluable source of information. Your stay includes an extensive Continental breakfast, lowcountry afternoon tea, and evening sherry. • *117 Broad Street, Charleston, SC 29401,* ☎ *(843) 720-2070 or 1-800-720-9812, www.governorshouse.com* • *$$$–$$$$*

The Inn at Middleton Place • Travel 25 minutes from Charleston's historic center and arrive miles back in time to a 17th-century rice plantation. Tucked into a pine and live oak forest on the grounds of Middleton Place (see *Plantations*), this architecturally stunning inn features 53 rooms, each with an entire wall of glass overlooking the Ashley River. Rooms include minimalist interiors of wood and tile with fireplaces, stocked refrigerators, and glass-block baths. Some have balconies. Included in your stay are kayaking, bicycling, guided nature hikes, access for two to the Middleton Place house museum and manicured gardens (worth $60), a hot breakfast cooked to order in the lake house, hors d'oeuvres in the lodge, and snacks and drinks in your refrigerator. Horseback riding is extra. Kayaking is especially pristine here. The Ashley River offers tidal creeks where paddlers can see herons, egrets, other wildlife, and even shipwrecks. The onsite restaurant overlooks a scenic pond and serves lowcountry-plantation fare for lunch and dinner. • *4290 Ashley River Road, Charleston, SC 29414,* ☎ *(843) 556-0500 or 1-800-543-4774, www.middletonplace.org* • *$$$$*

Planters Inn • The epitome of a first-rate, European-style hotel, Planters Inn has earned membership in the prestigious Relais &

Chateaux, an international collection of ultra-fine small hotels and restaurants. Large granite columns and steps welcome guests into the 1844 Federal-style building in the heart of Charleston's historic district. Tall, sunny windows framed by tasseled formal drapes border the comfortable parlor, where a hushed, elegant interior offers wonderful refuge from Charleston's busy streets. The 56 rooms and six suites feature richly upholstered furniture, beds with handmade lace canopies, and Roman-marble baths. The quietest rooms overlook the lovely courtyard garden with a fountain and reflecting pool. The inn's second "Piazza" building has a newer feel, but retains a sense of history. Amenities include afternoon sherry or port, a landscaped rooftop terrace, and some rooms with fireplaces and whirlpool baths. Breakfast, not included, is served on silver in your room. Planters Inn is also home to Peninsula Grille, one of Charleston's most-distinguished restaurants. • *112 North Market Street, Charleston, SC 29401,* ☎ *(843) 722-2345 or 1-800-845-7082, www.plantersinn.com* • *$$$$*

Two Meeting Street Inn • Built in 1892 as a wedding gift from father to daughter, this inn is as pretty as a spring bride. It is Charleston's oldest inn, yet kept forever young through the loving care of the family through whom it's passed over the years. Overlooking the Battery and Charleston Harbor, Two Meeting Street is one of very few inns in the fiercely guarded residential area south of Broad. The often-painted Queen Anne Victorian inn, skirted with wrap-around porches, features graceful arches and a fluted turret. The grounds include restful gardens with huge live oaks veiled in Spanish moss. Inside you'll find Tiffany glass, gleaming mahogany, waxed English oak, Oriental rugs, floral bou-

quets, and streaming sunshine that illumi-
nates not one mote of dust. The seven
rooms and two suites continue the elegance
with canopy beds, high ceilings, and spacious baths; some rooms have a fireplace, sitting area, and veranda. A favorite is the Spell
Room with its lovely turret window.
Innkeepers Pete and Jean Spell, natives of
Charleston, embody Southern grace and
hospitality, evident in their genteel, lowcountry afternoon tea and continental
breakfasts, which may include baked pear
chutney, oversized fresh muffins, and homemade applesauce. • *2 Meeting Street at the
Battery, Charleston, SC 29401,* ☎ *(843) 723-
7322, www.twomeetingstreet.com* • *$$–$$$$*

Vendue Inn & The Inn at Vendue • This
inn has two buildings with two names
across the street from one another. The
Vendue Inn houses the common areas,
where complimentary evening refreshments
and continental breakfasts are served, and 45
guest rooms of moderate size and décor. The
Inn at Vendue has 20 newer rooms and
suites with upgraded amenities such as ele-
gant, modern baths and fresh, interesting
furnishings. Guests enjoy a central location,
just steps from Charleston's Waterfront Park,
with a long, paved path ideal for walking or
jogging. • *19 Vendue Range, Charleston, SC
29401,* ☎ *(843) 577-7970 or 1-800-845-
7900, www.vendueinn.com* • *$$–$$$$*

Wentworth Mansion • Now here's a mansion that looks like a mansion, complete
with four grand stories, a mansard roof
with cast-iron railing, and a cupola with
windows overlooking the city. The interior
of this 1886 Georgian-style home is 90 percent original and features Austrian crystal
chandeliers, Tiffany stained-glass windows,

heart-pine floors, carved woodwork, and
colored tile. The 14 rooms and four suites
are all befitting a mansion—spacious with
high ceilings and luxurious baths that
include wonderful modern luxuries like
whirlpool tubs. Wentworth is set in a quiet
residential area, an easy 10-minute walk
from historic-district touring and shopping.
Complimentary breakfast consists of a
European-style buffet with server assistance.
Afternoon tea and lemonade are served, as
well as wine with hors d'oeuvres in the
evenings. On the grounds is the highly
touted Charleston restaurant, Circa 1886. •
149 Wentworth Street, Charleston, SC 29401,
☎ *(843) 853-1886 or 1-888-466-1886,
www.wentworthmansion.com* • *$$$$*

Woodlands Resort & Inn • If you're in the
mood for world-class pampering, here's your
spot. At the end of a long forested lane, this
1906 Revival-style home is a member of the
highly exclusive Relais & Chateaux association of fine inns. Accordingly, Richard Gere
and Harry Belafonte are among the noteworthy who've sought low-profile R&R among
Woodlands' 42 private acres. All of the 19
suites are grand; some are simply grander
than others. Suites vary, but include such
amenities as fireplaces, whirlpool tubs, heated towel racks, and the resort's signature yellow roses. The inn features subdued, traditional décor with a West-Indies influence.
Meals are an art form at Woodlands, home
to South Carolina's only AAA Five Diamond
restaurant. The grounds include a pool, tennis courts, croquet lawn, and loaner bicycles.
Your concierge is ready to help arrange day
excursions for touring, sailing, fishing,
horseback riding, and kayaking, as well as
hiking and canoeing in the nearby Francis
Beidler Forest. However, the danger here is

that you'll be reluctant to leave the cocoon of luxury. • *125 Parsons Road, Summerville, SC 29483,* ☎ *(843) 875-2600 or 1-800-774-9999, www.woodlandsinn.com* • *$$$$*

Other Recommended Downtown Inns

Elliott House Inn, 78 Queen Street, ☎ (843) 723-1855 or 1-800-729-1855, *www.elliotthouseinn.com,* $$–$$$; **John Rutledge House Inn,** 116 Broad Street, ☎

(843) 723-7999 or 1-866-720-2609 *www.johnrutledgehouseinn.com,* $$$–$$$$; **The Meeting Street Inn,** 173 Meeting Street, ☎ (843) 723-1882 or 1-800-842-8022, *www.meetingstreetinn.com,* $$–$$$

The John Rutledge House

D i n e   W e l l

Defining lowcountry cooking is like nailing Jell-o to a tree. Ten different people will give you ten different answers, but agreement seems to rest on a style that blends seafood, fruits, and locally harvested vegetables. With a multi-cultured heritage combining West Indies, African, Native American, and European influences, Charleston's cuisine is world-class. The city is teeming with great restaurants, from everyday eateries to haute cuisine, and the following list barely touches on the options. Reservations are required at some, recommended at all.

82 Queen • Set on land within the original walled city of Charles Town, 82 Queen features a verdant garden courtyard, greenhouse, and 10 private dining rooms serving the much-lauded lowcountry cuisine of Executive Chef Steve Stone. Using fresh, home-grown ingredients, Stone creates such appetizers as baked oysters with spicy sausage, crabmeat, and cornbread stuffing, smoked Gouda cheese and horseradish cream. Entrée choices range from black pepper-grilled rib eye with mashed red skin potatoes, caramelized onions, melted brie and asparagus, to crispy roasted duck with wild rice pilaf, cherry Grand Marnier glaze with haricot verts and baby carrots. A delectable dessert menu and award-winning wine

list are also available. Open daily for lunch and dinner. • *82 Queen Street, Charleston,* ☎ *(843) 723-7591 or 1-800-849-0082*

Charleston Grill • The soft sounds of the Frank Duvall Jazz Trio greet visitors upon entering this candlelit, wood-paneled dining room, while the aroma of French-trained Chef Bob Waggoner's cuisine sets the stage for an epicurean evening. The menu changes seasonally, but may include such appetizers as baked country rabbit, served with seared foie gras and vidalia onions with slivered mushrooms in a Hollywood sausage sawmill gravy, and such entrées as the grilled diver scallops over diced lobster, baby clam and smoked bacon orzo. Wine and dessert lists complement the meal, rounding out an evening of simple elegance. Open nightly for dinner. • *224 King Street, Charleston,* ☎ *(843) 577-4522*

Circa 1886 • Be careful whom you take to this five-star restaurant because you might be moved to propose. Expect small rooms with soft music, deep romantic booths, a 280-bottle wine list, and exceptionally attentive service. And then, of course, there's the food. Order Carolina crab cake soufflé with mango puree, pineapple relish, and crispy sweet potatoes to start; seared molasses lacquered duck breast with sweet potato hash and bourbon pan sauce as a main dish; and mango coconut cream soup to finish. Circa 1886 presents a changing seasonal menu of lowcountry cooking with a light, contemporary touch. Open for dinner, Monday–Saturday. • *149 Wentworth Street, Charleston,* ☎ *(843) 853-7828*

High Cotton • Step off Charleston's busy streets into this high-ceilinged dining room with gently paddling rattan fans and prepare for a spirited evening of good drink and fine food. Executive Chef Jason Scholz spit roasts and grills meats, game, and seafood that are all about great flavor without the fancy frills. Accompanied by a selection from the compelling wine list, meals are a complete experience in the best of American dining. Dinner served nightly; brunch served Saturday and Sunday. • *199 East Bay Street, Charleston,* ☎ *(843) 724-3815*

Hominy Grill • A favorite with locals, this little café features a simple, stylish décor inside and a patio bordered in tall, green bamboo outside. Chef and owner, Robert Stehling, serves up "Southern comfort food."

Spectacular shrimp and grits and one-of-a-kind cornbread are just two items that will have you purring with culinary comfort. Fun, imaginative vegetables, fish, crab, pork, duck, black-eyed pea croquettes—whatever you're in the mood for, Hominy Grill surely has it. A bit too far from Charleston's main historic district for a stroll but worth the five-minute drive. Parking available. Breakfast and lunch, Monday–Friday; dinner, Monday–Saturday; brunch Sunday. • *207 Rutledge Avenue, Charleston,* ☎ *(843) 937-0930*

Jestine's Kitchen • Fancy it's not, but Jestine's excels at homestyle food, including meatloaf, fried shrimp po boys, corn bread, fried green tomatoes, and even peanut butter and banana sandwiches. The selection is wide, the flavors are delicious, and there's plenty to fill you up. Come casual to this lively café and expect service that's friendly and prompt. Open for lunch and dinner. Closed Mondays. • *251 Meeting Street, Charleston,* ☎ *(843) 722-7224*

Magnolia's Uptown-Down South • Located on the site of Charleston's original Customs House, Magnolia's serves imaginative American cuisine with Down South zest in a high-ceilinged dining room with wood floors. The menu changes seasonally but may include such appetizers as pan-seared sea scallops on sweet corn hoe cakes with a caramelized, apple-smoked-bacon, cream and balsamic syrup, and such entrées as the grilled mahi mahi on a creek shrimp and pearl hominy succotash with blackened green tomatoes, lump crab, and tomato corn butter. Magnolia's features an award-winning wine list. Open daily for lunch and dinner, as well as for brunch on Sundays. • *185 East Bay Street, Charleston,* ☎ *(843) 577-7771*

Peninsula Grill • One of Charleston's most-celebrated restaurants (with good reason), Peninsula Grill prepares modern American cuisine with contemporary Southern flair. Translated, that means such fare as a grouper, shrimp, and salmon tart with sun dried tomatoes, goat cheese and herbed brioche crumbs, or perhaps benne crusted rack of New Zealand lamb with wild mushrooms, potatoes, and coconut-mint pesto. The wine steward will be happy to recommend vintages from the award-winning, 375-bottle wine list that includes both surprises and familiar favorites. The mood of the dining room is sophisticated with velvet, antiques, cypress woodwork, and a dominant painting of a plantation mule like no other. Alfresco dining takes place in the garden courtyard with a reflecting pool. Dinner served nightly. • *112 North Market Street, Charleston,* ☎ *(843) 723-0700*

Slightly North of Broad • Lively chatter and heavenly aromas define the dining room of this popular bistro. An eclectic décor is capped off at the rear with a huge brick arch through which Executive Chef Frank Lee cooks up lowcountry cuisine with a multicultural twist. A native South Carolinian with classic French training, Lee turns out flavors that are both robust and light. Emphasis is on regional seafood and vegetables. Entrées include shrimp and grits, house-cured and smoked, grilled pork loin, and Maverick beef tenderloin topped with deviled crab cake and béarnaise. Save room for dessert, as two outstanding choices are sour cream apple pie and crème brûlée. The restaurant has an outstanding and extensive wine selection. Dinner served nightly. Lunch served Monday–Friday. • *192 East Bay Street, Charleston,* ☎ *(843) 723-3424*

Sticky Fingers • Tuck in your bib for some finger-licking barbecue at Sticky Fingers, started locally by three school chums. Come as you are to this restaurant with its casual brick walls, wood booths, and blues music, and where the plate of ribs will conquer even the mightiest appetite. There's a whole selection of barbecue sauces from which to choose. Looking for lighter fare? Sticky Fingers also serves salads, sandwiches, and chicken. Lunch and dinner served daily. • *Two locations: 235 Meeting Street, Charleston,* ☎ *(843) 853-7427 and 1200 North Main Street, Summerville,* ☎ *(843) 871-7427*

Woodlands Resort & Inn Restaurant • There is just one opinion about South Carolina's only AAA Five Diamond restaurant: a meal here is nothing less than art. Executive Chef Ken Vedrinski has trained at so many Four- and Five-diamond restaurants that he's an atlas of food knowledge. To say the cuisine is "new American with a regional influence" doesn't tell the tale. Expect presentations almost too lovely to touch and flavors that range from impossibly delicate to positively enchanting. Menus change, but anticipate such selections as filet of Kobe beef with cippoline onion, fingerling potato, and a Barolo wine reduction, or a butter-poached Maine lobster with maitake mushroom "egg foo yong" and Asian spices. Diners can choose from a five-course tasting menu, or an à la carte menu. The full-time sommelier will ensure that you enjoy the appropriate wine with your selections. Leisurely meals take place in a sophisticated, two-level dining room overlooking the Woodlands' lawn and gardens. The restaurant is approximately 25 minutes from historic Charleston. Breakfast, lunch, and dinner served daily. Closed Sundays for dinner. • *125 Parsons Road, Summerville,* ☎ *(843) 875-2600*

Picnic Packing

Serving a variety of eggs, croissants, and homemade jams, **Baker's Café** 214 King Street, ☎ (843) 577-2694, *www.bakerscafe.com*, might lull you into thinking all they serve is breakfast. However, a long list of sandwiches, salads, and lunch entrées is also available, whether you're dining in or taking it to the beach. • **The Bookstore Café** 412 King Street, ☎ (843) 720-8843, *www.bookstorecafecateringandevents.com*, serves unique breakfasts all day, as well as gourmet sandwiches, salads, pastries, coffee, and more. Stop in and enjoy the rustic ambience or order one of their extraordinary boxed lunches for the road. • **Moose Mountain Coffee and Tea**, 50 North Market Street, ☎ (843) 853-0008, *www.moosemountain.com*, has a large selection of drinks and desserts, as well as soups, salads, and sandwiches.

Just Desserts

With all of that biking, hiking, walking, and kayaking, you'll need to add back a few calories. The popular recommendation for satisfying a sweet tooth in Charleston is **Kaminsky's,** 78 North Market Street, ☎ (843) 853-8270, where you'll find desserts from sundaes to countless, freshly made cakes and pies, including apple caramel spice cake, Italian cream cake, and caramelized banana buttercream cake. Good stuff. • Just on the other side of the street is **Ben and Jerry's,** 96 North Market Street, ☎ (843) 853-3888, if you're hankering for some hardcore ice cream. • Also, **The Sugar Plantation,** 48 North Market Street, ☎ (843) 853-3924, sells fudge, pralines, chocolates, and more.

A Long-Weekend Itinerary

Day One

After breakfast at your inn or B&B, head to **Coastal Expeditions** (page 196) in Mount Pleasant for a three-hour sea kayak tour of Charleston Harbor. Return to Charleston to have lunch at **Slightly North of Broad** (page 227). Walk Charleston Peninsula south to explore **White Point Gardens** (page 214), the Battery, and the city's most-aristocratic neighborhood, south of Broad Street. Work your way up the peninsula, stopping to photograph and visit **various churches** (page 212), **historic homes** (page 209), and **historic buildings** (page 207).

Return to your inn to shower and freshen up for dinner at **The Peninsula Grill** (page 227). Then join Anna Taylor Blythe for her **Ghost Walk** tour (page 220) of the city at night. Lights out.

Day Two

Linger over breakfast to soak in your vacation, and then drive north for some **back roads touring** on the National Scenic Byway, the **Ashley River Road** (page 203). Head to **Middleton Place** (page 204) to tour the house and gardens. Eat lunch at the restaurant at the **Inn at Middleton Place** (page 223). Then, rent bicycles to ride along the plantation's nature tours or join a guided horseback trail ride through Middleton Place's 200 acres.

Return to Charleston to shop at the **Old City Market** (page 218) before returning to your inn to shower and prepare for dinner at **Circa 1886** (page 226). Bring the day to a close with a romantic, horse-drawn carriage tour of downtown Charleston with **Charleston Carriage Company** (page 206).

Day Three

After breakfast at your inn, spend the morning in Charleston's **shops & stops** (page 218), **antiques dealers** (page 200), and **art galleries** (page 202). Take in a massage at **Stella Nova Spa Salon** (page 219) before swinging by **Baker's Café** to pick up a picnic lunch to take to **Beachwalker Park** (page 199) on Kiawah Island. Spend the remainder of your time on the beach, enjoying the sun, sand, and surf before showering up at the park and reluctantly returning home.

Additional Information

Charleston Area Convention and Visitors Bureau, 375 Meeting Street, Charleston, SC 29403, ☎ (843) 853-8000, *www.charlestoncvb.com* is open daily, 8:30 A.M.–5:30 P.M., except major holidays. A trained staff is available to answer questions and provide assistance. Free brochures, a courtesy phone, maps, local publications for sale, and restrooms are available.

Kiawah Island Visitor Center, 22 Beachwalker Drive, Kiawah Island, SC 29455, ☎ (843) 768-5116, *www.welcometokiawah.com*, is open weekdays, 9 A.M.–5 P.M. in the summer. Hours vary seasonally.

Mount Pleasant - Isle of Palms Visitor Center, 311 Johnnie Dodds Boulevard, Mount Pleasant, SC 29464, ☎ (843) 849-9172, *www.townofmountpleasant.com*, is open daily, 9 A.M.–5:30 P.M., except major holidays.

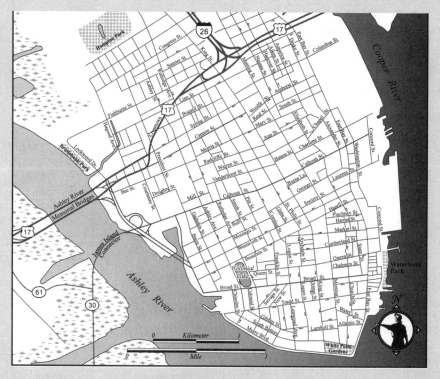

The Charleston Peninsula

Throughout the history of this city, it has risen again and again from the ravages of fires, earthquakes, hurricanes, and wars. And always Charleston rises like a lady, one who knows who she is and remains true to herself.

– Ann Dorer, Southern Lady Magazine

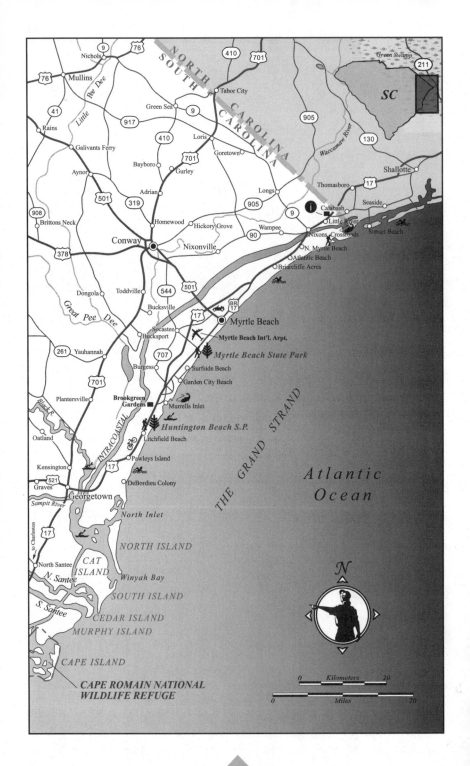

North Carolina
South Carolina

Nichols
76
9

Mullins
Pee Dee
76

41
Rains

Galivants Ferry

Aynor

501

908
Brittons Neck

378

Dongola

261 Yauhannah

701

Plantersville

Oatland

Kensington
521
Graves

Sampit River

Little

917

410

319

Adrian

Homewood

Conway

544

Great Pee Dee

Toddville

Bucksville

17
Socastee
Bucksport

707
Burgess

Brookgreen
Gardens

Green Sea
9

Loris
701
Goretown

Bayboro
Gurley

Longs
905

Hickory Grove
90
Nixonville

501

Tabor City

410
701

SC

905

Waccamaw River

130

Shallotte

Thomasboro
17

Calabash
Little River

Seaside

Nixons Crossroads
N. Myrtle Beach
Atlantic Beach
Briarcliffe Acres

Wampee

BR
17
Myrtle Beach
Myrtle Beach Int'l. Arpt.

Myrtle Beach State Park

Surfside Beach
Garden City Beach

Murrells Inlet

Huntington Beach S.P.
Litchfield Beach
Pawleys Island

DeBordieu Colony

THE GRAND STRAND

Atlantic
Ocean

Green Swamp
211

Sunset Beach

INTRACOASTAL

Georgetown

Black R.

North Inlet

to Charleston
17
North Santee
N. Santee

CAT
ISLAND

NORTH ISLAND

Winyah Bay

S. Santee

SOUTH ISLAND

CEDAR ISLAND
MURPHY ISLAND

CAPE ISLAND

CAPE ROMAIN NATIONAL
WILDLIFE REFUGE

N

Kilometers   20

0   Miles   20

Myrtle Beach and the Grand Strand, South Carolina

Including Georgetown, Pawleys Island, Litchfield Beach, Murrells Inlet, and North Myrtle Beach

Southern Carolina's 200-mile coast has two distinct regions marked by topographical, historical, and social differences. The Lowcountry, which encompasses roughly 140 miles from the Georgia State line north to Winyah Bay, stews slowly in its long, refined past. The fragmented coast is riddled with broad rivers, tidal creeks, vast marshes, and a scattershot of barrier islands. From Winyah Bay north, the coast spans 60 miles in a relatively unbroken stretch of beach to the North Carolina State line. This is the Grand Strand, essentially a long island bordered by the Atlantic Ocean to the east and the Intracoastal Waterway to the west. Gone, for the most part, are the islands, rivers, colonial history, and lazy, lowcountry pace—all replaced by a sprawl of 20th-century beach towns, glitzy resort developments, and the vibrant, superstore-sized vacation destination, Myrtle Beach.

Save for Florida's Disneyland and New Jersey's Atlantic City, no place on the East Coast draws as many visitors as the Strand. Each year, 13 million vacationers arrive, looking for low scores on the golf course, performances by big-name country music stars, fresh-seafood buffets, and of course, good tans. But there's more to the region than the go-go pace of Myrtle Beach. Traveling south on the coast toward Georgetown, the glitz decreases, particularly in the colonial resort Pawleys Island, the mid 20th-century Town of Litchfield Beach, and the still-developing pri-

Myrtle Beach Area CVB

A home in Georgetown's historic district

vate enclaves of Prince George and DeBordieu Colony, all of which welcome upscale beach and golf vacationers who rarely (if at all) visit Myrtle Beach during their stay.

The southern anchor of the Strand is Georgetown, South Carolina's third-oldest settlement founded in 1729 on Winyah Bay, where four rivers—the Sampit, Black, Pee Dee, and Waccamaw—converge to flow into the Atlantic. Once the epicenter of the state's colonial rice empire—vast plantations lined the surrounding rivers—Georgetown was a wealthy port with a fashionable downtown and cultured population. A well-preserved historic district and an attractive riverfront wharf remain today, tucked away from the city's hardscrabble steel and paper mills and commercial sprawl.

Native Americans were the first to settle the area. Various tribes—the Winyah and Waccamaw among them—established villages along the region's rivers. In fact, the Strand's primary highway, Route 17, follows an Indian trading path that connected these villages with those of Woodland tribes from the coastal regions of Virginia and further north. But the Native-American presence would diminish rapidly following the arrival of European explorers in 1521, when Spanish sailors began abducting Indians as slaves and introduced diseases against which the natives had no defense. From 1600 to 1715, more than 85 percent of South Carolina's coastal Indians disappeared.

English settlers began moving north from Charles Town in the late 17th and early 18th centuries to trade with the Winyah Bay tribes. The value of four large rivers converging in one bay was immediately apparent to the English and by 1729, Georgetown's founder, Elisha Screven, had laid out a plan for the city. (Georgetown's historic district adheres exactly to this plan; neither street names nor lot numbers have changed, and many original houses still stand.) Georgetown quickly became a valuable port as indigo and eventually rice and cotton from the plantations were floated downstream and placed on ships for export. Despite a short occupation by the British during the Revolutionary War, the port played key roles as a landing spot for the Marquis de Lafayette's army and as a supply center for Patriot General Nathaniel Greene.

Following the war, rice plantations continued production, generating great wealth for the 90 or so planters who

Hey Winyah, Wasya?

Whether or not American history began in Winyah Bay with a purported Spanish settlement in the 1520s is open to debate. Some historians believe that Spaniard Lucas Vasques de Allyon founded America's first European colony in 1526 on the Waccamaw Neck in Winyah Bay. Others aren't so sure, choosing to believe the Spanish explored the bay but did not put down roots. This much is certain. If the Spanish colonized the area, they didn't stay long. Had they, American history might have been quite different. Entienda?

owned land on the four Georgetown rivers and the Santee River 15 miles to the south. By the mid 1800s, half of the nation's rice output was produced by Georgetown plantations. An aristocratic culture developed that was nearly as extravagant as Charleston's and Beaufort's. Planters sent their sons to Europe to be educated and their daughters to private tutors. In the summer, the aristocratic families would move to comfortable beach homes on Pawleys Island—the furthest north any development had occurred

The Grand Strand just north of Winyah Bay

prior to the late 1800s—to escape malaria season and inland heat.

The region was spared any major fighting during the Civil War; however, Union forces occupied Georgetown, stabled their horses in the 1750 Prince George Winyah Episcopal Church, and ransacked the town upon leaving. The plantation culture collapsed after the war. Many of the region's plantations fell into disrepair, eventually being sold off as hunting preserves to wealthy residents of the North. Meanwhile, Georgetown turned to lumber mills as the base of their new economy, an industry that continues today.

Until 1900, the Grand Strand north of Pawleys Island was unsettled. At that time, South Carolina businessman F.A. Burroughs, who acquired beachfront land for a pittance in a deal for "more valuable" inland property, decided to develop it.

In an effort to make his new beach development sound appealing, F.A. Burroughs named the fledgling resort Myrtle Beach after the Crepe Myrtle Trees that bloomed in profusion. Some accounts suggest the name came from Burroughs' wife; others say it originated from a local newspaper contest. In 1901, he built the first hotel, the Seaside Inn, and charged $2 a night for a room.

Burroughs soon partnered with New York stockbroker S. G. Chapin to form Myrtle Beach Farms, a corporation that sold beachfront lots. In 1925, they convinced a Greenville textile magnate, John Woodside, to build a luxury resort, the Ocean Forest Hotel, complete with the area's first golf course. Woodside and a group of investors bought much of the town, built roads, and continued selling lots. Beach houses and small inns began to go up in Garden City,

Shagging, American Style

No kidding, the following description of South Carolina's official dance, the Shag, came from a government document: *The General Assembly by Act No. 329, 1984, designated the Shag as the official dance of the State. The Shag, one of the great developments of terpsichorean culture and native to this State, is performed to music known as rhythm and blues. Both the music and dance are structured on time signature and can be performed to almost any tempo, as long as the basic step is maintained and kept in time to the music.* Huh? To see what this really means, head to **Fat Harold's Beach Club,** 212 Main Street, North Myrtle Beach, ☎ (843) 249-5779, Tuesday-Saturday.

Families flock to the Grand Strand

Cherry Grove, and throughout Myrtle Beach. However, the 1929 Stock Market Crash halted development.

Following World War II, development picked up significantly, and the town began promoting the construction of motels to lure the growing number of Americans vacationing by car. Families poured onto the Grand Strand, as did teenagers and young adults drawn by the Myrtle Beach social scene. Days were spent on the beach and along the boardwalk, and at night, the young and the young-at-heart hit the dancehalls to do the Shag, a smooth and oh-so-cool dance that originated here in the 1940s.

In 1954, Hurricane Hazel blew through town, decimating Myrtle Beach. The rebuilding effort that commenced after Hazel has yet to stop and, as many would argue, is further decimating Myrtle Beach. The Grand Strand today is a morass of concrete development: high-rise condos, low-cost motels, outlet malls, Wal-Marts, themed restaurants, arcades, amusement parks, waterslides, and one mini-golf course after another. That said, upscale vacationers will indeed find lodging and dining gems tucked into the mix, though the majority exists in the southern reaches of the Strand.

What brings the Play Hard Rest Easy traveler here? Ultimately, it's the beach and the opportunities it presents: walking, jogging, fishing, swimming, pedaling, and paddling. But it's also the refined shopping available in the communities of Pawleys Island, Litchfield Beach, and Georgetown; the handful of interesting historic sites, plantations, public gardens, and state parks; and the restful peace that comes from simply staring out to sea.

The Way Around

To the south, the Grand Strand begins with **Georgetown,** or "Little Charleston," as it was once known. Georgetown's four-by-eight-block historic district—bordered by Wood, Church, Meeting, and Front streets—is on the National Register of Historic Places and includes numerous well-preserved homes with plaques listing their construction dates. Other notable historic stops in town include the Rice Museum, which depicts the area's plantation heritage, and the 1747 Prince George Winyah Episcopal Church, which was

Georgetown's boardwalk on the Sampit River

built with bricks used as ballasts in ships arriving from England.

Front Street is the town's main street, full of antiques stores, gift shops, bookstores, and art galleries. The town is also a popular stop for boaters on the Intracoastal Waterway, who tie up on the city's attractive boardwalk to dine in fine restaurants or load up on supplies from Kudzu Bakery, housed in a former antebellum horse stable.

Georgetown has its blemishes. A paper mill spills acrid effluent into the air, the largely blue-collar population has fallen on hard times with the Chapter 11 bankruptcy of Georgetown Steel, and Route 17 south passes through the town's unattractive commercial development.

Moving north from Georgetown, **Route 17** crosses Winyah Bay on arching concrete bridges and lands on the **Waccamaw Neck,** the southern portion of the Grand Strand from Winyah Bay to Murrells Inlet. The southern tip of the Strand is largely private, consisting of **Hobcaw Barony**, a wildlife refuge and research facility managed by Clemson University, and the exclusive resort enclaves of **Debordieu Colony** and **Prince George.**

A Friendly Ghost

Pawleys Island has a ghost to call its own: the mysterious, shadowy Gray Man, who walks the beach and enters homes to warn residents of forthcoming hurricanes. According to legend, the homes of residents who see the Gray Man are protected during the storm. Despite attempts by numerous insurance companies to capture and employ 'ole Gray, the man slips through every time.

The colonial resort **Pawleys Island** appears next. Accessed by either the North Causeway or South Causeway off Route 17, the four-mile-long barrier island has a small historic district comprised of 12 beach homes built between the late 1700s and mid 1800s by wealthy planters as summer homes for their families. (Pawleys calls itself the nation's oldest resort.) Long proud of its low-key demeanor—the island's unofficial motto is "arrogantly shabby"— homes here are primarily wood cottages with huge screened porches shaded by live oaks. There are no commercial ventures to speak of on the island, but the town, located along Route 17, features numerous elegant restaurants and upscale boutiques.

To the north, **Litchfield Beach** is home to the big resort village, Litchfield By the Sea, as well as to a number of large beach cottages lining North Litchfield Beach. The town was named for Litchfield Plantation, an antebellum rice plantation. The beach itself is pristine, beautiful, and among the widest in the state (though high tide throughout the Strand tends to swallow the beach whole). Immediately north of Litchfield, the 2,500-acre Huntington Beach State Park preserves the beach and surrounding maritime forest in their natural, undeveloped states.

North of the state park, Route 17 splits, with **Route 17-Business** veering right to the state's oldest fishing village, **Murrells Inlet.** Today this village is the region's seafood capital, where more than 40 seafood restaurants line a three-mile stretch of blacktop. Just north of Murrells Inlet, Route 17 splits again: the bypass veers north/northwest, and the business route becomes **Kings Highway,** providing access to the increasingly commercial beach towns of **Garden City, Surfside Beach,** and ultimately Myrtle Beach.

Beach houses along the Grand Strand

(Route 17-Bypass actually bypasses very little, lined as it is with mega-shopping centers, family attractions, and restaurants with improbably large facades.)

At last, you come to the grand dame herself...Myrtle. The heart and soul of the Grand Strand, **Myrtle Beach** makes no apologies. Sure, she's over-developed, over-crowded, over-loud, and at times, flat overwhelming, but she is what she is and she ain't 'a-changin'. (In personality, that is. Myrtle Beach does indeed change year-to-year, as more developments, restaurants, and attractions go up.) Simply put: Myrtle Beach is Americana-on-vacation.

The town's artery is **Ocean Boulevard,** which parallels the beach and passes the unofficial center of town, the **Pavilion,** once a dancehall and now an amusement park with pay-as-you-ride roller coasters, Ferris wheels, whirling dervishes, and candy apples shiny enough to tempt Eve into a second go round. In general, the southern reaches of Ocean Boulevard include rows of high-rise accommodations, the mid-section is full of attractions, and the northern stretch includes homes, condominiums, and motels.

One block west of Ocean Boulevard, also paralleling the coast, **Kings Highway** is a concrete apparition of beach shops, motels, restaurants, attractions, mini-golf

Of Cruising and Crawling

The highways and major roads along the Grand Strand are notorious for their miles-long backups, as traffic often slows to a crawl moving into and out of Myrtle Beach. Before you write letters to the editor berating the Strand's municipal traffic planners for negligence, consider that the # 1 culprit is as old as humankind: hormones. Cruising, or driving up and down the main drag, windows open, music blaring, and essentially seeing and being seen is as sure an occurrence here as the tides. To join the scene, head to **Ocean Boulevard.**

Golf in the Kingdom

For a mulligan, answer this: Which vacationers visit Myrtle Beach and never set foot in the sand or water, except to play an unfortunate lie? Golfers. And to them, Myrtle Beach, with its mild climate and more than 100 courses, is a kingdom by the sea. (Only Florida attracts more golfers.) There are courses for everyone, from duffers to scratch golfers, and most offer stunning scenery and the chance to see native wildlife. (The Hooters beverage cart, for example.) To name a few highlights: **The Legends,** ☎ 1-800-552-2660, features three courses from Pete Dye and Tom Doak; **Willbrook Plantation,** ☎ 1-800-344-5590, which is one of *Golf for Women* magazine's top 30 women-friend-ly courses; and **Barefoot Resort,** ☎ 1-888-557-6226, home to Davis Love III-, Tom Fazio-, Pete Dye-, and Greg Norman-designed courses. For a complete review of area courses, pick up a copy of Scott Martin's excellent *Insider's Guide to Golf in the Carolinas.*

Myrtle Beach Area CVB

courses, and more. Roughly three miles west of the beach, Route 17-Bypass rolls past gargantuan shopping centers, including Broadway at the Beach, a multiple-personality complex of more than 100 specialty shops, 10 nightclubs, 25 attractions (including Ripley's Aquarium), and—just in case you're too tired to drive out of the collosal parking lot—three onsite hotels.

The area incorporated as **North Myrtle Beach** encompasses the developments of Ocean Drive, Crescent Beach, Crescent Hill, and Cherry Grove, but good luck finding the lines separating them. Sadly, the lines between these communities and **Atlantic Beach** are fairly clear, as Jim Crow laws once designated Atlantic as the "black beach." (Chain link fence actually separated Atlantic from the "white beaches.") Today, Atlantic remains popular primarily with African Americans.

Popular North Myrtle sites include **Restaurant Row,** a stretch of Route 17-Bypass with one neon sign after another, promoting all-you-can-eat seafood buffets. Cherry Grove's **Hogg Inlet** is a prime spot for fishing and crabbing, while Cherry Grove is a prime fishing-for-the-opposite-sex spot during spring break and the week following high school graduations. The Strand ends at **Little River Inlet** and the Town of **Little River,** a historic fishing village that's become a center-of-sorts for the region's deep-sea-fishing charter industry.

Myrtle Beach Area CVB

The Pavilion on Ocean Boulevard

Weather

The Strand's temperate climate and annual average of 216 sunny days makes for pleasant year-round vacationing. Winters are mild, with highs in the mid 50s and overnight lows in the upper 30s. Spring and fall are comfortable; daytime highs are in the mid 70s, overnight lows in the lower 50s. Summer can be quite hot with daytime highs in the lower 90s, cooling at night to the mid to upper 70s. In the summer, sudden storms are a common afternoon occurrence.

Getting to the Grand Strand

By Air: The **Myrtle Beach International Airport,** ☏ (843) 448-1589, *www.myrtlebeachairport.com,* hosts most major airlines and car rental companies.

By Car: From Atlanta, take Interstate 20 east to Route 76 east to Route 576 east, which becomes Route 501 south to Myrtle Beach and Route 17. Expect a seven-hour drive. **From Charlotte,** take Interstate 77 south to Columbia, and then Interstate 20 east roughly 70 miles toward Florence. Follow signs for Route 76 east to Route 576 east. Route 576 becomes Route 501 south and leads directly to Myrtle Beach. Driving time from Charlotte is roughly four hours. **From Raleigh,** take Interstate 40 east to Interstate 95 south for roughly 100 miles to Exit # 181 and Route 38. Follow Route 38 east toward Marion, and then take Route 501 south into Myrtle Beach. Expect a four-hour drive.

P l a y   H a r d

W i d e   O p e n

Despite its prominence as a vacation destination, the Grand Strand has surprisingly few public, multi-sport, outdoor playgrounds. Except for the beaches, of course. The Strand's 60-mile coastline is popular with walkers, joggers, bicyclists, paddlers, surfers, anglers, and sailors. In addition to the sand and surf, there are two state parks with a smattering of nature trails.

Located three miles south of Murrells Inlet off Route 17, **Huntington Beach State Park,** 16148 Ocean Highway, (843) 237-4440, encompasses 2,500 acres of maritime forest, salt marsh, freshwater lagoon, and pristine beach. It's the former estate of Archer Huntington and his wife, American sculptress Anna Hyatt Huntington. Their former home, the 1930s Moorish castle, Atalaya, is a popular attraction. Park activi-

Huntington Beach State Park

For the Birds

Birding enthusiasts create quite a flap over Huntington Beach State Park, one of the premier spots on the Eastern Seaboard to sight great blue herons, snowy egrets, clapper rails, oystercatchers, eastern brown pelicans, and more. Bring your binoculars. Wear a hat.

ties include hiking the nature trails and fishing, sea kayaking, swimming, and collecting shells along the undeveloped, three-mile beach. Changing rooms and seasonal showers are available. Open daily, 6 A.M.–10 P.M., during the summer. Call for winter hours. Nominal day-use fee.

Four miles south of Myrtle Beach on Route 17-Business, **Myrtle Beach State Park,** 4401 South Kings Highway, (843) 238-5325, is a 312-acre natural oasis right in the middle of the Strand's commercial chaos. The land consists of a maritime forest full of live oaks, wax myrtles, hollies, and magnolias, plus a mile of beachfront accessed by several boardwalks. Popular pursuits include hiking, shell gathering, fishing, surfing, picnicking, and swimming. Amenities include a fishing pier, nature trail, campground, changing facilities, and cold-water showers. Open daily, 6 A.M.–10 P.M. Nominal day-use fee.

Dayhiking

Walking beside the Atlantic Ocean when the wind is strong and the sea has white-tipped waves makes for an excellent, exhilarating workout. Higher on the beach, the soft sand gives way, making your foot, calf, and leg muscles work harder. If your inn, hotel, or beach cottage doesn't provide access to the beach, don't sweat it. There are hundreds of public access points all along the Strand, most of which are clearly signed.

♦ You'll find two short trails at **Huntington Beach State Park,** 16148 Ocean Highway (Route 17), Murrells Inlet, (843) 237-4440. The easy, two-mile **Sandpiper Pond Trail** passes through several coastal ecosystems, including maritime forest, marsh, and beach. From the salt marsh boardwalk parking area, set out on the boardwalk over the spartina grass—look

for oysters and fiddler crabs in the mud—to the observation deck mid-way and then to the pier over Oaks Creek. Backtrack to pick up the trail through the maritime forest of red cedars and live oaks. You'll pass a saltwater pond with observation towers, where you may see ospreys, herons, and egrets. When you reach the beach, either retrace your steps to the car,

Up for a walk?

or add another six miles (roundtrip) by walking the beach to the Murrells Inlet Jetty. ◆ The 0.25-mile **Kerrigan Nature Trail** sets out from the campground parking area for an easy walk to a boardwalk that extends over a fresh-water lagoon. There's an observation deck, from which you'll lose count of the various species of birds.

Myrtle Beach Area CVB

Huntington Beach State Park

◆ The 0.75-mile **Sculptured Oak Nature Trail** at **Myrtle Beach State Park,** 4401 South Kings Highway (Route 17-Business), Myrtle Beach, (843) 238-5325, winds through a scenic maritime forest, densely foliated with magnolias, live oaks, wax myrtles, and hollies, and passes several boardwalks providing access to the beach. The trail starts across the street from the Nature Center parking area. After a short stretch, a spur trail departs right leading to a pond. The main trail continues straight, past another spur trail on the left (on which you'll return), to a park roadway paralleling the beach. Turn left on the road, continue past the beach board-walks, and turn left on the spur trail at the next parking area to close the loop.

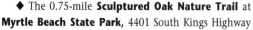

Bicycling

SC Division of Tourism

The nearest mountain is several hundred miles to the west, so mountain bikes are out; single-speed beach cruisers are in. In general, the roads just off the beach in smaller communities like Litchfield and Pawleys Island are safe and enjoyable routes; however, as you move north on the Strand toward Myrtle Beach, traf-fic picks up and most roads, even those closest to the beach, lose their lazy, sand-swept appeal.

◆ Portions of **Bike the Neck,** a paved, multi-purpose path that will eventually stretch 27 miles from Murrells Inlet to Georgetown beside Route 17, are complete in North Litchfield, Litchfield By the Sea, and between the North and South Causeways at Pawleys Island. Several miles of side trails are available off the main path. For example, at the Litchfield By the Sea intersection, a spur path extends west along Willbrook Boulevard.

◆ The best place to ride beach cruisers is, of course, on **the beach,** where for a couple of hours on either side of low tide, the sand near the water is firm enough to ride. Throughout the region, public access points and parking regulations are clearly signed. Even in more-private communities such as Pawleys Island and North Litchfield, public access points exist. On Pawleys, a public parking lot is located on the southern end. At North Litchfield Beach, more than 15 streets provide access off Parker Drive. In Myrtle Beach, nearly every road off Ocean Boulevard provides public beach access, though not all have public parking.

◆ Ride the shoreline at **Huntington Beach State Park,** 16148 Ocean Highway (Route 17), Murrells Inlet, (843) 237-4440, or along the four miles of road. (Bikes are not allowed on the nature trails.) ◆ You can also bike the roads inside **Myrtle Beach State Park,** 4401

South Kings Highway (Route 17-Business), Myrtle Beach, (843) 238-5325. Note that riding bikes on the beach is prohibited between 10 A.M.–3 P.M., June–September.

◆ Mountain bikers will want to drive south into the 250,000-acre **Francis Marion National Forest** to ride its forest roads and multi-use trails. See the Charleston chapter for coverage of the forest's trails.

Rentals

The following shops rent single-speed beach cruisers (a few rent mountain bikes.) Helmets and locks are typically included in the rental price. **Bicycles-n-Gear,** 515-C Route 501, Myrtle Beach, ☎ (843) 626-2453, *www.bikesngear.com;* ◆ **The Bike Doctor,** 315 Sea Mountain Highway, North Myrtle Beach, ☎ (843) 249-8152; ◆ **The Bike Shop,** 715 Broadway, Myrtle Beach, ☎ (843) 448-5335; ◆ **Mr. C's Bicycles,** 720 Route 17-Business, Surfside Beach, ☎ (843) 238-3222; ◆ **Pawley's Island Beach Service,** 9710 Route 17, Pawleys Island, ☎ (843) 237-4666. (Open seasonally.)

Paddling

Paddling waters along the Grand Strand are primarily the four rivers that flow into Winyah Bay—the Sampit, Black, Pee Dee, and Waccamaw—and the Atlantic Ocean. Compared to the shoreline around Charleston and Beaufort, the Strand's coastline is not fragmented with barrier islands, rivers, and creeks, so sea kayaking has not taken hold here as it has to the south. Despite this, Georgetown has one of the state's best full-service paddling outfitters, **Black River Outdoors**, 21 Garden Avenue, (843) 546-4840, *www.blackriveroutdoors.com,* located three miles north of town on Route 701.

Black River rents canoes and kayaks for individual use and operates a number of naturalist-led tours. Half-day and moonlight tours, lasting between three and four hours, and sum-

SC Division of Tourism

mer evening, 1.5-hour Georgetown Harbor tours are regularly scheduled. (Full-day excursions are available upon request.) The following tours include an introductory lesson and all equipment rentals. Costs range from $20 per person for the evening tours to $45 per person for the half-day and moonlight paddles. Call for full-day rates.

SC Division of Tourism

◆ Some of the popular tours Black River Outdoors offers include a paddle through the **Black River Cypress-Tupelo Swamp,** where tannic-stained water flows through the 1,300-acre Black River Nature Preserve. Possible wildlife sightings include alligators, deer, wild turkeys, otters, beavers, and water and woodland birds. ◆ The spartina-cordgrass marshes, creeks, and freshwater lagoons inside **Huntington Beach State Park** allow paddlers the chance to see bald eagles, porpoises, stingrays, and alligators. The tour also winds past Drunken Jack Island, where legend has it that Blackbeard stashed an as-yet-unfound treasure. (Bring a shovel.) ◆ The popular evening **Historic Harbor and Seaport of Georgetown** tour is a gentle paddle along the Sampit River, past the Front Street boardwalk and the million-dollar yachts moored to the docks. In addition to the paddling exercise, you'll learn some history about this colonial town, the state's third-oldest English settlement.

Black River Outdoors operates more organized tours. They're also happy to suggest routes to undertake on your own. The shop includes well-worn maps and guidebooks for use in planning paddling adventures, or you can purchase reference materials to carry with you.

◆ **Surf-the-Earth,** 47 Da-Gullah Way, Pawleys Island, (843) 235-3500, *www.surf-the-earth.com,* located on Route 17 a half-mile south of Pawleys Island's North Causeway, rents sit-on-top kayaks for ocean play and enclosed sea kayaks for exploring area waterways. The shop also operates guided paddling tours of the creeks and marshes nearby.

Deep Sea Fishing

Fishing—inshore and offshore—is serious sport along the Grand Strand, and the season, which lasts from spring through late fall, pulls anglers from across the Carolinas who come to cast in the surf, motor out to the Gulf Stream, troll the inlets, or to drop bait from one of the dozen or so piers extending out into the Atlantic.

Myrtle Beach Area CVB

Closer to shore, your catch may include flounder, Spanish and king mackerel, pompano, red drum, whiting, trout, and sheepshead. Head to the warm waters of the Gulf and you'll possibly reel in yellowfin tuna, blue marlin, amber jack, wahoo, sailfish, and more. The Grand Strand offers numerous fishing charters, many of which operate from **Little River**. Charters range from half- and full-day inshore and deep-sea trips to 12-hour Gulf Stream trips. Prices average $300 for half-day and up to $1,000 for 12-hour charters. Rates vary based on boat size, passenger load, and the type of fishing.

◆ Where to find the charters? Some good bets in order from south to north include: **Georgetown Charters,** Georgetown Landing Marina, Route 17 at the Black/PeeDee River Bridge, Georgetown, (843) 997-9842, *www.georgetowncharters.net;* ◆ **Capt. Dick's Deep Sea**

Fishing & Water Sports, 4123 Business Route 17, Murrells Inlet, (843) 651-3676 or 1-866-557-3474, *www.captdicks.com;* ◆ **Shallow Minded Inshore Charters,** 1 Harbour Place, North Myrtle Beach, (843) 280-7099, *www.fishmyrtlebeach.com;* and ◆ **Captain Smiley's Inshore Fishing Charters,** 4474 Water Front Avenue, Little River, (843) 361-7445 or (843) 222-1988, *www.captainsmileyfishingcharters.com.*

Horseback Riding

Inlet Point Plantation, 5800 Route 236, North Myrtle Beach, (843) 249-2989, *www.inletpointplantation.com,* offers beach and trail rides on a private island. Carriage rides are also available. ◆ **Best View Farm,** 6129 Best Western Trail, Myrtle Beach, (843) 650-7522, provides lessons and trail rides through the farm's 45 wooded acres.

Rainy Day Workout

When Mother Nature wreaks havoc on your outdoor-sport plans, head to **HealthPoint** 12965 Ocean Highway (Route 17), Pawleys Island, (843) 237-2205, a 40,000 square-foot facility, with nearly every kind of exercise and post-exercise amenity you can fathom. There's an indoor lap pool, warm-water exercise pool, whirlpool, indoor track, aerobics studio, and courts for basketball, volleyball, and racquetball. A large fitness room features a full assortment of cardiovascular and strength-training equipment, plus free weights. Locker rooms feature steam rooms, saunas, and showers. Also onsite: a deli and juice bar, plus a day spa with numerous treatments, including massage, body treatments, facials, manicures, and pedicures. Nominal day-use fee.

Sailing

With beautiful Winyah Bay, the Intracoastal Waterway, and the wide-open Atlantic Ocean, sailors have plenty of water to explore. The Grand Strand's myriad marinas are the best places to locate captains willing to motor out and raise the mainsail. Also, plenty of outfits rent Hobie Cats for personal use. The following charters and businesses are good places to begin.

◆ **Ocean Tours,** Cricket Cove Marina, 4495 Baker Street, Little River,

A Jolly Good Time

Reserve a place on the 80-foot tall ship *Jolly Rover,* ☎ (843) 546-8822 or 1-800-705-9063, which departs from the boardwalk in downtown Georgetown for two-hour sails of Winyah Bay. Expect the pirate-dressed captain to tell some scary ghost stories. For a more romantic sail, opt for the 2.5-hour evening sail. Trips depart at 10 A.M., 1 P.M., and 6 P.M., Monday-Saturday. Call for reservations.

(843) 446-7245, offers private, half- and full-day charters for up to six passengers on a 27-foot Stiletto Catamaran from April–November. Half-day charters include snacks and beverages, full-day trips include lunch. Call for costs. ◆ **Wallace Sailing Charters,** Broad and Front streets, Georgetown, (843) 902-6999, *www.wallacesailingcharters.com,* offers two-, four-, six-, and eight-hour trips for six passengers aboard a 40-foot Beneteau Oceanis 400. Trips may include visiting a Civil War shipwreck, the Georgetown Lighthouse at the mouth of Winyah Bay, or South Island, where you'll motor ashore to explore the small, secluded sand paradise. Call for rates and reservations.

◆ Sail your own Hobie Wave 14 (for novice sailors) or Hobie Cat 16 from **Downwind Sails of Myrtle Beach,** 2915 South Ocean Boulevard, Myrtle Beach, (843) 448-7245, *www.dwswatersports.com.* Rent by the hour or day, or make arrangements to have a staff member sail with you. The store also provides sailing lessons.

Swimming

Where not to swim? The 60 miles of beach along the Grand Strand and the temperate climate mean you can swim just about wherever and whenever you want. Want to bathe with a morass of humanity? Head to Myrtle Beach's Pavilion area. There are no public restrooms, but hotels must (by law) allow beachgoers to use their facilities. In North Myrtle, try **Oceanfront Park**, at First Avenue and South Ocean Boulevard, where there's parking, a seasonal concession stand, restrooms, and outdoor showers. Nothing beats the more-natural beach environment at **Myrtle Beach State Park,** 4401 South Kings Highway (Route 17-Business), (843) 238-5325, four miles south of town, and the three-mile stretch of undeveloped beach at **Huntington Beach State Park,** 16148 Ocean Highway

(Route 17), (843) 237-4440, three miles south of Murrells Inlet. Both parks feature restrooms, changing rooms, and shower facilities.

♦ Public beach access points are located throughout the Grand Strand, even in the more-private communities of **Pawleys Island,** where a public parking lot is located on the southern end, and **North Litchfield Beach**, where more than 15 streets provide access off Parker Drive. In **Myrtle Beach**, nearly every road off Ocean Boulevard provides public beach access, though not all have public parking. Throughout the region, public access points and parking regulations are clearly signed.

Local Outdoor Advice

Black River Outdoors • A one-stop paddling shop, Black River sells and rents canoes, kayaks, and paddling gear, and operates a number of naturalist-led kayak tours. Located three miles north of Georgetown on Route 701, the store welcomes folks looking for suggestions on where to play. • 21 Garden Avenue, ☎ (843) 546-4840, *www.blackriveroutdoors.com*

Surf-the-Earth • One-part surf-store and one-part full-service paddling outfitter, Surf-the-Earth sells gear, apparel, and accessories for surfing, skateboarding, and kayaking. Rentals include surfboards, sit-on-top kayaks for ocean play, and enclosed sea kayaks for exploring area waterways. The shop also operates guided paddling tours. • 47 Da-Gullah Way (off Route 17), Pawleys Island, ☎ (843) 235-3500, *www.surf-the-earth.com*

Kick Back

When the sun, sand, and sea have drained your energy or if Mother Nature fails to cooperate with your outdoor plans, the following laid-back pursuits offer plenty of ways to pass the time.

Antiques & Art Galleries

Serious buyers and casual browsers alike will find plenty of antiques shops and art galleries worth exploring throughout the Strand. In general, Murrells Inlet and Georgetown feature the most antiques dealers, and Pawleys Island and Georgetown have the greatest concentration of art galleries. Some recommended stops include the **Legacy Antique Mall,** 34420 Route 17 South, Murrells Inlet, (843) 423-1636, which specializes in estate jewelry, paintings, and silver. ◆ **Wachesaw Row Antique Mall,** 4650 Route 17 South, Murrells Inlet, (843) 651-7719, features a variety of dealers whose offerings range from furniture and decorative accessories to glassware, pottery, and jewelry.

◆ **Cheryl Newby Gallery,** 11096 Ocean Highway (Route 17), Pawleys Island, (843) 979-0149 or 1-800-435-2733, *www.cherylnewbygallery.com,* is a fine-art gallery specializing in antique prints and engravings, as well as paintings by regional and national artists. Other items on hand include 16th- to 19th-century antique maps and charts, as well as prints and lithographs of works by such well-known natural-history artists as John James Audubon. ◆

The Gullah O'oman Shop, Petigru Drive and Waverly Road, Pawleys Island, (843) 235-0747, features Gullah art, antiques, books, historic documents, and memorabilia. Owners Bunny and Andrew Rodrigues also give periodic seminars and lectures on Gullah contributions to Carolina culture. ◆ **Augustus and Carolina,** 830 Front Street, Georgetown, (843) 545-9000, offers a large selection of fine European antique furniture and art, as well as quality reproductions. ◆ The cooperative **Georgetown Art Gallery,** 732 Front Street, Georgetown, (843) 527-7711, features work by more than 20 artists in such media as photography, sculpture, watercolors, acrylics, and pastels.

The Burroughs-Chapin Art Museum

Art in Myrtle Beach goes beyond intricate tattoo design and velvet Elvis-es sold roadside thanks to the **Franklin G. Burroughs-Simeon B. Chapin Art Museum,** 3100 South Ocean Boulevard, ☎ (843) 238-2510, *www.myrtlebeachartmuseum.org,* which features an art gallery, education center, and gift shop. Housed in a former beach cottage, the 3,600 square-foot gallery has two permanent collections and displays rotating exhibitions of work by local, regional, and national artists. Also on display: a collection of antique maps and prints, including a hand-drawn map of Charleston Harbor created in 1861.

Amusements

It's easier to count bikinis in Myrtle Beach than to list all of the attractions found along the Strand. The following is but a start. ◆ Gentlemen, start your engines: **NASCAR SpeedPark,** Route 17 Bypass (across from Broadway at the Beach), Myrtle Beach (843) 626-8725, *www.nascarspeedpark.com,* is where drivers of various ages, sizes, and skills can live out their stock car racing dreams in one of more than 150 scaled-down race cars on seven tracks of varying sizes. If driving in circles doesn't dizzy you, the array of other activities onsite will. There's miniature golf, a climbing wall, bumper boats, an arcade, and more NASCAR memorabilia than you'd believe.

◆ One of South Carolina's most-popular attractions, **Ripley's Aquarium,** Broadway at the Beach, Route 17-Bypass, Myrtle Beach, (843) 916-0888 or 1-800-734-8888, *www.rip-leysaquarium.com,* features fish, fish, and fish in a variety of ocean and fresh-water habitats. Sharks, of course, take center stage (center-tank?), and highlights include standing on the moving walkway that passes UNDER the 750,000-gallon Dangerous Reef tank. Very cool.

A shark passes overhead at Ripley's Aquarium

Open daily, 9 A.M.–6 P.M. Admission charged. ◆ For a short and snappy trip, head to one of the world's largest reptile zoos, **Alligator Adventure,** Route 17 at Barefoot Landing, North Myrtle Beach, (843) 361-0789, *www.alligatoradventure.com.* Home to more than 800 alligators and an armada of Galapagos turtles, snakes, lizards, frogs, crocodiles, and Komodo Dragons, the park is sure to crawl inside your memory, especially when you step near the water. Live shows include the feeding and handling of gators and snakes. Open daily, though hours change according to season. Admission charged. ◆ The area's largest water park, **Myrtle Waves,** 3000 10th Avenue North (off Route 17-Bypass), Myrtle Beach, (843) 448-1026, *www.myrtlewaves.com,* features 20 acres of slip-sliding fun. The highlight is the 10-story Turbo Twister. Open daily at 10 A.M., late May–early September. Admission charged.

In the Beginning...

There was the **Myrtle Beach Pavilion Amusement Park,** 812 North Ocean Boulevard, ☎ (843) 448-6456, *www.mbpavilion.com,* and it's still going strong after more than 50 years of roller coasting, Ferris wheeling, carouseling, and carnavalizing visitors to the Strand. The highlight? "Hurricane Category 5," purportedly the biggest, baddest roller coaster in the state. The seasonal, pay-as-you-ride park sits on 11 acres in the center of Myrtle Beach and is typically open from early afternoon to late evening.

Boat Tours

The **Great American Riverboat Company**, Route 17 at Barefoot Landing, North Myrtle Beach, (843) 650-6600, *www.mbriverboat.com,* offers sightseeing, sunset, and dinner cruises aboard the ***Barefoot Princess Riverboat,*** a side-wheel riverboat that plies the Intracoastal Waterway for 1.5- and 2.5-hour journeys. ◆ If it floats, you can probably ride it at **Captain Dick's Marina**, Kings Highway South (Route 17-Business), Murrells Inlet, (843) 651-3676 or 1-866-557-3474, *www.captdicks.com,* where the menu of water tours ranges from the 2.5-hour "Saltwater Marsh Explorer Adventure" led by a marine biologist to the two-hour "Cruisin' The Beach" cruise on the Atlantic Ocean. There are plenty more tours from which to choose, as well as boats to rent for your own adventure. ◆ **Cap'n Rod's Lowcountry Plantation Tours**, 705 Front Street, Georgetown, (843) 477-0287, *www.lowcountrytours.com,* set out on a 56-foot, covered pontoon boat captained by native Rod Singleton. Choose from the three-hour Plantation River; Lighthouse-Shell Island; and the two-hour, Sunset Ghost Story/Harbor tours.

Brookgreen Gardens

Brookgreen Gardens, Route 17 between Murrells Inlet and Pawleys Island, ☎ (843) 237-4218 or 1-800-849-1931, *www.brookgreen.org*, is America's first and largest public sculpture garden. Covering 300 acres of the 9,000-acre Brookgreen Wildlife Sanctuary, the garden features more than 550 sculptures from such artists as Frederick Remington, Daniel Chester French, and Anna Hyatt Huntington. The centerpiece is a beautifully land-scaped garden of centuries-old live oaks and more than 2,000 species and subspecies of plants native and adapted to the Southeastern United States.

Begin your visit at the Welcome Center, where a 10-minute ori-entation film gives an overview, and the staff provides informa-tion about activities and programs onsite. The property also houses the **Lowcountry Center**, an exhibit-filled, ecology facil-ity; a 23-acre wildlife habitat with a 90-foot aviary built over a cypress swamp; an otter pond; raptor aviary; and alligator swamp. Also, the self-guided **Lowcountry Trail** winds through several ecosystems on the property. Nominal admission fee for a seven-day pass. Open daily, 9:30 A.M.–5 P.M., mid March-mid November. Closed Mondays in the winter.

Brookgreen Gardens

Country Music

♪ Myrtle Beach follows only Nashville and Branson, Missouri as a country-music desti-nation. People come to hear their favorite performers—Garth Brooks, George Jones, and Alan Jackson, among them—and to catch up-and-comers in any one of the numerous country-music theaters. The following are just a few of the Strand's entertainment hotspots.
♦ Opened in 1986 as the area's first large entertainment venue, **The Carolina Opry,** 82nd Avenue North, North Myrtle Beach, (843) 238-8888 or 1-800-843-6779, *www.cgp.net*, pro-duces a nightly, two-hour musical variety show, mixing Broadway and country music, dancing, comedy, and Vegas-style showmanship into a family-oriented spectacle. ♦ Founded by the group Alabama, the **Alabama Theatre** at Barefoot Landing, 4750 Route 17, North Myrtle Beach, (843) 272-1111 or 1-800-342-2262, *www.alabama-theatre.com*, fea-tures celebrity music and weekly comedy performances, as well as a musical variety show six nights a week. ♦ Dolly Parton's dinner theater, **Dixie Stampede,** 8901-B Route 17 North, Myrtle Beach, 1-800-433-4401, *www.dixiestampede.com*, serves up a mixture of music, comedy, Wild-West performances, and rodeo with a four-course, country-style meal.

Elvis Never Left the Building

The gang's all here: Elvis, Nat King Cole, Conway Twitty, Marilyn Monroe, even 'ole Blue Eyes. At **Legends in Concert,** 301 Route 17 South, Surfside Beach, ☎ (843) 238-7827 or 1-800-960-7469, *www.legendsinconcert.com*, you can catch an amazing ensemble of look-alike, sound-alike performers in a Vegas-style review of great tunes performed with a live orchestra.

Historic Sites & Museums

🏛 Styled after a Moorish castle, Archer and Anna Hyatt Huntington's former winter home, **Atalaya,** Huntington Beach State Park, Route 17, Murrells Inlet, (843) 237-4440, was built between 1931–1933 by local laborers and is today a National Historic Landmark. The castle by the sea features a tall tower and interior courtyard surrounded by 33 rooms. The home is not furnished. You can tour the castle seasonally on your own or with a guided tour. Nominal admission fee. Open daily, 9 A.M.–5 P.M.

Myrtle Beach Area CVB

Atalaya

◆ The **Kaminski House Museum,** 1003 Front Street, Georgetown, (843) 546-7706 or 1-888-233-0383, features a collection of 18th- and 19th-century antiques, plus a few older items, including a 15th-century Spanish wedding chest. The residence, built around 1769, has been home to a Confederate sea captain and three Georgetown mayors, including namesake Harold Kaminski, who governed in the early 1930s. Open daily, 10 A.M.–4 P.M.; Sundays, 1 P.M.–4 P.M. Nominal admission fee.

◆ Discover Georgetown's colonial and antebellum plantation history at the **Rice Museum,** Old Market Building, Front and Screven streets, Georgetown, (843) 546-7423, *www.ricemuseum.com,* where dioramas, old maps, artifacts, and a short film enlighten visitors about the importance of rice to the region's development. The Clock Tower building housing the museum is an exhibit itself: It was built in 1842 and features an 1878 addition. Open Monday–Saturday, 10 A.M.–4:30 P.M. Nominal admission fee.

◆ Georgetown's historic district is best explored on a guided tour. Join the **Georgetown Tour Company,** 627 Front Street, (843) 546-6827, for a one-hour tour aboard a tram.

Historic Churches

Two of the South's oldest Episcopal churches are on the Grand Strand. The Church of England established the Parish of Prince George in 1721 to serve the growing number of colonists in the area, and in 1747, the **Prince George Winyah Episcopal Church,** 300 Broad Street, Georgetown, ☎ (843) 546-4358, was built with bricks used as ballasts in ships arriving from England. Inside are original box pews and a stained-glass window behind the altar that came from a local slave chapel. The British occupied the church during the Revolutionary War, as did Union forces during the Civil War. The church graveyard is one of the oldest in the state, with burial markers dating to 1767. On Pawleys Island, **All Saints Episcopal Church,** 3560 River Road, ☎ (843) 237-4223, was established in 1767 to serve planters spending summers on the island. The church's stunning grounds feature moss-draped live oaks that shade the historic building and adjacent cemetery. Admission to both churches is free; donations are accepted.

Nature Preserves

The 17,500-acre **Hobcaw Barony,** Route 17 South, Georgetown, (843) 546-4623, *www.hobcawbarony.com,* is a wildlife refuge and environmental research facility housed on the former estate of the late financier and presidential advisor Bernard Baruch. Long before Baruch bought the property in the early 1900s, the land held several rice plantations. There's a visitor center—open 10 A.M.–5 P.M., weekdays—with exhibits detailing Hobcaw's history,

Hobcaw Barony

as well as salt- and fresh-water fish tanks. Make advance reservations to join a guided van tour of the estate, including former plantation-era slave cabins and Baruch's 1930 mansion. Admission to the visitor center is free; nominal fee for the tour.

◆ Accessible only by boat, **Sandy Island Preserve** is a ten mile-long, eight mile-wide island just west of Brookgreen Gardens and tucked between the Waccamaw and Great Pee Dee Rivers. Managed by the Nature Conservancy, it's the largest, undeveloped tract remaining in the Waccamaw Neck. In the 1800s, its 1,100 acres of wetlands along the Waccamaw River were used to grow rice. Dikes and several rice-cultivation structures still exist. Visitors are asked to stay away from the eastern end of the island, where a small community of slave descendents lives. To access the island, join a paddling tour operated by Black River Outdoors. See *Local Outdoor Advice.*

Plantations

Located off Route 17 on the North Santee River roughly 12 miles south of Georgetown, **Hopsewee Plantation**, (843) 546-7891, *www.hopsewee.com,* was the home of Thomas Lynch, a delegate to the first Continental Congress, and birthplace of Thomas Jr., a Declaration of Independence signer. The 1740 Hopsewee home is unique because it's been painstakingly preserved—not renovated. The mansion features a stunning Georgian staircase and numerous 18th- and 19th-century antique furnishings. Open Tuesday–Friday, 10 A.M.–4 P.M. Nominal admission fee.

◆ Roughly 15 miles south of Georgetown and just off Route 17, the 322-acre **Hampton Plantation State Historic Site**, (843) 546-9361, was once part of a vast rice plantation that belonged to several families before passing to Archibald Rutledge, a former South Carolina poet laureate. (He sold it to the state in 1971.) Located on the banks of the Santee River, the estate fea-

Library of Congress

Slave quarters on Hopsewee Plantation

tures the circa 1735, Georgian-style Hampton Mansion, originally a six-room house that was added on to twice before George Washington arrived to spend the night in 1791. Park interpreters conduct tours of the mansion. Visitors are welcome to explore the grounds adorned with towering live oaks, camellia gardens, and a separate kitchen building. Open daily, 9 A.M.–6 P.M. (grounds); 11 A.M.–4 P.M. (mansion) in the summer. Call for winter hours. Admission to the grounds is free; nominal admission fee for the house.

Shops & Stops

If there's a pursuit that exceeds all others in the Grand Strand—even visiting the beach—it's shopping. So prolific are the various retail venues that you'll wonder how they manage to stay in business. Not only do they stay afloat, but they also thrive. Each year, more retail centers go up with many, if not all, of the tenant spaces pre-leased. So grab your credit cards and prepare for a workout.

Shops line Front Street in Georgetown

◆ The largest shopping complexes are in the northern Strand, where you'll find such behemoths as the **Waccamaw Factory Shoppes,** Route 501 at the Intracoastal Waterway, Myrtle Beach, (843) 236-6152 or 1-800-444-8258, *www.waccamawfactoryshoppes.com,* and its three colossal malls on 500 acres. A few of the tenants include QVC Outlet, Liz Claiborne, The Linen Shoppe, and the massive Pottery at Waccamaw, where you can buy fine china, garden pottery, cookware, and more. ◆ **Barefoot Landing,** Route 17, North Myrtle Beach, (843) 272-8349, *www.bflanding.com,* is home to more than 100 specialty shops and a dozen factory direct stores, including Izod, Van Heusen, Bass, and Geoffrey Beene. The specialty shops sell everything from Gothic décor to peanuts to blown glass. ◆ Similar in scope is **Broadway at the Beach,** Route 17-Bypass, Myrtle Beach, (843) 444-3200 or 1-800-386-4662, *www.broadwayatthebeach.com,* which also features more than 100 shops, including boutiques like Noah & Friends and the Fun Art Gallery, as well as such national stores as the Discovery Channel Store, Harley Davidson Apparel, and Birkenstock. The Build-a-Bear Workshop is one of the most popular shops.

◆ South of the Goliaths, the **Pawleys Island Hammock Shoppes,** 10707 Ocean Boulevard, Pawleys Island, (843) 237-

Bang for your Buck

Along Route 17, especially in Myrtle Beach, signs promise cheap fireworks for sale. Inside these volatile shops, you'll find bottle rockets, spinners, jacks, firecrackers, and more. But before you go all giddy with a lighter, note that it's illegal to light fireworks within any city limits along the Strand.

8448 or 1-800-332-3490, features more than 20 specialty retailers, including the Original Hammock Shop, where the renowned Pawleys Island Hammock has been sold since 1930. Many of the shops, which offer fine jewelry, handcrafts, clothing, toys, and more, are housed in historic buildings.

◆ There's something for everyone at the **Shops at Oak Lea,** 11096 Ocean Highway, Pawleys Island. **The Joggling Board,** (843) 237-2631, carries children's clothing; **Lilly Pulitzer's Signature Shop,** (843) 237-2631, has apparel for women, men, and children; **Pawleys Pedalar,** (843) 237-2012, sells ladies shoes; and **The Men's Store,** (843) 237-2412, features fine apparel. Also onsite are a jewelry store and an art gallery.

◆ **Primarily Pine,** 11302 Ocean Highway, Pawleys Island, (843) 237-3562, features a great selection of reproduction furniture, including chests-of-drawers, armoires, and tables, as well as a variety of woven baskets. ◆ **Pawleys Playhouse,** 10707 Ocean Highway, Pawleys Island, (843) 235-2972, sells toys and children's books.

◆ Georgetown's **Front Street** features a number of charming shops that sell candy, books, antiques, art, children's clothing, kitchen accessories, and more. When you're ready for a break from shopping, stroll the boardwalk fronting the Sampit River. ◆ Gardening enthusiasts won't want to miss **Roycroft Daylily Nursery,** 942 White Hall Avenue, Georgetown, (843) 527-1533, a nationally known daylily garden. Roycroft specializes in modern hybrid daylilies that visitors may buy in pots or have shipped (bare-root). Located south of Georgetown off Route 17 (look for signs marking the left turn onto White Hall Avenue), the nursery is open March–October.

Beach Reading

The Strand has two outstanding independent bookstores. In a nondescript shopping center, **Litchfield Books,** Litchfield Landing, 14427 Ocean Highway, Pawleys Island, ☎ (843) 237-8138, *www.litchfieldbooks.com,* carries a carefully selected and good-sized inventory of fiction, nonfiction, and children's titles in an intimate store that was recently expanded to include a café and a children's room with a large aquarium. The store carries a number of South Carolina and regional titles. ◆ **Harborwalk Books** 723 Front Street, Georgetown, ☎ (843) 546-8212, *www.harborwalkbooks.com,* carries general fiction and nonfiction, but specializes in regional history and Civil War books. There's also an extensive selection of children's books, newspapers, and magazines, plus a few gift items and local artwork.

Spa & Massage

⬤ **Exclusively You Salon & Spa,** 3310 Route 17 South, North Myrtle Beach, (843) 361-8080, *www.exclusivelyyou.com,* offers an array of services, including massage, nail and hair treatments, and facials. Day spa packages range from two to six hours. ◆ **Her Body & Soul Spa & Fitness Center,** 8605 Montague Lane, Queens Harbor, Myrtle Beach, (843) 650-7685, *www.herbodysoul.com,* features a range of massage, skincare, and body treatments, plus a Health Café and women-only fitness center. Body treatments, such as wraps and salt scrubs, are done in a specially designed "wet room" under a Vichy shower.

R e s t   E a s y

S l e e p   W e l l

G rand Strand lodgings range from Georgetown's historic inns to Myrtle Beach's massive resorts and myriad motels. Play Hard Rest Easy guides focus primarily on inns, B&Bs, and unique, independently owned resorts, so more consideration is given to properties south of Myrtle Beach. At the end of these listings, you'll find a short list of some of the Strand's largest resorts. Also, many visitors choose to rent beach cottages or condominiums for a week or longer, and you'll find a rundown of the area's top rental agencies.

Accommodations Pricing

Less than $100	Inexpensive	$
$100-150	Moderate	$$
$151-200	Expensive	$$$
More than $200	Very Expensive	$$$$

Prices are per room, per night, based on double occupancy during peak seasons. Note that B&Bs and most country inns include breakfast in the rate.

DuPre House • Built around 1740 on Lot #53 in Georgetown's historic district, DuPre House features five large guestrooms, each individually decorated and with a private bath. Four rooms have queen-sized beds; one has two twins. Some rooms feature fireplaces, soaking tubs, and verandas. Common areas include parlors on the first and second floors and an elegant dining room, where a full, hot breakfast is served each morning. Throughout the property, you'll find 17th- to 19th-century antiques and artwork. Other amenities include a large swimming pool, poolside spa, well-tended gardens, and complimentary evening hors d'oeuvres. • *921 Prince Street, Georgetown, SC 29440,* ☎ *(843) 546-0298 or 1-877-519-9499, www.duprehouse.com* • *$$–$$$*

Harbor House Bed & Breakfast • Located on the banks of the Sampit River in Georgetown's historic district, this circa 1740 Georgian house features four bedrooms, each with a private bath and excellent harbor views. The three-story house, with its distinctive red roof (that sailors have used for navigation for centuries), sits on a bluff with mature live oaks and pretty magnolias, camellias, and hydrangeas. Inside are original heart-pine floors, eight fireplaces, colonial moldings, and antiques. The second floor also features a sitting room with a television. Guests are treated to a full breakfast, afternoon snacks, and a convenient wet bar. • *15 Cannon Street, Georgetown, SC 29440,* ☎ *(843) 546-6532 or 1-877-511-0101, www.harborhousebb.com* • *$$–$$$*

Litchfield Plantation • This 600-acre estate along the Waccamaw River was once a prosperous, mid-18th-century rice plantation. Today it's an achingly beautiful inn

with membership in the prestigious *Small Luxury Hotels of the World*. So it's no surprise that Litchfield Plantation, which guests reach by passing through wrought-iron gates and driving down a quarter-mile avenue of oaks, is one of the area's most unique and luxurious properties. There are four large suites in the 1750 plantation house, and five rooms and one deluxe suite in the brick and stucco guest house. All guest quarters are elegant. Save for the modern convenience of electricity, common areas feel as if the plantation's original owners just stepped out for a fox hunt. Tasteful period décor and furnishings exist throughout the property. Resort-like amenities include the onsite Carriage House Club, where a full breakfast is served, as well as dinner (see *Dine Well*); a beach club house on Pawleys Island; a private marina; a large, heated pool; two tennis courts; and temporary membership privileges at several area golf clubs. • *Kings River Road, Litchfield, SC 29585,* ☎ *(843) 237-9121 or 1-800-869-1410, www.litchfieldplantation.com* • *$$$$*

The antebellum Litchfield Plantation is now a luxurious inn

Live Oak Inn • A bevy of live oaks, including one estimated to be more than 700 years old, surrounds this relative newcomer to Georgetown's historic district, the 1905 Victorian Live Oak Inn. Five guestrooms

Rest Easy: Sleep Well

feature private baths, fireplaces, and period antiques and reproductions. Porches, beautiful backyard gardens, a comfortable parlor, and an elegant dining room comprise the common areas. A hot, gourmet breakfast is served with fresh bread and fruit each morning. • *515 Prince Street, Georgetown, SC 29440,* ☎ *(843) 545-8658 or 1-888-730-6004, www.liveoakinn.com* • *$–$$*

Mansfield Plantation • Set on more than 900 acres along the Black River, this former 18th-century rice plantation is so authentic that Mel Gibson shot the film *The Patriot* onsite. Eight guestrooms are spread among three historic buildings—an 1840 schoolhouse, the circa 1800 kitchen building, and the 1930s guesthouse—and each has a private bath, private entrance, and a fireplace with a carved mantle. Hearty breakfasts are served in the circa 1800 plantation house, furnished with antiques and 19th-century American paintings. Amenities include golf and tennis privileges at nearby Wedgefield Plantation. This pet-friendly inn is listed on the National Register of Historic Places. • *1776 Mansfield Road, Georgetown, SC 29440,* ☎ *(843) 546-6961 or 1-800-355-3223, www.mansfieldplantation.com* • *$$*

Sea View Inn • Not an ounce of pretension exists at this comfortable inn located on the beach at Pawleys Island. In fact, bare feet are encouraged. Surfside relaxation is the aim, and the Sea View Inn hits the mark in every way. Combined, the main house and adjacent cottage have 20 rooms, all of which have simple furnishings, overhead fans, cross-breezes, private half-baths—guests share six showers—and tremendous ocean or marsh views. The main-house living room features comfort-able furnishings and books of every type to enjoy on the beach or on the oceanfront porch lined with rockers. Three meals a day are included in the rate. • *414 Myrtle Avenue, Pawleys Island, SC 29585,* ☎ *(843) 237-4253, www.seaviewinn.net* • *$$$*

Serendipity Inn • Located on a residential side street just 300 yards from the beach, this small, Spanish-style inn offers a quiet, quaint option to most Myrtle Beach lodgings. The inn's 15 rooms are individually decorated to reflect specific historic eras. Many feature four-poster beds, and all have private baths. A continental breakfast, featuring cereals, baked pastries, fresh fruit, yogurt, and hardboiled eggs, is served daily in the wicker-filled Garden Room. Serendipity also has a pool • *407 71st Avenue North, Myrtle Beach, SC 29572,* ☎ *(843) 449-5268 or 1-800-762-3229, www.serendipityinn.com* • *$–$$*

Area Resorts

Litchfield Beach & Golf Resort, Route 17, Litchfield Beach, ☎ (843) 237-3000 or 1-888-766-4633, *www.litchfieldbeach.com,* features more than 500 rooms on a 4,000-acre campus with outdoor and indoor pools, 17 tennis courts, three 18-hole golf courses, a fitness club, full-service spa, and two miles of private beach. • **Kingston Plantation,** 9800 Queensway Boulevard, Myrtle Beach, ☎ (843) 449-0006 or 1-800-876-0010, *www.kingstonplantation.com,* and its sister property, Hilton Myrtle Beach Resort, feature more than 1,300 accommodations. This attractively landscaped, 145-acre property features a half-mile private beach, nine pools, a golf club, a colossal fitness facility, tennis courts, and six dining options. •

258

Barefoot Resort and Golf, 4980 Barefoot Resort Bridge Road, North Myrtle Beach, SC 29582, ☎ (843) 390-7999 or 1-888-557-6226, *www.bfresort.com*, is a 2,300-acre resort paradise for upscale travelers, especially golfers who will salivate over the four courses designed by Greg Norman, Davis Love III, Pete Dye, and Tom Fazio. Expected to be complete in 2005, there will be pools-galore, a private beach, marina, spa, and all manner of overnight accommodations.

Your Own Seaside Cottage

The majority of vacationers to the southern Grand Strand rents beach houses or condominiums. From late May to early September, rentals are primarily available on a weekly basis only. The following are just a few of the more-established rental agencies serving the Litchfield, Pawleys Island, and DeBordieu beaches: **The Dieter Co.** 13253 Ocean Highway, Pawleys Island, ☎ (843) 237-2813 or 1-800-950-6232, *www.dieter-company.com;* • **Pawleys Island Realty,** 88 North Causeway Road, Pawleys Island, ☎ (843) 237-4257 or 1-800-937-7352, *www.pawleysislandvacations.com;* and • **DeBordieu Rental Office,** 129 Luvan Boulevard, Georgetown, ☎ (843) 527-9894 or 1-800-797-3633, *www.debordieurentals.com*

Dine Well

The most challenging aspect of Grand Strand dining is choosing where to eat and in the case of the following suggestions, getting a table. Dining out is as much a part of beach vacations as is playing in the surf, so reservations are required to secure seating in the more-refined restaurants. Of course, if your mood leans toward frivolous fun, you won't need reservations at many of the more than 1,000 restaurants around Myrtle Beach. (Head to **Restaurant Row,** a stretch of seafood restaurants that lines both sides of North Kings Highway/Route 17-Business between Myrtle Beach and North Myrtle.) Throughout the Strand, seafood leads the culinary charge, and nearly all restaurants serve creative dishes featuring fresh shrimp, the local staple, as well as native flounder, swordfish, and salmon.

Austins at Pawleys • Expect innovative American cuisine (with a strong Southern influence) at this refined yet relaxed restaurant located on Route 17 in Pawleys Island. Chef/owner Bill Austin, a Culinary Institute of America grad, prepares such appetizers as the Southern fried green tomato tower (slices of fried green tomato stacked with fresh spinach and herbed Montrachet, topped with charred tomato basil vinaigrette) and such entrées as blackened

salmon over creamy cheddar grits and fried Vidalia onions. The restaurant features an extensive, carefully chosen wine list. Open nightly for dinner. • *11359 Ocean Highway, Pawleys Island,* ☎ *(843) 235-3800*

The Carriage House Club at Litchfield Plantation • Set in a historic English carriage house under a canopy of live oaks, this restaurant is the epitome of elegant, romantic dining. The creative menu changes regularly but typically embodies lowcountry cuisine with international flair. That translates into such starters as she-crab soup with aged sherry; and pan-fried grits with shrimp, fresh herbs and cognac sauce. Entrées may include beef tenderloin with wild forest mushrooms, port-shallot sauce, and blue cheese; and pan-seared salmon with bok choi, marinated artichoke hearts, and asparagus. Dress is business casual, though jackets are the norm. Easy on the palate (not necessarily the wallet), the Carriage House Club is ideal for special occasions. Open nightly for dinner by reservation only. • *King's River Road at Litchfield Plantation, Pawleys Island,* ☏ *(843) 237-9322*

Collector's Café • For a bit of culture amidst Myrtle Beach's glitz and neon, make reservations at this restaurant, modeled after 17th-century European salons, where painters sold art while feeding their patrons. Collector's Café began as a coffeehouse/gallery and evolved into a fine Mediterranean dining experience. Six dining rooms, each with unique décor, feature interesting, provocative art for sale. The cuisine is creative as well. Start with the black bean cakes with fresh tomato-jalapeno salsa, guacamole and sour cream; and then add heat to the fire with the Cajun-spiced shrimp, tossed with penne rigate in a jalapeno, fresh cilantro, and tomato broth. Order something cold for dessert. Dinner served Monday–Saturday; coffeehouse hours are noon–midnight. Closed Sundays. • *7726 North Kings Highway, North Myrtle Beach,* ☏ *(843) 449-9370*

The Dogwood Café • A relative newcomer to Georgetown's dining scene, this café serves up satisfying salads and innovative sandwiches for lunch and tasty lowcountry cuisine for dinner. Begin with the crab and cheese fondue or the barbecue bacon shrimp before moving on to the cashew-seared yellowfin tuna or the pecan and honey pan-seared chicken. Dine inside or out on the covered patio overlooking the Sampit River. Open Monday–Saturday for lunch and dinner. • *713 Front Street, Georgetown,* ☏ *(843) 545-7777*

Frank's & Frank's Out Back • With a nod from *Southern Living* readers as the "best small town restaurant" two years running, this restaurant combo is where the Debidue set dines when they're Debidone dining inside DeBordieu. In other words, this is amongst the finest upscale dining in the Strand. Housed in the 1930s-era Marlow's Supermarket, the more-formal Frank's fronts Route 17 and serves an eclectic dinner menu of steaks, chops, and fresh seafood. Start with the sautéed shrimp served with creamy grits and Andouille sausage and move on to the grilled mahi mahi served with spicy ginger cashew vinaigrette, roasted new potatoes, and crispy onions. Behind Frank's, Frank's Out Back features lighter fare for lunch and dinner. Dining is either indoors or in a covered garden surrounded by live oaks. (Garden dining is available year-round.) Both restaurants are open Monday–Saturday. • *10434 Ocean Highway, Pawleys Island,* ☏ *(843) 237-3030 or (843) 237-1581*

Greg Norman's Australian Grille • If you're looking for a cheesy, celebrity-chain restaurant, you won't find it here. This is PGA-superstar Norman's only restaurant, and his tastes are evident in the Australian décor featuring leather, hand-carved

Australian wood, a hand-painted ceiling, and Aboriginal art. The menu includes seafood, beef, pasta, and lamb, and the wine list has earned *Wine Spectator's* prestigious Award of Excellence. Dine inside, where numerous windows provide views of the Intracoastal Waterway, or outside on the waterfront deck. Open daily for dinner. • *4930 Route 17 at Barefoot Landing, North Myrtle Beach,* ☎ *(843) 361-0000*

Landolfi's Italian Bakery & Deli • This casual, genuine-Italian eatery serves the Strand's best brick-oven, thin-crust pizza, as well as large deli sandwiches and freshly made, mouth-watering desserts. (The profiteroles are magnifico.) Order takeout or come as you are to eat in the restaurant's small dining room or on the outside patio. • *9305 Route 17, Pawleys Island,* ☎ *(843) 237-7900*

Louis's at Pawleys • Lauded by the *New York Times* and other national media as one of the pioneers of lowcountry cuisine, native South Carolinian Louis Osteen left Charleston—where he ran the wildly successful Louis' Charleston Grill—to open this restaurant plus the adjacent Fish Camp Bar in 2002. Louis's excels at creative yet simple preparations of fresh seafood—garlicky steamed clams, local baby flounder with sweet onion jam, and crab-stuffed Blue Ridge rainbow trout, for example—accompanied by such traditional Southern sides as beer-braised collards and succotash. The cozy décor includes fireplace mantles that once graced local plantations, as well as walls and floors made with wood and bricks recovered from the Waccamaw River. The Fish Camp Bar features outstanding and reasonably priced soups, salads, and sandwiches. Both restaurants serve lunch and dinner daily. • *10880 Ocean Highway, Hammock Shops, Pawleys Island,* ☎ *(843) 237-8757*

The Rice Paddy • Located in a historic bank building, the Rice Paddy serves outstanding, right-off-the-boat seafood, as well as beef, lamb, and veal dishes in downtown Georgetown. Locals cheered the restaurant's 2002 relocation from the waterfront because the new space made for more room (though reservations remain a must). The regional, gourmet cuisine features such appetizers as soft-shell crab, and such entrées as linguini with shrimp, scallops, tomato, and basil with a cream and white wine sauce. The dinner atmosphere is casually elegant, hitting the right note for either a romantic dinner for two or an evening out with friends. Open Monday–Saturday for lunch and dinner. • *732 Front Street, Georgetown,* ☎ *(843) 546-2021*

The River Room • This Georgetown mainstay is all about seafood and great views of the Sampit River. Located on the wharf, the River Room's grilled fish, shrimp and grits, and McClellanville crab cake entrées are consistently outstanding. A warm atmosphere permeates, thanks to original heart-pine floors and exposed brick walls adorned with old, black and white photographs of historic Georgetown. Young children will love the large aquarium with colorful fish in the dining area, as well as the chance to explore the wharf while dinner is prepared. Open Monday–Saturday for lunch and dinner. • *801 Front Street, Georgetown,* ☎ *(843) 527-4110.*

Seafood Capital of South Carolina

More than 40 seafood restaurants line a three-mile stretch of Route 17-Business through the small fishing village of **Murrells Inlet,** and they're filled to capacity during summer dinner hours. The seafood doesn't get any fresher—boats pull in and unload within an angler's cast of the restaurants—nor does the atmosphere get any more casual than at these down-home, primarily family-run establishments. The cuisine is nearly the same at each: grilled, broiled, or fried seafood, including salmon, flounder, sea bass, trout, and shellfish. And hushpuppies, hushpuppies, hushpuppies. A few, especially noteworthy Murrells Inlet stops, all on Route 17-Business: **Admiral's Flagship,** ☎ (843) 651-3016; • **The Captain's Restaurant,** ☎ (843) 651-2416; • **Capt. Dave's Dockside Restaurant & Gazebo Bar,** ☎ (843) 651-5850; and • **Drunken Jack's Restaurant & Lounge,** ☎ (843) 651-2044.

Cafés & Picnic Packing

Front Street Deli, 809 Front Street, Georgetown, ☎ (843) 546-2008, serves an array of sandwiches on fresh-baked bread, plus soups, salads, and such entrées as lasagna. Add a brownie or piece of homemade pie to your picnic. Closed Sundays. • The quintessential gourmet market, **Kudzu Bakery & Market,** 120 King Street, Georgetown, ☎ (843) 546-1847, sells fresh-baked breads, muffins, croissants, cheese biscuits, and cakes, plus a variety of meats and veggies for "home-cooked" meals. Fill a picnic basket with made-to-order deli sandwiches, a bottle of wine, and one (alright, two) of Kudzu's chocolate chip or oatmeal raisin cookies. Closed Sundays. • **Perrrone's,** Live Oaks at Litchfield, Route 17, Litchfield, ☎ (843) 235-9193, is a gourmet food and wine market, specializing in pre-prepared meals to cook at home. Expect fresh-baked breads, soups, salads, and amazing chicken salad. Closed Sundays. • A favorite gathering place for Georgetown residents since 1929, **Thomas Café** 703 Front Street, Georgetown, ☎ (843) 546-7776, serves breakfast and lunch in a casual, diner-like space with large booths and a smattering of tables. The café's specialties are blueberry pancakes, Cajun omelets, and homemade biscuits for breakfast and Southern fried chicken for lunch. Open daily for breakfast and lunch; brunch served on Sundays.

Just Desserts

Harvest Moon Ice Cream Shop, 801 Front Street, Georgetown, ☎ (843) 527-4110, serves sundaes, shakes, malts, floats, and more than 20 flavors of ice cream. Order a couple of scoops on a freshly made waffle cone and walk the river wharf to watch boats tie up or set sail. Open daily, hours vary seasonally. • Words fail to capture the flavors of the bakery concoctions you'll find at **Landolfi's Italian Bakery & Deli,** 9305 Route 17, Pawleys Island, ☎ (843) 237-7900. Don't ask questions. Just go.

A Long-Weekend Itinerary

Day One

After breakfast at your inn, swing by **Kudzu Bakery** (page 262) in Georgetown to purchase a picnic lunch and then by **Pawley's Island Beach Service** (page 244) to rent beach cruisers before heading to **Huntington Beach State Park** (page 243). Ride the park's roads, hike the nature trails, explore Atalaya, and then picnic on the beach. Work off lunch by walking or riding the shoreline and then cool off in the surf. Shower at the park and cross Route 17 to **Brookgreen Gardens** (page 251) to check out the amazing sculptures.

Return your bikes and head to the **Hammock Shops** (page 254) and the **Shops at Oak Lea** (page 255) in Pawleys Island for some late-afternoon browsing. Return to your inn to freshen up for dinner at the **Rice Paddy** (page 261) in downtown Georgetown. After dinner, stroll the river boardwalk. Call it a day.

Day Two

Linger over breakfast to soak in your vacation, and then head to **Black River Outdoors** to join a guided paddle tour of the **Black River Cypress-Tupelo Swamp** (page 245). Next head to **Thomas' Café** (page 262) for some Southern fried chicken. Spend the early afternoon touring historic Georgetown with **Georgetown Tour Company** (page 252) or on your own, making sure to stop at the **Rice Museum** (page 252). Next head south on Route 17 to explore **Hopsewee Plantation** (page 253) or **Hampton Plantation State Historic Site** (page 253). On your return drive, stop by **Roycroft Daylily Nursery** (page 255) to purchase some plants as gifts from your trip.

Return to your inn to shower and to prepare for dinner at the **Carriage House Club at Litchfield Plantation** (page 259).

Still going after dinner? Head to the bar at **Frank's** (page 260) for a nightcap.

Alternate Day Two

After breakfast, fast track to the **NASCAR SpeedPark** (page 249) for some lead-foot action on one of the seven race courses. Hot on the heels of "just racing," cool off with a few spins on the Turbo Twister at **Myrtle Waves** (page 250). Time for some seafood: dine on Myrtle Beach's **Restaurant Row** (page 259), before hitting the beach in **Myrtle Beach State Park** (page 247) to digest and rest.

Shower off at the park and then do some late-afternoon shopping at **Broadway at the Beach** (page 254) before bellying up to the bar at **Greg Norman's Australian Grille** (page 260) for drinks and dinner overlooking the Intracoastal Waterway. End your day with a few carnival games at the **Pavilion** (page 250) or by catching **Legends in Concert** (page 251). Lights out.

Day Three

After breakfast at your inn, spend the morning either **shopping** (page 254), browsing the Grand Strand's **antiques shops & art galleries** (page 248); touring **Hobcaw Barony** (page 253); or doing nothing more strenuous than reading a book on the beach.

Head to **Louis's at Pawleys** (page 261) for lunch and then climb reluctantly into your car for the drive back to the real world.

Additional Information

Georgetown Convention & Visitors Bureau, 1001 Front Street, Georgetown, SC 29440, ☎ (843) 546-8436 or 1-800-777-7705, *www.georgetown-sc.com*, is open summer weekdays, 9 A.M.–5 P.M.; Saturdays, 10 A.M.–3 P.M. Call for winter hours.

Myrtle Beach Area Chamber of Commerce, 1200 North Oak Street Myrtle Beach, South Carolina 29577, ☎ (843) 626-7444 or 1-800-356-3016, *www.mbchamber.com*, operates three visitor centers, all of which are open weekdays, 8:30 A.M.–5 P.M. Weekend hours are 9 A.M.–5 P.M., March–mid October. Call for winter hours. Other locations are in **North Myrtle Beach** at 213 Route 17 North, ☎ (843) 249-3519; and in **Murrells Inlet**, 3401 Route 17 South, ☎ (843) 651-1010.

*Every time we walk along a beach some ancient urge
disturbs us so that we find ourselves shedding shoes
and garments or scavenging among seaweed and whitened
timbers like the homesick refugees of a long war.*

– Loren Eiseley

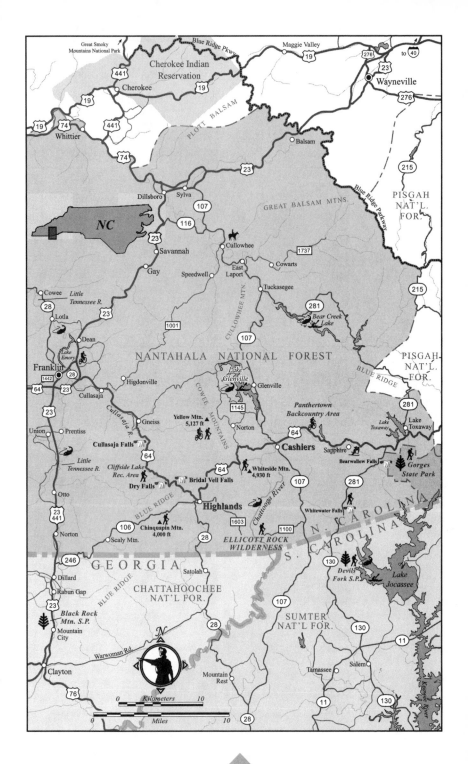

Highlands and Cashiers, North Carolina

A s if being squeezed by its narrowing borders, North Carolina becomes increasingly rugged moving west from Asheville. The Blue Ridge and Smoky Mountains brush together here, where deep valleys, dense forests, and high peaks define the landscape. Much of the western reaches of the state falls within the mammoth, 530,000-acre Nantahala National Forest. Named for a Cherokee word meaning "land of the noon day sun"—the deepest valleys receive direct sunlight only at mid day—the forest is a collection of ancient mountains and cascading waterways, where each spring, melting snow and heavy rains turn the region's 250-plus waterfalls into furious flumes. Save for a smattering of small, workaday mountain towns and such upscale, summer-resort towns as Highlands and Cashiers, the Nantahala is scarcely populated.

The Cherokee lived in these fertile valleys for centuries before Spanish explorer Hernando DeSoto came through in 1540, searching for gold. It wasn't until the 18th and 19th centuries, however, that pioneers began to push the frontier westward into Cherokee territory. Tensions ran high between the Native Americans and settlers and by the start of the American Revolution, the Cherokee were happy to align with the English in attacking pioneer settlements. That alliance cost the Indians dearly. After the war, the United States Government dealt a heavy hand in land negotiations with the tribe, pushing the Cherokee further westward until 1838, when an Act of Congress ordered all Native Americans east of the Mississippi to relocate to Oklahoma. That forced removal became known as the "Trail of Tears."

Around the same time, planters and wealthy merchants from South Carolina's Lowcountry discovered the area as a summer destination; the cool mountain air proved an ideal antidote to the heat and mosquito-born illnesses common along the coast. They purchased land, built large homes, and brought their families and domestic servants up the rough mountain roads by stagecoach for the summer. Both Cashiers, settled around 1839, and Highlands, founded in 1875, developed as seasonal resorts for wealthy "flatlanders."

Line of Reasoning

Legend has it that Highlands was settled after the town's founders, Samuel Kelsey and Clinton Hutchinson, drew a line on a map from New York to New Orleans, another from Chicago to Savannah, and decided to build a town where the lines intersected.

In 1911, President Taft signed the Weeks Act, allowing the U.S. Forest Service to purchase private land to provide a continuous supply of timber and to generate hydroelectric power. The law eventually led to the establishment of the Nantahala National Forest in 1920. Today the Forest Service manages public lands, including the Nantahala, with a more environmentally friendly focus: to sustain the use of natural resources; to protect biological diversity and natural wildlife habitats; and to provide venues for outdoor recreation.

NC Division of Tourism

The abundance of places to play outdoors is a major reason visitors flock to Highlands, Cashiers, and the Nantahala National Forest but certainly not the only one. North Carolina's southwestern mountains also feature a number of fine shopping outlets, cultural venues, and upscale lodging and dining establishments. Each season has its charms. Spring brings colorful flora and rushing whitewater, while summer delivers cool temperatures and endless green ridges. Fall's foliage dazzles with red, yellow, and orange leaves, and winter is when you'll find the least traffic and shortest lines at the grocery stores.

Autumn in the Western Mountains

The Way Around

The colossal **Nantahala National Forest** stretches from the western boundaries of the Pisgah National Forest near Sapphire to North Carolina's westernmost boundaries with Tennessee. This chapter focuses primarily on the southeast and south-central portions of the forest near the towns of Highlands, Cashiers, and Franklin. The chapter on the Great Smoky Mountains National Park covers the remaining areas of the forest. For more detail, see *Wide Open*.

NC Division of Tourism

Numerous golf courses line the hills around Highlands

Located only 10 miles apart, Highlands and Cashiers sit in a narrow depression surrounded by mountain peaks higher than 5,000 feet. Both remain primarily summer-resort, second-home villages, drawing the same visitors from Atlanta, Florida, and Charlotte each season. Of the two, **Highlands** is more posh. Set at 4,100 feet at the junction of Routes 64, 28, and 106, Highlands has a charming Main Street lined with art galleries, cafés, B&Bs, and boutiques. The town comes alive each summer when the year-round population of 3,000 expands to nearly 20,000.

East of Highlands at 3,500 feet, the more laid-back **Cashiers** (pronounced CASH-ers) surrounds the intersection of Routes 64 and 107. Locals call the intersection "the crossroads." Cashiers doesn't have the same pedestrian-friendly compactness that Highlands has, though the town is making improvements in providing a centralized shopping district. Here small shopping centers and freestanding buildings are home to restaurants, antiques shops, and crafts stores. Cashiers also has the Village Green, a two-acre park with a pavilion.

Just east of Cashiers on Route 64 are **Sapphire**, a year-round resort community, and **Lake Toxaway**, a private lake ringed with upscale homes and the classy Greystone Inn. North of Cashiers on Route 107, **Cullowhee** is home to Western Carolina University and the CulloWhee Arts Festival.

West of Highlands, Route 64 follows a serpentine route through stunning **Cullasaja Gorge** and its collection of roadside waterfalls to **Franklin**, a bustling mountain town that developed in the late 19th Century when rubies and other gems were discovered nearby. A number of gem mines operate in the area, including plenty open to the public. Franklin has several interesting museums as well.

Major roadways in the area include **Route 64**, which runs east-west, skirting North Carolina's southern borders with South Carolina and Georgia. The highway connects Sapphire, Cashiers, Highlands, and Franklin before continuing further west into Tennessee. Past Highlands, Route 64 doubles with **Route 28** through the Cullasaja Gorge. In Cashiers, **Route 107** travels north through Glenville and Cullowhee to Sylva.

The region's roadways will have your car's brakes begging for mercy. They are rarely flat or straight as they work their ways around the mountains. There are beautiful views from the roads throughout the area; however, be exceptionally careful taking your eyes off the road. Hairpin turns, narrow lanes, and oncoming traffic pose risks.

Deron Nardo

A waterfall in the Cullasaja Gorge

Weather

Summer is peak season in Highlands and Cashiers, when daytime highs reach the upper 70s and evening lows dip into the mid 50s. Spring and fall produce colorful scenes—wildflowers in May, turning leaves in October—and pleasant temperatures, with daytime highs in the mid 60s and overnight lows in the lower 40s. Winters are cold but not bitter. Expect average highs in the mid 40s, overnight lows in the mid 20s. Watch the weather carefully if you're heading outdoors, as heavy snowfalls can occur anytime between late November and March. Highlands is one of the wettest places in the East, with more than 90 inches of average annual rainfall.

Getting to Highlands & Cashiers

- **By Air**: Located about an hour's drive from Highlands, **Asheville Regional Airport**, ☎ (828) 684-2226, *www.ashevilleregionalairport.com*, hosts several national and regional air carriers, as well as most major car rental companies. Also an hour's drive, the **Greenville-Spartanburg International Airport**, ☎ (864) 848-6233, *www.gspairport.com*, is serviced by four major airlines and several commuter lines. Ground transportation and rental cars are available onsite.

- **By Car**: **From Atlanta**, take Interstate 85 north to Interstate 985 north to Gainesville, Georgia, where you catch Route 23 north (becomes Route 23/441). Follow Route 23/441 north to Dillard, South Carolina, where you turn right on Route 246 (becomes Route 106), which leads directly into Highlands. Expect a 2.5- to 3-hour drive. **From Charlotte**, take Interstate 85 south to Route 74 west to Interstate 26 west toward Asheville. Take Exit #18B for Route 64 west, which you follow to Cashiers and Highlands. Allow 3.5 hours for the drive. **From Raleigh**, take Interstate 40 west through Asheville to Exit #27, where you take Route 74 west toward Waynesville. Take Exit #81 and Route 441/23 south to Franklin, where you take Route 28/64 south to Highlands. Expect a six-hour drive.

Play Hard

Wide Open

Outdoor recreation is for breakfast, lunch, and dinner in the Highlands-Cashiers region, where the amount of public land on which to play is mind boggling. Here you can hike, bike, paddle, fish, swim, ski, and snowshoe to your heart's content. The big playground is the **Nantahala National Forest**. The forest's more than a half-million acres spread across a map of Southwestern North Carolina like an ink stain, from the Pisgah National Forest in the east to Tennessee's Cherokee National Forest in the west. The forest also abuts the Chattahoochee and Sumter national forests to the south and the Great Smoky Mountains National Park to the north.

NC Division of Tourism

Streams flow throughout the Nantahala National Forest

271

To manage this beast of a wilderness, the National Forest Service divides the Nantahala into four ranger districts—the Cheoah, Tusquitee, Wayah, and Highlands—only two of which include activities suggested in this chapter. The **Highlands Ranger District**, 2010 Flat Mountain Road, Highlands, (828) 526-3765, encompasses 116,000 acres of granite mountains, fast-flowing streams, and dramatic waterfalls from the national forest's eastern borders to the Franklin area. Topographic highlights inside the district include the Cullasaja Gorge, Panthertown Valley, and Whiteside Mountain, which some geologists consider the oldest peak in the world.

Within the Highlands District, the **Panthertown Valley Backcountry Area** is a 6,300-acre spread of deep valleys, rocky outcroppings, and sheer granite cliffs. More than 30 miles of trails and the headwaters of the Tuckasegee River make Panthertown perfect for hiking, biking, horseback riding, and fishing. To access the area, take Route 64 east two miles from Cashiers to Cedar Creek Road, onto which you turn left. Proceed roughly two miles and then bear right on Breedlove Road. After 3.4 miles, the road ends at a parking area for Panthertown Valley.

Inside Cullasaja Gorge and within the Highlands District, **Cliffside Lake Recreation Area**, (828) 526-3765, is a serene, lakeside picnic area popular for swimming, hiking, and fishing. Take Route 64 west from Highlands four miles to the recreation area on your right. In the summer, there's a nominal day-use fee.

The 135,000-acre **Wayah Ranger District**, 90 Sloan Road, Franklin, (828) 524-6441, is in the central portion of the Nantahala National Forest and includes sections of the **Appalachian** and **Bartram trails**, **Wayah Bald**, and the **Nantahala River**, including the spectacular 8.5-mile **Nantahala Gorge**, a whitewater haven for kayaking, canoeing, and rafting (covered in the chapter on the Great Smoky Mountains National Park).

Located along the North Carolina-South Carolina border, **Gorges State Park**, (828) 966-9099, is a rugged, 7,100-acre park with an extensive, well-blazed trail system for hiking, horseback riding, and mountain biking. Fly fishing for rainbow and brown trout is also popular in the park's rivers and creeks. From Highlands, travel east on Route 64 through Cashiers to Sapphire, and then turn right (south) on Route 281. The park's main entrance is less than a mile ahead on your left. Another park entrance—the Frozen Creek Road Access—is reached by continuing on Route 64 east eight miles past Sapphire to a right turn onto Frozen Creek Road. Drive for three miles to the parking area on the right.

The **Ellicott Rock Wilderness** is a federally managed, 8,274-acre spread of forest located south of Highlands where North Carolina, South Carolina, and Georgia meet. The rugged, mountainous terrain, which encompasses land from three national forests (Nantahala, Chattahoochee, and Sumter), includes dense woods, high cliffs, waterfalls, and the Chattooga River. Fishing and hiking are popular pursuits here.

In North Georgia, the 750,000-acre **Chattahoochee National Forest** borders North and South Carolina. In the forest, the

*The rugged
Ellicot Wilderness*

Tallulah Ranger District, 809 Highway 441 South, Clayton, GA, (706) 782-3320, a short, scenic drive from Highlands, is packed with hiking, horseback riding, and fishing opportunities. From Highlands, take Route 106 south (becomes Route 246 at the Georgia State line) to Route 15, which you take south to Clayton.

Other public lands a stone's throw from the Highlands area include South Carolina's **Sumter National Forest**, through which flows the **Chattooga River**, one of the few free-flowing rivers in the Southeast. Popularized (maligned, actually) by the movie *Deliverance*, the Chattooga defines the boundary between South Carolina and Georgia in 50-mile stretch that's salivated over by whitewater paddlers, fly fishermen, and hikers. The National Wild and Scenic River (federal designation given to exceptionally scenic, remote sections of river with recreational value) flows into Georgia's **Tugaloo Lake**.

South Carolina's **Devils Fork State Park**, 161 Holcombe Circle, Salem, SC, (864) 944-2639, is also nearby. This 633-acre park is named for the Devils Fork River, which flows into manmade Lake Jocassee. Paddling, swimming, and fishing are popular pursuits in the cold, crystal-blue water of the deep (more than 300 feet in places), large (7,565 acres) mountain lake. The park also has numerous hiking trails. From Highlands, take Route 64 east to Sapphire and Route 281 south, which turns into Route 130 in South Carolina. At Route 11, turn left, cross over Lake Jocassee, and then turn left into the park.

Dayhiking

With some of the most-dramatic landscapes east of the Mississippi, where scenic vistas and cascading waterfalls seemingly await around every bend, the Highlands-Cashiers area begs to be hiked. The following trails are some of the highlights; however, if this sampling fails to wear you out, the sources listed under *Local Outdoor Advice* will happily suggest more.

◆ Located between Highlands and Cashiers, the **Whiteside Mountain Recreational Trail** is a two-mile loop that climbs what some geologists consider the oldest mountain in the world, 4,930-foot Whiteside Mountain. The trail follows the mountain's ridge along precipitous cliffs (with safety rails) to stunning summit

Whiteside Mountain Recreational Trail

views of surrounding peaks and the Chattooga River far below. From the parking area, you can climb either the more gradual, old roadbed or the trail to the right of the roadbed, which ascends via stairs and switchbacks. Both routes climb along the edges of rocky outcroppings, where you'll find numerous places to stop, rest, and take in the views. Whiteside Mountain is one of the more-popular hikes in the area, so expect company, particularly on clear, pretty days. From Highlands, take Route 64 east for about five miles and turn right on Whiteside Mountain Road. Follow signs to the parking area on your left.

◆ There are several pleasant, short hikes at the **Cliffside Lake Recreation Area**, located four miles west of Highlands on Route 64. (Pick up a map when you pay the nominal day-use fee.) On warm summer days, you can hike a couple of miles and then cool off with a refreshing swim in Cliffside Lake. The one-mile **Cliffside Vista Nature Trail** is an interpretative trail that passes through a pine forest and climbs to a ridgetop gazebo with scenic views. Signs describe the foliage along the way. The 1.5-mile **Cliffside Vista Trail** follows the nature tail for the first mile to the rustic gazebo and then continues along the mountain ridge with periodic open views. The half-mile, easy **Skitty Creek Trail** leads from the recreation area to Route 64 near Dry Falls, where you can stand beneath the rock behind the falls (and stay relatively dry). The 0.75-mile **Cliffside Loop Trail**, which encircles Cliffside Lake, is another flat, easy trail.

Whitewater Falls

At 411 feet, **Whitewater Falls** is one of the highest waterfalls east of the Rockies, and several trails provide good vantage points. A short, paved walk from the parking area leads to the first viewing area. To the right of this area, a steep set of wooden stairs leads to a second platform with an even better view. From the platform, you can descend 600 feet to the Whitewater River on a steep, rocky half-mile trail. A shady spot near an old iron bridge waits at the bottom.

Whitewater Falls

Feeling adventurous? Continue on the **Foothills Trail** (a 76-mile hiking trail that passes Whitewater Falls and travels along the border between North Carolina and South Carolina) to Laurel Falls on Corbin Creek, just a mile beyond the iron bridge. Access the Whitewater Falls parking area by taking Route 107 south 9.3 miles from Cashiers into South Carolina, where you turn left at the sign to Whitewater Falls. Continue 2.3 miles to the intersection with Route 130, turn left (the road becomes Route 281 crossing back into North Carolina) and drive to Whitewater Falls on your right. Expect a nominal access fee in the summer.

◆ Two outstanding trails set out from the **Glen Falls Scenic Area**, just a short drive from Highlands. The strenuous **Glen Falls Trail** (departs left from the parking area) descends steeply for 1.4 miles, passing spur trails to stunning views of each of the three, scenic cascades that make up Glen Falls on the East Fork. Retrace your steps to the parking area. The **Chinquapin Mountain Trail** departs right from the parking area and gradually ascends over 1.6 miles to the summit of Chinquapin Mountain (4,160 feet), where you can look out over the Blue Valley into South Carolina. You'll have to cross the East Fork several times en route. Sample a few of the spur trails from the Chinquapin Mountain Trail for additional scenic vistas. To reach the trailheads, take Route 106 west 1.7 miles from Highlands to a road on the left marked by a sign for Glen Falls Scenic Area. The parking area is one mile ahead on this gravel road.

◆ For a strenuous hike to the summit of Yellow Mountain, where a fire tower provides 360-degree views, get thee to the **Yellow Mountain Trail**. The trail, which climbs nearly 2,000 feet along its 4.8 miles, is a day hike, with the emphasis on "day;" pack a picnic and allow yourself the better part of a day to enjoy this ten-mile out-and-back hike. En route to the summit from the trailhead at Cole Gap, you'll climb 4,600-foot Cole Mountain, 5,000-foot Shortoff Mountain, and 4,120-foot Goat Knob before the final 1,000-foot assault on 5,127-foot Yellow Mountain. (After which your two foot gonna hurt.) Yellow

Slippery Sirens

Waterfalls are tempting to approach but get too close and you could be slip slidin' away. Wet rocks are exceptionally slippery, and each year people are injured or killed getting too close to waterfalls in the Nantahala National Forest. Use extreme caution around waterfalls and keep a safe distance.

Mountain is one of the highest peaks in the Highlands District, and reaching the summit provides a nice rush. To reach the trailhead, take Route 64 east 2.7 miles from Highlands to Buck Creek Road, onto which you turn left and drive 2.3 miles to Cole Gap. Park on the shoulder of the road at the sign on the right for the trail.

◆ **Gorges State Park**, (828) 966-9099, located south of Sapphire, is a dayhiker's haven, with a wide range of trails to waterfalls, steep cliffs, and rugged river gorges. As North Carolina's newest state park (opened in 1999), Gorges has an exceptionally well-marked trail system; most trails feature blazes every 20 yards or so. Grab a trail map in the park office (located just east of the intersection of Routes 64 and 281 and open daily, 8 A.M.–5 P.M.), lace up your boots, and head to one of Gorges' two parking areas. (See *Wide Open* for directions.) A series of four trails set out from parking area off Route 281. **Buckberry Ridge Trail** is an easy .75-mile loop blazed with white circles. **Bearwallow Valley Trail**, blazed in red circles, is a 1.25-mile stroll through the forest that leads to the **Bearwallow Falls Trail**, a blue-circle-blazed, half-mile hike to the falls on Bearwallow Creek. Toward the end of the Bearwallow Falls Trail, you can access the 2.7-mile **Ray Fisher Place Trail**, blazed in green circles, which leads to Jake's Branch. From the Frozen Creek Road parking area, the **Canebrake Trail** is a 10-mile out-and-back hike that connects to the 76-mile Foothills Trail.

◆ **Devils Fork State Park**, 161 Holcombe Circle, Salem, SC, (864) 944-2639, which is part of Sumter National Forest in South Carolina, has a couple of short, easy hikes that wind their way through the forest and around Lake Jocasee. The 1.5-mile **Oconee Bell Nature Trail** is a loop named for an indigenous

wildflower, and the 3.5-mile **Bear Cove Trail** is a loop that offers scenic views of the Blue Ridge Mountains and Lake Jocasee. See *Wide Open* for directions.

◆ Other good hiking options nearby exist in the **Panthertown Valley Backcountry Area** and **Ellicott Rock Wilderness**. For trail maps and directions to these hiking areas, stop by the Highlands Ranger District office. (See *Local Outdoor Advice.*)

Mountain Biking

Mountain biking purists drive more than an hour to reach the **Tsali Recreation Area**, located on the southern shores of Lake Fontana, where a wicked system of challenging trails awaits. But the drive isn't necessary. If you're hoping to mountain bike around the Highlands area, you'll be glad to know there's a smattering of trails and many miles of forest roads you can ride. (Tsali is covered in the Great Smoky Mountains National Park chapter.)

◆ In the **Panthertown Valley Backcountry Area** (see *Wide Open* for directions), a combination of gravel roads and singletrack trails provides access to the entire valley. This area only recently became public land, and an extensive trail project is underway that will increase and improve the trails. (For current trail information, call the Highlands Ranger District at (828) 526-3765.) The most well-known rides are the 7.5-mile **Boggy Creek Loop** and the **7.5-mile Canaan Land Loop.** Each combines challenging climbs and descents with sublimely beautiful scenery. The drawback to Panthertown Valley? None of the trails is well marked. Unless you're riding with someone who knows the area, don't head in without a topographical map (available at the Highlands Ranger District) and compass. If your sense of direction or ability to remember the route you've ridden is strong, Panthertown is an excellent place to set out for some aimless exploration. In general, expect plenty of gutted gravel and dirt roads, numerous creek crossings, and a few open areas where power lines run. The Salt Rock access area is a good place to enter Panthertown. From Cashiers, take Route 64 east two miles to a left turn at Cedar Creek Road. Drive 2.3 miles to Breedlove Road. Turn right and continue the final 3.5 miles to the parking area.

NC Division of Tourism

◆ The **Round Mountain Ride** is on a gated, gravel logging road (Forest Road 88) that's closed to automobiles. The three-mile road features a couple of steep climbs, as well as occasional views through the leaves to South Carolina's Lake Jocasee and the Whitewater River corridor. From Cashiers, drive south on Route 107 roughly six miles to Forest Road 88 on the left, where limited parking is available at the gate.

◆ The **Brush Creek Ride** is another gated forest road popular with mountain bikers for its great mountain and valley views. The 12-mile out-and-back ride on the gravel road descends steeply from Cole Mountain Gap for a couple of miles (making for a tough climb on the return trip) into the Brush Creek area, then alternately climbs and descends Emmaline Gap. From Highlands, take Route 64 east three miles to Buck Creek Road and head north (left) on Buck Creek for two miles to Forest Road 4539. There is limited parking on the side of the road. Set out past the gate.

Bike 'n Hike

To combine a good ride with a short, strenuous hike, take the 3.5-mile ride from **Stewart Cove** to **Yellow Mountain Gap**, where you can lock up the bike and climb a mile to the summit of Yellow Mountain. The ride begins on Forest Road 4593, a gated logging road located two miles north of the Brush Creek Ride trailhead on Buck Creek Road. Park at the trailhead if there's no room, backtrack two miles on Buck Creek Road to Cole Mountain Gap to park and ride to Yellow Mountain Gap. (At the one fork on Forest Road 4593, bear right.) Then hoof the one-mile, 1,000-foot climb to the fire tower and 360-degree views atop Yellow Mountain. Retrace the route to your car.

◆ In **Gorges State Park**, mountain bikers can ride the **Auger Hole Trail**, which departs from the Frozen Creek Road parking area and stretches six miles to Turkey Pen Gap at the western boundary of the park. The multi-use trail—watch for hikers and horseback riders—descends to cross the Toxaway River, before flattening out and then  crossing Bear Wallow Creek. The red-square-blazed trail ends at Turkey Pen Gap, where you turn around to retrace your route. Follow directions to the parking area under *Wide Open*.

◆ In Franklin, the **Little Tennessee River Greenway** is a four-mile paved bicycling and walking path that follows the gentle Little Tennessee River through town. There are five parking areas along the trail and two bridges that cross the river. The easiest parking area to find is right off Northeast Main Street at the bridge across the river. This path makes for an ideal, slow-paced ride.

Bike Rentals

The Adventure Depot, 200 Yellow Mountain Road, Cullowhee, ☎ (828) 743-2052 or 1-800-903-4401, *www.adventuredepot.net*, rents front- and full-suspension mountain bikes and offers guided tours, complete with lunch. ◆ **Smoky Mountain Bicycles**, 3580 Georgia Road (Route 441/23), Franklin, ☎ (828) 369-2881, *www.smokymtnbikes.com*, rents mountain bikes by the hour, day, and week. Located three miles south of Franklin on Route 441/23.

Paddling

NC Division of Tourism

Paddling waters abound near Highlands

Highlands and Cashiers are within an hour's drive of two world-class whitewater rivers, the **Chattooga** and the **Nantahala**. Both rivers (and the outfitters that run rafting trips on them) are profiled in separate chapters. The North Georgia Mountains chapter covers the Chattooga, and the Great Smoky Mountains National Park chapter covers the Nantahala River. Paddling options in the immediate Highlands area are primarily on gentle rivers or on pristine mountain lakes.

◆ Located four miles north of Cashiers, **Lake Glenville** is a stunning, six-mile long, manmade lake that, at 3,500 feet in elevation, is the highest body of water its size in the Eastern United States. The nearly 1,500 acres of clear water and 26 miles of shoreline make for the perfect playground on which to paddle. ◆ North of Cashiers, just off Route 107, **Bear Creek Lake** and **Cedar Cliff Lake** are two serene, undeveloped mountain lakes with minimal boat traffic. Both offer rugged shoreline amidst scenic mountain views. To reach Cedar Cliff Lake, take Route 107 north 14 miles from Cashiers. Just before you reach Tuckasegee, turn right on Shook Cove Road, where a boat ramp provides access to the lake. For Bear Creek Lake, continue north on Route 107 past Shook Cove Road to Route 281, where you turn right and drive four miles to the lake's access area on the right.

◆ With more than 75 miles of shoreline, 7,500-acre **Lake Jocassee** is a serene mountain lake with clear, refreshing water, forested shores, and sweeping views of the surrounding Southern Appalachian Mountains. Formed in the 1970s for hydroelectric power, Lake Jocassee is more than 300 feet deep in places. **Devils Fork State Park** in South Carolina provides the best access to the lake. See directions under *Wide Open*.

Rentals

The Adventure Depot, 200 Yellow Mountain Road, Cullowhee, ☏ (828) 743-2052 or 1-800-903-4401, *www.adventuredepot.net*, rents canoes and kayaks and offers a variety of guided paddle tours. ◆ Located five miles north of Cashiers, **Signal Ridge Marina**, Route 107, Glenville, ☏ (828) 743-2143, *www.signalridgemarina.com*, rents canoes and sea kayaks for use on Lake Glenville. ◆ Located in Salem, South Carolina, **Hoyett's**, 516 Jocassee Lake Road, Salem, SC, ☏ (864) 944-9016, *www.hoyetts.com*, rents canoes and sea kayaks for use on Lake Jocassee.

Fly Fishing

With cool, mountain water knifing through the valleys of the Nantahala National Forest and settling in surrounding lakes, good fishing is never more than a cast away. Rainbow and brown trout are the most-popular river catches, while bass, crappie, and walleye frequent the area's pristine lakes. Popular fishing waters include the **Chattooga**, **Tuckasegee**, and **Little Tennessee rivers**; **Lake Jocassee**; **Cliffside Lake**; **Lake Glenville**; **Bear Creek Lake**; and **Cedar Cliff Lake**. The best way to fish these waters is with a guide. Fortunately, several good outfitters exist around Highlands and Cashiers to get you started. If you plan to fish without a guide, stop by one of the following shops for stream reports.

NC Division of Tourism

♦ As the area's only Orvis-endorsed shop, **Brookings-Orvis**, #3 Chestnut Square, Highway 64, Cashiers, (828) 743-3768 or 1-888-544-7343, *www.brookings-cashiersnc.com*, operates a full-service fly shop, a school offering casting and fly-tying instruction, and guide services on the Tuckaseegee and Davidson rivers. ♦ **The Highland Hiker**, 28 Church Street in Highlands, (828) 526-5298; and at the crossroads of Routes 64 and 107, Cashiers, (828) 743-1732, *www.highlandhiker.com*, is a full-service fly shop with a guide service and fly-fishing school. The store puts together all manner of fishing expeditions to the Nantahala, Tuckaseegee, Cullasaja, Chattooga, and Whitewater rivers, as well as into Panthertown Valley. ♦ **The Adventure Depot**, 200 Yellow Mountain Road, Cullowhee, (828) 743-2052 or 1-800-903-4401, *www.adventuredepot.net*, offers fly-fishing classes and guided trips.

The Laws of Fishing

Unless you want to meet the local game warden on less-than-ideal terms, you'll need a state fishing license to fish 'round here. To order one over the phone with a credit card, call the North Carolina Wildlife Resources Division, ☎ 1-888-248-6834, or stop by **Brookings-Orvis**, #3 Chestnut Square, Route 64, Cashiers, ☎ (828) 743-3768, or **Reeves Hardware**, 275 Main Street, Highlands, ☎ (828) 526-2157.

Horseback Riding

To saddle up and ride a powerful steed through the scenic mountains of Southwestern North Carolina, head to **Arrowmont Stables**, 276 Arrowmont Trail, Cullowhee, (828) 743-2762 or 1-800-682-1092, *www.arrowmont.com*, where you can select from a variety of trail rides across their 200 acres. Expect generous helpings of picturesque valleys, lakes, streams, and overlooks.

Rainy Day Workout

If the weather cancels your outdoor play, get a workout in at one of the following area fitness facilities, all of which accept guests for a nominal day-use fee. ◆ **Elite Fitness**, 460 Carolina Way, Highlands, (828) 526-9083, is a full-service gym with cardiovascular equipment and free weights. After throwing some weight around, take advantage of the onsite massage services. ◆ **Franklin Health & Fitness Center**, 1214 East Main Street, Franklin, (828) 369-5608, *www.franklinfitnesscenter.com*, presents its guests a number of options for getting the heart pumping, including cardio equipment, Nautilus, yoga, tai chi, and a junior Olympic pool. ◆ **Yoga Luna**, 265 Oak Street, Highlands, (828) 526-1022, *www.yogaluna.com*, welcomes you to drop in on any of their Hatha yoga classes for $12 per class.

Swimming

Deron Nardo

In the summer, nothing beats working up a sweat hiking or biking and then taking a refreshing swim in a cool, clear lake or mountain stream. The following swimming holes are some of the area's best. ◆ **Cliffside Lake Recreation Area**, located four miles west of Highlands off Route 64, has a lake for swimming, restrooms, a shower, and a picnic area. ◆ **Lake Jocassee**, accessed via South Carolina's **Devils Fork State Park**, features cool, clear water. See *Wide Open* for directions. ◆ The **Chattooga River** has many accessible swimming holes along its banks. The **Bull Pen Bridge** is a popular spot. Take Route 107 south from Cashiers approximately six miles,

Swimming in the Chattooga River

make a right on Bull Pen Road and drive roughly five miles to the iron bridge, where you park. Swim at the bridge or hike downstream for more privacy.
◆ **Sliding Rock**, a rock waterslide that spills into a chilly pool of water, is a popular swimming hole on the Chattooga. From Cashiers, take Route 107 south roughly a mile to Whiteside Cove Road and make a right. Follow the road until you come to a bridge over

the Chattooga River, park nearby, and walk upstream to Sliding Rock. ◆ Adjacent to Gorges State Park, **Turtleback Falls** is one of many falls on the Horsepasture River and it makes an excellent swimming hole, particularly after hiking the park's rugged trails. Follow directions in *Wide Open* to the park's entrance at Route 281. From the parking area, walk back to Route 281 and turn left. You'll soon come upon a gate and old path on your left. It leads to the Horsepasture River and Turtleback Falls. Hike roughly one mile to the river and then walk 200 yards downstream to Turtleback Falls.

Skiing

NC Division of Tourism

Sapphire Valley, 4350 Highway 64 West, Sapphire, (828) 743-1169, *www.skisapphire.com*, is a small ski resort with only two runs—one beginner and one intermediate—one chairlift, and a 200-foot vertical drop. The longest run is 1,600 feet. Despite such small-scale features, the resort is big on fun with a festive atmosphere. Instruction and ski and snowboard rentals are available onsite. There is only night skiing during the week—hours are 5 P.M.–10 P.M.—but weekend hours are 9 A.M.–10 P.M.

Local Outdoor Advice

Nantahala National Forest, Highlands Ranger District • One of four ranger stations to service North Carolina's largest national forest, the Highlands Ranger Office is located just east of Highlands off Route 64. The station is staffed Monday–Friday, 8 A.M.–4:30 P.M. • 2010 Flat Mountain Road, Highlands, ☏ (828) 526-3765

The Adventure Depot • A one-stop shop for mountain bike rentals and tours, canoe and kayak rentals and tours, and rock climbing and rappelling, the Adventure Depot also sells and rents many kinds of outdoor gear. Actually closer to Cashiers than Cullowhee, the Adventure Depot is reached by taking Route 64 west from Cashiers roughly three miles to Norton Road, onto which you turn right and drive two miles to Yellow Mountain Road. • 200 Yellow Mountain Road, Cullowhee, ☏ (828) 743-2052 or 1-800-903-4401, *www.adventuredepot.net*

Highland Hiker • Highland Hiker has two locations in the area, both of which feature the latest fly-fishing, hiking, camping, backpacking, and canoeing gear, as well as outdoor clothing and footwear. The staff in both locations will happily direct you to a great hike or fishing hole. • 601 East Main Street, Highlands, ☏ (828) 526-5298; and at the intersection of Routes 64 and 107 in Cashiers, ☏ (828) 743-1732; *www.highlandhiker.com*

K i c k   B a c k

Y ou can't fill your entire vacation with thigh-crunching hikes, epic mountain-bike rides, and frothy whitewater paddles, right? Fortunately, there's also sport in finding great shopping deals, a strong-handed masseuse, and a gourmet meal.

Antiques

Cashiers and Highlands list more than 30 antiques stores in their shopping guides, so bring your checkbook. In Cashiers, most antiques dealers are clustered around the intersection of Routes 64 and 107. Stop by the **Cashiers Antique Mall**, 31 Pillar Drive, at Route 107 South, (828) 743-3580, *www.cashiersantiquemall.com*, where 14 dealers are under one roof. Expect a variety of items, ranging from furniture and decorative accessories to antique glass and oil paintings. ◆ At **Lyn K. Holloway**, 25 Burns Street, (828) 743-2524, you'll find 4,500 square-feet of space filled with English, French, and Continental antiques. ◆ In Highlands, the majority of antiques dealers is on or near Main Street (Route 64). Try **Scudders Galleries**, 352 Main Street, (828) 526-4111, *www.scuddersgalleries.net*, for silver and crystal, chandeliers, oriental rugs, and American and English furniture; or ◆ **The Elephant's Foot Antiques**, Route 64 and Foreman Road, Highlands, (828) 526-5451, which carries French and English 18th- and 19th-century furniture.

Back Roads Touring

So many scenic, two-lane roads exist in Western North Carolina that numerous guidebooks focus just on driving tours through the region. Every road around the Highlands-Cashiers area serves up one stunning vista after another, so all you really need to piece together a route is a full tank of gas and a roadmap. The following are some of the area's highlights.

◆ The **Blue Ridge Parkway** is perhaps the most-beautiful stretch of road in the country, and it's no secret: 22 million people cruise sections of the 469-mile roadway each year. The parkway's southern terminus at the Great Smoky Mountains National Park is a little more than an hour's drive from Highlands and Cashiers. The quickest way to access

the parkway from Cashiers is to take **Route 107** north 27 miles (a beautiful drive, too) to Route 74 east. Take Route 74 east roughly 10 miles to the parkway, which you can drive either south to Great Smoky Mountains National Park or north to Asheville, the French Broad River, Mount Mitchell and points beyond.

◆ The **Mountain Waters Scenic Byway** is a state-designated, 61-mile drive from Highlands to Fontana Lake that winds through the Nantahala National Forest. Highlights include waterfalls, the Nantahala River, and pristine Fontana Lake. From Highlands, take Route 64 west through Franklin to a right turn on Old Route 64 and then a left turn on State Road 1310 (Wayah Road). For a stunning side trip, follow signs to Wayah Bald, a 5,385-foot, grass-covered mountain with 360-degree views. State Road 1310 passes Nantahala Lake and reaches the Nantahala River. At Route 19, turn right to follow the road north to Fontana Lake. ◆ The previous drive's first eight miles are through **Cullasaja Gorge** and past some of the state's most-scenic waterfalls on **Route 64**. See *Waterfalls* for more detail. ◆ The drive south from Highlands on **Route 28** to Walhalla, South Carolina passes several photogenic landscapes, including the Upper and Lower Satulah Falls, Satulah Mountain, and the Blue Valley Overlook.

Designated Driver

So you're on vacation and are suddenly struck with the urge to go bouncing through the Nantahala backcountry in someone else's Land Rover. What to do? Call **Highland Safari**, ☎ (828) 526-9268, *www.highlandsafari.com*, of course. This unique tour company takes up to nine passengers in its 1973 Series III Land Rover (shipped stateside from England) for off-road adventures through rugged, private land. In addition to the basic, three-hour safari, which includes local history, folklore, and light refreshments, other packages include a dinner safari (bring your own or let Highland Safari cook for you); a haunted safari (guides tell ghost stories); and a seasonal Christmas tree safari (cut your own Fraser fir for the holidays).

Galleries

NC Division of Tourism

Crafts shopping in Cashiers

"Upscale" and "fine art" go hand in hand, and Highlands and Cashiers are most certainly upscale. So it's no surprise that galleries command a lot of retail space here. Some of the better stops: ◆ **Summit One Gallery**, 4152 Cashiers Road, Highlands, (828) 526-2673, in the Apple Mountain Shops, displays work by regional artists in various mediums including pottery, oil, photography, and watercolors. ◆ **Bascom-Louise Gallery**, 554 Main Street, Highlands, (828) 526-4949, *www.bascom-louisegallery.org*, is a nonprofit art center featuring local and regional art in a rustic building that shares space with Hudson Library. The gallery has exhibits, events, and workshops throughout the year.

◆ **John Collette Fine Art,** 137 Main Street, Highlands, (828) 526-0339, imports and shows pieces from nationally renowned painters, sculptors, and glass-artists. ◆ The **Ann Jacob Gallery**, 394 Main Street, Highlands, (828) 526-5550, *www.annjacob.com,* presents portrait and still-life paintings, with an emphasis on oils, created by artists with both international and local roots. ◆ In an old Baptist church on Route 64 between Highlands and Cashiers, **Whiteside Art Gallery,** 1057 Route 64 East, Cashiers, (828) 743-2269, features the paintings of William Whiteside, the gallery's owner, as well as work by local artists. ◆ **White Moon,** 545 Route 107 South, Cashiers, (828) 743-6666, features oil paintings, blown glass, landscapes, pottery, photography, and calligraphy.

Gem Mines

In 1870, prospectors found what Hernando DeSoto could not more than three centuries before: precious stones. When large rubies and sapphires were found around Franklin, two large mining companies moved in. They later abandoned their operations when the source of the minerals was not found. What wouldn't support a large-scale mining effort is enough to satisfy thousands of tourists each year who head for the local gem mines to sort through buckets of ore and pan in water-flowing flumes. To try your luck, head to one of the following mines.

◆ At **Gold City Gem Mine**, 9410 Sylva Road, Franklin, (828) 369-3905, *www.goldcityamusement.com*, take your place along the flume to pan for rubies, sapphires, blue and silver topaz, amethysts, and emeralds.

◆ **Mason Mountain Mine and Cowee Gift Shop**, 5315 Bryson City Road, Franklin, (828) 524-4570, *www.masonmtnmine.org*, lets you choose what type of bucket you'll work from, ranging from the $2 general bucket to the $300 super bucket.

◆ Dig your own dirt (with gems?) or sort through pre-dug buckets of dirt at **Rose Creek Mine**, 115 Terrace Ridge Drive, Franklin, (828) 349-3774, where the rewards may include sapphires, rubies, quartz, and moonstones.

Can't Dig It?

Not in the mood for breaking a nail or freezing your hands in cold mountain water? You can still discover Franklin's mining heritage and see some of the amazing stones found in the area with a visit to the **Franklin Gem and Mineral Museum**, 25 Phillips Street, Franklin, ☎ (828) 369-7831. The museum is housed in an 1850s jail-you won't have far to go if you try to make off with some of the gems on display-and admission is free. Open Monday-Friday, Noon-4 P.M.; Saturday, 11 A.M.-3 P.M.

Museums

The **Scottish Tartans Museum & Heritage Center**, 86 East Main Street, Franklin, (828) 524-7472, *www.scottishtartans.org*, exhibits general Scottish history, with a special emphasis on the history of the tartan and kilt. The museum's large gift shop sells Scottish apparel, including kilts. Open Monday–Saturday, 10 A.M.–5 P.M. Nominal admission fee. ◆ **The Highlands Nature Center**, run by the Highlands Biological Research Station, 930 Horse Cove Road, Highlands, (828) 526-2623, has a series of trails that run through a botanical garden with more than 500 specimens of native North Carolinian plants. The garden borders small Lake Ravenel. In addition, there are educational exhibits that interpret the diverse flora of the Highlands area. Open daily, from sunrise to sunset. Free admission. ◆ **The Museum of American Cut & Engraved Glass**, 472 Chestnut Street, Highlands, (828) 526-3415, is a nonprofit displaying cut and engraved glass from the American Brilliant Period (1876-1916). Period pieces are for sale. Open Tuesdays, Thursdays, and Saturdays, 1 P.M.–4 P.M., from mid May–October. Admission is free.

Performing Arts

With a tradition dating to 1938, the **Highlands Playhouse**, 362 Oak Street, Highlands, (828) 526-2695, presents four productions by professional actors over a 10-week season beginning in June. The theater is on top of the hill at the corner of Oak and Third streets. Recent productions have included *Annie* and *The Odd Couple*. ◆ **The Highlands-Cashiers Chamber Music Festival**, PO Box 1702, Highlands, (828) 526-9060, *www.h-cmusicfestival.org*, runs for six weeks, July–August, with performances on Mondays and Saturdays at the Albert Carlton Library in Cashiers, and Sundays and Tuesdays at the Community Baptist Church in Highlands. The HCMF also showcases specific performers and ensembles in its Friday night "spotlight series." ◆ Each year, the **Highlands Community Players**, 507 Chestnut Street, Highlands, (828) 526-8084, *www.highlandscommunityplayers.org*, produce four, weekend-long runs of contemporary and classic plays. Recent productions include *Barefoot in the Park* and *Our Town*. Performances are in the Martin-Lipscomb Performing Arts Center.

Whee!

Plan your vacation properly and you may get to enjoy the two-day **CulloWHEE! Arts Fest**, held each June on Western Carolina University's campus in Cullowhee. Please your ears, eyes, and taste buds with live music on multiple stages, an arts village, and a wide variety of festival-type food. For information, call the CulloWHEE! Arts Fest at ☎ (828) 227-7722 or 1-866-928-3378, or check out *www.cullowheeartsfest.com*.

Spa & Massage

With all of the hiking, biking, and paddling in the area, some professional therapeutic work might come in handy. ◆ **The Day Spa on Spring**, 225 Spring Street, Highlands, (828) 526-8832, offers a variety of wraps and massages. Try the "Heavenly Bliss" treatment, which combines an aromatherapy massage, exfoliating body scrub, and an herbal bath blend package to take home. ◆ **Creative Body Works**, 459 Laurel Street, Highlands, (828) 526-3939, offers Swedish massage, reflexology, and a number of facial and body treatments. ◆ **Wendy's Studio**, Highway 107 South, Cashiers, (828) 743-0535, has massage therapy, as well as yoga classes for all levels.

Shops & Stops

A rainy weekend is not necessarily a wasted one: Your credit cards can get a workout in the area's boutiques. There are more cool stops than the following, but you won't want to miss these. ◆ Drop by **Cyrano's Bookstore**, 390 Main Street, Highlands, (828) 526-5488, for a carefully selected lineup of fiction and nonfiction. ◆ Just a few doors down, **Buck's Coffee Café**, 384 Main Street, Highlands, (828) 526-0020, offers a cozy spot to read, listen to occasional live music, and check out the original art adorning the walls. The café serves a number of hot drinks and wine by the glass. Expect a crowd at night; this is one of the area's few nightlife spots. ◆ The **Highlands Wine and Cheese Shop**, 561 East Main Street, Highlands, (828) 526-5210, at the end of Main Street, specializes in fine wines,

The Falls on Main is a small shopping venue in dowtown Highlands

cheeses, unique gifts, and wine accessories. ◆ **The Stone Lantern**, 309 Main Street, Highlands, (828) 526-2769, fills its store with all things Asian, including porcelains, bonsai plants, bronze Buddha statues, art, and antiques. ◆ For some alternative lighting, stop by **Chattahoochee Candle Company**, 216 South Fourth Street, Highlands, (828) 526-5448. ◆ In Cashiers, **Chapter 2 New and Used Books**, 60 Ingles Shopping Center (on Route 64), (828) 743-5015, offers new and used books, mainly paperbacks. ◆ **Southern Hands**, 1 Wright Square, Highlands, (828) 526-4807; and Route 107 North, Cashiers Commons, Cashiers, (828) 743-5499; *www.southernhands.com*, sells decorative crafts and accessories for the home. ◆ **Cottage Walk**, 46 Commons Drive, Cashiers, (828) 743-6728, *www.cottage-walk.com*, sells primarily new furnishings and accessories for the home, along with a small selection of antiques and reproductions.

Waterfalls

Deron Nardo

Dry Falls off Route 64

So many waterfalls exist in and around the Highlands-Cashiers area that you'll likely encounter one or two couples who are visiting just for the waterfalls. You don't have to hike to see them all. There are several by the roadside, including one you can drive under.

◆ Route 64 runs west eight miles through **Cullasaja Gorge** and passes a collection of scenic waterfalls. The first set of falls appears just 2.5 miles into the drive. **Bridal Veil Falls**, named for its resemblance to a bride's headdress, tumbles 120 feet next to the highway. A paved driveway detours off Route 64, allowing cars to drive behind the thin plume of water.

◆ One mile further west, **Dry Falls** is a 75-foot waterfall with a walking path behind the cascade, giving you the opportunity to view a waterfall from the inside-out.

◆ Another five miles past Dry Falls on Route 64, **Lower Cullasaja Falls** is a 250-foot waterfall you can photograph from your car.

◆ South of Cashiers, 411-foot **Whitewater Falls** is one of the highest waterfalls east of the Rockies. From Cashiers, take Route 107 south 9.3 miles into South Carolina, where you turn left at the sign to Whitewater Falls. Continue 2.3 miles to the intersection with Route 130, turn left (the road becomes Route 281 crossing back into North Carolina) and continue to Whitewater Falls on your right. (Nominal parking fee in the summer.)

R e s t   E a s y

S l e e p   W e l l

E nough of those nights spent on the mattress pad, shivering in your tent, as the chilly mountain air curls your toes. How about a soft feather-mattress, a full Southern breakfast, and a little heat? There are plenty of beds to choose from in Highlands and Cashiers. It's just a matter of finding the one to fit your mood.

Accommodations Pricing

Less than $100	Inexpensive	$
$100-150	Moderate	$$
$151-200	Expensive	$$$
More than $200	Very Expensive	$$$$

Prices are per room, per night, based on double occupancy during peak seasons. Note that B&Bs and most country inns include breakfast in the rate.

---

4 ½ Street Inn • This cozy inn, located between 4th and 5th streets, sits on a serene acre of land within a short stroll of Highlands' main drag. Owners Rick and Helene Siegel display their unique talents—Rick as landscape designer and Helene as chef—in the wonderfully restored 100-year-old house. The inn has 10 rooms, each with antique appointments and an elegant ambience. Request Room #2 for its queen-sized bed, fireplace, claw foot tub with shower, and access to a wraparound porch. Amenities include a full gourmet breakfast—the French toast strada with apple-cider syrup is exquisite—wine hour, fresh baked cookies, and an outdoor hot tub. • *55 4 ½ Street, Highlands, NC 28741, ☎ (828) 526-4464, or 1-888-799-4464, www.4andahalfstinn.com • $$–$$$*

Fire Mountain • If staying in your own elegant tree house isn't enough to entice you to Fire Mountain, perhaps the views from 4,000 feet, the walking and hiking trails at the top of the mountain, and the art gallery will convince you. Set on hundreds of acres, this upscale resort takes advantage of its natural surroundings; an abundance of windows, decks, and porches provide ample views. There are 15 guest accommodations—six rooms in the main inn, six cabins, and three tree houses (actually cabins built three floors up in the forest). All feature spacious baths, elegant furnishings, and tremendous views. Two highlights in the main inn: the Red Thunder room, with 180-degree views from its private deck; and the Satohla Room, with a native stone wood-burning fireplace and terraces on both the sunrise and sunset sides of the inn. The tree houses and cabins are exceptionally private. The hot gourmet breakfast includes ingredients from the inn's own organic gardens and orchards. Lunch and dinner are available by reservation. • *P.O. Box 2772, Fire Mountain, Highlands, NC, 28741, ☎ (828) 526-4446 or 1-800-775-4446, www.firemt.com • $$–$$$$*

Greystone Inn • With high tea in the afternoon, champagne cruises in the evening, and croquet, tennis, and golf nearby, the Greystone Inn feels as if its been torn from the pages of F. Scott Fitzgerald's novel *The Great Gatsby*. Originally built in 1915 as a second home on scenic Lake Toxaway, the Greystone Inn features 21 elegant rooms, some with such names as Rockefeller, Vanderbilt, and Wanamaker. Yet none is as grand as the Presidential Suite, with its 25-foot ceilings, massive stone fireplace, king-sized bed, and oversized Jacuzzi. If you can't get the Presidential Suite, don't fret—each room comes with a Jacuzzi and is uniquely appointed with period pieces and reproductions. A one-night stay includes a gourmet dinner, huge high-country breakfast, hors d'oeuvres, and an assortment of lake activities, including fishing, kayaking, and water skiing. The inn, which has a spa on the grounds, is a member of the inn association, the *Select Registry*. • *Greystone Lane, Lake Toxaway, NC 28747, ☎ (828) 966-4700 or 1-800-824-5766, www.greystoneinn.com • $$$$*

High Hampton Inn • The High Hampton Inn has a long history as a mountain retreat. Former South Carolina Governor Wade Hampton purchased the property in the 1830s and built a hunting lodge on the grounds. Fire destroyed the lodge, and in 1933 the current, chestnut-bark sided inn was completed. Today there are 117 guestrooms in the main inn and several cottages throughout the property, all with private baths.

(Rooms are free from modern intrusions like phones and televisions.) The property's décor is mountain-rustic. Rates include three daily meals, all of which are served buffet-style and consist of traditional Southern cuisine. (Coat and tie are required for gentlemen for dinner.) Amenities include a private, 35-acre lake with a small beach and sailboats for guest use; tennis courts; an 18-hole golf course; and onsite hiking trails. • *1525 Highway 107 South, Cashiers, NC 28717,* ☎ *(828) 743-2311 or 1-800-334-2551, www.highhamptoninn.com* • *$$$–$$$$*

Highlands Inn • Located on the corner of Main and Fourth streets in Highlands, this inn offers its guests a unique "downtown" view. Many of the rooms share the 133-foot balcony that stretches across the front of the inn, overlooking the hustle and bustle of Highlands. The décor in its 31 rooms features period pieces such as antique armoires and colonial paintings. Rates include a full, continental breakfast and cookies and tea in the afternoon. The inn's restaurant, Kelsey's Place, serves lunch and dinner to guests and to the public. For a little pampering, stay at the inn's Mountain Luxury Suites, located a few blocks away, which feature Italian-marble floors, Jacuzzi tubs for two, glass showers, and private balconies overlooking Mill Creek. • *420 Main Street, Highlands, NC 28741,* ☎ *(828) 526-9380, www.highlandsinn-nc.com* • *$–$$$$*

Inn at Half-Mile Farm • The Inn at Half-Mile Farm blends contemporary luxury with an air of simplicity. Lose yourself roaming the 14 acres of fields, forests, ponds, and streams, recollecting the outdoor spirit of Thoreau or Muir. But you'll quickly forget 'ol Henry and John when, upon returning to the inn, you enjoy complimentary evening wine and hors

d'oeuvres or a soak in your Jacuzzi tub. Or both. Many of the 15 rooms have stone fireplaces, whirlpool tubs, and private decks. The inn is only a half-mile from Highlands, but still peacefully off the beaten track. • *214 Half-Mile Drive, Highlands, NC 28741,* ☎ *(828) 526-8170 or 1-800-946-6822, www.innathalfmilefarm.com* • *$$$–$$$$*

Kelsey & Hutchinson Lodge • Named for the founders of Highlands, this brand new lodge (on the grounds of the original, which was destroyed by fire in 1982) opened in 1998, continuing a lodging tradition begun in 1890. Ideally located near Highlands' Main Street yet peacefully set on three-and-a-half acres, the lodge offers the best of rural and urban comforts. There are 33 rooms in several buildings. Rooms in the main inn (the Lee House) feature private balconies, whirlpool tubs, and gas fireplaces. The Cottage, Garden, and Terrace rooms are less expensive—some allow pets; others may have whirlpool tubs or gas fireplaces. A fireside appetizer and wine social awaits you in the evening, and a satiating continental breakfast is served each morning. • *450 Spring Street, Highlands, NC 28741,* ☎ *(828) 526-4746 or 1-888-245-9058, www.k-hlodge.com* • *$$–$$$$*

The Main Street Inn • Built in 1885 and lovingly restored in 1998, this Federal Farmhouse-style inn sits smack dab in the middle of Highlands and has welcomed visitors for more than a century. Antique appointments, cathedral ceilings, and a stone fireplace in the lobby greet guests upon arrival. Twenty cozy guestrooms, split between the main inn and guest houses, all have private baths. Request the Owners' Quarters, a deluxe room in a private wing with a king-sized bed, balcony, claw-foot tub, and cathedral ceilings. A hot, country buffet breakfast is served in the dining room, as is afternoon tea. • *270 Main Street, Highlands, NC 28741,* ☎ *(828) 526-2590 or 1-800-213-9142, www.mainstreet-inn.com* • *$–$$$*

Millstone Inn • Built in 1933 as a private home, the Millstone Inn's charm exudes from its exposed beam interior, cedar-shake exterior, and large stone fireplace in the lobby. The inn features seven rooms and four suites, all with impressive views of the countryside and Whiteside Mountain in the distance. Each room has period and antique furnishings; many feature private decks and sitting rooms. Rates include complimentary sherry, cookies, refreshments, and a full breakfast. • *119 Lodge Lane, Cashiers, NC 28717,* ☎ *(828) 743-2737 or 1-888-645-5786, www.millstoneinn.com* • *$$$–$$$$*

Toad Hall Inn • The reference is to *The Wind in the Willows* and Mr. Toad's waterfront estate, where he generously entertained guests. Similarly, you can expect generous service at this mountain lodge on the shore of a beautiful mountain lake at an elevation of more than 4,100 feet. Each of the five rooms in Badger Lodge features a private deck and Jacuzzi tub. The ultimate in privacy is the property's one-bedroom cottage, with a separate living room and fireplace. Toad Hall serves a hot breakfast each morning, complemented by stunning views of Lake Sequoyah. Wine and cheese are served in the afternoon. Guests may use the inn's canoes to paddle across the lake's smooth-as-glass water. • *61 Sequoyah Point Way, Highlands, NC 28741,* ☎ *(828) 526-3889, www.toadhallb-b.com* • *$$–$$$*

Dine Well

The Nantahala National Forest offers endless ways to burn calories, yet the area's restaurants assure you'll put them right back on. The town of Cashiers is officially "dry"—no alcohol is sold in restaurants or stores—but restaurants allow brown-bagging, usually for a small fee. Highlands, on the other hand, lets the wine flow freely, but does not sell liquor or beer. Again, brown-bagging is permitted for a small fee. Highlands and Cashiers are seasonal destinations, and most restaurants are closed or set limited hours November–April.

Horacio's Restaurant • Horacio Repetto, who hails from Vienna (via Florida), serves European and Northern Italian fare, including appetizers such as sautéed soft shell crab and entrées such as grilled sea bass and lobster and smoked venison tenderloin. The menu changes seasonally. Repetto prepares the cuisine in full view of the dining room, so he can watch his guests enjoy their meals. You can also sit on an outdoor patio, overlooking a small pond and Chestnut Square, a small cluster of shops. The restaurant is BYOB, so bring your favorite Italian red. Horacio's is on Route 64, just east of the Route 107 intersection. Open daily for lunch and dinner. • *Route 64 East, Cashiers,* ☎ *(828) 743-2792*

Lakeside Restaurant • Located just a block off Main Street in Highlands, Lakeside Restaurant is a small, intimate eatery with views of serene Harris Lake. Chef Marty

Rosenfield opened Lakeside in 1990 after working for 10 years in Atlanta. Expect creative preparations of fresh seafood, pasta, chicken, and veal. His wine list has received *Wine Spectator's* prestigious Award of Excellence. Open Tuesday–Saturday for dinner. • *531 Smallwood Avenue, Highlands,* ☎ *(828) 526-9419*

Lightwater Grille • In a rustic, inside dining area (or outside on the porch in season), this grill serves dishes such as vegetarian pasta, fresh mountain trout, and veal Sorentino in a casual setting full of mountain ambience. Stained glass and temporary art exhibitions add a nice touch to the décor, while views of the small pond next to the restaurant set a serene tone. Open daily for lunch and dinner. • *Highway 107 North, Cashiers,* ☎ *(828) 743-5410*

The Market Basket • It's not often you see a grocery store with a grand piano and full dining area. You'll find that and more at the Market Basket, where at night, the store becomes a restaurant with a menu of seafood, pasta, and steaks. "Hot Rocks" is the big draw. Cook your own shrimp, chicken, or steak on a super-hot slab of North Carolina granite. Enjoy live music while dining, Thursday through Sunday evenings, when pianist Cy Timmons tickles the ivories. Open daily for lunch and dinner. • *104 Route 107 South, Cashiers,* ☎ *(828) 743-2216*

On the Verandah • Set on the banks of scenic Lake Sequoyah, this popular, upscale restaurant offers a choice of settings: the verandah with views of the lake, or the elegant dining room, where you may enjoy the live piano music coming from the wine bar.

(This establishment knows its wines; its list of more than 200 vintages has received *Wine Spectator's* Award of Excellence annually since 1987.) Expect fresh fish and seafood specials. Menu standouts include the spicy Thai coconut ginger shrimp and tamarind soy-glazed lamb. The champagne brunch is a big draw on Sundays. Open daily for dinner. • *1536 Franklin Road (Highway 64), Highlands,* ☎ *(828) 526-2338*

Ristorante Paoletti • Firmly ensconced in the memory of past dinner guests, this Italian restaurant features more than 850 wines (recognized by *Wine Spectator's* Award of Excellence) and a menu with Italian seafood, steaks, and homemade pastas. Expect such traditional Italian entrées as chicken with prosciutto in a wild mushroom Marsala sauce, and creative preparations of fresh seafood. The yellowfin tuna with a ginger balsamic port wine reduction is superb. Open daily for dinner. • *440 Main Street, Highlands,* ☎ *(828) 526-4906*

Wild Thyme Gourmet • A favorite among locals, Wild Thyme Gourmet features a small, casual dining area inside and a tree-shaded courtyard outside. The cuisine is decidedly gourmet. Rather than presenting a menu with dozens of options, the café focuses on creative preparations of fewer dishes. The lump crab cakes rival anything you'll find in the Lowcountry, and the salmon baked in a Vidalia onion crust is excellent. Like its menu, the wine list is carefully chosen. Open daily for lunch and dinner. • *490 Carolina Way, Highlands,* ☎ *(828) 526-4035*

Wolfgang's on Main • Chef Wolfgang and his wife Mindy have used their talents—

Wolfgang in the kitchen and Mindy in the dining room—to create a fantastic culinary experience in the heart of Highlands. With a penchant for New Orleans- and Bavarian-style dishes—crawfish étouffee and schnitzel, for example—Wolfgang's entrées explode with flavor. Make reservations for one of several dining areas: a garden pavilion, an awning-covered deck, and a warm dining room with a fireplace. The restaurant's list of more than 650 vintages has earned awards from *Wine Spectator*. Open daily for dinner. • *474 Main Street, Highlands, ☎ (828) 526-3807*

Picnic Packing

The Market Basket, 104 Highway 107 South, Cashiers, ☎ (828) 743-2216, is part gourmet grocery, part delicatessen, and part restaurant. It's a particularly well-suited spot to grab a picnic lunch before venturing into the woods. • **Wild Thyme Bakery**, Village Walk, Highway 107 South, Cashiers, ☎ (828) 743-1065, has a number of gourmet sandwiches—chicken havarti, and a portabella with goat cheese and spinach, for example—to complete your picnic basket, or to enjoy on the deck. Also open for dinner. • **Fresser's Eatery**, 470 Oak Street, Highlands, ☎ (828) 526-8847, puts a healthy spin on carry-out food with soups, salads, and a complete menu of deli sandwiches ready for the trail. Try some basil chicken salad or a cool smoothie on a warm summer afternoon. • The **Highlands Hill Deli**, 115 North Fourth Street, Highlands, ☎ (828) 526-9632, has a full menu of sandwiches, salads, and hoagies.

Just Desserts

Try **Sweet Treats**, 11 Mountain Brook Way, Highlands, ☎ (828) 526-9822; and Village Walk, Cashiers, ☎ (828) 743-5452, for fudge, smoothies, ice cream, shakes, and handmade chocolates. • **Kilwin's of Highlands**, 370 Main Street, Highlands, ☎ (828) 526-3788 or 1-888-339-3788, *www.kilwinsofhighlands.com*, serves ice cream, homemade fudge, chocolate, caramel, pralines, and old-fashioned sodas and malts.

A Long-Weekend Itinerary

Day 1

After a hearty breakfast at your inn, lace up your hiking boots, drop by the **Market Basket** (page 293) for picnic supplies, and head to **Whitewater Falls** (page 274), where you can view the 411-foot waterfall and then continue on the **Foothills Trail** (page 274) to **Laurel Falls**, the perfect place to relax with a picnic. Head for a swim at **Cliffside Lake Recreation Area** (page 280) and continue your exploration of the area's **waterfalls** (page 287) along Route 64 through Cullasaja Gorge.

Return to your inn to shower, and then refuel with cappuccino from **Buck's Coffee Café** (page 286) before browsing the many unique **shops** (page 286) and **galleries** (page 283) on Highlands' Main Street. Don't miss the **Ann Jacob Gallery** (page 284) and **Cyrano's Bookstore** (page 286). Dine at **Ristorante Paoletti** (page 292) and soak in the tastes of Italy, right through to their hip-shaping desserts. Call it a day.

Day Two

Rise before the sun to hike **Whiteside Mountain** (page 273) for a glorious sunrise. Make your way back to the B&B and join the late-risers for breakfast. Grab a shower, and meet your guide from the **Highland Hiker** (page 279) for a day of fly fishing on the **Chattooga River**. (Ask that lunch be provided.) Get back to town just in time for a late-afternoon massage at **The Day Spa on Spring** (page 286). Spend the evening gazing out over Lake Sequoyah from your romantic table at **On the Verandah** (page 292) with a nice bottle of Chardonnay by your side. Lights out.

Day Three

Sleep in, savor your vacation, eat breakfast, and then check out the latest exhibits at **Summit One Gallery** (page 283) before you park in Cashiers and walk the antiques shops, among them the **Cashiers Antique Mall** (page 282). Grab lunch for the road at the **Wild Thyme Bakery** (page 293) before winding your way home.

Additional Information

For additional dining, accommodations, and sightseeing information including the dates of special events, contact:

Cashiers Chamber of Commerce, 202 Route 64 west, Cashiers, NC 28717, ☎ (828) 743-5941, *www.cashiersnorthcarolina.com*. Open Monday–Friday, 9 A.M.–5 P.M.; Saturday, 10 A.M.–4 P.M.

Franklin Chamber of Commerce, 425 Porter Street, Franklin, NC 28734, ☎ (828) 524-3161, *www.franklin-chamber.com*. Open Monday–Saturday, 9 A.M.–5 P.M.

Highlands Chamber of Commerce, 396 Oak Street, Highlands, NC 28741, ☎ (828) 526-2112, *www.highlandschamber.org*. Open Monday–Saturday, 9 A.M.–5 P.M.

And this our life, exempt from public haunt
Finds tongues in trees, books in the running brooks,
Sermons in stones, and good in everything
– William Shakespeare, As You Like It

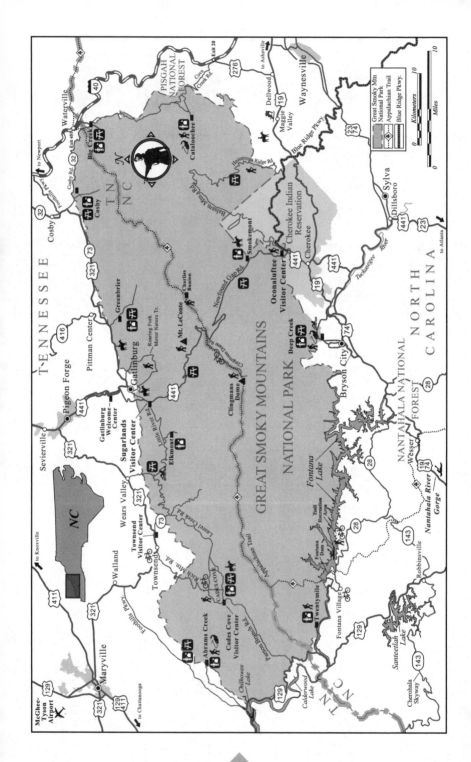

Great Smoky Mountains National Park, North Carolina

Moving west across North Carolina's Piedmont, the land begins to ripple gently in the foothills and then to rise dramatically to form the Appalachian Mountain Range. Created between 250 and 450 million years ago by a colossal traffic accident—tectonic plates smashed into each other and crumpled the land—the Appalachians were once as high as the Rockies. Today the average elevation of the range, which stretches from Georgia to Newfoundland, is 3,000 feet. In North Carolina, the mountains proved the most resilient; here you'll find some of the range's highest, most-rugged peaks.

The wide southern Appalachians feature several subranges—the Black, Balsam, Nantahala and Great Smoky mountains, among them. Though the East's highest peak, 6,684-foot Mount Mitchell, is in the Black Mountain Range, the Great Smoky Mountains feature the highest collection of peaks, including 17 more than 6,000 feet in elevation. With a 36-mile stretch of ridgeline above 5,000 feet, the Smokies form an impressive wall of ancient rock along the modern-day border of North Carolina and Tennessee. Today nearly the entire range exists within the 520,400-acre Great Smoky Mountains National Park.

Named an International Biosphere Reserve for the awesome variety of plant and animal life found here, the Great Smoky Mountains National Park (GSMNP) has more than 1,500 types of flowering plants and 100 species of native trees (more than any other national park), all nourished by rich soil and roughly 90 inches of annual precipitation. The park's wildlife is equally remarkable: 200 species of birds, 80 types of reptiles, and 50 species of mammals—including the nation's largest concentration of black bears—make their home here.

What created such diversity? The last ice age. Roughly 10,000 years ago, glaciers covered much of North America but did not reach as far south as the Smokies. Life continued in the

Haywood County Tourism

mountains, providing refuge for many species driven south. The dramatic variance in elevation aids in the diversity of flora and fauana, as well. From Cades Cove, a sweeping valley in the GSMNP, the land rises from 875 to 6,643 feet at nearby Clingmans Dome.

Hunter-gatherers roamed this area as many as 11,000 years ago; however, little evidence of their presence remains, nor of the subsequent Archaic Indians who settled small, seasonal villages along the high-plateau rivers. Much more is known about their ancestors, the Cherokee, who migrated to the region they called "shaconage," meaning "blue, like smoke," in the 14th and 15th centuries. The tribe lived relatively peacefully for generations, trading with Native Americans from as far away as the Gulf Coast and Ohio Valley, as well as hunting and farming the land that would become the Great Smoky Mountains National Park.

In the 17th Century, Europeans, primarily the English, began exploring the mountains to trade with the Native Americans. Over time, the continued presence of English traders and the encroaching western settlement boundary strained relations with the Cherokee, who sided with the French against the English in the French and Indian War. During the Revolutionary War, the tribe joined the English.

As the settlement frontier pushed westward into the mountains, the Cherokee were continually re-settled until the discovery of gold in Georgia's mountains prompted Congress to sign the 1830 Indian Removal Act. The legislation confiscated Cherokee land and forced the tribe's relocation to Oklahoma on the infamous "Trail of Tears."

Not all Cherokee relocated. A handful was allowed to stay under terms of previous treaties, and a small number hid in the surrounding mountains. Eventually the Cherokee that remained formed the eastern band of the tribe and were granted protected land in what was to be called the Qualla Band Reservation. Today the Town of Cherokee is the reservation's hub.

White settlement around the base of the Smokies occurred slowly due to the rugged land. A small number of farmers built homesteads in the region's valleys, including Cades Cove, on the Smokies' Tennessee side, in the early 19th Century. (Many of the original homesteads, grist mills, and farm buildings built throughout the valleys remain today.)

In the early 20th Century, logging companies set up camp in the Smoky Mountains, giv-

Two Sides

Following the 1830 Indian Removal Act, President Andrew Jackson stated that the act ".will place a dense, civilized population in large tracts of country now occupied by a few savage hunters." Pioneer explorer and Tennessee Congressman Davy Crockett disagreed, calling the forced removal "unjust, dishonest, cruel, and short-sighted in the extreme."

ing rise to a smattering of mill towns, including Gatlinburg, Townsend, and Bryson City. By 1920, nearly two-thirds of the timber in the Smokies had been felled. Meanwhile, national conservation sentiment was rising, fueled by the creation of three national parks in the West—Yellowstone, Sequoia, and Yosemite. Conservationists soon began scouring the East for lands to protect.

Several individuals played key roles in the formation of the GSMNP. North Carolina Senator Gifford Pinchot, who became the first director of the National Forest Service, rallied President Theodore Roosevelt around the value of conservation. Horace Kephart, a librarian from St. Louis, moved to the Smoky Mountains around 1900 and wrote eloquently about the area. His books and magazine articles included impassioned pleas to protect the land from logging. Meanwhile, wealthy Knoxville boosters recognized the economic benefit of creating a national park nearby and began promoting the idea.

Land ownership proved tricky. More than 6,000 parcels of land in the proposed park area belonged to private citizens, and vast tracts belonged to timber companies. Money and cooperation were needed to purchase the land, relocate the residents, and fight the powerful logging-industry lobbyists. Fortunately for park supporters, the nation's wealthiest man was also an ardent conservationist. John D. Rockefeller matched private and state donations by contributing $5 million to help create the park. In a 1940 ceremony on Newfound Gap Road, President Franklin D. Roosevelt dedicated the Great Smoky Mountains National Park.

The Civilian Conservation Corps built the park's infrastructure of roads, hiking trails, and campgrounds, which paved the way (literally) for the influx of tourists soon to arrive.

Meanwhile, the old mill towns surrounding the park transformed into thriving tourist stops for vacationers headed into the park.

Today nearly 10 million people visit the GSMNP each year, making it the nation's most-visited national park. There are three busy sea-

Cades Cove

sons: spring, when the profusion of flowering plants blooms; summer, when families flock to the campgrounds and surrounding villages; and autumn, when the leaves turn brilliant hues of gold, crimson, orange, and yellow. Of these, spring is the least crowded. But don't let the visitor numbers scare you; the majority never ventures far from their cars. You can visit the park during the height of fall, when traffic is at a standstill on Newfound Gap Road, and still be able to hike 15 minutes to a private piece of forested paradise.

The Way Around

In contrast to the go-go pace of Gatlinburg, Tennessee, towns surrounding the park on the North Carolina side are pleasantly subdued. To be sure, these mountain hamlets cater to visitors—there are country inns, B&Bs, hokey attractions, and numerous crafts shops—but the overall kitsch level is lower. The following towns are the primary tourism villages described in the chapter.

Editor's Note:

This chapter includes *Play Hard* activities in the national park in both North Carolina and Tennessee; however, most *Kick Back* and *Rest Easy* coverage is limited to North Carolina. Throughout the chapter, the Great Smoky Mountains National Park is abbreviated to GSMNP.

Located off Route 74, **Waynesville** is the county seat for Haywood County and the largest North Carolina town west of Asheville. With turn-of-the-century brick buildings and a Main Street lined with restaurants, coffee houses, bakeries, galleries, and antiques dealers, Waynesville positively bustles, particularly in the summer. Just down the hill from Main Street and around the historic train depot, Frog Level is a hip neighborhood with art studios and an eclectic offering of shops and cafés. Waynesville is the site of numerous festivals throughout the year.

Southwest of Waynesville on Route 23/74 at 3,550 feet sits **Balsam**, a small village popular with visitors off the

adjacent Blue Ridge Parkway and travelers who use the hamlet as a base for hiking adventures. Further along Route 23/74, **Sylva** is the county seat of Jackson County and home to many of the region's industries, as well as to one of the state's finest independent bookstores, City Lights. The city's Main Street is undergoing a revitalization effort. Merely a mile away, **Dillsboro** is full of art and crafts studios. Its train depot hosts the Great Smoky Mountain Railroad, the county's most-visited tourist attraction.

Northwest of Waynesville on Route 19, **Maggie Valley** is a resort town full of attractions along Soco Road (Route 19), which runs up the middle of the valley and climbs to one of the most-photographed views of

Haywood County Tourism

Downtown Waynesville

the Smokies just above the village. This is serious clogging country, as residents learn to walk and clog around the same time. The village was named for the daughter of its first postmaster in 1904.

West of Maggie Valley on Route 19 and the site of the GSMNP Oconaluftee Visitor Center, **Cherokee** is the closest North Carolina

Maggie Valley

comes to matching Gatlinburg for manic tourism. Cherokee is the "hub" of the Cherokee Indian Reservation (created in 1875 and also known as the Qualla Boundary), which encompasses more than 55,000 acres across five counties. Cherokee is home to Harrah's Cherokee Casino, a video-format gaming center, and an adjacent 15-story, 252-room hotel.

Further west on Route 19 on the Tuckasegee River, **Bryson City** is home to the Nantahala Outdoor Center, the state's most-comprehensive, outdoor-adventure outfit. The Great Smoky Mountain Railroad stops here, as do well-informed GSMNP visitors who appreciate the hiking opportunities departing from Deep Creek Campground.

West of Bryson City via Routes 74 and 28, **Fontana Village** is a resort community on the western end of Fontana Lake, a 30-mile-long, manmade lake created in 1944 by Fontana Dam on the Little Tennessee River. At 480 feet, Fontana Dam is the highest concrete dam east of the Rockies. Fontana Village originated as a village for the dam builders. Due south of Fontana (though accessed via Route 143 off Route 28), **Robbinsville** is the county seat of Graham County and home to the Joyce Kilmer Memorial Forest, Santeetlah Lake, and the start of the Cherohala Skyway, a national scenic byway.

Weather

The GSMNP features a wet and relatively mild climate. Summer is brilliant, with highs in the mid 80s and overnight lows in the upper 60s. The lower elevations tend to be more humid and hot. The colorful seasons of spring and fall feature crisp days with highs in the low to mid 60s and overnight lows in the mid 30s. Fall is the driest season, and spring is typically the wettest. Average winter highs are in the low to mid 40s, and overnight lows are in the upper 20s. Snowfall is common in the higher elevations and may occur beginning in November and end as late as May.

Getting to the GSMNP

By Air: The **Asheville Regional Airport,** ☎ (828) 684-2226, *www.ashevilleregion-alairport.com,* 60 miles east of Cherokee, hosts several major airlines. Ground transportation and rental cars are available onsite.

By Car: From Atlanta, take Interstate 85 north to exit #113, which leads to Route 985. Take Route 985 north to Gainesville, Georgia. From Gainesville, head north on Route 23, which turns into Route 23/441. Stay on Route 23/441 until you see signs for Route 74 west to Bryson City and Cherokee. From Route 74, turn on Route 441 north to the national park. Allow 3.5 hours for the drive. **From Charlotte,** take Interstate 85 south to Interstate 26 west in Spartanburg to Interstate 40 west. From Interstate 40, take Exit #27 and head west on Route 19, which goes through Maggie Valley before reaching Cherokee. In Cherokee, take Route 441 north into the park. Allow 3.5 hours for the drive. **From Raleigh,** take Interstate 40 west past Asheville to Exit #27 and follow signs for Maggie Valley (Route 19/74). Follow Route 19 west through Maggie Valley to Cherokee. Turn right onto Route 441 north in Cherokee to the Great Smoky Mountains National Park. Allow five hours for the drive.

---

*Thousands of tired, nerve-shaken, over-civilized people are
beginning to find out that going to the mountains is going
home; that wilderness is a necessity; and that mountain parks
and reservations are useful not only as fountains of timber and
irrigating rivers, but as fountains of life!*

– John Muir

P l a y   H a r d

W i d e   O p e n

Western North Carolina features a superstore-sized selection of wide-open, public land for adventurous outdoor play. You can spend a lifetime hiking, mountain biking, paddling, horseback riding, skiing, and snowshoeing through the mountains, valleys, forests, and rivers and still not explore it all. But don't let that stop you from trying.

The **Great Smoky Mountains National Park,** (865) 436-1200, *www.nps.gov/grsm/*, features 800 square miles, or 520,400 acres, of rugged mountainous land, with nearly equal parts in North Carolina and Tennessee. Ninety-five percent of the park is forested. There are two major entrances with large visitor centers. North Carolina's primary point-of-entry, the **Oconaluftee Visitor Center,** (828) 497-1900, is north of Cherokee on Route 441. From the park boundary, Route 441 becomes **Newfound Gap Road** and travels 33 miles northwest, bisecting the park en route to the GSMNP headquarters at Tennessee's **Sugarlands Visitor Center,**

Deron Nardo

Little River Road

(865) 436-1291, located two miles south of Gatlinburg. Both visitor centers feature rangers on staff, maps, brochures, and general information about the park.

More than 270 miles of paved and well-maintained gravel roads wind through the park. Finding your way is not difficult—few major roads run through the park—but making your way is another matter. With 10 million visitors a year, most of whom see the park from behind a windshield, no one goes anywhere quickly. For example, the drive on Newfound Gap Road takes just less than an hour in ideal conditions (good weather, little traffic). In the height of summer and fall, it can take several hours. The best advice? Enjoy the ride.

The park is described in more detail throughout the chapter, but the following provides an overview of the major roads and points of interest. Newfound Gap Road passes numerous pull-offs with tremendous views and access to hiking trails. The most popular is at 5,048-foot **Newfound Gap**, where a large parking area with restrooms provides access to the Appalachian Trail.

Clingmans Dome Road departs from Newfound Gap Road and climbs seven miles to just below the summit of Clingmans Dome. From the parking area at road's end, a steep, paved half-mile trail leads to the summit of the park's highest peak, 6,643-foot Clingmans Dome. (Clingmans Dome Road is closed in the winter.)

> ### How's the Weather Up There?
>
> With elevations ranging from 800 to 6,600 feet, the GSMNP can experience temperature variables of 18 degrees between its high and low points. Keep elevation in mind as you dress for the day; count on a three-degree difference every 1,000 feet in altitude.

From the Sugarlands Visitor Center in Gatlinburg, **Little River Road** departs west 18 miles along the Little River past scenic waterfalls and wildflower-filled pastures to an intersection with Route 73 near Townsend. Here the route changes names to **Laurel Creek Road,** which continues west seven miles to the start of one-way **Cades Cove Loop Road.** This 11-mile road goes through the park's most-popular area, **Cades Cove,** a large (6,800 acres) and exceptionally scenic mountain valley with a collection of historic log cabins and churches. The **Cades Cove Visitor Center** is located near the midpoint of Cades Cove Loop Road.

From Gatlinburg, **Cherokee Orchard Road** connects with the five-mile, one-way **Roaring Fork Motor Nature Trail,** a scenic route that winds past several historic homesteads and provides access to a number of hiking trails.

There are several small access points and recreation areas in the Tennessee portions of the GSMNP, including the **Elkmont/Tremont area** off Little River Road; the **Abrams Creek Campground Area**, northwest of Cades Cove; the **Greenbrier and Cosby areas,** located off Route 321 northeast of Gatlinburg; and the **Big Creek area,** located in the park's northeast corner near Waterville and off Interstate 40. Coverage of these areas is limited due to relative inaccessibility from North Carolina-based lodgings.

Smaller park access points in North Carolina include **Deep Creek,** a quiet recreational area less than two miles from Bryson City. (Take Locust Street to West Deep Creek Road north to the park entrance.) Numerous hiking trails set out from the area. Trout fishing is popular along Deep Creek, as is photographing the three nearby waterfalls: Juney Whank, Toms Branch, and Indian Creek falls. All are a short walk from the parking area.

Located west of Fontana Village off Route 28, the **Twentymile Ranger Station** provides access to several hiking trails, including the Twentymile Trail, which follows an old railroad grade beside portions of the cascading, trout-filled Proctor Branch on its way to the Appalachian Trail at Sassafras Gap.

Abrams Falls on Abrams Creek

East of the Oconaluftee Visitor Center, the 29-square mile **Cataloochee Valley** is a rugged, remote area with outstanding hiking, fishing, and horseback riding. Similar to Cades Cove, the area is full of abandoned homesteads, churches, and other vestiges of settlement. (The area was cleared out when the government purchased the land for the national park.) It's also home to a herd of wild elk. To get here, take Interstate 40 west to Exit #20 and Route 276 north for one tenth of a mile to Cove Creek Road, which leads into the valley. ◆ The **Balsam Mountain Campground Area**, reached via the Blue Ridge Parkway north of the Oconaluftee Visitor Center, provides another access point to the park. Take Heintooga Ridge Road off the BRP to Balsam Mountain Road, a one-way route through the park that connects with Straight Fork Road and then Big Cove Road to create a scenic driving loop.

If the GSMNP isn't enough space for your tastes, the 516,000 acres of the **Nantahala National Forest** add a wee-bit more room to play. To manage this colossal wilderness, which covers much of Western North Carolina, the National Forest Service divides the national forest into four ranger districts—the Cheoah, Tusquitee, Wayah, and Highlands—only one of which includes activities suggested in this chapter.

The **Cheoah Ranger District**, Route 1, Robbinsville, (828) 479-6431, maintains 120,000 acres immediately south of the GSMNP. Located in this district, the **Tsali Recreation Area** is a hiking, horseback riding, and wildly popular mountain biking destination that occupies a peninsula on the southern shores of Fontana Lake. Access Tsali by taking Route 19/74 south from Bryson City to Route 28. Take Route 28 north 5.5 miles to a right turn

Cataloochee Valley

NC Division of Tourism

Joyce Kilmer Memorial Forest

onto Forest Road 521 for 1.5 miles. Tsali has a nominal trail-use fee.

Located three miles from Fontana Dam on Route 28, the **Cable Cove Recreation Area** provides hiking trails and access to Fontana Lake. Also within the Cheoah district, the **Joyce Kilmer Slickrock Wilderness**, (828) 479-6431, encompasses more than 17,000 acres of undeveloped land, including the 3,800-acre **Joyce Kilmer Memorial Forest**, an old-growth forest with some of the largest trees in the eastern United States. There are more than 60 miles of hiking trails in the wilderness. From Robbinsville, take Route 129 north 1.5 miles north to a left turn onto Route 143, which you follow five miles to Kilmer Road. Turn right and drive roughly seven miles to the top of Santeetlah Gap and the junction with the Cherohala Skyway. Bear to your right and continue for another 2.5 miles to the entrance of the Joyce Kilmer Memorial Forest.

Dayhiking

While more than nine million people visit the GSMNP each year, a fraction of visitors lace up hiking books and venture into the woods. The rewards for the footloose are many: a quiet meadow, a private swimming hole at the base of a cascading waterfall, a mountaintop view, or a dense forest to call your own. In total, more than 850 miles of hiking trails wind through the GSMNP, including nearly 70 miles of the 2,100-mile Appalachian Trail (AT). In fact, the park's Clingmans Dome is the highest point on the entire AT.

In addition to the GSMNP trails, several hundred more miles of footpaths meander through the Nantahala National Forest. While many of the trails in the park and forest are long and demanding, there are numerous paths ideal for short hikes. The following trails, grouped by location, are merely a sampling of area hikes.

Newfound Gap Road

◆ The **Oconaluftee River Trail** is an easy, three-mile, out-and-back hike from Oconaluftee Visitor Center on Newfound Gap Road to the GSMNP entrance. The flat, gravel-surface path travels beside the Oconaluftee River through a hardwood forest. ◆ The two-mile **Kephart Prong Trail** is another easy hike that follows a branch of the Oconaluftee River. The trail, named for naturalist and early GSMNP supporter Horace Kephart, gradually climbs the flank of Kephart Mountain to an intersection with Sweat Heifer Creek Trail. Along the path, you'll pass remnants of an old fish hatchery and a Civilian Conservation Corps camp. The trailhead is located on the right side of Newfound Gap Road, approximately nine miles north of Cherokee.

◆ From the Newfound Gap parking area, the four-mile hike on the **Appalachian Trail** to

Deron Nardo

*Appalachian Trail to
Charlies Bunion*

the **Charlies Bunion** rock outcropping is a high-elevation ridge hike with wonderful views, especially from Charlies Bunion. (Horace Kephart named the craggy rock during a hiking expedition to the area in 1929 after noticing the hobbled gait of his friend Charlie Conner.) From the parking area, follow the AT north as it climbs at a moderate pace. You'll pass junctions with the Sweat Heifer Creek Trail and the Boulevard Trail, a popular route to the summit of Mount LeConte. From Charlies Bunion, retrace your steps to finish the eight-mile hike.

◆ One of the most-scenic trails in the entire park, the moderate **Alum Cave Bluffs Trail** climbs two miles to Alum Cave Bluffs, a huge slate ledge that hangs over the trail. (The trail continues another three miles to the summit of 6,593-foot Mount LeConte. Most people turn around at Alum Cave Bluffs for a 4.4-mile hike versus the 9.8-mile roundtrip trek to LeConte.) Features along the way include dense stands of mountain laurel and rhododen-dron; two unique rock formations caused by erosion (Arch Rock and Alum Cave Bluffs); and numerous scenic views, particularly beyond the bluffs. From the LeConte summit, you can see downtown Gatlinburg and, on a clear day, Knoxville. The trail starts from a large signed parking area on Newfound Gap Road, roughly 23 miles north of the Oconaluftee Visitor Center .

Deron Nardo

Clingmans Dome Road

◆ Clingmans Dome Road departs Newfound Gap Road roughly 20 miles north of the Oconaluftee Visitor Center and twists, turns, and climbs seven miles to a parking area just below Clingmans Dome. The road (closed November–April) provides access to several fine hiking trails, including a short, paved summit trail. (See "The Sweat-free Summit.") From the parking area, the 3.6-mile hike to Andrews Bald and back on the **Forney Ridge Trail** is an outstanding trek for a picnic. The trail descends a mile through a thick forest laced with ferns to a junction where the Forney Creek Trail veers right.

Hikers on Forney Ridge Trail

The Sweat-Free Summit

Climbing the highest peak in the Smokies and third highest east of the Mississippi doesn't require hiking boots thanks to Clingmans Dome Road, which stretches seven miles from Newfound Gap Road to a parking area just below the peak of 6,643-foot Clingmans Dome. From here, the paved **Clingmans Dome Trail** climbs the final, steep half mile to an observation tower on the mountain's summit, where stunning 360-degree views await.

Continue straight on the Forney Ridge Trail, which levels out before a brief climb and fall to the stunning, panoramic views on Andrews Bald. (Balds are grass- or heath-covered mountain summits.) Hike this trail in June, and you're in for an explosion of colorful azalea and rhododendron blooms. Refuel with a picnic and then start the strenuous climb back to your car.

Cades Cove Area

◆ En route to Cades Cove and just 3.7 miles from the Sugarlands Visitor Center on Little River Road, the **Laurel Falls Trail** is a pleasant, albeit popular, path to 75-foot Laurel Falls. The easy, 2.6-mile out-and-back hike climbs a mere 300 feet. From the parking area at Fighting Creek Gap, the paved trail climbs to a bench with beautiful views of Laurel Creek and the Little River Valley. From here, the trail continues to the cascading falls, where a cement bridge extends across their base to a shaded pool of water.

◆ For a serene, flat hike to a much-photographed waterfall, take the **Abrams Falls Trail** 2.5 miles to 20-foot Abrams Falls. Tucked in a narrow valley, this waterfall features a large flow of water plunging into a broad pool ideal for a quick dip. For most of its length, the trail winds along Abrams Creek through a rhododendron forest. You'll likely encounter anglers on their way to the "Horseshoe," a bend in the creek that's a popular fishing hole. Follow directions to the Cades Cove Loop in *Wide Open*. The clearly signed trailhead is between Signposts 10 and 11, roughly five miles into the one-way loop.

◆ **Gregory Bald** offers one of the most-scenic, panoramic views in the park and can be reached by hiking the strenuous, 5.5-mile **Gregory Ridge Trail** (11 miles roundtrip), which departs from the end of Forge Creek Road off Cades Cove Loop. The trail winds through an old-growth forest beside Forge Creek and then climbs aggressively to the high-meadow bald. This is an ideal hike for a picnic, especially in June when flame azaleas bloom on the bald and wild blueberry bushes ripen to provide dessert.

Roaring Fork Motor Nature Trail

◆ For the view from *behind* a waterfall, get thee to **Trillium Gap Trail** for a 2.8-mile roundtrip hike to **Grotto Falls,** where the trail passes behind the 25-foot waterfall. The trail makes numerous creek crossings early. If reaching the falls just whets your appetite for a

longer trek, continue on the trail 1.5 miles to 4,700-foot Trillium Gap. Still feeling strong? From Trillium Gap, a spur trail climbs another half-mile to the summit of bald **Brushy Mountain**, where tremendous views await. Hike the whole stretch and you've logged seven miles. To reach the trail,

Atop Andrews Bald

take Newfound Gap Road into Gatlinburg, where you turn right onto Route 321 (east) and drive to Stoplight #8. Turn right onto Historic Nature Trail Road, which becomes Cherokee Orchard Road in the park and then Roaring Fork Motor Nature Trail. The clearly signed parking area is roughly 1.5 miles along Roaring Fork Motor Nature Trail.

Twentymile Ranger Station

◆ For some of the most-remote hiking in the GSMNP, head to the Twentymile Ranger Station, west of Fontana Village off Route 28, where the 4.7-mile **Twentymile Trail** connects with the AT in Sassafras Gap. Part of this trail follows the stunning Proctor Branch, a cascading trout stream. Create a 6.5-mile loop by hiking the Twentymile Trail to the Wolf Ridge Trail on the left after the bridge, then taking a right onto the Twentymile Loop Trail, which intersects again with the Twentymile Trail, where you turn right to return to your car. Highlights include the Twentymile Cascades.

Deep Creek

◆ From the Deep Creek Campground just two miles north of Bryson City, the four-mile **Deep Creek Loop** combines portions of the Deep Creek, Indian Creek,

Thar's Bears in Thar

One of the nation's highest concentrations of black bears—perhaps as many as 1,600—exists in the GSMNP, so it's entirely possible you'll run across one while exploring the park. Here's what you need to know. First, don't feed a bear. Second, if you find bear cubs, leave the area slowly but steadily. A few more rules of engagement:

• Never run from a bear. Walk backwards slowly facing the bear. (Run and you look like prey.)

• If the bear charges, stand your ground and make yourself look big and mean by holding your arms above you, standing on a rock, or waving a stick. Chances are the bear is performing a "bluff charge" and will move on if you stay put.

• In the highly unlikely event a bear attacks you, fight back aggressively. Do not play dead.

and Loop trails and passes a couple of waterfalls and swimming holes. From the parking area (see directions under *Wide Open*), follow the Deep Creek Trail beside Deep Creek and past Tom Branch Falls to the intersection with Indian Creek Trail. Turn left and hike past Indian Creek Falls to the Loop Trail intersection, where you turn left for an aggressive climb along a ridge. When you reach the Deep Creek Trail, turn left for the gradual descent to the parking area.

◆ If time is short, take the half-mile out-and-back hike from the Deep Creek parking area to **Juney Whank Falls,** a pretty 90-foot waterfall.

Balsam Mountain Area

◆ The five-mile out-and-back hike on **Flat Creek Trail** to Heintooga Road is a relatively flat hike through wooded terrain beside Flat Creek. You'll pass a couple of open heath balds and plenty of wildflowers, as well as a spur trail to Flat Creek Falls. To get to the trailhead, take the Blue Ridge Parkway north from Route 441 at the Cherokee park entrance to Milepost 458, where a spur road leads to Heintooga Overlook and the trailhead. Roughly 2.5 miles into the hike, you'll reach Heintooga Road, the turnaround point.

Cataloochee Valley

More than 35 miles of trails wind through remote Cataloochee Valley. One of the most enjoyable is the 7.4-mile **Boogerman Trail Loop,** which features old-growth forest, scenic creeks and waterfalls, and pioneer history. Named for Robert "Boogerman" Palmer, an early pioneer settler, the trail passes Palmer's homestead (marked today by old fence posts and numerous stone piles) and through a forest of some of the region's largest trees. (Palmer didn't allow logging companies to cut on his land.) To reach the trailhead, follow signs on Cove Creek Road (see *Wide Open* for directions) to the Caldwell Fork Trailhead. Park here and cross Cataloochee Creek on the bridge. Continue on the Caldwell Fork Trail beside and frequently crossing gurgling Caldwell Fork past the first Boogerman Trail junction on the left. Roughly three miles into the hike, you'll reach the upper loop portion of the Boogerman Trail. Turn left here to pass through Palmer's homestead. The trail climbs along Snake Branch and then descends back to the Caldwell Fork Trail, where you turn right to return to your car.

Joyce Kilmer Memorial Forest

"I think I'll never see a poem as lovely as a tree," mused Joyce Kilmer, a poet killed in action in World War I. Whether or not Kilmer's poetry moves you, a visit to the Joyce Kilmer Memorial Forest most certainly will. This is one of the nation's old-growth forests, filled with more than 100 species of trees, many of which are more than four centuries old. A two-mile trail leads from the parking area and loops past the huge trees (some are 20 feet in circumference) to a memorial plaque and back. See *Wide Open* for directions.

Nantahala National Forest

◆ Looking for a subdued, short hike that's easy to follow? Try the 0.75-mile **Lewellyn Cove Nature Trail,** a quiet loop near Fontana Village with informative placards describing 50 different species of trees and shrubs. Steps make the few steep sections manageable. The trailhead is in a signed parking area just east of Fontana Village on Route 28.

Mountain Biking

While national forests have few qualms about mountain bikers on their multi-purpose trails, the National Park System isn't so enlightened. So, despite the 800 square miles of rugged land in the GSMNP, mountain bikes are not allowed on any of the park's trails. But fret not. **Tsali Recreation Area,** one of the Southeast's premier mountain biking destinations, is beside nearby Fontana Lake·in the Nantahala National Forest.

Managed by the Cheoah Ranger District, (828) 479-6931, Tsali features 42 miles of horseback and mountain biking trails. There are four main loops and a smattering of smaller loops. To keep equestrians and mountain bikers apart, the forest service swaps daily which trails are open to mountain bikes. On any given day, two loops are open to bikes and two are open to horses. (Check the schedule board at the trailhead.)

The Tsali trails are generally hard-packed dirt and not overly steep or technical, though enough root-strewn sections, banked turns, mud, and gravel exists to keep things interesting. Throughout, the trail system serves up outstanding scenery of the surrounding peaks and gorgeous Fontana Lake. All of the trails are accessible from the parking area (see *Wide Open* for directions), where you'll find a trail system map, restrooms, and a bike-cleaning station. There's a nominal day-use fee, which helps pay for trail maintenance.

Nantahala Outdoor Center

◆ The trails include the **Right Loop,** an 11-mile route of mostly singletrack that features several creek crossings, numerous stretches beside Fontana Lake, and a number of hills away from the lake. ◆ The 12-mile **Left Loop** is also mostly singletrack with numerous lakeshore stretches, plus a couple of steep climbs and descents on the interior of the peninsula away from the water. ◆ The 6.5-mile, singletrack **Mouse Branch Loop** follows the contours of a mountain and features a fast downhill section, plus great lake views as it winds through various coves. ◆ The 7.7-mile **Thompson Loop** features singletrack through a scenic forest with rhododendron stands. There are stream crossings, as well as several stretches beside the lake.

◆ Other trails in Tsali include the 1.5-mile **County Line Road,** a hard-packed dirt, double track trail; the steep and challenging two-mile **Overlook Loop;** and the one-way, 2.5-mile **Mouse Branch Overlook Loop.**

◆ There are 25 miles of difficult singletrack trails located near **Fontana Village** that many serious mountain bikers prefer to those in Tsali. A map of the trails is available from the bike shop at the Fontana Village Adventure Center (see "Rentals"). ◆ The five-mile **Flint Ridge Trail** is a technical singletrack route near the Nantahala River on the property of the **Nantahala Outdoor Center** (see "Rentals"). There's no fee for riding the trail. Ask for directions at the shop.

Rentals

Nantahala Outdoor Center, 13077 Route 19, Bryson City, ☎ 1-800-232-7238, *www.noc.com.* ◆ Summer rentals available from **Fontana Village Adventure Center,** Route 28, Fontana Dam, ☎ (828) 498-2211 or 1-800-849-2258.

Road Biking

With the exception of the Roaring Fork Motor Nature Trail, all GSMNP roads are open to bicycles; however, traffic and steep inclines make for challenging rides on most. That said, the flat, 11-mile **Cades Cove Loop Road** is exceptionally popular with cyclists because it's closed to automobiles Wednesdays and Saturdays from dawn until 10 A.M., the second week of May through the next to last Saturday in September. The stunning scenery through the valley, plus the possibility of wildlife sightings—black bears, red and gray foxes, raccoons, coyotes, and red wolves—make this ride an unforgettable experience. See *Wide Open* for directions.

♦ It's a tough climb, but you'll earn your afternoon beer after cycling the 14-mile roundtrip ride on **Clingmans Dome Road** from Newfound Gap to just below the Clingmans Dome summit. This is some of the highest-elevation riding the Smokies have to offer, as your lungs will quickly point out during the 1,500-foot ascent. Traffic can be intense, so it's best to ride the road early in the morning during the week.

Paddling

Whitewater paddling near the GSMNP centers on the dam-released **Nantahala River,** which tumbles through the nine-mile **Nantahala Gorge.** En route, expect plenty of Class II-III rapids, including Class III *Patton's Run,* Class II *Tumble Dry,* and the final rapid, Class III *Nantahala Falls.* The river-running season is March—October. While numerous outfitters run the river, the undisputed heavyweight is the **Nantahala Outdoor Center,** 13077 Route 19 West, Bryson City, 1-800-232-7238, *www.noc.com,* which operates a large campus of buildings—including a full-service paddling store—beside the river. The outfitter offers kayak and canoe instruction, and runs all manner of whitewater rafting tours on the Nantahala and five other Southeastern rivers.

Whitewater Rafting

♦ Other nearby whitewater paddling outfitters include **Endless River Adventures,** 14157 Route 19 West, Bryson City, (828) 488-6199 or 1-800-224-7238, *www.endlessriveradventures.com;* ♦ **Rafting in the Smokies,** 10811 Route 19 West, Bryson City, 1-800-776-7238, *www.raftinginthesmokies.com;* and ♦ **Wildwater Rafting,** 10345 Route 19 West, Bryson City, (828) 488-2384 or 1-800-451-9972, *www.wildwaterrafting.com.*

Fly Fishing

With more than 900 miles of streams in the GSMNP, fly-fishing opportunities for rainbow, brown, and brook trout are abundant. Popular rivers and streams in the park include **Deep Creek** just north of Bryson City, accessed from the Deep Creek Campground; **Cataloochee Creek** in the park's quiet northeast corner off Cove Creek Road; the **Little River** from the Elkmont Campground; the "Horseshoe" and Abrams Falls on **Abrams Creek;** and **Porters Creek** beyond the Greenbrier Ranger Station.

Fishing

♦ Such an abundance of fly-fishing waters begs for the services of a knowledgeable guide. Fortunately, there are several excellent fly-fish-ing operations in the area. Each carries equipment, apparel, and all manner of flies. Other services include fly-fishing instruction and guided trips, ranging from half- and full-day wading trips to full-day float trips. Outfitters with outstanding reputations include **Lowe Fly Shop,** 15 Woodland Drive, Waynesville, (828) 452-0039, *www.loweflyshop.com;* ♦ and **Outpost Fly & Tackle/High Country Outfitters,** 4768 Route 74, West Whittier, (828) 586-8400. ♦ William Cope's **Smoky Mountains on the Fly** (828) 586-4787, *www.smokyon-thefly.com,* in Sylva is also a well-respected guide service.

Read All About It

For a comprehensive list of GSMNP fishing regulations, plus a detailed map of the park's trout streams, pick up a copy of *Great Smoky Mountains Fishing Regulations,* a free brochure avail-able at all visitor centers and most local outfitters. The first thing you'll learn? You need a state fishing license, which you can order over the phone with a credit card by calling the North Carolina Wildlife Resources Division, ☎ 1-888-248-6834, or log onto *www.ncwildlife.org,* where you'll find a list of retailers authorized to sell licenses.

Horseback Riding

With roughly 550 miles of equestrian trails and three commercial stables within its borders, the GSMNP is wildly popular for riding horseback through high mead-ows, across rushing streams, and up steep mountain trails. Three stables provide trail rides inside the park: **Cades Cove,** Laurel Creek Road, (865) 448-6286; **Smoky Mountain Stables,** (865) 436-5634, on Route 321 at the border of the park in Gatlinburg;

Haywood County Tourism

and **Smokemont,** (828) 497-2373, located two miles north of the Oconaluftee Visitor Center on Newfound Gap Road. All three stables provide guided rides by the hour.

♦ Other area commercial stables include **Cataloochee Ranch,** 119 Ranch Drive, Maggie Valley, (828) 926-1401 or 1-800-868-1401, *www.cataloochee-ranch.com,* which offers hourly, half- and full-day rides on 1,000 acres of private land; ♦ **Hemphill Stables,** 32 Woods Road, Waynesville, (828) 926-0331, for two- and four-hour rides in the GSMNP by reservation; and ♦ **Fontana Riding Stables,** Route 28 in Fontana Village, (828) 479-8911, which has hourly or full-day rides in the park or to Fontana Dam.

Rainy Day Workout

The Great Smokies Fitness Center, 414 Skyland Drive, Sylva, (828) 586-8799, has a Nautilus circuit, free weights, and a cardio room equipped with bikes, stairs, and cross-trainers. Nominal day-use fee. ♦ Part of the Haywood Regional Medical Center, the **Haywood Regional Fitness Center,** 75 Leroy George Drive, Clyde, (828) 452-8080, features a full array of cardio and strength-building machines, as well as free weights, an Olympic-sized swimming pool, and an indoor track. Nominal day-use fee.

Swimming

While there are 900 miles of rivers, creeks, and streams in the GSMNP, the official park ranger recommendation is not to swim at all. Why? Partly because of people slipping and falling on slick rocks and partly because the water is always cold, which can lead to hypothermia, even in warm weather. But, swimming is not restricted, so when you find a suitable swimming hole, use caution if you choose to get wet. The following are some of the better swimming spots in the park.

Step Slowly

After building up a sweat on a long hike, it's easy to forgo common sense when planning a swim in an inviting mountain stream. So, to help remind you: Never dive into a creek or river. No matter how clear the stream appears, moving water is notoriously deceptive about depth and rock placement. Second, do not climb on or near waterfalls. The constant spray onto nearby rocks promotes the growth of moss or algae, which makes for super-slick surfaces. It's best to stick to the base of the falls. Whenever approaching a stream or pool of water, wade in slowly.

◆ **Deep Creek,** just north of Bryson City and accessed by the Deep Creek Trail from Deep Creek Campground, offers cool, refreshing water. The creek is popular with tubers. See *Wide Open* for directions. From the trailhead, hike upstream to find the best swimming holes.

◆ There are numerous swimming holes along the **Little River** off Little River Road west of Sugarlands Visitors Center. Popular spots traveling west include **Elkmont Campground** (reached via an access road); the **Metcalf Bottoms Picnic Area;** and the **Sinks,** a series of rapids where swimming is dangerous if the river's flow is strong. You can also hike downstream from the Sinks to find additional swimming holes. Finally, at the Townsend entrance to the park where Little River and Laurel Creek roads intersect, the **"Y"** is a broad, deep swimming hole at the bridge over the Little River.

Skiing

With an elevation roughly a mile high, **Cataloochee Ski Area,** 1080 Ski Lodge Road, Maggie Valley, (828) 926-0285 or 1-800-768-0285, *www.cataloochee.com,* is well-situated for making snow. The 740-foot vertical drop mountain has snow-making capability on all of its 10 trails, which are serviced by three chairlifts (a double, triple, and a quad) and one surface lift. The slopes are 25 percent beginner, 50 percent intermediate, and 25 percent advanced. Lessons and equipment rentals available onsite.

Local Outdoor Advice

Great Smoky Mountains National Park • Each of the park's visitor centers is staffed with friendly park rangers happy to suggest outdoor adventures suitable to your mood and energy level. The primary North Carolina stop is the Oconaluftee Visitor Center, ☎ (828) 497-1900, located north of Cherokee on Route 441/Newfound Gap Road. The park information line is ☎ (865) 436-1200. The park headquarters is located in the Sugarlands Visitor Center on Newfound Gap Road in Gatlinburg. • 107 Park Headquarters Road, Gatlinburg, TN, ☎ (865) 436-1291, *www.nps.gov/grsm*

Mast General Store • In addition to candy, candles, and candelabras, you can purchase excellent outdoor equipment, gear, and apparel from the Mast General Store and pick up some good advice on where to use it • 63 North Main Street, Waynesville, ☎ (828) 452-2101, *www.mastgeneralstore.com*

Nantahala Outdoor Center • This one-stop adventure outfitter operates a retail shop in Bryson City where you can purchase all manner of outdoor gear and apparel. The staff lives the outdoor life and will happily point you to nearby trails, creeks, and vistas. • 13077 Route 19 West, Bryson City, ☎ 1-800-232-7238, *www.noc.com*

Kick Back

Worn out from vigorous outdoor play? Kick back and enjoy some of the following laid-back approaches to the mountains.

Antiques

Antiquing is a popular pursuit in North Carolina towns surrounding the GSMNP. Wares typically include early American-Country furniture, home and kitchen furnishings, and general Americana. A few good stops: ◆ From knick knacks to fine furniture, you'll find something of value at **Barbers Orchard Antique Mall,** 36 Providence Place, Waynesville, (828) 456-7229, where nearly 65 dealers operate under one roof. ◆ Located in a former school

Going Once, Going Twice...

SOLD. Hear these words plus some fast, unintelligible talking at **Thad Woods Auction,** 25 Muse Business Park, Waynesville, ☎ (828) 456-3298, *www.thadwoodsauction.com,* where large, antiques auctions are held every Friday and Saturday night at 7 P.M. Even if you're not in the market for antiques, go to enjoy the show.

building, the **Old School Antique Mall,** 4704 Route 441, Sylva, (828) 586-8097, *www.old-schoolantiquemall.com,* sells antique furniture, glass, pottery, and jewelry.

Art & Crafts Galleries

You'll have no trouble finding unique, creative gifts in the North Carolina mountains; art and crafts galleries are prolific. In the towns surrounding the GSMNP, Dillsboro is the hostess-with-the-mostest. Don't miss the **Riverwood Shops,** founded by Robert and Ruth Morgan, whose **Riverwood Pewter Shop,** 17 Craft Circle, Dillsboro, (828) 586-6996, *www.riverwoodpewter.com,* opened in 1957 and kicked off the town's birth as an artisan village. Here metal workers hammer pewter into stunning jewelry, serving pieces, dinner plates, bowls, and more. Watch the artisans work Monday–Friday, 10 A.M.–3:30 P.M. ◆ Next door, one of the Morgans' daughters, Susan Leveille, operates the **Oaks Gallery,** 29 Craft Circle, (828) 586-6542, a cooperative that displays more than 100 artists' work, including paintings, jewelry, pottery, glass, metal, and textiles.

◆ Another cooperative, **Dogwood Crafters,** 90 Webster Street, Dillsboro, (828) 586-2248, *www.dogwoodcrafters.com,* is housed in a rustic-looking log cabin that showcases calligraphy, quilts, pottery, stained glass, textiles, and paintings created by artisans living within 75 miles of the shop. ◆ There's an open studio to watch potters work at **Mountain Pottery,** 150 Front Street, Dillsboro, (828) 586-9183, plus an extensive gallery with pieces ranging from functional pots and plates to sculptures and whimsical watchamacallits.

◆ Waynesville also has a concentration of galleries. **Twigs & Leaves,** 98 North Main Street, Waynesville, (828) 456-1940, *www.twigsandleaves.com,* features fine art and crafts, including paintings, needlework, pottery, jewelry, metal works, and handcrafted furniture. More than 150 artists are represented. ◆ Contemporary wood sculptures by Dennis Ruane are on display at the **Hardwood Gallery,** 102 North Main Street, Waynesville, (828) 456-3500, *www.woodart3d.com.* Ruane's work includes sculptures of humans and wildlife, as well as masks and wall pieces. ◆ **T. Pennington Art Gallery,** 15 North Main Street, Waynesville, (828) 452-9284, *www.tpennington.com,* features colored-pencil drawings of Western North Carolina scenes by artist Teresa Pennington.

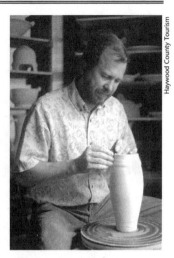

Haywood County Tourism

◆ In Cherokee, head to the **Qualla Arts & Crafts Mutual,** Route 4412 at Drama Road, Cherokee, (828) 497-3103, a cooperative displaying the work of hundreds of Cherokee craftspeople and including such items as pottery, wood carvings, baskets, and masks.

The Far Side of the Mountain

For an impressive crafts tour, head over the Smokies to tour the **Great Smoky Arts and Crafts Community's "loop,"** an eight-mile driving tour of artisans' shops, studios, and galleries on the outskirts of Gatlinburg. Every kind of collectible you can imagine is represented at the more than 90 stops along Buckhorn and Glades roads. Shop for candles, baskets, quilts, pottery, jewelry, dolls, ceramics, silver, leather, stained glass, wearable fashions, and fine photography. It's worth taking a day to drive. Even better, spend the night. Try Gatlinburg's **Eight Gables Inn,** 219 North Mountain Trail, ☎ (865) 430-3344 or 1-800-279-5716, *www.eightgables.com,* an upscale, Four-Diamond inn that also belongs to the *Select Registry.* For more information: ☎ 1-800-565-7330, *www.artsandcraftscommunity.com*

Back Roads Touring

So scenic is the GSMNP that a surprising number of the nine million annual visitors never get out of their cars, yet feel as if they've seen most of the park's beauty. They haven't, of course, but the park's roads do indeed pass through stunning scenery. In addition to the 33-mile **Newfound Gap Road,** which twists, turns, climbs, and falls through the center of the park, other drives include the seven-mile **Clingmans Dome Road** from Newfound Gap to a parking area just short of Clingmans Dome's summit. It's the highest

Deron Nardo

A deer in Cades Cove

road in the park. ◆ The 18-mile stretch of **Little River Road** from the Sugarlands Visitor Center near Gatlinburg to Cades Cove, provides numerous vistas of the Little River, waterfalls, dense forest, and pretty wildflowers.

◆ The one-way, 11-mile loop through **Cades Cove** is the park's most-celebrated scenic drive and with good reason. From the valley floor, expansive views of fields bordered by mountain peaks look like scenes from *Little House on the Prairie*. The abundance of wildlife and an unmatched collection of historic churches and cabins attract more than two million visitors every year, causing traffic jams to rival those of any major urban area. Stop at the Sugarlands or Oconaluftee visitor centers to pick up the self-guiding booklet, highlighting the historic sites along the road.

Hurry Up and Wait

In the summer and fall, traffic in the GSMNP slows to a crawl, particularly on Newfound Gap Road and the Cades Cove Loop. For example, a trip around the 11-mile, one-way Loop Road can take between two and four hours during the busy seasons. What to do? Start early, pack some good music, a snack, and a lot of patience.

◆ Other GSMNP roads with stand-up-and-applaud views include the one-way **Roaring Fork Motor Nature Trail,** which, when combined with **Cherokee Orchard Road,** creates an 11-mile loop through the park just southeast of Gatlinburg. You'll ride through hardwood forests with dozens of roadside streams, waterfalls, and gentle cascades, and past several historic homes of residents who lived here prior to the park's creation. To access the drive from Gatlinburg, turn right at Stoplight #8 onto Historic Nature Trail Road (formerly Airport Road). In the park, the road becomes Cherokee Orchard Road, which leads three miles to the start of the Roaring Fork Motor Nature Trail.

◆ If you're interested in exploring more of the park's scenic drives, stop by one of the visitor centers to purchase a copy of the GSMNP's official road guide, *Mountain Roads & Quiet Places,* or call (865) 436-0120. It costs $8.95.

◆ The southern terminus of the nation's most-popular scenic road, the **Blue Ridge Parkway,** (828) 298-0398, *www.nps.gov/blri,* is located near the Cherokee entrance to the GSMNP. From here, it travels north 469 miles along the Appalachian Mountain ridgelines to Virginia's Shenandoah National Park. Numerous overlooks, pull-offs, and various recreation areas line the road, which was built by the Civilian Conservation Corps in the 1930s and 1940s, in part to give work to men who'd lost employment during the Great Depression. To enjoy this road, pick up the free parkway map printed by the National Park Service and available free at the Oconaluftee Visitor Center.

◆ The 52-mile **Cherohala Skyway** is a National Scenic Byway that stretches from Robbinsville, North Carolina to the Tellico Plains in southeast Tennessee. The highway features long, sweeping curves and amazing views of the rugged Nantahala and Cherokee national forests. There are numerous overlooks, including spectacular Spirit Ridge at 4,950 feet. To access the road, take Route 143 north from Robbinsville 12 miles to the Cherohala Skyway at Santeetlah Gap.

The Blue Ridge Parkway

Historic Sites

There are more than 70 historic structures within the GSMNP, most of which are open for viewing. The largest concentration of historic buildings is in **Cades Cove,** where a working gristmill, three churches, cantilever barns, and homesteads stand as testament to 19th-century life in the broad valley. A self-guiding, auto-tour booklet that interprets the sites along the 11-mile Cades Cove Loop is available from any visitor center in the park. See *Wide Open* for directions to Cades Cove.

◆ **Cataloochee Valley** was a thriving agricultural center in the early 1900s, with numerous apple orchards lining the valley, when the Federal Government purchased the land to create the GSMNP. Today preserved structures include two churches, a school, and a cluster of houses. Purchase a self-guiding auto leaflet from a dispenser near the entrance to the valley. See *Wide Open* for directions.

◆ Located adjacent to the Oconaluftee Visitor Center on Newfound Gap Road north of Cherokee, the open-air **Mountain Farm Museum** features a variety of old farm buildings, including a log home, springhouse, apple house, smoke house, corn crib, blacksmith shop, and log barn. Pick up the self-guiding booklet detailing the lives of the early settlers from the visitor center. ◆ A half-mile north of the Oconaluftee Visitor Center on Newfound Gap Road, **Mingus Mill** is a gristmill powered by a 19th-century water turbine that grinds out corn meal and flour for sale to visitors.

◆ **The Oconaluftee Indian Village,** Route 441 North, Cherokee, (828) 497-2315 or (828) 497-2111 (off-season), *www.oconalufteevillage.com,* is a replica 18th-century Cherokee village, complete with a seven-sided council house and village homes. Cherokee guides in native costumes provide tours. Watch as tribesmen build canoes, mold pots and bowls from clay, and chip arrowheads from flint. Nominal admission fee. Open daily, 9 A.M.–5:30 P.M., May 15–October 25.

Mingus Mill

Museums

🏛 **The Museum of the Cherokee,** 589 Tsali Boulevard, Cherokee, (828) 497-3481, *www.cherokeemuseum.org,* uses high-tech exhibits (computer-generated imagery, special effects, and audio) along with an extensive collection of artifacts to present the story of the Cherokee Indians from roughly 10,000 years ago through the present day. Archives include more than 1,000 black and white photos from the 1880s–1930s, more than 4,000 books, and a collection of papers and diaries from 1834–1899. Open daily, 9 A.M.–5 P.M. Nominal admission fee.

Waiter, My Food's Moving

The **Great Smoky Mountains Railroad,** ☎ 1-800-872-4681, *www.gsmr.com,* departs from Dillsboro and offers a variety of full- and half-day scenic journeys through the valleys and gorges of the Great Smoky Mountains. For a unique, romantic experience, ride the rails on the four-course, gourmet-dinner train, or take in the excitement of the three-course, mystery-theatre dinner train. Dressy-casual attire required. Call for reservations.

NC Division of Tourism

◆ **The Museum of North Carolina Handicrafts,** 49 Shelton Street, Waynesville, (828) 452-1551, is a comprehensive exhibit of 19th-century crafts and furniture, including quilts, pottery, and hand-painted china. The museum, housed in the historic 1875 Shelton House, also features a collection of Native-American artifacts. Open Tuesday–Friday, 10 A.M.–4 P.M. Nominal admission fee.

Performing Arts

♪ The **Haywood Arts Repertory Theatre**, 250 Pigeon Street, Waynesville, (828) 456-6322, *www.harttheatre.com,* produces two main-stage musicals, five main-stage plays, and up to six studio-theatre shows each season, which runs year-round. Past performances include such classics as *The King and I, The Grapes of Wrath,* and *Jekyll and Hyde.*

◆ **Unto These Hills,** Route 441 North, Cherokee, (828) 497-2111 or 1-866-554-4557, *www.untothesehills.com,* is an outdoor drama depicting the plight of the Cherokee Indians from the time of their first contact with Europeans—the arrival of Hernando De Soto in 1540—to their banishment to Oklahoma on the 1838 "Trail of Tears." Evening shows run Monday–Saturday at 8:30 P.M. for 10 weeks from June–August.

NC Division of Tourism

Unto These Hills

◆ **Harrah's Cherokee Casino & Hotel,** 777 Casino Drive, Cherokee, 1-800-427-7247, *www.harrahs.com,* has a 1,500-seat pavilion with 20-foot projection screens and concert sound and lighting. Bill Cosby, Jay Leno, and Wayne Newton are just a few of the entertainers who've performed here. Call for event schedules and reservations. ◆ **Maggie Valley Opry,** 3605 Soco

Road, Maggie Valley, (828) 926-9336, is open nightly, May–October, and features the world-class banjo picking of Raymond Fairchild, as well as touring bluegrass and folk music acts.

Shops & Stops

In addition to the aforementioned antiques dealers and art and crafts galleries, numerous specialty shops exist in the towns surrounding the GSMNP. The largest concentrations are in Waynesville, where the historic downtown features an array of specialty shops facing brick-lined sidewalks; Dillsboro, a highly walk-able town with nearly 50 shops and businesses; and Sylva, a designated North Carolina Main Street town, where an increasing number of boutiques are opening.

◆ In Waynesville, highlights include a branch of the **Mast General Store,** 63 North Main Street, (828) 452-2101, *www.mastgeneralstore.com,* housed in a 1930s building with two floors full of clothes, outdoor gear, footwear, general mercantile items, and more than 5,000 pieces of hard candy. ◆ **Vicki and David's General Mercantile,** 48 North Main Street, Waynesville, (828) 452-2266, *www.vickianddavid.com,* carries such items as gourmet food, candles, personal care products, and housewares. ◆ The **Waynesville Book Company,** 184 North Main Street, (828) 456-8062, is a full-service bookstore with a strong emphasis on local and regional titles, including maps, hiking guides, fiction, and more.

◆ In Dillsboro, head to **The Kitchen Shop,** 18 Marsh Lilly Drive, (828) 586-4182, for anything and everything related to cooking. ◆ **The Nature Connection,** 150 Front Street, Dillsboro, (828) 586-0686, *www.nature-connection.com,* sells home, garden, and patio accessories, as well as art, crafts, jewelry, and music. ◆ **The Golden Carp,** 107 Webster Street, Dillsboro, (828) 586-5477, *www.thegoldencarp.com,* is a unique home furnishings and accessories store, carrying everything from French hotel clocks to bamboo birdcages.

◆ If you find yourself in Sylva without your fleece, head to **Blackrock Outdoor Company,** 570 West Main Street, Sylva, (828) 631-4453, for outdoor apparel and footwear. ◆ **City Lights Bookstore,** 3 East Jackson Street, Sylva, (828) 586-9499 or 1-888-853-6298, *www.citylightsnc.com,* is an wonderful bookshop stocked with current and classic fiction and nonfiction. The store has a paticularly strong lineup of books about Appalachian culture.

Lady Luck

A little slice of Vegas sits right in the heart of the Smokies at **Harrah's Cherokee Casino & Hotel,** 777 Casino Drive, Cherokee, ☎ 1-800-427-7247, *www.harrahs.com,* where such video format games as poker, craps, and blackjack await.

Spa & Massage

Serenity Salon & Day Spa, 1088 North Main Street, Waynesville, (828) 452-5182, has a full range of manicures, pedicures, facials, and massages. ◆ **The Day Spa at Lakeview,** Mile Marker 61, Route 74, Bryson City, 1-800-742-6492, *www.lakeviewnc.com,* welcomes the public for a full menu of massages (try the hot-stone massage), body treatments, and skin-care services.

R e s t   E a s y

S l e e p   W e l l

Lodging options in North Carolina around the GSMNP include full-service resorts, historic country inns, and charming B&Bs. Note that some lodgings have limited schedules during winter.

Accommodations Pricing

Less than $100	Inexpensive	$
$100-150	Moderate	$$
$151-200	Expensive	$$$
More than $200	Very Expensive	$$$$

Prices are per room, per night, based on double occupancy during peak seasons. Note that B&Bs and most country inns include breakfast in the rate.

Balsam Mountain Inn • Opened in 1908, the Balsam Mountain Inn sits on 24 scenic acres surrounded by mountain peaks. A spacious lobby with fireplaces and a library with more than 2,000 volumes are two of the amenities greeting guests upon arrival. Upstairs, 50 rooms, each with a private bath, are available in a variety of arrangements. Standard rooms have either two double or one king-sized bed; "bed-sitting rooms" feature living areas and primarily king-sized beds; and suites are spacious with two rooms, king-sized beds, and scenic views. A hearty, Southern breakfast, complete with fresh fruit and coffee, is served each morning. Dinner in the main dining room is also available at an additional cost. • *68-7 Springs Drive, Balsam, NC 28707,* ☎ *(828) 456-9498 or 1-800-224-9498, www.balsaminn.com* • *$$–$$$*

Blackberry Farm • Lodging coverage for this chapter is limited to North Carolina properties... with this exception. Located just northwest of Townsend, this Relais & Chateaux property sits on 2,500 acres of meadows, woods, and streams on the Tennessee-side of the Smokies. Amenities include miles of hiking and biking trails, fly fishing (with onsite instructors), horseback riding, and a full spa located in a 1870s farmhouse. Three gourmet meals are served daily (included in the rate, which starts at $545 a night based on a two-night minimum stay). Breakfast and candlelight dinners are served in the elegant dining room; lunch is packed for the trail. And then there are the rooms, all of which are appointed with antique furnishings and fine art and represent the utmost in elegance and comfort. • *1471 West Millers Cove, Walland, TN 37886,* ☎ *(865) 380-2260 or 1-800-648-2348, www.blackberryfarm.com* • *$$$$*

Folkestone Inn • Built as a farmhouse in the 1920s, this inn is ideally located less than one mile from the Deep Creek Campground in the GSMNP. Folkestone features a cozy atmosphere in common areas such as parlors and porches, while period furnishings help the inn maintain much of its original charm. There are ten rooms—nine have queen-sized beds, one has a king-sized bed—each with private bath, including an old-fashioned clawfoot tub and shower. Some rooms have balconies, decks, or private entrances. Try the Wrens & Warblers (a nod to the variety of birds that visit the inn) Room, which features French doors opening to a private balcony with tremendous views of the Smokies. Breakfast is served each morning and includes such specialties as country sausage and raspberry pancakes. • *101 Folkestone Road, Bryson City, NC 28713,* ☎ *(828) 488-2730 or 1-888-812-3385, www.folkestoneinn.com* • *$–$$*

Fryemont Inn • Nestled into a mountain-shelf overlooking GSMNP, the historic Fryemont Inn offers serene luxury at an affordable price. The spacious lobby has a massive stone fireplace with eight-foot logs, and the rocking chair-lined porch serves up spectacular views. The are 37 rooms, each with a private bath, chestnut paneling, and large windows. There are also three fireplace suites in separate buildings, with king-sized beds, living rooms, wet bars, and more. A two-bedroom, 1.5-bath log cabin with a wood stove and gas grill is also available. Rates include breakfast and dinner, served in the dining room, which features a full-service bar and pool table. • *245 Fryemont Road, Bryson City, NC 28713,* ☎ *(828) 488-2159 or 1-800-845-4879, www.fryemontinn.com* • *$$*

Old Stone Inn • Located on six acres filled with century-old oaks and stands of mountain laurel and rhododendron, the Old Stone Inn is a "country retreat" in the middle of town. Its 22 guest rooms are spread across seven buildings. A sampling of the choices: The 1947 Oak Terrace Lodge features rooms with private baths, hardwood floors, and porches; the Rhododendron Lodge has larger rooms with king-sized beds, spacious bathrooms, vaulted ceilings, and covered porches; and the Main Lodge features two chestnut suites with queen-sized beds, sitting areas, and gas log fireplaces. Breakfast is served fireside and typically includes freshly baked breads, fresh fruit, eggs, smoked trout, and the morning paper. • *109 Dolan Road, Waynesville, NC 28786,* ☎ *(828) 456-3333 or 1-800-432-8499, www.oldstoneinn.com* • *$–$$$*

Prospect Hill B & B • Located on an acre and a half at the top of the hill on Waynesville's Main Street, this century-old Victorian inn features a sprawling front porch, antique furnishings, and original artwork. Five guest rooms, each with private bath, are in the main house. The Savannah Room is popular for its mountain views, lace-canopied, king-sized, poster bed, and two-person whirlpool tub. Two, one-bedroom apartments are located in a cottage behind the main house and feature king-sized feather beds, kitchenettes, picture windows, and a shared porch. Breakfast is included for guests of the main house, optional for those in the cottage. • *274 South Main Street, Waynesville, NC 28786,* ☎ *(828) 456-5980 or 1-800-219-6147, www.mountaininns.com* • *$$–$$$*

The Swag • This spectacular retreat on 250 acres sits on a mountain summit above 5,000 feet and adjacent to the GSMNP. The 50-mile views are magnificent. So, too, are the amenities, accommodations, and service. The 11 guestrooms, one suite, and three private cabins are individually decorated with rustic antiques and original artwork. Many of the rooms feature private balconies, steam showers, and large fireplaces. The cabins have sitting rooms and private porches. Included in the rate is a buffet-style, hot breakfast; lunch packed for the trail or served in the lodge; and a festive, gourmet dinner, complete with hors d'oeuvres and place cards. Amenities include a 2.5-mile nature trail and a redwood sauna and spa. The Swag is a member of the distinguished *Select Registry* and has earned Mobil's demanding Four-Star award. • *2300 Swag Road, Waynesville, NC 28786,* ☎ *(828) 926-0430 or 1-800-789-7672, www.theswag.com* • *$$$$*

Windsong Mountain Inn & Llama Farm •

This rustic inn sits on 24 acres at an elevation of 3,000 feet and is surrounded by forest laced with miles of hiking trails. Amenities include a swimming pool, tennis court, poolroom, hot tub, and a farm with llamas and pygmy goats. Hot, gourmet breakfasts are served on fine china and with the inn's own blend of coffee. Lunch and dinner llama treks are also available (for an extra fee). The five guestrooms feature queen-sized beds, full baths, and decks or patios with tremendous views. Most rooms have two-person tubs and wood-burning fireplaces. The Pond Lodge is 200 yards up the mountain, and has two suites, each with two bedrooms, full kitchens, wood-burning stoves, private decks with grills, and more. (Continental breakfast served for suite guests.) • *459 Rockcliffe Lane, Clyde, NC 28721,* ☎ *(828) 627-6111, www.windsong-bb.com* • *$$–$$$*

The Yellow House • There are seven, richly decorated suites and a two-bedroom, two-bath cottage at this elegant retreat located at 3,000 feet with views of rolling meadows, green pastures, and the Blue Ridge Mountains. Suites, which reflect the innkeepers' worldly tastes (and travels), feature individual décor with strong French and Dutch influences. Each has a private bath and king- or queen-sized bed, and may also include such features as a whirlpool tub, balcony or terrace, and fireplace. The Carriage House Suite has them all. The scenic grounds feature two ponds, and perennial, herb, and bird gardens. There is also a two-bedroom, two-bath cottage on the grounds, with two fireplaces and a French country kitchen. Breakfast and hors d'oeuvres are included in the rate. The Yellow House belongs to the *Select Registry* association. • *89 Oakview Drive, Waynesville, NC 28786,* ☎ *(828) 452-0991 or 1-800-563-1236, www.theyellowhouse.com* • *$$$–$$$$*

Dine Well

Cuisine in the villages around the GSMNP ranges from country cooking with biscuits and gravy, fried chicken, and farm vegetables to gourmet cuisine prepared by graduates of the nation's finest culinary schools. In general, the area's best restaurants are a part of inns and resorts and require reservations to secure a seat. The following is merely a sampling of the region's finest restaurants.

Dillsboro Smokehouse • With a menu including (but not limited to) barbecued beef, chicken, and pork, this casual eatery is anything but casual in their approach to 'cue. Try the baby back ribs—the tender meat falls off the bones. Side dishes like Texas toast (cheese toast), hush puppies, yams, and BBQ beans are also available, along with plenty of extra napkins. Open daily for lunch and dinner. • *403 Haywood Road, Dillsboro,* ☎ *(828) 586-9556*

The Fryemont Inn • Expect hearty portions of Southern cooking in a huge, rustic, country dining room with an enormous stone fireplace, hardwood floors, and a vaulted ceiling. Entrées include braised lamb shanks slow-cooked with garlic, oregano, and tomatoes; and almond-crusted fresh rainbow trout in a white wine sauce. Soup, salad, family-style side dishes, and dessert are included in the entrée price. A complete wine list and full bar are also available. Open daily for breakfast and dinner, April–Thanksgiving. • *245 Fryemont Road, Bryson City,* ☎ *(828) 488-2159 or 1-800-845-4879*

The Jarrett House • Built in 1884, the Jarrett House originally served as a popular dining spot for Western North Carolina Railway workers and passengers. Today it maintains its reputation for good, Southern food. Family-style dinners are served in a spacious dining room. Expect such entrées as mountain trout, fried chicken, and mountain country-cured ham, accompanied with sides like cole slaw, candied apples, pickled beets, green beans, and hot biscuits. From December–April, open Monday–Saturday for lunch; Friday and Saturday for dinner; and

Sunday for brunch. In the summer, open daily for lunch and dinner. • *100 Haywood Road, Dillsboro,* ☎ *(828) 586-0265 or 1-800-972-5623*

Lomo Grill • Waynesville may not seem a likely spot for outstanding Mediterranean-Argentinean cuisine, but you'll find just that in a renovated 1920s red brick building with hardwood floors and a tin ceiling. A member of the Parisian gourmet food and wine society, Chaine de Rotisseurs, Chef Ricardo frequently changes the menu but regularly offers such appetizer favorites as calamari bruschetta (calamari rings sautéed in white wine, garlic, tomato, and parsley over crispy pan rustique) and such entrées as involtine di melanzane (grilled eggplant rolled with sun-dried tomatoes, spinach, fresh basil, calamata olives and goat cheese, drizzled with roasted red pepper coulis). A European-style bakery and espresso and wine bar are also onsite. The restaurant is open for lunch daily, and dinner Monday–Saturday. Call for winter hours. • *44 Church Street, Waynesville,* ☎ *(828) 452-5222*

Lulu's on Main • Centrally located on Sylva's Main Street, Lulu's offers creative American cuisine in a hip, casual atmosphere. Considered by many locals one of the region's best eateries, Lulu's has nightly features that always include at least one fresh-seafood choice. For starters, try the portabella mushroom marinated in a citrus basil sauce and served with a hot baguette and creamy gorgonzola dressing, and follow it with the roasted mozzarella basil ravioli topped with roasted red pepper cream sauce, parsley, and parmesan. An extensive beer selection and a well-chosen wine list complement the menu. Open Monday–Saturday for lunch and dinner. • *612 West Main Street, Sylva,* ☎ *(828) 586-8989*

Nantahala Village Restaurant • Housed in the immense, 200-acre Nantahala Village Resort, the Nantahala Village Restaurant offers everything from traditional Southern favorites to innovative cuisine. The main dining room features a locally crafted, stone fireplace, and the outdoor deck serves up gorgeous mountain views. Along with nightly dinner and vegetarian specials, the menu includes such entrées as the village rib-eye, seasoned with a blend of spices and topped with lemon-parsley butter; and the wild forest pasta (linguini tossed with mushrooms, zucchini, tomatoes, artichoke hearts, onions, parmesan cheese, herbs, and butter, and topped with an alfredo sauce). Full wine and beer lists are also available. The restaurant is open for breakfast, lunch, and dinner, late March–November, but hours vary weekly. Call for reservations. • *9400 Highway 19 West, Bryson City,* ☎ *(828) 488-2826 or 1-800-438-1507*

The Old Stone Inn • Candlelight dinners, slow-cooked and served by the stone fireplace, make The Old Stone Inn a favorite for romantic, intimate dining. The menu, which changes seasonally to include the freshest available ingredients, features entrées of beef, pork, lamb, and seafood. Favorites include appetizers such as the fresh mushroom soup and such entrées as the escalopes of pork tenderloin with rosemary, served over lemon-scented rice. A well-matched wine list and delicious desserts complete the meal. Open April–Thanksgiving, Monday–Saturday for dinner; reservations required. • *109 Dolan Road, Waynesville,* ☎ *(828) 456-3333*

The Spring Street Café • Sharing a space with City Lights Bookstore, The Spring Street Café offers an eclectic menu with numerous vegetarian dishes. Seafood and chicken keep traditionalists happy, but more adventurous epicureans will want to try the spicy jerk string beans and wakame salad. Open Tuesday–Saturday for lunch and dinner, as well as for Sunday brunch. • *3 East Jackson Street, Sylva,* ☎ *(828) 586-1800*

Picnic Packing

Stretch out on the patio or pack a sandwich for your hike from the **Patio Bistro and Coffee Shop,** 26 Church Street, Waynesville, ☎ (828)454-0070, which serves a selection of deli sandwiches, wraps, melts, and salads. • **The Well House,** 65 Craft Circle, Dillsboro, ☎ (828) 586-8588, features gourmet deli sandwiches, served hot or cold.

Just Desserts

Dillsboro Chocolate Factory & Espresso Bar, 28 Church Street, Dillsboro, ☎ (828) 631-0156, sells homemade fudge, chocolates, smoothies, and an assortment of coffee drinks. • **Sweet Dreams Bakery and Café,** 894 East Main Street, Sylva, ☎ (828) 586-0939, offers pastries, cakes, and pies, as well as soups and sandwiches for lunch. • **Timothy's,** 112 North Main Street, Waynesville, ☎ (828) 456-3883, features a dessert café.

A Long-Weekend Itinerary

Day One

After breakfast at your inn, swing by the **Patio Bistro and Coffee Shop** (page 327) to purchase a picnic lunch and then head into the **GSMNP** to drive **Newfound Gap** and **Clingmans Dome roads** (page 317). Walk the half-mile **Clingmans Dome Trail** (page 307) to the summit, take in the views, and return to the parking area to hike the **Forney Ridge Trail** (page 307) to Andrews Bald. Picnic on the bald, and then return to your car to head to Waynesville to tour some art and crafts galleries, including **Twigs and Leaves** (page 317) and **Hardwood Gallery** (page 317). Return to your inn to shower before a quiet dinner at **Lomo Grill** (page 326). Call it a day.

Day Two

Rise early for breakfast and head to the **Nantahala Outdoor Center** (page 311) to rent mountain bikes and a car rack for the trip to **Tsali Recreation Area** (page 310). Don't forget your camera, as the views of Fontana Lake are stunning. Or, if you're not up for mountain biking, join one of NOC's three-hour **Nantahala River** (page 312) rafting trips. When you finish riding or rafting, head back for a shower, and then grab lunch at Sylva's **Spring Street Café** (page 327) before browsing through the selections at **City Lights Bookstore** (page 321). Spend the afternoon in Cherokee at **Oconaluftee Indian Village** (page 319) and in the **Museum of the Cherokee** (page 320). Enjoy dinner at the **Jarrett House** (page 325). Lights out.

Day Three

Linger over breakfast to soak in your last day of vacation. After checking out of your inn, take time to browse the area's **shops** (page 321), **antiques shops** (page 316), and **art & crafts galleries** (page 316). Grab lunch at **The Well House** (page 327), and some chocolate and coffee at **Dillsboro Chocolate Factory & Espresso Bar** (page 327) for the ride home.

Additional Information

For additional dining, accommodations, and sightseeing information including the dates of special events, contact:

The Haywood County Tourism Development Authority runs the **Balsam Visitor Center,** 20525 Great Smoky Expressway, Waynesville, NC 28786, ☎ (828) 452-7307, *www.smokeymountains.net.* Open daily, 9 A.M.–5 P.M.

Jackson County Chamber of Commerce, 773 West Main Street, Sylva, NC 28779, ☎ (828) 586-2155 or 1-800-962-1911, *www.mountainlovers.com.* The visitor center is open spring through fall, Monday–Saturday, 9:30 A.M.–5:30 P.M., and Sunday 1:30–4:30 P.M. Winter hours are Monday–Friday, 9:30 A.M.–5:30 P.M., Saturday, 10 A.M.–3 P.M. Closed Sunday.

Swain County Chamber of Commerce, 16 Everett Street, Bryson City, NC 28713, ☎ 1-800-867-9246, *www.greatsmokies.com.* The office is open from Monday–Saturday, 9 A.M.–5 P.M. in season, which runs from spring until the end of leaf season (which varies year by year).

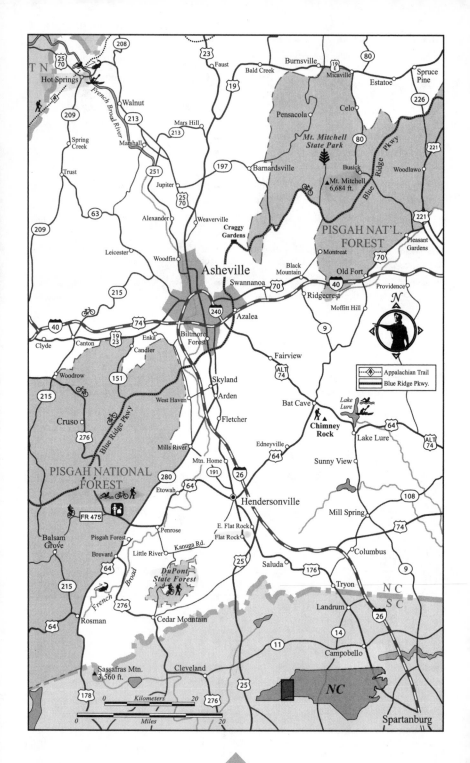

Asheville, North Carolina

Including Black Mountain, Brevard, Flat Rock, Hendersonville, Hot Springs, and Lake Lure

The Appalachian Mountain Range, which stretches from Georgia to Newfoundland, formed between 250 and 450 million years ago as tectonic plates surfed Earth's liquid core, smashed into each other, and pushed the land skyward. At birth, the peaks were as high and craggy as the Rocky Mountains are today, but time softened their edges, eroding them to a present average elevation of 3,000 feet. In North Carolina, the mountains proved the most resilient. This is where you'll find the range's highest and most-jagged peaks. And here, surrounded by these ancient mountains and spread across a high-plateau valley at the junction of the French Broad and Swannanoa rivers, is the free-spirited City of Asheville.

Sixty-eight thousand residents do indeed make a city, but Asheville's diverse and colorful population—mountain settlers' descendents, craftspeople, sophisticates, alternative types, and everyday folks—challenges the notion of cities as pretentious, impersonal, and buttoned-up. Alternately tradition-bound and New Age, fastidious and unkempt, cosmopolitan and rural, Asheville has a long history as a meeting point between cultures. In fact, the former frontier town developed around the intersection of pre-historic Native-American trading paths.

The earliest settlers were the Connestee, hunter-gatherers who traded locally mined mica for pottery, flint, copper, and tools with tribes as far away as the Gulf Coast

Downtown Asheville

The Appalachians are among the world's oldest mountains

and Ohio. Excavations of an 1,800-year-old Connestee village on the present-day grounds of the Biltmore Estate have turned up artifacts more than 6,000 years old. The Connestee descendents were the Cherokee, a powerful tribe that numbered perhaps 20,000 in the 16th Century when the first Spanish explorers trudged through the area in search of gold. Cherokee society, with its own government, laws of progeny, and rich mythology, was advanced, and while inter-tribal skirmishes broke out over hunting lands and trade practices, the tribe essentially lived in peace. That is until the first white settlers made their way into the mountains in the 18th Century. Land negotiations favored the settlers and continually pushed the Cherokee west until the discovery of gold in Georgia prompted the 1830 Removal Act that sent all Native Americans east of the Mississippi to Oklahoma on the "Trail of Tears."

In the late 18th Century, the first pioneers settled the fertile Swannanoa Valley, which they called "Eden Land." By 1791, enough settlers had arrived that the State Assembly established Buncombe County, named in honor of the Revolutionary hero, Colonel Edward Buncombe. Soon thereafter, a log courthouse was built in Pack Square. In 1793, John Burton became the settlement's first developer. He purchased 200 acres of land surrounding the courthouse, subdivided it, named the development Morristown, and sold 42 half-acre lots for $2.50 each. In 1797, Morristown honored then-Governor Samuel Ashe by incorporating the land as Asheville.

The Pre-Jet Set

George Vanderbilt, E.W. Grove, Zelda and F. Scott Fitzgerald, Calvin Coolidge, Franklin and Eleanor Roosevelt, Henry Ford, Thomas Edison, Will Rogers. These are just a few of the folks who rode the rails into Asheville in the early 20th Century to enjoy the city's sparkling social climate. Many of them stayed at the palatial Grove Park Inn, which from its opening in 1913 through the Roaring Twenties, was one of the "in spots" for the nation's glitterati.

By the mid 1800s, the area's cool summer climate had begun to attract seasonal visitors, but it wasn't until the arrival of the railroad in the 1880s that the city took off as a tourist destination. The fresh air, expansive mountain views, and proximity of numerous hot sulfur springs attracted travelers, as well as tuberculosis patients whose doctors recommended Asheville as a geographic remedy. The city constructed hotels, boardinghouses, and sanitariums to host the influx. (Novelist Thomas Wolfe was born here in 1900 and grew up in a boardinghouse run by his mother for such visitors. His autobiographical novel, *Look Homeward Angel*, was set in Asheville.)

George Vanderbilt visited with his mother in 1880 and decided to build a "country home" on the outskirts of town. He purchased 125,000 acres and in 1890 began construction on the Biltmore, a 250-room French château. E.W. Grove, another wealthy visitor, arrived from St. Louis in the early 20th Century to build the Grove Park Inn and several buildings downtown, including Grove Arcade, one of the country's first indoor shopping malls. Flush with cash from tourism and willing to hedge bets on future growth, Asheville erected a glittering downtown full of Art-Deco and Gothic buildings. The grand party, however, was headed for an

The 250-room Biltmore House

Alka Seltzer. The Great Depression levied a sobering toll on the wealth that fueled Asheville's good times, and the city that was so dependent upon seasonal visitors spiraled deep into debt.

Ironically, Asheville's gargantuan debt saved its downtown architecture from the wrecking ball. Without the funds to "modernize," the city let its buildings sit until the late 1980s, when town officials recognized the value of preserving and revitalizing its center. The result is a vibrant downtown district with hip retailers, restaurants, and cafés housed in distinctive buildings. (In the Southeast, only Miami Beach has more Art-Deco buildings than Asheville.)

The outdoors permeates the region. The Blue Ridge Parkway, Appalachian Trail, Pisgah National Forest, and French Broad, Nolichucky, and Pigeon rivers surround the city. From *Bike* magazine's "Top 15 North American Cities for Mountain Biking" to *Canoe & Kayak's*

"Top 10 Paddle Towns in the U.S.," Asheville regularly appears on the national outdoor media's radar.

Asheville really isn't like anywhere else. The mix of rich history, interesting architecture, indigenous art and crafts, Biltmore Estate, museums, bistros, and shops, and outdoor playgrounds without limit, make this region one of the finest Play Hard Rest Easy destinations in the Southeast.

The French Broad River

The Way Around

The cultural and economic hub of Western North Carolina, **Asheville** is Buncombe County's biggest city (68,000 residents), complete with urban sprawl and its own bypass, **Interstate 240,** which loops north from Interstate 40 to lasso the city's downtown area. **Downtown Asheville** is the city's heart with shops, restaurants, art galleries, eclectic architecture, and attractions. It's best to walk downtown given the city's slightly dysfunctional street system (roads change names without warning). Metered parking spots are abundant.

NC Division of Tourism

Asheville's vibrant downtown

There are municipal parking decks at the Civic Center, on Rankin Avenue, and on Wall Street.

Pack Square and nearby South Pack Square make up the city's center. Located at the intersection of College Street, Broadway, and Biltmore Avenue, Pack Square features the 75-foot Vance Monument, a granite obelisk erected in 1896 to honor North Carolina Governor Zebulon Vance; the cultural arts center, Pack Place; and the city's first skyscraper, the Jackson building. The streets surrounding Pack Square feature museums, shops, restaurants, and municipal buildings.

Biltmore Avenue, which extends south from Pack Square, is home to art galleries, cafés, and thrift shops. Eventually, this road leads to the Biltmore Estate and **Biltmore Village,** where you'll find pleasant shopping and dining on cobbled sidewalks. Biltmore Avenue continues north of Pack Square as **Broadway,** a bustling, commercial street with coffee and retail shops. Other major streets downtown include **Lexington Avenue,** a popular antiques corridor; **Wall Street**, a one-block road full of interesting specialty shops and cafés; **Battery Park Avenue,** parallel to Wall Street and also full of shops, cafés, and the indoor mall, Grove Park Arcade; **Haywood Street**, another stretch of retailers, plus the Pack Memorial Library; and **Market Street**, a cobble-stoned road with restaurants, the Thomas Wolfe Memorial Home, and a commanding view of the Jackson Building.

Cosmopolitan, yet Cosmological

Dreadlocks, Birkenstocks, "river rats," hikers, tourists, shopkeepers, bankers, poets, painters ... there is no single Asheville type. "Live and let live" is the open-minded attitude that makes Asheville a haven for free spirits and friendly people.

From downtown, both Haywood Street and **Patton Avenue** extend across the **French Broad River** to **West Asheville**, once a separate township that today is experiencing a rebirth as a hip area full of funky shops and cheap eats. Northwest of downtown just across Interstate 240, the **Montford Historic District** is Asheville's oldest neighborhood with many attractive Victorian homes, a number of which are bed and breakfasts. **Montford Avenue** is the neighborhood's main thoroughfare. North of downtown, Broadway becomes **Merrimon Avenue/Route 25** and travels a mere six miles through posh neighborhoods into **Weaverville.** Weaverville is small community that's been popular with artists for some time but is increasingly luring young professionals and families who work in Asheville but prefer to live in a slower, more-rural area.

Located north of Asheville in rural, rugged Madison County, **Hot Springs** became popular in the mid 19th Century with travelers seeking the restorative benefits of its mineral springs. Today the small town attracts rafters, hikers, and bathers headed to the private Hot Springs Spa. The French Broad

Gordon Smith

The Wright Inn in Asheville's Montford neighborhood

River and the Appalachian Trail pass through town. To get to Hot Springs from Asheville, take Route 19/23 north to the Marshall Exit, and then Route 25/70 north roughly 30 miles.

Just a 20-minute ride from Asheville east on Interstate 40, **Black Mountain** was established in 1893 as a summer resort for flatlanders and today is a major religious retreat town and home to private Montreat College. Artisans, craftspeople, and travelers populate the lovely downtown with its collection of shops and cafés set against a Blue Ridge backdrop.

Southwest from Asheville in Transylvania County, **Brevard** is a scenic hideaway reached by taking **Interstate 26** east to Exit #9, where you take **Route 280** south to **Route 64** into town. Its location on the eastern edge of the **Pisgah National Forest** provides miles of nature to explore. The more than 250 waterfalls nearby have earned Transylvania County the moniker, "Land of Waterfalls." Incorporated in 1868, Brevard is now a popular community for retirees, drawn here for the intellectual stimulation provided by the renowned Brevard Music Festival and private Brevard College. The town's busy **Main** and **Broad streets** have numerous unique shops, galleries, and cafés. You can look up and down the intersection of the two and see the mountains just outside of town.

Downtown Hendersonville

Located southeast of Asheville off Interstate 40, **Hendersonville** is a large mountain town with a busy **Main Street** lined with benches, boutiques, antiques shops, art galleries, restaurants, and even an old-style soda shop where you can enjoy a frothy fountain malt. The town supports a large seasonal retirement community. Each summer, the population swells with seniors from Florida who travel north for the cooler air and rich cultural activities. Nearby is the delightful Village of Flat Rock. Sometimes called the "little Charleston of the mountains," **Flat Rock** was originally populated by lowcountry planters escaping the heat and mosquitoes. Today the town is best known for the acclaimed Flat Rock Playhouse and the historic Carl Sandburg Home. There are numerous upscale inns and restaurants leading into town along **Route 25**.

Traveling east of Asheville roughly 25 miles on **Route 64/74A**, you'll enter **Hickory Nut Gorge**, a 14-mile-long canyon, in which you'll find gorgeous **Chimney Rock Park** and **Lake Lure** of *Dirty Dancing* fame. Chimney Rock Park is private but worth every dime of the admission for its well-maintained hiking trails and for the quick 26-story elevator ride to the top of the Chimney for 75-mile views. Hidden among the towering Blue Ridge peaks, Lake Lure is a shimmering jewel.

Weather

A city for all seasons, Ashville comes to life with spring flowers and bright green in mid April, gently migrates to bumblebees and brilliant wildflowers in summer, and bursts with fiery autumn color during its peak fall season, before curling up for a quiet winter with just the occasional dusting of snow. Average winter daytime highs are 47 degrees with overnight lows in the upper 20s. Average summertime highs are in the mid 80s, cooling to the lower 60s at night. Fall is cool and crisp with average daytime highs in the lower 60s. Spring is even cooler with average high temperatures in the mid 50s. Elevation makes a difference; a general rule is the air is three degrees cooler for every 1,000-foot rise in elevation.

Getting to Asheville

By Air: The **Asheville Regional Airport**, ☎ (828) 684-2226, *www.ashevilleregion-alairport.com*, services several major airlines and offers both rental cars and ground transportation.

By Car: From Atlanta, take Interstate 85 north to Greenville, where you take Route 25 north to Interstate 26 west. Expect a four-hour drive. **From Charlotte,** take Interstate 85 south to Route 321, which you take north to Interstate 40 west into Asheville. The drive should take between two and 2.5 hours. **From Raleigh,** take Interstate 40 west for the 4.5-hour drive to Asheville.

I am two with nature.

– Woody Allen

P l a y   H a r d

W i d e   O p e n

Asheville is a cosmopolitan city at the doorstep of the rugged outdoors. It's not unusual to see adventurers in full-regalia—hikers in mud-splattered boots or river runners in Teva's glittering with mica—browsing the downtown shops and galleries like cultured frontiersmen on a break from the wild. Where have they been playing? Probably in one of the following outdoor wonderlands.

The **Pisgah National Forest** is a 505,000-acre beast of a place that the government could tame only by dividing it into three ranger districts. And "tame" is the wrong word. While there are kinder, gentler portions of the forest, it is primarily pure, unadulterated wilderness. As such, prudence is advised when entering Mother Nature's turf; don't head for Pisgah's furthest reaches without a first-aid kit, an eye on the time, and a partner. The national forest stretches across much of Western North Carolina, from the South Carolina State line well up into the High Country around Blowing Rock. South of Asheville, the **Pisgah Ranger District** encompasses

Many Asheville residents are equipped to play hard

157,000 acres of forest with numerous waterfalls, rivers, and rugged mountain peaks ranging from 2,000 to 6,410 feet in elevation. More than 400 miles of trails for hikers and mountain bikers wind through the district, and it's also a popular spot for climbers, paddlers, fly fishermen, and sweaty tourists hoping to cool off in any one of the many swimming holes.

Bisected by the Blue Ridge Parkway, the district includes the 18,500-acre **Shining Rock** and the 7,900-acre **Middle Prong wilderness areas**, as well as the former forestry school, the **Cradle of Forestry.** The Pisgah Ranger District's office, 1001 Pisgah Highway, Pisgah Forest, (828) 877-3265, is near Brevard on Route 276, 1.5 miles north of Route 280. A popular multi-sport launching point is the parking lot at the **Pisgah Fish Hatchery** off Forest Road 475. To get here, take Route 276 north 5.5 miles from Route 280 near Brevard to Forest Road 475 on the left, which you take two miles to the fish hatchery on the left.

The National Forest Service operates the **Bent Creek Research Forest** within the Pisgah District with land open for horseback riding (18 miles of trails), mountain biking (23 miles of trails), and hiking on the horseback and biking trails. To get here, take Interstate 26 east to Route 191 south for four miles, and then follow signs. ◆ With nominal day-use fees, two recreation areas within Bent Creek are also notable. The **Lake Powhatan Recreation Area** is popular with anglers and swimmers, and there are numerous hiking and mountain biking trails throughout. From Asheville, take Interstate 26 east to Route 191 south for four miles, and then turn right on Forest Road 806. The parking area is 3.5 miles ahead. ◆ The **North Mills River Recreation Area** has trails for mountain biking, horseback riding, and hiking, and the river is a good fishing spot. From Asheville, take Interstate 26 east to Route 191 south for 13.3 miles. Turn right on State Road 1345 and drive five miles to the parking area.

Also within the Bent Creek area, the **North Carolina Arboretum**, 100 Frederick Law Olmstead Way, Asheville, (828) 665-2492, *www.ncarboretum.org*, is a 400-acre spread (only 60 acres are developed) with gardens, a greenhouse, interpretative trails, and wilderness open to hikers and mountain bikers. There is a nominal parking fee. To get there from Asheville, take Interstate 26 east to Route 191 south for two miles. Follow signs to the Arboretum, which is on the right.

The Bear Facts

Black bear sightings in the Pisgah National Forest are relatively rare, but enough bears live around Asheville that you'll want to know the following rules of engagement. First, don't ever feed a bear. Second, if you find bear cubs,  leave the area slowly but steadily. A few more:

• Never run from a bear. (Run and you look like prey.) Walk backwards slowly facing the bear.

• If the bear charges, stand your ground and make yourself look big by holding your arms above you, standing on a rock, or waving a stick. Chances are the bear is performing a "bluff charge" and will move on if you stay put.

• In the highly unlikely event a bear attacks you, fight back aggressively. Do not play dead.

Waterfall in the Pisgah District

After a recent reorganization, the National Forest Service consolidated two ranger districts—the French Broad and the Toecane—into the **Appalachian Ranger District.** The original districts are now known as "stations." ◆ Northwest of Asheville, the 80,000-acre **French Broad Station,** 88 Bridge Street, Hot Springs, (828) 622-3202, encompasses some of the most remote, rugged terrain in the Pisgah National Forest. Rocky cliffs, deep gorges, and narrow hollows define this wilderness along the Tennessee border. ◆ The **French Broad River** bisects the area and draws canoeists, kayakers, and rafters to its whitewater and quickwater sections. ◆ More than 80 miles of the **Appalachian Trail** wind through the district up and over numerous peaks, including **Max Patch,** one of the most-scenic mountains on the entire 2,100-mile footpath. To get to Max Patch from Hot Springs, head south on Route 209 for 7.3 miles to Meadow Fork Road (State Road 1175), onto which you turn right and drive 5.4 miles to State Road 1181. Turn right here and follow the road to its end at State Road 1182. Turn right and drive to the Max Patch parking area.

Six miles downstream on the French Broad from Hot Springs, the **Murray Branch Recreation Area** is a favored spot for anglers, canoeists and kayakers. From Hot Springs, take Route 25/70 across the French Broad River, turn left immediately after the bridge, and then right on State Road 1304 (River Road) for four miles to the parking area. ◆ The **Rocky Bluff Recreation Area** features fishing spots and hiking trails. From Hot Springs, take Route 209 south for 3.3 miles to Rocky Bluff.

The bald on Max Patch

The **Toecane Ranger Station,** Route 19-East Bypass, Burnsville, (828) 682-6146, oversees more than 75,000 acres of the Pisgah National Forest northwest of the Blue Ridge Parkway from Asheville to Blowing Rock and along the Tennessee State line. Much of this district is covered in the High Country chapter, but the southern end of the district includes several outdoor sites near Asheville, not the least of which is 6,684-foot **Mount Mitchell,** the highest peak east of the Mississippi. ◆ **Mount Mitchell State Park,** Route 128, Burnsville, (828) 675-4611, features nearly 20 miles of hiking trails, a paved road to the summit, and a concrete observation tower near the peak with views on clear days of up to 70 miles. From Asheville, take the Blue Ridge Parkway north to Milepost 355, then turn right on Route 128, which leads to the park.

Located southeast of Brevard, the **Dupont State Forest,** (828) 877-6527, is a 10,400-acre wonderland of granite mountains, dramatic waterfalls, and forested valleys in the Little River Valley. There are more than 90 miles of well-marked trails for mountain bikers, horseback riders, and hikers, plus many more miles of dirt and gravel roads. The forest's slick-rock trails

earned it the moniker "Moab of the East." It's one of the finest mountain biking destinations in the Carolinas. Five parking areas provide access to the forest, but this chapter describes only trails from the Corn Mill Shoals parking area. (See *Mountain Biking.*) To discover the rest of the forest, pick up a free trail map available from most of the sources listed under *Additional Information.* Or log onto *www.dupontforest.com* to view the map.

The 469-mile **Blue Ridge Parkway** (BRP) passes through Asheville, and along the road in both directions, you'll find ample opportunities for outdoor play, including hiking, mountain biking, horseback riding, and climbing. The road itself is popular with cyclists who endure long ascents and outrageous descents.

Dupont State Forest

Dayhiking

Lucky are the residents of Asheville who, when having a bad day, can drive 15 minutes to hike their concerns away. Don't let the dense forests and craggy mountains mislead you into believing that only serious Alpinists would lace up a pair of boots here. There are plenty of trails for all abilities, and while there are trails that call for backcountry experience, most require merely a little fitness and an adventurous spirit. The following hikes, grouped by area, are just a sampling. If these don't suit your mood, stop by any of the sources under *Local Outdoor Advice* for more trail options.

Pisgah National Forest: Pisgah District

Malcolm Campbell

◆ There are more than 40 miles of hiking trails that wind over and around the rugged Shining Rock Ridge inside **Shining Rock Wilderness Area.** Named for the ridge's distinctive quartz outcropping that reflects the sun, the wilderness area features dense forests, open-shrub patches, grassy balds, the Pigeon River, and five peaks higher than 6,000 feet. Numerous parking spots provide access to the area. One of the easiest to reach is the **Black Balsam parking area**, located off BRP Milepost 420.2. From the parkway, take State Road 816 north approximately a mile to the road's end. Four trails begin here: **Ivestor Gap, Flat Laurel Creek, Sam Knob,** and **Sam Knob Summit.**

◆ The **Sam Knob Summit Trail** is a moderate 2.5-mile hike that leaves Black Balsam parking area on the gated road behind the restroom facilities. Roughly a half-mile

Winter hiking in the Pisgah District

along the flat roadbed, a large meadow appears at the end of which is the hike's official trailhead on the right. The trail climbs via switchbacks until reaching an intersection where a right turn delivers you to the southern summit of Sam Knob and a left climbs to the northern summit. Both are worth visiting. On a clear day from the northern summit, you can see the highest mountain in the East, Mount Mitchell, nearly 50 miles away. Retrace your steps to return to your car.

◆ The **Flat Laurel Creek Trail** stretches 3.7 miles from the Black Balsam parking area to a parking area off Route 215. The orange-blazed trail departs from the southern end of the parking area along a roadbed and continues roughly a third of a mile until the path narrows to a trail. Along this route, you'll hike past some outstanding waterfalls and swimming holes, as well as through a high-elevation bog, a spruce-fir forest, and a beech-tree forest. There are excellent views of Sam Knob along the trail. If you're not up to the entire 7.4-mile out-and-back hike, stop at any point and retrace your steps.

◆ From the **Big East Fork parking area** off Route 276 roughly a mile north of BRP Milepost 412, you can piece together a whopping seven-mile loop to the summit of **Shining Rock** and back. The **Shining Creek** and the **Old Butt Knob trails** set out together from the parking area to Shining Creek Gap, roughly 0.75-miles into the hike. At this point, the Old Butt Knob Trail

Day-use Areas

Three Pisgah National Forest day-use areas near Asheville have many trails to explore. All three have nominal parking fees. Directions to all three are in *Wide Open*. ◆ The **Lake Powhatan Recreation Area** has a swimming area that, in warm months, is perfect for cooling off after hiking any of the surrounding trails. Ask for specific trail suggestions at the gate. ◆ The **North Mills River Recreation Area** also has a number of good trails that you can inquire about when paying your day-use fee. ◆ There are more than ten hiking trails at the **North Carolina Arboretum,** most of which are easy. Pick up a map when you arrive.

Looking Glass Rock

departs right and stretches 3.6 miles along Chestnut Ridge over Old Butt Knob, through Spanish Oak Gap, and over Dog Loser Knob before reaching a spur trail on the right to the summit of 5,940-foot Shining Rock. (If you miss this trail and end up at Shining Rock Gap, climb the short distance north on the Art Loeb Trail from the gap to the summit.) After summiting, take the Art Loeb Trail south to Shining Rock Gap, where the 3.4-mile Shining Creek Trail closes the loop and returns to the parking area. Highlights on the return trip include several swimming holes in Shining Creek.

♦ Just north of Brevard in the **Davidson River Valley,** the **Daniel Ridge Loop** is an easy four-mile hike with pleasant river and waterfall views. To get to the trailhead, follow directions to the Pisgah Fish Hatchery (see *Wide Open*) but continue another two miles on Forest Road 475 past Cove Creek Campground to the parking area on the right at gated Forest Road 137. The trailhead is on the left past the gate and over the bridge. The red-blazed trail follows the Davidson River upstream for the first stretch before turning right and climbing a mile to an intersection with the **Farlow Gap Trail.** Stay to the right, following the red blazes through a young forest that, depending on the season, may offer scenic views of Pilot Mountain, Cedar Rock, and Looking Glass Rock. You'll pass through a nice stretch of wildflowers, mountain laurel, and rhododendron before coming to a gravel road. Turn left to view a 90-foot waterfall, then backtrack and hike the gravel road to return to your car.

♦ Looking Glass Rock, which gets its name from the way it reflects light when water flows down the granite face and freezes, has the popular **Looking Glass Rock Trail,** a strenuous, six-mile out-and-back hike that rises 1,300 feet to the summit. To get to the trailhead, take Route 276 north 5.5 miles from Route 280 near Brevard to Forest Road 475 on the left, which you take 0.4 miles to the signed parking area on the right. The yellow-blazed trail begins with a pleasant wooded section before climbing steadily via switchbacks to the two-mile mark, where the path levels out. You'll soon reach an open rock section with the letter "H" painted on it. (Your helicopter will land here should you join the motley crew of hikers who ignored warnings that Looking Glass is slick and steep.) From the landing area, the trail resumes a steep ascent to the summit. The cliff face, just beyond the summit, offers tremendous views of the forest and of the Blue Ridge Parkway. *Remember: The cliff does not have a guardrail. If you slip and fall, nothing will stop you from going over the edge, so exercise extreme caution, particularly if the rock is wet.* Backtrack to return to your car.

♦ For an excellent workout plus great views of Looking Glass Rock, pack a picnic

Real Men Read Maps

It's one thing to ask driving directions in the civilized world—no self-respecting man does that—but quite another to consult a map in the woods. Should you get lost, a good topographical map and a compass are your tickets back to the evening's Cabernet. While the hikes in this guidebook are chosen for being easy to follow, we recommend carrying a copy of **National Geographic's** *Pisgah Ranger District Map* with you. This waterproof, tear-resistant map includes the hikes listed here and many more. It'll set you back roughly ten bucks but will send you forward armed with excellent directions. Available from most area outfitters and bookstores.

Hiker atop John Rock

and head for the **Cat Gap Loop** and the **John Rock trails**. When combined, these routes create a 6.2-mile loop that begins and ends in the Pisgah Fish Hatchery parking lot off Forest Road 475. (See directions under *Wide Open*.) From the eastern end of the parking lot (furthest from the hatchery), set out on the orange-blazed Cat Gap Trail beside the Davidson River. After a couple of creek crossings, the trail leaves the river's side and begins climbing. It crosses a forest road and continues to an intersection with John Rock Trail on the right. Take this yellow-blazed trail up to John Rock, a granite outcropping with outstanding views of Looking Glass Rock, the Blue Ridge Parkway, and the hatchery directly below. This is a nice place to picnic. Though the rock face is not as steep as Looking Glass, there's no guardrail, so be careful, especially if it's wet. To continue, cross back into the tree cover and follow the yellow blazes to an intersection with the Cat Gap and Cat Gap Bypass trails. Take the orange-blazed Cat Gap Trail through all intersections to descend to your car.

Blue Ridge Parkway Trails

♦ North and south of Asheville on the Blue Ridge Parkway, there are dozens of hikes to scenic overlooks, waterfalls, and mountain summits. Some of these hikes are inside Pisgah National Forest but are listed here because the trails are accessible directly from the parkway. The following hikes are just a few of the trails along the parkway.

♦ Several hiking trails provide expansive views from the summit of 6,684-foot **Mount Mitchell** in Mount Mitchell State Park. (See *Wide Open* for directions.) After paying the entrance fee, drive to the summit where you can hike out-and-back on the various trails that begin or end at the peak, including the **Old Mount Mitchell Trail**, a two-mile path that originates from the summit of Mount Hallback; the **Balsam Trail**, a 0.75-mile, self-guiding nature trail; the mile-long **Camp Alice Trail**, which leads to a campground; and the 5.4-mile **Deep Gap Trail**, which departs from Mitchell and climbs four 6,500-foot-plus peaks—Mount Craig, Big Tom, Balsam Cone, and Cattail Peak—en route to Deep Gap. You can also descend on the **Mount Mitchell Trail**, a 5.6-mile path that originates from the Black Mountain Recreation Area. (See "Because It's There" on the next page.)

♦ A 15-minute drive north of Asheville between Mileposts 364 and 369, the 700-acre **Craggy Gardens Area** is a grassy bald mountain full of wildflowers. June is high season when the innumerable, purple rhododendrons burst into bloom. Craggy Gardens features a picnic area (Milepost 367.5), visitor center (Milepost 364.6), and a few

An Appalachian Graveyard

Mount Mitchell's flanks are full of dead and dying fir and spruce trees, all victims of acid rain, high ozone levels, ice storms, and ravenous insects. It's sad to see the old growth expire but also encouraging to find young trees and shrubs, including blueberries and blackberries, thriving on the mountain.

Asheville CVB

Graggy Gardens

short hiking trails. The half-mile **Pinnacle Trail** switchbacks from the Craggy Dome parking lot (Milepost 364.1) to the 5,840-foot summit for 360-degree views. The 0.8-mile **Craggy Gardens Self-Guiding Trail** departs from the visitor center parking lot and leads to the picnic area. En route, signs identify the various plants living on the heath and explain the delicate balance in which they live.

◆ The mountain for which the national forest is named is 5,721-foot Mount Pisgah. Legend has it that James Hall, a Presbyterian minister, climbed the mountain in the late 18th Century, took in the expanse of the French Broad River valley, and likened it to the promised land Moses saw from Mount Pisgah overlooking the Jordan River. To make your own proclamation from the summit, head to Milepost 407.6, where the **Mount Pisgah Trail** departs from the parking lot for a strenuous but short (1.2-mile) climb to the summit. At the top there's an observation platform and ungainly radio tower, yet the 360-degree views of the French Broad River Valley, surrounding mountains, and Asheville (on clear days) are spectacular. To complete the 2.5-mile hike, retrace your steps. ◆ As its name implies, the **Devil's Courthouse** recounts a Cherokee legend about a devil named Judaculla who held court inside this craggy mountain. But the only plea you'll enter is "please slow down" to your hiking partner should he or she set off too quickly on the steep, strenuous half-mile climb through a forest of spruce and fir trees. At the 5,462-foot summit on a clear day, views stretch into three states: South Carolina, Georgia, and Tennessee. The trailhead is at the parking area at Milepost 422.4.

Because It's There.

Want your own mini-Everest experience? Eat your Wheaties and set out early on the **Mount Mitchell Trail**, a grueling 5.6-mile hike from the Black Mountain Campground up 3,600 feet to the summit of the East's highest peak. Most fit hikers can make the summit in three to four hours. You'll have time to eat a picnic lunch and either beg for a return ride in someone's car or descend the way you came. To reach the trailhead, exit the BRP at Milepost 346 and take Forest Road 2074 north 2.5 miles to the intersection with Forest Road 472. Stay on Forest Road 2074 and follow signs to the campground. The blue-blazed trail is well-marked.

Pisgah National Forest: Appalachian District, French Broad Station

◆ For some of the region's most remote and rugged hiking, head north to Hot Springs and the French Broad River, where the 2,100-mile Appalachian Trail (AT) winds through the area on its way north from Georgia to Maine. Numerous trails intersect with the AT for great loop possibilities. An excellent example within spitting distance of downtown Hot Springs is the 5.6-mile loop created by the **Appalachian Trail** and the **Pump Gap Loop** and **Lover's Leap trails**. A highlight is the final leg along Lover's Leap Ridge with its outstanding views of the French Broad River and Hot Springs 1,000 feet below. (A Cherokee legend recounts that a young maiden leapt to her death from the ridge after learning of her brave's death.) From Hot Springs, take Route 25/70 across the French Broad River, turn left immediately after the bridge, and then left again on River Road. Follow signs to the Silvermine Trailhead, where you park. From the parking area, follow the Lover's Leap Trail to the first major switchback where you take the yellow-blazed Pump Gap Trail straight. At the next trail intersection the Pump Gap Trail splits (the loop begins here). Veer left and hike to the intersection with the AT in Pump Gap. Turn left onto the AT for the commanding views along the ridge. The AT descends steeply to the parking area.

◆ So scenic is the grassy bald atop 4,629-foot **Max Patch Mountain** that you almost expect Julie Andrews to twirl by,

Hot Springs from Lover's Leap Ridge

singing *The Sound of Music*. From the summit, you're treated to jaw-dropping, unobstructed

360-degree views of the surrounding Tennessee and North Carolina mountains. There are two **Max Patch loop** trails to hike. The shorter 1.4-mile loop crosses the summit; the longer 2.4-mile loop encircles the bald. (The **Appalachian Trail** also crosses the mountain's summit.) Another route to Max Patch's summit is on a 0.25-mile grass and dirt path from the parking area. See directions in *Wide Open*.

High atop Max Patch

Mountain Biking

News of the area's mountain biking scene is spreading fast, thanks to national attention like *Bike* magazine naming Asheville one of the nation's top five mountain biking cities. What's the draw? More than 200 miles of trails in the Pisgah National Forest and nearby Dupont State Forest, plus many more miles of forest roads. Riders of all abilities can find terrain to explore. The one constant regardless of where you ride? The consciousness-awakening scenery of the North Carolina Mountains. Some of the better rides follow, grouped by area.

South of Asheville: Dupont State Forest

◆ To ride a **slickrock loop,** head to **Corn Mill Shoals** parking area. From Asheville, take Interstate 240 west to Interstate 26 east to Exit #9 for the Asheville Airport and Route 280. Take Route 280 south 16 miles into Brevard. (At the intersection with Route 64/276, continue straight into downtown Brevard. Note: Route 280 ends.) In town, turn left to follow Route 276 for 10 miles to Cascade Lake Road, onto which you turn left. The parking area is about two miles ahead on the left.

Unloading at Corn Mill Shoals

Atop Big Rock

Mountain Bike Nirvana

Mention North Carolina slickrock to mountain bikers, and they'll know you're referring to one of two trails at **Dupont State Forest**. The renowned **Big Rock** and **Cedar Rock trails** include long stretches of exposed rock leading to the summits of Big Rock and Cedar Rock, where there are unobstructed views of the surrounding mountains. And these two trails are just the beginning of the love you'll feell inside Dupont. In total, there are 98 named trails—singletrack, doubletrack, and forest roads—that climb, fall, twist, and twirl through the forest. Two features make Dupont's trails especially inviting: sand is part of the soil, so there's less mud, and the hills, while steep in sections, are not as long as those in the national forest. Add the ability to ride past several impressive waterfalls, and you've got the recipe for an entire vacation's worth of fat-tire exploration.

The **Corn Mill Shoals Road Trail** starts across the road from the parking lot. Turn right on the dirt and rock Corn Mill Shoals Road and bear left at the intersection with **Bridal Veil Trail.** (If you continue on Corn Mill Shoals, you'll come to an attractive rock and stream crossing.) Follow Bridal Veil past the first Cedar Rock trailhead on the left to the second intersection further ahead, also on the left. Take **Cedar Rock Trail** over rocky terrain to the slickrock ride along the summit. (If you have to dismount climbing the creek bed up Cedar Rock, don't turn around. This technical section is short.) The intersection with the **Big Rock Trail** is at the summit. You can take this trail right to continue over Big Rock or descend on Cedar Rock Trail. (Cedar Rock descends to Bridal Veil Trail, where you turn right to complete your ride). Continuing on Big Rock Trail, you'll ride more slickrock with tremendous, 360-degree views. The trail eventually descends to Corn Mill Shoals Road Trail. Turn left to return to your car. The descents on both Big Rock and Cedar Rock trails offer tight, slalom-like turns, and depending upon your speed, big bumps for plenty of air. A rider of any ability can ride (or walk portions of) these trails. But ride slowly at first to get familiar with the terrain.

◆ Other highlights of Dupont State Forest trails include rides to **Hooker Falls** and **Triple Falls.** The best way to explore these and the 90-plus miles of trails here is to pick up either the free trail map published by the Division of Forest Services or the larger, waterproof map published by Friends of Dupont Forest, available for $8 from most local outdoor and biking shops. For directions to the remaining four parking areas with access to the trails, visit *www.dupontforest.com.*

South of Asheville: Bent Creek Area

◆ Excluding forest roads, the majority of mountain biking trails inside the **Pisgah National Forest** is in the Pisgah District between Brevard and Asheville. In general, the trails are rocky and root-strewn with

Hawkeye was here

We're not talking Alan Alda but rather actor-turned-shoe-cobbler-turned-actor-again, Daniel Day Lewis, who played the original Hawkeye in the film, *Last of the Mohicans*. Numerous scenes were shot in Dupont State Forest on the Little River at four of its dramatic waterfalls: Triple Falls, High Falls, Bridal Veil Falls, and Hooker Falls.

A forest road in Pisgah National Forest

tight singletrack on thigh-crunching climbs and screaming descents. Most are not recommended for beginner riders. With a few exceptions noted below, novice mountain bikers will want to fashion routes out of the dazzling array of **forest roads**, all of which sacrifice nothing in the way of mountain and forest scenery. There are three primary riding areas within the Pisgah District: the Bent Creek area (including Lake Powhatan Recreation Area); the North Mills River Recreation Area; and the Davidson River Valley.

◆ Most of the 11 mountain bike trails and forest roads inside **Bent Creek Research and Development Forest** are within 15 minutes of Asheville. In warm weather, you can ride the trails and roads to exhaustion, ending up at Lake Powhatan for a swim to cool down and clean up. For a novice rider, the two-mile **Boyd Branch Loop** offers a good workout, as well as a brief section of singletrack. To reach the trailhead from Asheville, take Interstate 26 east to Route 191 south past Biltmore Square Mall to Bent Creek Gap Road on the right. After 0.2 miles, the road forks. Bear left and drive two miles to the paved parking area at the **Hard Times Trailhead.** This is a good place to park for many of Bent Creek's trails; however, you can drive a short distance further to a better parking area for the Boyd Branch Loop. From the Hard Times parking area, continue 0.2 miles to a gravel road on your right. Take this road to the bottom of the first hill where there's a small parking area across from a gated forest road. Begin by riding past the gate and up **Boyd Branch Road,** which climbs moderately beside Boyd Branch Creek. The road ends at the highest point of the ride in a grass clearing. Take the singletrack trail on the right that descends into the woods and eventually crosses Boyd Branch Creek. The trail, which changes from rocky and root-strewn to packed dirt, soon intersects with the gravel **Bent Creek Gap Road**, where you turn right to return to your car.

◆ The four-mile **Sidehill Trail Loop** offers a pleasant mix of gravel roads with some moderately challenging singletrack and stream crossings. This loop begins at the Hard Times Trailhead (see directions in previous ride). From the parking lot, turn left and then right at the first road on your right. The surface changes to gravel before reaching the next gated road on your right, **Ledford Branch Road** (Forest Road 479E). Ride past the gate and uphill beside Ledford Branch creek to Ledford Gap, where you turn left onto the yellow-blazed, singletrack **Sidehill Trail.** The trail climbs and falls along the side of the mountain with periodic stream crossings. At the first trail intersection, continue over the gap, following the yellow blazes. The descent is fairly steep and rocky, but by maintaining an easy speed, novice riders will find it enjoyable. The trail reaches a grassy clearing where the singletrack gives way to a gravel road. At this point, look for an unnamed singletrack trail on your left that descends

Take Care of the Trails

Help keep the trails in the Pisgah National Forest open to mountain bikes by staying off trails closed to bikes and by practicing smart trail maintenance: Avoid muddy trails and dismount to carry your bike over wet patches where bike tires will harm the trail. Finally, be mindful of hikers and horseback riders. Yield to both.

into the woods. This trail crosses a stream before inter-secting with gravel Bent Creek Gap Road. Turn right and follow this road straight at all intersections (you'll ride around several forest service gates), past Lake Powhatan, and over the dam to Hard Times Road on your left. Follow this road back to the parking area.

♦ Other great trails include the 1.5-mile **Ingles Field Gap Trail;** the four-mile **North Boundary Trail;** and the one-mile **Homestead Trail.** If you're loathe to buy a map and don't want to tote this book on the ride, Bent Creek is the kind of place where you can park, unload, and set off without a specific route in mind. Trails closed to bikes are marked as such.

Mountain biking Pisgah National Forest

South of Asheville: North Mills River Area

♦ The **North Mills River Recreation Area** features a mix of routes, from gently graded forest roads to radical singletrack. A good beginning loop is the 9.5-mile **Fletcher Creek Trail Loop**, a moderately challenging ride of forest roads and singletrack. To reach the trail-head, take Interstate 26 east to Exit #9 for Route 280 south to Route 191. Follow Route 191 south less than half a mile to North Mills River Road (Forest Road 1345) on the right. Take this road five miles to Wash Creek Road (Forest Road 5000). Turn right and drive roughly 2.5 miles to the **Trace Ridge parking area** on the left (a half-mile past the concrete bridge). From the parking area, ride past the gate onto Forest Road 5097. The road climbs gradually as it winds around Coffee Pot Mountain. Five miles into the ride, you'll reach the blue-blazed Fletcher Creek trailhead on the left, which you take as it drops through a mead-ow, past several trail intersections, and through a hardwood forest. After the Spencer Trail intersection, the Fletcher Trail climbs at a moderate incline before dropping over a rocky stretch and ending at Forest Road 142. Turn left to ride 1.5 miles to your car.

South of Asheville: Davidson River Valley Area

♦ South of the North Mills River area and north of Brevard, the **Davidson River Valley** is the most-visited area of the Pisgah District, yet it still affords the adventurous ample, accessible solitude. In addition to numerous well-known mountain biking trails—**Farlow Gap, Daniel Ridge,** and **Sycamore Cove trails**, among them—the Davidson River Valley has an extensive network of **forest roads**, providing more exploration possibilities than your legs or the waning daylight will allow. Another benefit to riding here is the number of waterfalls and swimming holes throughout. All are ideal places to rest, soak your feet, or take a dip.

♦ A number of great rides originate from from the **Pisgah Fish Hatchery** parking lot on Forest Road 475. See directions under *Wide Open*. Perfect for the beginner, the 14-mile **Gumstand Gap/Sliding Rock/Looking Glass Falls loop** is on gravel forest roads and paved Route 276. From the parking area, turn left on **Forest Road 475** and ride the short distance to the fork, where Forest Road 475B veers right. Take this road for a strenuous three-mile climb to Gumstand Gap where you'll find a parking area. From here, the road descends and soon intersects with another forest road from the left. Keep to the right and ride three miles to the intersection with **Route 276,** where you turn right. Two miles later, you'll reach the **Sliding Rock Recreation Area,** where there is a naturally occurring, 60-foot, granite waterslide emptying into a seven-foot deep pool. (Cost is $1 per person.) Two miles beyond Sliding Rock on Route 276, you'll pass a parking area on the left for **Looking Glass Falls,** where the Davidson River spills 60 feet over a rocky cliff. To close the loop, continue on Route 276 for a half-mile to Forest Road 475 on the right, turn here, and ride the final two miles back to your car. Take two Advil. *Note: Route 276 can be exceptionally busy during the tourism seasons (foliage and summer) when mountain bikers should be on the lookout for the most dangerous form of wildlife: inattentive drivers.*

North of Asheville: Hot Springs Area

◆ Much less known than the Pisgah District, the Appalachian District's French Broad Station oversees a handful of great mountain biking trails. In addition to the following rides, there are more than 150 miles of **forest roads** that snake through every reach of the Pisgah National Forest, opening up tremendous views of the mountains, valleys, and French Broad River. The 3.5-mile **Mill Ridge Bike Trail** winds around some high-elevation fields with panoramic views of the surrounding countryside. To reach the trailhead from Hot Springs, take Route 25/70 south (toward Asheville) 3.5 miles to Tanyard Gap, where the Appalachian Trail crosses above the road on a concrete bridge. Turn left just after the bridge and left again at the next intersection to cross over Route 25/70. Follow this road (Forest Road 113) to the trailhead (marked by a sign) at the end of the road. The trail begins by descending along an old roadbed and turns left at the bottom of the hill to become a single-track trail. It winds through a clearing and then enters the gated Forest Road 113A, which climbs gradually back to Forest Road 113. Turn left at the road to return to your car.

◆ The easy 3.6-mile **Laurel River Trail** is a delightful ride along an old railroad bed paralleling Big Laurel Creek as it flows toward the French Broad River. To reach the trail from Hot Springs, take Route 25/70 south to its intersection with State Road 208 at Big Laurel Creek, where you turn right (continuing on Route 25/70) and drive 100 yards to the park-

Bike Rentals

The following businesses rent mountain bikes, and in some instances, touring bikes. Several also conduct mountain bike tours. **Backcountry Outdoors,** 18 Pisgah Highway, Pisgah Forest, ☎ (828) 884-4262, *www.backcountryoutdoors.com;* ◆ **Bio Wheels,** 76 Biltmore Avenue, Asheville, ☎ (828) 232-0300 or 1-888-881-2453, *www.biowheels.com;* ◆ **Liberty Bicycles,** 1378 Hendersonville Road, Asheville, ☎ (828) 274-2453, *www.libertybikes.com;* ◆ **Ski Country Sports,** 1000 Merrimon Avenue, Asheville, ☎ (828) 254-2771 or 1-800-528-3874, *www.skicountrysports.com;* ◆ **Sycamore Cycles,** 112 New Hendersonville Highway, Pisgah Forest, ☎ (828) 877-5790, *www.sycamorecycles.com*

ing area on the right. The trail begins just past the gate at the end of the parking area. The first mile passes through private property, so stay on the trail. Thereafter, you enter the Pisgah National Forest. The trail continues to the French Broad River at the town of Runion. To return, retrace your route.

Road Biking

While Lance Armstrong prefers the High Country roadways around Boone and Blowing Rock, cycling superstar Greg Lemond once called the Asheville region one of the best training locations in the world. Who can argue with either? Both areas have rural roads with long hills and sizzling descents through spectacular mountain scenery, and both straddle the Blue Ridge Parkway. From the bustling city of Asheville, you can soon be pedaling past weathered barns, mountain farms, and rushing streams.

Lighten Up

Blue Ridge Parkway regulations require cyclists to have a light or reflector visible at least 500 feet to the front and a red light or reflector visible at least 200 feet to the rear during periods of low visibility, between the hours of sunset and sunrise, and when traveling through a tunnel.

For the most part, the area is bike-friendly, and local drivers are courteous and safe. But watch for tourists who are not necessarily watching the road as they pass scenic overlooks. Your best bet? Ride defensively at all times. Also, remember that while there are flat stretches of road to enjoy, you are, after all, in the mountains, and roads go up, up, up and down, down, down. You'll want to downsize your normal mileage to account for the hills.

◆ So, where to ride? The **Blue Ridge Parkway** is an obvious choice, combining undeveloped mountain, valley, and pastoral scenery with slow-moving traffic (speed limit is 45 mph). It's an officially designated bicycling route, so you won't be the first cyclist to roll its asphalt. From Asheville, you can travel north or south on the roadway and track your mileage easily with the highly visible mileposts. From Asheville, the ride north toward **Craggy Gardens** is a 30-mile stretch that, if begun early in the morning, is a full-day's ride. ◆ Another long parkway segment is from Craggy Gardens at Milepost 364 north 25 miles to **Crabtree Meadows** at Milepost 340. The ride passes through Beetree Gap (4,900 feet), over Green Knob (4,760 feet), and through Buck Creek Gap (3,373 feet). Long uphill sections and seemingly shorter downhill sections line the route. Crabtree Meadows has public pay phones, just in case you're too pooped to finish.

◆ South of Asheville near Brevard are two state scenic byways popular with cyclists, Routes 276 and 215. **Route 276** enters the Pisgah National Forest from Route 280 and climbs 15 miles past Looking Glass Falls, Sliding Rock, the

Mountain roads are rarely flat or straight

Cradle of Forestry, and Pink Beds (an upland bog full of pink rhododendrons that flower in June) to the Blue Ridge Parkway. Ride early in the day during the busy summer and fall seasons. Route 276 continues north beyond the parkway another 18 miles past rural villages and farms to the small community of Bethel. ◆ From the town of Rosman, North Carolina Scenic Byway **Route 215** rolls north along the North Fork of the French Broad River eight miles to the small community of Balsam Grove. From here, it's another eight miles to the Blue Ridge Parkway. If you're feeling frisky, keep pedaling Route 215 north past the parkway to the town of Bethel. The 18-mile route from the parkway to Bethel climbs to nearly 6,000 feet and passes mountain farms, cascading streams, and the West Fork of the Pigeon River.

◆ Other scenic routes include **Route 25/70** near Hot Springs, **Route 209** south from Hot Springs, **Route 251** between Alexander and Marshall, and gated **Old Route 70** from Old Fort to the road's end. For additional rides and current road conditions, stop by any of the bike shops listed under rentals in *Mountain Biking*. Another source: the **Blue Ridge Bicycle Club**, *www.blueridgebicycleclub.org*, a group that organizes weekly rides.

Paddling

From quickwater and whitewater sections on the French Broad, Nolichucky, and Pigeon rivers to serene flatwater on numerous mountain lakes, paddling destinations surround Asheville. So when your legs tire from biking or hiking, give your back, arms, and shoulders a workout while appreciating the beauty of the Appalachians from the water. The area has plenty of places to rent canoes and kayaks, and many tour operators offer whitewater rafting, canoeing, tubing, and kayaking adventures. The following are the major waters in the area.

◆ Named in the 18th Century by colonial settlers because the wide river flowed toward French-held territory, the **French Broad** offers a range of paddling options from quietwater suitable for novice canoeists to Class II–V whitewater for experienced paddlers. From its headwaters in Rosman where the North, West, and Middle forks come together, the French Broad is calm as it flows past farms and through the Pisgah National Forest to

NC Division of Tourism

Serious Training Waters

Asheville's **Ledges Park** is an important training area for serious whitewater paddlers, including many Olympic hopefuls. Located on the French Broad, the park has a number of "play holes" and eddy lines, as well as a full slalom course. It's not just for experts. Beginners can put in at Ledges and float downstream for miles to any one of numerous takeouts. To get to the park, take Route 19/23 north to the UNC-Asheville Exit and turn left at the bottom of the ramp onto Broadway. Bear right at the intersection of Broadway and Route 251/River Road. Ledges Park is seven miles down Route 251. (You'll have to turn left at one T-intersection to remain on Route 251.)

Asheville. Downstream from Asheville, the river turns frothy through Barnard en route to Hot Springs. Downstream of Hot Springs, the river returns to an easier pace. The river's biggest whitewater is in the spring and early summer.

There are access points along the river from its headwaters to Hot Springs and beyond, the most convenient being public parks and national forest lands. Popular spots south of Asheville include: **Champion Park** on Route 64 in Rosman, south of Brevard; **Island Ford Access Area** off Route 64 just outside Brevard (10 miles downstream from Champion Park); and **Hap Simpson Park,** Route 276 two miles south of Brevard (20 miles downstream from Champion Park). Downstream from Asheville the water is quick enough that, unless you have significant whitewater experience, you'll want to navigate with a river guide. South of Hot Springs the **Murray Branch Recreation Area** is a favored spot to launch kayaks and canoes or to float in tubes. See directions under *Wide Open.*

◆ Less-known and less-crowded than the French Broad, the **Nolichucky River** is a wild whitewater river northeast of Asheville along the remote Tennessee border. The section from Poplar, North Carolina into Tennessee has numerous frothy rapids, ranging from Class III–Class IV. The scenery in North Carolina is awe-inspiring as the river flows through one of the state's steepest gorges. The rafting season runs March–October, and because the river is not damned, water levels depend upon rainfall. (For flow information, call the Tennessee Valley Authority, 1-800-238-2264.) The put-in is off Route 197 in Poplar but the take-out eight miles downstream in Erwin is tough to find. You'll want to hire a shuttle service. (See tour operators below.) ◆ Other navigable rivers around Asheville include stretches of the **Davidson** and **Pigeon rivers,** as well as sections of the **North Broad.** You'll find coverage of the **Chattooga** and **Nantahala rivers** in the North Georgia and Great Smoky Mountains National Park chapters, respectively.

◆ Surrounded by mountains, **Lake Lure** is a gorgeous lake with 27 miles of shoreline. While lake homes line the shore, you can still find ample solitude in secluded coves, far from the whizzing ski boats. And such is the beauty that despite development, *National*

Tour Operators & Boat Rentals

The following businesses operate river-running tours March–October, and most also run river shuttles and rent kayaks and canoes for personal use: **Appalachian River Adventures,** 172 Charlotte Street, Asheville, ☎ (828) 230-9380, *www.appalachianriveradventure.com;* ◆ **French Broad Rafting Expeditions,** Route 25/70, between Marshall and Hot Springs, ☎ (828) 656-2978 or 1-877-265-6867, *www.frenchbroadrafting.com;* ◆ **Headwaters Outfitters,** Route 64, Rosman, ☎ (828) 877-3106, *www.headwatersoutfitters.com;* ◆ **Huck Finn River Adventures,** Route 25/70, Hot Springs, ☎ 1-877-520-4658, *www.huckfinnrafting.com;* ◆ **USA Raft,** Route 25/70 between Marshall and Hot Springs, ☎ (828) 649-0560 or 1-800-872-7238, *www.usaraft.com.*

Geographic saw fit to name Lake Lure "one of the ten most beautiful man-made lakes in the world." For canoe rentals, head to **Lake Lure Marina,** Route 64/74A East, 1-877-386-4255, *www.lakelure.com.* From Asheville, take Interstate 40 to Route 74A (Exit #53A) east 22 miles.

◆ **Lake Julian,** in Lake Julian Park, is a thermal lake used to cool the power plant that lurks on one side of the lake, so the water is always warm. (Even in winter, it rarely dips below 50 degrees.) You can rent a paddleboat or launch your own canoe or sea kayak for a fee of $2. To reach the park from Asheville, take Interstate 26 east to Exit #6 and turn left onto Long Shoals Road. The park is one mile ahead on the right.

Fly Fishing

 With one of Trout Unlimited's Top 100 trout streams—the **Davidson River**—plus many more rivers, creeks, and streams, the Asheville area lures fishermen from far and wide. Other popular rivers around the greater Asheville area include the **North Mills, Laurel, Pigeon,** and **French Broad rivers,** plus numerous tributaries of each. Depending on the river, local catches may include brook, brown, and rainbow trout; smallmouth bass; crappie; and the occasional muskie. The best way to fish these waters is with a guide. Fortunately, several world-class fly fishing operations are here to ensure you'll be on your way to hooking the wily ones in no time.

Got a License to Use That?

If you plan to fish around Asheville, you'll need a North Carolina fishing license. To order one over the phone with a credit card, call the **North Carolina Wildlife Resources Division,** ☎ 1-888-248-6834. Or log onto *www.ncwildlife.org,* where you'll find a list of retailers authorized to sell licenses, as well as more information on catch limits and release policies.

◆ **Davidson River Outfitters,** 4 Pisgah Highway, Pisgah Forest, (828) 877-4181 or 1-888-861-0111, *www.davidsonflyfishing.com,* is a full-service fly shop, guide service, outfitter, and fly-fishing school. Located a stone's throw from the Davidson River, this outfit offers classes in fly-tying, casting, and fishing, and puts together all manner of fishing expeditions, from half-day wading trips to full-day river floats. ◆ **Hunter Banks Company,** 29 Montford Avenue, (828) 252-3005 or 1-800-227-6732, *www.hunterbanks.com,* operates a full-service fly shop, a school offering casting and fly-tying instruction, and guide services for half- and full-day walk, wade, and float trips. ◆ Dozens of fishing guides operate in and around Asheville. A sampling: Bruce Harang's **Beaucatcher,** (828) 230-0450, *www.beaucatcher.com;* **Brookside Guides,** 1-877-298-2568, *www.brooksideguides.com;* and **Joe Whisnant's Big Foot Guides**, (828) 891-2784, *www.bigfootguides.com.*

Trout waters near Asheville

Horseback Riding

Berry Patch Stables, 300 Baird Cove Road, Asheville (828) 645-7271, promises tame horses (and frisky ones, too) for its one- to two-hour trail rides. Berry Patch also offers riding lessons. ◆ Merely 10 minutes from downtown Asheville, **Fordbrook Stables,** 120 Fordbrook Road, (828) 667-1021, offers trail rides for all levels of riders. One ride climbs through several alpine pastures and woods before reaching a mountain clearing at 3,000 feet in elevation with panoramic views of Asheville, the majestic Grove Park Inn, and the surrounding mountains. ◆ **Sandy Bottom Trail Rides,** Caney Fork Road, Marshall, (828) 649-3464 or 1-800-959-3513, *www.sandybottomtrailrides.com,* offers two-, three-, and four-hour trail rides, as well as all-day and overnight backcountry rides. They also offer a popular three-hour ride to Long Pine Gem Mine.

Rainy Day Workout

When the rain clouds are out but you must get your workout in, head to one of the following indoor fitness facilities, which admit visitors for nominal day-use fees. **The Sports Center** at the **Grove Park Inn,** 290 Macon Avenue, Asheville, (828) 252-2711 or 1-800-438-5800, *www.groveparkinn.com,* features a cardio room with bikes, elliptical trainers, treadmills, and stair climbers, plus a weight-training room with free weights and resistance-training machines. Choose from a selection of aerobics classes. Your day fee also includes access to the indoor pool, locker rooms, and towel service. ◆ Sporting the "largest selection of cardio equipment in Asheville," the **Asheville Racquet Club**, 200 Racquet Club Road, (828) 274-3361, *www.wncfitness.com,* is a tennis facility (26 courts, including six indoor) with an extensive fitness area. Expect more than seven tons of free weights, cardio and weight machines, an outdoor pool, and a basketball court. The club offers all manner of aerobics classes, and the men's and women's locker rooms each have saunas and showers.

Rock Climbing

With miles of routes for novice to advanced climbers, **Looking Glass Rock** is one of the premier climbing destinations in the North Carolina Mountains. Some of the climbing faces on this granite monolith are more than 500 feet high. On the easier end, the **South Face** appeals to instructors working with beginners, while the **North Face**, which has been likened to Yosemite, is where the instructors head when their classes are over. In total, there are five climbable "sections" on the mountain and more than 25 routes, each of which has an intriguing name: *Short Man's Sorrow, Safari Jive,* and more than a few we can't print here. The mountain is a popular nesting area for Peregrine Falcons, and many routes are closed from mid January–mid August. ◆ If you've never strapped on a harness or opened a carabineer, you'll find the Asheville area's climbing shops and guide services to be great places to learn the art of this vertigo-defying sport. In downtown Asheville, **Climbmax**, 43 Wall Street, (828) 252-9996, *www.climbmaxnc.com,* is an indoor climbing facility that offers instruction as well as guided tours. You can't miss the Climbmax outdoor climbing wall, which towers above the sidewalk and street below. ◆ **Black Dome Mountain Sports**, 140 Tunnel Road, Asheville (828) 251-2001 or 1-800-678-2367, *www.blackdome.com,* is an outdoor outfitter with an extensive selection of climbing gear. The business also operates a guided climbing tour service and offers rock-climbing instruction.

Swimming

From large lakes to small river pools no larger than a bath tub, swimming spots are found throughout the area. So pack your swim trunks for your hike or bike and check out some of the following. ◆ South of Asheville in the Pisgah District of the Pisgah National Forest, Lake Powhatan in the **Lake Powhatan Recreation Area** is a small, scenic lake with a beach area, restrooms, and lifeguards in-season. The recreation area charges a nominal day-use fee. See *Wide Open* for directions. ◆ Perhaps the most popular swimming area (and thus the most crowded) south of Asheville is **Sliding Rock,** a huge granite slab of rock over which thousands of gallons of cool mountain water pour each minute. Handrails along the side of the rock allow you to climb to the top where you sit on your rump and slide down to the seven-foot pool at the bottom. There are restrooms, observation areas, and lifeguards on duty during the summer months. From Route 280 near Brevard, take Route 276 north for 7.6 miles to the parking area on the left. Cost to enter is $1 per person.

◆ Several small swimming holes are found along **Route 276** between Route 280 and the Blue Ridge Parkway, including one at the Davidson River Campground. You'll have to pay to play (the campground charges a nominal entrance fee). The "Riverbend" swimming

hole in the **Davidson River** is wide and deep, and the current is slow. To get to the camp-ground, take Route 276 north one mile past the forest entrance. ◆ Further ahead on Route 276, you can get your feet wet at the base of **Looking Glass Falls,** where the water fills a wide basin at the foot of the falls. It's only four

Asheville CVB

Sliding Rock

feet deep but plenty cool and clear enough to refresh your spirit. To access the falls, take Route 276 into the national forest roughly five miles from Route 280 near Brevard. A sign on the right directs you to the parking area.

◆ To combine an outstanding hike or mountain bike loop with a cool swim, head to **Daniel Ridge Falls** in the Davidson River Valley area. To access the area, follow directions under *Dayhiking* to the Daniel Ridge Falls Loop. You'll find several swimming holes in the Davidson River along the trail. ◆ Along its length from south of Asheville north to Hot Springs and into Tennessee, the **French Broad River** offers many swimming holes, from **Champion Park** in the town of Rosman on Route 64 south of Brevard to the **Murray Branch Recreation Area** south of Hot Springs. See *Wide Open* for directions to Murray Branch.

◆ Roughly 25 miles southeast of Asheville on Route 64/74, **Lake Lure** has a swimming beach and a quasi-amusement area called Water Works, which features water slides, bumper boats, and all manner of 'get-wet' equipment, plus restrooms with showers, a picnic area, and a snack stand. Nominal admission fee.

Skiing

Despite Asheville's location in the mountains, most of the state's ski resorts are more than an hour's drive and are profiled in the High Country chapter. But two resorts are less than 40 miles from Asheville. ◆ Just 25 miles from downtown Asheville, **Wolf Laurel,** Route 3, Mars Hill, (828) 689-4111 or 1-800-817-4111, *www.ski-wolflaurel.com,* has 54 acres of skiable terrain spread amongst 15 trails, the majority of which is ranked intermediate. The mountain's modest 700-foot vertical drop allows for a couple of expert runs: the *Flame Out* and *Upper Streak* trails. There's also a snow-tubing park. Two surface lifts, plus one double chairlift and one quad, service the trails, which are lit for nighttime skiing. The resort has a 26,000-foot lodge where you can rent skis and snowboards. ◆ With an elevation a mile high, **Cataloochee Ski Area,** 1080 Ski Lodge Road, Maggie Valley, (828) 926-0285 or 1-800-768-0285, *www.cataloochee.com,* is well-situated for making and keeping snow. The 740-foot vertical drop mountain has snowmaking capability on all of its 10 trails, which are serviced by three chairlifts (a double, triple, and a quad) and one surface lift. The slopes are 25 percent beginner, 50 percent intermediate, and 25 percent advanced.

Local Outdoor Advice

Pisgah Ranger District Office, Pisgah National Forest • Located on Route 276 roughly 1.5 miles from Route 280 near Brevard, this office is a clearing house of information about outdoor opportunities in the 157,000 acres of the Pisgah District. Forest rangers staff the office and happily recommend their favorite hikes and swimming holes.

Numerous free brochures are available, plus a variety of area maps and guidebooks are for sale. Also, there are restrooms, a gift shop, exhibits, and a nature trail that sets out from the parking area. • 1001 Pisgah Highway, Pisgah Forest, ☎ (828) 877-3265

French Broad Station, Pisgah National Forest • As one of two stations in the colossal Appalachian Ranger District, the French Broad Station in the center of Hot Springs oversees the 80,000 acres of rugged forest land along the Tennessee State line. The office provides a variety of brochures on mountain biking, hiking, and horseback riding trails in the area. Rangers will gladly help you select an outdoor adventure. • 88 Bridge Street, Hot Springs, ☎ (828) 622-3202

Backcountry Outdoors • This full-service outdoor store sells all manner of gear, apparel, and footwear; plus they operate a bicycle shop that rents and sells mountain bikes. Located at the entrance to the Pisgah National Forest, Backcountry Outdoors is staffed by serious outdoor enthusiasts happy to point you to their favorite spots for hiking, mountain biking, and paddling. • 18 Pisgah Highway, Pisgah Forest, ☎ (828) 884-4262, *www.backcountryoutdoors.com*

Black Dome Mountain Sports • This large Asheville store carries gear, apparel, and footwear for nearly every kind of outdoor pursuit. The shop specializes in hard-to-find rock- and mountain-climbing equipment, and the staff is exceptionally well-informed about the area's outdoor offerings. Also at Black Dome: guide services and instruction for climbing and spelunking. • 140 Tunnel Road, Asheville, ☎ (828) 251-2001 or 1-800-678-2367, *www.blackdome.com*

Bluff Mountain Outfitters • A serious trail shop for thru-hikers on the Appalachian Trail, Bluff Mountain sells anything and everything you might want for your trip into the woods. They sell outdoor gear and apparel, guidebooks, maps, and a complete selection of trail food, including organic health foods. • 152 Bridge Street, Hot Springs, ☎ (828) 622-7162

Looking Glass Outfitters • Located near the Route 276 entrance to the Pisgah National Forest, this shop sells gear, apparel, and footwear for paddling, hiking, climbing, and backpacking. The staff welcomes drop-ins looking for trail recommendations and directions. • 90 New Hendersonville Highway, Pisgah Forest, ☎ (828) 884-5854, *www.lookingglassoutfitters.com*

Kick Back

What to do when your muscles cry "no more" or the weather plays foul? Check out the following laid-back pursuits in Asheville and the surrounding towns.

Attractions

◆ Founded in 1960, the **Botanical Gardens at Asheville,** 151 W.T. Weaver Boulevard, Asheville, (828) 252-5190, *www.ashevillebotanicalgardens.org,* fills 10 acres with trees, shrubs, vines, wildflowers, herbs, and other plants native to the Southern Appalachians. In total, there are approximately 700 species of plants. A walking path winds through the gardens and two meadows, as the birds trilling overhead re-set your stress level to "subdued." Grounds are open daily, sunup to sundown; gift shop and botany center open daily, 9:30 A.M.–4 P.M., March–mid November. Admission is free, but donations are appreciated.

◆ The **North Carolina Arboretum,** 100 Frederick Law Olmstead Way, Asheville, (828) 665-2492, *www.ncarboretum.org,* brings people and plants together. The 426-acre public garden features greenhouses, several garden areas, trails for hiking and mountain biking, and a 25,500-square-foot education center where lectures, clinics, and events are held. Pick up a map of the grounds from the information desk in the education center. Nominal parking fee, but entrance to the facilities and grounds is free. Grounds are open daily. Property hours are 8 A.M.–9 P.M., April–October; 8 A.M.–7 P.M., November–March. The Visitor Education Center is open Monday–Saturday, 9 A.M.–5 P.M.; Sunday, Noon–5 P.M.

◆ The 6,500-acre **Cradle of Forestry,** Route 276, Pisgah Forest, (828) 877-3130, *www.cradleofforestry.com,* is where the nation's forestry and conservation efforts began in the late 19th Century. Here, on land belonging to George Vanderbilt, Dr. Carl A. Schenck founded the nation's first forestry school, the Biltmore Forest School, in 1898.

Packed In

Downtown Asheville's star is the 92,000 square-foot cultural facility, **Pack Place Education, Arts and Science Center,** 2 South Pack Square, ☎ (828) 257-4500, *www.packplace.org.* Housed within it are five major Asheville attractions: The **Asheville Art Museum** (see *Art Galleries);* the **Colburn Gem and Mineral Museum,** ☎ (828) 254-7162, *www.colburnmuseum.org,* which displays thousands of Carolina gems and minerals; **Health Adventure,** ☎ (828) 254-6373, *www.health-adventure.com,* a hands-on health and science museum; the 500-seat **Diana Wortham Theatre,** ☎ (828) 257-4530, *www.dwtheatre.com;* and the **YMI Cultural Center,** ☎ (828) 252-4614 *www.ymicc.org,* an African-American center that hosts exhibits, lectures, performances, and other cultural programs.

Sandy Kolman

Pack Place

Vanderbilt had hired Schenck to manage the Biltmore Estate's land. Located onsite, the **Forestry Discovery Center** features exhibits on conservation and forestry, plus a brief film on the Cradle's history. Other sites on the historic campus include an old sawmill, a 1915 Climbmax logging locomotive, a gift shop, and café. Open daily, 9 A.M.–5 P.M., mid April–early November. Nominal admission fee.

NC Division of Tourism

Chimney Rock Park

◆ Located 25 miles southeast of Asheville, **Chimney Rock Park,** Route 64/74A, Chimney Rock, (828) 625-9611 or 1-800-277-9611, *www.chimneyrockpark.com,* is a privately owned, 1,000-acre park with a number of interesting rock formations; a 404-foot waterfall, Hickory Nut Falls; a nature center; a moonshiner's cave with a replica of a still; and more than 3.5 miles of nature trails, ranging in difficulty from easy to moderate. The park's crowning attraction is the Chimney, a 315-foot monolith with tremendous views that stretch more than 75 miles from its 2,280-foot summit. (You can walk to the summit or take a 26-floor elevator ride.) The beautiful scenery in the park has drawn filmmakers; numerous scenes from *The Last of the Mohicans* with Daniel Day Lewis and *Firestarter* with Drew Barrymore were shot in the park. There's enough to do here to fill a full day, so if you think you'll return, purchase a season pass, which at $22 is less than the price of two $14 one-time passes. Open daily (weather permitting), 8:30 A.M.–4:30 P.M. (until 5:30 P.M. during daylight savings).

Get Rich (Not So) Quick

Rockhounds flock to the Appalachian Mountains to hunt for valuable stones, including sapphires, rubies, and emeralds created a few hundred million years ago as friction from tectonic plate collisions exposed igneous rock to enormous heat. Get in on the action at the **Old Pressley Mine,** 240 Pressley Mine Road, Canton, ☎ (828) 648-6320 or 1-877-903-4754, *www.oldpressleymine.com,* where the 1,445-carat "Star of the Carolinas" blue sapphire was found. Be forewarned: Gem hunting requires patience, and while you may find a precious stone or two, the chances of finding a stone to fund your retirement are slim.

Antiques

Antiques shops abound in Asheville, with the largest concentrations along **Lexington Avenue** in downtown Asheville, in the **Biltmore Village**, and in **Weaverville**, just seven miles north of Asheville. In addition to period styles you'd expect of a mountain community—Early American Country, for example—a surprising collection of shops sell European antiques. For example, **King-Thomasson Antiques,** 65 Biltmore Avenue, (828) 252-1565, *www.king-thomasson.com,* specializes in furniture made from native English woods. Items include Windsor chairs, dressers, chests-of-drawers, and cupboards from the 17th–19th centuries. ◆ With 12,000 square feet of retail floor, **Village Antiques**, 755 Biltmore Avenue, Asheville, (828) 252-5090, *www.villageantiquesonline.com,* features 17th

through 19th-century furniture, artwork, and decorative accessories. ◆ With kudos from *Southern Living* and *Southern Accents* magazines, **Fireside Antiques and Interiors,** Biltmore Village, 30 All Souls Crescent, Asheville, (828) 274-5977, has four galleries of exquisite European furniture made from mahogany, pine, and walnut, as well as decorative porcelain accessories. ◆ Downtown Asheville's **Lexington Park Antiques,** 65 Walnut Street, (828) 253-3070, is a large antiques mall with more than 90 dealers spread over 26,000 square feet. Items on hand range from Americana collectibles to European fine art.

◆ In Weaverville, **Elkins' Antiques,** 99 Silverwood Farm Road, (828) 645-5285, *www.elkinsantiques.com,* specializes in fine American Southern Country furniture. Their inventory includes cupboards, hutches, armoires, wardrobes, tables, and desks. ◆ Looking for an antique door knob, door, sink, toilet, or fireplace mantel? Head to **Preservation Hall,** 55 North Main Street, Weaverville, (828) 645-1047, *www.preservation-hall.com,* where you'll find all manner of antiques salvaged from old homes. Even if you have no idea what you might want, chances are you'll find something old to make new in your home. There are three floors and more than 5,000 square feet of retail space. ◆ Numerous fine antiques shops line Cherry Street in **Black Mountain** and North Main Street in **Hendersonville.**

Art & Crafts Galleries

So rich are its art and crafts offerings that Asheville was recently included in *American Style* magazine's list of the Top 25 Arts Destinations in the nation, along with such art behemoths as New York City, Chicago, and Santa Fe. The following are some highlights.

◆ Founded in 1930, the **Southern Highland Craft Guild,** *www.southernhighlandguild.com,* is a collective of more than 800 Southern Appalachian craftspeople whose work ranges from traditional quilting to contemporary glass. You can view members' work—woodwork, pottery, basketry, textiles, furniture, metal, and more—just a few minutes from Asheville at the

guild's headquarters, the **Folk Art Center,** BRP Milepost 382, (828) 298-7928, or purchase select pieces from **Allanstand,** a retail crafts shop inside the center. Admission is free. ◆ The **Appalachian Craft Center,** 10 N Spruce Street, Asheville, (828) 253-8499, *www.appalachiancraftcenter.com,* displays and sells work by more than 100 area artisans working primarily with clay, but also with fiber, jewelry, wood, and glass. ◆ Located in a former industrial area of town along the French Broad River, Asheville's **Historic River District** is home to more than 30 working artists' studios. Potters, sculptors, and blacksmiths are just a few of the craftspeople here. Wander past the studios—primarily on Riverside Drive, Roberts Street, and Clingman Avenue—and chances are good you'll find several open with the artists working inside.

An art gallery in Brevard

◆ Traditional art also thrives in Asheville at the **Asheville Art Museum** at Pack Place, 2 South Pack Square, (828) 253-3227, *www.ashevilleart.org.* This visual-arts facility features more than 1,500 pieces of 20th-century American fine art, with a particular emphasis on work by Southeastern artists. Included in the collection are paintings by Romare Bearden and Jacob Lawrence, plus contemporary abstract work by Asheville natives Kenneth Noland

and Donald Sultan. ◆ **Blue Spiral 1,** 38 Biltmore Avenue, Asheville, (828) 251-0202, *www.bluespiral1.com,* presents contemporary fine art and crafts by Southeastern artists in a three-floor space that's a work of art itself. Of special note is a gallery dedicated to the works of Will Henry Stevens (1881-1949), an early 20th-century American artist.

◆ The **Black Mountain Center for the Arts**, 225 West State Street, Black Mountain, (828) 669-0930, exhibits paintings and clay, fiber, and wood crafts by well-known regional and national artists. ◆ Also in Black Mountain, **Seven Sisters Gallery**, 117 Cherry Street, (828) 669-5107, is a laid-back place featuring clay, textiles, beads, metal, oils, pastels, and more by local and regional artisans. ◆ Downtown Hendersonville features a number of crafts studios. One you shouldn't miss is **WICKWIRE fine art/folk art**, 330 North Main Street, (828) 692-6222, *www.wickwireartgallery.com,* where fine art by established and emerging artists hangs alongside traditional and contemporary mountain crafts. ◆ In Brevard, **Number 7 Arts, A Fine Arts & Crafts Cooperative**, 7 East Main Street, (828) 883-2294, showcases basketry, jewelry, textiles, metal, paintings, and sculptures by more than 20 area artists.

Back Roads Touring

Of course, the mother of all scenic roadways in the area, indeed in the nation, is the **Blue Ridge Parkway** (see *Blue Ridge Parkway*). But many more area roads are worth exploring. The Pisgah National Forest publishes *Forest Heritage National Scenic Byway,* a small brochure detailing a 79-mile loop through the national forest. Suggested stops along the way include Looking Glass Falls, Sliding Rock, the Cradle of Forestry, Pink Beds Scenic Area, and Lake Logan. Pick up a copy from the Pisgah District office on Route 276 (see *Local Outdoor Advice*). The drive runs the length of **Route 276** west through the forest, past the Blue Ridge Parkway, and into the small town of Bethel, where you take **Route 215** south back across the parkway to the intersection with Route 64 in Rosman. Take **Route 64** east through Brevard to close the loop.

◆ Combine a daytrip to the Hot Springs area with the pleasant **Hot Springs Loop**, which heads north from Asheville on **Route 19/23** to connect with **Route 25/70** north to Hot Springs. The drive is largely rural and becomes particularly mountainous as you approach Hot Springs. To return, take **Route 209** south from Hot Springs to the town of Trust, where you take **Route 63** south into Asheville. ◆ From Hot Springs, driving to **Max Patch** is exceptionally scenic. At the mountain, you can park and walk a quarter-mile uphill to tremendous 360-degree views of the Tennessee and North Carolina mountains. See directions for this drive under *Wide Open*. ◆ The Madison County Tourism bureau publishes a free brochure entitled *Madison County Driving Tours*, which details two loops through the county's rural scenery of rolling hills, rugged mountains, cows, pastures, barns, and roadside streams. Historical commentary explains the sights. The Asheville Visitor Center has copies of the brochure (see *Additional Information*) or you can pick up a copy at the **Madison County Visitor Center,** 72 South Main Street, Mars Hill, 1-877-262-3476. To reach Mars Hill from Asheville, take Route 19/23 north.

Biltmore Estate & Biltmore Village

Once the country home for George Vanderbilt, and today one of the most-visited attractions in the United States, the **Biltmore Estate,** 1 Approach Road, Asheville, (828) 225-1333 or 1-800-624-1575, *www.biltmore.com,* stands as a testament to the colossal wealth generated by the 19th-century American industrialists. George

NC Division of Tourism

Vanderbilt's grandfather, Commodore Cornelius Vanderbilt, made millions as a railroad and steamship baron, and his son, William, expanded the Vanderbilt fortune. So did William's three oldest sons. However, his fourth son, George Washington Vanderbilt, was content to spend. And spend he did. A world traveler, multi-linguist, cultured intellectual, and overall bon vivant, George arrived in Asheville in the 1880s at age 25. Attracted by the surrounding countryside, he purchased 125,000 acres on which to build Biltmore. After Vanderbilt's death, the government purchased much of the land to form the Pisgah National Forest. Today the estate, which remains privately owned by Vanderbilt's heirs, encompasses approximately 8,000 acres of forest, meadow, and landscaped gardens.

Construction on the home took five years (1890–1895) and the effort of more than 1,000 laborers to complete. The result was (and is) the largest private residence in the

Visiting Biltmore

A three-mile driveway from the entrance to the house gives you an idea of the scale of Biltmore, so you'd do well to devote a full day to visiting the home, gardens, and winery. Daytime admission is not cheap (nearly $40 per adult), but the ticket is good for a self-guided visit through four floors of the Biltmore House; entrance to the acres of gardens and walking trails; entrance to the **Biltmore Winery,** including tours of the production areas and a complimentary wine tasting (for guests 21 and older); and parking onsite. The self-paced audio tours for rent are an excellent way to learn about the estate. To reach Biltmore Estate from downtown Asheville, follow Biltmore Avenue to Route 25 south, which leads to the entrance.

United States: a 250-room French Renaissance château. Here are the numbers: 34 bedrooms, 43 bathrooms, 65 fireplaces, three kitchens, a library with more than 20,000 books in seven languages, and 250 acres of landscaped gardens designed by Frederick Law Olmstead, who also designed New York City's Central Park. More than 70,000 furnishings purchased by Vanderbilt on his world travels and original to the house remain, including oriental rugs, paintings—we're talking Renoir, Sargent, and Pellegrini—porcelains, bronzes, and furniture. So many items of note are in the house that merely mentioning a few—a chess set and gaming table that belonged to Napoleon and Chinese goldfish bowls from the Ming Dynasty—does little justice to the historic art on display.

Adjacent to Biltmore Estate is **Historic Biltmore Village,** *www.biltmorevillage.com*, a community planned and built by Vanderbilt and his friend, Biltmore architect, Richard Hunt. Constructed in the late 19th and early 20th centuries, the buildings are in architectural concert with Biltmore Estate. Nearly all of the original structures remain standing, including the heart of the village, the **Cathedral of All Souls,** 3 Angle Street. Today shops, galleries, and restaurants line the village. Learn more about the area at the **Biltmore Village Museum,** 7 Biltmore Plaza, (828) 274-9707, which presents the history of the village from the late 1800s to the present through photographs, maps, antique post cards, and artifacts. Open Monday–Saturday, 12:30 P.M. – 4:30 P.M. Free admission.

Blue Ridge Parkway

The **Blue Ridge Parkway,** (828) 298-0398, *www.nps.gov/blri*, is the nation's most popular scenic highway (more than 21 million visitors a year drive portions of the road), and it passes just south of Asheville. (Take Biltmore Avenue/Route 25 south to the parkway.) Stretching 469 miles from Virginia's Shenandoah National Park to North Carolina's Great Smoky Mountains National Park along ridgelines of the Appalachian Mountains, the BRP rolls past stunning scenery that invites leisurely driving. Numerous overlooks, pull-offs, and recreation areas line the road, which was built by the Civilian Conservation Corps in the 1930s and 1940s, in part to give work to men who'd lost employment during the Great Depression. To take a drive, pick up the free parkway map printed by the National Park Service (available from all sources listed under *Additional Information*). Concrete mileposts mark

The Blue Ridge Parkway

every mile, beginning with Milepost 0 in Virginia and ending with Milepost 469 in North Carolina. All the major sites on the parkway within a reasonable drive from Asheville are listed in this chapter with milepost locations.

Cool Movie House

Want to catch a flick more intellectually satisfying than *Terminator 7*? Head to Asheville's **Fine Arts Theatre,** 36 Biltmore Plaza, (828) 232-1536, *www.fineartstheatre.com,* an immaculately restored downtown Art-Deco wonder that shows first-run art and independent films. In addition to films featuring indie stars like Chloe Sevigny and Benicio Del Toro, the theatre offers "undiscovered" independent filmmakers a venue in which to show their work and talk with the audience.

From the Farm

Farms stretch in all directions outward from Asheville, and the fruit (and vegetables) of their labor appear at the region's many roadside stands and farmers markets. The big market is the **Western North Carolina Farmers Market,** 570 Brevard Road, (828) 253-1691, roadside on Route 191 southeast of Asheville. Overflowing with vegetables, fruits, baked goods, plants, honey, and crafts, the market sits on 36 acres filled with rows of wooden tables outdoors and several large buildings with indoor tenants. Open daily, year-round (8 A.M.–6 P.M. April–October, 8 A.M.–5 P.M. November–March). ◆ The **Henderson County Curb Market,** at the corner of 2nd Avenue and Church Street, Hendersonville, (828) 692-8012, sells goods and crafts, including produce, baked goods, jellies, plants, flowers, and toys. Open Tuesday, Thursday, and Saturday, 8 A.M.–2 P.M., May–December; Tuesday and Saturday, 8 A.M.–2 P.M., January–April.

Keep the Doctor Away

If there's one fruit that most epitomizes the North Carolina Mountains, it's the apple. Apple trees thrive in the cool summer nights and long sunny days, and no less than 14 juicy, crisp, and sweet varieties grow in the state. You can purchase apples from the farmers that grow them, or better yet, pick your own. Autumn is harvest time, and the best place to begin is in **Henderson County,** where a whopping 75 percent of the state's apples are grown. The largest concentration of roadside stands and pick-your-own orchards exists on Route 64 east of Hendersonville.

Historic Sites & Museums

Nearly all of downtown Asheville's 19th- and early 20th-century buildings remain standing (see "Frozen in Time"), so strolling the city's center provides a historic architectural perspective. The following are just the highlights. If you're interested in knowing more, stop by the Visitor Center on Haywood Street (see *Additional Information*) to request a printout with the complete list of buildings and their histories. (It costs $0.25.)

◆ The **Grove Arcade,** built between 1926–1929 by E.W. Grove as the state's first indoor mall, occupies a full city block along Battery Park Avenue. Today it houses a collection of boutiques and dining choices. Cream-glazed terra cotta covers this imposing Neo-Tudor Gothic building designed by Charles N. Parker. Don't miss the winged Griffin statues guarding the Battle Square entrance. ◆ Built in 1909, the **Basilica of Saint Lawrence,** 97 Haywood Street, is a Spanish Baroque Revival-style Catholic Church. Designed by world-renowned architect Raphael Guastavino, the red-brick church features two five-story towers that bookend its façade and an entirely self-supporting dome believed to be the largest of its type in North America. There are no wood or steal beams in the entire structure; everything is constructed out of tiles and other masonry materials.

Asheville CVB

Grove Arcade

◆ In Pack Square, the 13-story **Jackson Building,** designed by Ronald Greene, went up in 1925 as the state's first skyscraper. ◆ Built between 1926–1928, the **Asheville City Building**, 70 Court Plaza, is an Art-Deco masterpiece designed by architect Douglas Ellington. It is set on a marble base and crowned by a pink- and green-tiled octagonal, pyramid-style roof. ◆ Also designed by Douglas Ellington, the Art-Deco **S&W Cafeteria** building, 56 Patton Avenue, was built in 1929 for the cafeteria chain. The two-story building features a multi-hued, terra-cotta façade. Inside, Art-Deco decorations separate the interior lobby from the dining rooms. ◆ At the entrance to Wall Street and located at 10-20 Battery Park Avenue, the **Flatiron Building** is a wedge-shaped, eight-story, tan-brick building built in 1926. ◆ On the outskirts of town, E.W. Grove's **Grove Park Inn,** 290 Macon Avenue, went up in 1913 and was meant to emulate a Yellowstone Park mountain lodge Grove once visited. Designed by Grove's son-in-law (who had no architectural experience), the hotel features native timber and uncut granite boulders on a poured-concrete base. The distinctive red roof comes from red-clay tiles produced in Tennessee. Even if you're not a guest, visit the inn for coffee, tea, or dinner, so you can see the massive 120-foot by 80-foot main lobby, bookended by fireplaces so large you could park a VW Bug inside.

◆ As the second most-visited attraction in Asheville (the Biltmore is #1), the **Thomas Wolfe Memorial Home**, 48 Spruce Street, (828) 253-8304, *www.wolfememorial.com,* was the boyhood home of the famous author. Immortalized as "Dixieland" in Wolfe's autobiographic novel, *Look Homeward Angel,* the 19-room, Queen Anne-style boardinghouse was run by his mother for middle-class guests visiting Asheville. "Dixieland was a big cheaply constructed frame house of eighteen or twenty drafty high-ceilinged rooms: it had a rambling, unplanned, gabular appearance, and was painted a dirty yellow," wrote Wolfe. Prior to a

Frozen in Time

Downtown Asheville's architecture is like a freeze-frame of the good times the city enjoyed leading up to the Stock Market Crash of 1929. As a 19th- and early 20th-century vacation destination for wealthy sophisticates like Henry Ford, Thomas Edison, and F. Scott Fitzgerald, Asheville spared no expense on its buildings. Without a unified style—Art-Deco stands next to Classical, for example—the eclectic mix might have been ripe for the wrecking ball in the homogenous 1950s had the city been able to afford the demolition. Buried under tremendous debt, Asheville let its city-center sit, and as a result, the National Trust for Historic Preservation named Asheville one of 12 best-preserved and unique communities in the nation.

Grove Park Inn

The Grove Park Inn

devastating fire in 1998, the house had been preserved nearly intact with original furnishings. After the fire, many items were salvaged, and the home underwent a $2.1 million restoration for the May 2004 grand re-opening. A modern **visitor center,** 52 North Market Street, exhibits personal items from the home, the author's New York City apartment, and his father's stonecutting shop. Catch the short film about the writer and browse the onsite gift shop. Open Tuesday–Saturday, 9 A.M.–5 P.M.; Sunday, 1 P.M.–5 P.M., from April–October. Winter hours are Tuesday–Saturday, 10 A.M.–4 P.M.; Sunday, 1 P.M.–4 P.M. Moderate admission fee.

♦ The oldest surviving structure in Asheville, the red-brick **Smith-McDowell House**, 283 Victoria Road, (828) 253-9231, was built around 1840 by James McConnell Smith, one of the first settlers born west of the Blue Ridge Mountains. Today period antiques furnish the house, and exhibits provide interesting details about Victorian life in Asheville. Rooms include a kitchen from the 1840s, an 1850s bedroom, and an 1890 dining room. The home also features gardens designed by Frederick Law Olmstead, the landscaper of Biltmore Estate and New York City's Central Park. Also on the grounds is the Buncombe County Civil War Memorial. Open Tuesday–Saturday, 10 A.M.–4 P.M., Sunday, 1 P.M.–4 P.M., April–December. Closed Sundays and Mondays, January–March.

♦ Just north of downtown Asheville, the **Montford Historic District** is an attractive residential neighborhood of more than 200 turn-of-the-century homes. Here you'll find a large concentration of bed and breakfasts, as well as **Riverside Cemetery,** 53 Birch Street, where many of Asheville's best-known citizens are buried, including writers Thomas Wolfe and O. Henry, and North Carolina Governor Zebulon Baird Vance.

♦ Just north of Asheville in Reems Creek Valley, the **Vance Birthplace,** 911 Reems Creek Road, Weaverville, (828) 645-6706, is a pioneer farmstead where three-time North Carolina Governor Zebulon Baird Vance was born in 1830. Vance, who also served as a Civil War officer and United States Senator, was the third child of early Buncombe County settler David Vance. The homestead includes various outbuildings and a reconstructed log home built around the original chimneys. Period antiques furnish the homestead; museum exhibits depict early pioneer days in the mountains. Open Monday–Saturday, 9 A.M.–5 P.M. Free admission.

♦ In Flat Rock, the **Carl Sandburg House,** 1928 Little River Road, (828) 693-4178, *www.nps.gov/carl,* was home to Pulitzer-Prize

A Museum Without Walls

To discover Asheville's cultural and historic heritage, walk the **Asheville Urban Trail,** an interpretative trail downtown marked by sculptures, plaques, and granite markers. There are 30 "stations," each of which highlights an important site, building, or person from the city's past. Five trail segments represent key historic periods: the Pioneer Period, the Gilded Age, the Times of Thomas Wolfe, the Era of Civic Pride, and the Age of Diversity. The 1.7-mile trail takes two hours to walk. Pick up a trail brochure from the Asheville Visitor Center, 151 Haywood Street.

The Estes-Winn Museum

winning poet, author, biographer, folksinger, and humorist Carl Sandburg after he moved from Michigan in 1945. Widely considered a voice for the American people, Sandburg, along with his wife, spent more than 20 years on the farm named Connemara, and it was here that he wrote more than one-third of his life's work. The grounds include the circa 1838 home, a dairy barn, and various sheds. Also, there are two small lakes, an orchard, gardens, and walking trails. The home is open for guided, 30-minute tours offered daily beginning at 9:30 A.M. and ending at 4:30 P.M. Nominal admission fee.

◆ **Historic Downtown Hendersonville** offers a free brochure, *Art & History: A Hendersonville Walking Tour,* available from the visitor center at 201 South Main Street. The tour highlights nearly 30 notable sites and buildings, including the 1847 **Shepherd-Riley Building,** an antebellum commercial building; the 1850 **Ripley Building,** another rare, antebellum commercial building; and the 1882 **Oakdale Cemetery,** site of **"Wolfe's Angel,"** the sculpture Wolfe made famous in *Look Homeward Angel.*

Planes, Trains, and Automobiles

Transportation-history buffs can check out three separate museums focusing on cars, trains, and airplanes. The **Estes-Winn Antique Automobile Museum,** 111 Grovewood Road, Asheville, ☎ (828) 253-7651, features a collection of more than 30 antique cars dating from 1905. ◆ The first train pulled into the **Historic Hendersonville Depot,** Maple Street off 7th Avenue, Hendersonville, ☎ (828) 698-0052, in 1879, though the present structure dates to 1902. Of note in the depot's baggage room: a model train with 500 feet of track. ◆ The state's first flight museum, the **Western North Carolina Air Museum,** 1340 Gilbert Street, ☎ (828) 698-2482, at Hendersonville's airport, houses a collection of restored vintage airplanes.

Hot Air Ballooning

For an uplifting experience and a unique way to see the mountains, get above it all in a hot air balloon. Two outfits provide rides in the area. ◆ **Mt. Pisgah Balloons,** 1410 Pisgah Highway, Candler, (828) 667-9943, floats over the Pisgah National Forest and the French Broad River. You'll be treated to great views of the mountains and the city of Asheville. ◆ **Transylvania Balloon Company,** 40 Pole Miller Road, Brevard, 1-877-500-0506, *www.transylvaniaballoonco.com,* flies over the apple orchards and scenic valleys of Henderson County.

Performing Arts

♪ So many theatrical, musical, and dance opportunities exist in the mountains that the following list captures just the highlights. In addition to contacting the groups directly, pick up a copy of *The Asheville Citizen-Times* or the weekly alternative paper, the *Mountain Xpress*, for show listings.

♦ Founded in 1946, the **Asheville Community Theatre,** 35 East Walnut Street, Asheville, (828) 254-1320, *www.ashevilletheatre.org,* performs six productions a year, including classics, musicals, and comedies. Recent shows were *The Sound of Music, Death of a Salesman,* and *Look Homeward Angel.* Performances are in the Heston Auditorium, named for Charlton Heston, who launched his career here with wife, actress Lydia Clark, in a 1947 production of Tennessee Williams' *The Glass Menagerie.* ♦ **The Montford Park Players,** (828) 254-5146, *www.montfordparkplayers.org,* is Asheville's Shakespeare-in-the-park troupe. The all-volunteer acting and technical crew produces two plays—a comedy and a tragedy—by the Bard each summer. Free performances are in the outdoor Hazel Robinson Amphitheater, 34 Pearson Drive, in the Montford Historic District.

♦ The **North Carolina Stage Company**, (828) 669-4367 or (828) 350-9090 for tickets, *www.ncstage.org,* presented its first full season in 2003-2004 with productions of the Pulitzer Prize-winning play *Proof* and Shakespeare's *Twelfth Night.* The new troupe focuses on producing classics (with an emphasis on Shakespeare), as well as compelling modern plays. Performances are held in the Earth Guild Building, 33 Haywood Street, accessed via an alley off Walnut Street.

Other regional theatre troupes include: ♦ **Brevard Community Theatre Company**, (828) 884-2587, *www.brevardlittletheatre.com,* which performs three to four plays a year in the Barn Theatre, on the campus of Brevard College; ♦ **Hendersonville Little Theatre,** (828) 692-1082, *www.hendersonvillelittletheatre.org,* which produces four plays a year in The Barn on State Street, a converted riding stable between Kanuga and Willow streets in Hendersonville; and ♦ the **Southern Appalachian Repertory Theatre,** (828) 689-1239, which produces traditional summer stock, plus one original script a year, in the historic Owen Theatre on the campus of Mars Hill College in Mars Hill.

♦ The **Asheville Symphony Orchestra**, (828) 254-7046, *www.ashevillesymphony.org,* performed

All the World Knows This Stage

With a history dating to 1937 and an international reputation for outstanding productions of modern and classic dramas, musicals, and comedies, the **Flat Rock Playhouse,** 2661 Greenville Highway (Route 25), Flat Rock, ☎ (828) 693-0403 or (828) 693-0731 for tickets, *www.flatrockplayhouse.org,* is a major performance venue under contract to the Actors' Equity Association. Eight productions each summer and fall are performed over seven months on an enchanting, barn-like stage. Recent performances included *Singing in the Rain, The Jungle Book,* and the British comedy, *Brush with a Body.* Tickets are generally between $25 and $30 for adults. Evening performances are at 8:15 P.M., Wednesday–Saturday. Matinee showings are at 2:15 P.M. on Wednesday, Thursday, Saturday, and Sunday.

The lawn at the Brevard Music Center

its 43rd season in 2003-2004 of classical, pops, and choral works (in conjunction with the **Asheville Symphony Chorus**). The well-known orchestra performs in Asheville's Civic Center, 87 Haywood Street, and really shines with its Masterworks series of classical works by such composers as Beethoven, Mozart, and Brahms. ◆ The **Asheville Chamber Music Series,** (828) 298-5085, is a volunteer music organization that produces between four and six programs a year at Asheville's Unitarian Universalist Church, 1 Edwin Place. Visiting trios, quartets, and quintets include many of the nation's finest musicians. ◆ With the accompaniment of the Asheville Symphony Orchestra, the **Asheville Lyric Opera,** (828) 236-0670, *www.ashevillelyric.org,* performs two major operas a year in Asheville's 500-seat Diana Wortham Theatre, 2 South Pack Square. Recent productions were *Don Pasquale, La Bohème,* and *Madama Butterfly.* ◆ Founded in 1932 as the Asheville Civic Music Association with the goal "to bring better music to Asheville," **Asheville Bravo! Concerts,** (828) 299-0820, *www.ashevillebravoconcerts.org,* delivers top-notch classical music performers, operas, ballet troupes, and more to the Thomas Wolfe Auditorium at the Asheville Civic Center, 87 Haywood Street. Recent performers included violinist Robert McDuffie with the Philharmonia of the Nations, the Moscow Festival Ballet, and pianists Katia and Marielle Labèque.

Eat, Breathe, & Sleep Music

One of the nation's best-known music camps and festivals for pre-professional musicians is the **Brevard Music Center,** 1000 Probart Street, Brevard, ☎ (828) 862-2100 or 1-888-384-8682, *www.brevardmusic.org,* where for seven weeks each summer, 400 students "eat, breathe, and sleep music." They receive instruction from the professional faculty and help perform in more than 80 public concerts, operas, and musicals. Their efforts are to your gain, as the quality of music is outstanding. Concerts are on campus in an open-air auditorium; seating is covered or on the lawn.

◆ Brevard College's **Paul Porter Center for Performing Arts**, 400 North Broad Street, (828) 884-8330, hosts numerous outstanding musical performances throughout the year by the college's nationally recognized music department. ◆ Founded in 1979 as Western North Carolina's first modern dance troupe, the **Asheville Contemporary Dance Theatre,** 28 Commerce Street, Asheville, (828) 254-2621, *www.acdt.org,* performs a varied repertoire, pulling from both traditional and experimental forms of modern dance. Performances are in either the Bebe Theatre, 28 Commerce Street, or the Diana Wortham Theatre, 2 South Pack Square.

Shops & Stops

$ The combination of historic architecture and pedestrian-friendly streets makes shopping **downtown Asheville** particularly pleasant. In keeping with the city's creative

Gordon Smith

Inside the Grove Arcade

flair, expect generous helpings of galleries, antiques dealers, new-age boutiques, and funky apparel shops. A rough generalization: exotic retailers are on **Wall Street, Lexington Street** is the antiques corridor, and galleries line the sidewalks along **Biltmore** and **Broadway avenues.** ◆ **A Far Away Place,** 11 Wall Street, (828) 252-1891 or 1-888-452-1891, promises "gifts from the heart of the world." Indeed, you're far from Kansas when you step inside this fragrant-smelling shop with its collection of world art, clothing, religious artifacts, and global knick-knacks. ◆ The non-profit **Ten Thousand Villages,** 10 College Street, Asheville, (828) 254-8374, *www.villagesasheville.com,* sells crafts made by Third World artists who receive income from your purchases to care for their families. ◆ To find something you didn't know you wanted, head to **The L.O.F.T. of Asheville,** 53 Broadway Avenue, (828) 259-9303, *www.loftofasheville.com.* The L.O.F.T. ("lost objects found treasures") sells funky furniture, paper journals, French soaps, scented candles, pottery, garden stuff, and more. ◆ **The Mast General Store,** 15 Biltmore Avenue, (828) 232-1883, *www.mastgeneralstore.com,* operates an outpost in Asheville, where you'll find everything from old-timey mercantile items (wind-up toys and Radio Flyer red wagons, for example) to clothing and outdoor gear. ◆ The **Grove Arcade Public Market,** 1 Page Avenue, Asheville, (828) 252-7799, *www.grovearcade.com,* is home to more than 30 specialty food, crafts, and service retailers in the renovated 1929 Grove Arcade building.

◆ South of downtown, **Biltmore Village** features more than 50 unique shops, galleries, and restaurants, many of which are in historic buildings along brick-paved sidewalks. Don't miss **Interiors Marketplace**, 2 Hendersonville Road, Asheville, (828) 253-

Positively Bookish

The Asheville region loves its bookstores—the number of independent and chain bookstores rivals that of much larger cities. ◆ **Malaprops Bookstore/Café,** 55 Haywood Street, Asheville, ☎ (828) 254-6734, *www.malaprops.com,* is as much a reading center as a bookstore, given the café is packed with tables full of customers sipping coffee and losing themselves in books. Malaprops carries fiction, poetry, and nonfiction, with a notable selection of work by Southern writers. ◆ **Accent on Books,** 854 Merrimon Avenue, Asheville, ☎ (828) 252-6255 or 1-800-482-7964, *www.accentonbooks.com,* carries religion, spirituality, psychology, gay & lesbian issues, and health titles. There's also a great children's selection. ◆ **The Captain's Bookshelf,** 31 Page Avenue, Asheville, ☎ (828) 253-663, is an interesting used bookstore with a large selection of first editions and autographed books. ◆ Located opposite Brevard College, **Highland Books,** 480 North Broad Street, Brevard, ☎ (828) 884-2424, carries a wide selection of new fiction and nonfiction, with special emphasis on regional titles, including outdoor and travel books. ◆ In Hendersonville, **Mountain Lore,** 555 North Main Street, ☎ (828) 693-5096, carries new fiction, poetry, and nonfiction with a special emphasis on regional titles.

2300, *www.interiorsmarketplace.com,* for all manner of art, antiques, and furniture. ◆ **The Compleat Naturalist,** 2 Biltmore Plaza, (828) 274-5430 or 1-800-678-5430, *www.compleat-naturalist.com,* is a nature store and wildlife gallery.

◆ Downtown Hendersonville has a great mix of apparel, jewelry, music, toy, art, and antiques shops spread across a six-block area. Park anywhere along Main Street or in one of the municipal lots on Church or King streets. In addition to another outpost of the **Mast General Store,** 527 Main Street, (828) 696-1883, notable stops include: ◆ the **Purple Sage,** 416 North Main Street, (828) 693-9555, for gourmet cooking items, including cookware, cookbooks, fine food, and wine; and ◆ **Dancing Bear Toys**, 418 North Main Street, (828) 693-4500, *www.dancingbeartoys.com,* an independently owned toy shop.

◆ **Black Mountain** offers art galleries, antiques shops, and gift boutiques, particularly along Cherry and State streets. Two neat stops include: ◆ **Town Hardware & General Store,** 103 West State Street, (828) 669-7723 or 1-800-669-7723, *www.townhardware.com,* an old-fashioned hardware and general store with tools, garden and home accessories, toys, and antique replicas of hand-crank ice-cream churners and apple peelers; and ◆ **Song of the Wood,** 203 West State Street, (828) 669-7675, *www.songofthewood.com,* which sells hammer dulcimers, bowed psalteries, and other traditional mountain instruments constructed by owner Jerry Read Smith, a legend in mountain-instrument making. The shop also carries numerous CDs by folk musicians.

◆ The downtown area of **Brevard** along Main and Broad streets is packed with cool boutiques and galleries, all set against the backdrop of the mountains. **The White Squirrel Shoppe**, 2 West Main Street, Brevard, (828) 877-3530 or 1-888-729-7329, *www.whitesquirrelshoppe.com,* is an interesting general merchandise and gift shop located in the historic 1899 McMinn Building. ◆ A couple of storefronts down, **Celestial Mountain Music,** 16 West Main Street, Brevard, (828) 884-3575, *www.celestialmtnmusic.com,* sells all manner of stringed instruments, including Cedar Mountain banjos, as well as accessories, sound equipment, and recordings.

◆ The **Chimney Rock area** has a number of shops worth exploring. Check out **Edie's Good Things,** Route 64/74A, Chimney Rock Village, (828) 625-0111, *www.ediegoodthings.com,* for handmade basketry, jewelry, pottery, glass, carved wood, and metal pieces, plus a collection of cards and music.

Downtown Brevard

Spa & Massage

Housed in a historic home one minute from downtown Asheville, **The Asheville Oasis,** 73 Merrimon Avenue, (828) 257-2570, *www.theashevilleoasis.com,* offers facials, pedicures, manicures, and massage services. ◆ S-t-r-e-t-c-h your vacation out at

Fire, Water, Rock, Light

Grove Park Inn

Travel + Leisure calls the $42 million, 40,000-square foot, subterranean **Grove Park Inn Spa**, 290 Macon Avenue, Asheville, ☎ (828) 252-2711 or 1-877-772-0747, *www.groveparkinn.com,* one of the world's best spas. We agree. The architectural theme of fire, water, rock, and light plays out through five fireplaces, two waterfalls, a lap pool, mineral pool, whirlpool, and coldwater plunge. Light from glass skylights illuminates the rock walls. The atmosphere alone soothes your spirit, yet the real renewal begins in the spa's 24 treatment rooms, where dozens of massage and salon services are offered. Try the most popular treatment, "Fire, Rock, Water & Light," which includes a full body exfoliation; buttermilk and honey whirlpool bath; cream body wrap; waterfall massage; and more.

Asheville Yoga Center, 239 South Liberty Street, Asheville, (828) 254-0380, *www.youryoga.com,* a community center offering all styles of hatha yoga. The center holds classes for all levels of practitioners in a room with soothing colors, high ceilings, and natural light. ◆ The **Hot Springs Spa**, 315 Bridge Street, Hot Springs, (828) 622-7676 or 1-800-462-0933, *www.hotspringsspa-nc.com,* has several outdoor hot tubs filled with 104-degree water from a natural mineral spring. Tubs are drained and re-filled after each use. Request Tub #5 bordering Spring Creek's intersection with the French Broad River. The spa also offers massage services.

More massage therapists than you can throw a loufa at work in and around Asheville. Two worth mentioning: ◆ Bob Counts of **Healing Essence Massage,** 1208 Conner Road, Lake Lure, (828) 286-1926, offers numerous forms of massage, including Kaya Regeneration Therapy, an ancient, Indian massage technique using hot oil pouches that promote relaxation, weight loss, and an increase in muscle mass. ◆ In Asheville, **Healing Hands,** 233 South French Broad, (828) 628-4075, offers a variety of massage options, as well as aromatherapy and energy-balance therapies.

Tours

To get oriented to Asheville and hear some anecdotes about the city's history, join **Asheville Trolley Tours**, 1-888-667-3600, *www.ashevilletrolleytours.com,* for a vintage trolley ride (on wheels) to all the major points of interest in town. Stops include the Grove Park Inn, Biltmore Village, the Thomas Wolfe Memorial, the historic downtown shopping district, and the Asheville Museum. The flexible tours allow you to get off to shop, dine, or sightsee, and then re-board to continue the tour. ◆ **Lake Lure Tours,** 2930 Memorial Highway, Lake Lure, (828) 625-1373 or 1-877-386-4255, *www.lakelure.com,* operates a tour of scenic Lake Lure from a covered pontoon boat. The ride goes past numerous locations used during the filming of the movie *Dirty Dancing,* as well as past stretches of gorgeous mountain scenery.

R e s t   E a s y

S l e e p   W e l l

With a long history of hosting travelers, the Asheville region has a rich offering of upscale resorts, country inns, and B&Bs. The following list includes options in Asheville proper and in the surrounding towns.

Accommodations Pricing

Less than $100	Inexpensive	$
$100-150	Moderate	$$
$151-200	Expensive	$$$
More than $200	Very Expensive	$$$$

Prices are per room, per night, based on double occupancy during peak seasons. Note that B&Bs and most country inns include breakfast in the rate.

The Cottages at Spring House Farm • Ninety-two acres, five cottages, and wild birds too numerous to count—the Cottages at Spring House Farm are all about getting away. Situated 45 minutes east of Asheville in a rural farming community, this pro-ecology property features phone-less "cottages"—actually large, elegant log cabins—locally crafted with creative detail. (For example, porch beams were hewn from different types of trees fallen on the property, including oak, pine, walnut, cherry, and locust.) Cabin amenities include large decks with enormous hot tubs, serene forest views, gas grills, full kitchens, fireplaces, TVs with VCRs (but no cable), canoes, fishing gear for trout and bass, and breakfast provisions. (Innkeepers Zee and Arthur Campbell provide dinner provisions like steaks, chops, shrimp, or salmon, and veggies from the garden for an added fee.) Check-in is at the main house, a beautifully preserved 1836 post-and-beam farmhouse. Walking trails on the farm climb a mountain and wind past ponds, creeks, and flower meadows, including a sunflower field where flocks of goldfinch roost. • *219 Haynes Road, Marion, NC 28752,* ☎ *1-877-738-9798, www.springhousefarm.com* • *$$$-$$$$*

Cumberland Falls Inn • Every detail of this B&B proves restful, from its location in Asheville's quiet Montford neighborhood to the serene walk to the front door. (You'll pass flowers, evergreens, koi ponds, and hear the music of a pleasant waterfall.) The Cumberland Falls Inn is a turn-of-the-century house lovingly restored with such details (all original to the home) as quilted maple woodwork, pine and fir floors, high ceilings, bay windows, and a wood-burning fireplace. The five spacious rooms include amenities like whirlpool tubs, fireplaces, robes, TV/VCRs, and turndown service with bedside chocolates. Innkeepers Patti and Gary Wiles prepare a delicious gourmet breakfast featuring such items as Belgian waffles, Eggs Benedict, muffins, and fresh-squeezed juice. Early risers can take their coffee to the front or back sitting porches overlooking the property's extensive gardens. • *254 Cumberland Avenue, Asheville, NC 28801,* ☎ *(828) 253-4085 or 1-888-743-2557, www.cumberlandfalls.com* • *$$$-$$$$*

Grove Park Inn • Set high above downtown Asheville on Sunset Mountain, this inn stands nearly as majestic as the surrounding mountains. Simply put, the Grove Park Inn is one of America's grand old resorts. There are 510 rooms available in different configurations in three buildings: the 1913 Main Inn and two more recent additions, the Vanderbilt and Sammons wings. All feature comfortable furniture, private baths, televisions, coffee makers, and more. The inn's impressive past—the guest list reads like a who's who of 20th-century politics and celebrity—infuses the present, and it's easy to imagine yourself an important dignitary as you read the paper in the 120-foot by 80-foot main lobby bookended by two-story fireplaces. Service from the hotel's large staff is what you'd expect from such a lauded resort: attentive when you need help, out of sight when you don't. A sampling of amenities includes one of the nation's finest spas; indoor and outdoor pools; a century-old, Donald Ross-designed golf course; tennis courts; a full sports complex with a fitness facility; shops; and commanding views of the Asheville skyline. • *290 Macon Avenue, Asheville, NC 28804,* ☎ *(828) 252-2711 or 1-800-438-5800, www.groveparkinn.com* • *$$-$$$$*

Highland Lake Inn • Bordered by a cascading waterfall, the entrance to Highland Lake Inn is a picturesque welcome to this 27-acre country retreat with its main lodge, guest house, and numerous cabins and cottages. A winding lane takes you back in time to childhood summer camp at the lake, complete with fireflies, cozy cabins, and rope swings. In fact, the Highland Lake Inn was once a camp, but it's highly unlikely former campers would recognize the nicely appointed lodgings available today. In total, there are more than 70 rooms, ranging from simple to deluxe. The finest are the 16 guestrooms in the Woodward House, but even the rustic cabins prove restful. Property amenities include a fine restaurant with an award-winning wine list, Highland Lake, canoes, bicycles, a tennis court, and outdoor pool. A hot country breakfast with selections from the inn's large organic garden is included for all but the cabins. Highland Lake Inn is close to the DuPont State Forest and downtown Hendersonville. • *Highland Lake Road, Flat Rock, NC 28731,* ☎ *(828) 693-6812 or 1-800-762-1376, www.hlinn.com* • *$–$$$$*

The Inn on Biltmore Estate • Set upon a ridge above the Biltmore Estate Winery with stand-up-and-applaud views of the surrounding mountains, this inn is the only way to sleep over on the 8,000-acre Biltmore Estate. This Mobil Four-Star, AAA Four-Diamond property is what George Vanderbilt himself would have built, had his original intention of constructing an inn on the estate been realized during his lifetime. There are 204 guestrooms, plus nine suites; all are elegantly appointed with French- and English-manor décor. Rooms feature grand beds, comfortable reading chairs, marble-accented bathrooms, custom robes and slippers, and Web TV with wireless keyboards (trust us, it's cool). Property amenities include an outdoor pool and hot tub, a fitness room, a stunning library, and numerous outdoor activities such as hiking, mountain biking, horseback riding, and paddling. The main dining room serves breakfast, lunch, afternoon tea, and dinner. Admission to Biltmore Estate is not included in the rates, but the inn offers complimentary shuttles to the Biltmore House, Gardens, and Winery. • *1 Antler Hill Road, Asheville, NC 28803,* ☎ *(828) 225-1660 or 1-800-858-4130, www.biltmore.com* • *$$$–$$$$*

Ivivi Mountain Lake & Lodge • Awaken to a panorama of misty mountains reflected upon smooth-as-glass Lake Lure. Ivivi is South African for "renewal," and you'll experience just that at this contemporary glass and wood lodge on a forested peak overlooking what *National Geographic* calls one of the world's five most-beautiful lakes. Fine African art and artifacts imported by the inn's German owner create a smooth, soothing, and elegant effect in both common areas and the seven rooms. All guest rooms feature fine linens, silk bedspreads, soft bathrobes, satellite TV, and private baths so spectacular they belong in an interior design magazine. Most rooms feature a private balcony or stone terrace. Every evening, guests are treated to a leisurely boat ride across Lake Lure for breathtaking views that include multi-million-dollar, shore-front homes nestled among the trees. The innkeepers prepare a fresh-cooked breakfast, ever-present snacks, afternoon hors d'oeuvres, and evening wine, all included in the rate. • *161 Waterside Drive,*

Lake Lure, NC 28746, ☎ (828) 625-0601 or 1-866-224-7740, *www.ivivilodge.com* • *$$$$*

The Lodge at Lake Lure • As the only inn directly on Lake Lure, this property boasts unrivaled views of golden sunlight twinkling off the water. After stepping through the entrance arch, covered with fragrant jasmine and roses, you'll become enchanted by this impeccable lodge, where a recent $1.5-million renovation created the perfect marriage of rustic lakeside serenity and luxurious modern-day comforts. Beautiful wormy-chestnut paneling remains in the 1920 main lodge with many other charming features, including the occasional creak of original floorboards. However, the 16 guestrooms—12 in the main lodge, four in the adjacent "Shared Dreams" house—feature such contemporary amenities as whirlpool tubs, all-glass showers, fireplaces, televisions, and private terraces. Each evening guests are treated to an hour-long boat tour of Lake Lure and its stunning mountain vistas. Also included is a fresh breakfast cooked to order and afternoon wine and hors d'oeuvres. (On a limited schedule, the inn serves lunch and dinner for an additional fee. Call for details.)

Gordon Smith

The Lodge at Lake Lure's boathouse

Terraced gardens lead from the inn to the boathouse where you can take a swim, go for a paddle in a canoe, or read the paper on the deck. Overseeing the inn's operations is grand dame Giselle Hopke, originally from Germany's Black Forest, who has a gift for making guests feel utterly pampered. • *361 Charlotte Drive, Lake Lure, NC 28746,* ☎ *(828) 625-2789 or 1-800-733-2785, www.lodgeonlakelure.com* • *$$–$$$$*

Mountain Magnolia Inn & Retreat • Jaded guidebook authors view plenty of before and after pictures displayed by proud innkeepers. When Karen and Pete Nagle show theirs, the only appropriate response is WOW. After purchasing the Victorian 1868 James H. Rumbough House, the Nagles enclosed the entire structure in a giant tent and went about transforming the grand home into the impressive inn it is today. The main inn has five guest rooms, each with private bath and several with gas fireplaces and private balconies overlooking the mountains. Miss Peggy's Suite works well for families or two couples traveling together—the suite has two bedrooms, plus a common sitting area with a gas fireplace. Also on the grounds, the Garden House has three bedrooms, two baths, and a fully equipped kitchen. Breakfast is hot, creative, and outstanding, as is dinner in the inn's highly regarded restaurant. A recent addition to the Nagle's lodging lineup, Fowler's Bend, is a former general store restored as a guesthouse. Located just two miles from the main hotel, Fowler's Bend overlooks Spring Creek and features two suites, both of which have two bedrooms with king beds and gas fireplaces, two baths, a deck, a den, and a kitchen and dining area. • *204 Lawson Street, Hot Springs, NC 28743,* ☎ *(828) 622-3543, www.mountainmagnoliainn.com* • *$$–$$$$*

Richmond Hill Inn • For the experience of a more genteel era when elegant surroundings, impeccable service, and exquisite dining were the way of Southern ladies and gentlemen, plan a visit to this 1899 Queen Anne-style Victorian mansion. Period décor and luxury amenities adorn each of the 36 rooms—12 in the mansion, nine in the Garden Pavilion, and 15 in the Croquet Cottage—available in several classes. (Even the least-expensive rooms make guests feel like royalty.) Nearly 50 acres of estate grounds feature sweeping Blue-Ridge views, walking paths, numerous sitting areas, several formal gardens and natural areas with more than 1,000 varieties of plants, a mountain brook that cascades through several pools to a nine-foot waterfall, and a perfectly tended croquet court. There's also an onsite exercise room. Afternoon tea with attentive waiters, cloth-covered tables, and delightful homemade treats is included, as is a full breakfast ordered from a menu with such selections as Eggs Benedict. The Inn's restaurant, Gabrielle's, is among the region's finest. A perennial AAA Four-Diamond, Mobil Four-Star property, the Richmond Hill Inn is the epitome of excellence in a serene setting. • *87 Richmond Hill Drive, Asheville, NC 28806,* ☎ *(828) 252-7313 or 1-888-742-4536, www.richmondhillinn.com* • *$$$–$$$$*

Sourwood Inn • In perfect harmony with its 100 acres of secluded surroundings, the impeccable Arts & Crafts-style Sourwood Inn blends excellent taste with gracious warmth in its 12 rooms. Each has a balcony with a sweeping mountain view, a sitting area, period furniture, a natural wood fireplace, and a bathroom that deserves a paragraph all its own. (For starters, picture a frosted-glass door, pristine tile work, walk-in shower, towel warmers, and an elevated tub with a picture window overlooking the mountains.) Common areas—the lobby, library, game room, and numerous porches with rockers—are both spacious and intimate. Also onsite is the Sassafras Cabin, a lovely, two-level hideaway with two baths, a kitchen, a loft bedroom, and a pullout sofa in the living area. Grounds include two miles of groomed walking trails along which you can either work off the hot, made-to-order Southern breakfast or build an appetite for the delicious complimentary afternoon tea, cookies, and snacks. (Ask about the fixed-price, three-course dinners served Thursday–Sunday, prepared by Chef Kacia Duncan, a New England Culinary Institute grad.) It's hard to imagine how innkeepers, Susan and Jeff Curtis and Anne and Nat Burkhardt, could possibly do more to make guests feel welcome and utterly pampered. The inn is closed December 21–February 1; open Thursday–Sunday in February; and open full-time beginning March 1. • *810 Elk Mountain Scenic Highway, Asheville, NC 28804,* ☎ *(828) 255-0690* • *www.sourwoodinn.com* • *$$–$$$*

WindDancers Lodge and Llama Treks • Set on 270 secluded acres of mountainous land just a short drive west from Asheville, this unique property features nine spacious suites in three lodges. The artfully decorated rooms have such amenities as whirlpool tubs for two with separate showers, fireplaces, comfortable sitting areas, and balconies with log rocking chairs. (Two lodges—the Hickory and Maple—feature kitchens fully stocked for make-your-own breakfasts, while guests in the Llama Lodge are served a hot breakfast.) Balcony views are of pastures dotted with llamas against a panoramic backdrop of seven misty mountain ridges. WindDancers keeps the llama herd for its trekking service. These shy, gentle animals carry provisions for guided lunch, dinner, or overnight hikes, all of which are available for a reasonable charge. (Don't overlook this lodge just because you don't go for llamas. When you first meet one, it's hard not to be fascinated by their huge, expressive eyes, downy wool, and gentle ways.) WindDancer's finest feature is the graciousness of its hosts. The Livengood's (Donna & Gale, plus son Greg & his wife, Susan) are some of the warmest, most knowledgeable, and helpful innkeepers you'll encounter. • *1966 Martins Creek Road, Clyde, NC 28721,* ☎ *(828) 627-6986 or 1-877-627-3330, www.winddancersnc.com • $$–$$$*

The Wright Inn • Situated in Montford, Asheville's neighborhood of grand historic homes, The Wright Inn is a Queen Anne-style Victorian home as lovely now as when it was built in 1899. Surrounded by award-winning gardens, the inn welcomes visitors with a wraparound porch and spacious gazebo. A step inside is a step back in time, as period antiques, rich furnishings, and fresh flowers from the garden adorn the inn. Of the 11 rooms, three are suites and include fireplaces, whirlpool baths, CD players, TVs, and high-speed Internet connections. All rooms have a private bath. Behind the home, the three-bedroom carriage house features two full baths, dining and living rooms, and a galley kitchen, making it ideal for families or couples seeking space and solitude. Innkeepers Mark and Vicki Maurer offer a warm welcome with an afternoon wine social. They also prepare a hot, three-course breakfast each morning. Guests are welcome to use the inn's bicycles. • *25 Pearson Drive, Asheville, NC 28801,* ☎ *(828) 251-0789 or 1-800-552-5724 • www.wrightinn.com • $$–$$$$*

Dine Well

Downtown Asheville has an excellent mix of restaurants, ranging from traditional, upscale, watch-your-manners dining to unusual, even funky, spots nurtured by the city's free-thinking (and acting) community. Put this outstanding cuisine together with the city's strollable streets and you have a recipe for a great evening out. If you're staying in Asheville, you'll still want to consider the great restaurants in nearby towns, where the cuisine and service are just as special.

Early Girl Eatery • Nestled among the row of galleries and shops on Wall Street, Early Girl Eatery is just the spot for a pause during your stroll through the fabulous art of Asheville. The fare—call it nouveau-Southern—features traditional Southern elements with unusual twists. For example: Aunt Mabel will love the biscuits yet may raise an eyebrow at the vegetarian herb-cream gravy smothering them. (One bite and she'll be hooked.) All food is made from scratch with fresh produce and organic ingredients. In addition to a full range of breakfasts, Early Girl offers homemade soups, salads, and sandwiches, as well as such tempting dinner entrées as shrimp rice and okra beignets, and pan-fried mountain trout. The setting is relaxed and casual. • *8 Wall Street, Asheville,* ☎ *(828) 259-9292.*

Gabrielle's at Richmond Hill • Thought by many to serve the finest cuisine in the region, Gabrielle's is set in the grand Richmond Hill Inn. Chef Perry Hendrix offers Modern-American cuisine on a seasonal menu, with such selections as striped bass roasted with salsa, asparagus, lobster, and meyer lemon; and roasted duck breast with wild risotto, rosemary poached pear, and black pepper foie gras sauce. Accompanying such fare is a selection of more than 200 vintages. (The list has earned *Wine Spectator's* prestigious Award of Excellence.) Dessert? How does apple 'Tarte Tatin' with buttermilk ice cream and Earl Grey caramel sound? The food is exceptional, and the service is top-notch. Diners can view the mountains and city in a serene atmosphere, thanks in part to a pianist who plays most evenings. Jackets recommended, reservations required. Open daily for dinner except Tuesdays. • *87 Richmond Hill Drive, Asheville,* ☎ *(828) 252-7313*

Horizons • The Grove Park Inn's formal dining room provides a total-sensory experience, including smell, taste, hearing (the hushed silence of people dining in a historic setting), and sight (the nighttime view of downtown Asheville in the valley below). Expect an elegant evening: white linen service, fine china, and a wine selection that's earned *Wine Spectator's* exclusive Award of Excellence. Horizons serves a prix fixe, four-course menu with seasonal selections. Starters may include items like roasted Vidalia onion, served with sweetbreads, morel mushrooms, and Clemson Blue Cheese; two soup options, including Horizons' signature lobster bisque; and several salad choices. Entrées include fish, game, beef, and vegetarian ingredients. (If it's on the menu, try the salmon crusted with whole grain mustard and served with beet couscous.) For dessert try the Rose Hip Brûlée, which is, in a word, divine. Dress well—jackets required for men • *290 Macon Avenue, Asheville, NC 28804,* ☎ *(828) 252-2711.*

Laughing Seed • Meat-eaters who swallow their prejudices and sample the entirely vegetarian fare at this Asheville institution have the last laugh over those who dismiss the café without investigation. Laughing Seed's food is outstanding, with flavors that dance on your pallet like a happy child. The creative menu includes dishes like "Thai Red Curry," which is a spicy vegetable and tofu dish in a red-curry and coconut-milk sauce served over brown rice. Included in the mix are broccoli, carrots, red and green bell peppers, and shitake mushrooms. The "Laughing Chili Bowl" is a black bean chili served over a bed of brown rice and topped with organic smoked yogurt cheese. It comes with a corn bread muffin and can be spiced to your liking with the café's "five-alarm salsa." The menu is extensive, with numerous appetizers, soups, salads, sandwiches, entrées, and even treats from the juice bar. Expect a wait. Open for lunch and dinner daily except Tuesdays. • *40 Wall Street, Asheville,* ☎ *(828) 252-3445.*

The Market Place Restaurant • With nods from such media as the *New York Times, Food & Wine,* and *Southern Living,* this restaurant is one of Asheville's finest choices for an elegant, sophisticated meal. Owner Mark Rosenstein opened Market Place in 1979 and continues, day after day, to serve meals that add to the restaurant's reputation. The seasonal menus are built on classic cuisine. Expect dishes that use ingredients found in the Western North Carolina Mountains. For example, you may find meats and game smoked with local apple wood or desserts topped with Biltmore Estate berries. Appetizers include the renowned "Market Place Crispy Potato Cake" made with goat cheese, quince and mustard applesauce, and topped with a garlic cream sauce. Try the sautéed halibut entrée, served with risotto cake, seasonal vegetables, and an organic apple and carrot sauce. Honored by *Wine Spectator* magazine, Market Place Restaurant has hundreds of exquisite vintages. Reservations recommended but not required. Open for dinner daily except Sunday. • *20 Wall Street, Asheville,* ☎ *(828) 252-4162*

Mount Pisgah Inn Restaurant • The food is good, the location even better. Set 5,000 feet above sea level on the Blue Ridge Parkway, this restaurant features glass walls in the main dining room that serve up panoramic scenes of the mountains. The casual atmosphere makes this a convenient stop for travelers on the parkway, and a steady stream of hungry folks flows in for breakfast, lunch, and dinner. Entrées include fresh mountain trout baked or charbroiled in lemon butter sauce and filleted at your table, and fettuccini tossed in a garlic butter sauce with chicken, spinach, tomatoes, and mush-

rooms. The lunch menu includes a number of sandwiches and salads. Open seven days a week, from 7:30 A.M.–9 P.M., April–October. (Call for April and May hours). • *BRP Milepost 408, Waynesville,* ☎ *(828) 235-8228*

Mountain Magnolia Inn • Dining in this lovingly restored 1868 Victorian house feels like being a guest in a good friend's home. There are far fewer tables than you'll find in most restaurants, and the relatively small number of patrons, combined with the soft lighting—provided in part by the fireplace and candles—makes for an intimate evening. (Warm-weather dining on the outdoor patio is a pleasure, too.) Add in the cuisine and wine selection and you have a recipe for a memorable evening. Touting "creative American cuisine," Mountain Magnolia prepares a variety of appetizers, soups, salads, entrées, and desserts made fresh daily, many with locally grown ingredients. The inn's popular "Mountain Magnolia Trout" is especially rewarding—locally grown trout sautéed with white-wine butter, mushrooms, tomatoes, and green onions and served with herb-smashed potatoes and French-cut green beans with sautéed onions and toasted almonds. Make reservations well in advance. • *204 Lawson Street, Hot Springs,* ☎ *(828) 622-3543*

Point of View • With seating for just 75 guests, reservations go quickly at this popular Hickory Nut Gorge restaurant. While the restaurant may not win any awards for interior design, it might just capture one for its signature "Mountain Trout Meuniere," a fresh-caught trout pan-sautéed in a lemon-butter sauce and topped with roasted almonds. Other selections include beef, lamb, veal, and fowl. Owners Rhonda Boyd and Brenda Hoyle proudly cook up these hot, fresh entrées as guests enjoy the lovely view of Lake Lure and the surrounding mountains. Dinner served nightly and reservations are suggested. • *Route 64/74A, 1.5 miles east of Route 9 at Buffalo Shoals Road, Lake Lure,* ☎ *(828) 625-4380*

Rezaz • Conveniently located at the edge of Biltmore Village, Rezaz serves up Mediterranean cuisine in a stylish, contemporary-bistro atmosphere. Appetizer selections include the divine shitake potato gnocchi, and "Merguez" (grilled lamb and currant sausage with a roasted-grape and port-wine sauce). For an entrée, order the "Paella Catalonia," which is saffron rice topped with shrimp, mussels, clams, braised duck, and chorizo tossed in soffrito & grilled lemons. Other dinner entrées include a range of sea and land dishes, and the wait staff is exceptionally knowledgeable about recommending the correct Spanish wine to complement the meal. Open for lunch and dinner Monday–Saturday. (The lunch menu is lighter with sandwiches, salads, and less-filling entrées.) • *28 Hendersonville Road, Asheville* ☎ *(828) 277-1510.*

Salsa • Definitely not your corner Mexican joint, Salsa serves up heaping portions of Mexican and Caribbean cuisine creatively prepared to order and served with an exciting array of salsas. This place is authentic. Explore items such as patacones and empanadas, or opt for a new approach to old favorites like burritos, quesadillas, and tostadas. This cheerful, colorful, casual café always includes a variety of vegetarian

selections in its daily specials. Arrive early or expect a big wait at this popular eatery, as it's just a few steps around the corner from Pack Place, and there are only 75 seats. If there's a line, join it. The food and friendly service will make the wait worthwhile. Open for lunch and dinner, Monday–Saturday. • *6 Patton Avenue, Asheville,* ☎ *(828) 252-9805.*

Tupelo Honey Cafe • A big hit with locals, Tupelo Honey is a taste of upscale Southern cooking in the heart of downtown Asheville. Lively chatter and clatter set the tone in the Charleston-esque café. The menu—put together by owner Sharon Schott and executive chef, Brian Sonoskus—features traditional Southern fare with a twist. For example, the entrée, Country Catfish, is a Cajun catfish topped with green tomato salsa and served over summer succotash. Other enticing selections include "Eggs Crawley" (sautéed crab cakes topped with poached eggs, asparagus, and hollandaise); a grilled peanut butter and banana sandwich; and a shrimp and grits dish with goat cheese. Breakfast and lunch are served daily beginning at 9 A.M., except for Monday when the restaurant is closed. Dinner is served only on Friday and Saturday nights. The breakfast menu, including the wildly popular Sweet Potato Pancakes, is available throughout the day. Reservations are not accepted, so come early. • *12 College Street, Asheville,* ☎ *(828) 255-4863.*

Zambra • Slip into the sultry Moroccan atmosphere of Zambra and lose yourself in tapas and entrées from faraway lands. Order the peppercorn-encrusted flank steak topped with a tomato and herb-beurre bane

Beer Here?

Yep. And how. Asheville is home to several fine microbreweries that produce outstanding ales in small batches. A few eatery/brewery combinations worth sipping, er...slipping, into include **Jack of the Wood**, 95 Patton Avenue, Asheville, ☎ (828) 252-5445; and **Asheville Pizza and Brewing Company**, 675 Merrimon Avenue, Asheville, ☎ (828) 254-5339. In addition, two microbreweries, **Highland Brewing** and **French Broad River Brewing,** offer a fine selection of stouts and ales available from many area restaurants and bars.

and served over oranges and roasted sweet potatoes, or the sautéed scallops with crushed chilis, smoked bacon, shitake, peas, and tomatoes tossed with a blue-cheese beurre blanc. The crisp calamari is also outstanding. The interior is gypsy hideaway, the taste is wonderfully exotic, and the location is downtown Asheville. Reservations recommended but not required. Open Monday–Saturday for dinner. • *85 West Walnut Street, Asheville, ☎ (828) 232-1060.*

Picnic Packing

• Locals love the **Blue Moon Bakery & Café,** 60 Biltmore Avenue, Asheville, ☎ (828) 252-6063, and it's no wonder. Ultra-fresh breads, sandwiches, soups, pizza, focaccia, and oh-so-irresistible desserts. Sit inside or outdoors to watch the world go by in downtown Asheville, or have your sandwiches packed for the trail. • Everything served at the **West End Bakery,** 757 Haywood Road, in West Asheville, ☎ (828) 252-9378, is made from scratch with 100% organic flour and the freshest ingredients available. Sandwiches are available on a wide variety of breads, and the bakery packs a mean picnic for the trail, including delicious dessert selections.

Just Desserts

The **Old Europe Coffee House,** 18 Battery Park Avenue, Asheville, ☎ (828) 252-0001, on the west side of downtown serves up homemade European desserts on silver trays. The chocolate selection is delightful. • Chocoholics in recovery had better steer clear of **The Chocolate Fetish**, 36 Haywood Street, Asheville, ☎ (828) 258-2353, an award-winning chocolate shop that serves American- and European-style truffles homemade with fresh ingredients. Little-known fact: the word "decadent" was first uttered here. • **True Confections,** Grove Arcade, 1 Page Avenue, Asheville, ☎ (828) 350-9480, sells an amazing selection of cookies, cakes, pies, and sweet breads baked in the shop. The desserts go perfectly with the shop's locally roasted coffees, espressos, and whole-leaf teas. • While they don't serve desserts, they make delicious coffees at Asheville's **Double Decker Coffee Co.,** 41 Biltmore Avenue, ☎ (828) 255-0441, housed in a red, English double-decker bus.

A Long-Weekend Itinerary

Day One

After breakfast at your inn or B&B, swing by **Blue Moon Bakery & Café** (page 382) to purchase a picnic lunch and liquid refreshments. Then take your supplies and fresh legs to hike the six-mile loop on the **Cat Gap Loop** and the **John Rock trails** (page 343) in the Pisgah National Forest. Picnic on the summit of John Rock. After lunch, work up a good sweat completing the hike, and then head to **Sliding Rock** (page 355) for some wet, refreshing fun.

When you tire of sunning yourself, getting wet, then sunning some more, pack up and spend the remainder of the afternoon browsing the shops in scenic **Brevard** (page 371) or touring the historic **Cradle of Forestry** (page 358). Return to your inn and prepare for dinner at **Salsa** (page 381). After dinner, take in the vibrant city streets of downtown Asheville before returning to your inn to retire for the day.

Day Two

After an early breakfast at your inn, head to **Backcountry Outdoors** (page 349) south of Asheville to rent mountain bikes and grab a map of **Dupont State Forest**, where you can ride either the slickrock on the **Big Rock** and **Cedar Rock** trails (page 346) or along Dupont's many forest roads. After a couple of hours, return the bikes and grab an early lunch at Asheville's **Laughing Seed Café** (page 379).

Head down Biltmore Avenue with a quick stop at **Double Decker Coffee Co.** (page 382) en route to the **Biltmore Estate** (page 362), where you'll spend the remainder of the day. Been there, done that? Then, give your feet a rest and do some **back roads touring** (page 361) in your car. Try the **Hot Springs Loop** (page 361) with a detour to **Max Patch** (page 362) for tremendous summit views.

As the sun wanes, return to your inn to shower and prepare for dinner at **Gabrielle's at Richmond Hill** (page 379). Hit the hay.

Asheville CVB

Be sure to shop Wall Street in Asheville

Day Three

Linger over breakfast to soak in your vacation, and then head to the **Grove Park Inn Spa** (page 372) for their "Fire, Rock, Water, & Light" treatment. Fully refreshed, return to downtown Asheville to browse the city's **antiques shops** (page 359), **art & crafts galleries** (page 360), as well as its many **shops** (page 369). Break for lunch at **Tupelo Honey Café** (page 381) and continue your retail therapy until it's time to return to the real world.

Additional Information

For additional dining, accommodations, and sightseeing information, including the dates of special events, contact:

The Asheville Convention & Visitors Bureau operates the Asheville Visitor Center, 151 Haywood Street, Asheville, NC 28801, ☎ (828) 258-6103 or 1-800-280-0005, *www.exploreasheville.com*, at Exit #4C off Interstate 240, which is fully stocked with brochures, fliers, and an exceptionally helpful staff. Open Monday–Friday, 8:30 A.M.–5:30 P.M.; Saturday and Sunday, 9 A.M.–5 P.M.

Black Mountain-Swannanoa Chamber of Commerce operates a visitor center, 201 East State Street, Black Mountain, NC 28711, ☎ (828) 669-2300 or 1-800-669-2301, *www.blackmountain.org*, open Monday–Saturday, 9 A.M.–5 P.M., except from November–March. Call for winter hours.

The **Visitor Information Center for Historic Hendersonville & Flat Rock,** 201 South Main Street, Hendersonville, North Carolina 28792, ☎ (828) 693-9708 or 1-800-828-4244, *www.historichendersonville.org*, is open weekdays 9 A.M.–5 P.M.; weekends, from 10 A.M.–5 P.M.

The **Transylvania County Tourism Development Authority** operates a visitor center at 35 West Main Street, Brevard, NC 28712, ☎ 1-800-648-4523, *www.visitwaterfalls.com*, open weekdays, 9 A.M.–5 P.M.; Saturday, 10 A.M.–4 P.M.

The **Hot Springs Information Center,** on Bridge Street across from the post office, is housed in a red caboose and is open Monday–Thursday, 8 A.M.–3:30 P.M. For more information, call ☎ 1-888-446-8774.

*Nature is the one place where miracles not
only happen, but happen all the time.*

– *Thomas Wolfe*

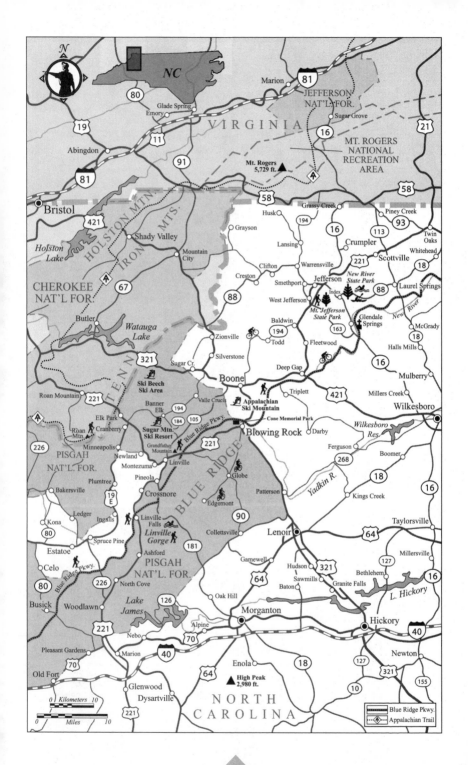

The High Country, North Carolina

Including the Blue Ridge Parkway, Blowing Rock, Boone, Valle Crucis, Banner Elk, Grandfather Mountain, Linville, and West Jefferson

Tucked into North Carolina's northwestern corner, the High Country is a rugged region of steep mountains, deep gorges, dense forests, and fast-moving streams that form the headwaters of four of the state's major rivers: the Watauga, New, Yadkin, and Catawba. With valleys ranging in elevation from 3,000 to 3,700 feet and peaks rising above 5,000 feet, the High Country is aptly named. You'll find little land that's flat here. The terrain is constantly rising and falling—most often in dramatic leaps—and on bike, foot, or by car, you can expect to grit your teeth as you go up, up, up and then down, down, down.

Bordered by Tennessee to the west, Virginia to the north, and the North Carolina foothills and Piedmont to the east and south, the region's remoteness, which made for slow settlement in the 18th and 19th centuries, is what draws many travelers here today. In fact, Watauga County, the center of tourism activity in the region, takes its name from a Cherokee word meaning "land of the beyond." Here the only skyscrapers are the Blue Ridge Mountains; suburban sprawl, stultified city air, and the pressed daily grind exist as mere memories from a distant place.

The first permanent settlers were the Cherokee, who farmed the rich, loamy soil of the valley

Linville Peak in the rugged High Country

Hugh Morton

Malcolm Campbell

The Blue Ridge Parkway passes through the High Country

floors and traded extensively with other tribes from as far away as the Ohio River Valley and Gulf Coast. By the mid 18th Century, the first white pioneers began settling the region. Known informally amongst settlers as "The Lost Province," the High Country became home to fiercely independent, self-sufficient people who in 1772—four years before Thomas Jefferson's *Declaration of Independence*—drafted the *Articles of the Watauga Association* to create the first majority-rule system of American democracy. Accordingly, mountain settlers weren't keen on answering to the English Crown. During the Revolutionary War, men from the area joined settlers from the Tennessee Mountains to form the Overmountain Men, a brigade that marched down into the Piedmont to defeat the British at Kings Mountain in 1780.

The 19th Century brought more permanent settlers to the area, as well as the first summer residents, wealthy "flatlanders." These seasonal visitors built summer homes or boarded in large resort hotels or boarding houses in villages like Blowing Rock, Linville, and Banner Elk. The Civil War had far less effect on this region than elsewhere in the Carolinas. The independent spirit of the mountaineers and the fact that few residents of the High Country had slaves explain why a number of men refused to take up arms for the Confederacy. In fact, some mountain residents must have known and ignored the fact that the surrounding craggy peaks and dense forests served as hiding places for escaped slaves traveling on the Underground Railroad.

By the late 19th Century, the bounty of hemlock, oak, hickory, and chestnut trees drew the logging industry, which wasted little time felling the old-growth timber. Railroads built lines into the mountains to transport this wood, as well as minerals and ore mined from the hillsides. By the start of World War II, however, the trains stopped running because the lumber resources were exhausted and better roads had been built.

The Boonies

The same characteristics that slowed settlement of the High Country—rugged land and a hostile Indian presence—are what drew early American trailblazer Daniel Boone here. Boone kept a hunting cabin on what is today the campus of Appalachian State University, and he earned income leading early mountain settlers over the Wilderness Road, a route he helped forge.

Today tourism is a major industry, and the area draws vacationers year-round. Summer is full of concerts and festivals; fall and spring dazzle with kaleidoscopes of colors; and winter bustles with skiers. Throughout the year, you'll find Charlotteans & Atlantans "in the know," as well as visitors from much farther away who discovered the area while touring the Blue Ridge Parkway.

With ample public land—the Pisgah National Forest, several large rivers, and four ski resorts—the High Country abounds with outdoor sports, while the pleasures of town—galleries, museums, shops, and restaurants—are just as plentiful. Resting after an active day comes naturally in the fresh mountain air. Here you can rock gently on one of the region's many front porches or in front of a wood fire before retiring for a restful night's sleep.

The Way Around

The High Country is home to dozens of small and even-smaller towns. While isolated communities remain (particularly in the Northern High Country), much of the area has opened to tourism. The High Country Host (a visitors bureau) identifies six counties as the High Country, but this chapter focuses primarily on three—Watauga, Ashe, and Avery. Here you'll find the major vacation villages of Linville, Blowing Rock, Boone, and Banner Elk, as well as the majority of lodging, dining, and shopping options.

Just a short drive apart, Boone and Blowing Rock are the heart of the region. The national media regularly lists both among "America's best small towns;" however, they are actually quite different. As the county seat and largest town in the region, **Boone** is the area's commercial center. But rest assured that the commercial sprawl you encounter along Route 321

Boone CVB

Watch for traffic

southeast of town is not all there is. Boone's real character appears in its historic downtown, centered primarily on **King** and **Depot streets**, where there are good restaurants, artists' studios, crafts galleries, and unique shops.

Boone is named for Daniel Boone, who kept a hunting cabin in the late 1700s on the present-day grounds of Appalachian State University. The town evolved slowly. In 1800, an early settler named Jordan Council opened a general store just beneath Howard's Knob, but it wasn't until 1850 that Boone had enough settlers to found the Boone Post Office. Officially, Boone didn't incorporate until 1872. Today, as home to the university and its 12,000 students (who endow the town with vibrant hipness), Boone positively bustles.

The resort town of **Blowing Rock** is just a few miles south of Boone on Route 321. If Boone has a few hairs out of place, Blowing Rock is perfectly coiffed. To many of its well-dressed, credit-card-at-the-ready visitors, Blowing Rock *is* the High Country. Indeed, this village was founded for the same reason many people visit today: vacationing. Beginning in the mid 1800s and hitting full steam in the 1880s, lowcountry planters and wealthy flatlanders began visiting in the summer to escape the heat and pesky mosquitoes. By the turn of the century, Blowing Rock had several large hotels and a full, summer social calendar. A similar migration occurs today. The village's year-round population of 1,500 climbs to more than 6,500 each summer and fall.

Blowing Rock sits on a high ridge that straddles the Eastern Continental Divide, a serrated, north-south-running bump that "divides" streams flowing east from those flowing west.

The actual Blowing Rock

Named for a rock formation that juts out over the Johns River Gorge and that catches winds funneling up the gorge, the village of Blowing Rock is actually separate from the rock, which is just south of the village on Route 321. To see the village's namesake, you'll have to pony up an admission fee; the rock is privately owned. The views are sublime, but if you don't make it, you're not alone. Many Blowing Rock visitors never visit the attraction, enchanted as they are with the great restaurants, shops, and galleries lining **Main Street**.

Northwest of Boone and Blowing Rock on Route 194, **Valle Crucis** (Latin for "valley of the cross") is a small village tucked into the surrounding mountains and rolling hills. In the late 1700s, early settlers Samuel Hix, Joseph Mast, and Dr. Ezekial Baird came to the area to build farmsteads and churches, some of which stand today. The village has a number of buildings on the National Register of Historic Places, and the entire valley is a North Carolina Rural Historic District (the state's first). Originally known as the Baird Community, the settlement changed names to Valle Crucis in 1842, when Stillman Ives, an Episcopalian bishop, climbed a ridge, looked down on the valley, and noted that the streams and land formed the shape of a crucifix. Ives, who came to the area to start a divinity school, purchased 3,000 acres and launched the first Anglican monastic order since the Reformation in the 1500s. The school and monastery disbanded in 1852, but the Episcopalian presence continued. Today several religious retreats operate in the valley.

What's Happening?

Upon arrival, pick up a copy of the *Mountain Times,* a free weekly covering community news and entertainment happenings in the High Country. It's distributed everywhere in boxes, as well as on counters in shops, inns, and restaurants. Content is also online at: *www.mountaintimes.com.*

Valle Crucis has several bed and breakfasts—some with fine dining—and a smattering of artists' studios. The big draw is the Mast General Store, a National Historic Landmark and a destination unto itself. This old-timey mercantile store carries everything from dime-store candy to high-end shoes.

West of Valle Crucis on Route 194, **Banner Elk** is an attractive village that serves as base camp to North Carolina's two largest ski areas—Beech Mountain and Sugar Mountain. First settled around 1825, Banner Elk became a tourist destination around the turn of the century as flatlanders constructed summer homes or visited newly built hotels and boarding houses. Today in the winter, skiers and snowboarders populate the shops, restaurants, and lodgings lining the valley and in the summer, you'll find golfers, rafters, and cyclists doing the same.

Named for its resemblance to a reclined, bearded man, **Grandfather Mountain** is off of Route 221 just southwest of Blowing Rock. This privately owned mountain—held in the MacRae family since 1885—is

Sugar Mountain

a scenic attraction, nature preserve, and International Biosphere Reserve. (More than 40 rare or endangered species live in the 16 ecosystems on the mountain.) Grandfather Mountain also has a nature museum; a wildlife habitat with black bears, mountain lions, and deer; and a suspension bridge across an 80-foot chasm.

A mountain lion on Grandfather Mountain

A number of small villages make up the **Southern High Country,** including **Linville, Pineola, Crossnore, Spruce Pine,** and **Little Switzerland**. There are many upscale condominium resorts, golf courses, country clubs, and second-home communities here, plus a smattering of shops and inns. A handful of gem mines surround Spruce Pine, home to the North Carolina Museum of Minerals.

The **Northern High Country** is a broad but sparsely populated area where tourism plays second fiddle to agribusiness. Rural scenery—pastures, woods, weathered barns—reigns supreme, and life is measured by planting seasons rather than by Daytimer pages. The state's largest concentration of Christmas tree farms is here, and the big harvest season is

Christmas trees in the Northern High Country

just after Thanksgiving. The **New River** flows slowly north through the northern High Country into Virginia. Located on Route 221, **West Jefferson** is the largest town in the area with just more than 1,000 residents. The town is home to a small gathering of excellent antiques and crafts shops, as well as to the Ashe County Cheese Company, the state's only cheese-making operation. Nearby, **Jefferson** features a 1904 courthouse that operates as a visitor center and museum. East of Jefferson and close to the Blue Ridge Parkway, the area around **Glendale Springs** annually attracts thousands of visitors to the Churches of the Frescoes, two small Episcopal churches with frescoes painted by Ben Long.

Weather

In addition to the natural beauty and slower pace of life, the weather is a primary reason why the High Country is such a popular destination. Summertime is practically mosquito-free, and daytime temperatures rarely exceed the mid 80s, with evening lows in the upper 50s. Fall is spectacular with clear, crisp days. Highs are in the lower 60s with overnight lows around 40, making for perfect fire weather. Cold winter temperatures make the area a draw for skiers, with January highs averaging in the 30s and overnight lows dipping into the low 20s. While snow cover is not guaranteed in the winter, you should be prepared for frozen precipitation during your stay. Spring comes late with daytime temperatures not reaching the 60s until May.

Getting to the High Country

✈ **By Air:** The **Asheville Regional Airport**, ☎ (828) 684-2226, *www.flyavl.com*, features nonstop flights to and from six major airports on various commuter airlines, plus USAirways. Rental cars and ground transportation are available; the airport is roughly 100 miles from Boone, about a 2.5-hour drive. ◆ An easier and slightly shorter drive (only two hours) is from **Charlotte Douglas International Airport**, ☎ (704) 359-4013, *www.flycdia.com*, which is served by all major airlines and rental car companies.

🚌 **By Car: From Atlanta,** take Interstate 85 north to Spartanburg, SC, where you take Interstate 26 west to Route 74. Follow Route 74 east to Route 221 north into Linville, where you take Route 105 north to Boone. Expect a five-hour drive. **From Charlotte,** take Interstate 85 south to Route 321 north into Blowing Rock and Boone. Expect a two-hour drive. **From Raleigh,** take Interstate 40 west to Winston-Salem and then Route 421 north to Boone. Expect a 3.5-hour drive.

P l a y   H a r d

W i d e   O p e n

Thank your lucky stars if you plan to hike, bike, paddle, ski, swim, climb, or ride horses in the High Country; numerous outdoor playgrounds exist to pursue these and many other adventurous sports. The following are the area's major, multi-sport public lands.

The 505,000-acre **Pisgah National Forest** stretches from south of Asheville to the High Country. To manage this vast wilderness, the National Forest Service divided the land into three "bite-sized" ranger districts, two of which are at your doorstep. The **Grandfather Ranger District,** 109 East Lawing Lane, Nebo, (828) 652-2144, encompasses 189,000 acres of some of the East Coast's most-scenic and rugged terrain, particularly in **Linville Gorge,** the deepest gorge east of the Mississippi River. Formed by the scouring action of the **Linville River,** the gorge measures 12 miles long with sides that tower more than 1,900 feet above the river. The federally protected, 12,000-acre **Linville Gorge Wilderness Area** has nearly 40 miles of hiking trails along the steep walls of the gorge and

Linville Gorge

Who was Linville?

Linville, Linville Falls, Linville Gorge...the High Country pays hefty tribute to William Linville, one of its earliest white explorers. Linville and his family settled the area in the mid 18th Century, though not to the pleasure of the Cherokee. The tribe attacked William and his son, John, in 1766 in the gorge that bears his name. William died but John survived.

down to the Linville River below. The eastern wall of the gorge, formed by Jonas Ridge, is more popular, and hikers and climbers go bananas over the various trails and rock formations at **Table Rock.** To reach Table Rock Picnic Area, exit the Blue Ridge Parkway at Milepost 312 and take Route 181 south. At the intersection with Route 183, continue south on Route 181 three miles to Gingercake Road/Forest Road 210. Turn right and keep to the left at the first fork through the Gingercake Acres neighborhood. Forest Road 210 turns to gravel and continues to an intersection with Forest Road 99, where you turn right to reach Table Rock.

Other outdoor playgrounds in the Grandfather Ranger District include **Wilson Creek Wilderness Area,** a 5,000-acre spread of rugged land with numerous streamside trails. **Wilson Creek**, which forms on the flanks of Calloway Peak (the highest peak on Grandfather Mountain), is a National Wild and Scenic River that flows 23 miles through a narrow, rocky valley to the Johns River in Caldwell County. Paddlers are awed by the spring flows on Wilson Creek, while hikers and mountain bikers are drawn to the more than 75 miles of backcountry trails. This is also a popular fishing area. There is a new visitor center, (828) 759-0005, located on Brown Mountain Beach Road in Collettsville. The center is closed in winter.

The **Appalachian District's Toecane Ranger Station**, Route 19-East Bypass, Burnsville, (828) 682-6146, oversees more than 75,000 acres of national forest land along the Tennessee

State line. Much of this district, including 6,684-foot **Mount Mitchell**—the highest peak east of the Mississippi—is profiled in the Asheville chapter, but 6,285-foot **Roan Mountain** is closer to the High Country than to Asheville. This stunning, bald ridgeline straddles Tennessee. In fact, **Roan Mountain State Park**, 1-800-250-8620, is located on Route

The balds on Roan Mountain

143 in Tennessee. The area is popular with hikers, cyclists, and cross-country skiers. The 2,100-mile **Appalachian Trail** passes over the mountain. To reach Roan Mountain, take Route 194 west from Boone to Banner Elk, and then Route 19E north into Tennessee, where you'll turn left on Route 143 to Roan Mountain. (You can also reach the mountain by taking Route 261 north from Bakersville, and then Route 143 north.)

> **The Color Purple**
>
> Each spring, more than 600 acres of Catawba rhododendron, the largest patch of wild rhododendron in the world, explode in purple on Roan Mountain. The one-mile **Roan Mountain Gardens Trail** winds through the colorful plants.

Several parks along the **Blue Ridge Parkway** offer multi-sport adventures. **Moses H. Cone Memorial Park** (Milepost 294) has 3,500 acres of land and more than 26 miles of historic carriage roads for hiking, horseback riding, and cross-country skiing. **Julian Price Memorial Park** (Milepost 297) features 4,300 acres at the base of Grandfather Mountain, with miles of hiking trails, and paddling opportunities on 47-acre Julian Price Lake. The 440-acre **Linville Falls Recreation Area** has a visitor center located on an access road off Milepost 316 with restrooms, a small gift shop, and a large map outlining three hiking trails that lead to views of the spectacular upper and lower waterfalls. North from Blowing Rock on the parkway between Mileposts 238 and 244, **Doughton Park** is a 7,000-acre spread of pastures, valleys, and ridgelines with more than 30 miles of trails for hikers and several creeks popular with anglers. There are also horseback trails in the park.

The 1,500 acres of rugged, rural land in the **New River State Park**, Wagoner Access Road, Jefferson, (336) 982-2587, surround the New River, which is actually the world's second-oldest river. (Egypt's Nile River is older.) There are hiking trails, but the big sports are paddling, tubing, swimming, and fishing in the gentle current. To reach the park, take Route 221 north through Jefferson to Route 88, onto which you turn right to travel east. Cross the New River and turn left on Wagoner Access Road (State Road 1590), which leads to the park office.

Mount Jefferson State Natural Area, State Road 1152, Jefferson, (336) 246-9653, is a 541-acre park dominated by Mount Jefferson, which rises more than 1,600 feet above the surrounding land. Mount Jefferson provides hikers, cyclists, and cross-country skiers a serene place to catch sunsets from the summit, where unobstructed views stretch across rural pastures, woods, and distant mountains. To reach the park, take Route 221 north to West Jefferson. After passing State Road 163 on the right, watch for the park sign on the right. Turn right onto Mount Jefferson State Park Road (State Road 1152) and continue 1.5 miles to the park entrance.

Mose H. Cone Memorial Park

Dayhiking

The High Country is a hiker's paradise. With so many great walks and hikes in every direction, you can't travel far without stumbling across a foot path.

Blue Ridge Parkway Trails

♦ Some of the easiest trails to reach from Boone and Blowing Rock are just off the Blue Ridge Parkway. While some of these hikes are in the Pisgah National Forest, they're listed here because the trailheads are in parking areas on the roadway. The following is just a sampling of trails that intersect with the parkway.

♦ Just south of Blowing Rock at Milepost 294, the **Moses H. Cone Memorial Park** is an excellent place to combine sightseeing with an easy hike along more than 25 miles of carriage roads. The carriage paths are multi-use—hikers, cross-country skiers, and horseback riders use them—and are wide enough for pleasant side-by-side walking. The paths wind through the estate's 3,500 acres of pastures, woods, and mountain ridges. Optimum times to visit are late spring and early summer, when the multitude of mountain laurel and rhododendron blooms with pink and purple flowers. Bring a picnic; the scenic land begs for a blanket. Park at the Moses H. Cone Manor and pick up the free trail map from the park ranger information desk inside.

♦ While the trail map is sufficient to create a full day's worth of loops within the park, a recommended hike is the six-mile out-and-back **Duncan Carriage Trail** down to Bass Lake. The mileage includes a 0.8-mile loop around picturesque Bass Lake, a 22-acre pond at the bottom of the 2.5-mile descent from Cone Manor. From the lake, you can look across the expansive pastures to the white, 20-room house high above. To begin the hike from the manor's front porch, turn right (facing downhill) on the paved trail and follow it to the signed intersection where you keep to the left on the dirt-and-rock path. Loop around Bass Lake and then retrace your steps to the parking area. The return trip is uphill; gauge your energy level before descending the entire way. To hike this trail going up for the first half, you can park at the **Bass Lake**

The Tanawha Trail

The 13.5-mile **Tanawha Trail**, which parallels the Blue Ridge Parkway from Price Lake to Beacon Heights (Milepost 304), provides excellent out-and-back hiking options from points along the parkway. "Tanawha" is Cherokee for "fabulous hawk," which is what the Native Americans called Grandfather Mountain. For a short, strenuous workout with excellent views, park at Wilson Creek Overlook near Milepost 303 and hike the Tanawha to Raven Rocks Overlook and back. Signs with feather icons show the way.

Entrance to the park, accessed off Route 221, roughly a mile south of Blowing Rock.

◆ On the opposite side of the Blue Ridge Parkway from Cone Manor, the three-mile **Flat Top Mountain** hike climbs past the Cone Family Cemetery to the summit of 4,558-foot Flat Top Mountain, where a lookout tower provides tremendous views of the surrounding mountains. To start, follow the road from Cone Manor past the stables to the parkway underpass. Turn right beyond the underpass and follow the carriage path through the pasture. Roughly a mile into the hike, you'll come across a short trail on the left that leads to the Cone Cemetery. The climb continues to the summit and the lookout tower that Moses Cone built for his wife's enjoyment. Retrace your steps to the car.

◆ The 4,300-acre **Julian Price Memorial Park** (Milepost 297) has a number of excellent hiking trails, ranging in difficulty from easy to strenuous. Pick up a free trail map from the ranger desk at Cone Manor (Milepost 294). The 2.5-mile **Price Lake Loop** is an easy, well-graded path around Price Lake that crosses several streams as it winds through an oak and pine forest. Rhododendron and mountain laurel line portions of the path, which is damp in places near the lake. ◆ From the Sim's Pond parking area (Milepost 296), the **Green Knob Trail** is a moderately strenuous, 2.3-mile loop that follows Sim's Creek, climbs through a pasture, and ascends 3,920-foot Green Knob. Fine views of Grandfather Mountain and Price Lake open up en route. After reaching the summit of Green Knob, continue the loop by descending a steep hill back to the parking area.

◆ The 5.5-mile **Boone Fork Trail** is a moderately strenuous loop that serves up generous helpings of open pastures, dense woods, rock outcroppings, and clear mountain streams. The trail, which starts at the Price Park picnic area (Milepost 296), ambles along Boone Fork, named for Jesse Boone (Daniel's nephew who settled here in the early 19th Century). Set out across the footbridge over the picturesque creek to the trail map sign, and head left on the trail for a counter-clockwise loop. The trail climbs through the woods to the Price Park Campground and continues to a fork where the Tanawha Trail breaks to the left. Bear right at all trail intersections to close the loop and to return to the parking area. En route, you'll cross several streams as you climb toward a rocky area that's great for a picnic.

◆ Further south on the Blue Ridge Parkway at Milepost 316, the **Linville Falls Recreation Area** offers a few short but rewarding hikes to outstanding views of Linville Falls. From the visitor center, the **Erwins View Trail** (a.k.a. the Linville Falls Trail) is a moderate 0.8-mile climb to Erwin's View. En route, you pass four overlooks. A half-mile up the trail, **Upper Falls Overlook** offers a view of the wide, gentle upper falls. After the Upper Falls, the Linville River fills a broad pool before narrowing into a rocky chute and dropping out of sight. Two-tenths of a mile further is the second overlook, **Chimney View,** where you catch the first glimpse of the 45-foot lower falls. This is a good spot to photograph both the upper and lower falls. The Erwins View Trail con-

NC Division of Tourism

Price Lake

NC Division of Tourism

Linville Falls

Some Grand Hikes

Grandfather Mountain, 2050 Blowing Rock Highway, Linville, ☎ (828) 733-2013 or 1-800-468-7325, *www.grandfather.com*, maintains 12 miles of hiking trails that wind

through the 3,000-acre, privately owned nature preserve. Several begin at the mountain's base on the Blue Ridge Parkway and climb to the summit of 5,964-foot Calloway Peak, the highest peak in the Blue Ridge Range. For a classic day hike—one guaranteed to burn off breakfast—try the 5.2-mile, out-and-back hike on the **Daniel Boone Scout Trail** to Calloway Peak. This path rises 2,000 feet over 2.6 miles. Near the top, ladders and metal rungs help hikers make it to the rocky summit. Park at Boone Fork Parking Area (Milepost 300) and follow the Tanawha Trail left for the trailhead. You'll need to purchase a $6 permit, available from Footsloggers in Boone or Blowing Rock (see *Local Outdoor Advice*) or from Grandfather Mountain (take Route 221 one mile south from Milepost 305). The permit comes with a map detailing the park's other trails. If you visit Grandfather Mountain, your admission is good for hiking the trails.

tinues to a fork to the left of which **Erwins View** provides a long-range vista of the falls and of Linville Gorge. To the right, **Gorge View Overlook** features a spectacular view of the Linville River flowing through Linville Gorge. ◆ You can also hike the one-mile **Plunge Basin Overlook Trail** and the 1.4-mile **Linville Gorge Trail**, which leads to the base of the falls. Both trails start on the opposite side of the Linville River from the visitor center.

◆ North of Blowing Rock, **E.B. Jeffress Park**, BRP Milepost 272, has two short hiking trails: the 1.2-mile **Cascades Nature Trail**, a self-guiding loop from the parking area through a hardwood forest to a waterfall on Falls Creek (exercise caution on the rocks at the top of the waterfall); and the short **Tompkins Knob Trail**, a half-mile loop from the parking area that encircles the historic, mid-19th-century Cool Spring Baptist Church. This log-constructed, open-air church was the scene of many 19th- and early 20th-century revivals, and the nearby Jesse Brown Cabin (circa 1850) was where the traveling evangelists would sleep.

◆ **Doughton Park**, between Mileposts 238 and 244, has more than 30 miles of trails through its 7,000 acres. This area was home to the Brinegar family in the late 19th and early 20th centuries, until the National Park Service acquired the land for the parkway. Their cabin remains and is popular with summer visitors who stop to see old hand-loom weaving demonstrations. There are several long trails within the park, including the strenuous 4.2-mile **Cedar Ridge Trail** and the moderate 7.5-mile **Bluff Mountain Trail**, both of which depart from the parking area. Also in the park: the five-mile **Flat Rock Ridge Trail**, the 3.3-mile **Basin Cove Trail**, and the 6.5-mile **Grassy Gap Fire Road Trail**.

Pisgah National Forest: Grandfather District

♦ The nearly 40 miles of trails in the **Linville Gorge Wilderness Area** wind through pure, rugged wilderness. There are good hiking trails on both the eastern and western rims of the gorge, as well as straight up the canyon along the Linville River. If you're up for a strenuous challenge, head to the Table Rock Picnic Area (see *Wide Open* for directions) and set out on the 5.6-mile **Shortoff Mountain Trail.** This rugged path passes the Chimneys, a popular rock-climbing area, and then winds through dense laurel and rhododendron before reaching a ridge-

The Hiker's Bible

Planning to do a lot of hiking in North Carolina? Pick up the definitive state hiking guide, *North Carolina Hiking Trails* by Allen de Hart (AMC Books). This $18.95 book is available in local bookshops.

line with expansive views. The trail drops steeply before entering the woods where it climbs again. Eventually, you'll reach rocky Shortoff Mountain, where you can look out across Linville Gorge and see Table Rock Mountain, your starting point, in the distance. To complete the 11.2-mile hike, retrace your steps. ♦ From the same picnic area, the two-mile, out-and-back **Table Rock Trail** to the summit of 3,909-foot Table Rock Mountain rewards you with outstanding 360-degree views of Linville Gorge. ♦ Also at the Table Rock Picnic Area, the 1.5-mile **Table Rock Loop Trail** is a moderate hike around Table Rock.

♦ The easiest trail into the gorge from the eastern rim is the **Spence Ridge Trail,** which departs from a parking area off Forest Road 210. This 1.7-mile trail descends steeply to the Linville River and the intersection with the **Linville Gorge Trail,** an 11.5-mile path that extends the length of the gorge. (The trail is on the far side of the river, so you'll have to wade across to hike it.) After hiking down and exploring the river's edge, retrace your steps to the car. To reach the Spence Ridge trail-head, follow directions to Table Rock (*Wide Open*) but instead of driving eight miles on Forest Road 210, drive roughly four miles to the parking areas on both sides of the road.

Malcolm Campbell

♦ **Wilson Creek Wilderness Area,** with its 75 miles of trails, is another excellent place to hike within the Grandfather District. While most trails have trailhead signs, few are blazed throughout their length, so be sure to travel with a map and compass as you head into this wild and scenic watershed. You'll have little trouble following the popular, six-mile **Wilson Creek Trail** as it winds through Wilson Creek Gorge with sheer rock cliffs high above. When it's hot, this is an excellent hike because of the many swimming holes along its length. The trailhead is on Route 90 north of Edgemont on the left. There's a signed parking area from which you set out.

♦ Other popular trails in the Wilson Creek Wilderness Area include the three-mile **Lost Cove Trail** and the 6.5-mile **Harper Creek Trail** to Harper Creek Falls. The best way to hike these and other trails here is to pick up a free map from the **Wilson Creek Wilderness Area Visitor Center**, (828) 759-0005, located on Brown Mountain Beach Road in Collettsville. (Closed in the winter.) You can also get trail information from any of the Pisgah National Forest ranger districts listed under *Local Outdoor Advice.*

Pisgah National Forest: Appalachian District, Toecane Ranger Station

♦ The Pisgah National Forest's Appalachian District borders Tennessee. Nowhere in the district is the hiking as scenic as it is on Roan Mountain, especially during late spring/early summer when the mountain laurel and rhododendron bloom. Located 45 minutes from Boone (see *Wide Open* for directions), **Roan Mountain** and the **Roan Mountain Highlands** feature several trails across the balds and through rhododendron patches. The 2,100-mile **Appalachian Trail** passes directly over the 6,285-foot summit and makes for outstanding out-and-back hikes from the parking area. (The trail south along the ridgeline into North Carolina serves up one expansive view after another.) ♦ For an easy stroll from the parking area, try the **Roan Mountain Gardens Trail,** a one-mile, partly paved loop through the rhododendron gardens. ♦ From the summit of Roan Mountain, the three-mile **Cloudland Trail** follows the crest of the mountain past the site of the Cloudland Hotel, which was built near the summit in 1885. The building fell into disrepair, and all that remains are a few scattered rocks from the foundation.

A Hike from Town

Need a break from shopping in Blowing Rock? Hit the village's **Glen Burney Trail**, a scenic, 1.6-mile path from Annie Cannon Park through the woods to Glen Mary Falls, a 55-foot waterfall. The trail also passes two smaller waterfalls—the Cascades and Glen Burney Falls—during its steep descent beside New Year's Creek. (The trail drops 800 vertical feet into the Johns River Gorge.) From Glen Mary Falls, retrace your steps to complete the 3.2-mile hike. To reach the trailhead from Main Street, take Laurel Lane to the parking area on the left just past the four-way stop.

Other Hiking

♦ In the northern High Country, **Mount Jefferson State Natural Area,** State Road 1152, Jefferson, (336) 246-9653, has two scenic trails worth exploring. The 0.3-mile **Summit Trail** departs from the parking area and ascends to the summit of 4,684-foot Mount Jefferson. From the summit, you can connect with the 1.1-mile **Rhododendron Trail,** a self-guiding trail with numbered stations highlighting various points of interest. (Pamphlets at the trailhead provide descriptions corresponding to the station numbers.) The loop begins at the summit and stretches along a ridge to Luther Rock, a rock outcropping with spectacular views of neighboring valleys and peaks. The trail then loops to return to the summit.

Mountain Biking

Mountain biking options on public land in the High Country range from forest roads to singletrack trails, all sharing a common denominator: They are rarely flat. In addition to trails on public land, there are popular places to ride on private land, but guidebooks generally do not mention them due to liability issues. So if the following sampling of rides fails to satisfy, ask the gear heads at the local bike shops for more options.

Sugar Mountain Resort, Inc.

◆ The **Pisgah National Forest** offers a number of great rides on forest roads, especially in the **Linville Gorge Wilderness Area.** Bikes are not allowed within the gorge itself. No matter: The forest roads are so steep in places that you'll get as much of a workout as you would on many singletrack trails. The long, winding forest roads on the eastern side of the gorge leading to the **Table Rock Picnic Area** are perfect for non-technical mountain biking. (See directions in *Wide Open.*) Except for occasional dust storms kicked up by passing motorists, the ride on **Forest Roads 210** and **99** through the forest along Jonas Ridge is pure pleasure. Gingercake Acres Road (Forest Road 210) is paved at first, then turns to gravel and dirt for eight miles to the intersection with Forest Road 99. Park at any of the small parking areas along Forest Road 210 and start pedaling. The final stretch on Forest Road 99 to the Table Rock Picnic Area is paved but steep. (You'll likely have to walk.) This is an excellent place to lock your bikes and hike the short distance to the summit of Table Rock for a picnic.

◆ On Linville Gorge's western side, the eight-mile **Wiseman's View Ride** follows the Kistler Memorial Highway (a.k.a Old Highway 105) from Route 183 in Linville Falls to this popular overlook. It's roughly four miles to the turn-off on the left to Wiseman's View, where the observation area features a great view across the gorge to Hawksbill and Table Rock mountains. Pack snacks and plenty of water. The ride begins at the Linville Falls parking area, located roughly a mile south of Linville Falls on Route 183.

◆ If you had two helpings of Wheaties for breakfast and you're up for an epic ride, then add another 12 miles to the Wiseman's View Ride by continuing six miles on Kistler Memorial Highway to Pinnacle Rocks Overlook. The 20-mile **Pinnacle Rocks Ride** serves up the same fare—grueling climbs, white-knuckle descents, and stunning views—but in super-sized portions. At the midway point, the observation platform looks out over Linville Gorge and the northern tip of Lake James. You'll see Table Rock, Hawksbill, and Shortoff mountains on the far side of the gorge.

◆ The 5,000-acre **Wilson Creek Wilderness Area** is increasingly popular with

The Long & Winding (Forest) Road

Perfect for non-technical mountain biking, **Kistler Memorial Highway** departs from Route 183 in Linville Falls and skirts the western rim of Linville Gorge. "Highway" may be one of the biggest misnomers this side of the Mississippi. This is a long, winding, dirt and gravel forest road, where the hills are strenuous but the views sublime.

mountain bikers drawn to the rugged beauty of the watershed and its challenging rides. Trails open to mountain bikes include **Thorps Creek Trail,** which can be combined with **Schoolhouse Ridge Trail** to create a six-mile loop. The loop begins at the Mortimer Campground & Recreation Area. To get there from Linville, take Roseboro Road (State Road 1511) south. At 1.5 miles, the paved road turns to dirt (after passing beneath the Blue Ridge Parkway). Continue roughly nine miles to the T-intersection with State Road 90. Turn right and drive two miles to the campground area. The singletrack trail sets out from the campground beside Thorps Creek and ascends 2.4 miles to the creek's headwaters at Wilson Ridge. Bear left at each intersection to connect with Schoolhouse Ridge Trail and to return to the campground. ◆ Also in Wilson Creek, the six-mile **Greentown Trail** makes for an excellent 12-mile bike ride along an old logging road. The trail sets out through an apple orchard and descends to Upper Creek before riding beside Burnthouse Branch to Forest Road 198. Turn around here to retrace your route and complete the ride. To reach the trailhead, take Route 181 south nine miles from Pineola to the Greentown Trail parking area.

◆ Boone's **Greenway Trail** leaves the Watauga County Recreation Complex and winds six miles through the countryside, passing through thick stands of rhododendron and crossing the South Fork of the New River several times on wooden bridges. The six-mile ride traverses gravel and dirt surfaces at an easy grade, so it's perfect for a first-time mountain biker. To get to the trail, travel a half-mile south on Route 221 in Boone from the intersection of Routes 221 and 321. Turn left onto State Farm Road and drive one mile to the recreation complex.

Gnarly singletrack

Shrinking Violets Need Not Apply

Sugar Mountain Resort off of Route 194 in Banner Elk, ☎ (828) 898-4521, flips the switch on the Gray chairlift for mountain bikers on weekends, July–September, providing access to more than 20 miles of singletrack and doubletrack trails. The views from the mountain are tremendous, but keep your eyes on the trail during the screaming descents. (Not one of which is officially sanctioned by the Association of Shrinking Violets.) Lift tickets run $20 for an all-day pass. Forgo the lift access

and you can ride the trails for free. Similarly, you can ride more than 40 miles of trails for free on nearby **Beech Mountain,** but no lift service is offered. For a trail map, visit Beech Mountain Sports listed under "Rentals."

Rentals

The following businesses rent mountain bikes; some offer guided mountain-bike tours. **Beech Mountain Sports,** 325 Beech Mountain Parkway, ☎ (828) 387-2373, *www.beechmountain-sports.com;* ◆ **Boone Bike & Touring**, 899 Blowing Rock Road, Boone, ☎ (828) 262-5750; ◆ **High Mountain Expeditions**, 915 Main Street, Blowing Rock, ☎ (828) 295-4200 or 1-800-262-9036, *www.highmountainexpeditions.com;* ◆ **Ski Country Sports**, Route 184 (across from Sugar Mountain), Banner Elk, ☎ (828) 898-9786 or 1-800-528-3874, *www.skicountrys-ports.com;* ◆ **Wahoo's Adventures**, Route 321 one mile south of Boone, ☎ (828) 262-5774 or 1-800-444-7238, *www.wahoosadventures.com;* ◆ **Magic Cycles**, 140 South Depot Street, #2, Boone, ☎ (828) 265-2211, *www.magiccycles.com,* does not rent bikes but welcomes cyclists for free route suggestions.

◆ For an easy, eight-mile ride on a flat dirt road, head to the village of Valle Crucis, north of Boone on Route 194, to ride the **Watauga River Road.** This pleasant route beside the beautiful Watauga River includes rolling pastures with weathered barns against a mountainous backdrop. To get underway, take Route 194 a quarter-mile north of the Mast General Store to Watauga Road on the left. Park at the bridge on Watauga Road and pedal four miles to the road's junction with Route 321. Turn around and retrace your route.

Road Biking

Where did Lance Armstrong find the will—and the wind—to recover from cancer and return to cycling to win the Tour de France five times in a row? Right here in North Carolina's High Country. Long-known to local and regional cyclists as one of the best places to ride, word spread worldwide when Armstrong praised the mountains around Boone in his memoir *It's Not About the Bike.* Here hundreds of miles of paved roads wind through stunning mountain scenery. The region has become so popular with cyclists that most local drivers know to expect them on the roads; however, tourists flock to the area in the summer and their driving can be hazardous. Be prudent and ride defensively at all times.

◆ So, where to ride? The **Blue Ridge Parkway** is an obvious route of choice. An officially designated bicycling route, the BRP combines pristine mountain scenery with slow-moving traffic. From

Boone CVB

NC Division of Tourism

Blowing Rock, you can travel north or south on the parkway and easily track your mileage with the highly visible mileposts. The ride north toward **Doughton Park** has fewer popular stops than the ride south toward **Linville Falls**, which can be to a cyclist's advantage. Regardless, the parkway is punishing in either direction with long climbs, screaming descents, and weather that changes by the hour. Parkway regulations require that cyclists have a light or reflector visible at least 500 feet to the front and a red light or reflector visible at least 200 feet to the rear during periods of low visibility, between the hours of sunset and sunrise, and while traveling through a tunnel.

♦ You can ride the 40-mile **Parkway Loop** from Blowing Rock by taking the Blue Ridge Parkway south to Milepost 305, where you pick up Route 221 to ride north back to Blowing Rock. This ride includes the Linn Cove Viaduct, a concrete bridge that snakes around Grandfather Mountain. Built from the top down to minimize impact on the mountain, the viaduct is an awesome architectural wonder. The open views from the viaduct are sublime and give cyclists the sensation of pedaling through air.

Buy the Book

If you're serious about cycling or planning to get serious and want to explore all the routes the High Country has to offer, pick up a copy of Tim Murphy's *Road Cycling the Blue Ridge High Country* (John F. Blair, $14.95). Available at most local bookstores and bike shops, this handy book details 26 rides and more than 800 miles of cycling routes, ranging in difficulty from relatively easy to downright difficult.

♦ The **Todd to Fleetwood Ride** is unique because it's the only long, flat, paved ride in the area. This gorgeous 10-mile stretch on Railroad Grade Road beside the New River is ideal for a day when you want to be outdoors but don't want to muster the energy for a Lance-attack on some unsuspecting mountain. The rural scenery is of Christmas-tree farms, woods, and fields. To reach the ride's start, take Route 194 roughly 10 miles from Boone to the village of Todd, where you turn right onto Railroad Grade Road. Leave your car at the park across from the Todd General Store.

♦ Also, check out **Route 194** west from Valle Crucis through Banner Elk; **Route 221** north from Blowing Rock; **Route 105** from Boone to Valle Crucis; and **Old Route 421** from Sugar Grove to Zionville.

This Road's a Beech

Serious cyclists, or those hoping to repeat Lance Armstrong's "I-found-myself-again-on-Beech-Mountain" ride, can tackle **Route 184** for the punishing 3.5-mile climb up the mountain to the Town of Beech Mountain. (At 5,085 feet, it's the highest town in the Eastern United States.) Park in Banner Elk, and ride Route 194 north to Route 184 on the right. Good luck.

Paddling

Bob DeCamara

Several rivers in and near North Carolina's High Country promise wet and wild good times. While experienced paddlers bring their own boats to hit the rapids of Wilson Creek and the Watauga River or the gentle waters of the New River, the uninitiated will be glad to know that numerous paddling outfitters offer expeditions ranging from gentle inner-tube floats to frothy whitewater rafting trips on the following major waterways.

♦ Despite its name, the **New River** is believed to be the second-oldest river in the world behind the Nile. (Thomas Jefferson's dad, Peter, named the river by default: "Hey we found a new river!" Another account suggests the elder Jefferson named it for a Mr. New, who drowned in it.) More than 300 million years old, this gentle, wide river has its headwaters near Blowing Rock. Two forks—the North and the South—meet near the Virginia State line and continue north into Virginia and West Virginia. Twenty-six miles of the **South Fork** in Ashe and Alleghany counties make up the **New River State Park,** Wagoner Access Road, Jefferson, (336) 982-2587. This National Wild and Scenic River is popular with canoeists, beginner kayakers, and folks interested in an easy inner-tube float. See *Wide Open* for directions to the park.

♦ The **Watauga River** forms on Grandfather Mountain and flows through the High Country, gently at first with Class I and II rapids near Valle Crucis, and then much more aggressively downriver as it enters Watauga Gorge, a six-mile, rocky chute with high canyon walls. With names like *Hydro, Knuckles, Heavy Water,* and *Edge of the World* (a 10-foot waterfall), these Class IV–V rapids have created their own mythology. The upper section around Valle Crucis is popular with canoeists, beginner kayakers, and folks floating in tubes, while the Watauga Gorge is the domain of expert kayakers, white-water canoeists, and guide services running rafting tours. The river flows into Tennessee and the manmade Watauga Lake. The river is dam controlled, and the rafting season runs from Memorial

Paddling Outfitters

Edge Of The World Outfitters, Route 184 in downtown Banner Elk, ☎ (828) 898-9550 or 1-800-789-3343, *www.edgeoworld.com;* ♦ **High Mountain Expeditions**, 915 Main Street, Blowing Rock, ☎ (828) 295-4200 or 1-800-262-9036, *www.highmountainexpeditions.com;* ♦ **New River Outfitters,** 10725 Route 221, Jefferson, ☎ (336) 982-9192 or 1-800-982-9190, *www.canoethenew.com;* ♦ **Wahoo's Adventures,** Route 321 one mile south of Boone, ☎ (828) 262-5774 or 1-800-444-7238, *www.wahoosadventures.com;* ♦ **Zaloo's Canoes,** 3874 Route 16 South, Jefferson, ☎ (336) 246-3066 or 1-800-535-4027, *www.zaloos.com.*

Todd Bush

Day–Labor Day. Stop by any of the paddling outfitters for directions to put-ins and take-outs.

♦ **Wilson Creek** flows 23 miles from its headwaters on Grandfather Mountain to the Johns River in Catawba County. The natural-flowing National Wild and Scenic River has two sections popular with paddlers in the spring, when water levels are highest. The first is from Mortimer Recreation Area in the Pisgah National Forest to the forest's outer boundary, where primarily Class II rapids attract beginner white-water paddlers. The section of river from Wilson Creek Gorge to Brown Mountain Beach Road gets downright freaky, especially through the 2.5-mile gorge, where Class III, IV, and V rapids (some with ominous names like *Boat Buster* and *Thunderhole*) await. Stop by any of the paddling outfitters for directions to put-ins and take-outs.

♦ Scenic flatwater paddling options in the area include 47-acre **Price Lake** in Julian Price Park, BRP Milepost 297. You can rent canoes by the hour from the campground in the summer. ♦ Though it's located in Tennessee, **Watauga Lake** is easily accessible from Boone (45 minutes west on Route 321) and is ideal for stunning flatwater canoeing. This pristine lake sits at an elevation of 2,000 feet, covers 6,430 acres, and has more than 100 miles of shoreline. Most recreational facilities for renting canoes and other watercraft are located on Route 321 along the lake's southern shores.

Rock Climbing

The High Country offers some of the best climbing faces in the Southeast, most of which are in the **Linville Gorge Wilderness Area**. (Most climbing routes in Linville Gorge are closed from January 15–August 15 to protect peregrine-falcon nesting sites.) The major action goes down (if you're rappelling) or up (if you're climbing) along **Jonas Ridge**, which forms the gorge's eastern rim. From the Table Rock picnic area (see *Wide Open* for directions), climbers have access to nearly 100 traditional climbing routes of varying difficulties.

Rock Ratings

The **Yosemite Decimal System** is the primary system for rating the difficulty of climbing routes. Any rating beginning with the number five denotes a free climb and the numbers following the decimal denote difficulty. A rough breakdown: 5.0 to 5.4 is easy; 5.5 to 5.8 is intermediate; 5.9-5.10 is advanced; and 5.11 and above is expert.

♦ The primary climbing face for beginners on **Table Rock Mountain** is the **East Face**, where several "easier" routes to the summit make fine practice grounds. If you're just learning the sport, chances are your guide will lead you up *The Cave Route 5.4* or *Jim Dandy 5.4*, which are the least-challenging climbs on the mountain. In total, there are 54 climbing routes on Table Rock.

Boone CVB

◆ As its name suggests, **Little Table Rock** is smaller than Table Rock. But the cliffs on this face present nine good climbing routes, primarily for intermediate to advanced climbers. Two of the most challenging climbs are *League of Gentleman 5.11a* and *License to Dog 5.11a.*
◆ **The Devil's Cellar** is a deep chasm formed by Table Rock and a huge stone buttress. There are nine routes for beginner to advanced climbers. ◆ Other climbing areas in Linville Gorge are the **Amphitheater,** where you'll find 38 routes, as well as the **Mummy Buttress**, a monolith with two of the gorge's most popular climbs: *The Mummy 5.5* and *The Daddy 5.6;* the **North Carolina Wall** with 33 climbing routes; **Shortoff Mountain** with 57 climbing routes; and the 43 routes on **Hawksbill Mountain**.

For a Good Climb, Call...

...a High-Country guide service. Rock climbing doesn't afford many second chances if you make a big mistake, so unless you're a seasoned climber, join one of the region's outfitters. Each employs expert guides practiced in safe-climbing techniques. Some of the better known outfits: ◆ **Edge Of The World Outfitters**, Route 184 in downtown Banner Elk, ☎ (828) 898-9550, *www.edgeoworld.com;* ◆ **High Mountain Expeditions**, 915 Main Street, Blowing Rock, ☎ (828) 295-4200, *www.highmountain-expeditions.com;* and ◆ **Wahoo's Adventures,** Route 321 one mile south of Boone, ☎ (828) 262-5774, *www.wahoosadventures.com.* ◆ For climbing practice or instruction, head to **Footsloggers,** 139 South Depot Street, Boone, ☎ (828) 262-5111, *www.footsloggers.com,* where you can learn the basics on their 35-foot climbing tower.

Fly Fishing

Rules to Fish By

Unless you want to meet the local game warden on less-than-ideal terms, you'll need a state fishing license to fish 'round here. To order one over the phone with a credit card, call the **North Carolina Wildlife Resources Division**, ☎ 1-888-248-6834, or log onto *www.ncwildlife.org*, where you'll find retailers authorized to sell licenses, as well as information on state fishing regulations, including catch limits and release regulations for specific rivers.

Welcome to Trout Country, where rainbow, brown, and brook trout populate local rivers and streams. Popular fishing waters include the **North Toe, South Toe, Linville,** and **Watauga rivers**, along with the **North Fork** of the **New River**. Dozens of creeks throughout Ashe, Avery, Alleghany, and Watauga counties draw anglers as well, including the river-curiously-called-a-creek **Wilson Creek.** Also within the Wilson Creek Wilderness Area are four major trout creeks—**Andrews, Lost Cove, North Harper, and South Harper**—each teeming with wily ones awaiting just the right fly. In general, rainbow and brown trout are found throughout the region; brook trout are primarily found at higher elevations.

♦ Such an abundance of rivers and streams begs for the services of a guide who knows the waters. Fortunately, fly shops and guide services are much easier to find than are the easily spooked brook trout. The major, full-service fly shops carry equipment, apparel, and hundreds of flies. Other services include fly-fishing instruction and guided trips, ranging from half- and full-day wading trips to full-day float trips. Full-service outfitters include Boone's **Appalachian Angler,** 174 Old Shulls Mill Road, (828) 963-8383, *www.appalachi-anangler.com;* and ♦ the two locations of Orvis-endorsed **Foscoe Fishing Company & Outfitters,** *www.foscoefishing.com,* 150 Sunset Drive, Blowing Rock, (828) 295-7636 and Shoppes at Tynecastle, 4533 Tynecastle Highway, Banner Elk, (828) 898-7555.

Horseback Riding

Located just outside of Blowing Rock, **Blowing Rock Equestrian Preserve**, 2880 Laurel Lane, (828) 295-4700, offers mountain trail rides, April–November, along the 26 miles of carriage trails in Moses H. Cone Memorial Park. ♦ **The Chadi Farm**, Route 194, Valle Crucis, (828) 963-5399, has thirty acres lined with equestrian trails that, in the summer, fill with young riders attending the Mountain Riding Academy. The farm offers trail rides exploring the private property, which includes a mountain with excellent summit views of Calloway Peak and Table Rock. ♦ **Banner Elk Stables,** 796 Shomaker Road, off Route 194, Banner Elk, (828) 898-5424, offers guided trail rides, ranging from one hour to overnight trips. Rides are offered year-round.

Boone CVB

Rainy Day Workout

Westglow Spa, 2845 Route 221 South, Blowing Rock, (828) 295-4463 or 1-800-562-0807, *www.westglow.com,* features a wide range of cardiovascular machines, free weights, and Cybex weight-training equipment. A variety of aerobics classes is also offered. When you're done, take a dip in the indoor pool or hit the whirlpools or sauna. Nominal day-use fee.

♦ **The Inn at Yonahlossee**, 226 Oakley Green, Boone, (828) 963-6400 or 1-800-962-1986, *www.yonahlossee.com,* has two fitness centers, one in the inn and the other at the resort's indoor tennis facility. The inn's facility is newer, yet both feature cardiovascular equipment (treadmills, elliptical cross trainers, stationary bikes), circuit weight-training equipment, and free weights. The tennis facility also has a 75-foot, enclosed swimming pool, plus six outdoor and three indoor tennis courts.

Swimming

When warm weather spreads over the High Country, residents and visitors alike take to the water in dozens of swimming holes found in rivers, creeks, and lakes. The Wilson Creek Wilderness Area is full of great places to cool off, especially along the lower 15 miles of **Wilson Creek**, where you'll find numerous swimming holes accessible from Ralph Winchester Road, which parallels the river. To get here, take Route 181 south from Linville to Route 2, turn left and drive roughly five miles to a left turn onto Ralph Winchester Road. Park at any of the pull-offs along the road and amble down to the river.

♦ **Wilson Creek Gorge** is so flooded with swimming holes that you're virtually assured of finding a private spot. Rocks line the river's path through the 2.3-mile gorge, creating pools of slow-moving, slightly swirling water. Use extreme caution swimming in moving currents or getting too close to the bases of ledges, where the force of falling water can push you under. The Wilson Creek Gorge Day Use Area is located along Ralph Winchester Road, beginning three miles north of Route 2.

♦ Also in Wilson Creek Wilderness Area, **Upper Creek Falls** is a popular cascading waterfall with an excellent swimming hole at its base. You'll have to hike nearly a mile on a steep trail to reach the falls, but that's a good thing. It's best to be hot before dipping into the cool mountain water. To reach the trailhead, take Route 181 south from the Blue Ridge Parkway near Milepost 315. Travel roughly 7.5 miles to Forest Road 982 on the left. Take this dirt road 100 yards to the trailhead parking area. Grab your towel and swimsuit and start hiking.

♦ You can't swim in Linville Falls but you can get wet further downstream in the **Linville River** in Linville Gorge. The only way to get to the river is by foot, and one of the better routes down into the gorge is the 1.35-mile **Conley Cove Trail,** located on the western rim. (From Linville Falls, take Route 183 south one mile to the Kistler Memorial Highway, a dirt road, which you follow roughly 4.5 miles to the Conley Cove Trailhead.) Swim in the river at the base of the trail or hike in either direction along the river to find other swimming holes. The drawback? After feeling refreshed and clean, you've got to hike up and out of the steep canyon.

♦ The stunning, 50-foot **Elk Falls** has a deep pool its base. To get there, take Route 194 west from Banner Elk to Route 19E, which you take north. Just less than a mile after turning onto 19E, take a sharp right onto State Road 1303. Shortly, you'll come upon Elk River Road (State Road 1305) on the left, which you take four miles to the small parking area and picnic grounds. A trail leads a quarter-mile to the falls. ♦ The gentle flow

Your own, private swimming hole

of the **New River** makes it perfect for swimming. Head to the New River State Park, Wagoner Access Road, Jefferson, (336) 982-2587. See *Wide Open* for directions.

♦ Located in Tennessee, **Watauga Lake** is an unspoiled mountain lake that's only 45 minutes from Boone. Take Route 321 west from Blowing Rock to the numerous public access areas along Route 321, including the **Watauga Point Recreation Area** and the **Shook Branch Recreation Area**, both of which have designated swimming areas.

Downhill Skiing

With the highest-elevation skiing in the eastern United States (Beech Mountain) and one of the Southeast's greatest vertical drops (Sugar Mountain), North Carolina skiing presents its share of challenging slopes. When combined with the outstanding ski schools and well-groomed beginner and intermediate slopes,

you have every kind of terrain you'll need to progress through the sport. As with all eastern ski resorts, the impact of global warming makes each season a game of cross-your-fingers-for-a-cold-and-wet-winter. Regardless, snowmaking is a perfected science here, and seasons generally last Thanksgiving–mid March. The following ski resorts have lodges with beverage and food services, equipment rentals, and instructional facilities.

♦ The state's largest ski area, **Sugar Mountain Resort,** 1009 Sugar Mountain Drive, Banner Elk, (828) 898-4521 or 1-800-784-2768, *www.skisugar.com,* has 20 trails (40 percent novice, 40 percent intermediate, and 20 percent expert) spread across 115 acres of terrain, 100 of which are lighted for night skiing. Beginners take it slow on *Easy Street* while advanced skiers carve turns on black-diamond *Tom Terrific, Boulder Dash,* and *Whoopdedoo.* One triple chair and four double chair lifts whisk skiers to the summit, 1,200 vertical feet above, while two lifts have stops mid-ride. Skiers and snowboarders alike are welcome on all trails; Sugar also has snowboarding and tubing parks.

Learn Here, Ski Anywhere

There's a proud adage that if you learned to ski in North Carolina, you can ski anywhere, such are the conditions in this Mother Nature-challenged state where warm daytime temperatures often melt snow patches that re-freeze at night. Consider yourself warned: sharpen your edges and reflexes for those dull-gray, ice spots that can drop you like an anchor.

♦ **Ski Beech,** 1007 Beech Mountain Parkway, Beech Mountain, (828) 387-2011 or 1-800-438-2093, *www.skibeech.com,* has 14 trails (30 percent beginner, 40 percent intermediate, 30 percent advanced) across 95 acres of skiable terrain, plus tubing and snowboard terrain parks. The vertical drop from the 5,506 summit is 830 feet, and you'll white-knuckle every foot of it on the black-diamond *Upper* and *Lower White Lightning* trails. There are six double chairs, one high-speed detachable quad, and three surface lifts. The slopes are closed between 4:30 P.M.–6 P.M. for grooming for the night-skiing session.

At the base of the mountain, Beech Tree Village is an alpine-style community, with shops and restaurants surrounding an ice skating rink.

◆ Just outside of Blowing Rock and two miles off of Route 321, **Appalachian Ski Mountain,** 940 Ski Mountain Road, (828) 295-7828 or 1-800-322-2373, *www.app-skimtn.com*, is a small, family-friendly ski resort with nine slopes (two novice, four intermediate, three advanced) open to skiers and snowboarders and served by two quads, one double chair, and two surface lifts. While advanced skiers will feel their runs are over before they begin—the vertical drop is 360 feet and there are 17 acres of skiable terrain—the resort feels huge to a beginner. An excellent place to learn, the mountain's French-Swiss Ski College emphasizes smaller classes to insure you'll get the individual attention needed to keep you upright on the slopes. There's an outdoor skating rink at the base of the mountain.

◆ Located between Boone and Banner Elk on Route 105, **Hawksnest Golf & Ski Resort,** 2058 Skyland Drive, Banner Elk, (828) 963-6561 or 1-800-822-4295, *www.ski-hawk.com,* features 12 slopes (20 percent beginner, 40 percent intermediate, 40 percent advanced) open to skiers and snowboarders, a 619-foot vertical drop, and 20 acres of ski-able terrain. There are two double chair lifts and one surface lift serving the slopes and the snowboard terrain park. All trails are open for nighttime skiing.

Cross-Country Skiing & Snowshoeing

When a major winter storm dumps on the High Country, the adventurous take to the Blue Ridge Parkway and Pisgah National Forest on cross-country skies or snowshoes. Popular places to explore include all the trails listed under *Dayhiking* and *Mountain Biking* in the **Wilson Creek** and **Linville Gorge wilderness areas.** Be advised that in heavy snow, it's safer to stick to forest roads than it is to bushwhack or to follow a backcountry trail. Of particular note: the **Kistler Memorial Highway** along the western rim of the Linville Gorge, and **Brown Mountain Beach** and **Ralph Winchester roads** in the Wilson Creek Wilderness Area.

◆ The National Park Service closes sections of the **Blue Ridge Parkway** in inclement weather, making for an excellent and relatively safe place to ski or snowshoe. For news of road closings, contact the parkway office at (828) 298-0398. Just a stone's throw from Blowing Rock, the 26 miles of carriage trails in the **Moses H. Cone Memorial Park** are the perfect place to shush through the silent land. If the parkway is closed, take Route 221 south from Blowing Rock to the park's Bass Lake entrance on the right.

◆ The higher elevations are more likely to have snow, so if you're interested in snowshoeing or Nordic skiing and the lower elevations aren't white enough, head for **Roan Mountain** where you may well find enough snow. Directions are under *Dayhiking*.

◆ It's hard to find businesses that rent snowshoes or cross-country skis, given the area's natural snow cover doesn't warrant enough demand. So unless you already own a pair, you'll either have to borrow or purchase the equipment. **Sugar Mountain Resort**, 1009 Sugar Mountain Drive, Banner Elk, (828) 898-4521 or 1-800-784-2768, *www.skisugar.com*, is the exception. The mountain offers guided snowshoe tours with equipment rentals included. Depending upon snow cover, you may explore the resort's mountain biking trails, the sides of the ski slopes, or a nearby golf course.

Local Outdoor Advice

Grandfather District, Pisgah National Forest • If you're heading into Linville Gorge or the Wilson Creek Wilderness Area, make a point of stopping at this ranger station to get the latest information on trail closures, nesting peregrine falcon information, and suggestions on scenic trails. The rangers are patient and helpful in providing suggestions on where to spend time in the district's more than 189,000 acres of land. • 109 East Lawing Lane, Nebo, ☎ (828) 652-2144

Footsloggers • With Boone and Blowing Rock locations, Footsloggers is a full-service outdoor store that sells all manner of gear, apparel, and footwear. The staff at both locations consists of serious outdoor enthusiasts who will gladly point you to the hot spots for hiking, mountain biking, paddling, and climbing. In fact, the store prints a free brochure listing some of the area's hiking trails and climbing spots. The Boone store has a 35-foot climbing tower, as well as a paddle shop located directly behind the main store. There is also an Outdoor Outlet, which carries name-brand outdoor gear and apparel at steep discounts. • Boone location: 139 South Depot Street, ☎ (828)-262-5111; Downtown Blowing Rock location: Village Shoppes On Main, Main Street, ☎ (828) 295-4453; *www.footsloggers.com*

Mast General Store • Along with candy, candles, and candelabras, you can purchase excellent outdoor equipment, gear, and apparel from the Mast General Store's various locations, as well as pick up some good advice on where to use it. In addition to the flagship store in Valle Crucis, try the Boone location at 630 West King Street, ☎ (828) 262-0000 • Route 194, Valle Crucis, ☎ (828) 963-6511, *www.mastgeneralstore.com*

Kick Back

Not everything in the High Country proceeds at the pace of the Linville River rushing over Linville Falls. When you're ready to relax, try the following laid-back pursuits.

Antiques

Antiquing in the High Country combines scenic driving from village to village with ample opportunities to discover rare treasures. The following is just a sampling of the dozens of shops throughout the region. ♦ The **Blowing Rock Antique Center**, Route 321 Bypass, Blowing Rock, (828) 295-4950, features roughly 50 antiques dealers, selling original art, collectibles, garden accessories, furniture, and home décor items. ♦ Open for more than 25 years, **Village Antiques & Gifts,** 1127 Main Street, Blowing Rock, (828) 295-7874, sells antique silver, estate jewelry, modern and antique glass, custom pine furniture, and handcrafted copper lights. ♦ In nearby Banner Elk, **The Gilded Age Antiques,** 10890 Route 105 South, Banner Elk, (828) 963-8633, *www.gildedageantiques.com*, sells 17th- to 19th-century English and European furniture and accessories. The shop boasts one of the nation's largest selections of Victorian majolica. ♦ If there's a center to the region's antiques action, it's Route 105 in Foscoe, where upscale dealers line both sides of the road. An example: **Staffordshire Antiques,** 8599 Route 105, Foscoe, (828) 963-4274, which carries a large collection of antique English chimney pots manufactured between 1840 and 1880. ♦ In Boone, **Timeless Treasures Antiques Depot**, 199 Howard Street, (828) 262-1957, and **Old Boone Antique Mall**, 631 West King Street, (828) 262-0521, are two antiques malls with extensive varieties of vendors. ♦ West Jefferson's **Old Hotel Antiques,** 6 Jefferson Avenue, (336) 246-2004, *www.oldhotelantiques.com,* is a large cooperative with 11 rooms of items, ranging from glassware to antique furniture.

Art & Crafts Galleries

Located in Flat Top Manor in the Moses H. Cone Memorial Park (BRP Milepost 294), the **Parkway Craft Center,** (828) 295-7938, *www.southernhighlandguild.org,* features handcrafted works from Southern Highland Craft Guild members. Expect a variety of crafts, including glass, clay, jewelry, metal, fiber, wood, and paper. It's possible your visit will coincide with a demonstration by one of the guild's artists on the porch. Open March–November. ♦ **Traditions Pottery,** 4443 Bolick Road, Blowing Rock, *www.traditionspottery.com*, (828) 295-5099, offers a large selection of decorative and functional pottery from Mike and Janet Calhoun. Janet is a sixth-generation potter of the renowned Owens family of potters from Seagrove, NC. ♦ The family also operates **Traditional Owens Pottery** in the Wilcox Emporium, 161 Howard Street, Boone, (828) 262-1221, where you'll find a delightful variety of bowls, plates, cups, and decorative accessories. ♦ **IAGO,** 1165 Main Street, Blowing Rock, (828) 295-0033, *www.iagoblowingrock.com*, features work by national and international artists. Items include jewelry, metalwork, blown glass, pottery, and home furnishings.

♦ The big visual-arts buzz in the High Country centers aroud Appalachian State University's **Turchin Center for Visual Arts,** 423 West King Street, Boone, (828) 262-3017,

Art in the Park

One Saturday each month from May–October, hundreds of artisans travel to Blowing Rock for **Art in the Park**, a juried art show held in Blowing Rock Memorial Park on Main Street. Most of the work, which includes basketry, weavings, paintings, pottery, sculpture, leatherwork, wood carvings,

photographs, quilts, and jewelry, is available for purchase. For the current or upcoming schedule, call the Blowing Rock Chamber of Commerce at ☎ (828) 295-7851 or 1-800-295-7851, *www.blowingrock.com.*

www.turchincenter.org, which opened in 2003 as the largest visual arts center in Northwestern North Carolina, Eastern Tennessee, and Southwestern Virginia. The large facility includes the **Martin & Doris Rosen Galleries,** where exhibits display the work of regional, national, and international artists. Also onsite: a community arts school and gift shop. Admission is free, donations are accepted, and the gallery is open year-round. ◆ In Boone, the **Hands Gallery**, 543 West King Street, (828) 262-1970, is a crafts cooperative gallery with jewelry, pottery, metalwork, and woodwork from some of the area's best artisans, one of whom staffs the gallery each day.

◆ Located in a historic stone cottage on the grounds of the private Crossnore School, **Crossnore Weaving Room & Gallery,** 205 Johnson Lane, Crossnore, (828) 733-4660 or 1-800-374-4660, *www.crossnoreschool.org,* preserves the craft of weaving on turn-of-the-century, foot- and hand-powered floor looms. Mary Martin Sloop, who founded the children's school and home in 1913 for impoverished mountain children, opened the Weaving Room to provide income for mountain families and to pass the craft on to young Crossnore residents. In addition to the hand-woven clothing and home furnishings, the gallery sells locally made pottery and other crafts.

◆ In Valle Crucis, visit the **Mark W. Read Studio**, 1898 Broadstone Road, Valle Crucis, (828) 963-8191, *www.markreadstudio.com,* to view fine custom jewelry, sculp-

Pass It On

NC Division of Tourism

In 1923, an Episcopalian school teacher named Lucy Morgan established the Penland Weavers to revive and to preserve hand weaving as a craft and to provide local women a source of income. She invited expert weavers as guest instructors, and word of the learning opportunities soon spread, resulting in students arriving from afar. From that influx, the Penland Weavers evolved into the **Penland School of Crafts,** Penland Road (off Route 19E south of Spruce Pine), Penland, ☎ (828) 765-6211 or 1-800-227-3912, *www.penland.org,* which today is a national center for crafts education in more than a dozen disciplines, including ceramics, drawing, glassblowing, metalworking, photography, printmaking, textiles, and woodworking. Students visit for one- to eight-week workshops, where they learn from master craftspeople. On campus, the **Penland Gallery** exhibits and sells work by current and former students. Call for hours and for information about touring the school's 400-acre campus.

tures, and architectural pieces. Read's work has been exhibited in the Smithsonian Institute in Washington, DC, among other museums and galleries across the country. ◆ Take a view of the High Country home with you from the **Kevin Beck Studio,** Route 194 South, Valle Crucis, (828) 295-6868, *www.kevinbeck.com,* where you'll find the artist's oil and pastel paintings of various mountain

scenes. ◆ West Jefferson's **Ashe County Arts Center,** 303 School Avenue, (336) 246-2787, *www.ashecountyarts.org,* includes a gallery and gallery shop exhibiting art and crafts in a 1930s building constructed by the Works Progress Administration.

Attractions

At 5,964 feet, **Grandfather Mountain,** 2050 Blowing Rock Highway, Linville, (828) 733-2013 or 1-800-468-7325, *www.grandfather.com,* is the highest peak in the Blue Ridge Mountain Range and also a 4,500-acre privately owned park. One of the most-visited attractions in Western North Carolina, Grandfather Mountain features a paved road up part of the mountain that passes two billion-year-old rock formations, Split Rock and Sphinx Rock; a nature museum with natural history exhibits; a quarter-mile paved trail through a wildlife habitat, with black bears, mountain lions, deer, river otters, bald eagles, and more; and a suspension bridge across an 80-foot chasm at an elevation of more than a mile. There are numerous hiking trails throughout the park, and the entire mountain is an International Biosphere Reserve that's home to 47 rare or endangered species of plants and animals. To get to Grandfather Mountain, take Route 221 one mile south from BRP Milepost 305.

◆ Between Blowing Rock and Boone, you'll find North Carolina's first amusement park, **Tweetsie Railroad**, Route 321, Blowing Rock, (828) 264-9061 or 1-800-526-5740, *www.tweetsie.com.* The family-oriented park opened in 1957 and is still chugging along, thanks to its

Hugh Morton

NC Division of Tourism

Tweetsie Railroad

centerpiece, a 1912 coal-fired, steam-engine locomotive named for its shrill whistle. Tweetsie travels on a three-mile track through the mountain woods and into "bad-guy" territory, where lo and behold, train robbers climb aboard with evil thoughts in mind. You'll be thankful for the good marshal—the one in the white hat, lest there be any doubt—who puts-a-hurtin' on the would-be train robbers. The park's theme harkens back to the Wild West—can-can showgirls, cow pokes, and gunslingers—and it features amusement rides, live entertainment, and an authentic Old West main street. Tweetsie Railroad is a National Historic Landmark. In October, the venerable engine dons a ghoulish mask and becomes...Ghost Train™. Open April–October. Admission fee. Bring the kids, or the kid in you.

◆ Not the kind of place you want to visit after a couple of beers, **Mystery Hill,** 129 Mystery Hill Lane (off Route 321), Blowing Rock, (828) 264-2792, *www.mysteryhill-nc.com,* is an attraction where, in the Mystery House, you can stand at a 45-degree angle, see water flow uphill, and marvel over objects that seem to fall up. (Apparently, the house experiences a stronger-than-usual pull to the north resulting in some odd effects on the laws of physics.) You'll find enough optical illusions and hands-on experiments to entertain kids for a couple of hours, adults for much fewer.

What Lies Beneath

Depending on your approach to the High Country, you may have passed billboards promoting one of the region's better-known attractions, the subterranean **Linville Caverns,** Route 221 between Linville and Marion, ☎ (828) 756-4171 or 1-800-419-0540, *www.linvillecaverns.com.* These limestone caverns deep in Humpback Mountain are pretty cool literally (year-round temp is a static 52 degrees) and figuratively (hey, you're *inside* a mountain). While Native Americans knew of the caverns long ago, it wasn't until the 1880s that white men "discovered" them. (They were puzzled over the sight of trout swimming "into" the mountain.) The caverns feature an interesting array of stalactites and stalagmites, as well as an underground stream in which blind fish swim. Half-hour guided tours explain the cavern's history and geology. Open daily, March–November; weekends only, December–February. Nominal admission fee.

◆ At the **Blowing Rock,** off Route 321 south of Blowing Rock, (828) 295-7111, *www.theblowingrock.com,* a northwest wind blows up the rocky walls of the Johns River Gorge with enough force to return handkerchiefs or other light objects dropped from the cliff. The attraction plays off the legend that a Cherokee brave leapt to his death from the rock because he was conflicted about leaving his Chickasaw maiden to return to his tribe. The maiden prayed to the Great Spirit, and a gust of wind blew the brave up and into the maiden's arms. (Don't try this yourself.) There's a self-guiding trail around the property and magnificent views from the rock and from an observation tower built over the gorge. Open daily, April–October; weekends, November–March (weather permitting). Nominal admission fee.

Back Roads Touring

With no interstate and relatively few four-lane highways slicing through the High Country, the roads around Boone and Blowing Rock offer gorgeous, mountain countryside that makes driving anywhere a scenic journey. If your legs are tired or the weather isn't cooperating with your outdoor plans, simply grab a road map and hit the surrounding two-lane blacktops for some touring. If you prefer your routes a little more planned, some of the following picturesque highways are worth exploring.

♦ The king of all scenic roadways in the area is the Blue Ridge Parkway (see *Blue Ridge Parkway*), but there are many more roads worth exploring, including **"the Little Parkway,"** a.k.a. **Route 221** between Blowing Rock and Linville. Prior to the 1987 completion of the Linn Cove Viaduct, the last-remaining section of the parkway, the 18-mile "Little Parkway" circumvented Grandfather Mountain to connect the two parkway segments. The highway twists and turns past waterfalls, rock formations, and the base of Grandfather Mountain. En route, it also passes Linville Falls, Linville Caverns, and an entrance to the Moses H. Cone Memorial Park.

♦ An 18-mile stretch of **Route 194** west from Vilas (north of Boone) to the small community of Cranberry is a North Carolina Scenic Byway. The drive passes through Valle Crucis, Banner Elk, and Elk Park. Highlights include the Watauga River Valley, the state's first Rural Historic District centered around Valle Crucis; the heart of North Carolina Ski Country in Banner Elk; and the scenic Elk River Valley.

♦ **Route 194** (east of Boone) and **Route 88** (west of Jefferson) constitute another North Carolina Scenic Byway called the **New River Valley Byway.** This 41-mile drive passes through Christmas tree country and skirts and crosses the world's second oldest river, the New River. The drive begins in Boone and follows Route 194 east into the New River Valley and the village of Todd. From here, the drive continues on **Route 221** north to West Jefferson, where you'll find the state's only cheese-manufacturing facility, the Ashe County Cheese Company (see *Shops & Stops*). Continue through Jefferson on Route 221 to the Route 16/88 intersection, where you take **Route 88** east into the heart of New River paddling country. The 10-mile drive from here to Laurel Springs passes through Ore Knob, a mining community with several copper mines. The drive ends in Laurel Springs, just a couple of miles short of the Blue Ridge Parkway, which makes an excellent return route. For more information on the state's scenic byways, log onto *www.byways.org* and follow the links to North Carolina.

♦ The Blowing Rock Chamber of Commerce provides a free brochure entitled *Three Scenic Tours* that suggests a variety of driving itineraries from Blowing Rock. Choose from the **"Frescoes Tour,"** which

A roadside apple stand

NC Division of Tourism

417

details a 70-mile driving route along the Blue Ridge Parkway and other rural highways and recommends various stops. Included among them are the Holy Trinity Church in Glendale Springs and St. Mary's Church in West Jefferson, where you can view frescoes created by North Carolina-native and world-renowned artist Ben Long (see "Churches of the Frescoes"); the **"Attractions Tour,"** a 20-mile itinerary with stops at various attractions like Tweetsie Railroad, Flat Top Manor, and the Daniel Boone Native Gardens; and the **"Blue Ridge South Tour,"** a 65-mile drive along and off the Blue Ridge Parkway from Price Park south to Linville Caverns.

Blue Ridge Parkway

The nation's most-popular scenic highway, the venerable **Blue Ridge Parkway**, (828) 298-0398, *www.nps.gov/blri*, passes through the region (125 miles of the road's 469 miles is in the High Country). In fact, Blowing Rock is the only full-service town directly on the parkway.

Hugh Morton

Built in the 1930s and 1940s by the Civilian Conservation Corps, the road follows ridge lines of the Appalachian Mountains, connecting the Shenandoah National Park in Virginia to the Great Smoky Mountains National Park in North Carolina. Its singular intent is recreation. The 45 mile-per-hour speed limit encourages leisurely driving, and the stunning scenery—easily enjoyed from numerous overlooks, pull-offs, and recreation areas—invites stopping.

Concrete mileposts mark every mile beginning with Milepost 0 near Shenandoah National Park and ending with Milepost 469 at the Great Smoky Mountains National Park. Blowing Rock and Boone provide access to the parkway at Milepost 292. The National Park Service offers free maps available from any visitor center on the parkway. (The closest to Blowing Rock is the park ranger desk at Flat Top Manor in Moses H. Cone Memorial Park at Milepost 294. Maps are also available from the sources under *Additional Information*.) All of the major parkway sites within a reasonable drive from Asheville are listed with milepost locations throughout the chapter.

The Linn Cove Viaduct on the Blue Ridge Parkway

Got Kilt?

Be ye Scot, or be ye not, you're invited to join the nation's largest gathering of Scottish clans at the **Grandfather Mountain Highland Games,** held each summer at MacRae Meadow on Grandfather Mountain. More than 30,000 people—many of them wearing kilts and whatever Scotsmen do or do not wear underneath—arrive the second full weekend in July for a rousing celebration of Celtic culture and competition. The games open to a bagpipe-led procession and the unfurling of nearly one hundred tartan banners. There are drum and bag-piping competitions, Scottish folk music concerts, Celtic-music jams, hammer throws, Highland wrestling, foot races, sheep-herding contests, and numerous dances held during the weekend. The games, which began in 1956, draw more than 135 clans, including Campbells, MacDonalds, McColls, and more. Call (828) 733-1333 or visit *www.gmhg.org* for event schedules and ticket information.

Hugh Morton

From the Farm

Beginning at 7 A.M. and continuing until "sellout" on Saturdays, May–October, and Wednesdays, July–August, the **Watauga County Farmers Market**, 891 Horn in the West Road, Boone, *www.wataugacountyfarmersmarket.org,* is where you'll find fresh mountain produce—organically grown vegetables, fruits, berries, herbs, and flowers—and other products of the region's farms, including cider, honey, butter, mustard, jams, eggs, and fresh-baked breads. The biggest find? Some of the nicest, most-genuine folks you'll ever encounter. ◆ The folks are just as friendly and the produce and other products just as fresh at the smaller **Ashe County Farmers Market**, 2nd Street, West Jefferson, (336) 219-2650. Open Wednesdays, 8 A.M.–2 P.M.; and Saturdays, 8 A.M.–1 P.M., April–autumn.

Boone CVB

Sin by the Bushel

If you think apples are the fruit of original sin, you can get into a whole heap of trouble at the **Orchard at Altapass**, 1025 Orchard Road, Little Switzerland, ☎ 1-888-765-9531, *www.altapassorchard.com.* First planted in 1908, Altapass' orchards straddle both sides of the Blue Ridge Parkway at Milepost 328.3. The trees start bearing fruit in early July and continue through the fall, the ideal time to visit. Open seasonally, seven days a week.

Gardens

The **Daniel Boone Native Gardens,** 651 Horn in the West Drive, Boone, (828) 264-6390, presents three acres of gardens as they might have appeared in the 18th Century. Trails wind past native North Carolina plants, including many rare species. The beautiful grounds contain ponds, wooden arbors, a wishing well, the Meditation Maze, and a reflection pool. Each season presents a different show of color—dogwoods and azaleas in the spring, rhododendrons in the summer, and hardwood leaves in the fall. The wrought iron gates at the entrance were made by Daniel Boone VI, the pioneer's direct descendent. Open daily, May–September, weekends in October. Nominal admission fee.

♦ In Blowing Rock off Laurel Lane, the **Annie Cannon Memorial Gardens** features pretty walking trails past the small but picturesque Broyhill Lake. These gardens also contain the entrance to the Glen Burney Trail. (See *Dayhiking*.)

Churches of the Frescoes

Each year, thousands of visitors take a brief detour off the Blue Ridge Parkway at Milepost 259 to visit two small Episcopalian churches, where renowned artist and North Carolina native Ben Long painted frescoes. (A fresco is a painting on wet plaster that requires inordinate planning and patience to apply the pigments at the right level of moisture.) Merely 12 miles apart, **Holy Trinity Church**, 120 Glendale School Road (Route 16), Glendale Springs, ☎ (336) 982-3076, and **St. Mary's Church**, 400 Beaver Creek School Road (Route 194), West Jefferson, ☎ (336) 246-3552, are open daily, 24 hours a day. Long, who apprenticed in Italy to learn the ancient art of fresco, painted three frescoes—"Mary Great with Child," "John the Baptist," and "The Mystery of Faith"—at St. Mary's between 1974-77, often working during worship services. The artist's pregnant wife served as the model for "Mary Great with Child." For "The Last Supper," painted on an entire wall behind the altar inside Holy Trinity in 1980, Long turned to local parishioners as models for the apostles. The churches, which share a parish, have established a Ministry of the Frescoes and parish members are trained as docents to assist visitors. Admission is free but donations are welcome. Sunday services alternate between the two churches.

NC Division of Tourism

Gem Mines

The ground beneath Western North Carolina is a gem superstore with pockets of valuable stones—rubies, emeralds, and sapphires, for example—waiting to be discovered. Get in on the hunt at one of several area gem mines open to the public. Mining methods vary—panning in flumes or creek beds or sifting through buckets of mining ore, for example—but most mines offer gem cutting and jewelry-setting services onsite. In general, the season runs April–November. Expect to pay by the bucket, with prices ranging from $6–$500 per bucket depending on the value of the ore. A sampling of area mines includes **Rio Doce Gem Mine/Jerry Call, Inc.,** 14622 Route 226 South, Spruce Pine, (828) 765-2099, *www.riodoce.com*, which guarantees you'll find gems in each bucket of ore. ◆ Run by two families who have mined the area since 1810, **Spruce Pine Gem & Gold Mine**, 15090 Route 226, Spruce Pine, (828) 765-7981, features year-round mining: outdoors in the warm months and indoors with a heated flume in the winter. ◆ **The Emerald Village**, 321 McKinney Mine Road, Little Switzerland, (828) 765-6463, *www.emeraldvillage.com*, is home to three mines, including the underground Bon Ami Mine, which features such historic mining equipment as lamps, dynamite plungers, and rail cars.

Historic Wanderings

The **Hickory Ridge Homestead**, 891 Horn in the West Road, Boone, (828) 264-2120, is a living history museum with eight log cabins that date from 1785 to the early 1930s. With the exception of the smokehouse, each historic structure stood in Watauga County prior to being relocated here. (The smokehouse was constructed onsite with 18th-century tools.) Inside each cabin, costumed docents portray either the owners of the cabin or people from the time periods. The lesson? Living in the mountains in the late 1700s and early 1800s was tough. Mountain settlers had to be entirely self sufficient. In addition to growing or hunting their food, settlers made their own clothes and presumably spent a lot of time by the fire in winter. There's a weaving house on the grounds with a 200-year-old human-powered loom made from chestnut. Visitors are welcome to attend workshops on weaving, candle making, and tin-smithing. Open year round. Free admission, but a $2 donation is suggested.

◆ The restored **Brinegar Cabin,** which dates from the early 1880s, and the one-room **Caudill Family Homestead,** are in **Doughton Park**, BRP Milepost 238.5. For more information, see *Dayhiking*. ◆ **Flat Top Manor,** BRP Milepost 294, (828) 295-3782, was built on 19th-century textile

Flat Top Manor

NC Division of Tourism

The Mast General Store in Valle Crucis

A Retail DyMASTy

A cross between a history museum and a profit-amassing retail enterprise, the **Mast General Store**, Route 194, Valle Crucis, ☎ (828) 963-6511, *www.mastgeneralstore.com*, first opened in 1883. In 1887, Henry Taylor sold a half-interest to W.W. Mast, a descendant of Joseph Mast, one of the valley's earliest settlers. In 1913, Mast purchased the rest of the enterprise and endeavored to sell anything his customers might need. Promising everything "from cradles to caskets," Mast General Store became a legend. Today the store is a National Historic Landmark and still very much in business. Stop by to purchase traditional mercantile goods, clothing, and outdoor gear; to use the antique post office; and to warm up beside the potbellied stove. There are other store locations in **Boone:** 630 West King Street, ☎ (828) 262-0000; **Waynesville, Hendersonville, Asheville,** and **Greenville, SC.**

magnate Moses H. Cone's 3,500-acre estate. Cone, who was known as the "Denim King" because of the high-quality denim his mills produced, built the 20-room mansion to live in with his wife as their health declined. He lived out his days here as a farmer, philanthropist, and conservationist. You can follow in the footsteps of the Cones' daily morning walks on the Craftsman's Trail and then tour the grand home, where you'll find a visitor center and the Parkway Craft Center. The park is open year-round, but the Manor and visitor center are only open late March–early January. Free admission.

♦ The village of **Valle Crucis** along Route 194 in the Watauga River Valley constitutes North Carolina's first Rural Historic District. Many of the farm buildings and churches in the area are listed on the National Register of Historic Places, including the **Mast Farm** (see *Sleep Well*), the original **Mast General Store** (see "A Retail DyMasty"), and the **Mission School Conference Center,** a small campus of turn-of-the-century buildings that belong to the Episcopal Church. It was here, in 1842, that an Episcopalian bishop, Stillman Ives, founded the **Society of the Holy Cross,** the first monastic order in the Anglican Church since the Reformation in the 1500s. Church bureaucracy deemed the monastery too "Roman" and ordered it disbanded in 1852. Also on the campus: Bishop Ives' 1840s log cabin and the 1925 **Church of the Holy Cross**.

Museums

With a focus on the people and history of the Appalachian Mountains, the **Appalachian Cultural Museum,** University Hall Drive, Boone, (828) 262-3117, *www.museum.appstate.edu*, features permanent exhibits on many subjects, including Native-American ancestry, the Civil War, NASCAR, the Blue Ridge Parkway, and the Craft Renaissance. The museum is also home to an extensive collection of self-portraits by North Carolina artists. Open Tuesday–Saturday, 10 A.M.–5 P.M.; Sunday, 1 P.M.–5 P.M. Nominal admission fee, except Tuesdays, when admission is free. ◆ Located in the 1903 home built for D.D. and B.B. Dougherty, the two brothers who founded Appalachian State University, **the Appalachian Heritage Museum,** 175 Mystery Hill Road, Blowing Rock, (828) 264-2792, is a living history museum that portrays life at the turn of the century for a prominent mountain family. The home was the first in the area to have electricity and running water. ◆ In the same location, the **Native American Artifacts Museum** features more than 50,000 authentic Native-American artifacts, including arrowheads, spears, stone tools, pottery, jewelry, and eating utensils. A nominal admission fee serves both museums. Open daily, 8 A.M.–8 P.M. in the summer; 9 A.M.–5 P.M., the rest of the year.

◆ The **North Carolina Museum of Minerals,** BRP Milepost 331, Spruce Pine, (828) 765-2761, has an excellent presentation on the significance of mining to the state and to the mountain counties in particular. Visitors learn about geological history, including how gems formed, and about early mining ventures. Also on display is a broad array of locally found gems and minerals. Revolutionary War buffs will appreciate that the museum is in Gillespie Gap, which was a key stop for the Overmountain Men who descended from the mountains to defeat the British at the Battle of Kings Mountain. Open daily, 9 A.M.–5 P.M.

Performing Arts

♪ No one describes the area's cultural scene better than the tourism bureau, the High Country Host: "From banjos to violins, dosie-does to pirouettes, local storytellers to Neil Simon plays, and hand-thrown pottery to towering steel sculpture, the High Country offers a unique blend of traditional and modern culture." The following is a sampling of the region's performing-arts offerings.

◆ Described as the closest thing to Spoleto you'll find in North Carolina, **An Appalachian Summer Festival,** (828) 262-6084 or 1-800-841-2787, *www.appsummer.org,* is a month-long, multi-arts festival held each July on Appalachian State University's campus. Renowned musicians and vocalists from such genres as bluegrass and classical; dance companies with styles ranging from folk to modern; and actors, playwrights, and directors all converge in Boone to produce an amaz-ing assortment of performances, most of which are held on campus in either Rosen Concert Hall or Farthing Auditorium. There's also a visual arts component with the annual Rosen Outdoor Sculpture Competition. ◆ The High Country's professional theater company is **Blowing Rock Stage Company,** 152 Sunset Drive, Blowing Rock, (828) 295-9627, *www.blowingrock-*

Scott Sharpe

Picking in Valle Crucis

Outlasting the Energizer Bunny

The nation's third-oldest, continually running outdoor drama, *Horn in the West*, 591 Horn in the West Road, Boone, ☎ (828) 264-2120, begins each June, as it has every summer since 1952. The production tells how Daniel Boone and the fiercely independent pioneers who settled this remote area rebelled against British oppression and helped create a new nation. The production employs music, dancing, drama, comedy, and pyrotechnics on three stages. Shows are nightly except Mondays, late June–early August, in an outdoor theater. Call for exact dates and performance times.

stage.com, which performs a variety of musicals, comedies, and romances. Founded in 1986, the troupe has staged well-known productions and world premieres, including the musicals of North Carolina native, Robert Inman. Typically upbeat and entertaining, performances have included such productions as *Ain't Misbehavin'*, *Godspell,* and *Shirley Valentine.* In late 2004, the company moves into the new **Blowing Rock Community Arts Center**, (828) 295-0112, *www.brcac.org,* on Route 321 Bypass. The 25,000-foot facility will also host dance and musical performances, and visual arts exhibitions.

◆ Mountain music is nearly as old as the hills, and numerous venues feature live performances of bluegrass, folk, and country music. Every Friday night, there are country and bluegrass jams at the **Todd General Store,** 3866 Railroad Grade Road, Todd, *www.toddgeneralstore.com,* (336) 877-1067. This 1914 store is a gathering point for pickers—fiddlers, and banjo, dulcimer, and guitar players—and up to as many as 40 enthusiastic audience members. Performances are casual and free. In the summer on Saturday afternoons, the store also offers mountain music concerts. ◆ **Mountain Music Jamboree,** 9331 Route 16, Glendale Springs, (336) 384-4079 or 1-800-803-4079, *www.mountainmusicjamboree.com,* is a music and dance show featuring bluegrass music, old-time bands, clogging, and square dancing. Performances are Saturday nights, 7 P.M.–11 P.M., year-round.

◆ If country music is your taste, git' up and go to the **High Country Roundup**, 200 Den-Mac Drive, Boone, (828) 265-4604, *www.HCRoundup.com,* a three-hour, musical variety show featuring country, bluegrass, gospel, and oldies music. After dinner and the show, there's dancing for everyone. Shows begin at 7 P.M. on Friday and Saturday nights.

An Americana Music Celebration

Each spring, acoustic music fans flock to the campus of Wilkes Community College off Route 421 in Wilkesboro for **MerleFest,** ☎ (336) 838-6267 or 1-800-343-7857, *www.merlefest.org,* one of the premier bluegrass, folk, gospel, blues, Cajun, jazz, and Celtic music festivals in the country. Merle Watson, the son of legendary guitarist and Grammy Award-winner Doc Watson, was a respected folk musician who died in a tractor accident in 1985. Friends of Doc Watson convinced him to organize a musical tribute to his son. Since the first show in 1988, the festival has grown to draw more than 75,000 fans and such artists as Alison Krauss, Bela Fleck, Dolly Parton, Vince Gill, Willie Nelson, Earl Scruggs, and Doc Watson, of course. There are 15 stages, as well as impromptu jams throughout the school's campus during the four-day celebration. Tickets sell out months in advance. Call or visit the website for festival dates, scheduled performers, and ticket prices.

Shops & Stops

Boone CVB

Shopping is a serious sport in the High Country, and the Western North Carolina Mountains have more unique boutiques than you can wave a Ben Franklin at. It'd be a folly to list them all, so the following provides general descriptions of retail hot spots, plus a few suggested stops. ◆ When you visit **Blowing Rock's Main Street,** you'll notice park benches along the sidewalks. Is this just smart municipal planning to encourage people to linger near retailers? Perhaps. But it's our observation that the benches are really there for those who shop until they literally drop. Main Street is the quintessential, upscale shopping area in the region, where you can find antiques, crafts, art, apparel, outdoor gear, home furnishings, and dozens of smaller items, from elegant accessories to commemorative knick knacks.

Suggested Blowing Rock stops include: ◆ **DeWoolfson Down,** 304 Sunset Drive, (828) 295-0504 or 1-800-554-3696, where you'll find the same down comforters and pillows that your upscale inn most likely uses. ◆ **Cabin Fever,** 915 North Main Street, (828) 295-0520, for rustic furnishings and decorative accessories for mountain getaways, lake houses, and deep woods cabins. ◆ **My Favorite Kitchen Things**, 1098 Main Street, (828) 963-2710, for anything and everything related to the kitchen. ◆ **neaco,** 1081 Main Street, (828) 295-0709, for hip, decorative home accessories. ◆ **Skyland Books,** 1116 Main Street, Martin House Cottage, (828) 295-4231, for a large selection of bestsellers, children's books, fiction, and nonfiction. ◆ And **Tanger Shoppes On The Parkway,** Route 321, Blowing Rock, (828) 295-4444 or 1-800-720-6728, for more than 30 factory outlet stores, including Gap, Jones New York, London Fog, Nautica, Ralph Lauren, Coach, and Seiko.

◆ **Boone's historic downtown** around West King and Depot streets has rows of specialty stores, galleries, and antiques marts, as well as bistros and coffee houses for refueling when your energy runs low. Suggested Boone stops include **Heavenly Chocolates,** 691 West King Street, (828) 963-1826, for thousands of unique gifts, such as cards, picture frames, and as the store promises, "the hottest candles in the country used by Hollywood stars." Of course, there are chocolates and truffles as well. ◆ **Farmer's Hardware,** 661 West King Street, (828) 264-8801, sells a complete selection of Americana, plus general hardware products in a historic store with an ambiance that Home Depot can't touch. ◆ **Espresso News/Mosaic Books**, 267 Howard Street, Boone, (828) 264-8850, carries a fine selection of new fiction and nonfiction and has an in-house coffee shop.

◆ The **Wilcox Emporium Warehouse,** 161 Howard Street, Boone, (828) 262-1221, claims you can "shop the entire High Country under one roof." The historic, 60,000 square-foot warehouse features 240 merchants and three restaurants. ◆ For an unbelievable selection of maps—USGS topographical maps, trail maps, raised-relief maps, travel maps, and antique reproduction maps—find your way to the **Blue Planet Map Company,** Shops at Shadowline, 240 Shadowline Drive, Boone, (828) 264-5400 or 1-800-810-6277. Blue Planet also carries an excellent selection of guidebooks, plus various tools for exploration, including compasses, altimeters, atlases, and more.

◆ **Blue Moon Books,** 271 Oak Avenue, Spruce Pine, (828) 766-5000, offers a wide selection of new and used books, with a special focus on both regional fiction and history. ◆ If you like to browse, you'll find nice collections of shops in **Banner Elk** along Tynecastle Highway, and **Valle Crucis,** along Route 194.

General Stores

The High Country's rugged terrain and sparse population have kept huge retailers like Wal-Mart from establishing a big-scale presence here, allowing general stores that carry a wide variety of products to prosper. One-part retailer and one-part community center, these general stores are a unique pleasure to visit. Inventory and services range from groceries, hardware items, mountain crafts, and video rentals to outdoor equipment, clothing, newspapers, and books. The best-known general store is the Mast General Store in Valle Crucis (see "A Retail DyMasty" under *Historic Wanderings*), but there are many more in the area, including the **Todd General Store,** 3866 Railroad Grade Road, Todd, ☎ (336) 877-1067, which opened in 1914; ◆ the **Old Hampton Store,** 77 Ruffin Street, Linville, ☎ (828) 733-5213, which opened in 1920 at the foot of Grandfather Mountain; ◆ and the most-recent addition to the High Country's general-store community, **Fred's General Mercantile,** 501 Beech Mountain Parkway, Beech Mountain, ☎ (828) 387-4838, which opened in 1979.

Spa & Massage

Westglow Spa, 2845 Route 221 South, Blowing Rock, (828) 295-4463 or 1-800-562-0807, *www.westglow.com,* is a European-style spa that offers numerous facial and body treatments. A complete list of services would take pages. A sampling of selections includes: antioxidant and oxygen facials, aromatherapy massage, body wraps, reflexology, raindrop therapy, and several chocolate treatments. Westglow also offers hair

styling, manicures and pedicures, and classes for healthy cooking and personal stress management. There's a full fitness facility onsite (see *Rainy Day Workouts*) with personal trainers, an indoor pool, and wet/dry saunas. ◆ The **Spa at Chetola Resort**, North Main Street, Blowing Rock, (828) 295-5565 or 1-800-243-8652, *www.chetola.com,* is on the picturesque, private, 87-acre resort located a short walk from downtown Blowing Rock. Rejuvenating services include Swedish and deep-tissue massage, herbal body wraps, various facial treatments, and reflexology.

A pastoral scene at Westglow Spa

Rest Easy

Sleep Well

While you'll find a variety of accommodations in the High Country, a few generalizations about the lodging scene can be made. More upscale inns and B&Bs are found in villages like Blowing Rock and Valle Crucis, and more motel and hotel chain choices are located in Boone for people visiting Appalachian State University. Around Banner Elk, expect a higher concentration of no-frills, ski-lodge-style accommodations. The mountains are also full of cabin and condominium rental options; contact the chambers of commerce or tourism bureaus listed at the end of the chapter for more information. Be aware that as the leaves fall in October and early November, both the demand for lodging and the room rates go up. Make your reservations months in advance and expect to pay a premium.

Accommodations Pricing

Less than $100	Inexpensive	$
$100-150	Moderate	$$
$151-200	Expensive	$$$
More than $200	Very Expensive	$$$$

Prices are per room, per night, based on double occupancy during peak seasons. Note that B&Bs and most country inns include breakfast in the rate.

Baird House • One of the saddest sounds you'll hear is the crunch of dirt under your tires on the Watauga River Road as you pull away from this intimate mountain farm bed and breakfast. Set upon 16 acres fronting the Watauga River with spectacular views in every direction, the historic Baird House has seven rooms—four in the main house and three in the carriage house— each with a private bath. Built in 1790 by Dr. Ezekial Baird and his wife, Susanna, along the main route into Tennessee, the Baird House is one of the oldest homes in Watauga County. It has been carefully restored and includes many of the home's original features, including hand-planed doors, antique nails, and several original glass panes. Guestrooms have sitting areas, comfortable appointments like goose-down comforters, and each room in the main inn has a fireplace. The hot country breakfast will more than satisfy you. • *1451 Watauga River Road, Valle Crucis, NC 28691,* ☏ *(828) 297-4055 or 1-800-297-1342, www.bairdhouse.com • $$–$$$*

The Eseeola Lodge at Linville Golf Club • Bestowed with Mobil's four-star rating, the Eseeola embodies hushed ease. It's a golf-shirt-by-day, coat-and-tie-by-night affair, where evening perfume mixes with after-dinner cigar smoke in the cool mountain air. Built in the late 19th Century, the first lodge burned in the 1930s but was quickly replaced by the current lodge, a handsome, rustic-looking building with chestnut-bark siding. The property features 24 rooms in the main lodge, available in two configurations—suites are larger than deluxe rooms and have separate living rooms and porches—as well as a cottage with two bedrooms, two bathrooms, a living room, and full kitchen. All guestrooms at the resort have private baths, plus appointments like handmade quilts, antiques, and such modern features as cable TV. The inn's grounds are impeccably kept, and the lodge sits amidst thousands of acres that invite exploration. If at first the rates seem walloping, consider that they include daily breakfast and dinner in the lodge's famous dining room. Guests may use the outdoor heated pool, eight tennis courts, and fully equipped fitness facility. While you can use the resort as a home base for further High-Country exploration, you'll be in the minority. Most guests treat the Eseeola Lodge as a destination unto itself. The lodge is open seasonally from April–October. • *175 Linville Avenue, Linville, NC 28646,* ☏ *(828) 733-4311 or 1-800-742-6717, www.eseeola.com • $$$$*

Gideon Ridge Inn • True to its name, Gideon Ridge Inn rests atop a secluded knoll of the Blue Ridge Mountains on the outskirts of the charming village of Blowing Rock. Up a narrow lane and past a high hedgerow, this 1939 English Cottage-style mountain retreat warmly greets its guests. The experience is one of being transported to a time before TVs, telephones, Palm Pilots, and dawn-to-dusk pressures. Gideon Ridge Inn is one big, relaxed sigh. On the property, patios, lawns, stone paths, and terraced gardens feature entrancing views and silky breezes carrying the season's blossom scent. The inn's interior is equally inviting. Listed in the distinguished *Select Registry*, Gideon Ridge maintains fine standards, with such amenities as marble walk-in showers, soaking tubs, balconies, room refrigerators, and towel warmers. Common areas are furnished with deep, cushioned furniture, period antiques, and original work from mountain artisans. Though there are just 10 rooms and suites, the inn has a lovely rambling feel with nooks in which to curl up and read. The main sitting room features a grand piano and a six-foot stone fireplace. A hearty breakfast and afternoon tea are included. Dinner is served some evenings for an additional fee. (See *Dine Well*.) • *202 Gideon Ridge Road, Blowing Rock, NC, 28605,* ☎ *(828) 295-3644* • *www.gideonridge.com* • *$$$–$$$$*

The Inn at Ragged Gardens • On Sunset Drive just a block off Blowing Rock's Main Street, this handsome, bark-sided manor sits back from the sidewalk across a verdant lawn with fragrant, well-tended gardens. (There are also "ragged" or informal gardens onsite.) The inn was originally a seasonal cottage. In 1996, the owners restored the circa 1900 property to a state luxurious enough to join the prestigious *Select Registry* association of distinguished inns. There are 12 rooms, each decorated with a garden theme. Among the common appointments are queen- or king-sized beds with goose-down comforters and pillows, private baths with bathrobes, and fireplaces. Most have sitting areas, whirlpool baths, and private balconies. Public spaces are elegant, and highlights include the granite staircase in the grand hall and the chestnut-paneled walls in the living room. Hot gourmet breakfasts are served in the glass-enclosed dining room, which operates in the evenings as Heirlooms Restaurant, one of Blowing Rock's fine dining establishments. • *203 Sunset Drive, Blowing Rock, NC 28605,* ☎ *(828) 295-9703, www.ragged-gardens.com* • *$$$–$$$$*

Lovill House Inn • Tucked discretely away on 11 acres of gorgeous mountain land, complete with its own stream and waterfall, this inn has five rooms in the main farmhouse and one in the Spring House, a separate cottage directly behind the inn. Each room has a private bath. The spacious Hickory Room has a two-room bath. Once the home of Confederate War hero and North Carolina State Senator Captain Edward F. Lovill, this 1875 home underwent a careful restoration that created a comfortable, welcoming retreat. You can wander the grounds, sit under the gazebo, or relax on the inn's wraparound porch. The wood-burning fireplace in the living room makes this a fine place to read after breakfast or in the evening before retiring to bed. The full country breakfast is hot and satisfying, as you'd expect from a property that's earned AAA's Four-Diamond award. • *404 Old Bristol Road, Boone, NC 28607,* ☎ *(828) 264-4204 or 1-800-849-9466, www.lovillhouseinn.com* • *$$–$$$*

Maple Lodge • It's hard to be more centrally located in Blowing Rock than at the Maple Lodge's location just a half-block from Main Street's shops and galleries. This property was built in the mid 20th Century specifically for accommodating visitors to Blowing Rock. The cheerful, yellow, two-story house is surrounded by a white-picket fence that encloses several well-tended perennial gardens. There are 11 guest rooms—three on the main floor and eight on the second floor—each with private bath and individually decorated with antiques and reproductions. Public spaces include two parlors downstairs with comfortable chairs and couches and a handsome library with wood-paneled walls and a wood-burning stone fireplace. You'll be served a hot breakfast—think blueberry pancakes with sausage or orange-pecan waffles—in the bright dining room overlooking a wildflower garden. • *152 Sunset Drive, Blowing Rock, NC 28605,* ☎ *(828) 295-3331, www.maplelodge.net • $–$$$*

Mast Farm Inn • With an 1880s farmhouse, an acclaimed restaurant (see *Dine Well*), a wine bar & espresso café, a gift shop, and several cabins and cottages for accommodating guests, the Mast Farm has come a long way from its late 18th-century settlement by Joseph Mast. Named in 2000 as one of *Travel + Leisure's* 10 favorite B&Bs in the entire country, the Mast Farm Inn knows how to make your stay memorable. It's had practice: The farmhouse has hosted guests since the turn of the century. There are eight large, comfortable rooms in the farmhouse, each with a private bath. Several rooms have fireplaces. Also onsite are seven private cottages, some of which are new, while others have been renovated from existing historic buildings on the property. For example, the 1812 Loom House was originally a two-room log cabin built on the farm. Josie Mast, a later owner of the farm, used the cabin for weaving on her loom. Today it's a romantic cottage for two guests with the original wood-burning fireplace, a massage tub for two, a wet bar, a comfortable bedroom, and a private porch with rockers. The bucolic grounds are stunning and feature organic flowers, vegetable and herb gardens, and grand views of the surrounding mountains. Included in your stay is a delicious, hot country breakfast. Mast Farm Inn belongs to the *Select Registry* association of upscale inns. • *2543 Broadstone Road, Valle Crucis, NC 28691, (828) 963-5857 or 1-888-963-5857, www.mast-farminn.com •* ☎ *$$$–$$$$*

A patio at Gideon Ridge Inn

D i n e   W e l l

Dining choices in the High Country range from home-style restaurants serving country cooking to fine dining rooms serving haute cuisine, with many variances in between. Inexpensive pizza and Mexican restaurants cater to Appalachian State University students in Boone, while chefs get creative with their cuisine in the villages of Blowing Rock, Banner Elk, and Valle Crucis. Throughout the High Country, you'll find outstanding dining in the many inns and small resorts that serve both overnight guests and the general public. Always call to make sure they're serving dinner on any given night and to make reservations.

Canyons • Looking to dine over a good view? You'll be satisfied at this casual restaurant, which overlooks an endless roll of mountains stretching to the horizon. (Want proof? Visit their website for live views from their webcam: *www.canyonsbr.com*) You can't pass this restaurant with its large parking lot on Route 321 just south of town without thinking, "Now that would be a fine place to have a drink and watch the sunset." And indeed it is. The American, Asian, and Southwestern items on the menu are reasonably priced and fairly good, but it's the view that takes top billing. The restaurant becomes a popular watering hole at night and often features live music. • *Route 321 South, Blowing Rock,* ☎ *828-295-7661*

Crippens Country Inn & Restaurant • Crippens fuses country charm with elegance in a low-ceilinged dining room where the youthful yet attentive staff delivers a variety of game, fish, and vegetarian fare. As soon as you sit down, your server brings a variety of fresh-baked breads with a couple of spreads to sample as you look over the menu. The menu changes daily, but you can count on (and should order) whichever horseradish-encrusted fish the

chef is serving that day. (On one visit, it was oven-roasted Maine salmon with mirin butter sauce, wasabi mash, and crispy soy-fried shallots.) For starters, try the spinach salad with crispy pancetta, oven-dried tomatoes, pine nuts, goat cheese, and balsamic vinaigrette. For dessert, order the warm apple tart with caramel sauce and homemade cinnamon ice cream. Open daily for dinner. Reservations recommended. • *239 Sunset Drive, Blowing Rock,* ☎ *(828) 295-3487 or 1-877-295-3487*

Daniel Boone Inn Restaurant • Housed in a white-washed building that was home to Boone's first hospital, this High Country institution has been serving heaping portions of country-home cooking since its opening in 1959. The atmosphere is decidedly casual, yet you'll see diners from all walks of life digging into the large serving bowls and platters of such foods as country-style steak, fried chicken, mashed potatoes, country ham biscuits, green beans, creamy corn, coleslaw, and fresh-stewed apples. In the summer, lunch and dinner are served daily. In the winter, dinner begins at 5 P.M. during the week, and lunch and dinner are both served on Saturday and Sunday, starting at 11 A.M. Throughout the year, you can sit down for a family-style country breakfast from 8–11 A.M. every Saturday and Sunday. Reservations recommended. • *130 Hardin Street, Boone,* ☎ *(828) 264-8657*

The Gamekeeper • With a menu primarily consisting of wild game, including many unusual meats (ostrich, boar, and bison, for example), this upscale restaurant, housed in an attractive stone building, is true to its name. Rest assured The Gamekeeper is not putting novelty ahead of your palate; all of the game dishes are marvelously prepared and not one will have you uttering, "It tastes just like chicken." The menu changes daily, but sample starters may include baked double-cream brie crusted with mixed nuts and served with dried fruit, vanilla, lavender honey, thyme compote, and water crackers, as well as cream of new-potato soup with apple-smoked bacon and green onions. A recent entrée entitled "Field & Stream" featured grilled buffalo flank steak and fried crawfish tails with spicy steak fries and Gamekeeper barbeque sauce. For dessert, try the white-Russian cheesecake. The Gamekeeper also serves daily vegetarian selections. All food is prepared from scratch, and much of it is grilled over a hickory-wood fire. Open Thursday–Monday for dinner in the summer and fall, and for dinner in the winter only on Friday and Saturday. Reservations recommended. • *3005 Shull's Mill Road, Boone,* ☎ *(828) 963-7400*

Gideon Ridge Inn • There's just one seating each evening at this intimate restaurant in an English Country-style inn, where the chef prepares a prix fixe menu with five courses. Promptly at 7:30 P.M., the chef joins

diners to describe the menu and answer any questions. Menus offer such starters as pan-seared shrimp with yellow-tomato hoisin glaze, or crabmeat wrapped in phyllo with fresh basil aioli. Entrées may include such items as New Zealand lamb tenderloin en brochette with an East Indian spice rub and coconut curry sauce, or a grilled veal chop with morel mushroom sauce, topped with goat cheese. The expansive wine menu is well suited to the evening's fare, and the chef is happy to make recommendations. The cuisine is imaginative and the views of the velvety Blue Ridge Mountains are always stunning. Expect fresh ingredients, impeccable service, and a cozy atmosphere with only 24 fellow diners. Reservations required. Open Tuesday–Saturday, spring through fall, and Thursday–Saturday in the winter. • *202 Gideon Ridge Road, Blowing Rock,* ☎ *(828) 295-3644*

Heirlooms • Housed in the handsome Inn at Ragged Gardens, Heirlooms is a fine-dining experience that serves innovative, contemporary American cuisine in one of several intimate dining rooms: the sun porch, the garden, parlor, or the wine-cellar. Regardless of where you're seated, the food is delicious. For starters, try the pan-seared scallops served with fennel-leek red onion slaw and Pernod fume, or the lobster corn chowder, which features a poached medallion of lobster tail meat in a cilantro-crème fraîche. Recent entrées included grilled North Carolina mountain trout filled with lemon thyme, Southern wild rice, and a sweet-corn bourbon cream sauce, and "Low Country Black & Bleu Pasta," which is Gulf shrimp, andouille sausage, and fresh flounder lightly blackened and served with a bleu cheese cream sauce over fresh linguini.

Complement your meal with a vintage from the wine list, which has received *Wine Spectator's* prestigious Award of Excellence. Save room for dessert. The cognac crème brûlée served with fresh berries and home-made chewy gingersnap cookies is the ideal way to end your marvelous meal. Dinner served Tuesday–Saturday. Reservations recommended. • *203 Sunset Drive, Blowing Rock,* ☎ *(828) 295-9703*

Louisiana Purchase • Louisiana Purchase serves up a festive atmosphere, as well as delicious Cajun, Creole, and French cuisine. From walls lined with murals of the Big Easy to jazz music floating throughout the restaurant (live on the weekends, recorded otherwise), this restaurant permeates the senses with all things 'Nawlins. For starters, try the pan-seared jumbo diver scallops with tabouleh and mango sweet chili sauce before moving on to the "Mumbo Gumbo," a traditional Creole gumbo with chicken, okra, and andouille sausage, served with seasoned rice and topped with gumbo filé. Owner Mark Rosse is a serious wine connoisseur, and his wine list is regularly honored by *Wine Spectator* magazine. Once a month, the restaurant has a "special wine dinner," when Rosse invites a noted vineyard to host a seven-course meal. Do yourself a flavor and find out if one of these dinners is scheduled during your vacation. There's also a wine bar in a loft above the dining room that serves wines by the glass. Open for dinner daily except Mondays. Reservations recommended. • *3984 Shawneehaw Avenue, Banner Elk,* ☎ *(828) 898-5656*

Mast Farm Inn • With a reputation for outstanding cuisine served in an elegant but relaxed atmosphere, the Mast Farm Inn draws dinner guests from throughout the High Country. It's worth the trip, whether you're descending the stairs from your room in the inn or driving from Blowing Rock or Banner Elk. Chef Matt Johnston prepares seasonal menus that change daily, but you'll typically find creative preparations of game, beef, and fish, as well as vegetarian dishes. There are always several tempting appetizers, but our money is on the warm spinach salad with apple-wood bacon, caramelized onions, and grilled Portobellos, served with poppyseed vinaigrette. For dinner, try the grilled tournedos of beef tenderloin, served with garlic-mashed potatoes and topped with a cabernet peppercorn sauce. The restaurant's carefully selected wine list complements the fare. Dinner is served daily (except Wednesdays) in the summer and fall and on Fridays and Saturdays in the winter. Reservations recommended. • *2543 Broadstone Road, Valle Crucis,* ☎ *(828) 963-5857 or 1-888-963-5857*

Village Café • Wandering Main Street in Blowing Rock, you'll come upon a walkway beside Kilwins Fudge & Ice Cream, which if you follow it, leads to the outdoor garden patio of the delightful Village Café. You can dine outdoors or inside the historic 1907 Randall Memorial Building, a pretty cottage that has served over the years as a crafts shop, public library, community club, and summer home. At one time, noted writer and artist Elliott Daingerfield worked in a studio on the second floor. But that's all in the past. What's important today is that this is an excellent place for a satisfying gourmet breakfast or lunch. Many of the menu items include fugasa, a traditional Argentine sour dough bread, made from scratch and baked daily. For breakfast, you might try the

French toast, made with fugasa bread and served with pure Vermont maple syrup, or the "Montrachet Eggs Florentine," which is three eggs scrambled with Montrachet goat cheese and fresh spinach. Lunch entrées are similarly innovative. Sandwiches include such varieties as pan-seared mountain trout on toasted fugasa with lettuce, tomato, and aioli; and a grilled Portobello with grilled onion, lettuce, tomato, and aioli. The café also offers a serious dessert selection, so save room or plan to stop back by for a mid-afternoon pick-you-up. If you visit in the winter, beeline for a seat indoors where you'll find Blowing Rock's largest, free-standing fireplace. Open daily, 8 A.M.–3 P.M. • *Off Main Street, Blowing Rock,* ☎ *(828) 295-3769*

Woodlands BBQ and Pickin' Parlor • Located on Route 321 Bypass, this lively BBQ joint serves up classic beef and pork barbecue (chopped and sliced), barbecued chicken and ribs, and a variety of Mexican dishes. The "pickin' parlor" refers to the nightly live entertainment that makes Woodlands' lounge a popular watering hole throughout the year. True BBQ aficionados will tell you this is some of the best BBQ in the mountains, and we're inclined to agree. • *8304 Valley Boulevard (Route 321 Bypass), Blowing Rock,* ☎ *(828) 295-3651*

Picnic Packing

Blowing Rock Market, 990 Main Street, Blowing Rock, ☎ (828) 295-7373, operates a full-service deli with Boar's Head meats, carries more than 900 wines, and sells a variety of picnic supplies. • **Kojay's Eatery,** 1132 Main Street, Blowing Rock, ☎ (828) 295-0015, is a delightful dine-in place or a picnic-supply stop where you can pick up cool wraps and sandwiches for the trail, plus a variety of delectable desserts. Kojay's also has a location in Banner Elk at 4533 Tynecastle Highway, ☎ (828) 898-3388. • In Boone, **Our Daily Bread,** 627 West King Street, ☎ (828) 264-0173, makes specialty sandwiches and includes a generous selection of vegetarian and vegan menu items. • There's a fine deli that'll pack picnics to go in the **Mast General Store,** Route 194, Valle Crucis, ☎ (828) 963-6511.

Just Desserts

No directions are needed to **Kilwin's Fudge & Ice Cream,** 1103 South Main Street, Blowing Rock, ☎ (828) 295-3088. Just follow your nose right up to the door and inside, where you'll find blocks of most every kind of homemade fudge. The cheerful counter staff is happy to cut samples. Also, try a taste of their many other candies and dipped ice cream in enough flavors to make decisions maddening. • Just a few door down is **Sunset Café,** 1117 Main Street, Blowing Rock, ☎ (828) 295-9326, which is actually a walk-up window. Here you'll also find lots of ice cream along with tasty quick lunches like grilled cheese, burgers, and hot dogs. Out back is a pretty, shaded garden for seating.

A Long-Weekend Itinerary

Day One

After breakfast at your inn, stop by Blowing Rock's **High Mountain Expeditions** (page 403) to rent mountain bikes and then pick up some picnic supplies across the street at **Blowing Rock Market** (page 434) before heading off to Linville Falls to park the car and ride **Kistler Memorial Highway** to **Wiseman's View** (page 401). On the ride back, stop at the **Conley Cove Trailhead** (page 409) to hike down to the **Linville River** for a picnic and swim. Hike back out of the gorge and ride back to your car to return your bikes.

Return to your inn to shower and dress for a relaxing afternoon in the **galleries** (page 414) and **shops** (page 426) of Valle Crucis, including the historic **Mast General Store** (page 422). Head for cocktails and dinner at the **Mast Farm Inn** (page 433).

Return to your inn for a restful night's sleep.

Day Two

After breakfast, head to **Kojay's Eatery** (page 434) to purchase a picnic lunch and then head to **Moses H. Cone Memorial Park** (page 395) to visit **Flat Top Manor** and **the Parkway Craft Center** (page 413). After touring the home, pack your picnic for the six-mile **Duncan Carriage Trail** (page 396) hike. Picnic at the bottom of the hill around scenic Bass Lake. Retrace your steps to the top and climb back into the car to drive the **Blue Ridge Parkway** (page 418) south across the Linn Cove Viaduct en route to **Grandfather Mountain** (page 415). Visit the museum and wildlife habitats and walk across the mile-high swinging bridge.

Climb back into your car and continue south on the Blue Ridge Parkway to **Linville Falls Recreation Area** to hike the **Erwins View Trail** (page 397) and to photograph the upper and lower falls. Spend the remainder of the day doing some **back roads touring** (page 417) before returning to you inn to shower and dress for dinner at the **Gamekeeper** (page 432).

Hit the hay.

Stroll the trails at Cone Manor

Day Three

After breakfast, spend the morning browsing the High Country's **antiques shops** (page 413), **art & crafts galleries** (page 413), and **shops** (page 425).

Head to **Westglow Spa** (page 426) for a massage and relaxing sauna. Finally, enjoy a casual lunch at Blowing Rock's **Village Café** (page 433) before reluctantly returning to the real world.

Additional Information

For additional dining, accommodations, and sightseeing information including the dates of special events, contact:

North Carolina's High Country Host, 1700 Blowing Rock Road, Boone, NC 28607, ☎ (828) 264-1299 or 1-800-438-7500, *www.highcountryhost.com*, operates a visitor center open Monday–Saturday, 9 A.M.–5 P.M.; Sunday, 9 A.M.–3 P.M.

Ashe County Chamber of Commerce & Visitor Center, 6 North Jefferson Avenue, West Jefferson, NC 28694, ☎ (336) 246-9550, *www.ashechamber.com*. Open Monday–Friday, 9 A.M.–5 P.M.

Avery-Banner Elk Chamber of Commerce, 4501 Tynecastle Highway, Banner Elk, NC 28604, ☎ 1-800-972-2183, *www.banner-elk.com*, is open Monday–Friday, 9 A.M.–5 P.M. From May–October, Banner Elk opens a visitor center at the intersection of Routes 221, 105, and 181 in Linville, Monday–Friday, 10 A.M.–4 P.M.; Saturday, 10 A.M.–5 P.M.; Sunday, 1 P.M.–5 P.M.

Beech Mountain Chamber of Commerce, 403-A Beech Mountain Parkway, Beech Mountain, NC 28604, ☎ (828) 387-9283 or 1-800-468-5506, *www.beechmtn.com*, is open Monday–Friday, 9 A.M.–5 P.M.; Saturday, 9 A.M.–4 P.M.

Boone Area Chamber of Commerce, 208 Howard Street, Boone, NC 28607, ☎ (828) 262-3516 or 1-800-852-9506, *www.boonechamber.com* or *www.visitboonenc.com*. Open weekdays, 9 A.M.–5 P.M., the Boone Chamber offers brochures, information on area activities, and maps of the community.

Blowing Rock Chamber of Commerce, 132 Park Avenue, Blowing Rock, NC 28605, ☎ (828) 295-7851 or 1-800-295-7851, *www.blowingrock.com*, is open Monday–Thursday, 9 A.M.–5 P.M.; Friday and Saturday, 9 A.M.–5:30 P.M.

For in the true nature of things,
if we rightly consider, every green tree
is far more glorious than
if it were made of gold and silver.

– Martin Luther

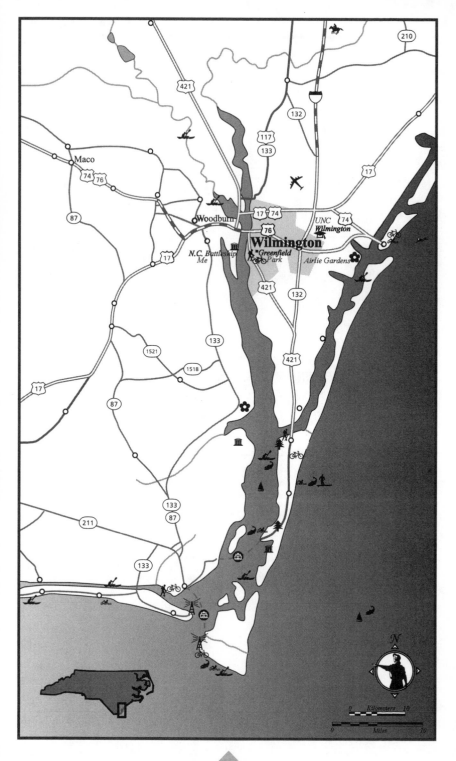

Wilmington,
North Carolina

Including Wrightsville Beach, Carolina Beach, Kure Beach, Southport, Oak Island, and Bald Head Island

From its headwaters near Greensboro, North Carolina, the Cape Fear River flows southeast more than 200 miles through the Piedmont and coastal plain, past the historic City of Wilmington, and to the state's southernmost cape where it meets the Atlantic Ocean. It is North Carolina's only river to empty directly into the sea. At the river's mouth and stretching miles out to sea, a series of sandbars—the treacherous Frying Pan Shoals—prompted early European sailors to call the area "Cape of Feare."

Tidal creeks, rivers, low-lying marshlands, and barrier islands make up the deceptively fragile-looking area surrounding Wilmington, the state's largest coastal city. Though 30 miles upriver from the ocean, Wilmington's position on a peninsula bordered by the Cape Fear River to the west and the Atlantic to the east means the city is concerned with all things water, from the path of the next hurricane to the latest trend in water sports. Indeed, the river and ocean have defined the region's settlement history from the beginning.

The area's first inhabitants were the Cape Fear Indians, who fished along the river and its tributaries in dugout canoes through the early 18th Century. In contrast to the well-established coastal tribes in South Carolina and Georgia, the Cape Fear tribe was small, and after losing a brief skirmish with early European settlers in 1715, the Native Americans left the area for good.

Europeans began plying the waters off Cape Fear as early as 1524, when Giovanni de Verrazano led a French expedition up the

Downtown Wilmington

439

Deron Nardo

A downtown monument to Wilmington's Confederate soldiers

Eastern seaboard from North Carolina to Nova Scotia; however, it was another 200 years before the first permanent settlers arrived. In 1726, English colonists from South Carolina founded Brunswick Town on the west bank of the lower Cape Fear River. The location proved vulnerable to pirates and coastal storms, and by 1729, another settlement had begun further upriver on a bluff on the east bank. Initially called Newton, the settlement was founded as Wilmington in 1739 and quickly grew to be the center for commerce for the region.

An abundance of pine forests along the river made transporting commercial products—lumber, tar, turpentine, and pitch—easy. Wilmington was the world's largest exporter of naval stores in the 18th and 19th centuries, and was also the site of the world's largest cotton exchange. The waterfront bustled with activity leading up to the Revolutionary War, and the town, which drew a brazen group of colonists, was the site of several colorful protests to British rule. The region saw bloodshed only once during the war in a quick but decisive victory for the American patriots in 1776 at Moore's Creek, about 20 miles north of Wilmington. Despite this victory, the British eventually occupied Wilmington in 1781 from January through October, when Lord Charles Cornwallis surrendered at Yorktown.

Wilmington prospered following the war, as slaves provided labor necessary for the grueling work on area plantations. The burgeoning slave trade, booming rice and cotton markets, and easy transportation provided by the Cape Fear River brought a great deal of wealth to town and drove construction of many fine homes and civic buildings. The opening of the Wilmington & Weldon Railroad in 1840 further helped boost the economy, as well as Wilmington's national influence, by providing local merchants an alternate means of moving commercial goods.

Wilmington was the South's most important port in the Civil War. The treacherous Frying Pan Shoals and two forts—Fisher on the Cape Fear's east bank and Anderson on the west bank—kept Union ships from entering the port and allowed blockade runners to sail through and supply Confederate troops. So valuable was Wilmington that when Fort Fisher eventually fell to Union troops, the South surrendered soon after.

Following the Civil War, Wilmington's port once again brought a measure of economic success, as textile and tobacco

Firestarter

In 1983, Hollywood producer-director Dino De Laurentiis sparked a new industry in Wilmington when he arrived to film *Firestarter* starring Drew Barrymore. Favorable weather and inexpensive labor costs soon drew more producers and directors, earning Wilmington the nickname, "Hollywood East." It's not unusual to see celebrities shopping or dining in town or to find a city street blocked by large cranes and glaring lights as a crew films on location. Among the movies filmed here: *Blue Velvet, Crimes of the Heart, Lolita, 28 Days,* and *The Divine Secrets of the Ya-Ya Sisterhood.* Wilmington also doubled as Capeside, the fictional Massachusetts town for the popular television show, "Dawson's Creek," which ended a six-year run in 2003. To tour the nation's largest motion picture facility outside of California, visit **Screen Gems Studios,** 1223 North 23rd Street, Wilmington, ☎ (910) 343-3433, *www.screengemsstudios.com.*

exports flowed through. During World War II, the city hosted a military base for training soldiers and a merchant ship-building facility; however, the war's end and the 1960 relocation of the Atlantic Coast Line Railroad's headquarters from Wilmington to Florida pummeled the local economy. The historic district fell into shambles, and much of downtown became a red light district.

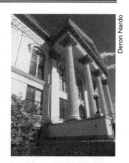

As concerned citizens watched this decline, a preservation movement began in the 1970s and accelerated in the 1980s, as developers and individuals purchased historic properties for renovation. Downtown revitalization efforts on abandoned buildings like Chandler's Wharf and the Cotton Exchange encouraged restaurants,

Flush with cash, Wilmington built Thalian Hall in the mid 19th Century

shops, and galleries to open around the waterfront, and tourists began to visit. In 1983, the film industry arrived (see sidebox, "Firestarter") and effectively transformed Wilmington's image from utilitarian port town to hip coastal community. Today, tourism is an important contributor to the region's economy.

Why should you visit? To play hard—paddling, swimming, fishing, or bicycling—in the natural beauty of the surrounding barrier islands and waterways, and then to rest easy, enjoying the upscale shopping, dining, and lodging in Wilmington's historic waterfront area.

The Way Around

Located on the Cape Fear River, Wilmington is a thriving city that is most attractive near the waterfront, where there's a dazzling array of shops, museums, galleries, B&Bs, and restaurants. With more than 230 blocks of restored buildings and homes, Wilmington's **historic district** is one of the largest on the National Register of Historic Places. Despite its size, the area is eminently walkable.

Navigating downtown is fairly straightforward. **Water Street** runs along the Cape Fear River, paralleled by **Front Street,** one block removed from the waterfront. Both streets bustle with shops and restaurants. **Market Street** runs perpendicular to Front and Water streets and is the main thoroughfare leading from the greater city to the riverfront. **River Walk** is a boardwalk along the Cape Fear River with benches and scenic views.

Market Street (Route 17/74) east of downtown passes through the greater Wilmington area, an indistinctive stretch of shopping centers, commercial development, and neighborhoods until **Route 74/Eastwood Road** veers right to

Wilmington's River Walk on the Cape Fear River

Wrightsville Beach

Harbor Island, a small residential island just short of the larger barrier island, **Wrightsville Beach.** Though full of homes, cottages, and a sprinkling of resorts, this five-mile-long island maintains small town charm through strict zoning laws preventing extensive commercial development. Summer is high season, as tens of thousands of vacationers join several thousand permanent residents. Attractions such as the expansive beach, Johnny Mercer Pier, Wrightsville Beach Park, and a 2.5-mile, multi-use trail provide extensive outdoor opportunities, while the island's fine restaurants and lodgings make Wrightsville a destination unto itself.

Two barrier islands north of Wrightsville Beach—Figure Eight and Topsail—attract beach vacationers primarily in the summer. The first island directly north of Wrightsville, **Figure Eight Island,** 1-800-279-6085, *www.figure8island.com,* is privately owned and has roughly 400 high-end homes for rent but no commercial venues. A security gate provides access to the island. **Topsail Island** includes the towns of North Topsail Beach, Surf City, and Topsail Beach. The island's population swells in the summer months from roughly 400 residents to more than 8,500. High-rise development is prohibited, so the island and its towns have a pleasant, low-key demeanor.

Brother, Can You Spare a Dime...

...for the parking meter? Parking in Wrightsville Beach can be downright brutal in the summer, particularly on weekends, because of extra traffic and a relative lack of public parking. From 9 A.M.–6 P.M. (March 1–October 31), you have two options: metered parking spaces or parking lots with pay stations. Metered spaces on public streets take coins ($1.25 an hour); pay stations accept dollar bills but will soon take credit cards. Parking lots are on the north end of the island; at Wynn Plaza; and between Iula and Nathan Streets. Streets with enforced pay station parking are West Salisbury, East Salisbury, and the 100 block of South Lumina. Your best bet is to arrive early in the day, as spots fill fast. Finally, don't risk getting towed. Restaurant and shopping area parking lots are closely watched for beach-trippers.

To the south of Wrightsville Beach, undeveloped **Masonboro Island** (see *Wide Open*) separates Wrightsville from **Pleasure Island**, a large barrier island where you'll find Carolina Beach, Kure Beach, and the Fort Fisher State Recreation Area. (From Wilmington, take Route 421 south 15 miles.) Located at the northern end of Pleasure Island, **Carolina Beach** is a seasonal beach community with extensive residential and tourism-based development. There are numerous vacation cottages, motels, beach shops, and commercial attractions like mini-golf, waterslides, and an amusement park. **Carolina Beach State Park,** a popular outdoor venue, is also here.

Further south on Route 421 as you enter **Kure Beach,** the island narrows—from the road you can see the Cape Fear River on your right and the Atlantic Ocean on your left—and traffic moves more slowly past the motels, tackle shops, and small mom-and-pop restaurants that fill this family-oriented beach town. Fewer visitors make it this far south from Wilmington, so the beach is less crowded. If you take Route 421 to its end, you'll reach the **Fort Fisher State Recreation Area** and its undeveloped, seven-mile beach. (See *Wide Open*.) Also here is the **Southport-Fort Fisher Ferry Terminal,** where ferries depart for the quick ride across the Cape Fear River to Southport.

Southport is also accessible by land. Take Route 17/74 west from downtown Wilmington across the Cape Fear River to Route 133, which you follow south 25 miles. (En route, you'll pass signs for Orton Plantation Gardens, a 1725 former rice plantation surrounded by expansive gardens, and Brunswick Town, the site of the first permanent settlement on the Cape Fear River.) Located at the mouth of the Cape Fear River, **Southport** is a small, cozy village that dates to 1792. Shaded by 200-year-old live oaks, the village has a number of historic churches,

Ferry Crossings

Two ferries ply the waters of the Cape Fear area, providing a relaxing and scenic means of getting around. **The Southport-Fort Fisher Ferry,** ☎ (910) 457-6942 or 1-800-368-8969, *www.ncferry.org,* crosses the Cape Fear River in both directions (from Southport and Fort Fisher) every 45 minutes in the summer from 8:30 A.M.–4:45 P.M. ($5 for cars, $2 for bicycles, and $1 for pedestrians.) Take Route 421 south to its end to reach the Fort Fisher terminal on the southern tip of Pleasure Island. The Southport terminal is just north of town on Ferry Road off Route 211. The **Southport-Bald Head Island Ferry,** ☎ (910) 457-5003, *www.baldheadisland.com,* departs from Indigo Plantation (on West 9th Street, off Route 211) in Southport on the hour and from Bald Head Island on the half-hour in the summer between 8 A.M.–11 P.M. ($15 round-trip for an adult, $8 for children under 12, and $15 for a bicy- cle.) Call for the winter schedules for both ferries.

NC Dept. of Transportation

Victorian homes, and a five-block downtown district lined with antiques shops, wonderful restaurants, and B&Bs, many of which overlook the Cape Fear River.

The **Southport-Bald Head Island Ferry** (see "Ferry Crossings") connects Southport to the southernmost island at the mouth of the Cape Fear River, **Bald Head Island,** 1-800-234-1666, *www.baldheadisland.com.* Accessible only by boat, Bald Head features attractive, upscale homes and neighborhoods developed in concert with the island's 10,000 acres of protected salt marsh and tidal creeks. A 14-mile sand beach and an extensive maritime-forest preserve round out Bald Head's natural offerings, while a couple of B&Bs, restaurants, and the marina line the island's main harbor. An ecologist's dream, Bald Head prohibits automobiles on the island, making bicycles, golf carts, and feet the primary means of getting around.

South of Southport and accessed by Route 133, **Oak Island** is a thin barrier island with a 13-mile, south-facing shoreline and two municipalities, **Oak Island** and **Caswell Beach.** Both are quiet beach communities with numerous vacation cottages and year-round homes. The main attraction is the beach, which features more than 50 public access points, most of which are located along Beach Drive. In general, the beaches on the island's western end are less crowded. To reach Beach Drive, take Route 133 across the Intracoastal Waterway onto

NC Division of Tourism

Bald Head Island

the island. Turn right onto Oak Island Drive and continue west to 58th Street, where you take a left toward the ocean. Just short of the beach, turn right onto Beach Drive.

Major roadways into Wilmington include **Interstate 40** from the north and **Routes17/74/76** from the west, which enter town on the **Cape Fear Memorial Bridge.** In downtown Wilmington, **Third Street** becomes **Route 421** as it heads south. **Market Street** heads east from downtown and becomes **Route 17/74** until the roads split and **Route 74/Eastwood Road** veers right toward Wrightsville Beach. **Route 17** cuts north toward Topsail Island. **Route 421** departs from downtown Wilmington and heads south through Carolina and Kure beaches to its end at Fort Fisher. Routes 17/74/76 west from downtown Wilmington cross the Cape Fear River on the Cape Fear Memorial Bridge and then intersect with **Route 133,** which travels south to Southport and Oak Island.

Weather

The warm Gulf Stream, which flows some 45 miles offshore from Cape Fear, moderates Wilmington's weather, producing a mild climate with four distinct seasons. Summers can be hot with average August temperatures in the upper 80s during the day, cooling to the lower 70s at night. (Even when the mercury hits the 90s, ocean and river breezes moderate the heat.) Average high temperatures in January are 55 degrees with only occasional overnight dips into the 20s. Spring is perhaps the finest time to visit, as azaleas and other flowers explode into color, filling the warm, 70-degree days with pleasant fragrances. Similarly, average temperatures in autumn are in the mid 70s with overnight lows in the lower 50s.

Getting to Wilmington

By Air: Wilmington International Airport, ☎ (910) 341-4333, *www.flyilm.com,* is served by several major airlines and most major car rental companies. Drive times from the airport range from 10 minutes to downtown Wilmington to 20 minutes to Wrightsville Beach.

By Car: From Atlanta, take Interstate 20 east to Florence, South Carolina, where you take Interstate 95 north. Just outside Lumberton, take Exit #14 for Route 74 east to Wilmington. Expect a six-hour drive. **From Charlotte,** take Route 74 (Independence Boulevard) all the way to Wilmington. Drive time is approximately 4.5 hours. **From Raleigh,** take Interstate 40 east directly to Wilmington. Expect a 2.5-hour drive.

P l a y   H a r d

W i d e   O p e n

Public access to wild, unspoiled settings in and around Wilmington makes the Cape Fear Region an outdoor sports capital. From miles of beach and protected marshlands on the surrounding barrier islands to the ever-present flow of the Cape Fear River, there are outdoor venues to suit everyone. The following are some of the area's major, multi-sport playgrounds.

A rock's skip from Wilmington's historic district, **Greenfield Park**, Willard Street (off South Third Street), (910) 341-7855, includes Greenfield Lake, a 150-acre lake surrounded by moss-covered cypress trees. Walkers, joggers, and cyclists make use of the five-mile, multi-use path that winds around the shoreline, especially in the spring when the park's myriad azaleas bloom, turning the scene into a color Rorschach blot. To get to the park from downtown Wilmington, take Third Street (Route 421) south roughly a mile to a large sign for the park on your left. Turn left onto Willard Street and continue to the parking area on the right.

Michael Wolf

Paddling is a serious sport around Wilmington

Twelve miles east of Wilmington, **Wrightsville Beach,** (910) 256-7900, *www.townofwrightsvillebeach.com,* has five miles of sand fronting the Atlantic Ocean, which invites beachcombers, joggers, surfers, paddlers, anglers, and sailors. Numerous public access areas to the beach are described in the individual sport sections. ◆ Just south of Wrightsville and accessible only by low-draft boat or kayak, **Masonboro Island,** (910) 772-8007, *www.masonboroisland.com,* is undeveloped with 5,000 acres of tidal salt marsh, mud flats, and nearly eight miles of sandy beach. Part of the National Estuarine Research Reserve, Masonboro is home to a bevy of wildlife, including raccoons, terns, river otters, gray foxes, and University of Wilmington college students. It's also a major nesting area for loggerhead turtles. The island is popular with kayakers, who paddle along the island's western shoreline on the Intracoastal Waterway, and with surfers, beachcombers, and anglers who land on the island to spend the day. There are no facilities on Masonboro and whatever you take to the island must make the return trip, including trash. To access the island, check with one of the rental sources under *Paddling.*

Carolina Beach State Park, 1010 State Park, Carolina Beach, (910) 458-8206 or (910) 458-7770 (marina), contains more than 750 acres of one of the most ecologically diverse tracts in North Carolina. Six miles of hiking trails wind across sand ridges, over brackish marsh, and through maritime forest full of live oaks. The park's most-unique feature is its population of the carnivorous Venus flytrap plant, which grows wild here. The park's full-service marina provides access to the Cape Fear River and Intracoastal Waterway; both waterways make for great paddling and angling adventures. Stop by the park's visitor center at the entrance for a map and suggestions on where to play. To get to the park from Wilmington, take Route 421 south roughly 15 miles to where the road forks. Veer right onto Dow Road and follow signs to the park just ahead on the right. ◆ The shoreline along **Carolina** and **Kure beaches** provides more opportunity for walking, fishing, swimming, surfing, and bike riding. Public access areas are described in the individual sport sections.

What's Bugging You?

Warm weather brings out a variety of biting insects—mosquitoes, horseflies, and sand gnats, among them—and there's no faster way to turn a pleasant day at the beach or park into a miserable experience. Your best defense? Bug spray. Don't leave your inn without it.

At the southernmost point of Pleasure Island, **Fort Fisher State Recreation Area,** 1610 Fort Fisher Boulevard South, Kure Beach, (910) 458-5538, features more than seven miles of beach fronting the Atlantic Ocean, as well as salt marshes, tidal creeks and mud flats on the western edge of the park facing the Cape Fear River. There's a short hiking trail along the marsh, but the park is most popular with beachcombers, surfers, and anglers who are allowed to pull four-wheel drive vehicles onto the beach. Take Route 421 south 20 miles from Wilmington to Loggerhead Road on the left. Take Loggerhead Road to the visitor center parking area on the left. The North Carolina Aquarium and the remains of the Confederate Fort Fisher, which stood guard at the mouth of the Cape Fear River, are also here.

Zeke's Island is another National Estuarine Reserve property and is actually comprised of three islands: Zeke's, No Name, and North. Located directly south of Pleasure Island, the islands are most popular with kayakers who paddle the calm lagoon area created by a three-mile rock jetty that disrupts the flow of the Cape Fear River. The surrounding waters and tidal flats are full of fish, bottlenose dolphins, shrimp, crabs, and aquatic birds like ibis and egrets. The islands can only be accessed by boat, and of the three, only North Island is large enough to allow much exploration on foot. Unless you're an experienced sea kayaker, the best way to explore the lagoon is with one of the paddling outfits described in *Paddling*.

A great variety of outdoor activity exists on **Bald Head Island,** 1-800-234-1666, *www.baldheadisland.com*, where miles of paved roads free from automobile traffic make great cycling, running, walking, and rollerblading routes, and where the 14 miles of beach are enough to exhaust even the most-energetic explorers. Paddlers take to the more than 10,000 acres of protected tidal creeks and marshes; steady winds push sailors along; and fertile waters keep the anglers casting in search of 'the big one.'

Carolina Beach State Park

Dayhiking

The flat, coastal landscape around Wilmington doesn't offer much in the way of rigorous hiking; however, there are plenty of trails and paths for those who enjoy pleasant walks in the woods or along the coast. The most popular walking destinations are the area beaches. You'll also find a smattering of municipal paths through coastal communities and in local parks. The following hikes present a sampling of the region's offerings.

◆ Located less than a mile from downtown Wilmington off Route 421 South (see

The Wrightsville Beach Loop

Wide Open for directions), **Greenfield Park,** (910) 341-7855, features a five-mile, paved path around stunning Greenfield Lake and beneath cypress trees with shawls of Spanish Moss. In the summer, the best time to walk is as the sun is rising when the air is still cool and the trees cast long shadows across the water. In the spring, blooming azaleas make this walk a colorful and fragrant treat for the senses. ◆ Wrightsville Beach maintains **the Loop**, a 2.5-mile paved path for walking, jogging, and rollerblading that winds around Wrightsville Beach Park, along North Lumina Avenue, and across Banks Channel to Harbor Island. Park at the Wrightsville Beach Museum on Harbor Island off Route 74 and set out.

◆ Several trails crisscross the 750 acres of **Carolina Beach State Park,** 1010 State Park, Carolina Beach, (910) 458-8206, and while none is challenging, each provides an interesting overview of the park's ecological treasures. (See *Wide Open* for directions to the park.) Blazed with orange circles, the three-mile **Sugarloaf Trail** departs from the marina parking lot and traverses a tidal marsh, pine forest, and the edge of the Cape Fear River en route to Sugarloaf Dune. You'll see ample wildlife, including aquatic birds, fiddler crabs, and possibly a foraging raccoon (at low tide). The return portion of the trail passes Cypress, Lilly, and Green ponds. ◆ The half-

Now Showing: JAWS

Certainly one of the most intriguing members of the plant kingdom, the carnivorous **Venus flytrap** is indigenous to the Cape Fear Region and can be seen along a handful of walking trails around Wilmington. The best place to spot these plants is along the **Flytrap Trail** in Carolina Beach State Park, but you may also happen upon them in Greenfield Park and Airlie Gardens. In case you've forgotten your 7th-grade science, the plant, which grows to a foot in height and features between four and eight sets of leaf traps, attracts insects to the inside of the trap with its red coloring. Within 1/30th of a second after the insect crawls in, the jaws snap shut. Stiff bristles keep the prey from escaping, while digestive enzymes dissolve the bug. Each leaf of the flytrap repeats this process three times every eight to 10 days before dying. While it's tempting to 'tease' the plants by tickling inside their jaws, please don't. They're becoming increasingly rare and interference weakens their health.

mile **Flytrap Trail** is a short loop that winds past an abundance of the rare, insect-eating Venus flytrap plants. Stay on the orange diamond-blazed path to avoid damaging these fragile plants. To access this trail, turn onto the first road on the left inside the park and drive the short distance to the parking area at the end. ◆ Other trails in the park include the one-mile, blue circle-blazed **Campground Trail;** the 0.75-mile, red circle-blazed **Swamp Trail;** the half-mile, red diamond-blazed **Snow's Cut Trail;** and the 0.25-mile, blue diamond-blazed **Oak Toe Trail**. All of the trails may be combined to create longer loops. When you arrive, stop at the park office for a trail map.

◆ In addition to the seven miles of undeveloped beach fronting the Atlantic Ocean at **Fort Fisher State Recreation Area,** 1610 Fort Fisher Boulevard South, Kure Beach, (910) 458-5538, the one-mile **Basin Trail** combines a scenic marsh walk with a bit of history. You'll pass the earthen remains of the 1861 Fort Fisher as well as a World War II bunker en route to Basin Overlook, a small bluff with views of Zeke's Island. The blue-blazed trail departs from the park's visitor center parking area. Stop in for a trail map. See *Wide Open* for directions to Fort Fisher.

◆ In **Southport,** take the relaxing, one-mile **Southport Trail** through the town's charming historic waterfront. Pick up a brochure for this self-guided trail from the Southport Visitor Center, 113 West Moore Street. The loop through the village and along the waterfront features a number of highlights, including City Hall, Franklin Square Park, and the Old Brunswick Jail.

◆ Six miles of paved roads without cars and 14 miles of stunning beach make **Bald Head Island,** 1-800-234-1666, *www.baldheadisland.com,* an ideal destination for the footloose. After disembarking from the ferry (see *The Way Around* for directions), pick up an island map at the ferry terminal and set out. A suggested six-mile loop through maritime forest and past upscale homes: From the ferry terminal, follow West Bald Head Wynd to the right (the beach will be on your right) as it gently curves left to become South Bald Head Wynd. Continue on South Bald Head Wynd to the intersection with Federal Road, where you turn left. Federal Road returns to the ferry terminal, though the road's name changes to North Bald Head Wynd en route.

◆ Bald Head's beach is ideal for invigorating walks or jogs. From the main harbor, rent a golf cart at Island Passage, 1 Marina Wynd, (910) 457-4944, ($25 for first hour, $10 per hour thereafter, or $55 per day) and take North Bald Head Wynd (which becomes Federal Road) to South East Beach Drive, where you turn left. Make a right on Station House Way, where three beach access points lie within a few hundred yards of each other. Park and set out to the left (north) for more deserted shoreline or to the right (south) to reach Cape Fear Point, which you can follow around the bend to South Beach. With your cart rental, you'll receive an island map detailing many more beach-access areas.

◆ Also on Bald Head Island and maintained by the Bald Head Island Conservancy, the half-mile **Kent Mitchell Nature Trail** is a boardwalk and trail through salt marsh and maritime forest located off Federal Road between Muscadine Wynd and Maritime Way. Another conservancy property, **Bald Head Woods** is a 173-acre site of maritime forest off Federal Road in which you'll find a mile-long interpretive trail with signs identifying the plant and animal life. "Baldy," a huge live oak tree, is at the entrance to the trail.

◆ Other excellent walking beaches include the five-mile stretch of sand on **Wrightsville Beach**; and the 13 miles of south-facing beach on **Oak Island.**

The remains of Fort Fisher

Bicycling

Bicycling opportunities in the greater Wilmington area are a mixed bag. The flat terrain makes pedaling easy—no true "mountain" biking here—but many of the area's roads have too much traffic for safe riding. That said there are several paths in area parks, a few lightly traveled roads, and many miles of beach to explore on a beach cruiser. The following are some of the better places to ride. For longer routes, ask for suggestions from any of the sources listed under "Rentals."

◆ The five-mile paved path around Greenfield Lake at **Greenfield Park,** Willard Street (off South Third Street), Wilmington, (910) 341-7855, is a serene ride. The easy, flat path winds past stately moss-covered cypress trees, towering live oaks, magnolias, redbuds, crepe myrtles, and dogwoods, along with thousands of jonquils, daffodils, and tulips. Spring is the primary blooming season. See *Wide Open* for directions to the park.

◆ From **Carolina Beach State Park,** 1010 State Park, Carolina Beach, (910) 458-8206, you can pedal a 16-mile out-and-back route to **Fort Fisher State Recreation Area,** where you can visit the Aquarium, walk the park's trails, picnic, or take a swim before riding the eight miles back. From Carolina Beach State Park (see *Wide Open* for directions), take the lightly traveled Dow Road south. En route to Kure Beach, the road provides occasional views of the Cape Fear River to your right. In Kure Beach, Dow hairpins left to become Avenue K, which you follow to its junction with Route 421. Turn right on Route 421 and ride to Fort Fisher. Once beyond Kure Beach, the speed limit increases to 55 mph, but the highway has a designated bike shoulder on which to ride. During this 3.5-mile stretch, you're treated to views of the Atlantic Ocean to the left and Cape Fear River to the right. (Note: this area is prone to cross winds, so if it's a particularly windy day, choose another ride.) After relaxing at Fort Fisher, retrace your route to Carolina Beach. To extend your adventure, catch the Fort Fisher-Southport Ferry from the end of Route 421 to explore Southport before catching the return ferry and riding back to your car.

◆ The quiet, live oak-lined streets and attractive waterfront of **Southport** are excellent places to explore on a bike. Traffic moves slowly in town, but you'll still want to ride defensively at all times. The town's historic district is small enough to explore without a map, but if you prefer more direction, stop by the Southport Visitor Center, 113 West Moore Street, for a town map. Be sure to ride along the waterfront on Bay Street. Also, visit **Waterfront**

Park (Bay Street between Howe and Davis streets) where a line of benches overlook the mouth of the Cape Fear River, and **Keziah Park** (corner of Lord and Moore streets) which has the Indian Trail Tree, a live oak believed to be 800 years old.

◆ The Town of Oak Island publishes a free brochure entitled *Bicycle Trail Maps* that details 11 bicycling routes of varying lengths on **Oak Island.** (Pick up a free copy at the Oak Island Recreation

Cypress Trees surround Greenfield Lake

Center, 3003 East Oak Island Drive, Oak Island, (910) 278-5518.) The brochure includes maps, mileages, and special notes for each ride. Included in the rides is the 3.2-mile **Heron Loop Trail,** which begins at Heron Park on 40th Street SE (from Route 133 turn right onto Oak Island Drive and travel to 40th Street, where you turn left to reach the park). From the park, take East 40th Street north (away from the ocean) to East Yacht Drive where you turn left. Ride 40 blocks west on Yacht Drive to Middleton Drive, where you turn left to ride toward the ocean. At Beach Drive, turn left and ride the bike pathway east to 40th Street, where you turn left to close the loop by riding to the park. ◆ A couple of hours on either side of low tide, you can ride beach cruisers along the beaches on Oak Island and on Wrightsville Beach.

◆ What's a cyclist's dream? Miles of paved roads free from automobile traffic. You'll find just that on **Bald Head Island,** 1-800-234-1666, *www.baldheadisland.com,* where cars are prohibited and cyclists share the roads with golf carts, rollerbladers, and pedestrians. Pick up a copy of the flyer entitled *Go the Distance*—available from the ticket window at Indigo Plantation in Southport and in the Chandler Building (on your left exiting the ferry) on Bald Head—which details the island's major roads with point-to-point mileage information. While all of the island's roads are pleasant to ride, highlights include the

maritime forest preserve on **Federal Road,** and along **South Bald Head Wynd** with its tremendous views of the Atlantic Ocean. You'll have to take the ferry from Southport to Bald Head Island (see *The Way Around* for directions), at a cost of $15 per person roundtrip. Rent your bike on Bald Head at Island Passage (see *Rentals*), because the ferry system charges an additional $15 per bike roundtrip.

Oak Island Lighthouse

NC Division of Tourism

Rentals

The Adventure Company, 807-A Howe Street, Southport, ☎ (910) 454-0607, *www.theadventurecompany.net,* rents beach cruisers and offers guided bicycle tours of Southport for groups of four or more. ◆ **Island Passage,** 1 Marina Wynd, Bald Head Island, ☎ (910) 457-4944, rents beach cruisers for use on the island. ◆ **Pleasure Island Rentals,** 2 North Lake Park Boulevard, Carolina Beach, ☎ (910) 458-4747, *www.pleasureislandrentals.com,* rents beach cruisers and tandem bikes. ◆ **Southport Bicycles,** 417-B North Howe Street, Southport, ☎ (910) 457-1878, *www.southportbicycles.com,* rents beach cruisers for travel around Southport. ◆ **Two Wheeler Dealer,** 4408 Wrightsville Avenue, Wilmington, ☎ (910) 799-6444, *www.bikesarefun.com,* is a full-service bike shop that rents mountain and road bikes. ◆ **Wheel Fun Rentals** has two locations—107 Carolina Beach Avenue, Carolina Beach, ☎ (910) 458-4545; and 14 Market Street, Wilmington, ☎ (910) 763-6565, *www.wheelfunrentals.com*—that rent cruisers, mountain bikes, and four-wheeled bikes.

Paddling

With a superstore-sized selection of scenic waterways—tidal rivers, creeks, sounds, salt marshes, the Intracoastal Waterway, and the Atlantic Ocean—the Cape Fear Region is a major paddling destination. Sea kayaks are the boats of choice for most paddlers. Sleek, stable, and able to navigate in mere inches of water, a kayak allows you to float silently at water level and to observe dolphins, shore and aquatic birds, and other wildlife up close.

The following provides general descriptions of the best paddling spots. Unless you're an experienced paddler, consider joining a guided tour. Enough water challenges exist (see "Up the Creek") that relying on an experienced guide is a prudent step. What's more, your outfitter will tote your boat and provide transportation to and from the put-in and take-out points. If you choose to go it alone, stop by any of the outfitters below to get directions to the best put-ins based on current conditions.

NC Division of Tourism

♦ On the western side of **Wrightsville Beach**, extensive marshes make excellent paddling grounds. The calm, tidal waters teem with marine life, creating a major feeding area for birds—look for herons, ospreys (the ones toting wriggling fish in their claws), snowy egrets, terns, and pelicans.

♦ A popular paddle from the Wrightsville Beach area is to **Masonboro Island,** an undeveloped barrier island with 8,000 acres of salt marshes and mud flats teeming with brown pelicans, royal terns, and laughing gulls. After paddling the island's western banks facing the **Intracoastal Waterway**, you may choose to explore the island by foot or to plunk a towel down on the pristine, eight-mile beach.

Up the Creek

As in, don't get caught there without the proverbial paddle. For all of their beauty and allure, the area's paddling waters pose some tricky challenges, including tidal fluctuations, currents, wind, and sudden storms. Unless you know the local waters well, start with a tour offered by one of the local paddling outfitters. It's the most-assured means of enjoying your excursion and taking in the sights versus standing in a mud flat wondering where all the water went and who called in the mosquitoes.

♦ Paddling through the **Basin** to **Zeke's Island,** a barrier island just south of the Fort Fisher State Recreation Area, is a pleasant trip. The Basin is a large, protected body of water between the Cape Fear River and Atlantic Ocean. A three-mile rock jetty keeps the currents of the Cape Fear River from swirling into the basin and the bay's shallow depth prevents motorboats from venturing in, so this is a popular place for beginners to learn the basics of sea kayaking. Zeke's Island is an undeveloped, 42-acre island surrounded by extensive marshes and tidal flats. In addition to being home for dozens of species of birds, this area is an important nursing ground for crabs, shrimp, and fish.

♦ Canoeists and sea kayakers have more than 24 miles of water trails to explore on **Oak Island.** The **Oak**

Island Trail System features four trails that make use of the winding waterways through and along Oak Island. Highlights include wildlife sightings—keep an eye out for great blue herons, snowy egrets, and scores of jumping fish—as well as plenty of pleasant, easy paddling. Trails include the blue-blazed, 4.2-mile **Lockwoods Folly Trail**; the white-blazed, seven-mile **Montgomery Slough Trail**; the red-blazed, 6.5-mile **Howells Point Trail**; and the orange-blazed, six-mile **Davis Creek Trail**. With the exception of Davis Creek, all trails begin at the **Blue Water Point Marina**, 5 Northwest 57th Place, on Oak Island. (The Davis Creek Trail begins at the intersection of the Montgomery Slough Trail and Davis Creek.) For a free map of the water trails, stop by the **Oak Island Parks & Recreation Department**, 3003 East Oak Island Drive, (910) 278-5518.

Free Paddling Map

Yours for the asking: a free, color map showing the general location of all of North Carolina's mapped paddle trails along the coastal plain, including many around Wilmington. *The North Carolina Coastal Plain Paddle Trails Guide* is a 38" by 26" map with trail names, difficulty ratings, skill levels, time and distance estimates, access points and trail contact information. To request the map, call the state's Division of Parks and Recreation, ☎ (919) 778-9499, or visit: *www.ncsu.edu/paddletrails*.

◆ A sampling of other paddling spots includes the numerous tidal creeks and marked water trails on **Bald Head Island;** and the **Cape Fear River,** which tends to attract more advanced paddlers because of the tides, currents, and commercial shipping traffic. (Give a wide berth to ocean-going ships.) The Cape Fear has dozens of navigable tributaries, many of which are brackish or blackwater creeks. ◆ Roughly an hour from Wilmington, the sublime **Black River** is a protected tributary of the Cape Fear River on which you'll find a blackwater swamp full of old-growth cypress trees. ◆ **Rice Creek** and **Town Creek** are both pristine tributaries of the Cape Fear River that connect with one another. Town Creek stretches 25 miles inland through maritime forest, marshland, and open pastures. The water changes from brackish near the Cape Fear to fresh blackwater the further inland you paddle. Both creeks present opportunities to see wildlife like osprey, owls, snakes, and possibly an alligator.

◆ Paddling out into the **Atlantic Ocean**—assuming it's relatively calm—presents a challenge for the more-experienced sea kayaker due to the potential for high winds, riptides, and sudden storms. If you've never been in open water before, stick to the protected waterways. Open-water paddling requires better boat handling skills and experience in self-rescue maneuvers like the "wet exit." You might also explore renting a sit-on-top kayak for paddling in the surf.

Yak Yak Yak

If paddling sounds like fun, but you came to Wilmington to enjoy the beach and can't tear yourself away from the surf, mix your pleasures by renting a **Funyak,** or sit-on-top kayak. These super-stable, plastic boats are great beach toys. Climb aboard with a lifejacket and paddle past the breakers—you won't capsize if you keep the boat perpendicular to the waves—to float on the gentle swells or to use the boat as a surfboard. To get started, get thee to **Pleasure Island Rentals**, 2 North Lake Park Boulevard, Carolina Beach, ☎ (910) 458-4747, *www.pleasureislandrentals.com*.

Paddling Outfitters

Numerous paddling outfitters exist in and around Wilmington. Some good bets include the **Adventure Company,** 807-A Howe Street, Southport, ☎ (910) 454-0607, *www.theadventurecompany.net,* which rents canoes and kayaks, and offers paddling instruction and a variety of two-hour, four-hour, full-day, and overnight tours. ◆ **Carolina Coastal Adventures,** 1337 Bridge Barrier Road, Carolina Beach, ☎ (910) 458-9111, *www.carolinacoastaladventures.com,* rents kayaks, provides instruction, and offers a range of guided tours, including sunrise and sunset tours. ◆ On Bald Head Island, **Island Passage,** 6 Maritime Way, ☎ (910) 454-8420, *www.islandpassage.net,* rents canoes and kayaks. ◆ **Pro Canoe & Kayak,** 435 Eastwood Road, Wilmington, ☎ (910) 798-9922 or 1-888-794-4867, *www.procanoe.com,* rents kayaks and canoes, plus offers instruction. ◆ In Wrightsville Beach, the **Salt Marsh Kayak Company,** 222 Old Causeway Drive, Wrightsville Beach, ☎ (910) 509-2989 or 1-866-655-2925. *www.saltmarshkayak.com,* offers kayak rentals, instruction, and paddling tours.

Fishing

With the Gulf Stream just 45 miles offshore, the greater Wilmington area sports an active deep-sea fishing industry. Numerous marinas host charter operations that promise productive trips into mackerel (Spanish and king), grouper, snapper, and mahi mahi waters. Plenty of big fish—tuna, shark, wahoo, and marlin, among them—wait offshore, as well. Inshore fishing on the region's sounds, creeks, and rivers may turn up such catches as flounder, mullet, spot, red drum, and more. You can fish year-round, but the primary offshore season runs March–November. July–October is the best time to fish closer to shore.

So many charter operations and guide services exist that you'll have little trouble finding

NC Division of Tourism

a captain ready to motor to the fruitful inshore and offshore fishing grounds. Should you opt to venture to the Gulf Stream, you'll spend a minimum of eight hours on open water and roughly $500 for a guided charter for two people. (On average, charters take six people; most boats operate "split charters," meaning they'll pair you with four or more other anglers.) Half-day rates are approximately $300.

One way to find a boat is to visit the area's many marinas (see "Marinas") and to talk with the captains to find one you like. The following charters are just a few of region's best. ♦ Jimmy Vass' company, **Hunter Charters**, (910) 791-6414, *www.fortunehuntercharters.com*, operates several boats from the Seapath Yacht Club, 328 Causeway Drive, on Wrightsville Beach. Vass and his crew of Coast Guard-licensed captains specialize in light-tackle, half- and full-day charters. ♦ Captain Robbie Wolfe's 42-foot *Whipsaw,* (910) 791-0555, *www.fishwhipsaw.com*, departs from Wrightsville Beach's Bridgetender Marina, 1418 Airlie Road, for half-, three-quarter-, and full-day charters. ♦ At Carolina Beach, **Captain John's Fishing Charters,** 1337 Bridge Barrier Road, (910) 458-9600, *www.fishing-carolinabeach.com*, features three boats for inshore, near-shore, and offshore charters. ♦ **Carolina Beach Fishing Charters,** 1-800-288-3474, *www.carolinabeachfishing.com*, operates the 49-foot *Flap Jack* and the 35-foot *Sea Trek* from Carolina Beach's Municipal Marina, 207 Canal Drive.

♦ To load up on fishing gear, secure the services of a guide, and swap big-fish stories, stop by Wilmington's **Intracoastal Angler,** 7220 Wrightsville Avenue, Suite A, Wilmington, (910) 256-4545, *www.intracoastalangler.com*. This full-service, saltwater tackle shop and outfitter offers an extensive lineup of gear, accessories, and apparel. The shop also offers fly-fishing clinics year-round.

Marinas

Public marinas are the places to find fishing and sailing charters; sunset, dinner and nature cruises; parasailing boats; and Wave Runner, Sunfish, and small-motorboat rentals. The following are just some of the many marinas around Wilmington: **Seapath Yacht Club and Marina**, 328 Causeway Drive, Wrightsville Beach, ☎ (910) 256-3747 ♦ **Carolina Beach Municipal Marina**, 207 Canal Drive, Carolina Beach, ☎ (910) 458-2540, *www.carolinabeachfishing.com* ♦ **Blue Water Point Marina Resort,** 57th Place and West Beach Drive, Oak Island, ☎ (910) 278-1230, *www.bluewaterpointmotel.com* ♦ **Southport Marina**, 606 West West Street, Southport ☎ (910) 457-9900, *www.southportmarina.org* ♦ **Bald Head Island Marina,** 1 Marina Wynd, Bald Head Island, ☎ (910) 457-7380.

Horseback Riding

Open seven days a week, **Desperado Horse Farm,** 7214 Route 210, Rocky Point, (910) 675-0487, *www.desperadohorsefarm.com*, offers trail rides through the woods or on Topsail Beach (September–March only). Guided rides range from one hour to all day, and the stable also features moonlight rides. Expect to pay roughly $25 an hour. Rides are available by appointment only, so call ahead. To reach the stables from

Wilmington, take Interstate 40 north to Route 210 (Exit #408), which you take east six miles to the farm's entrance on the left at Running Deer Road. Drive time is approximately 20 minutes.

Rainy Day Workout

When the rain clouds are out, head for a workout at one of several area fitness facilities. The following allow guests for a nominal day-use fee. **The Wilmington Athletic Club,** 2026 South 16th Street, Wilmington, (910) 343-5950, *www.wilmingtonathleticclub.com,* is a decidedly modern and spacious exercise facility with a full cardio room, free weights, Nautilus equipment, and basketball and racquetball courts. Pilates, yoga, and aerobics classes are offered, as are massage and day-spa services. In addition to men's and women's locker rooms with saunas and steam rooms, there's a lounge with a juice bar. ◆ **The Spa Health Club,** 2250 Shipyard Boulevard, Wilmington, (910) 392-4210, features a full cardio section, Paramount weight-training machines, free weights, an indoor track, lap pool, steam room, and sauna.

Sailing

The **Atlantic Ocean**, **Cape Fear River**, and **Intracoastal Waterway** make fine sailing grounds, and numerous charters set sail from local marinas. You can also rent your own boat or take a lesson. In fact, one of the nation's finest sailing schools is located here. A five-time recipient of the American Sailing Association's "School of the Year" award, **WaterWays Sailing & Charters**, 2030 Eastwood Road, Suite 12, Wrightsville Beach, (910) 256-4282 or 1-800-562-7245, *www.sailwaterway.com,* offers lessons for all levels, from beginners to more advanced sailors. The full-service sailing operation also provides captained charters from the **Seapath Yacht Club,** 328 Causeway Drive, Wrightsville Beach, (910) 256-3747, for three and six hours. Their popular sunset cruises promise ideal positioning for watching the day's light fade against a backdrop of Wrightsville Beach lighting up for the evening.

◆ Want to skipper your own boat? Stop by either Wrightsville Beach's **Salt Marsh Kayak Company**, 222 Old Causeway Drive, (910) 509-2989 or 1-866-655-2925, *www.saltmarshkayak.com,* which rents three sizes of sailboats, including 16-foot Hobie Cats, and offers instruction; or ◆ Carolina Beach's **Pleasure Island Rentals,** 2 North Lake Park Boulevard, (910) 458-4747, *www.pleasureislandrentals.com,* which rents an ultra-stable sailboat, the Escape Mango, that's a perfect toy for novice sailors.

NC Division of Tourism

Scuba Diving

The waters off the Cape Fear Coast feature more than two dozen shipwrecks within an easy trip from shore. All support underwater ecosystems as fascinating as anything you'll find on land. In general, the further offshore you go, the better the visibility. One of the better-known dive sites is the *Alexander Ramsey*, a clipper ship sunk in 1974 as an artificial reef three miles from Wrightsville Beach. The boat rests in 50 feet of water and is especially popular when rough seas prevent divers from venturing further out to sea. Barracuda and Spanish mackerel are abundant here. ◆ Sunk in March 1942 by a German torpedo, the 528-foot tanker *John D. Gill* sits in 90 feet of water 25 miles offshore and is home to sea turtles, barracuda, rays, scores of tropical fish, and an occasional shark. ◆ Several local dive operations will help you get to the bottom of things by providing instruction, gear rentals, and passage to area wrecks. Wilmington's **Aquatic Safaris,** 5751-4 Oleander Drive, (910) 392- 4386, *www.aquaticsafaris.com,* charters two 30-foot boats for day- and night-time dives. Trip prices range from $40–$130, depending on how far offshore you travel. Walk-ins welcome. ◆ **Bottom Time Charters,** 6014 Wrightsville Avenue, Wilmington, (910) 397-0181, *www.bottomtime.com,* offers inshore, offshore, and full-day trips, predominantly along the underwater ledges off Topsail Beach.

Hang Ten

In general, the north-south-running beaches off the Cape Fear Coast (from Topsail Island to Carolina and Kure beaches) produce wave action decent enough to keep most locals happy. But when a storm passes offshore, swells roll in that pull surfers from across the Carolinas. Popular breaks on Wrightsville Beach include **Crystal Pier,** near 703 South Lumina Avenue; **Johnny Mercer Pier,** 23 East Salisbury Street; and the end of **Columbia Street** (a.k.a. "C" Street). Note: Town regulations prohibit surfing in swimming-only areas during the summer. Heed all signs. The best advice, of course, comes from a surf shop, of which there are many. Try **Sweetwater Surf Shop,** 10 North Lumina Avenue, Wrightsville Beach, ☎ (910) 256-3821, *www.sweetwatersurfshop.com.*

Deron Nardo

Swimming

Sure, Wilmington has history, culture, and great shopping, but the area's big draw is the Atlantic Ocean with its many miles of sandy beaches. From the middle of spring to late fall, the water is ripe for swimming. In general, the local waters are calm. Throughout the region, public beach access areas are marked by orange and blue signs. Grab your towel, sunscreen, refreshments, and pulp fiction on the way to one of the following paradises. ♦ **Wrightsville Beach** features five miles of sand patrolled by lifeguards Memorial Day–Labor Day. Arrive early in the day to avoid parking headaches (see "Brother Can You Spare a Dime?" in *The Way Around*).

A public beach access

♦ The four miles of shoreline along **Carolina** and **Kure beaches** are easily accessed, with numerous metered parking spots available along side streets. Crowds pick up around Carolina Beach's boardwalk, where you'll find concessions and seaside shops. In general, Kure Beach is more subdued. ♦ **Fort Fisher State Recreation Area's** seven-mile beach is less crowded than Carolina and Kure beaches. See *The Way Around* for directions. ♦ The **Town of Oak Island** maintains more than 50 public access areas for its east-west running beaches, all marked by orange and blue signs. ♦ The 14-mile beach on **Bald Head Island** can be divided into three sections. The white sand beach on the island's east side is largely undeveloped and less crowded. The more-popular south beach has numerous beach access points, and the west beach faces the confluence of the Atlantic Ocean and the Cape Fear River.

Local Outdoor Advice

Two Wheeler Dealer • This full-service bike shop rents and sells road and mountain bikes, as well as cycling-related accessories and apparel. The friendly staff will happily point you to the area's finest trails. • 4408 Wrightsville Avenue, Wilmington, ☎ (910) 799-6444, *www.bikesarefun.com*

Carolina Coastal Adventures • An adventure outfitter and retail shop that sells kayaks, paddling accessories, and various outdoor gear, CCA is also the place to rent kayaks and sign up for kayaking, fishing, and sightseeing tours. Owners Angela and John Pagenstecher know the area exceptionally well and welcome drop-ins looking for outdoor suggestions. • 1337 Bridge Barrier Road, Carolina Beach, ☎ (910) 458-9111, *www.carolinacoastaladventures.com*

Great Outdoor Provision Co. • This full-service outfitter sells all manner of outdoor gear, apparel, and footwear. The Wilmington store—one of seven locations in the Carolinas—is staffed with friendly, knowledgeable outdoor enthusiasts. • Hanover Center, 3501 Oleander Drive, Wilmington, ☎ (910) 343-1648, *www.greatoutdoorprovision.com*

K i c k   B a c k

W hen rain threatens your outdoor plans or your body needs to rest from yesterday's play, let the following activities in and around Wilmington fill your day.

Antiques

As a port city with a long history, Wilmington has a number of antiques shops downtown, particularly along Front Street. Some of the better bets in Wilmington include: **Michael Moore Antiques,** 20 South Front Street, (910) 763-0300, where 10 dealers sell furniture, handmade rugs, decorative accessories, silver, and more on two floors; ◆ **River Galleries,** 107 South Front Street, (910) 251-2224, for a variety of high-end antiques, including furniture, china, fine art, and glassware; and ◆ **Celestial Antiques,** 143 North Front Street, (910) 362-0740, *www.celestialantiques.com,* which houses an array of furniture carved in the Far East, as well as nautical instruments and antique tools.

◆ In Historic Southport, **Southport Antiques,** 105 East Moore Street, (910) 457-1755, *www.southportantiques.com,* displays and sells furniture, quilts, silver, china, and nautical antiques.

Art & Crafts Galleries

With more than 35 privately owned galleries in the area, the Wilmington region is rich in visual-arts opportunities. The greatest collection of art and crafts galleries is in Wilmington's historic district, particularly along Water and Front streets. You'll also find several excellent galleries in Southport, primarily on Howe Street, and in Wrightsville Beach. A sampling of Wilmington's best stops: ◆ The **Wilmington Gallery,** 225 South Water Street, (910) 343-4370, *www.wilmington-art.org,* is a co-operative that displays and sells work by more than 70 local and regional artists. Expect crafts like textiles, pottery, and paper, as well as oils, watercolors, and pastels. The gallery is housed in a

The Cameron Art Museum

Formerly the St. John's Museum of Art, the 42,000-square foot **Louise Wells Cameron Art Museum**, 3201 South 17th Street at Independence Boulevard, Wilmington, ☎ (910) 395-5999, *www.cameronartmuseum.com,* is dedicated primarily to collecting and exhibiting North Carolina art. Among its permanent collection are color prints by Mary Cassatt, ceramic pieces by potter Ben Owen, and paintings by Romare Beardon. The gallery also hosts three to four traveling exhibitions at any one time. There's an onsite restaurant, bar, and gift shop. Open Tuesday–Saturday, 10 A.M.–5 P.M.; Sunday, 10:30 A.M.–4 P.M. Nominal admission fee.

restored 1884 warehouse in downtown Wilmington's Chandler's Wharf. ◆ **New Elements Gallery,** 216 North Front Street, (910) 343-8997 or 1-888-817-0834, *www.newelements-gallery.com*, features continually changing displays of fine art and crafts by regional and national painters, sculptors, potters, glassmakers, and woodworkers. ◆ Located near Wrightsville Beach, **Fountainside Gallery**, 1900 Eastwood Road, Suite 44, Wilmington, (910) 256-9956, *www.fountainsidegallery.com*, displays and sells fine art, including bronze sculptures, oil paintings, water colors, acrylics, and pastels in a 3,200-square foot gallery. ◆ **The Gallery at Racine,** 203 Racine Drive, Wilmington, (910) 452-2073, *www.racinecenter.com*, is a large art gallery inside the Racine Center for the Arts, a multi-discipline arts facility and school. The gallery features an astonishing variety of art pieces and crafts. Exhibitions change every six to eight weeks. Also within the arts center, **Blue Moon Showcase,** is a co-operative with booths selling work by local artists and craftspeople. This is an excellent place to purchase gifts. ◆ You'll find many forms of African art, including woodcarvings, masks, swords, and textiles at **Charles Jones African Art,** 311 Judges Road 6-E, Wilmington, (910) 794-3060, *www.cjafricanart.com*. Though the gallery focuses primarily on traditional West African art, work from other regions, including the Congo, Ethiopia, Sudan, and Tanzania, is represented as well.

Gardens

Located off Route 133 roughly 18 miles south of Wilmington, **Orton Plantation Gardens**, 9149 Orton Road SE, Winnabow, (910) 371-6851, *www.ortongardens.com*,

features 20 acres of formal and informal gardens open to the public. (The plantation home is a private residence.) Set on the grounds of a former 1725 Cape Fear rice plantation, the gardens include azaleas, camellias, crepe myrtles, flowering peaches, and numerous other perennials and annuals. Walking paths wind through the gardens, beneath pine and oak trees, and past several lakes and lagoons. The whole scene is as splendid as a movie set, which in fact, it's been. More than 40 major films have been shot on location at Orton, including *The Road to Wellville* and *Firestarter*. To catch the gardens at their peak (when the azaleas and dogwoods bloom) visit in the spring. Open daily, March–August, 8 A.M.–6 P.M.; and daily, September–November, 10 A.M.–5 P.M. Nominal admission fee.

Orton Plantation

◆ For an Eden-like experience just across the causeway from Wrightsville Beach, visit **Airlie Gardens,** 300 Airlie Road, Wilmington, (910) 798-7700, *www.airliegardens.org*, where European-style formal and informal gardens are laid out over 67 acres. A one-mile, self-guiding walking path meanders past two freshwater lakes and dozens of plant varieties, including camellias and azaleas. Of note: Airlie Oak, a tree more than 450 years old. Open from late February–October, Tuesday–Saturday, 9 A.M.–5 P.M.; Sunday, 11 A.M.–5 P.M. Nominal admission fee.

Presenting Queen Azalea

The first weekend of each April, Wilmington celebrates **The North Carolina Azalea Festival,** a celebration of the city's gardens, arts and cultural offerings, and history. Founded in 1948, the festival draws more than 250,000 people and has become one of the Southeast's major events. The fun kicks off with the arrival of Queen Azalea and her court. Following the ceremonial start, more than 125 events fill the four-day festival with fun, food, and music. Highlights include a three-day riverfront street fair; continuous live entertainment; a spectacular parade with floats, bands, clowns, animals, and celebrities; garden and home tours; a circus; and evening fireworks. For information, call ☎ (910) 794-4650 or visit *www.ncazaleafestival.org.*

Historic Homes

When British forces overran Wilmington in 1781, their leader, Lord Charles Cornwallis, established his headquarters in the 1770 **Burgwin-Wright House,** 224 Market Street, Wilmington, (910) 762-0570, a handsome, Georgian-style home built upon the foundation of a colonial jail. Originally built for planter and early colony treasurer John Burgwin, the fully restored house is open today as a museum. Inside there are 18th- and early 19th-century furnishings, as well as exhibits detailing the lives of previous residents. Seven formal, tiered gardens surround the house. Open Tuesday–Saturday, 10 A.M.–4 P.M., with guided tours on the hour. Nominal admission fee. Colonial cooking demonstrations are held one Saturday each month. (Call for schedule).

◆ The 22-room Italianate **Bellamy Mansion,** 503 Market Street, Wilmington, (910) 251-3700, *www.bellamymansion.org,* was built in 1859 for Dr. John Bellamy, a prominent planter, and his wife and nine children. During the Union occupation of Wilmington in the Civil War, General Joseph Hawley stayed here and liked it so much, he refused to give it up after the war. (Dr. Bellamy traveled to Washington to secure a pardon from President Andrew Johnson. As a result, Hawley got the boot.) Also on the property: a two-story brick slave quarters, a beautiful Victorian garden, and a carriage house that's been converted into a gift shop and visitor center. Hour-long

Cape Fear Coast CVB

The Burgwin-Wright House

tours detail the home's architectural and historical significance. Open Tuesday–Saturday, 10 A.M.–5 P.M., and Sunday, 1 P.M.–5 P.M. Nominal admission fee.

◆ Another Italianate mansion, the 14-room **Zebulon Latimer House**, 126 South Third Street, Wilmington, (910) 762-0492, *www.latimerhouse.org,* was built in 1852 for a wealthy merchant. Today the mansion is home to the Lower Cape Fear Historical Society, which has converted it into a museum depicting Victorian life for wealthy Wilmingtonians. More than 600 historical objects and antique furnishings, many of which belonged to the Latimer family, remain. The house and gardens are open Monday–Friday, 10 A.M.–4 P.M.; Saturday, noon–5 P.M. Nominal admission fee. The historical society conducts two-hour walking tours of downtown Wilmington that depart from the home. Hours vary by season; call for details.

◆ Located roughly 10 miles northeast of Wilmington, **Poplar Grove Historic Plantation**, 10200 Route 17, (910) 686-9518, *www.poplargrove.com,* is an 1850 Greek Revival manor house on 16 acres. The plantation was originally a 630-acre farm that grew corn, beans, and peas. Following the Civil War, the plantation grew only peanuts. The two-story frame house operates as a museum with period furnishings and exhibits. Costumed docents lead tours of the manor house. The grounds feature several outbuildings, including an outdoor kitchen, tenant farmer's cabin, and blacksmith shop. Period crafts demonstrations and classes are held on the property. Call for a schedule. Open Monday–Saturday, 9 A.M.–5 P.M.; Sunday, noon–5 P.M. Nominal admission fee.

Historic Sites

Founded in 1726 on the western bank of the Cape Fear River, **Brunswick Town,** 8884 St. Philips Road SE, Winnabow, (910) 371-6613, served as an early port for exporting such naval supplies as turpentine and lumber to Europe. Wilmington's rise as a larger center of commerce siphoned off most of Brunswick Town's residents until early in the American Revolution when British forces burned the settlement to the ground. In 1862, Confederate forces constructed Fort Anderson here to protect Wilmington. Today the site

A 37,400-ton Veteran

Moored directly across from downtown Wilmington as discreetly as a nine story-tall battleship can be, the **Battleship North Carolina**, Battleship Drive, Eagle Island, ☎ (910) 251-5797, *www.battleshipnc.com,* is a 729-foot, 37,400-ton gorilla of a ship that served in every major offensive in the Pacific during World War II. Fully restored and open for self-guided tours, the *North Carolina* features audio stations to aid your understanding of what life was like onboard during World War II. Wear comfortable shoes; the ship is massive, and the tour goes up and down narrow flights of stairs. Open daily, 8 A.M.–8 P.M., May–September; 8 A.M.–5 P.M., the rest of the year. Moderate admission fee. Access the battleship by car or by the water-taxi that departs from Front and Water streets. (Nominal fee for the taxi.)

NC Division of Tourism

includes the remains of St. Philips Anglican Church, built in 1754; the earthen remains of Fort Anderson; and a visitor center with interpretive displays of the town and fort. Open Monday–Saturday, 9 A.M.–5 P.M.; Sunday, 1 P.M.–5 P.M., April–October; and Tuesday–Saturday, 10 A.M.–4 P.M.; Sunday, 1 P.M.–4 P.M., November–March. Free admission.

NC Division of Tourism

Brunswick Town

◆ Located 20 minutes northwest of Wilmington on Route 210, **Moore's Creek National Battlefield**, 200 Moore's Creek Road, Currie, (910) 283-5591, celebrates the site of the patriot's first victory in the Revolutionary War. Here in 1776, using the ingenuity that helped win the war, colonists greased the logs on Moore's Creek Bridge. As the British redcoats crossed and scrambled for footing, the patriot's fired, decimating the confused loyalists. There's a visitor center with exhibits and two short, self-guiding trails. Open daily, 9 A.M.–5 P.M. Free admission.

◆ As the last major stronghold of the Confederacy, Fort Fisher kept the port of Wilmington open for blockade runners that supplied Robert E. Lee's troops to the north. Just how important was the fort to the Confederacy? When it fell into Union hands in 1865 after 2.5 days of continuous bombardment, the Confederacy fell soon after. You can learn much more about the fort's significance at the **Fort Fisher State Historic Site**, 1610 Fort Fisher Boulevard South, Kure Beach, (910) 458-5538, where roughly 10 percent of the original earthworks fort remains. A visitor center features interpretive exhibits and an audiovisual presentation. Open Monday–Saturday, 9 A.M.–5 P.M.; Sunday, 1 P.M.–5 P.M., April–October; and Tuesday–Saturday, 10 A.M.–4 P.M.; Sunday, 1 P.M.–4 P.M., November–March. Admission is free.

Museums

Established in 1898 as a Confederate museum, Wilmington's **Cape Fear Museum,** 814 Market Street, (910) 341-4350, *www.capefearmuseum.com,* presents a detailed history of the events and people important to the Cape Fear region. Exhibits range from displays of the area's natural history to memorabilia on Wilmington native son and basketball legend Michael Jordan. Open Tuesday–Saturday, 9 A.M.–5 P.M.; Sunday, 1 P.M.–5 P.M. During the summer, the museum

Hisssss...

With movie-set attention to detail (the habitats are, in fact, the work of set designers) the **Cape Fear Serpentarium**, 20 Orange Street, Wilmington, ☎ (910) 762-1669, *www.bushmastersonline.com,* presents a fascinating variety of reptiles from around the globe. More than 80 species of snakes, including Black Mambas and spitting cobras, are on display alongside lizards and a crocodile. Each habitat features a placard describing the species, where it lives, and how venomous it is. From rattlesnakes to the deadly bushmaster, the slippery serpents will likely curl up in your memory long after you leave.

The Underwater World

To learn what creatures are enjoying the surf with you, stop by the **North Carolina Aquarium,** 900 Loggerhead Road, Kure Beach, ☎ (910) 458-8257 or 1-866-301-3476, *www.ncaquariums.com,* which interprets the fresh and saltwater habitats of the Cape Fear region. After extensive renovation that tripled its size, the new 84,000-square foot aquarium opened in 2002 with, as its centerpiece, a two-story, 235,000-gallon tank with 50 different species, including sharks, lobsters, moray eels, sea turtles, and a variety of colorful reef and ocean fish. The multiple windows of this spectacular, 24-foot-deep aquarium offer splendid views of nearly 500 saltwater creatures. Located 15 miles south of Wilmington on Route 421, just beyond Kure Beach and north of the Fort Fisher Ferry Terminal. Open daily, 9 A.M.–5 P.M. Nominal admission fee.

also opens Mondays, 9 A.M.–5 P.M. Nominal admission fee. ◆ In Southport, there's a branch of the **North Carolina Maritime Museum,** 116 North Howe Street, (910) 457-0003, where interesting exhibits depict the extensive nautical history of the lower Cape Fear area. A 12-station, self-guiding tour takes you from the time of the earliest settlers to modern sailors. Displays range from scale models of ships to a video depicting pirate activity off North Carolina's coast. Open 9 A.M.–5 P.M., Tuesday–Saturday. Nominal admission fee.

◆ If the sound of a far-off train stirs your blood, make some fast tracks to the **Wilmington Railroad Museum,** 501 Nutt Street, Wilmington, (910) 763-2634, *www.wrrm.org,* which highlights in photographs and exhibits how the Wilmington & Weldon Railroad impacted the area. (Short answer: first it caused a boom, then a bust in the local economy.) When completed in 1840, the 161-mile railroad was the longest continuous line in the world, and it helped connect Eastern North Carolina to points north like Richmond. Over time, the railroad became the behemoth Atlantic Coast Line Railroad. In 1960, the company moved its headquarters to Jacksonville, Florida, taking an enormous number of local jobs with it. Open 10 A.M.–5 P.M., Monday–Saturday; 1 P.M.–5 P.M., Sunday. (Closed Sundays, mid October–mid March.) Nominal admission fee.

◆ **The Wrightsville Beach Museum of History,** 303 West Salisbury Street, Wrightsville Beach, (910) 256-2569, *www.wbmuseum.com,* details the interesting past of this coastal community, including its role in the Civil War. Of particular note is the story of Hurricane Hazel, which blew ashore in 1954 and caused extensive damage.

Cape Fear Coast CVB

Wrightsville Beach Museum

Performing Arts

♪ Built in 1858 and listed on the National Register of Historic Landmarks, **Thalian Hall for the Performing Arts,** 310 Chestnut Street, Wilmington, (910) 343-3664 or 1-800-523-2820, *www.thalianhall.com,* features three separate theaters—the Main Stage, Grand Ballroom, and Studio Theatre—which host a variety of live musical, theatrical, and dance events, as well as film presentations. A typical week includes

Thalian Hall

foreign or independent films shown Monday–Wednesday evenings, and then live arts performances from Thursday–Sunday. The Main Stage has a handful of seats with semi-obstructed views, particularly in the balcony, so ask in advance at the box office to avoid these seats. ◆ **The Wilmington Symphony,** (910) 962-3500 or 1-800-732-3643, *www.wilmingtonsymphony.org,* performs classical orchestral and pops works in Kenan Auditorium, 601 South College Road, on the campus of the University of North Carolina at Wilmington. Directed by Steven Errante, the symphony is made up of faculty, students, and local amateur and professional musicians.

Spa & Massage

⬤ Located in downtown Wilmington, **Nirvana European Day Spa & Salon,** 224 South Water Street, Wilmington, (910) 342-9186, offers full- and half-day packages, as well as an array of massage and hydrotherapy treatments. ◆ A few miles from downtown in The Forum (see *Shops & Stops*), **Ki Spa Salon,** 1125-Q Military Cutoff Road, Wilmington, (910) 509-0410, *www.kispasalon.com,* pampers guests with such services as aromatherapy steam baths, heated stone pedicures, and a variety of facials and massages. Browse the shop's extensive selection of bath and body products. ◆ **The Harbour Club Day Spa and Salon,** 1904 Eastwood Road, Suite 101, (910) 256-5020, offers a number of spa services, but our money is on the seven-hour VIP package, which includes a detox masque, Swedish massage, facial, light spa lunch, manicure, pedicure, scalp massage, shampoo, and style.

Shops & Stops

$ So many interesting retailers exist in the greater Wilmington region that you could fill a week with daily sessions of retail therapy and still not visit them all. Numerous upscale

NC Division of Tourism

Chandler's Wharf

shopping areas exist in the historic downtowns of Wilmington and Southport, as well as along the Eastwood Road/Military Cutoff Road corridor between Wilmington and Wrightsville Beach. The following is merely a sampling of the area's retail offerings.

◆ More than 100 retailers fill Wilmington's historic district, especially along Water, Front, and Second streets. On the southern end of downtown, **Chandler's Wharf,** 225 South Water Street, (910) 343-9896, is a small shopping district around a restored 19th-century river wharf building with an extensive collection of boutiques and restaurants. The two-block area fronts the Cape Fear River and features cobblestone streets and picket fences. Some of the better shops at Chandler's Wharf include **Azalea Coast Gifts and Flowers,** (910) 815-0102 or 1-866-815-0100, *www.azaleacoastflorist.com,* which sells soaps, lotions, candles, and gift baskets; and ◆ **The Gifted Gourmet,** (910) 815-0977, which stocks everything related to fine cooking, including gourmet jams, preserves, and more than 200 sauces. ◆ Across the street from the wharf building, **A Proper Garden,** 2 Ann Street, Wilmington, (910) 763-7177, *www.apropergarden.com,* sells such yard and garden accessories as hammocks and fountains.

◆ At the northern end of downtown, the **Cotton Exchange,** 321 North Front Street, (910) 343-9896, *www.shopcottonexchange.com,* is a restored 19th-century warehouse that once was a holding area for cotton to be exported. (The building was owned by the largest cotton exporter in the world.) Today the huge brick building houses 30 specialty shops and restaurants. Photos depicting the history of the building line the walls in the common areas. Some shops of note: ◆ **Two Sisters Bookery,** 318 Nutt Street, Wilmington, (910) 762-4444, is filled with local history books, classic fiction, and journals, as well as gifts and accessories. ◆ For unique jewelry, handcrafts, and pottery, **East Bank Trading Co.,** 321 North Front Street, Wilmington, (910) 763-1047, is a good bet.

◆ The **Old Wilmington City Market,** 119 South Water Street, has 10 shops in the heart of Wilmington with an open-air feel, minus the open air. Here you'll find **Barouke,** (910) 762-4999, a shop filled with such hand-crafted-wood gift items as wine racks, games, and jewelry boxes.

◆ Located on the way to Wrightsville Beach, **Lumina Station,** 1900 Eastwood Road, Wilmington, (910) 256-0900, *www.luminastation.com,* is an upscale shopping center with more than 15 specialty shops and restaurants. Shops of note include **Bristol Books,** 1908 Eastwood Road, Suite 116, (910) 256-4490, *www.bristolbooks.com,* an independent bookstore featuring a wide range of fiction, nonfiction, and children's books. The store specializes in regional titles and also carries journals

Michael Wolf

and stationery. ◆ For bedding, linens, the Shabby Chic line of furniture, and other home accessories, visit **Airlie Moon,** 1938-B Eastwood Road, 1-800-524-6507, *www.airliemoon.com.*

◆ Another upscale collection of specialty shops is at **The Forum,** 1125 Military Cutoff Road, Wilmington, *www.shoptheforum.com,* where more than 20 boutiques and a handful of eateries await. They include: **NOFO,** (910) 256-5565, *www.nofo.com,* which carries an eclectic mix of gift items, ranging from kitchen and bath items to books. **Scarpa,** (910) 509-9772, specializes in women's casual and dress shoes from top designers.

◆ Other shops of note in Wilmington: ◆ **Daughtry's Old Books,** 22 North Front Street, Wilmington, (910) 763-4754, is known for its collection of hard-to-find literature and first editions. ◆ **Italian Gourmet Market,** 22 South Front Street, Wilmington, (910) 362-0004 or 1-800-311-5202, *www.italiangourmet.us,* carries "all you need to prepare an authentic Italian feast." Choose from a selection of Italian wines, olive oils, pastas, and specialty foods. ◆ **The Wilmington Espresso Co.,** 24 South Front Street, Wilmington, (910) 343-1155, has standard coffeehouse fare, including pastries, muffins, and an assortment of lattes and espressos.

◆ Southport's compact shopping district is a pleasure to browse. Two stops worth making: **Waterfront Gifts & Antiques,** 117 South Howe Street, (910) 457-6496, for antiques, sculptures, and gift items all under one roof. Off the historic waterfront (but worth visiting), **Books N' Stuff,** 4961-11 Live Oak Village Shopping Center, Long Beach Road, (910) 457-9017, sells new, used, and collectible books.

Tours

There's no quicker way to become familiar with an area than by taking a narrated tour, and Wilmington has a number of tour outfits with knowledgeable, entertaining guides. ◆ To take in the sites of historic Wilmington accompanied by the soothing clip-clop of hooves on pavement, make plans for a carriage tour with **Horse Drawn Tours,** Market and Water streets, (910) 251-8889, *www.horsedrawntours.com.* ◆ **The Wilmington Trolley Company**, Dock and Water streets, Wilmington, (910) 763-4483, *www.wilmingtontrolley.com,* conducts eight-mile, 45-minute sightseeing tours on a motorized trolley car. ◆ Learn who (or what) haunts downtown Wilmington on the **Ghost Walk of Old Wilmington,** Market and Water streets, Wilmington, (910) 602-6055, *www.hirchak.com,* which departs in the evenings to explore alleys, homes, and haunted landmarks while local ghost hunters weave spooky tales of Wilmington's dark side. ◆ **Cape Fear Riverboats,** Wilmington, (910) 343-1611 or 1-800-676-0162, *www.cfrboats.com,* conducts tours aboard the *Henrietta III,* North Carolina's largest riverboat.

Michael Wolf

The Henrietta III riverboat

R e s t   E a s y

S l e e p   W e l l

To keep up with the Spielbergs, so to speak, Wilmington's lodging scene improved dramatically following its growth as a major film center. Throughout downtown, you'll find upscale inns and B&Bs in historic homes, while the surrounding barrier islands also have a number of unique properties. The following is merely a sampling of the region's offerings.

Accommodations Pricing

Less than $100	Inexpensive	$
$100-150	Moderate	$$
$151-200	Expensive	$$$
More than $200	Very Expensive	$$$$

Prices are per room, per night, based on double occupancy during peak seasons. Note that B&Bs and most country inns include breakfast in the rate.

C.W. Worth House • Innkeepers Margi and Doug Erickson lay out the red carpet for guests of this 1893 Queen Anne-style home surrounded by attractive, landscaped gardens. There are seven guestrooms, each individually decorated and with a private bath. The Rose Suite has a king-sized, four-poster bed, and a bathroom with a claw-foot tub and separate shower, while the Hibiscus Room has a cozy turret nook, plus a two-person whirlpool bath. If you hope to watch TV in your room, request the Louisiana Room, as all the others are TV-free. Common areas include a spacious Southern porch, formal Victorian parlor, a second-floor veranda with wicker furniture, and a third-floor sitting area. The Worth House has a collection of unique items on display, including antique cameras, an old gramophone from the Philippines, and a Weaver pump organ. A full, hot breakfast is served every morning in the formal dining room. Entrées might include banana oat pancakes or artichoke-mushroom quiche, accompanied by gourmet coffee, juices, and homemade muffins. • *412 South Third Street, Wilmington, NC 28401, ☎ (910) 762-8562 or 1-800-340-8559, www.worthhouse.com* • *$$–$$$*

Four Porches • "Pet-friendly" and "smoker-friendly" are not terms often associated with charming B&Bs, particularly one as old (c. 1847) and inviting as Four Porches, but they apply here. Indeed, there are four porches on this Italianate home—a Queen Anne-style wing was added later—as well as four guestrooms. The Garden Room can be connected via a bathroom to the Harlequin Room to make a suite (perfect for couples with children), while the Jungle Room features a mahogany bed and claw foot tub. The Beach Room has a king-sized canopy bed with bright colors and décor. Each morning, expect a hot, gourmet breakfast served with pastries, coffee, and fresh fruit. Tucked into Wilmington's historic district, Four Porches is nearby to shopping, dining, and downtown attractions. Guests are welcome to use the inn's bicycles to explore town. • *312 South Third Street, Wilmington, NC 28401, ☎ (910) 342-0849, www.4porches.com* • *$$*

Front Street Inn • You'll find 12 spacious suites, each with private bath, in this attractive, red-brick building built in the 1920s as the offices for the Salvation Army of the Carolinas. Though they fully renovated the building, innkeepers Stefany and Jay Rhodes chose to keep architectural elements like brick walls, maple floors, and arched doorways to complement the inn's charm. The most popular room is the Hemingway Suite, which features a king-sized sleigh bed, wood-burning fireplace, large bath with a spa tub for two, wet bar, and French doors that open to a private balcony with a view of the Cape Fear River. Breakfast is a relaxed buffet, where offerings may include such items as fresh fruits, biscuits, whole-grain muffins, smoked salmon, and a variety of juices. In the evenings, sip a glass of wine from the Sol y Sombra (sun and shade) bar in the lobby, or head down to the playroom for a quick game of nine ball. Located a half-block from Chandler's Wharf. • *215 South Front Street, Wilmington, NC 28401, ☎ (910) 762-6442 or 1-800-336-8184, www.frontstreetinn.com* • *$$–$$$*

Graystone Inn • Considered one of the most luxurious inns in Wilmington, the Graystone is a grand, neo-classical mansion built in 1905 for the widow of Preston

Bridgers, whose father founded the Wilmington & Weldon Railroad. The 14,300 square-foot inn features seven large suites, ranging in size from the 350 square-foot de Rosset Bedroom to the 1,300 square-foot Bellevue Suite. The Bellevue features 18-foot ceilings and an outstanding view of the Cape Fear River. All rooms are elegantly appointed and feature private baths. Common areas include a library with Honduras-mahogany paneling, a spacious sitting area, and an exquisite verandah with views of the inn's gardens. A full, hot breakfast is served in the formal dining room, which, in keeping with the rest of the inn, is decorated with turn-of-the-century antiques. The Graystone carries AAA's distinguished Four-Diamond rating. • *100 South Third Street, Wilmington, NC 28401, ☎ (910) 763-2000 or 1-888-763-4773, www.graystoneinn.com • $$$–$$$$*

The Graystone Inn

Murchison House Bed & Breakfast • After six arduous years of refurbishment, Ron and Sherry Demas have opened their home, the 1878 Murchison House, as a bed and breakfast. Wilmington and its guests couldn't be happier. This Second Empire-style house features bold colors, high ceilings, and enormous windows that bathe the house in light. Grounds include a Koi pond, three waterfalls, two fountains, and a brick and cobblestone courtyard. The first-floor parlors, library, and dining area provide guests with ample space to relax, although leaving your room may prove difficult. There are five elegant guestrooms, each individually decorated and with a private bath. A hot, gourmet breakfast and afternoon treats are served daily. • *305 South Third Street, Wilmington, NC 28401, ☎ (910) 762-6626, www.murchisonhouse.com • $$$$*

Theodosia Inn • Arriving on Bald Head via the Southport Ferry, you'll immediately see this grand, purple, Victorian Inn overlooking the harbor. There are 14 rooms—eight in the main inn, two in the carriage house, and four in the cottage—each of which features a private bath, elegant furnishings, and views of the water. The Coral Honeysuckle Room (a.k.a. the Honeymoon Suite) has a two-person Jacuzzi tub with a separate shower and a private porch ideal for watching both the sunrise and sunset. Hot, gourmet breakfasts—we're talking perfectly prepared Eggs Benedict and Bananas Foster pancakes—are served each morning, as are complimentary hors d'oeuvres in the evening. Room rates include access to the Bald Head Island Club's golf course, swimming pool, tennis courts, and elegant dining club. Upon checking in, you'll receive keys to your own golf cart. • *Harbour Village, Bald Head Island, NC 28461, ☎ (910) 457-6563 or 1-800-656-1812, www.theodosias.com • $$$–$$$$*

The Verandas • Built in 1853, this four-story, 8,500 square-foot Italianate mansion was a private home until a fire caused extensive damage in 1992. Dennis Madsen and Charles Pennington bought the property, gutted it, and spent more than a year renovating. The results are spectacular. There are eight spacious corner rooms to choose from, each with a marble-floored bathroom and large soaking tub. Second-floor rooms have access to two verandas; third-floor rooms have access to a spiral staircase that leads to the fourth-floor cupola and its tremendous views. Common areas include four verandas, two grand parlors, a formal living room, a piano room, and a dining area that's an entertainer's dream. With a full, gourmet breakfast—think eggnog French toast or a salmon omelet, perhaps—and a stocked butler's pantry in the breakfast room, you'll not go hungry. Listed in the distinguished *Select Registry*, the Verandas has also earned AAA's coveted Four-Diamond rating. • *202 Nun Street, Wilmington, NC 28401,* ☎ *(910) 251-2212, www.verandas.com* • *$$–$$$*

Dine Well

Cuisine in Wilmington ranges from Southern to French, with many options in between. Seafood dominates area menus, and most restaurants offer their own take on crab cakes and grilled salmon. There are many more fine establishments than those listed here, but the following sampling will remove any guesswork. Reservations are recommended at each.

Caffe Phoenix • Located in a restored 1899 Italianate building on Front Street, this chic restaurant serves Mediterranean cuisine in a setting as creative as the menu and award-winning wine list. High ceilings draw your gaze upward to a narrow balcony encircling the room, and a rotating collection of original art hangs on the walls. Caffe Phoenix is renowned for fresh soups and salads, complemented by five breads baked daily on the premises. The menu changes reguarly with new appetizers, entrées, and wines reflecting seasonal harvests, but recent selections included seafood risotto and rack of lamb. For dessert, try the cheesecake with blackberry sauce. Open daily for lunch and dinner. • *9 South Front Street, Wilmington,* ☎ *(910) 343-1395*

Caprice Bistro • You can spend an entire evening in this decidedly hip French restaurant, first basking in the culinary skills of chef/owner Thierry Moity, and then absorbing the social scene upstairs in the sofa-lined martini bar. The downstairs dining room—decorated with faux-finish walls, simple décor, and hardwood floors—serves traditional French cuisine. Start with the homemade French country paté, before moving on to steak au poivre served with a cognac sauce. Open daily for dinner • *10 Market Street, Wilmington,* ☎ *(910) 815-0810*

Circa 1922 • Exposed brick walls with large paintings of the Roaring Twenties and low, elegant lighting make for a warm environment in which to dine on this restaurant's renowned tapas. (Tapas are small-portion dishes; order several to make a meal.) Choices include creative preparations of pasta, meat, sushi, cheese, salad, and seafood. If they are on the menu, try the crab and avocado California roll with wasabi, pickled ginger, and soy; or the lobster ravioli. For dessert, try the Bananas Foster with Myers Dark Rum. Open daily for dinner. • *8 North Front Street, Wilmington,* ☎ *(910) 762-1922*

The Cottage • Housed in a 1916 crafts-style bungalow, this unpretentious beach restaurant serves simply prepared cuisine with an emphasis on fresh seafood. Dine inside or on the patio outdoors. Start with the crab dip served with pita bread before ordering any of their fresh fish entrées. If you forgo the crab dip appetizer, order the entrée-serving of crab cakes, which has made this restaurant an institution. Save room for their tart-to-perfection key lime pie. Open for lunch and dinner, Monday–Saturday. • *One North Lake Park Boulevard, Carolina Beach,* ☎ *(910) 458-4383*

Deluxe • With natural wood floors, exposed brick walls, and décor that runs the gamut from abstract to art deco, Deluxe is a feast for the eyes and the palate. The attentive wait staff delights in reciting nightly specials and in recommending vintages from the restaurant's wine list. Start with the mussels with fresh crabmeat in a sun-dried tomato sauce and move on to the five-spice tuna over crunchy lo mien noodles served with a plum sauce. Cross your fingers and hope the spiced-pumpkin ice cream with vanilla praline, homemade caramel glaze, and whipped cream is on the night's dessert menu. Open daily for dinner. • *114 Market Street, Wilmington,* ☎ *(910) 251-0333*

Freddie's Restaurante • A local favorite, Freddie's serves Italian fare excellenté, with a special penchant for creatively prepared

pork chops. Try the firehouse chop, cooked with mushrooms, peppers, and onions, and smothered in mozzarella cheese. Not in the mood for pork? There also are pasta, chicken, seafood, and steak dishes. For dessert, try the fried cheese-cake, a finger dessert that's topped with any of a half-dozen sauces, such as chocolate or raspberry. For the most privacy, request the table just inside the door to the right. Open Tuesday–Sunday for dinner. • *At the Pier, 111 Avenue K, Kure Beach,* ☎ *(910) 458-5979*

Jerry's • Owner Jerry Rouse's fascination with flight is evident from the photographs of planes lining the walls of his restaurant. Despite his skyward inclination, you'll be glad his feet are planted on the ground in the kitchen, where he turns out outstanding continental cuisine with a special emphasis on fresh seafood. Try the prosciutto-wrapped jumbo scallops or goat cheese-encrusted grouper. The wine list is strong on California wines, and the freshly made desserts change daily. Open daily for dinner. • *7220 Wrightsville Avenue, Wilmington,* ☎ *(910) 256-8847*

The Oceanic • If you'd like to enjoy a romantic, moon-lit dinner on a pier jutting out over the crashing waves of the Atlantic, put a dinner at the Oceanic on your to-do list. Everything about the place is big; the views, the menu, and the fact that it seats 400. Fresh seafood dominates the menu, and all three floors feature old photographs of Wrightsville Beach. Reservations are accepted for parties of eight or more in season, but the pier is seated on a first-come, first-served basis and is in high-demand during the summer months. Open daily for lunch and dinner. • *703 South Lumina Avenue, Wrightsville Beach, (910) 256-5551*

Pilot House • Predominantly a Southern seafood restaurant—think sweet potato grouper, and grilled salmon with grits—the Pilot House also offers such entrées as duck, lamb, and filet mignon. There are nightly specials and a well-rounded wine list. Whatever you are wearing—as long as it is not a sand-caked bathing suit—will work in this delightfully casual restaurant. Request a window seat to enjoy the river view or an outside table to catch a breeze. Open daily for lunch and dinner. • *Chandler's Wharf, 2 Ann Street, Wilmington,* ☎ *(910) 343-0200*

Port Land Grill • With an "open door" approach to cooking—from the bar area, you have a full view of the chefs at work—Port Land Grill promises "progressive American regional cuisine." That equates to such entrées as the peanut ginger-crusted Chilean sea bass served over wasabi-whipped potatoes, seared snow peas, and a spicy-peanut sauce. There are also seasonal game and vegetarian dishes along with nightly specials. A *Wine Spectator* award-winning wine list assures the perfect vintage to complement your meal. Save room for the roasted apple tiramisu. Located in the Lumina Station Shopping Center en route to Wrightsville Beach. Open Monday–Saturday for dinner. • *1908 Eastwood Road, Suite 111, Wilmington,* ☎ *(910) 256-6056*

Picnic Packing

Located on the way to Wrightsville Beach, **The NOFO Café**, 1125 Military Cutoff Road, Forum Shopping Center, Wilmington, (910) 256-5565, *www.nofo.com*, is a great place to grab deli sandwiches. • **Sweet & Savory Bake Shop & Café**, 1611 Pavilion Place, Wilmington, (910) 256-0115, supplies many local restaurants with fresh-baked breads and desserts. In addition, the café is open for breakfast and lunch and offers fish and veggie sandwiches served on its fresh bread.

Just Desserts

Indulge your sweet tooth at the delicious downtown Wilmington **Candy Bar,** 112 Market, Street, (910) 762-0805, where you'll find high-quality European chocolates, Joseph Schmidt truffles, old-fashioned fudge, and a large selection of regular and sugar-free candies. • **Bella's Sweets and Spirits,** 19 Market Street, Wilmington, (910) 762-2777, is a sweet shop, coffeehouse, and bar wrapped into one location. Choose from wine, beer, cookies, cakes, pies, and a variety of coffees and teas.

A Long-Weekend Itinerary

Day One

Rise early for a big breakfast, but don't be late for your reservation with **Kayak Carolina** (page 454) for a half-day paddle trip to **Zeke's Island** (page 452), where you can explore the waters surrounding this pristine island teeming with wildlife. Upon returning, grab lunch at **The Cottage** (page 472) in Carolina Beach, and then return to Wilmington for an afternoon browsing the **shops** (page 465) and **galleries** (page 459) of the historic district, making certain to visit **Chandler's Wharf** (page 466). Return to your inn to shower and prepare for an early dinner at **Deluxe** (page 472) and a performance afterward at **Thalian Hall** (page 465).

Day Two

After breakfast at your inn, swing by **Two Wheeler Dealer** (page 451) to rent bikes and a car rack, and then pick up a picnic lunch from **NOFO Café** (page 473) and drive to **Carolina Beach State Park** (page 450), where you'll make the eight-mile bicycle ride to the **Fort Fisher State Recreation Area** (page 448). After walking along Fort Fisher's beach,

Dine at The Cottage

catch the **Fort Fisher-Southport Ferry** (page 443) with your bike to **Southport** (page 449) to explore this historic fishing village. Have lunch in one of the city's parks before returning on the ferry to Fort Fisher, where you retrace your route to Carolina Beach State Park. Return to your inn for some Advil and a shower, and then it's off to **Port Land Grill** (page 473) for dinner. Hit the hay.

Day Three

Linger over breakfast at your inn to soak in your last day and then head to **Greenfield Park** (page 448) to take a nice walk around the lake before arriving for your well-deserved massage at **Nirvana European Day Spa & Salon** (page 465). Head to **The Pilot House** (page 473) for lunch, sitting on the deck to take in the relaxing pace of the Cape Fear River. On your way out of town, hit the **Louise Wells Cameron Art Museum** (page 459) to fuel a discussion of the work of Mary Cassatt for the ride home.

Additional Information

For additional dining, accommodations, and sightseeing information, including the dates of special events, contact:

The Cape Fear Coast Convention & Visitors Bureau, 24 North Third Street, Wilmington, NC 28401, ☎ (910) 341-4030 or 1-800-222-4757, *www.cape-fear.nc.us,* operates a visitor center open Monday–Friday, 8:30 A.M.–5 P.M.; Saturday, 9 A.M.–4 P.M.; and Sunday, 1 P.M.–4 P.M. The bureau also operates a riverfront booth at the foot of Market Street and Water Street from May–October.

Pleasure Island Chamber of Commerce, 1121 North Lake Park Boulevard, Carolina Beach, NC 28428, ☎ (910) 458-8434, *www.pleasureislandchambernc.org,* operates a visitor center open Monday–Wednesday 9 A.M.–5 P.M.; Thursday and Friday, 9 A.M.–7 P.M.; Saturday 9 A.M.–4 P.M.; and Sunday 10 A.M.–2 P.M.

The Southport Visitor Center, 113 West Moore Street, Southport, NC 28461, ☎ (910) 457-7927, (located just off the main traffic light in town) is open in the summer Monday–Saturday, 9:30 A.M.–4:30 P.M.; and Sunday, 1 P.M.–4 P.M. Call for off-season hours.

Southport-Oak Island Area Chamber of Commerce, 4841 Long Beach Road SE, Southport, NC 28461, ☎ (910) 457-6964 or 1-800-457-6964, *www.southport-oakisland.com,* runs a welcome center open to visitors Monday–Friday, 8:30 A.M.–5 P.M.; and on Saturday, March–November, 9 A.M.–4 P.M.

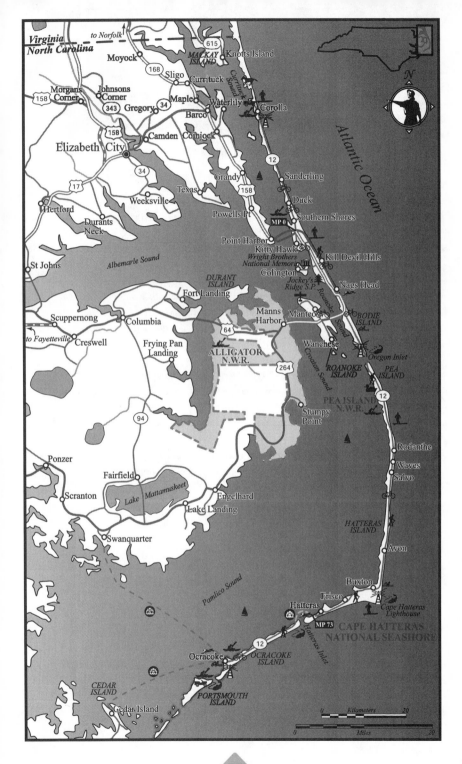

The Outer Banks, North Carolina

The Outer Banks is a series of barrier islands, stretching from Virginia more than 100 miles south to Ocracoke Island. Separated from the mainland by five vast sounds—Currituck, Albemarle, Croatan, Roanoke, and Pamlico—the islands are rarely more than a mile wide. But frail, they are not. As if to goad the sea, the Outer Banks elbows farther into the Atlantic than any point on the East Coast, and despite repeatedly enduring the fury of numerous hurricanes and Nor'easters, the scrappy spits of land always emerge ready for another round.

How does such a thin line of sand sustain the constant forces of wind, tides, and waves? By continually adapting and changing shape. The islands' landscapes are a mix of beaches, dunes, marshes, and woodlands, all of which are relatively malleable. What isn't malleable, of course, are the manmade structures, as Hurricane Isabel—and countless previous storms—pointed out in 2003, when she swept homes and roads out to sea, breached Hatteras Island (forming a new inlet), and wracked up nearly $1 billion in damages.

Hatteras Island is whole once again—the US Corps of Army Engineers dredged sand to fill the gaps—and it's likely that most, if not all, of the lost homes will be replaced because the Outer Banks is, after all, one of the nation's great vacation destinations. Connected to the real world by only a few bridges and ferries, the islands fill each summer with up to four million visitors, many of whom have been here before or will soon return.

Historians believe that Paleo-Indians roamed the islands as many as 10,000 years ago; however, the islands' earliest permanent settlers were Croatan Indians, members of the Algonquin Nation. They had lived in small villages near Cape Hatteras for 500 years by the time the first European explorers passed through in the early 16th Century. In 1524, Italian explorer Giovanni de Verrazzano landed on the Outer Banks and mistakenly believed the chain of

Cape Hatteras Lighthouse

islands to be an isthmus dividing the Atlantic and Pacific Oceans.

Sixty years later, English explorers successfully navigated an entrance through the islands and landed on Roanoke Island, where they found the friendly Croatan Indians. Encouraged by this news, Sir Walter Raleigh dispatched three ships with 117 colonists, including men, women, and children, to form the New World's first English-speaking settlement. The colony pre-dated Jamestown by 22 years.

One month after their arrival, Virginia Dare was born as the first English child on American soil. Soon thereafter, Governor John White left the settlement to secure more food, supplies, and colonists from England. The English war with Spain delayed his return for three years, and when he returned, the colony had disappeared.

England's colonization efforts continued. As ships sailing off the Outer Banks increased in number, the treacherous waters earned the respect and fear of mariners. Wide shoals, violent storms, and relentless wind took down many boats, earning the Outer Banks' coastline the moniker, "Graveyard of the Atlantic." (To date, more than 1,000 ships have sunk here.)

An Age-old Whodunnit

Three years later than planned, John White returned to Roanoke Island to find his family and the other colonists had vanished without signs of a struggle. White did find two cryptic carvings in separate trees: "CRO" scratched into one, "CROATAN" into another. For more than 400 years, historians have debated what happened to the Lost Colony. Questions abound. Were the colonists killed by the Croatans? Did they try to sail back to England and go down at sea? Or did they move west and disappear in the mainland? Roanoke Island knows, but as Paul Green, the Pulitzer Prize-winning playwright who penned the symphonic drama, *The Lost Colony*, suggested, the "muted tongueless shores" aren't likely to tell.

Such foreboding seas made the area an ideal haven for pirates. During the 1700s, notable scoundrels who pilfered ships offshore included Stede Bonnet, Calico Jack, Ann Bonney, and Blackbeard, who was beheaded on Ocracoke Island. Meanwhile, the federal government sought to make navigation easier off the Outer Banks and in 1794, it authorized construction of the

Deron Nardo

What the ocean wants, the ocean gets

Chicamacomico Lifesaving Station

barrier islands' first lighthouses. (Four remain operational today.)

The inlets of the Outer Banks played important roles in the Civil War. The Union Army defeated heavily encamped Confederate forces in a battle for Roanoke Island in 1862. Then Union held the Outer Banks for the remainder of the conflict. Following the war, freed slaves migrated to the islands and formed a government-sanctioned colony, later called the Freedman's Colony.

The United States Coast Guard originated along the Outer Banks in 1874, when seven lifesaving stations were established to help save sailors' lives and to salvage ships. Manned primarily by Outer Bank natives known as surfmen, the stations saved an unknown number of sailors whose ships had run aground. One of the most-dramatic rescues in Outer Banks' history occurred in 1918 after a German submarine torpedoed the British tanker *Mirlo*. Members of the Chicamacomico Lifesaving Station pulled most of the crew safely to shore from the fiery tanker.

On December 17, 1903, man first broke his bond to the earth when Orville Wright climbed into a glider he built with his brother, Wilbur, and flew 12 seconds and 120 feet from a sandy dune in Kill Devil Hills. There were four flights that first day. The final flight took 59 seconds and carried Wilbur 852 feet.

Though Nags Head was a popular tourist destination in the late 19th Century, it wasn't until after the early to mid 20th Century that tourism began to take off. The National Park Service designated the Cape Hatteras National Seashore, preserving the land for recreation, and in the 1930s, the first bridges were built from the mainland.

Adjacent to the natural wonders— maritime forests, gorgeous beaches, the tallest sand dunes on the East Coast, and the massive estuary formed by the

Man's first flight at Kill Devil Hills

Albemarle and Pamlico sounds—development ranges from such historic, laid-back fishing villages as Ocracoke to the imposing, million-dollar mansions in Duck.

The active traveler can choose from endless forms of outdoor fun and more-refined means of passing time. Whether you prefer to rest on the beach or play in the waves, catch your own dinner or be catered to in a restaurant, the islands have all the necessary elements for a fine getaway. Perhaps the most interesting draw to the area is that it's as much a state of mind as a specific place. Here time is as fluid as the islands' ever-changing shapes, and while you can leave the islands of the Outer Banks, it's unlikely they'll leave you.

The Way Around

Navigating the Outer Banks can be easy or frustrating mess of snarled traffic, depending on when you visit. On weekends from Memorial Day–Labor Day, **Route 12**, which runs the length of the Outer Banks from Corolla to Ocracoke, fills with a parade of brake lights. Without traffic, the trip from Corolla to Ocracoke, including the 35-minute ferry from Hatteras Village to Ocracoke Island, takes roughly three hours.

Fortunately for the navigationally impaired, you need to know only two major roads in addition to Route 12 to explore the Outer Banks. **Route 158** crosses from the mainland onto Bodie Island at Kitty Hawk and parallels Route 12 south to Whalebone. Here's the confusing part: Route 12, which is closest to the beach, is also called **South Virginia Dare Trail,** or simply **Beach Road**. Route 158, which is closest to the sound, is also called **North Croatan Highway,** or simply **the Bypass**.

The following lists the islands and villages on the Outer Banks, traveling south to north. **Ocracoke Island** is a 13-mile-long island of which 12 miles comprise the undeveloped, protected land of the **Cape Hatteras National Seashore**. At the island's southern end, Ocracoke

Milepost System

Driving on Bodie and Hatteras islands, you'll notice milepost signs, and businesses often provide directions by mentioning which milepost they're closest to. Traveling south from Kitty Hawk on either Route 158 or Route 12, you'll come upon the start of the milepost system, beginning with Milepost 1. The last milepost is Milepost 73, in Hatteras Village, just before the Ocracoke Island ferry terminal.

Village is a fishing town built around Silver Lake Harbor. A thriving art scene exists, and the town has a pleasant mix of unique galleries, shops, restaurants, and inns. A free ferry connects Ocracoke with Hatteras Island to the north.

Also part of the Cape Hatteras National Seashore, **Hatteras Island** is 33 miles long and is lined with seven small villages. The ferry from Ocracoke arrives in **Hatteras**, a quiet fishing village with a smattering of lodgings and restaurants. From here, Route 12 travels north to **Frisco**, another quiet village with beach cottages, art galleries, a pier, and limited lodging and dining choices. To the north of Frisco is **Buxton**, the commercial village for Hatteras Island, with more inns, restaurants, and shops. The Cape Hatteras Lighthouse, the nation's tallest brick lighthouse, towers above Buxton and shines 20 miles out to sea.

Further north, **Avon** also features several commercial businesses, including a large grocery

Ocracoke's Silver Lake Harbor

store, several hotels, restaurants, and a multitude of beach cottages for rent. Moving north from Avon, Hatteras Island is undeveloped for roughly 10 miles—the land belongs to the National Park Service—and in places, the road appears like an asphalt ribbon cutting through a valley of sand dunes. The beach-cottage communities of **Salvo**, **Waves**, and **Rodanthe** are often referred to as the Tri-Village area. Borders between them are difficult to distinguish. Of the three, Rodanthe has the largest commercial infrastructure, with a few shops, restaurants, and convenience stores. A portion of the Cape Hatteras National Seashore, the 6,000-acre Pea Island

You *Can* Get Something for Nothing

The only way to access Hatteras Island from Ocracoke Island is to board the free auto-ferry, which departs Ocracoke every 30 minutes from 8:30 A.M.–7 P.M.; and every hour from 5 A.M.–8 A.M. and 8 P.M.–midnight. (From Hatteras, departures are every half-hour, 7:30 A.M.–7 P.M.; and every hour, 5 A.M.–7 A.M., and 8 P.M.–midnight. Note that reservations are not accepted, and the ferry can be extremely crowded in the summer. (You may have to sit through two or three boat departures before boarding.) For more information call ☎ (252) 225-3551 for the Ocracoke station or ☎ (252) 986-2353 for the Hatteras station, or visit *www.ncferry.org*.

Outer Banks Visitors Bureau

National Wildlife Refuge, stretches 12 miles north from Rodanthe to the end of Hatteras Island and a three-mile bridge across Oregon Inlet.

Route 12 continues north to **Whalebone Junction**, where Route 64/264 travels west to Roanoke Island. **Roanoke Island** was the site of England's first attempt to colonize the New World in 1587. Manteo and Wanchese, two historic villages named for Croatan

NC Division of Tourism

Bodie Island Lighthouse

*The Wright Brothers
National Memorial*

Indians who proved helpful in European settlement, are on the small island. Each is distinct in character. **Wanchese** is a commercial fishing village that annually processes millions of pounds of seafood; **Manteo** draws visitors with its historic waterfront, upscale shopping opportunities, and numerous attractions.

Back across the causeway, Route 12 reaches **Nags Head**, the Outer Banks' first and best-known vacation destination. Here streets are lined with weathered beach homes, strip malls, motels, restaurants, and kitschy tourist elements—an amusement park, miniature golf courses, and brightly lit superstores, for example. Jockey's Ridge State Park, with the tallest sand dunes in the East, is located here.

North of Nag's Head, **Kill Devil Hills** continues in the same commercial vein with small shopping centers, surf shops, and motels lining Beach Road and the Bypass. The Outer Banks' first incorporated town, Kill Devil Hills is a family-oriented beach community and site of the Wright Brothers National Memorial, which draws throngs of tourists each summer. **Kitty Hawk**, just north of Kill Devil Hills and separated by little more than a sign, is also commercially developed. Kitty Hawk is a favorite vacation spot for families renting beach cottages.

Moving further north, the neon signs give way to the more subdued, upscale village of **Southern Shores**, the region's first planned community. This small residential area has million-dollar beachfront homes, a golf course, and two marinas, all designed in concert with the land. **Duck** appears next on Route 12. This upscale, thriving village features outstanding views of the water from town, many good restaurants and shops, and numerous high-dollar homes for rent. North of Duck, **Sanderling** is a quiet, upscale community.

Corolla is the Outer Banks' northern-most town and is full of upscale developments, large beachfront homes, and unique shopping and dining. The road literally ends north of Corolla, where Route 12 gives way to sand and the wild ponies that grace the northern, uninhabited reaches of the islands.

Wild ponies roam the beaches north of Corolla

Weather

The weather on the Outer Banks is generally mild year round. Summer highs average in the mid to upper 80s, with overnight lows in the upper 60s to low 70s. Spring and fall are the most-pleasant times to visit, when temperatures rarely rise above the mid 70s, and overnight lows range from the mid 50s to low 60s. Winter highs are in the lower 50s with overnight lows in the upper 30s. Winds are generally calmest during the summer and early autumn, with wind speeds averaging around 12 mph. At any point during the year winds can gust between 60 and 80 miles per hour and not raise a fuss amongst locals. Surf temperatures are generally comfortable from late May to mid October.

Getting to the Outer Banks

By Air: Norfolk International Airport, ☎ (757) 857-3351, *www.norfolkairport.com*, hosts most major airlines and car rental companies. Expect a two-hour drive to the Outer Banks.

By Ferry: The **North Carolina Ferry System**, ☎ 1-800-293-3779, *www.ncferry.org*, operates two ferries from the mainland to the Outer Banks, both arriving on Ocracoke Island. The **Swan Quarter-Ocracoke Island Ferry** takes roughly 2.5 hours to cross. Swan Quarter is accessible by taking Route 264 east from Interstate 95. The **Cedar Island-Ocracoke Island Ferry** also takes 2.5 hours to cross. Cedar Island is accessible just off Route 12 east of Morehead City. Reservations are strongly recommended. Both run year-round and cost $15 each way per automobile, or $1 per pedestrian. Call ahead: the schedule changes with the seasons and is subject to weather conditions.

By Car: From Atlanta, take Interstate 85 north to Interstate 40 east toward Raleigh. In Raleigh, take Interstate 440 north to Exit #13, where you follow Route 64 east across Roanoke Island and into Nags Head. Allow 9.5 hours for the drive. **From Charlotte**, take Interstate 85 north to Interstate 40 east toward Raleigh. From there, take Interstate 440 north to Exit #13, where you follow Route 64 east across Roanoke Island and into Nags Head. Allow seven hours for the drive. **From Raleigh**, take Route 64 east across Roanoke Island and into Nags Head. Allow 4.5 hours for the drive.

Deron Nardo

The only way to access the beach north of Corolla is by 4WD

P l a y   H a r d

W i d e   O p e n

More water than banks, the Outer Banks specializes in aquatic sports—fishing, surfing, swimming, windsurfing, and kayaking—though you'll be surprised by the number of places to hike and ride bikes. The following are the major outdoor playgrounds.

♦ The nation's first designated national seashore, the **Cape Hatteras National Seashore**, (252) 473-2111, extends from South Nags Head to Ocracoke Inlet and totals more than 70 miles and 30,000 acres. Visitors can pick a beach and surf, swim, walk, and fish in relative isolation. On the

Cape Hatteras National Seashore

sound, kayakers find seclusion with just a few paddle strokes, while windsurfers, sailors, and kiteboarders find the shallow waters and steady winds of Pamlico Sound irresistible.

Deron Nardo

Jockey's Ridge State Park

◆ Located between Rodanthe and Oregon Inlet, the **Pea Island National Wildlife Refuge**, Route 12, (252) 473-1131, encompasses 6,000 acres of land teeming with local and migratory birds. Walking platforms enable you to birdwatch, while the surrounding waters provide a serene place to kayak and fish.

◆ Located off Route 158 at Milepost 12, **Jockey's Ridge State Park** in Nags Head, (252) 441-7132, *www.jockeysridgestatepark.com*, is a 426-acre park with two self-guiding trails and the largest sand dune on the East Coast. Depending on shifting winds, it's typically between 80 and 140 feet high. Hang-gliding and hiking are popular activities in the park.

◆ **Alligator River National Wildlife Refuge**, Route 64, Manteo, (252) 473-1131, has more than 150,000 acres of wetlands for kayaking, canoeing, and fishing. There are also hiking trails and observation platforms for land-based adventures. Wildlife you may see include deer, alligators, black bears, and wolves. To get here, take Route 64 west from Manteo, where you'll see signs for the refuge before crossing Albemarle Sound.

◆ Operated by the Nature Conservancy, **Nags Head Woods Preserve**, 701 West Ocean Acres Drive, (252) 441-2525, is a 1,400-acre maritime forest with five miles of hiking trails. Kayaking and canoeing are also options. To reach the preserve from Route 158 in Kill Devil Hills, turn west near milepost 9.5 onto Ocean Acres Drive and drive one mile past the subdivision to the visitor center. Admission is free, but donations are appreciated.

◆ The **Currituck National Wildlife Refuge**, (252) 429-3100, is located 0.75 miles beyond the end of Route 12 in Corolla and encompasses 4,100 acres of sandy beach, grassy dunes, maritime forest, shrub thickets, and fresh and brackish marsh.

Dayhiking

On Ocracoke Island just north of Ocracoke Village, the 0.75-mile **Hammock Hills Trail** winds through salt marsh and maritime forest. Look for road signs marking the parking area off Route 12. ◆ The **Buxton Woods Nature Trail** is a mellow, 0.75-mile walk starting from the Cape Point Campground Picnic Area (off Route 12 in Buxton near the Cape Hatteras Lighthouse) and winding through maritime forest and over a freshwater marsh. The self-guiding trail features signs explaining the coastal ecosystem.

◆ On Hatteras Island's north end, the **Pea Island National Wildlife Refuge**, Route 12 between Rodanthe and Oregon Inlet, (252) 473-1131 or (252) 987-1118, has a short half-mile hike, the **North Pond Wildlife Trail**, which stretches between North Pond and New Field Pond. Bring your camera. There are prime vantage points from which to photograph aquatic birds and waterfowl.

◆ The 1.5-mile **Tracks in the Sand Nature Trail** is a self-guiding route through **Jockey's Ridge State Park**, Milepost 12, Route 158, Nags Head, (252) 441-7132. The trail sets out from the park's main parking area. The one-mile **Soundside Nature Trail** departs from the soundside parking area and leads to an overlook on Roanoke Sound. Both trails are described in the free brochure available from the park's visitor center.

Walking path on Hatteras Island

♦ A series of trails spread through the 1,400-acre maritime forest at **Nags Head Woods Preserve**, 701 West Ocean Acres Drive, Nags Head, (252) 441-2525. All present good opportunities to view the more than 300 species of plants and 150 species of birds that reside here. The **Center Trail** is a quarter-mile loop that introduces hikers to the forest. The two-mile **Sweetgum Swamp Trail** climbs over several steep ridges and through a variety of plant environments. The **Blueberry Ridge Trail** is a 1.5-mile loop that departs from the Sweetgum Swamp Trail and leads to a pond with scenic vistas. **The Roanoke Trail** is a 1.5-mile out-and-back hike through a salt marsh to the property's kayak site on Roanoke Sound. Located at the preserve's southern end, the 1.6-mile **Nags Head Town Trail** departs from the municipal park on Barnes Street (off Route 158), climbs several ridges, and then ends at Roanoke Sound's shoreline. Before you set out, pick up the free trail guide from the visitor center. See *Wide Open* for directions.

♦ **Cape Hatteras National Seashore**, which stretches across three islands—Bodie, Hatteras, and Ocracoke—encompasses more than 70 miles of undeveloped seashore. Along Route 12, there are numerous parking areas—many with restrooms and bathhouses—that are great starting points for lengthy, scenic walks.

Bicycling

The few roads that span the Outer Banks pose challenges to bicyclists. What the islands lack in elevation change they make up for in wind resistance. Also, traffic can be thick, especially on Route 12. Despite "Share the Road" signs posted along its 120 miles, the highway often fills with impatient drivers. Ride defensively at all times.

♦ For slower-paced touring, various multiuse paths wind beside major roads and/or through wooded areas. For example, the five-mile **Southern Shores Path** parallels Route 158 from Kitty Hawk Elementary School to the Southern Shores Town Hall, and then heads north beside Route 12 to the Duck Village line. ♦ The **Duck Path** extends the Southern Shores path another mile into Duck Village. ♦ The five-mile **Sanderling Path** parallels Route 12 from Duck to Sanderling.

♦ In Kitty Hawk, a two-mile path parallels **Woods Road**. ♦ The **Kill Devil Hills Path** begins at West First Street in Kill Devil Hills, follows Colington Road (by the Wright Memorial), and then continues east to Route 12. ♦ The **South Nags Head Multiuse Path** runs from Loggerhead Road on the ocean side of Route 12 south to the end of Old Oregon Inlet Road in South Nags Head, a span of nearly 10 miles. ◆ The six-mile **Roanoke Island Path** extends from Washington Baum Bridge to Manns Harbor Bridge. The scenic, well-shaded path is a pleasant way to tour downtown Manteo and other historic sights on Roanoke Island.

◆ All villages on the Outer Banks feature scenic neighborhood roads that are enjoyable to explore by bicycle.

Rentals

The following businesses rent single-speed beach cruisers. **The Bike Barn**, 1312 Wrightsville Blvd, Kill Devil Hills, ☎ (252) 441-3786; ◆ **Duck Village Outfitters**, 1207 Duck Road, Duck, ☎ (252) 261-7222, *www.duckvillageoutfitters.com*; ◆ **Island Cycles**, in the Food Lion Shopping Center on Route 12, Avon, ☎ (252) 995-4336 or 1-800-229-7810, *www.islandcycles.com*; ◆ **Ocean Atlantic Rentals**, ☎ 1-800-635-9559, *www.oar-nc.com*, has four locations on the Outer Banks to rent bicycles: Corolla Light Village Shops, Route 12, Corolla, ☎ (252) 453-2440; 1194 Duck Road, Duck, ☎ (252) 261-4346; Milepost 10, Virginia Dare Trail, Nags Head, ☎ (252) 441-7823; and Route 12, Avon, ☎ (252) 995-5868; ◆ **Shore Gear**, Route 12, Ocracoke, ☎ (252) 928-7060; and ◆ **The Slushie Stand**, Route 12, Ocracoke, ☎ (252) 928-1878.

Paddling

Paddling the sounds on the western side of the Outer Banks in a sleek, stable sea kayak offers great exercise, scenery, and opportunities to see such wildlife as ibis, egrets, ospreys, and herons. There are numerous public launch sites throughout the area. (They're listed in the free Outer Banks travel guide, available from any visitor center. See *Additional Information*). But your best bet, unless you're familiar with the local waters, is to join a guided paddling tour. Tides, ocean currents, wind, and sudden storms can make unguided paddling an unwelcome adventure.

The following provides general descriptions of the best paddling spots. If you're joining a tour, you'll meet your tour outfitter at the launch point, or they'll provide transportation from their location. If you're alone, check with the rental sources below for directions to the best put-ins based upon current conditions.

◆ With an abundance of wildlife and miles of soundside shoreline protected by a natural sand reef, **Ocracoke Island** is a kayaker's paradise. The island's **Silver Lake Harbor** is worth exploring on its own, though you'll want to be wary of boat traffic, especially large ferries. A short paddle to the right from the mouth of Silver Lake Harbor brings you to

Horsepen Point, where scenic marshland is filled with egrets, ibis, and herons.

♦ Paddling along Ocracoke's western shoreline in **Pamlico Sound** takes you past numerous coves that once harbored pirates. Paddle in and explore as many as you have the energy for. Note that red markers designate the shipping channels where

Paddling Manteo's waterfront

larger boats pass. Many outfitters offer an overnight kayak trip to **Portsmouth Island**, a settlement established in 1753 and now a deserted village.

♦ **Roanoke Sound**, on the western side of Bodie Island, features shallow waters, marshes, and small islands that make for interesting scenery. Historic Manteo's waterfront is also a fun place to explore. ♦ The **Alligator River National Wildlife Refuge**, just west of Roanoke Island, features more than 150,000 acres of wetland habitats and a tremendous variety of wildlife species, from wood ducks and alligators to black bears and red wolves. There are four marked trails on **Milltail Creek**, ranging from 1.5 miles to 5.5 miles. Each is marked with a particular color. The **Red Trail** is a 1.5-mile loop, while the two-mile **Green Trail** takes you to **Sawyer Lake**. Because of their lengths, the 5.5-mile **Blue Trail** and four-mile **Yellow Trail** have signs designating the routes' mid-points for paddlers too pooped to continue. All of the trails are protected from wind by a maritime forest. On the downside, the relatively stagnant air invites mosquitoes.

♦ On the north end of Hatteras Island, **Pea Island National Wildlife Refuge** has no marked trails, just an array of pristine canals and marshes to explore. ♦ In Kitty Hawk, the

Currituck Sound

Safari River Maritime Forest presents an easy launch into a reddish-colored creek lined with live oaks. It's a great area for beginners to hone paddling skills while exploring a unique marsh ecosystem. ♦ Another popular paddling area in the northern Outer Banks is **Currituck Sound**, located north of Corolla.

♦ The popularity of sea kayaking in the Outer Banks means you'll have little trouble finding an outfitter offering kayak rentals, instruction, and guided tours. The following are just a few of the better operations: ♦ **Ocracoke Adventures**, Route 12 and Silver Lake, (252) 928-7873, offers guided tours and rents equipment. ♦ **Ride the Wind**, Route 12, Ocracoke, (252) 928-6311, *www.surfocracoke.com*, rents kayaks and offers tours. ♦ **Kitty Hawk Kites/Carolina Outdoors**, Hatteras Landing, Hatteras, 1-877-359-8447, *www.kittyhawk.com*, features numerous locations along the Outer Banks that rent sea kayaks and provide guided tours. ♦ **Corolla Outback Kayak Tours**, 107 Austin Street, Corolla, (252) 453-0877, *www.kayak-corolla.com*, offers guided kayak tours. ♦ **Duck Village Outfitters**, 1207 Duck Road, Duck, (252) 261-7222, *www.duckvillageoutfitters.com*, rents kayaks and offers guided tours.

Scuba Diving

With good underwater visibility, the warm Gulf Stream current just offshore, and more than 1,000 shipwrecks on the ocean floor, the Outer Banks is one of the world's great wreck-diving destinations. Examples of some of the more-popular sites include the *Proteus*, sunk in 1918 while attempting to avoid a German sub; the *Isle of Iona*, which ran aground in heavy fog in 1914 and rests in only 25 feet of water; the *Hesperides*, which scraped its keel on Diamond Shoals and sunk in 1897; and the *USS Huron*, a Federal Gunship steamer that ran aground in 1877 and rests off Nags Head in 25 feet of water.

◆ To get to the bottom of things, head to one of the many dive shops located throughout the Outer Banks. Good bets include **Outer Banks Diving**, Route 12, Hatteras Village, (252) 986-1056, *www.outerbanksdiving.com*; ◆ **Outer Banks Dive Center**, 3917 South Croatan Highway, Nags Head, (252) 449-8349, *www.obxdive.com*; and ◆ **Sea Scan Dive Centre**, 2600 South Virginia Dare Trail, Nags Head, (252) 480-3467, *www.wreck-dive.com*.

Get the Hang of It

Tall sand dunes, soft landing spots, and brisk winds make **Jockey's Ridge State Park** in Kitty Hawk a popular hang-gliding spot. **Kitty Hawk Kites**, ☎ (252) 441-4124, *www.kittyhawk.com*, operates a training and instruction facility with classes for all levels, including novices. The beginner "demo lesson" starts at $69. Aero-towing is another option for which no experience is necessary. An ultralight tows you and an instructor—you're hooked into the glider together—from 1,500 feet to a mile high before releasing you for the majestic flight back to Earth.

Jockey's Ridge State Park

Outer Banks Visitors Bureau

Fishing

The Outer Banks is an angler's paradise. You can fish the Atlantic Ocean from more than 100 miles of sandy beaches, from any one of eight piers, and from one of countless deep-sea fishing boats. Similarly, charter boats also ply the inlets, sounds, and local rivers inshore.

◆ For those inclined to stay on land, the Outer Banks features some of the East Coast's greatest surf-fishing spots. Experienced anglers load up four-wheel drive vehicles and head to **Ocracoke Inlet**, **Hatteras Inlet**, **Oregon Inlet**, and **Cape Point**, though you can cast into the sea from anywhere along the shore and stand a good chance of reeling some-

thing in. Big drum, cobia, trout, flounder, Spanish mackerel, and bluefish are some of the fish you may catch from the shore.

♦ Deep-sea fishing is a religion off the Outer Banks, especially when the big fish are running, which tends to be from March–November. Offshore charters troll for blue marlin, sailfish, wahoo, and the elusive bluefin tuna. It would be a laughable task to list all of the deep-sea charters operating here. Your best bet is to head to a local marina to talk with the captains about prices and availability. In general, full-day charters taking six people cost between $700 and $1,200. The boats leave the docks around 6 A.M. and return by 4:30 P.M.

♦ Stop by the following marinas. The **Anchorage Inn & Marina**, located off Route 12 in Ocracoke, (252) 928-6661, *www.theanchorageinn.com*, is home to two deep-sea charter boats. ♦ Roughly 20 charter boats base their operations in **Hatteras Harbor Marina**, Route 12, Hatteras, (252) 1-800-676-4939, *www.hatterasharbor.com*. ♦ **Oregon Inlet Fishing Center**, Route 12 (eight miles south of Whalebone Junction), South Nags Head, (252) 441-6301 or 1-800-272-5199,

www.oregon-inlet.com, is a full-service marina with more than 45 charter boats. ♦ Located on the causeway between Manteo and Whalebone Junction, **Pirates Cove Marina**, Route 64/264, Manteo, 1-800-367-4728, *www.fishpiratescove.com*, hosts a charter fleet of more than 20 charter boats.

Rainy Day Workout

The Spa at Sanderling, 1461 Duck Road, Duck, (252) 261-4111, *www.thesander-ling.com*, features a large fitness facility with cardiovascular machines, Cybex resistance machines, free weights, an indoor pool, and a yoga and Pilates studio. Locker rooms have saunas, steam rooms, and showers. Nominal day-use fee. ♦ **The Elizabethan Inn**, 814 Route 64, Manteo, (252) 473-2101, *www.elizabethaninn.com*, operates a complete fitness center open to the public for a nominal day-use fee. There are outdoor and indoor pools, aerobics classes, free weights, weight-resistance equipment, and cardiovascular machines, including treadmills, Stairmasters, and stationary bikes.

Swimming

With more than 100 miles of sandy beaches, you can get wet just about anywhere along the Outer Banks. But always exercise caution. No matter how inviting the ocean looks, it's no wave pool. The waters here are famous for rip tides and strong undertows. Do not swim alone. Note that red flags flying along the beach indicate that dangerous currents and rough seas are at work. *It is illegal to swim at such times.*

Roving lifeguards patrol the Outer Banks' beaches Memorial Day–Labor Day, while the more popular spots feature permanent lifeguard stands. With few exceptions—Duck, for example—there are dozens of public beach access areas throughout the islands. A list of all access areas is in the official Outer Banks' travel guide, available free from area visitor centers. (See *Additional Information*.)

Outer Banks Visitors Bureau

◆ A few of the larger, more-popular spots with lifeguards, listed south to north: **Ocracoke Beach**, on Route 12, features paved parking and a wooden walkway to the beach. ◆ **Frisco**, just south of the Frisco Pier off Route 12, features paved parking and a bathhouse. ◆ There's paved parking and beach access at the **Cape Hatteras Lighthouse** off Route 12. ◆ Roughly two miles north of Oregon Inlet off Route 12, **Coquina Beach** features a bathhouse and paved parking.

◆ At the end of **Prospect Avenue** in Kill Devil Hills, there's paved parking, plus a wooden walkway to the beach and a shower. ◆ The **Kitty Hawk Bathhouse** near Kitty Hawk Road off Route 12, features paved parking, showers, and a bathhouse. ◆ In general, most streets perpendicular to the beach in Nags Head, Kill Devil Hills, and Kitty Hawk provide public beach access points, though not all feature lifeguards.

Keep Your Cool

Riptides—fast moving currents heading out to sea—can occur anywhere along the Outer Banks and can carry even the strongest swimmers quickly seaward. If you find yourself in a riptide, do not swim against it. Instead, swim parallel to the shore to reach the edge of the riptide, where you'll be able to swim back to shore.

Windsurfing, Surfing, Sailing, & Kiteboarding

Tasty waves, waist-deep water, and wicked winds draw the adventurous-fringe to the Outer Banks, where windsurfing, surfing, and kiteboarding are all the rage. The best way to get started in these sports—assuming you're not already a convert—is to take lessons from one of the many surf shops and adventure outfitters. The following businesses, which cater to novices and pros alike, are just a sampling of the Outer Banks' water-sports specialists.

◆ Barton Decker's **Hatteras Island Sail Shop**, Route 12, Waves, (252) 987-2292, *www.hiss-waves.com*, offers windsurfing, sailing, and kiteboarding instruction, as well as board rentals. Check into both private and group lessons. ◆ **Windsurfing Hatteras**, Route 12, Avon, (252) 995-5000, *www.windsurfinghatteras.com*, runs a windsurfing academy, and rents boards and sea kayaks.

◆ Aspiring surfers can learn the mechanics and art of both long- and short-board surfing at **Duck Village Outfitters**, 1207 Duck Road, Duck, (252) 261-7222, *www.duckvillage-outfitters.com*. ◆ **Whalebone Surf Shop**, 2214 North Croatan Highway, Nags Head, (252) 441-6747, *www.whale-bonesurfshop.com*, rents surf boards and offers surfing lessons Monday–Friday, 8 A.M.–11 P.M.

NC Division of Tourism

◆ A one-stop water-sports shop, **Nor'banks Sailing**, 1308 Duck Road, Duck, (252) 261-4369, *www.norbanks.com*, offers private and group lessons in sailing and windsurfing, and rents sailboats, wind surfboards, and kayaks. ◆ **Kitty Hawk Watersports**, Route 158, Milepost 16, Nags Head, (252) 441-2756, *www.khsports.com*, rents Hobie Cats and offers sailing instruction.

Local Outdoor Advice

Cape Hatteras National Seashore • The National Park Service operates three visitor centers where you can pick up brochures and get personalized advice on where to play. They are: **Bodie Island**, Route 12 roughly 6.5 miles south of Whalebone Junction, ☎ (252) 441-5711; **Hatteras Island**, at the Cape Hatteras Lighthouse, ☎ (252) 995-4474; and **Ocracoke Island**, located near the ferry docks, ☎ (252) 928-4531. All three visitor centers are open daily, 9 A.M.–5 P.M., and until 6 P.M. in the summer. • Headquarters, 1401 National Park Drive, Manteo, ☎ (252) 473-2111

Duck Village Outfitters • Whether you're looking or join a kayak tour or to rent a bike, kayak, or surfboard, this hip retail outfit stands ready to help. The seasoned staff knows the outdoor opportunities well and will happily point you to places to play. • 1207 Duck Road, Duck, ☎ (252) 261-7222, *www.duckvillageoutfitters.com*

Kitty Hawk Kites • You can't go far without running into one of the 12 locations of this full-service adventure outfitter. If you're interested in hang gliding, kite boarding, kayaking, surfing, parasailing, jet skiing, and more, Kitty Hawk Kites is the place to stop. • Across from Jockey's Ridge State Park, Nags Head, ☎ 1-877-359-8447, *www.kittyhawk.com*

Kick Back

After you've had your fill of wind, surf, and sun, shower up and chill out with the following laid-back activities. Note that the Outer Banks remains primarily a summer destination. Most businesses operate on scaled-back schedules (if at all) during the winter. If you're visiting from December through March, call ahead for shop and attraction hours.

Antiques

Manteo features an impressive collection of antiques shops, all within walking distance of one another. Two notables include **Outer Banks Quilts & Antiques**, 108 Sir Walter Raleigh Street, Manteo, (252) 473-4183, which has nine dealers under one roof, offering a mix of collectibles, antiques, and quilts; ◆ and **Muzzies Antiques and Gifts**, #3 Magnolia Market Square, Manteo, (252) 473-4505, which specializes in estate and heirloom jewelry, plus hand-painted and French furniture. ◆ On Ocracoke Island, stop by the **Blue Door**, 165 Lighthouse Road, (252) 928-7216, for a large collection of quilts and antique furniture. ◆ **Ocracoke Restoration Company**, Route 12, Ocracoke, (252) 928-2669, *www.ocracokerestoration.com*, specializes in English stained glass, but also sells furniture, doors, art, and a number of accessories from British pubs.

Aquarium

With a focus on the "Waters of the Outer Banks," the **North Carolina Aquarium on Roanoke Island**, 374 Airport Road, Manteo, (252) 473-3494, *www.ncaquariums.com*, showcases local marine life in a number of exhibits, including the state's largest saltwater tank. More than 1,000 creatures—fish, turtles, sharks, eels, crabs, and more—live inside the 285,000-gallon tank. Outside, a boardwalk and nature trail lead to an archaeological site, where visitors can dig for fossilized shark teeth. Open daily, 9 A.M.–5 P.M. year-round. Nominal admission fee.

Art Galleries

In addition to displaying work by regional painters and printmakers, **Greenleaf Gallery**, 1169 Duck Road, Duck, (252) 261-2009, *www.outer-banks.com/greenleaf*, exhibits such crafts as glass, fine ceramics, woodwork, and designer jewelry. Greenleaf also hosts temporary exhibits.

◆ **Seaside Art Gallery**, Milepost 11, 2716 Virginia Dare Trail, Nags Head, (252) 441-5418, *www.seasideart.com*, offers a variety of original animation art, pencil drawings, and hand-painted limited editions by Disney, Warner Brothers, and Hanna-Barbera. The gallery also displays antique porcelains, glass, bronzes, marble sculptures, handmade Russian boxes, and estate and Mexican jewelry.

◆ Nestled in the historic Manteo waterfront district, the **John Silver Gallery**, 101-A Fernando Street, Manteo, (252) 475-9764, *www.johnsilvergallery.com*, showcases the work of several local painters and artisans, including owner John Silver, who specializes in vibrant oil and watercolor seascapes.

◆ **Browning Artworks**, 53321 Route 12, Frisco, (252) 995-5538, *www.browningartworks.com*, sells metalwork, photography, stained glass, handwovens, pottery, and distinctive jewelry, all created by North Carolina artists.

Boat Tours

Discover the area's maritime history and local aquatic life, including playful bottlenose dolphins, on a boat tour of the Outer Banks. For a romantic end to your day, opt for a sunset cruise. Note that most vessels sail only during the summer and fall seasons. The following are just a few of the tour outfits. ◆ Fishing-boat-by-day, twilight-cruising-vessel-by-night, the 65-foot *Miss Oregon-Inlet*, Oregon Inlet Fishing Center, Route 12, Bodie Island, (252) 441-6301, motors through soundside waters for a 1.5-hour sunset tour most summer evenings. ◆ The *Downeast Rover*, Manteo Waterfront Marina, Manteo, (252) 473-4866, *www.downeastrover.com*, is a 55-foot topsail schooner that plies the calm waters of

Guided ATV Tours

The best way to see the less-inhabited parts of the Outer Banks is on an all-terrain vehicle. A handful of outfitters operate four-wheel drive tours north of Corolla to see the wild mustangs and ponies that inhabit the barren beach. For information about guided eco-tours of the Currituck National Wildlife Refuge, check with the folks at **Backcountry Outfitters and Guides**, located in the Corolla Light Village Shops, ☎ (252) 453-0877, *www.wildhorsesafari.com*; or ◆ **Corolla Outback Adventures**, Winks Shopping Center, Corolla, ☎ (252) 453-4484, *www.corollaoutback.com*.

Roanoke Sound for two-hour sails during the day and two-hour sunset cruises in the evening. ◆ The **Nags Head Dolphin Watch**, 7517 South Virginia Dare Trail, (252) 449-8999, *www.dolphin-watch.com*, is operated by a research team that studies these intelligent mammals and features tours on a large pontoon boat led by naturalists. You'll meet "the regulars," dolphins the staff knows by name. Three daily tours are available during the summer, as well as a sunset cruise each evening. Reservations are strongly recommended.

Historic Sites & Museums

As the site of the first English settlement in the New World, Roanoke Island is steeped in history. The best place to begin is the 513-acre **Fort Raleigh National Historic Site**, 1401 National Park Drive, Manteo, (252) 473-5772, located three miles northwest of Manteo on Route 64/264. Created in 1941 to honor the first English-speaking colonists in the New World, it now also preserves the region's Native-American culture, Civil-War involvement, and the Freedman's Colony. An onsite museum has exhibits, a short film, and artifacts excavated from the settlement site. There's also an Elizabethan room, removed from a 16th-century estate in England, that highlights the disparity of living conditions between the English nobility, who funded exploration of the New World, and the first colonists. Outdoors, a handful of interpretative trails explore and explain the grounds. The two-mile Freedom Trail commemorates the site of a colony for freed slaves. Open daily, 9 A.M.–5 P.M. Free admission.

◆ The nation's longest-running, outdoor drama (begun in 1937), *The Lost Colony*, Fort Raleigh National Historic Site, (252) 473-3414, *www.thelostcolony.org*, is an entertaining way to learn about Sir Walter Raleigh's attempt to colonize the island. *The Lost Colony* combines drama, music, and dance to tell the story of the 117 English colonists who mysteriously disappeared more than 400 years ago. The show is performed nightly at 8:30 P.M., June–August (excluding Sundays). Bring a sweater and bug repellant.

◆ Before leaving the Fort Raleigh National Historic Site, stop and smell the roses at the **Elizabethan Gardens**, Manteo, (252) 474-3234, *www.elizabethangardens.org*, a memorial to the first colonists. Modeled after England's Elizabethan-era formal gardens, the 10.5-acre site features such highlights as a sunken garden with an antique Italian fountain; a marble statue of Virginia Dare, carved by Italian sculptress Maria Louisa Lander; a Shakespearean herb garden; and the Queen's Rose Garden. Throughout are hundreds of varieties of trees, shrubs, plants, and flowers. Open daily at 9 A.M. Closing times vary but are typically 8 P.M. in the summer (7 P.M. Sundays). Nominal admission fee.

NC Division of Tourism

Elizabethan Gardens in Manteo

♦ Located on a small island across from Manteo's historic waterfront, Roanoke Island's 27-acre **Festival Park**, (252) 475-1500, *www.roanokeisland.com*, features a number of attractions that bring 400 years of history to life . An interesting, self-guiding tour delivers you to the main attractions, including the *Elizabeth II,* a replica of a 16th-century sailboat; a re-creation of Roanoke's first settlement site, complete with costumed actors; the Roanoke Adventure Museum, which presents Outer Banks' history; and a 50-minute, docu-drama film, *The Legend of Two Path,* which depicts the tumultuous changes the island's Algonquin Tribe underwent following the arrival of English settlers. Open 10 A.M.–7 P.M. in the summer. Closing times vary during the rest of the year. Nominal admission fee. (Inquire about the Attractions Pass and Queen's Pass programs, which include admission fees to other sites, such as the Elizabethan Gardens and the production of *The Lost Colony*.)

Up, Up and Away

The **Wright Brothers National Memorial**, Route 158-Bypass, Milepost 8, Kill Devil Hills, ☎ (252) 441-7430, *www.nps.gov/wrbr*, commemorates the site of man's first flight. A visitor center features full-scale reproductions of Orville and Wilbur Wright's 1902 glider and 1903 "flying machine," as well as exhibits that tell how the brothers got off the ground on December 17, 1903. Outside, monuments mark where the first flight took off and where each of the four attempted flights landed. Open daily, 9 A.M.–5 P.M., (until 6 P.M. in the summer). Nominal admission fee.

♦ In 1874, 12 lifesaving stations—staffed by native islanders—lined the shores of the Outer Banks for the purpose of saving sailors' lives, as well as for salvaging ships run aground. The most famous of these, the **Chicamacomico Lifesaving Station**, Route 12, Rodanthe, (252) 987-1552, is on the National Register of Historic Places and features a variety of exhibits related to maritime rescue. Watch a simulated 19th-century shipwreck rescue every Thursday at 2 P.M. in the summer. Open Tuesday–Saturday, 9 A.M.–6 P.M., Easter–Thanksgiving. Free admission.

♦ The **Frisco Native American Museum & Natural History Center**, Route 12, Frisco, (252) 995-4440, *www.nativeamericanmuseum.org*, houses a nationally recognized collection of Native American art and artifacts, including pottery, spears, walking sticks, baskets, and blankets. Exhibits provide information on Native Americans across the United States. Also on display are artifacts from early Native-American life on Hatteras Island, including a dug-out canoe discovered on museum property. The museum grounds have a scenic, self-guiding nature trail. Open 11 A.M. – 5 P.M., Tuesday – Sunday. Nominal admission fee.

♦ Adjacent to the Hatteras-Ocracoke Ferry and housed in a building designed to look like a ship, the **Graveyard of the Atlantic Museum**, 59159 Coast Guard Road, Hatteras, (252) 986-2995, *www.graveyardoftheatlantic.com*, preserves the maritime history of the Outer Banks from the 16th Century to the present. Three galleries divide the area's shipwrecks into boats that went down while exploring, transporting passengers, and carrying goods. The museum is partially open while fundraising is completed. The grand opening is scheduled for late 2004. Call for hours and admission policies.

Currituck Lighthouse

Lighthouses

Four historic lighthouses stand along the Outer Banks, all of which still guide ships at sea. Once manned by light keepers, the lighthouses are automated today. Located in Ocracoke Village, the 1823 **Ocracoke Lighthouse** is the nation's second oldest lighthouse. The white-brick structure measures 76 feet in height and shines more than 14 miles out to sea. It is not open for tours. ◆ Located six miles south of Whalebone Junction, the 150-foot **Bodie Island Lighthouse** has black-and-white horizontal bands and a beam visible 19 miles out to sea. The 1872 lighthouse is not open for climbing, but the adjacent former-keeper's home is a visitor center, (252) 441-5711. Open daily, 9 A.M.–6 P.M. Free admission.

◆ The Outer Banks' northernmost lighthouse is the **Currituck Lighthouse**, which was constructed in 1875 to fill an 80-mile "dark spot" between Bodie Island and Cape Henry, Virginia. The red-brick structure stands 162 feet high and has a beam visible for 18 miles. For a nominal fee, you can climb 214 steps to the top for incredible views. The lighthouse and adjacent visitor center are open daily, 9 A.M. – 6 P.M. During Daylight Savings Time, the facility closes at 5 P.M.

Still Standing Tall

At 208 feet, the **Cape Hatteras Lighthouse**, with its barbershop black-and-white stripes, is the tallest brick lighthouse in the nation. It shines 20 miles out to sea. Erected between 1869–1870, it was moved a half-mile inland in 1999 to save it from the eroding shoreline. The adjacent **Museum of the Sea**, housed in the keeper's quarters, features exhibits about lighthouses and the dangerous Diamond Shoals. Weather permitting and for a nominal fee, you can climb the lighthouse's 268 steps to an impressive view. Twenty-minute tours begin daily at 9 A.M. (last tour starts at 4:40 P.M.) from the Friday before Easter–Columbus Day. For more information, call the Hatteras Visitor Center, ☎ (252) 995-4474.

Shops & Stops

Shopping on the Outer Banks runs the gamut from tourist-souvenir shops to high-end, apparel boutiques. A few generalizations about the towns: Ocracoke Village is walkable and an excellent place to park and browse the unique shops that catch your eye. Hatteras Island lacks a central shopping area and offers only a few notable stops. You'll find the bulk of beach- and tourist-oriented shops in Nags Head, Kill Devil Hills, and Kitty Hawk. Discerning shoppers will want to spend time in Manteo, Duck, and Corolla.

◆ The following suggestions are a sampling of numerous shops worth visiting. In Ocracoke Village, head for **Albert Styron's Store**, Lighthouse Road, Ocracoke, (252) 928-6819, which opened in 1920 at its current location. Inside this general store, you'll find a variety of lighthouse-related gifts, T-shirts, wines, and picnic supplies. ◆ The **Ocracoke Island Hammock Company**, British Cemetery Road, Ocracoke, (252) 928-4387, *www.ocracokehammocks.com*, manufactures and sells hand-woven rope hammocks, chairs, and swings.

◆ In Hatteras Village, head for **Hatteras Landing**, next to the Hatteras-Ocracoke Ferry landing on Route 12, for a collection of specialty shops, galleries, adventure outfitters, and cafés. ◆ In Rodanthe, stop by **Exotic Cargo**, 1-800-950-7292, located in the Pamlico Station Shops on Route 12, for indoor and outdoor teak furniture, hand-painted ceramics, primitive masks, celestial mirrors, bronze and aluminum art, woodcarvings, and jewelry. Many of the items are from Thailand, India, Mexico, Guatemala, and Indonesia. The Rodanthe store is one of Exotic Cargo's five locations on the Outer Banks.

◆ On the waterfront in downtown Manteo, stop by **Sleeping In, Ltd.**, 207 Queen Elizabeth Avenue, (252) 475-1971 or 1-866-409-1971, *www.sleepinginltd.com*, for luxury linens, lingerie, and bath and body products. ◆ For such creative home and garden accessories as wind chimes, mosaics, and fountains, stop by **Garden Alchemy**, 105 Fernando Street, Manteo, (252) 475-1262.

◆ For nautical-themed apparel, clocks, home accessories, books, lamps, and music, head to **Island Nautical**, 3810 North Croatan Highway, Kitty Hawk, (252) 261-6799, *www.nauticalsource.com*. ◆ In Duck, the **Waterfront Shops**, just north of the water tower, has 14 specialty shops selling apparel, lingerie, shoes, books, jewelry, gifts, and toys. ◆ In Duck's Scarborough Faire shopping village on Route 12, **The Culinary Duck**, 1-800-617-6260, *www.culinaryduck.com*, sells anything and everything related to the kitchen, including utensils, pots, pans, spices, cookbooks, and gourmet foods. ◆ In Corolla overlooking Currituck Sound, **Timbuck II**, Route 12, *www.timbuckii.com*, is a complete shopping and entertainment village with restaurants, adventure outfitters, attractions, and more than 60 specialty shops. Open summers only.

Beach Reading

What's a visit to the beach without a good book? Stock up on pulp or classic fiction at one of the following fine, independent bookstores. **Books to be Red**, 34 School Road, Ocracoke, ☎ (252) 928-3936; ◆ **Java Books**, 226 Back Road, Ocracoke, ☎ (252) 928-3937; ◆ **Manteo Booksellers**, 105 Sir Walter Raleigh Street, Manteo, ☎ (252) 473-1221, *www.manteobooksellers.com;* and ◆ **The Island Bookstore**, 1177 Duck Road, Duck, ☎ (252) 261-8981; and 1130 Corolla Village Road, Corolla, ☎ (252) 453-2292.

Spa & Massage

The **Spa at The Sanderling**, 1461 Duck Road, Duck, (252) 261-4111, *www.thesanderling.com*, features a full menu of massages, body treatments, and skin-care services. For the ultimate, try the 90-minute "Cleopatra's Treatment," where two therapists work in tandem, one providing a hydrating facial and the other massaging your arms and feet, while you soak in a hydro-tub filled with a milk and honey solution. Next up is a sugar body scrub, followed by a soothing yogurt wrap, at which point you'll be good enough to eat. The treatment ends with a scalp massage and Vichy tropical rain shower rinse.

Rest Easy

Sleep Well

The majority of Outer Banks visitors lease cottages or condominiums, but the number of vacationers who choose to stay in an inn or B&B is sufficient enough to keep a sizeable number of lodging businesses in operation. Accommodations here range from beach-casual to outright luxurious. Not surprisingly, the most-difficult time to find a room is between Memorial Day and Labor Day. During the off-season—November through March—call ahead for reservations, as many inns close or operate on limited schedules.

Accommodations Pricing

Less than $100	Inexpensive	$
$100-150	Moderate	$$
$151-200	Expensive	$$$
More than $200	Very Expensive	$$$$

Prices are per room, per night, based on double occupancy during peak seasons. Note that B&Bs and most country inns include breakfast in the rate.

Southern Outer Banks

The Castle Bed & Breakfast • Built in 1954 as a retreat for its original owner to entertain business associates, this inn overlooks Silver Lake Harbor and features 10 guestrooms and one suite, all individually decorated and with private baths. Breakfast consists of a hot entrée with an assortment of breads and fruits served in the country kitchen or dining room. Eight courtyard villas with separate entrances, kitchenettes, and bedrooms are out back. Amenities include a heated pool, marina, sauna, and steam rooms. • *Silver Lake, Ocracoke, NC 27960,* ☎ *1-800-471-8848, www.thecastlebb.com* • *$$$–$$$$*

The Cove Bed & Breakfast • This attractive property features four rooms and two suites, all of which are individually decorated and feature private baths and private, furnished balconies. Both suites feature Jacuzzi tubs and offer views of Portsmouth Island, Pamlico Sound, and the Ocracoke Lighthouse. Hosts Jim and Mary Ellen Piland serve a full, hot breakfast and complementary wine in the afternoon. Bicycles are available for inn guests. • *21 Loop Road, Ocracoke, NC 27960,* ☎ *(252) 928-4192, www.thecovebb.com* • *$$$–$$$$*

The Island Inn • This Ocracoke mainstay has been hosting guests since 1901. The 35 rooms are of various shapes and sizes, and all are comfortable with country-inn atmospheres. Some offer pleasant views of the harbor. The Crow's Nest offers a view of, well, pretty much everything. The restaurant is perhaps the best on the island, especially for breakfast (try the crab omelet). •*Route 12, Ocracoke, NC 27960,* ☎ *(252) 928-4351 or 1-877-456-3466, www.ocracokeislandinn.com* • *$–$$*

Roanoke Island Inn • Built in the 1860s for the current innkeeper's great-great-grandmother, this casual inn has undergone tremendous renovation since but has retained its historic charm. There are eight guestrooms, each with a separate entrance and private bath. Most have king-sized beds, and all have access to the rocking chair-lined breezeway overlooking Roanoke Sound. Guests have free reign of the innkeeper's pantry (located in the lobby), stocked with beverages and snacks and refreshed each morning with muffins and coffee. The inn is within walking distance of the waterfront, though bikes are available for guests. • *305 Fernando Street, Manteo, NC 27954,* ☎ *(252) 473-5511 or 1-877-473-5511, www.roanokeislandinn.com* • *$$–$$$*

White Doe Inn • This luxurious, turn-of-the-century, Queen Anne-style inn features eight guestrooms, each with a private bath and plush bathrobes, sitting room, and gas fireplace. Common areas include the chandelier-lit foyer, study, parlor, and dining room, as well as a tranquil garden and wraparound porch. A three-course breakfast is served on the veranda, providing a great start for touring the historic Manteo waterfront, just a short walk away. Bicycles are available for guests. • *319 Sir Walter Raleigh Street, Manteo, NC 27954,* ☎ *(252) 473-9851 or 1-800-473-6091, www.whitedoeinn.com* •*$$$–$$$$*

Northern Outer Banks

Advice 5 Cents • Set in the quiet Sea Pines neighborhood in Duck, Advice 5 Cents features four guestrooms and one suite, each with a private bath and a deck. Innkeepers Nancy Caviness and Donna Black are of the belief that vacations are not for sitting in front of a TV. They offer "afternoon tea" with tasty gingersnaps and plenty of puzzles, games, and books for entertainment. Guests also have access to the Sea Pines swimming pool and tennis courts, as well as the private walkway to the beach. Beach chairs and towels are provided. Breakfast features baked-from-scratch scones, muffins, fresh fruit, and juices. •*111 Scarborough Lane, Duck, NC 27949, ☎ (252) 255-1050 or 1-800-238-4235, www.advice5.com • $$$–$$$$*

Cypress House Inn • Built in 1947 as a hunting and fishing lodge, this inn is named for the tongue-and-groove soft cypress walls original to the house. There are six guestrooms, all with private baths and cable TV. White wicker furniture adorns most rooms. The ocean is merely 150 yards away, and the inn provides beach towels, beach chairs, and bicycles. Innkeepers Karen and Leon Faso rise early to serve a home-cooked hot breakfast. • *500 North Virginia Dare Trail, Kill Devil Hills, NC 27948, ☎ (252) 441-6127 or 1-800-554-2764, www.cypresshouseinn.com • $–$$*

First Colony Inn • Built in 1932 and moved to its present location in 1988, this inn is listed on the National Register of Historic Places. There are 27 individually decorated guestrooms, each with English antiques, a television, refrigerator, and private bathroom, featuring a tiled bath and heated towel bar. Luxury rooms have wet bars and kitchenettes; some have Jacuzzi tubs, sitting rooms, or private, screened porches. Among the inn's many amenities are a pool, a gazebo atop a nearby dune, a croquet lawn, and wraparound verandas.

Continental breakfast and afternoon tea are included. • *6720 South Virginia Dare Trail, Milepost 16, Nags Head, NC 27948, ☎ (252) 441-2343 or 1-800-368-9390, www.firstcolonyinn.com • $$$–$$$$*

The Sanderling Inn • With 88 rooms split between three buildings, a full-service spa, and two restaurants—one located in a restored lifesaving station and the other with a sprawling view of the Currituck Sound—this upscale resort is a destination unto itself. Guestrooms and suites come with a variety of features, but all have kitchenettes, wet bars, and plush robes. Other amenities may include Jacuzzi tubs, parlors, and private porches with fantastic views. There are also four oceanside villas with either three or four bedrooms, Jacuzzi tubs, porches, covered garages, and more. The inn's Eco-Center provides guests with a choice of adventures, ranging from kayak tours of Currituck Sound to nature walks and bird watching. • *1461 Duck Road, Duck, NC 27949, ☎ 1-800-701-4111, www.sanderlinginn.com • $$$$*

White Egret Bed & Breakfast • This cozy property overlooks beautiful Colington Bay in Kill Devil Hills. There are three rooms, each with a king-sized bed, antique furnishings, and a private bath with Jacuzzi tub. Homemade muffins, fresh fruits, cereals, and daily specials are served in an elegant dining room or in your room, at your request. Amenities include an extensive video collection in an upstairs common area, beach towels and chairs for use on the beach, and bikes for guests' use. • *1057 Colington Road, Kill Devil Hills, NC 27948, ☎ (252) 441-7719 or 1-888-387-7719, www.whiteegret.com • $$*

Dine Well

Countless big-city chefs looking for quality-of-life changes have ventured to the Outer Banks, and the result shows in the tremendous cuisine. The following are just a few of the region's best spots. Note that many restaurants operate on limited schedules or close entirely for the winter. Reservations are recommended (if not required) at all establishments. Also, liquor laws vary from town to town—Roanoke, Hatteras, and Ocracoke Islands do not serve mixed drinks. Some establishments have permits that allow brown bagging. Call ahead to be sure.

Southern Outer Banks

1587 • On the waterfront in historic Manteo, this restaurant (part of the Tranquil House Inn) serves outstanding cuisine with Southern influences. One of the most-elegant restaurants on the Outer Banks, 1587 exudes cosmopolitan class in a softly lit, warm dining area. The menu changes but may include such appetizers as bourbon-sautéed shrimp with fire-roasted peppers, caramelized onions, and spinach atop a sweet grit cake, and such entrées as asiago risotto with sea scallops, shrimp, and vegetables surrounded by crawfish gumbo. An award-winning wine list complements the menu. Open daily for dinner in season. Call for off-season hours. • *405 Queen Elizabeth Street, Manteo,* ☎ *(252) 473-1404*

Austin Creek Grill • Awaiting your departure from the Ocracoke Ferry on Hatteras Island is Austin Creek Grill, a contemporary, waterfront bistro adjacent to the ferry docks. Specializing in Southern cuisine and seafood, this casual restaurant offers spectacular sunset views. Dishes like the pan-roasted Ocracoke flounder or the red chili-rubbed, wood-grilled salmon are popular choices. It ought to be illegal to leave without trying

the dark-chocolate, molten-lava cake. Open Monday–Saturday for dinner in season. Call for off-season hours. • *Route 12, Marina Way, Hatteras,* ☎ *(252) 986-1511*

The Back Porch • Situated in a cozy house with a screened-in porch, this restaurant is a favorite with locals and vacationers alike. Choose from fresh local seafood as well as steaks, chicken, and chops. Start with the crab cakes with red pepper sauce, and move on to the sauté of shrimp with artichoke hearts, sun dried tomatoes, and fresh mozzarella over penne. Indoor and outdoor seating available. Open daily for dinner in season. Call for winter hours. •*110 Back Road, Ocracoke,* ☎ *(252) 928-1981*

Café Atlantic • Café Atlantic serves a pleasant array of seafood and pasta dishes in a cozy, two-story restaurant with a pretty view of Ocracoke Island's marshes and dunes. Natural wood floors and original artwork adorn the walls, but the real star is the food, particularly the crab cakes. You can't go wrong with any of the baked, sautéed, or grilled seafood dishes. Save room for their homemade desserts. Open daily for lunch and dinner, and for Sunday brunch from early March–October. Call for winter hours. • *Route 12 just outside Ocracoke Village,* ☎ *(252) 928-4861*

Howard's Pub and Raw Bar • Everyone on Ocracoke, from locals to tourists, ends up at Howard's Pub eventually. It's open every day of the year in every kind of weather. Even if a hurricane knocks out power, generators keep the beer cold, which is a good thing— there are more than 200 kinds. Burgers, chowders, chili, and low-key seafood make up the menu, and it's all cooked to order. A giant wrap-around porch holds Adirondack chairs that offer views of the ocean. There are plenty of games to occupy your time, and occasional live music. • *Route 12, Ocracoke,* ☎ *(252) 928-4441*

Northern Outer Banks

Blue Point Bar & Grill • In retro-diner ambience, the Blue Point prepares its "Southern coastal cuisine" with a simple yet artistic air. The menu changes but may include such appetizers as BBQ duck confit on green chili corn bread with golden-pineapple salsa, and such entrées as Cornmeal-crusted, Southern-fried Carolina catfish with fresh shrimp, crab and tasso ham jambalaya. The sound-front location offers a perfect view of the sunset. Open year-round for lunch and dinner. • *1240 Duck Road, Duck,* ☎ *(252) 261-8090*

Carolina Blue • With room for just 35 diners, this elegant restaurant in The Marketplace prepares eclectic Continental cuisine, with primarily French influences. The menu changes, but if it's available, order the salmon covered with horseradish and served with organic root vegetables and fresh herb gnocchi. Fresh flowers and lit candles adorn the white-linen tabletops, making for a romantic evening out. Open Tuesday–Sunday for dinner in the summer; Wednesday–Sunday in the offseason. • *5589 North Croatan Highway, Southern Shores,* ☎ *(252) 255-1543*

Colington Cafe • The Colington Cafe will eventually lose its claim as the best kept secret on the Outer Banks if it keeps appearing in the pages of *Southern Living* as "best restaurant for the best price" on the Outer Banks. The restaurant is located in a classic Victorian house off the beaten path in Kill Devil Hills. Dishes such as pistachio-encrusted salmon with jumbo lump crab meat and desserts like key lime cannoli with fresh fruit and a mango coulis are favorites with regulars. Open daily for dinner, April–November. Call for off-season hours. • *1029 Colington Road, Kill Devil Hills,* ☎ *(252) 480-1123*

Elizabeth's Café & Winery • With an exceptionally long wine list, white-lace tablecloths, and fine French and Californian cuisine, this restaurant has earned a long list of awards, most notably the International Restaurant & Hospitality's Millennium Award of Excellence as one of America's top 100 restaurants. For an unforgettable experience, choose the prix fixe, six-course wine dinner, which pairs savory dishes with a separate vintage for each course. Open daily for dinner in season. • *Scarborough Faire Shops, 1177 Duck Road, Duck,* ☎ *(252) 261-6145*

The Lifesaving Station • Housed in a restored 1899 lifesaving station (registered as a Historic Landmark), this restaurant at The Sanderling Resort serves contemporary

American cuisine with an emphasis on regional seafood. Start with the shrimp, crab, and corn chowder, and then move on to the grilled beef ribeye steak served with mashed potatoes, tobacco onions, and horseradish cream. Original lifesaving-station artifacts and nautical antiques complement the early 1900s architecture. Open for breakfast, lunch, and dinner year-round. Resort-casual attire is required (i.e. no jeans for dinner). • *1461 Duck Road, Duck,* ☎ *(252) 262-4111*

Ocean Boulevard & Martini Bar • For a slice of Manhattan located in a converted hardware store, this richly decorated restaurant serves a seasonal menu that may include such appetizers as basmati-crusted, pan-fried oysters and such entrées as the chef's simply prepared, fresh-fish selection, served with a grit cake, pancetta, rock shrimp, Crimini mushrooms, local greens, and root vegetables. With exposed brick, golden walls, and a great selection of contemporary fixtures, Ocean Boulevard feels slightly like an upscale jazz club. The Concrete Martini Bar serves dinner and a full selection of martinis. Open daily for dinner in the summer. Call for off-season hours. • *Milepost 2.5, Route 12, Kitty Hawk* ☎ *(252) 261-2546*

Outer Banks Brewing Station • For those days when you just want to kick back and enjoy a cold beer and casual food, look no further than this brew pub. Eight 100-gallon batches of beer—from Hefewiezen to Pale Ale—are made onsite, and are served with a relatively limited but well-chosen menu. Dishes vary from seafood to burgers to pasta. Try the porterhouse pork chop or the three-cheese ravioli. There's a nice wine

selection, as well. Enjoy live music Monday evenings in season. Open for lunch and dinner daily in season. Call for winter hours. • *Milepost 8 1/2, Route 158, Kill Devil Hills,* ☎ *(252) 449-2739*

Roadside Bar & Grill • The high-traffic location of the Roadside Bar & Grill (next to the multi-use path along Duck Road) makes it an ideal spot to wander in for a lunchtime sandwich or to people-watch over dinner on the deck. A local favorite for its warm, welcoming feel, the Roadside offers a good selection of beer and wine by the glass. For lunch, try the crab cake sandwich or tuna melt. If the sun has set and your appetite is hearty from a day on the beach, order the filet mignon with spinach and garlic mashers or any one of the fresh-fish selections. Take in live jazz on the patio Tuesdays and Thursdays during the summer months. Open daily for lunch and dinner in season. • *1193 Duck Road, Duck,* ☎ *(252) 261-5729*

Sanderling Left Bank • The Left Bank, whose name is inspired by its location on the Outer Banks as well as Paris' Left Bank, serves three- and five-course meals in an expansive, formal dining room overlooking Currituck Sound. Recent menu offerings include Massachusetts Wellfleet oysters with 50-year-old sherry mignonette as an appetizer, and seared Arctic char with a sauté of escarole and roasted cipollini onions as an entrée. An award-winning wine list complements the menu. Save this restaurant for a special occasion. Open daily for dinner and for brunch on Sundays. Reservations are required, as are jackets for men. • *1461 Duck Road, Duck,* ☎ *(252) 261-4111 or 1-800-701-4111*

Cafés & Picnic Packing

Bacchus Wine & Cheese Deli, 887 Albacore Street, Corolla, ☎ (252) 453-4333, *www.bacchuswineandcheese.com*, serves nearly 30 specialty sandwiches and sells more than 700 wines and imported beers. • The crew at the **Buxton Munch Company**, Route 12, Osprey Shoppes, Buxton, ☎ (252) 995-5502, provides laughs as the side dish to some great sandwiches, including chiliburgers and a huge variety of wraps. Its motto: a groovy little place with a whole lot of taste. • In Manteo, the **Full Moon Café**, Manteo Waterfront, Roanoke Island, (252) 473-6666, serves wraps, quesadillas, sandwiches, and burgers with a great view of Shallowbag Bay and the historic *Elizabeth II*. • The yummy part of Albert Styron's General Store in Ocracoke Village is the **Cat Ridge Deli**, Corner of Lighthouse Road and Creek Road, Ocracoke Village, Ocracoke, ☎ (252) 928-3354, where the menu includes baked goods, wraps, deli sandwiches, and an assortment of salads and fresh produce.

Just Desserts

Lighthouse Delights, 295 Lighthouse Rd, Ocracoke, ☎ (252) 928-3760, is a sweet shop with treats such as root beer floats, banana splits, and frozen chocolate-covered bananas. Enjoy your calories in this cute house with the vine-covered doorway. • **Half Moon Junction Ice Cream Parlor**, 208 Queen Elizabeth Avenue, Manteo, ☎ (252) 473-5554, features hand-dipped gourmet ice cream in 20 flavors.

Long-Weekend Itineraries

Southern Outer Banks

Day One

After breakfast, join a guided kayaking tour of Pamlico Sound with **Ocracoke Adventures** (page 488). Back on shore, head to lunch at **Howard's Pub** (page 503), and then stroll Ocracoke Village, checking out its **antiques shops** (page 493), **art galleries** (page 494), and numerous **shops** (page 497). Catch the **Ocracoke-Hatteras Ferry** (page 481) for the 45-minute voyage to Hatteras Island. Dine at **Austin Creek Grill** (page 502). Call it a night.

Day Two

Before breakfast, catch the sunrise over the Atlantic along the **Cape Hatteras National Seashore** (page 484). Return to your inn for breakfast and then head into historic Manteo to browse downtown before heading to the **Fort Raleigh National Historic Site** (page 495) to discover the region's rich heritage. Next stroll through the **Elizabethan Gardens** (page 495). Pick up lunch from the **Full Moon Café** (page 505) on Manteo's historic waterfront and head to the beach to spend the afternoon resting, swimming, and shell-collecting. Return to your inn to shower up for dinner at **1587** (page 502). Lights out.

Day Three

Linger over breakfast, and then head out, camera in hand, to photograph the **Cape Hatteras Lighthouse** (page 497) and to visit the **Chicamacomico Lifesaving Station** (page 496). Take a final dip in the sea, before showering off, checking out of your inn, and grabbing a light lunch in Manteo before heading home.

Northern Outer Banks

Day One

After breakfast, grab a beach towel from your inn, purchase a picnic lunch from **Bacchus Wine & Cheese Deli** (page 505) and then head to Duck's beaches to stroll the sand, rest on a towel, swim, and collect shells. After lunch and maybe a mid-day snooze (lather up on sunscreen), head to **Duck Village Outfitters** (page 487) to rent beach cruisers and ride the area's pathways. Return the bikes and hit the shower at your inn to prepare for the acclaimed, six-course wine dinner at **Elizabeth's Café & Winery** (page 503). Call it a day.

Day Two

After breakfast, head to **Corolla Outback Kayak Tours** (page 488) to join their paddling tour along the northern Currituck beaches. Afterward, head to the **Roadside Bar & Grill** (page 504) for lunch, and then meet the folks at **Kitty Hawk Kites** in **Jockey's Ridge State Park** (page 489) for your introductory hang-gliding lesson. Next up, stop at the **Wright Brothers National Memorial** (page 496) and then head to the beach for a late-afternoon swim. Shower up and head to dinner at **The Lifesaving Station** (page 503). Lights out.

Day Three

After a late breakfast, do some upscale **shopping** (page 497) in Duck and Corolla before your massage and spa-services appointments at the **Spa at The Sanderling** (page 498). Enjoy lunch at **Blue Point Bar & Grill** (page 503) before climbing into your car for the reluctant drive home.

Additional Information

The Outer Banks Visitors Bureau, One Visitor Center Circle (at the foot of the Virginia Dare Bridge), Manteo, NC 27954, ☎ 1-877-629-4386, *www.outerbanks.org*. Open daily, 9 A.M.–5:30 P.M. The organization also operates the **Aycock Brown Welcome Center**, Route 158, Milepost 1.5, Kitty Hawk, NC 27949, ☎ (252) 261-4644. Open daily, 9 A.M.–5:30 P.M.

Currituck Outer Banks Visitor Center, Ocean Club Centre, 500 Hunt Club Drive, Corolla, NC 27927, ☎ (252) 453-9612 or 1-877-287-7488, *www.currituckchamber.org*, is open daily, 9 A.M.–5 P.M.

Wilderness Smarts

What To Carry

Carry the following items with you on every venture into the woods, regardless of the duration.

- **Water:** Carry at least one quart per person for short hikes (1–2 hrs) and three quarts per person for long hikes. Don't skimp on water. Dehydration can sneak up on you.
- **Food:** A picnic lunch is one of the pleasures of a full-day hike. For shorter hikes, bring a high-energy snack like fruit, trail mix, or a power bar.
- **Extra clothing:** Be prepared for sudden shifts in the weather. Carry a waterproof jacket for rain.
- **First aid kit:** First aid supplies to tend to minor problems like insect bites, wounds, blisters, and sunburns are worth every ounce of their weight. Adventure Medical Kits, 1–800–324–3517, *www.adventuremedicalkits.com*, manufactures a complete line of first aid kits, including the Day Tripper, a lightweight kit designed exclusively for explorers out just for the day.
- **Map and compass:** A compass can get you home, if you know how to use it. A trail map provides an overview of your location and let's you make informed decisions on which way to go, if you get lost.
- **Extra moleskin for foot protection:** No first aid kit can come with enough.
- **Pocket knife.**
- **Waterproof matches.**
- **Emergency blanket.**
- **Small flashlight.**
- **Sunscreen.**
- **Insect repellant.**
- **Whistle.**
- **Cell phone:** If you have a cell phone with network access in the area, carry it with you for use in emergencies.
- **Daypack:** Carry all of the above in either a fanny pack, which carries the weight on your hips, or a daypack, which offers more room and disperses most of the weight across your shoulders and back.
- **Hunting calendar:** Before you venture into the woods, check to see if hunters will be in the woods as well. If so, wear blaze orange.

What to Wear

Even in the summer, mountain temperatures can get quite cool, particularly on top of a summit on a cloudy, windy day. Always be prepared for chilly or inclement weather. In hot temperatures, cotton is an excellent fabric because of its cooling properties; however, it will not keep you warm when wet from rain or sweat. You're better off wearing a lightweight synthetic fiber, like polypropylene that retains warmth when soaked. Even on hot days, you should carry a lightweight Gore-Tex® jacket to keep you warm in the event of a sudden change in weather.

For cooler temperatures, wear clothes in layers so you can remove or add as necessary. Against your skin, wear a fabric that wicks moisture away, such as polypropylene. The best insulator is air, which layering traps against the body for warmth. Fabrics such as loose-fitting fleece act as great insulating layers. Your final layer should be wind and waterproof. Breathable nylon or Gore-Tex® make safe bets for your outer layer. In the cold, always carry a hat and wear it to retain body warmth. Likewise, carry and wear gloves or mittens. (Mittens will keep your hands warmer than gloves.)

On your feet, wear a thin liner sock made of polypropylene to wick moisture away and prevent blisters. Wear a thick wool or wool-blend hiking sock on top. If you suffer from weak knees or ankles, wear two pairs of socks for comfort and additional shock absorption.

If you don't already own a pair of hiking boots, invest in a good pair before your next dayhike. Your feet and ankles will thank you. If your primary activity will be limited to day-hikes, you can purchase a good pair of lightweight hiking boots for the same cost as a nice pair of running shoes. A proper fit is essential in hiking boots, so wear your hiking socks when trying on new boots. Lightweight boots may feel comfortable immediately, but you should wear them a few days around the house before hitting the trail. (If you wear them outdoors, you won't be able to return them.) If you'll be snowshoeing or skiing in deep snow, invest in a pair of gators to keep snow out of your boots.

On The Trail
Some general backcountry wisdom:
- **Don't hike, bike or ski alone** in unfamiliar territory.
- **Stay on marked trails**.
- **Stay alert at all times.** Should you encounter any wildlife, give it lots of room.
- **Know your limits.** When you're in the wilderness, listen to the voice of caution.
- **Pace yourself** so as not to tire too quickly. Find a rhythm you're comfortable with and stick to it.
- If anything goes wrong, **remain calm.** If you begin to panic, stop yourself by breathing deeply and repeating, "breathing in, I know I am breathing in. Breathing out, I know I am breathing out." Your common sense will return.
- Practice **low-impact** backcountry exploration:
  - Carry out what you carry in.
  - Pick up litter along the way.
  - Know local backcountry rules and obey them.
  - *Leave only footprints. Take only memories. Kill only time.*

Recommended Gear
The authors and staff at Walkabout Press are all experienced outdoorspeople and enjoy sharing apparel, footwear, and gear suggestions with one another and our readers. For a free list of equipment suppliers we've tested and trust, write to the email below. This is not an endorsement deal—just a list of our favorites: *gearideas@walkaboutpress.com*

Index

Index

About Walkabout Press

Founded in 2000 and located in Charlotte, NC, Walkabout Press publishes books and web content for soft-adventure travel, sports instruction, and outdoor recreation. Publisher Malcolm Campbell named the company after the Australian Aboriginal custom of walkabout, whereby an Aborigine disappears into the bush to follow his heart and walks for weeks or months on end without a destination in mind. The Aborigine follows "songlines," or paths embedded in the earth that only he can see. The journey is, of course, one of self-discovery and of living fully in the present. Walkabout Press strives to publish books and web content that encourage people to take walkabouts from their busy lives—through travel, exercise, and exploration of the great outdoors.

Our company's mission is: *to produce and sell outstanding books that deliver exactly what they promise to the reader; continue to sell year after year; and earn our competition's respect.* When we make a profit, we share our success by donating 1% of annual pre-tax profits to the National Center for Family Literacy (*www.famlit.org*), an organization that promotes parents reading to their children. In years that we do not make a profit, we contribute a baseline amount. So, thanks for buying our books and helping support this important cause.

Ordering & Contact Information

Look for our books in your local bookstore, outdoor shop, or on the Web at your favorite Internet retailer. No luck? Order directly from us:

Walkabout Press
P.O. Box 11329
Charlotte, NC 28220
1-800-231-3949
www.walkaboutpress.com

Ask about our ultra-cool, 100%-cotton, **Play Hard Rest Easy** T-shirts. Available in small, medium, large, and extra-large sizes for $12.95, plus shipping & handling.

For Booksellers

Our titles are available from Ingram, Baker & Taylor, and John F. Blair. If you're interested in having an author for an event, contact Walkabout Press directly.

Meet the Authors

Malcolm Campbell is a native of Charlotte, North Carolina and author of *Play Hard Rest Easy: New England*. Before founding Walkabout Press in 2000, he worked as an adver-

tising account executive, ad copywriter, travel marketing director, and senior editor for *Selling Power*, a national business magazine for which he profiled such people as former General Electric CEO Jack Welch; America Online Chairman Steve Case; and professional golfer Mark O'Meara. He lives in Charlotte with his wife, Lauren, sons, McLean and Elliott, and Bird, the family dog, whose ability to snore through the most-stressful of publishing deadlines is awe-inspiring and, perhaps, instructive.

Born and raised in Yardley, Pennsylvania, **Deron Nardo** received his BS in marketing from Loyola College in Maryland and is currently completing a masters degree in communications

at the University of North Carolina at Charlotte. An avid snowboarder, Deron has lived in Sun Valley, Idaho and Denver, Colorado. His passion for the outdoors was piqued during a summer-long, solo drive across the western United States, during which he camped, biked, and hiked to his heart's content. Deron currently lives in Charlotte, North Carolina with his dog, Fiya, who in two short years has proven to be his favorite conversationalist. (She always listens.) Forays into the freelance writing world have landed Deron in *Charlotte* magazine and on WFAE in Charlotte as an NPR commentator.